World Religions in Practice

A Comparative Introduction

Paul Gwynne

Second Edition

WILEY

This second edition first published 2018

Edition History: Blackwell Publishing Ltd (1e, 2009)
(Hardback: 978-1-4051-6702-4 / Paperback: 978-1-4051-6703-1)

Registered Offices
John Wiley & Sons, Inc., 111 River Street, Hoboken, NJ 07030, USA
John Wiley & Sons Ltd, The Atrium, Southern Gate, Chichester, West Sussex, PO19 8SQ, UK

Editorial Office
9600 Garsington Road, Oxford, OX4 2DQ, UK
For details of our global editorial offices, customer services, and more information about Wiley products visit us at www.wiley.com.

Wiley also publishes its books in a variety of electronic formats and by print-on-demand. Some content that appears in standard print versions of this book may not be available in other formats.

Library of Congress Cataloging-in-Publication Data

Names: Gwynne, Paul, 1957– author.
Title: World religions in practice : a comparative introduction / Paul Gwynne.
Description: 2nd edition. | Hoboken, NJ : John Wiley & Sons, 2017. | Includes bibliographical references and index.
Identifiers: LCCN 2017006967 (print) | LCCN 2016059938 (ebook) | ISBN 9781118972267 (pbk.) | ISBN 9781118972281 (Adobe PDF) | ISBN 9781118972274 (ePub)
Subjects: LCSH: Religions.
Classification: LCC BL80.3 .G89 2017 (ebook) | LCC BL80.3 (print) | DDC 200–dc23
LC record available at https://lccn.loc.gov/2017006967

Cover Image: © Bazuki Muhammad / Reuters
Cover Design: Wiley

Set in 10/12pt Warnock by SPi Global, Pondicherry, India
Printed in Singapore by C.O.S. Printers Pte Ltd

10 9 8 7 6 5 4 3 2 1

Contents

List of Boxes

List of Tables

List of Figures

Preface

The second edition of *World Religions in Practice* retains most of the key features of the original edition. It remains a comparative study of a sample of major religions based on a set of practical themes. What is new in this edition is the inclusion of a sixth religious tradition – Daoism – and, consequently, a slight reduction in the number of themes in order to maintain the length of the book. The addition of Daoism means that the sample now includes one of the principal ingredients of Chinese religious culture, which is an eclectic mix of popular folk traditions and the "Three Teachings": Daoism, Confucianism and Buddhism. Whilst Buddhism has an Indian provenance, Daoism and Confucianism originated in China and, in introductory works on world religions, are often dealt with under the umbrella term "Chinese religion". The decision to focus on Daoism alone, rather than include all elements of Chinese religious practice, is not intended as a value judgment on those other elements but simply to ensure that a manageable, working comparison is achieved.

The addition of this extra material meant that the chapter entitled Day has been omitted, although some of its time-related contents have been incorporated into the chapter entitled Year, which looks at the annual calendars. It also meant that, in each chapter, the original sections on the five religions have been trimmed to provide a more succinct presentation. Finally, the inclusion of Daoism has also affected the order in which the religions are covered in each chapter. As explained in the first edition, this order is not random. Rather, it has been designed to highlight similarities and connections between religions on the theme in question, thus producing a useful spectrum of comparative analysis each time. In other words, Daoism has now joined the "dance" of the religions across the themes. Hopefully, these changes have resulted in a tighter, more representative comparison of the fascinating interplay between six of the world's major religious traditions.

Note on Scriptural References

The following versions of scriptural and traditional texts have been used:

Access to Insight: Readings in Theravada Buddhism, ed. John Bullitt, sutta translations by the Venerables Bhikkhu Bodhi, Acharya Buddharakkhita, Bhikkhu Khantipalo, Nanamoli Thera, Ñanavara Thera, Narada Thera, Nyanaponika Thera, Soma Thera, Thanissaro Bhikkhu (Phra Ajaan Geoff), and Sister Vajira; I. B. Horner, John D. Ireland, K. R. Norman, and F. L. Woodward. At www.accesstoinsight.org.

Babylonian Talmud, ed. Rabbi Dr Isidore Epstein. London: Jews' College. Also available at www.come-and-hear.com/talmud.

Bhagavad Gita, trans. Laurie L. Patton. London: Penguin, 2008.

The Holy Bible: New Revised Standard Version with Apocrypha. New York: Oxford University Press (1991).

The Hadith, USC-MSA Compendium of Muslim Texts, University of Southern California, at www.usc.edu/dept/MSA/fundamentals/hadithsunnah.

The Holy Koran, trans. Mohammed H. Shakir. New York: Tahrike Tarsile Qur'an Inc., 1983. Also available at www.usc.edu/dept/MSA/fundamentals/hadithsunnah.

Translations of the Daode jing and other Daoist texts are taken from Louis Komjathy (2013). *The Daoist Tradition*. London: Bloomsbury.

The Pinyin system has been used for transliterations of Chinese words.

Words in **bold type** are included in the Glossary at the end of the book.

Acknowledgments

I wish to thank the following academic colleagues for their invaluable feedback on the draft manuscript:

Professor John D'Arcy May, Irish School of Ecumenics, Trinity College, Dublin

Associate Professor Douglas Pratt, Department of Philosophy and Religious Studies, University of Waikato, New Zealand

Dr Heather Foster, School of Education, University of South Australia, Adelaide

Peta Jones Pellach, Director of Adult Education, Shalom Institute, Sydney

Associate Professor Mehmet Olzap, Charles Sturt University

Amna Hansia and the staff of the Australian Islamic College, Perth

Associate Professor Constant Mews, Director of Centre for Studies in Religion and Theology, Monash University, Melbourne

I am also very grateful for the professional advice and support of the Blackwell staff and their associates for this second edition, especially Rebecca Harkin, Ruth Swan, Vimali Joseph and Georgina Colby. I also wish to thank my wife, Kim Host, for her proof-reading of the manuscript.

Paul Gwynne
Sydney

Introduction

Few would deny that religion constitutes a vital piece of the jigsaw when it comes to fully understanding human societies and their members, both past and present. It is a key influence on a host of cultural activities around the globe, from weddings and funerals to public holidays and festivals. Religious belief is frequently a source of inspiration for works of literature, art and architecture, and can significantly shape everyday life at the level of diet and clothing. Even in highly secularized Western society, the legacy of centuries of religious tradition has left its distinctive and enduring mark on language, symbol and custom. Sadly, religious motives are also an ingredient in many political conflicts and even acts of terrorism that currently dominate the world stage. For better or for worse, religion is still very much a part of the human story and cannot be ignored if we hope to explain fully what makes individuals and communities think and act in the way that they do.

Moreover, the contraction of the world from an array of far-flung continents to a single global village has brought a wide spectrum of religious beliefs firmly within our horizon, wherever that may be. In Western societies, mass immigration programs have meant a reversal of colonial times and the arrival of large numbers of adherents of "other faiths." The world has come to us and its religions are no longer exotic phenomena in distant lands, but the defining worldviews of neighbors and work colleagues. Conversely, the relative ease and affordability of travel provides an unprecedented opportunity for today's tourist to visit cultures where ceremonies, festivals, artworks and buildings express religious ideas in both recognizable and unrecognizable ways.

In such a world, an appreciation of different religious traditions is arguably more pertinent than ever. Without diluting or compromising one's own fundamental philosophical, spiritual or religious persuasions, an interested and respectful study of different religious systems affords an opportunity to complete the picture. The comparative study of religion provides the broader context into which more familiar faith systems can be situated and, thus, better understood. It can highlight the distinctive features that render each religion truly unique, while at the same time revealing fascinating areas of intersection between faiths.

This book is an attempt to explore those similarities and differences, hopefully contributing something to the quest for a deeper understanding and a more profound appreciation of the common ground between all religions. To this end, a phenomenological approach has been adopted. In other words, it is not primarily concerned with the veracity or credibility of the religious claims involved. Nor is it about demonstrating that one religion is more advanced or complete than another. Although absolute objectivity is an impossible ideal in any discipline, apologetic issues are deliberately set aside in an attempt to present each religion in a respectful and accurate manner.

World Religions in Practice: A Comparative Introduction, Second Edition. Paul Gwynne.

The major religions dealt with in this book are Hinduism, Buddhism, Daoism, Judaism, Christianity and Islam. The decision to restrict the study to these six in no way implies that the list is exhaustive. There are other religious and quasi-religious systems that could be considered global such as Confucianism, Sikhism, Jainism, Baha'ism and Zoroastrianism but the scope and approach of the book meant that a limit had to be imposed at some point. The six that have been chosen are frequently the subject of textbooks and courses on "world religions" and for good reason. Four of them represent the largest religious denominations according to approximate current statistics: Christianity (2.2 billion), Islam (1.5 billion), Hinduism (1 billion), and Buddhism (380 million). With about 14 million adherents, Judaism admittedly involves much smaller numbers, but it is included in the main six due to its significant age, widespread influence and fundamental links to the other two Abrahamic faiths, Christianity and Islam. Providing a meaningful figure for Daoism is more complex and messy. Although there is Daoist philosophy, Daoist rituals and Daoist priests and monks, it is unclear whether there are actually any "Daoists" in the sense of a community of believers who identify themselves as such in distinction from Confucians or Buddhists. On the contrary, it is more accurate to speak of drawing on Daoist, Confucian, Buddhist and popular folk traditions to various degrees as simply part of being Chinese.

The approach taken in this book is somewhat different from that of standard works in two ways. First, most introductory works on the world's major religions adopt a serial approach whereby the author outlines the key features of each religion in turn. Thus, chapters tend to be organized according to the religions themselves and the reader is escorted on a journey of discovery through various aspects of the faith system in question. The bibliography at the end of this book contains many such examples. The advantage is that a reasonably coherent overview of each religion is provided in discrete units. However, an alternative method has been used for this work. Rather than organizing religions in linear fashion and treating each one as a separate whole, a more lateral approach has been adopted whereby a range of general themes is explored across the religions. The result is a series of cross-sections that reveal how a particular theme, such as sacred writing or holy days, is expressed in each religion. Such an approach is able to generate greater levels of explicit comparison between the religions, uncovering not only the unique qualities that differentiate them, but also an assortment of interesting overlaps and connections.

Second, most books on the world's major religions tend to focus on either their historical development or their theological beliefs while (with a few exceptions) paying little or no attention to the actual living out of the faith. Several decades ago, Ninian Smart proposed that all religions contain, to a greater or lesser extent, seven fundamental dimensions: doctrinal–philosophical; experiential–emotional; mythical–narrative; ethical–legal; social–institutional; practical–ritual; and material. The themes chosen for this book belong primarily to Smart's last two categories (with one chapter devoted to the ethical dimension). Thus, we will be looking mainly at how the six religions are expressed in practice. Our principal interest lies more in customs than in creeds, in external actions than in inner attitudes. Nevertheless, an examination of the ritual and material dimension of these six religions inevitably touches on Smart's other dimensions, including the doctrinal–philosophical. A study of religious practices cannot avoid consideration of the theological foundations that underpin them. The practical features of religions, such as the use of images and texts in worship, the donning of special clothing, or the design of sacred buildings, reflect deeper doctrinal positions regarding the world and our place in it. In this respect, the old Latin adage rings true: *lex orandi lex credendi* ("the law of praying is the law of believing"). In other words, the practical is a mirror to the theoretical. Religious custom is a reflection of religious belief and vice versa.

The 11 practical themes are themselves arranged and linked under an overarching motif: the sanctification of the ordinary. As Smart rightly pointed out, religion is a complex, multi-dimensional phenomenon that has proved to be notoriously difficult to pin down. This is clear from the myriad of definitions available (for a sample see Box 0.1). Some definitions stress the individual while others stress the social; some the psychological, others the cultural; some the moral, others the political. However, most definitions of religion contain the reference to a reality beyond time and space, which can be denoted in many ways: "the divine"; "the sacred"; "the supernatural"; "the spiritual"; "Ultimate Being"; "God"; "Allah"; "Brahman"; "the Dao"; "eternal dharma"; and so forth. Whether this reality actually exists or is merely the product of the human imagination is one of the most burning of all philosophical issues. But apart from the question of its factual or fictional status, faith in transcendent reality clearly has a profound impact on the way in which believers interpret and live out human existence. Whatever the designation, Hindus, Buddhists, Daoists, Jews, Christians and Muslims all see it as the answer to the most important questions of all: Where did we come from? Why are we here? And where are we going?

Box 0.1 Some Definitions of Religion

The belief in a superhuman controlling power, especially in a personal God or gods entitled to obedience and worship. *(Concise Oxford Dictionary)*

A belief system that includes the idea of the existence of an eternal principle that has created the world that governs it, that controls its destinies or that intervenes in the natural course of its history. *(Random House Dictionary)*

Homo religiosus always believes that there is an absolute reality, the sacred, which transcends this world but manifests itself in this world, thereby sanctifying it and making it real. *(Mircea Eliade)*

Religion, in the largest and most basic sense of the word, is ultimate concern. It gives us the experience of the Holy, of something which is untouchable, awe-inspiring, an ultimate meaning, the source of ultimate courage. *(Paul Tillich)*

A system of symbols which acts to establish powerful, pervasive and long-lasting moods and motivations in men by formulating conceptions of a general order of existence and clothing these conceptions with such an aura of factuality that the moods and motivations seem uniquely realistic. *(Clifford Geertz)*

Religion implies that human order is projected into the totality of being. Put differently, religion is the audacious attempt to conceive of the entire universe as being humanly significant. *(Peter Berger)*

Religious ideas are illusions, fulfillments of the oldest, strongest and most urgent wishes of mankind. Thus, the benevolent rule of a divine Providence allays our fear of the dangers of life; the establishment of a moral world-order insures the fulfillment of the demands of justice, which have so often remained unfulfilled in human civilization; and the prolongation of earthly existence in a future life provides the local and temporal framework in which these wish-fulfillments shall take place. *(Sigmund Freud)*

Religion is the sigh of the oppressed creature, the heart of a heartless world, just as it is the spirit of a spiritless situation. It is the opium of the people. The abolition of religion as the illusory happiness of the people is required for their real happiness. *(Karl Marx)*

Consequently, belief in transcendent reality casts a new light on all aspects of life, even the most mundane. Ordinary realities such as food and clothing, birth, marriage and death, even time and space itself, are given a more profound, extraordinary meaning through the eyes of religious faith. Familiar objects, activities, moments and places become part of the provision of ultimate meaning and, thus, take on a sacred, transcendent quality.

The 11 themes are organized into three clusters which constitute the three sections of the book. Part 1 looks at two principal religious ways in which the reality that lies "beyond time and space" can be accessed: the visual image and the written or spoken word. The use (or non-use) of these two bridges to transcendent reality not only constitutes an important starting point for our comparison of practice but also reveals something about how each religion understands transcendent reality itself. Part 2 focuses on human existence "within time and space." It opens with a brief survey of moral duty in each religion and then proceeds to examine three main rites of passage (birth, death and marriage) that are frequently marked by religious ritual. This section also takes the two most basic necessities of life (food and clothing) and examines how they are also given sacred meaning by religious faith. Part 3 looks at the very fabric of spatial–temporal existence, and explores how each of the six religions sanctifies time and space itself. Themes of the annual calendar, the sacred building and spiritual pilgrimage are examined in each religion. Of course, the choice of these 11 themes does not imply that the list is complete. There are other practical themes that could be added such as healing, initiation and prayer. However, these 11 themes resonate effectively across the six religions, thus representing a useful sample that serves well the comparative and practical purpose of the book.

Given the limited size of such a book, there is simply not enough space to delve into the intricate details of the chosen themes. The beliefs and practices discussed here are merely the tips of many icebergs that can be adequately fathomed only in more specialized works. Moreover, the six religions themselves are far from monochrome, consisting of a spectrum of subdivisions, sects and traditions whose beliefs and practices can vary significantly at times, especially in the case of Hinduism. Moreover, as we noted above, Chinese religious practice is an eclectic mix of Daoism, Confucianism, Buddhism and folk religion. Thus, the danger of generalization hovers constantly over such a project, including the inherent limitations of the term "world religion" itself. Consequently, the author has endeavored to focus on broadly typical characteristics of each major religion, accompanied by the acknowledgment of variations and exceptions where relevant. Admittedly a picture painted with broad brush strokes must ignore small things, but there is some value in stepping back at times and taking a more panoramic view. In short, this book is more concerned with forests than trees, especially what the forests look like from above and where their boundaries touch.

The primary audience of the book is the tertiary or senior secondary student in religious studies courses as well as the layperson who has an interest in major religions and their interrelationship. Although the book is introductory in nature, a basic familiarity with the six religions will be advantageous since each religion is encountered thematically along with others. Accordingly, a brief vignette and timeline for each religion has been provided at the end of this Introduction. The effect of the comparative approach is akin to a thematic tour, but the road is more reminiscent of a meandering track than a straight highway. The order in which we travel through the six religions will vary from chapter to chapter, depending on where the bridges seem to occur naturally. It should be noted that the particular order in which the religions are dealt with in each chapter is not intended to imply any kind of priority or superiority, nor is it the only possible one. The tour itinerary is not binding, but hopefully it is one that will provide fresh views and interesting landscapes.

HINDUISM ॐ	
Key facts	
No. of adherents (approx.)	1 billion
Origins	Hinduism has no historical founder but its origins are usually linked to the Aryan invasion of the Indus Valley civilization around 1500 BCE, which resulted in a socio-religious **caste** system and the emergence of the **Vedas** as primary sacred texts.
Subdivisions	Hinduism is a general term embracing a complex spectrum of religious sects. It can be subdivided according to the principal form of **Brahman** which is worshiped: • Vaishnavism (650 million): worship of **Vishnu** and his incarnations such as **Krishna** and **Rama**; • Shaivism (250 million): worship of **Shiva**; • Shaktism: worship of **Shakti** (**Mother Goddess**) and her manifestations such as **Parvati**, **Durga** and Kali. There are also many recent movements such as the **Arya Samaj**, which was founded by Dayananda Saraswati in the late nineteenth century.
Transcendent reality	The term Brahman refers to the one absolute reality that embraces the entire cosmos. Brahman is beyond all finite categories but is manifest and worshiped in the form of different gods and goddesses such as Vishnu, Shiva, or the Mother Goddess. Thus, Hinduism is difficult to classify and is described variously as **polytheistic**, **henotheistic** or **monistic**.
Human existence	Hindus believe in **samsara** (reincarnation) whereby the **atman** (soul) of the deceased is reborn into the world according to the law of **karma**. The cycle can last hundreds or thousands of lifetimes but it is hoped that all individuals will eventually be released from the cycle of rebirth and attain **moksha** (final liberation). For some Hindu philosophers, such as **Shankara**, moksha involves the dissolution of the atman back into Brahman. For others, such as Ramanuja, the liberated atman retains some degree of individual existence in perfect communion with Brahman and other beings. There are three main paths to moksha: • jnana-marga: the path of knowledge and meditation; • karma-marga: the path of moral action; • **bhakti**-marga: the path of devotion and worship of a particular deity.
Sacred texts	There are two main categories of Hindu sacred writings: • **shruti** (primary revelation): the Vedas and the **Upanishads**; • **smriti** (secondary revelation): there are many works in this category of which the most prominent are the two great epics (the **Mahabharata** and the **Ramayana**), the poetic **Puranas**, and legal codes such as the **Laws of Manu**.
Key rituals	The 16 traditional life-cycle rituals (**samskaras**) include many prenatal and childhood ceremonies, as well as initiation into adulthood (sacred thread), marriage and funeral rites.

BUDDHISM	
Key facts	
No. of adherents (approx.)	380 million
Origins	**Siddhartha Gautama** (c.560–480 BCE) was born into the royal family of the Sakya kingdom (near the current Indian/Nepal border). He married and had a son, but upon experiencing the Four Sights (old age, sickness, death and a holy man) left his family and spent seven years as a wandering ascetic. Meditating under a tree at Bodhgaya, he grasped the **Four Noble Truths** and became **Buddha** (Enlightened One). He delivered the First Sermon to his five companions at Sarnath and thereafter traveled around northern India, teaching and attracting followers until his death at Kusinagara.
Subdivisions	• **Theravada** (Way of the Elders) has about 150 million followers located mainly in Sri Lanka, Myanmar, Thailand, Cambodia and Laos. It is sometimes called Hinayana (Lesser Vehicle) by the Mahayana tradition. Theravada Buddhism stresses the importance of the monastic community and the need for self-discipline in order to attain **nirvana**. • **Mahayana** (Greater Vehicle) has approximately 200 million followers located mainly in China, Mongolia, Japan, Korea and Vietnam. It has more readily incorporated elements from local cultures and stresses compassion, especially in the form of the **bodhisattva**, a holy person who postpones nirvana to assist others. • Vajrayana (Diamond Vehicle) has about 20 million adherents and is the dominant form of Buddhism in Tibet. It is characterized by mystical rituals and elements including **tantras**, **mantras** and **mandalas**.
Transcendent reality	Buddha rejected the Hindu concepts of Brahman (transcendent being) and atman (soul). The main focus of his teaching is on personal liberation from craving (greed, hatred and ignorance) which binds us to the wheel of reincarnation. Thus, many argue that Buddhism should not be classified as a religion, although it has many features that are similar to other religions.
Human existence	Buddhists believe in reincarnation according to the law of karma. However, the self is illusory and what is reborn each time is a reconfiguration of basic energies. Liberation from the wheel of samsara is attained by embracing the Four Noble Truths: 1) suffering is universal; 2) the root of suffering is craving for transient things; 3) nirvana is the end of suffering and reincarnation; 4) the way to nirvana is the Noble Eightfold Path: right knowledge, right attitude, right speech, right action, right livelihood, right effort, right mindfulness, and right meditation. The **Pancasila** (Five Precepts) is the Buddhist list of fundamental ethical principles that should be followed.

Key facts (Continued)	
Sacred texts	The **Tipitaka** (**Three Baskets**) is a threefold collection of the Buddha's sayings, the monastic rule, and a philosophical system. It is the most important text in Theravada Buddhism. Other texts are given equal or greater status in Mahayana and Vajrayana schools, such as Lotus Sutra and the Tibetan Book of the Dead.
Key rituals	Buddhism has no universal ceremonial system. Its rites of passage are profoundly influenced by local culture and custom. Monastic life involves ordination ceremonies, alms rounds and a range of meditation practices.

DAOISM	
Key facts	
No. of adherents (approx.)	It is difficult to provide a meaningful number because Daoists do not self-identify as in other religions. Rather, Daoism, along with Confucianism, Buddhism and folk religion, is part of being Chinese.
Origins	The origins of Daoism are usually linked to the legendary figure of **Laozi** ("Old Master") who was a contemporary of Confucius (sixth century BCE). It is said that he was a court official who wrote a short treatise called the **Daode jing**, which he gave to the Guardian of the Pass, before disappearing from society. However, the first organized forms of Daoism only emerged in the first century CE (late Han Dynasty) with the deification of Laozi as Lord Lao, ritual practice and new movements such as the Tianshi (**Celestial Masters**) and the Yellow Turbans.
Subdivisions	Today, the two main forms of Daoism in mainland China and among Chinese communities elsewhere are the Zhengyi and Quanzhen movements. • The **Zhengyi** (Orthodox Unity) movement dates to the eleventh century CE and was prominent in southern China. It is characterized by a married priesthood and community rituals such as exorcisms and healings. It is also called the **Tianshi** (Celestial Masters) movement since its highest authority is the Celestial Master who traditionally resided at Dragon Tiger Mountain until the 63rd Master fled to Taiwan in 1949. • The **Quanzhen** (Complete Perfection) movement was founded in the twelfth century CE. Historically dominant in northern China, it emphasizes asceticism, mystical experience and self-preservation practices. It has been heavily influenced by Buddhism and has celibate, vegetarian monk-priests. Its headquarters is the **White Cloud Monastery** in Beijing but the Quanzhen branch also has official jurisdiction over most Daoist pilgrimage sites in mainland China.

Key facts (Continued)	
Transcendent reality	The Daoist pantheon consists of a multitude of gods who form a heavenly, bureaucratic hierarchy. At the highest level are the **Three Pure Ones** (**Sanqing**) who presided over the formation of the cosmos, the appearance of **yin and yang** and the emergence of human civilization. Above and beyond the Three Pure Ones lies the elusive **Dao** ("Way") – a term that signifies several ideas: unfathomable mystery; all-pervading divine presence; the absolute origin and destiny of all beings. A principal Daoist aim is to harmonize one's thoughts and actions effortlessly with the Dao.
Human existence	In contrast to the reincarnational models of Hinduism and Buddhism, Daoism teaches that humans live only once. At physical death, the body decays but the person lives on as an ancestral spirit for a number of generations before being reabsorbed back into the cosmos. Many Daoist practices are aimed at enhancing one's physical and spiritual health, as well as extending one's lifespan in this life and the next.
Sacred texts	The **Daozang** (Treasury of the Dao) is a medieval collection of over 1400 sacred scrolls, organized into three sections (called "caverns"). Different Daoist schools prioritize different writings within this collection, but most schools acknowledge the importance of two of the earliest texts: the Daode jing (by Master Laozi) and the **Zhuangzi** (by **Master Zhuang**).
Key rituals	Daoism has many forms of official ritual including offering, petition, purification, initiation, consecration and ordination ceremonies.

JUDAISM	
Key facts	
No. of adherents (approx.)	14 million
Origins	Judaism traces its origins to the covenant between God and **Abraham** (c.1800 BCE) who left his homeland in Mesopotamia and settled in the land of Canaan (Israel). The covenant was passed on to his son (**Isaac**) and his grandson (**Jacob**). The most important event in Jewish history is the miraculous escape (the Exodus) of the Israelites from Egypt (c.1250 BCE) under the leadership of **Moses**. The **Torah** (Law) was subsequently revealed to Moses on **Mount Sinai**. After 40 years in the wilderness, the people entered the land of Canaan and established an independent kingdom with priesthood and temple.

Key facts (Continued)	
Subdivisions	• **Orthodox Judaism** upholds the value of tradition, stressing the ongoing importance of biblical **commandments** such as those pertaining to diet and the **Sabbath**. It is the official form of Judaism in Israel. • **Reform Judaism** is more liberal toward contemporary culture and, thus, more willing to adapt traditional teaching to new situations. For example, it allows vernacular language in worship and women's ordination. • **Conservative Judaism** takes a middle position between the Reform and Orthodox movements. There are also Jewish cultural streams such as **Ashkenazi** (from central and eastern Europe) and **Sephardic** (from the Iberian peninsula, northern Africa and the Middle East).
Transcendent reality	Judaism professes faith in one, supreme, personal God who created the universe. God has revealed his will via Moses and the **prophets**, and has intervened at key moments in history to save his chosen people. God is infinite and utterly beyond human imagination; thus idolatry is a grave sin and a constant danger.
Human existence	Humans are created in the image of God, and their destiny is to share eternal happiness with their creator in heaven. Most Jews believe that human persons are born and die just once, after which everyone faces divine judgment although some accept a limited form of reincarnation (gilgul). Jews are required to keep the divinely revealed Law, especially the 613 explicit commandments found in the Torah.
Sacred texts	The Jewish Bible, or **Tanach**, consists of the 5 books of the Law (Torah), the 8 books of the Prophets (Neviyim), and the 11 books of the Writings (Ketuvim). The **Talmud** is a detailed commentary on Tanach composed in two main forms around 500 CE.
Key rituals	The main rites of passage are circumcision, **bar mitzvah**, marriage and the funeral service. The sabbath (Saturday) is set aside as a day of strict rest.

CHRISTIANITY	
Key facts	
No. of adherents (approx.)	2.2 billion
Origins	**Jesus of Nazareth** (c.6 BCE–30 CE) is considered by Christians to be the long-awaited Jewish **Messiah** and also the incarnate Son of God. In a short public life that began with his baptism in the Jordan, Jesus preached the imminent coming of the kingdom of God in which sinners would find divine mercy and forgiveness. He is said to have worked many miracles in the tradition of **Moses** and **Elijah**, especially healing the sick. His message and person aroused serious opposition from the religious and political leadership and he was condemned to death by crucifixion. Christians believe that he was raised from the dead and appeared to his followers, commissioning them to continue his message and work.
Subdivisions	The main subdivisions of Christianity are a result of two historical moments: • Eastern Christianity (centered on Constantinople) and **Western Christianity** (centered on Rome) formally separated in the Great Schism of 1054. The Eastern churches are now known collectively as **Orthodox Christianity** (300 million). • The sixteenth-century Reformation led to a further division of Western Christianity into the (Roman) **Catholic Church** (1.1 billion) and many Protestant churches (850 million) such as the **Lutheran**, **Anglican**, **Calvinist** and **Baptist** traditions.
Transcendent reality	Christianity is essentially **monotheistic** in that it professes faith in one, supreme, personal God. However, the belief that Jesus is the human incarnation of God led to the concept of the **Trinity**: three divine persons, or modes of existence (Father, Son, and Holy Spirit) in the one divine essence (God).
Human existence	Human persons are born and die once, after which they face divine judgment. The virtuous enjoy heaven, which is a state of perfect, eternal bliss in communion with God and other beings. The wicked are condemned to hell, which is a state of eternal alienation from the creator. Christianity accepts the ongoing validity of the **Ten Commandments** as a fundamental moral guide but interprets them as imitation of Jesus who is the supreme model for human life.
Sacred texts	The Christian Bible consists of the Jewish Tanach (renamed as the **Old Testament**) and the 27 Christian books of the **New Testament**. Catholic and Orthodox Bibles also include some books found in the ancient Greek version of the Jewish Bible (the Septuagint) but not in Tanach.
Key rituals	Catholic and Orthodox churches recognize seven **sacraments** that are considered to have been established by **Christ**: **baptism**, confirmation, the **Eucharist**, holy orders, marriage, reconciliation and anointing of the sick. Protestant churches tend to recognize only two such rituals as having an explicit basis in the New Testament: baptism and the Eucharist.

ISLAM	
Key facts	
No. of adherents (approx.)	1.5 billion
Origins	**Muhammad** (c.570–632 CE) was a successful merchant based in **Mecca**. When he was about 40 years old, he received the first of a series of divine revelations, which continued until his death. Muhammad's monotheistic message met with opposition in Mecca, and eventually his small community was forced to migrate to **Medina** in 622 CE (the **Hijra**). Muhammad proved to be a successful leader in Medina where Islam consolidated and grew. After a series of battles, Mecca surrendered in 630 CE and Muhammad transformed its central shrine, the **Ka'bah**, into a symbol of the new faith. He died in 632 and is buried in Medina. His companion **Abu Bakr** was elected as the first **caliph**.
Subdivisions	The main subdivision in Islam is between the **Sunni** majority (1.3 billion) and the **Shi'ite** minority (250 million). Sunnis accept the election of Abu Bakr and his three successors (**Umar**, **Uthman** and **Ali**) as legitimate leaders (caliphs) of the early community. Shi'ites claim that the leadership should have passed immediately to Ali, who was Muhammad's son-in-law and cousin. Thus Ali, his wife (**Fatima**), his sons (**Hasan** and **Hussain**), and the line of true leaders (**imams**) have an important status in Shi'ite Islam.
Transcendent reality	Islam stresses the absolute oneness and transcendence of God (**Allah**). Thus, idolatry (**shirk**) is one of the gravest sins for a Muslim. God reveals his will through the prophets, of whom Muhammad is the last and greatest. God's will is encapsulated in the Qur'an.
Human existence	Islam believes that humans are born and die once. On the day of judgment at the end of the world, all will be held accountable: the just will be rewarded with the joys of Jannah (Paradise) while the wicked will be punished in Jahannam (hell).
Sacred texts	The holiest text in Islam is the **Qur'an**, which is a collection of the revelations received by Muhammad during his lifetime. The Qur'an is considered to be the literal word of God. Its authority is complemented, but not rivaled, by official collections of the sayings and example of the Prophet, which are known as **hadith**.
Key rituals	Islam ritually marks key moments in life such as birth, marriage and death. The Five Pillars of Sunni Islam are also an important aspect of practice: • **shahadah**: declaration of faith in God and his Prophet; • **salat**: formal prayers five times per day; • **zakat**: a percentage of income given to the poor; • **sawm**: daylight fasting during the month of **Ramadan**; • **hajj**: pilgrimage to Mecca.

ISLAM	
Key facts	
No. of adherents (approx.)	1.5 billion
Origins	Muhammad (570–632 CE) was a successful merchant based in Mecca. When he was about 40 years old, he received the first of a series of divine revelations, which continued until his death. Muhammad's monotheistic message met with opposition in Mecca and eventually his small community was forced to migrate to Medina in 622 (the hijra). Muhammad proved to be a successful leader in Medina, and Islam consolidated and grew. After a series of battles, Mecca surrendered, c. 630 CE, and Muhammad transformed its central shrine, the Ka'bah, into a symbol of the new faith. He died in 632 and is buried in Medina. His companion Abu Bakr was elected as the first caliph.
Subdivisions	The main subdivision in Islam is between the Sunni majority (1.3 billion) and the Shi'ite minority (250 million). This is about the election of Abu Bakr and his three successors, Umar, Uthman and Ali, elected imams/leaders of the early community. Shi'ites claim that the leadership should have passed immediately to Ali, who was Muhammad's son-in-law and cousin, that Ali, his wife Fatima, his sons Hasan and Husayn, and the line of the leaders or Imams, have an important status in Shi'ite Islam.
Transcendent reality	Islam stresses the absolute oneness and transcendence of God (Allah). This unity (tawhid) is one of the great tenets for a Muslim. God reveals his will through the prophets, of whom Muhammad is the last and greatest. God's will is recorded in the Qur'an.
Human existence	Islam believes that men and women will die and be raised on the day of judgment at the end of the world. All will be held accountable; the just will be rewarded with the joys of Jannah (Paradise), while the wicked will be punished in Jahannam (hell).
Sacred texts	The holiest text in Islam is the Qur'an, which is a collection of the revelations received by Muhammad during his lifetime. The Qur'an is considered to be the literal word of God. Its authority is complemented, but not rivalled, by official collections of the sayings and example of the Prophet, which are known as hadith.
Key rituals	Islam primarily marks key moments in life, such as birth, marriage and death. The Five Pillars of Sunni Islam are also an important aspect of practice: • shahadah: declaration of faith in God and his Prophet; • salat: formal prayers five times per day; • zakat: a percentage of income given to the poor; • sawm: daylight fasting during the month of Ramadan; • hajj: pilgrimage to Mecca.

Part I

Beyond Time and Space

1

Image

World Religions in Practice: A Comparative Introduction, Second Edition. Paul Gwynne.

CONTENTS

1.1 Introduction

At the heart of religion lies the belief in a transcendent reality that provides an overarching context for human life and all that it contains. Seen through religious eyes, this visible world is not the full story. There is a dimension beyond the visible that holds the key to the origin, the purpose and the ultimate destiny of the cosmos and its inhabitants. Where religions tend to diverge is on the specific nature of this dimension. Is it personal or impersonal? Is it one or many? Is it masculine or feminine? Is it fundamentally similar to or different from us? The answers to such questions can be found by investigating one of the principal practical ways in which Hindus, Buddhists, Daoists, Jews, Christians and Muslims access the transcendent – their use or non-use of the sacred image.

1.2 The Second Commandment

One of the most fundamental guides for religious and ethical life in Judaism is a list of ten commandments that Jews believe were revealed by God in ancient times.[1] The first commandment on the list consists of the simple statement "I am the Lord your God," which Jews interpret to mean that one must have religious faith. Belief in God is the first and foremost step. But it is the second commandment that holds the key to the Jewish understanding of the nature of divine reality. It begins with the phrase: "You shall have no other gods before me." This statement could be interpreted to mean that there are many gods but that the Jews should ensure that their god has priority: a position known as henotheism. However, the traditional Jewish interpretation has been that only one, true God exists. In other words, this is a monotheistic religion and one of the most serious sins is the interposing of "other (false) gods" before the One – idolatry.

The monotheistic bedrock of Judaism is manifest in a host of religious writings and practices, a classical example of which is the 13 Principles of the Jewish Faith (Box 1.1) enumerated by the outstanding twelfth-century philosopher **Maimonides**. His summary of the key elements of Jewish faith was converted into a poetic version known as

Box 1.1 The 13 Principles of the Jewish Faith (Maimonides)

1) God exists.
2) God is one.
3) God is incorporeal.
4) God is eternal.
5) God alone should be worshiped.
6) God has communicated through the prophets.
7) Moses was the greatest of the prophets.
8) The Torah is the word of God.
9) The Torah is authentic and cannot be changed.
10) God is aware of all of our actions.
11) God rewards the just and punishes the wicked.
12) The Messiah will come.
13) The dead will be resurrected.

Box 1.2 The Shema

Hear, O Israel: The Lord is our God, the Lord alone. You shall love the Lord your God with all your heart and with all your soul and with all your might. Keep these words that I am commanding you today in your heart. Recite them to your children and talk about them when you are at home and when you are away, when you lie down and when you rise. Bind them as a sign on your hand, fix them as an emblem on your forehead, and write them on the doorposts of your house and on your gates. (Deuteronomy 6:4–9).

the Yigdal hymn, which has been included in the daily worship service. Each morning in **synagogues** across the world, Jews chant:

> Exalted be the Living God and praised.
> He exists – unbounded by time in His existence.
> He is One – and there is no unity like His Oneness.
> Inscrutable and infinite is His Oneness.

Another striking statement of monotheism in the daily liturgy is the prayer that is considered by many to be the most important in Judaism: the **Shema** (Box 1.2). It opens with the declaration "Hear, O Israel: The Lord is our God, the Lord alone." The text goes on to exhort believers to love the one God with all of their being and to bring these words to mind "when you lie down and when you rise." In obedience to the command, the **rabbinic** tradition has incorporated the Shema into official evening and morning prayers. As the sun rises and sets each day, God's oneness is proclaimed by Jews at prayer in all corners of the world.

The Shema is not only verbally expressed on a regular basis at prayer, but is also literally worn on the body and fixed to doorways as a constant reminder of the divine unity. The same Deuteronomy text exhorts the believer to bind these words "as a sign on your hand, fix them as an emblem on your forehead and write them on the doorposts of your house and on your gates." Once again, in literal obedience to the divine command, the Shema is inscribed in black ink on parchment and placed inside special containers known as the tefillin and the mezuzah. The tefillin are small black boxes that are strapped to the forehead and left arm at weekday morning prayers, while the mezuzah is fixed to the doorposts of Jewish homes at eye level as a constant reminder of the oneness of God each time the believer passes. So essential is the idea of God's unity that it is placed before the Jewish mind and heart when they are stationary in prayer or on the move with their ordinary daily routine.

Given that Judaism is committed to belief in one God, how do Jews conceive of the deity? What images come to mind? The next line of the Yigdal hymn provides the beginning of an answer: "He has no semblance of a body nor is He corporeal; nor has His holiness any comparison." Although the Jewish scriptures and the Talmud occasionally refer to God's hands, eyes, mouth and other bodily parts, Jewish theology insists that such anthropomorphisms are metaphorical in nature and in no way imply that God is actually physical in any sense. Maimonides stressed the point by including the statement "God is incorporeal" among his 13 fundamental principles. The principle itself is concise, but Maimonides dedicated the first book in his major work, *Guide for the Perplexed*, to outlining the figurative nature of such language and insisting on the absolute difference between the Creator and creation. Human minds may legitimately use familiar concepts such as bodily features to imagine the divine, but to interpret that language literally would be to fail to appreciate the otherness of God and fall into idolatry. It would be to project finite qualities onto the infinite. God is, by definition, divine not human.

The principle that it is absolutely beyond our ability to express the fullness of God in word or form stands behind the remainder of the second commandment:

> You shall not make for yourself an idol, whether in the form of anything that is in heaven above or that is on the earth beneath or that is in the water under the earth. You shall not bow down to them or worship them; for I, the Lord your God, am a jealous God.[2]

The prohibition on images is not only aimed at avoiding worship of other gods, which would naturally undermine the monotheistic principle, but is also concerned with flawed attempts to depict the one true God. The ultimate mystery that shrouds the deity should never be forgotten. Among the world religions, Judaism in particular stresses the otherness and invisibility of God, which is the original meaning of the term kadosh, usually translated as "holy" but perhaps more accurately rendered "different." The God of Judaism is truly transcendent and any attempt to depict the Holy Other is doomed to failure. It can only lead to misinterpretation and idolatry. The biblical episode that perhaps best captures the Jewish concern not to reduce God to something finite via an image or idol is when Moses destroys the golden calf that the Israelites had fashioned while he was on the heights of Sinai. The text tells us that not only does Moses melt the statue, but he also grinds it into powder and casts the remains into the waters, which the sinful community must then drink.[3] The point is thrust home in graphic fashion that any form of idolatry is intolerable.

Thus, it is not surprising that one will never see statues, paintings, or similar realistic imagery of God in Jewish synagogues and homes. As for creatures, the **Shulhan Aruch** allows two-dimensional, but not three-dimensional, human and animal images, and even then it prefers that only part of the human figure be depicted.[4] As a result, Jewish art has understandably focused on more abstract patterns and elaborate decorations. Artists poured their aesthetic energies into ceremonial objects such as candelabra, scrolls and containers. All of these can be an aid to prayer but, when a Jew turns to worship, there is no mediating image or tangible object that represents God or connects the believer with the divine. At the far end of a synagogue, towards which the congregation faces, there is no statue or painting or altar (Figure 1.1). Instead, there is a receptacle, decorated and marked by a burning candle, inside which are kept the scrolls of the Jewish scriptures: divine words not divine images.

The synagogue itself is usually oriented toward the holy city, **Jerusalem**, where the **Temple** once stood. The last Temple was destroyed by the Roman armies in 70 CE. There is a legend that when the Roman general, Titus, entered its inner sanctum, called the Holy of Holies, he expected to find either immense treasure or a statue of some sort that portrayed the God of this stubborn, resistant people. Instead he found nothing: the room was empty. The God of Israel is one and transcendent, indivisible and invisible.

In fact, the Holy of Holies did once house an important object that disappeared into the mists of history long before Titus arrived on the scene. It was a rectangular chest known as the **Ark of the Covenant**. Over it were fixed two winged seraphs facing each other from either end, creating a space above the lid, which was known as the Seat of Mercy. According to Jewish belief, the Ark contained the very tablets that Moses received from God on Sinai with the Ten Commandments inscribed on them: again,

Figure 1.1 Interior of a Jewish synagogue.
(Reproduced with kind permission of iStock.)

divine words not divine images. As for the symbolic seat between the seraphs, on which the God of Israel was "enthroned" as king – it was empty. No man-made image was ever placed there. For the Jewish faith, past and present, God is indivisible and invisible. But Judaism is not the only religion in which empty space stands as the most appropriate symbol of the divine transcendence. Something very similar can be found in the town of Mecca.

☪ 1.3 Shirk

In the center of the courtyard of the great mosque of Mecca stands one of the most recognizable structures in the Islamic world – the Ka'bah. As the name vaguely suggests, it is cubic in shape, standing about 50 feet above a marble base. Constructed from gray stone, it is usually covered by the kiswa, a black cloth embellished with golden calligraphy. Islamic tradition tells us that it was built by Adam based on a heavenly prototype and subsequently rebuilt by Abraham and his son, **Ishmael**, after being destroyed in the waters of the Flood. In Muhammad's day, the Ka'bah was the focus of religious practice in pre-Islamic Arabia. Local tribes would make annual pilgrimages to the shrine which contained, at the time, more than 300 statuettes representing the pantheon of local gods.

In the year 630 CE, when Muhammad returned triumphant to his native town after nearly a decade as governor of Medina, he ordered all the statuettes to be destroyed. But the Ka'bah was retained and transformed into the axis of a new religious world. Five times a day, every day of the year, over one billion Muslims recite their daily prayers facing toward the Ka'bah as they fulfill one of the most fundamental requirements of their religion. It is a powerful global gesture unifying worshipers across a myriad of cultures and nations. The question is: What are they all facing? With what symbol did Muhammad replace the hundreds of pre-existing pagan statues inside the Ka'bah? The answer is illuminating – nothing. Apart from some hanging lanterns and a small table for perfumes, there is no sacred object or religious icon of any sort that attempts to portray God.[5] Like the Holy of Holies in the ancient Jewish Temple, at the core of Islam lies an indivisible and invisible mystery.

Muhammad's destruction of the many statues in the Ka'bah reflects the first key theological principle concerning the nature of God in Islam. It is a principle succinctly expressed in the shahadah – the first of the Five Pillars of Islam (Box 1.3) and its fundamental credal statement.

Box 1.3 The Five Pillars of Sunni Islam

Shahadah	the witness of faith
Salat	the five daily prayers
Zakat	the religious tax
Sawm	the Ramadan fast
Hajj	the pilgrimage to Mecca

> I bear witness that there is no god but God;
> I bear witness that Muhammad is His prophet.[6]

In direct and unambiguous terms, the shahadah announces Islam's unshakeable belief in the oneness and uniqueness of God – the principle known as tawhid. Alongside the Jewish faith, Islam stands as a resolute voice of unqualified monotheism, asserting that there is only one Absolute Being and that it is by nature undifferentiated and without equal. It is no coincidence that such a bedrock article of faith is woven inextricably into daily practice. The shahadah itself constitutes a key component of the haunting call from the tops of mosques that beckons Muslims to turn from their mundane activities and face Mecca in daily prayer. The same assertion of monotheism constitutes the gateway to Islam, since to utter the shahadah with clear-minded intention before two witnesses is sufficient for one to convert to Islam. Embracing the concept of tawhid is the key to joining the Muslim religious community. Tawhid is also one of the major recurring themes in Islam's holiest book, the Qur'an. An oft-quoted text is the brief 112th chapter:

> Say: He is Allah, the One,
> Allah is He on whom all depend,
> He does not beget, nor is He begotten,
> And (there is) none like Him.[7]

The converse of tawhid is shirk, which literally means "making a partner or an equal" and is conventionally translated into English as "idolatry." The attribution of partners or equals to Allah is to deny the principle of God's uniqueness and unity, undermining the very foundations of the religion. As such, shirk is one of the gravest sins in Islam.[8]

The pre-Islamic Arabic religious pantheon is a classical example of shirk, against which Muhammad's monotheistic message was aimed. The smashing of the idols of the Ka'bah is symbolic of the assertion of God's utter uniqueness over any form of polytheism. Furthermore, theologies of God that seem to compromise the inner unity of the godhead, such as the Christian Trinity, are also rejected as shirk by the Qur'an.

> O followers of the Book! Do not exceed the limits in your religion and do not speak (lies) against Allah, but (speak) the truth. The Messiah, Isa son of Marium is only an apostle of Allah and His Word which He communicated to Marium and a spirit from Him; believe therefore in Allah and His apostles and say not Three. Desist, it is better for you; Allah is only one God.[9]

The dangers of idolatry are not restricted to other religions that speak of many gods or a plurality within the godhead. It can happen within Islam itself. For many Muslims the sin is committed even when one approaches Allah via the intercession of another being.[10] In the strict Saudi Arabian **Wahhabi** school, shirk can occur when Muslim pilgrims display excessive devotion at the graves of saints, including Muhammad's tomb in Medina. Even the Birthday of the Prophet, a festival that the outsider might expect to be one of the most celebrated in the Islamic calendar, has no special prayers or services and is downplayed for fear of deifying Muhammad. The founder of Islam is considered to be the Seal of the Prophets and the greatest human ever to have lived, but in the end he is human not divine. There is no God but Allah, and Muhammad is his Prophet – nothing more.

The insistence on the unity of God does not imply that there is no richness in God. Islamic tradition stresses the simplicity of God but also speaks of the 99 divine "names" – a litany of qualities that traditionally begins with the two attributes that preface every chapter of the Qur'an: "In the Name of Allah, the most compassionate, the most merciful." The 99 names are recited in private meditation by Muslims with the assistance of the tasbih with its 33 beads. As in the case of Catholic and Buddhist rosaries, the beads are turned as the believer mentally moves along the list, although the tasbih today often serves more secular purposes such as worry beads for restless hands or as a fashion accessory.

If Muhammad's destruction of the idols of the Ka'bah reflects the key Islamic principle of monotheism, his decision not to replace them with any tangible symbol or icon reflects another key principle: **aniconism**. Allah is beyond all images. The prohibition of shirk means not only that there is no equal to God but also that there can be no finite image or object that is worthy of representing the Infinite One or through which the worshiper seeks a more palpable experience of the deity's presence. When Muslims enter into the sacred moment of official prayer five times a day, the only physical requirements are that they stand on clean ground and face Mecca. There is no icon or statue or altar between them and the focus of their adoration. Even if the prayers are recited inside a mosque, the only tangible object toward which the congregation faces is a decorated niche in the wall known as the mihrab. The mihrab is usually designed in the shape of a doorway or an arch but it does not lead to any room or inner sanctum. It is basically an architectural device indicating the **qibla** – the direction of Mecca. The minds of the worshipers who stand before the mihrab focus beyond the walls of their mosque to the distant Ka'bah, which itself is devoid of any sacred symbol or object. The God of Islam lies beyond any earthly horizon, rendering our attempts to portray him futile.

As in Jewish synagogues, a visitor to a mosque might be struck by the notable absence of religious images, pictures, statues and icons. The rejection of any artistic form that can lead to idolatry is manifest in the ambience of Muslim places of prayer. Instead of portraits and anthropomorphic figures, one finds instead more abstract themes such as geometric forms, floral designs and calligraphic patterns (Figure 1.2). The latter typically draw on verses from the Qur'an and other Islamic literature, capitalizing on the graceful, flowing style of Arabic script. The aesthetic dimension is far from absent in Islamic culture, but it tends to be expressed in written rather than pictorial form.

A striking example of the Islamic duty to avoid all potential forms of shirk in its sacred buildings is the case of the Hagia Sophia (Holy Wisdom) in Istanbul. Originally constructed as a Christian basilica, its internal walls were adorned with a magnificent array of holy mosaics. When the city fell to the Ottoman Turks in 1453, the building was converted into a mosque and, because of the **iconoclastic** demands of the new faith, its mosaics covered in plaster. One must admire the broadmindedness of the Ottoman sultans who periodically removed the plaster in order to maintain the artwork beneath.[11] The initial decision to cover the icons was not based on an inherent Islamic disdain for art or beauty as such, but rather on a deep-seated conviction that there can be no images in a house of prayer. With regard to the insistence on strict monotheism and the general ban of images in worship, Jews and Muslims are in fundamental agreement – God is utterly one and ultimately transcendent. But what is the position of the original Christian builders of the Hagia Sophia?

Figure 1.2 Interior of the Blue Mosque, Istanbul.
(Reproduced with kind permission of iStock.)

1.4 Incarnate Son

In the year 726 CE, the Byzantine Emperor Leo III published an edict declaring that all holy images were in direct contravention of the second commandment and, as idols, should be destroyed. Soldiers immediately began to implement his orders. Their removal of a popular image of Christ from the gate of the imperial palace in Constantinople sparked a general riot and constituted the first act in what historians call the Iconoclastic Controversy. The term iconoclast literally means "image-breaker," and the controversy itself refers to two distinct periods of Byzantine imperial opposition to the veneration of religious images during the eighth and ninth centuries. Coincidentally, it was the female regent who brought an end to the conflict in both periods. In 787 CE the Empress Irene organized a council of bishops that condemned iconoclasm as heresy. The decision was endorsed by the papacy and the council came to be recognized by most Christians as the seventh and last **ecumenical council** of the Church.[12] Similarly in 843 CE it was the Empress Theodora who restored the icons to churches and, since that date, **Eastern Christianity** has commemorated the event on the First Sunday of Greater Lent, which is known as The Triumph of Orthodoxy.

Historians suggest that there were a number of reasons for Leo's initial move against religious icons including his desire to control the monasteries, which were bastions of icon veneration. But behind the political motive was the theological argument that the veneration of images violated the second commandment. Although it eventually dispensed with many of the ritual obligations contained in the Jewish scriptures, Christianity never abandoned the essence of the religious and moral principles given to Moses on Sinai. Thus, it was argued that the ban on making and revering images remained in force. It was presumed that Christians shared the same conviction as Muslims and Jews: that God is utterly transcendent and beyond any visual depiction. So how did the opponents of iconoclasm possibly counter such an argument and prevail?

The key protagonist against the ban on icons was a monk living in Muslim-controlled Bethlehem named John of Damascus. John argued that the commandment forbidding images of God had been superseded by nothing less than the Incarnation. What did John mean by that? Something about the Christian understanding of divinity itself overturns the once valid biblical conviction that God cannot be portrayed in any finite material manner. For Christians, something has actually changed in God and it is here that Christianity begins to part ways with its monotheistic cousins, Judaism and Islam.

The Christian modification of traditional Jewish monotheism was not a sudden decision or a smooth journey. It took several centuries for Christians to agree on both the concept itself and the most appropriate language to express it. One of the most widely accepted and frequently recited versions of the eventual redefinition of God is found in the words of the **Nicene Creed** (Box 1.4).[13] What strikes the reader is that apart from four short assertions at the end, the entire Creed is concerned with the true identity of Jesus and his relationship to the one God of Israel, designated by Christians as "the Father."

For many the answer to the question of the founder's identity is summed up in his most common epithet, which now functions as a surname: Christ. The Greek word *Christos* literally means "anointed one" and is a direct translation of the Hebrew term *Masiah* (Messiah). The identification of Jesus as the Messiah constitutes one of the most fundamental differences between Christianity and Judaism, but it does not quite explain why the Christian idea of divinity and the use of images in worship vary from the Jewish and the Islamic vision of one invisible God. Ultimately, the Jewish Messiah is a human figure, a descendant of King **David** who, in the last days, will restore Israel to its former glory and righteousness. But the Nicene Creed goes much further than this. It states that Jesus is an incarnation of the divine Son who existed from before creation itself ("eternally begotten of the Father") and who is as fully divine as the Father ("God from God"; "of one being with the Father"). This belief was not based on the title Christ but on another title given to Jesus by the early Christians: *Kyrios* ("Lord"). This was the same term used in Greek translations of the Jewish scriptures for the Hebrew word *Adonai*: a sacrosanct title reserved exclusively for the one God.

Box 1.4 The Nicene Creed

We believe in one God,
the Father, the Almighty,
maker of heaven and earth,
of all that is, seen and unseen.

We believe in one Lord, Jesus Christ,
the only son of God,
eternally begotten of the Father,
God from God, Light from Light,
true God from true God,
begotten, not made,
of one being with the Father.
Through him all things were made.
For us and for our salvation
he came down from heaven:
by the power of the Holy Spirit
he became incarnate from the Virgin Mary,
and was made man.
For our sake he was crucified under Pontius Pilate;
he suffered death and was buried.
On the third day he rose again
in accordance with the Scriptures;
he ascended into heaven
and is seated at the right hand of the Father.
He will come again in glory
to judge the living and the dead,
and his kingdom will have no end.

We believe in the Holy Spirit, the Lord, the giver of life,
who proceeds from the Father (and the Son).
With the Father and the Son
he is worshiped and glorified.
He has spoken through the Prophets.
We believe in one holy catholic and apostolic Church.
We acknowledge one baptism for the forgiveness of sins.
We look for the resurrection of the dead,
and the life of the world to come. AMEN.

One can see the tension building as the Creed progresses. Christians believe in one God but are compelled to say more. The assertion of the full divinity of Jesus leads naturally to a revision of their understanding of God. There is talk of a divine Son who is distinct from the divine Father and who, unlike the Father, becomes enfleshed as a human person in time and space. Something of God remains utterly transcendent (Father) while something becomes incarnate (Son). The Creed goes on to complete the classical picture by introducing the third element (Spirit) who is described by many Christian theologians as the perfect reciprocal love between the other two divine "persons."

God is one and yet God is also three: Father, Son and Holy Spirit. This is the essence of the Christian doctrine of the Trinity and it is a direct consequence of the declaration of Jesus's divine status. Christians still count themselves as monotheists alongside Jews and Muslims, but belief in a God who is simultaneously one and three makes it a modified monotheism.

Despite the esoteric nature of the doctrine of the Trinity and the struggle by generations of Christian theologians to make sense of this mystery of mysteries, it is very much woven into everyday Christian language and practice. Many churches, colleges and other Christian institutions around the world bear the name "Trinity." Catholic and Orthodox Christians make a sign of the cross during private and public prayer by touching their forehead and each shoulder in turn with accompanying words that signify the Father, Son and Holy Spirit.[14] Christian clergy bless their congregations with the same cruciform gesture in the name of the three divine persons. Young and old neophytes are baptized into the Christian faith with water and an ancient formula that makes specific reference to the Trinity.

However, the Trinity has never been a major theme in Christian art and when it is the subject of a painting or icon, or more rarely a statue, problems quickly arise. The artist usually has no difficulty in portraying the Son but it is a different matter when it comes to the other two persons. While Orthodox Christianity forbids any attempt to depict the Father,[15] the Catholic tradition has allowed the use of a gray-bearded man and a dove to represent the Father and the Spirit respectively. For many it is poor theology. Strictly speaking, only the Son should be depicted in finite worldly form since only the Son becomes part of the finite world.

It was the doctrine of the Incarnation that John of Damascus appealed to in his battle with the iconoclasts. In response to the accusation that the veneration of sacred images was a violation of the second commandment, John argued that the prohibition of holy images had been abrogated by the Incarnation itself. If the Son of God has truly taken on human nature and become a part of the created world in a real sense, then the images are legitimate. They depict not an idol but the reality of the God-man. In John's thinking, the real danger of iconoclasm was that it failed to grasp the significance of the most important event in human history. For the Christian, the invisible, transcendent God had become visible and incarnate. God now had a human face.

It was not the last time in the Christian story that iconoclasm was an issue. Sixteenth-century Protestant reformers such as Calvin and Zwingli expressly condemned the potential idolatry linked to the use of statues, relics and other holy objects.[16] The climax of Reformation iconoclasm was the Beeldenstorm when, in the summer of 1556, several monasteries were attacked and statues destroyed in what is now the Netherlands and Belgium. Protestant Christianity is still wary and its preference for churches without statues and icons is reminiscent of the synagogue and the mosque. On the other hand, Orthodox and Catholic Christianity embraced the eighth-century victory over iconoclasm and their churches are typically characterized by mosaics, murals, stained-glass windows, frescoes, paintings and statues. Many of these may depict human figures such as Mary and the saints, but the most prominent place is usually reserved for an image of Christ. It may be as an infant at his mother's breast, dying victim on the cross or glorious risen Lord but the principle is the same – the incarnate Son is the visible icon of the invisible God (Figure 1.3).

Figure 1.3 Christian mosaics in the Hagia Sophia, Istanbul.
(Reproduced with kind permission of iStock.)

Although it is often categorized together with the other monotheistic faiths of Judaism and Islam, on closer inspection Christianity has a different hue. In the sense that it admits a plurality within the one godhead, the conceivability of divine incarnation in human form and the widespread use of sacred images in worship, it actually resembles not so much its cousin religions of the Middle East but that ancient religious system of the Orient, beyond the Indus River.

ॐ 1.5 Murti

In the ancient Hindu texts known as the Shilpa Shastras, one finds highly detailed instructions on how to design and make a sacred statue. Prescriptions depend upon the divine subject whose image is being created, and include meticulous guidelines with regard to posture, shape, features, hand gestures, color, symbols and so forth. Once complete, the image is still not ready for use in worship until a special consecration ceremony is held. Priests recite the blessing formula and purify the image with substances such as honey and butter. By touching various parts of the statue and breathing into it, the sacred minister facilitates the "installation" of divine presence in the object. The high point comes when the priest uncovers the sealed eyes, often with a special ceremonial needle. The entire ritual is appropriately named prana pratishta – the infusion of breath. From this moment, what was merely dead wood or stone becomes for the worshiper a sacred icon and a channel for divine blessings – a **murti** (Figure 1.4).

Figure 1.4 Sacred image (murti) of the Hindu goddess Durga.
(Reproduced with kind permission of iStock.)

For many Hindu schools, it is almost impossible to envisage worship without the murti.[17] In most Hindu traditions, the sacred image is an integral component of ritual adoration whether in the public space of a temple or the private sphere of a home. It is the center of attention and the heart of all symbolic acts during the service. Typically a statue will be kept concealed in the inner sanctum of a temple or behind a simple curtain or cabinet door in homes. At the time of worship, a portable murti will be brought out into a special viewing room in the temple, or simply uncovered in the domestic context.

The fact that the climax of the consecration ceremony involves uncovering the eyes indicates the importance of the visual for the Hindu. Seeing is all important and the eyes of the murti are often disproportionately large or highlighted in some way. In fact, Hindus often refer to the practice of worshiping before a murti as darshana, which literally means "an audience." The believer comes to the deity just as a humble subject might come before the king, in the hope that they will be granted a hearing for their concerns. The royal encounter theme is also reflected in the ritual actions performed on the murti during worship. Each gesture is meant to represent the cordialities that one would normally extend to an important visitor in one's house. First, the face, arms and feet of the statue are washed or sprinkled with water, just as a weary traveler might cleanse and refresh themselves after a tiring journey. The murti is then dressed in splendid clothing and adorned with jewelry, flowers and perfumes. Finally a meal is prepared and placed before the special guest for their consumption. Moreover, the term darshana can also connote religious vision; it is the fervent hope of the worshiper to actually "see" the deity through the image in a powerful, mystical sense.

Given the prominent role that the murti plays in Hindu worship, it is not surprising that adherents of the monotheistic religions have often branded the practice as idolatrous. However, the Hindu devotee is fully aware that the infinite cannot be captured or exhausted by a finite man-made statue. The murti itself is not the object of adoration and prayer, but functions as a tangible sign of the presence and power of transcendent reality. For the Hindu, the murti is the physical channel of divine energy, a visible point of access between heaven and earth. Although Hindus would agree with Jews and Muslims that the Absolute is beyond all worldly forms, nevertheless, along with many Christians, they also assert that it can be effectively encountered via sacred symbols and images.

In Hindu theology, the justification for the use of visible images to symbolize invisible divinity is based on the twin concepts of nirguna and saguna. The former refers to the utterly transcendent nature of the Absolute, which is beyond any attribute or quality that can be envisaged by the human mind. Nirguna is the ineffable, incomprehensible, elusive nature of the Absolute that remains forever shrouded in mystery. However, in order for the human mind to approach and worship ultimate mystery, it is appropriate to symbolize it in concrete form – saguna. In this way what is abstract and transcendent is conceived of and worshiped in a form that is more recognizable such as the human-like deities Vishnu, Shiva, or the Mother Goddess. For the various Hindu traditions that worship one of these main manifestations of the Absolute, there is both dissimilarity and similarity between transcendent reality and the empirical world. Divinity will always transcend the image depicted by the murti, but something of divinity is authentically captured in the artistic representation as well.

The difference–likeness tension is also reflected in the features of the murti itself. Sometimes the object is non-anthropomorphic such as sacred stones or the phallic **linga** of Shiva. More often the murti is anthropomorphic and each particular deity is identifiable by symbols and features specified in the Shilpa Shastras.[18] Even though the Hindu deity is generally portrayed as human-like, there are also non-human and superhuman features such as the elephant head of the popular Ganesha or the many arms that hold various objects – another reminder that there is still a significant difference between the divine and the human.

Mention of Vishnu, Shiva and the Mother Goddess raises another aspect of Hinduism that is often of concern to monotheistic outsiders: its apparent polytheism. The full Hindu pantheon is said to total over three hundred million gods. However, things are not always as they seem, especially in the Hindu universe. In practice, individual Hindus tend to devote themselves to one particular divine figure or ishta devata, rather than worship the entire pantheon. For example, in the **Shaivite** and **Vaishnavite** traditions, the figure of Shiva or Vishnu respectively is considered to be the one true divine being while other deities are secondary spirits, incapable of bringing definitive liberation. So, although the heavens are full of various quasi-divine beings, there are traditions within

Hinduism that profess an ultimate single deity who is the proper object of worship above them all.

In the other major Hindu theological tradition, the Advaita, each of the many gods provides an insight into the one ultimate mystery. In this school, divine figures such as Shiva, Vishnu, or the Mother Goddess are like the multiple colors of a beam of light refracted through a prism. Each captures something of the richness of transcendent reality. The term in Hinduism that best denotes the One is Brahman. It is the one ultimate source of all truth and goodness, one fundamental ground of all existence, the origin and end of all things. It is even beyond personification and is better understood as an impersonal Absolute rather than a personal God as in the Abrahamic religions.[19]

Just as the concept of Trinity suggests that Christianity is not simply monotheistic, so too the concepts of ishta devata and Brahman suggest that the many traditions that are categorized under the generic title of Hinduism cannot simply be described as polytheistic. Both religions acknowledge a mix of singularity and plurality within transcendent reality. Unity and differentiation coincide within absolute being.

This is not the only interesting connection between Hinduism and Christianity with regard to practical worship and its implications for a theology of transcendent reality. The widespread use of sacred images in both faiths presumes a fundamental similarity between divinity and humanity. This similarity is expressed in concrete terms via the notion of incarnation. In Christianity, the incarnation of a divine person in human nature has occurred once, and only once, in all of history. It is a salvific event of unparalleled proportion that has transformed both divine and human nature forever. In Vaishnavite Hinduism, there has been a series of incarnations as part of the gracious activity of Lord Vishnu who takes on creaturely form in times of crisis in order to save the world:

> I come into being from age to age with the purpose of fixing dharma – as a refuge for those who do good and as a doom for those who do evil.[20]

Hindus call these incarnations the **avatars** of Vishnu. Over 20 are mentioned in Hindu literature, but tradition highlights nine major ones, with a tenth expected at the end of this age. Commentators have noted how the list seems to reflect an evolutionary progress from sea creature to terrestrial animal to human (Box 1.5). Although there are clear differences between the 10 mythological avatars of Hinduism and the claim to a

Box 1.5 The 10 Avatars of Vishnu

1) Matsya, the fish
2) Kurma, the tortoise
3) Varaha, the boar
4) Narasimha, the man-lion
5) Vamana, the dwarf
6) Parashurama, the hero with the ax
7) Rama
8) Krishna
9) Buddha (or Balarama)
10) Kalki, the one to come

single historical incarnation in Christianity, nevertheless both religions accept the notion that the infinite gulf between the divine and the human can be bridged by the gracious descent of the former into our world. Just as Jewish and Islamic iconoclasm underlines the fundamental difference between the divine and the human, the Christian icon and the Hindu murti attest to a genuine similarity as well.

A pantheon of gods who are approached via sacred images that are awakened through a special ritual and an ultimate formless One that cannot be depicted in pictorial manner are key characteristics not only of the Hindu faith. They are also features of that ancient Chinese religious tradition whose temples are filled with statues and paintings of its many gods but which takes its name from a mysterious reality that lies beyond all images.

1.6 Opening the Radiance

There are many forms of Daoist worship rituals but one of the most common is performed before a sacred altar located in a temple, shrine or even in the private space of one's own home. Typically, the worshiper will present gifts such as flowers, fruit or tea but a key aspect is the raising of an incense (joss) stick with palms pressed together and eyes closed. Bodily gestures may include standing, kneeling, bowing or prostrating on a special mat while the smoke of the burning sandalwood wafts upward as a sign of reverence and petition. In temples, altar attendants may ring bells as the visitor bows, allowing the sound to end naturally just as it is appropriate not to extinguish the joss stick but to allow it to burn down without interference. The arrangement of Daoist altars varies across schools and according to the particular ritual being performed but there is usually a standard set of symbolic objects. These include: an incense burner; five bowls of fruit and food; three cups containing water, tea and rice grains; two candles; and a sacred lamp. Behind all of these symbols, occupying central place on the altar, is an image of the particular deity being worshiped and petitioned (Figure 1.5). In other words, one of the most important ways in which divinity can be accessed is via the use of the sacred image.

The image itself may be a two-dimensional painting on a special scroll or a three-dimensional statue, typically made of wood or clay. Often they are constructed in portable form so that they can be carried in formal procession out of the temple and through the neighborhood. As with the Hindu murti, these objects serve a profoundly religious purpose in Daoism and, not surprisingly, there is a hallowed and ancient tradition of consecrating sacred images, especially statues. The ritual is known as kaiguang, which literally means "opening the radiance."[21] As the word suggests, the principal aim of the verbal invocations and physical actions is to invite the deity to enter into the object and infuse it with the numinous cosmic energy known as **qi** (pronounced "chee"). In one sense, the statue is activated so that it is no longer an empty shell but a conduit for divine power and favor. A common way to symbolize the empowering of the image is for the priest to paint a third eye on the statue's forehead with cinnabar. Such a rite is appositely described as an "eye-opening" ceremony, implying that through this material channel, the person can now be seen and heard clearly by the deity whose undivided attention is being sought.

So who precisely is depicted by these holy, consecrated images? The answer is that an altar image could be any one of the hundreds of gods that inhabit the Daoist pantheon.

Figure 1.5 Daoist images on an altar.
(Reproduced with kind permission of iStock.)

Many of these beings are humans who were elevated to divine rank because of their heroism or outstanding acts; others are gods who began their existence in these celestial realms. The point is that there is certainly more than one god. At first glance, Daoism, like Hinduism, appears to be unmistakably polytheist. As with other religious traditions, individual gods can be identified by the conventional iconographic symbols used for their images.

Moreover, these gods are not of equal status or importance. Again, as with Hinduism, they are ranked according to a definite heavenly hierarchy, which mirrors the bureaucracy of imperial China. This ranking is reflected in the position given to a god within the temple layout. The higher the rank, the more central the location. Popular Daoist deities include: the Primordial Goddess of the Cerulean Mists (Bixia yuanjun) who protects women and children; the Dipper Mother (Doumu) who is a salvific figure like the Buddhist **Guanyin**; the God of Thunder (Leigong) who is associated with exorcism and purification; the God of Literature (Wenchang) who watches over scholars and students; and the God of Medicine (Yaowang) who is the patron of physicians. Presiding over all of these deities is the **Jade Emperor** (Yuhuang dadi). He is a sort of cosmocrat whose chief function is to dispense justice by reward and punishment. In this task he is assisted by other gods who report to him as officials might report to the earthly emperor. The Jade Emperor is typically seated on a throne with imperial robes, wearing a flat-topped crown embedded with pearls, and holding a tablet in both hands.

Although the Jade Emperor is the high god of the traditional Chinese pantheon, Daoism historically installed several deities above him in the hierarchy. Thus, at the centre of a Daoist temple, one would usually find images of three bearded men seated on thrones, each holding their personal iconographic symbol and wearing a distinctive colored robe. Described in popular literature as the "Daoist Trinity", they are The Three Pure Ones (Sanqing).[22] Each of them is entitled tianzin ("heavenly elder") and occupies his own particular heavenly realm. The central figure – the position of host in Chinese culture – is Yuanshi tianzun (Lord of First Matter). Robed in blue, he holds a flaming pearl that represents the first phase of the beginning of the cosmos. On his left – the position of the first guest – is Lingbao tianzun (Lord of the Spiritual Jewel). Robed in red, he carries the ruyi – an ancient Chinese scepter that symbolizes authority. Lingbao is associated with the second phase of creation, namely the separation of yin and yang from the primordial matter. On the right of Yuanshi – the position of the second guest – is Daode tianzun (Lord of the Way and its Virtue). Robed in yellow, he is usually depicted with white hair and holding a fan that symbolizes the third phase of creation, namely the spread of truth and order. In order to teach living beings the truth, Daode tianzun occasionally becomes incarnate in human form, including the founding figure Laozi.

The Three Pure Ones and the objects that they hold represent the three initial stages of creation according to Daoist cosmogony. But what came before them? According to the classical text, the Daode jing: "The Dao generated One; the One generated Two; the Two generated Three; the Three generated the myriad beings."[23] So, prior to the emergence of the Three Pure Ones, there existed, and still exists, Absolute Reality itself. This is the ultimate source of all being, the primordial non-differentiation (wu wuji) from which all reality emanates: the Dao. This is not a personal Creator God as in the Abrahamic religions, but it is infinite, unfathomable mystery. The Dao pervades all things in the universe but it also lies beyond all things as ultimate origin and end. In many ways the Dao resembles Brahman in Hinduism and, like Hinduism, Daoism is both polytheistic and monistic. There are myriads of gods but behind them all is the Dao.

In fact, the word Dao is insufficient to capture the mystery, which is formless and ineffable. As the Daode jing states in its opening line: "The Dao that can be spoken is not the constant Dao."[24] Hence, the Three Pure Ones are the highest form of divinity that can be legitimately depicted through a finite image; the Dao cannot. As with the invisible God of the Abrahamic faiths and the formless Brahman of Hinduism, the Dao, as Ultimate Reality, rightly has no iconography.

The term Dao is often translated as the Way or the Path. In this sense, the term means the natural patterns of this universe, which emanate from Ultimate Reality. This second meaning is more about cosmology than cosmogony; more about the way the world works than how it came into existence. It is the task of all followers of the Dao to be aware of these innate patterns in the world and ensure that they live their lives in harmony with them. This is the fundamental goal that shapes the vast array of Daoist practices, ranging from gymnastics and dietetics to divination and meditation. At this level, there is a symbol that profoundly expresses the most basic pattern in the universe: the harmonious balance of opposites. Known as **taijitu** (literally "diagram of the supreme ultimate"), it depicts the dynamic, complementary relationship between yin and yang, which is found in all natural phenomena (Figure 1.6). The origin of the yin–yang concept is a hill with one side in shade (yin) and the other in sunshine (yang). The yin–yang pattern is typically applied to other dualities such as female–male, earth–heaven, moon–sun, dark–light, cold–heat, low–high, heavy–light, inward–outward and so on. The taijitu replaced the older image of a tiger and a dragon: the pair of animals that can still be seen guarding Daoist temple gates today.[25] The taijitu itself not only functions as the widely accepted

Figure 1.6 The Taijitu. (Reproduced with kind permission of Fotolia.)

badge of Daoism, but it can be found in many areas of practical Daoism – such as on flags, logos, temple floors and clerical robes – reminding believers of the fundamental balance between opposites that is necessary to be in harmony with the Dao.

The Daoist mix of polytheistic iconography and monistic iconoclasm is strongly reminiscent of the Hindu tradition and its attempts to balance nirguna and saguna. Yet both religions have intersections with the second great Indian religious tradition. As noted earlier, the ninth avatar of Vishnu is often listed as the former Indian prince who found enlightenment in the forest, whilst the Daoist hierarchy includes the goddess Guanyin who is also a popular heavenly figure in Buddhism.

1.7 The Three Bodies

The first period of explicit Buddhist art commences with the reign of the Mauryan emperor **Ashoka** (c.273–232 BCE), who converted to Buddhism and promoted the new faith through extensive construction projects. What is striking in this earliest period is the absence of any human representations of the founder. Typically, the Buddha is represented by abstract symbols such as a wheel (symbolizing his teaching), the bodhi tree (under which he received **Enlightenment**), a lion (a popular theme under Ashoka), a lotus plant (Buddha's purity in a soiled world), a footprint (his impact on the world) or even an empty throne (his absence). Some speculate that the early avoidance of any likeness springs from the Buddha's own wish that there be no representations of his physical form after his death. The trend changes dramatically in the first century CE in northern India when anthropomorphic statues and sculptures suddenly begin to appear. To this day tens of millions of Buddha images adorn temples and homes throughout the world.

The most common posture for the Buddha image is a meditation position with legs crossed (Figure 1.7), although sometimes he is depicted reclining in death, sitting on a chair or walking on a missionary journey. The facial expression is usually one of serenity and calm, a result of the advanced state of mind that comes from enlightenment. At first, the sitting Buddha images may look monotonously identical but, upon closer inspection, the onlooker notices that the positions of the hands vary. These are the **mudras** of a Buddha statue and, like the posture, they carry different meanings: resting in the lap (meditating); holding a bowl (seeking alms); touching the earth (resisting temptation); and raised in front of the chest (teaching).

All of these are natural human features, but there is also a supernatural aspect to the Buddha statues that reflects the special status of their subject. According to tradition, a Buddha has the 32 major and 80 minor marks of a superior being. For example, one of these marks is the ushinisha – a bump on the top of the head in either the form of fire, representing spiritual energy, or the shape of stubble resulting from the cutting of his hair on the night he renounced his old life. Another example is the urna, which is a mark in the center of the forehead symbolizing the third eye of wisdom. The images of an eight-spoked wheel are also found on the soles of the feet, indicating the Noble Eightfold Path to final liberation.

Figure 1.7 Buddha statue at Kamakura, Japan. (Reproduced with kind permission of iStock.)

So the question arises: who is the subject depicted by these images that blend natural and supernatural qualities? The immediate answer is the sixth-century BCE figure named Siddhartha Gautama, at times referred to as **Sakyamuni** ("Sage of the Sakya People") but better known as the Buddha. Like the term Christ, Buddha is not a surname but an epithet, in this case meaning Enlightened One. However, in Buddhist thinking there is more than one Buddha. The Theravada tradition speaks of 27 Buddhas prior to Buddha Gautama, who is the Buddha for our age. In the Mahayana tradition there is not only a series of Buddhas throughout the great ages but also a host of celestial figures known as Buddhas and bodhisattvas, all of whom are vividly portrayed in statues and images across the Buddhist world. Some of these heavenly figures reside in a "**pure land**" where believers go after death provided they have faithfully expressed their devotion during this life. The pure land is not quite final liberation, but is the penultimate stage of the spiritual journey, because there are no further impediments to complete enlightenment in such a perfect world.

Tibetan Buddhism has developed the notion of the Five Wisdom Buddhas who inhabit pure lands at the cardinal points of heaven: north, south, east, west and center (Table 1.1). Each Buddha is recognizable by a particular color, mudra, symbol, cosmic element, vehicle, and so on. Arguably the most popular of these celestial Buddhas, not only in Tibet but throughout Asia in general, is the Buddha of the Western Pure Land – **Amitabha**.[26] The second most eminent religious figure in Tibet, the **Panchen Lama**, is considered to be his incarnation. In fact, so popular was Amitabha that historical tensions have arisen between Buddhist schools over whether Amitabha or the historical Gautama is more important and thus the true center of devotional practice.[27]

Each of the Five Wisdom Buddhas is accompanied by a bodhisattva. These are beings that have gained perfection and are ready for final liberation. However, they postpone nirvana out of compassionate concern and linger in this world in order to assist with the liberation of others. The ideal of selfless consideration embodied in the bodhisattva reflects the notion that spiritual liberation has a communitarian dimension. It is about us rather than just me. Moreover, the idea that there are generous, caring beings available to help is a deeply consoling one for struggling believers.

The most popular bodhisattva is **Avalokiteshvara**, companion to Amitabha of the Western Pure Land. Personified as the female Guanyin in China and the male Kwannon in Japan, Avalokiteshvara is the one who looks down in compassion.

Table 1.1 The Five Wisdom Buddhas of Tibetan Buddhism.

	North	South	East	West	Center
Name	Amoghasiddhi	Ratnasambhava	Akshobhya	Amitabha	Vairocana
Color	green	yellow	blue	red	white
Element	air	earth	water	fire	ether
Hand position	protection	giving	touching earth	meditation	teaching

In Buddhist art, he/she is usually portrayed in Hindu style, with thousands of arms, capable of reaching all in need. Indeed, the **Dalai Lama** of Tibet is believed to be an incarnation of Avalokiteshvara and the most popular Tibetan mantra, uttered by millions every day, is addressed to this bodhisattva: Om Mani Padme Hum ("Hail to the Jewel in the Lotus").

So the serene Buddha figures that are found in temple and home might represent a historical human figure or a group of transhistorical heavenly beings. But are they in any way divine images like the Christian icon or the Hindu murti? Are the celestial Buddhas in some sense gods like the Hindu deities who manifest a particular aspect of infinite Brahman? Is the historical Buddha Gautama some sort of divine incarnation, similar to how Hindus understand him to be the ninth avatar of Vishnu?

On one hand, the answer to such questions must be negative. Buddhism is generally considered an exceptional case among the six major world religions in that it is not clear whether Buddhists actually believe in a Supreme Being. In this sense Buddhism is oxymoronic – a non-theistic religion – which is why some prefer to categorize it as a philosophy. According to the sources, Buddha Gautama was silent on the question of the existence of God. The core of his message, summarized as the Four Noble Truths (see Chapter 3), provides a diagnosis of the source of human suffering as well as a lasting remedy. His primary concern is to map out a reliable path to ultimate liberation from all forms of suffering – physical or psychological. This path does not require belief in or devotion to a Supreme Being and this seems to be a far cry from Judaism and Islam. If they are religions of one God and no images, Buddhism is a religion with images but no God.

On the other hand, there is a doctrine in Buddhism that not only outlines the deeper theological significance of the Buddha images but also points to a concept that is very close to divinity. It is the teaching of the Three Bodies or Trikaya. According to this concept, a Buddha has three bodies, each reflecting the level of understanding attained by the observer. The first is the "created body," meaning the actual physical body of Buddha Gautama that was eventually cremated. The second is the "enjoyment body," which is usually depicted via Buddha statues. It has a combination of human and superhuman qualities that symbolize the superior nature of the enlightened ones. This is reputed to be what is seen in advanced states of meditation. The third is the "reality body," which is an abstract and absolute principle beyond any historical or trans-historical figure – the **dharma** or Buddha-truth. The Indian prince known as Buddha Gautama, the many heavenly figures that await us in their pure lands, and the bodhisattvas who come to our aid and accompany us to those lands are all manifestations of one supreme dharma truth in spatio-temporal form. That ultimate transcendent reality is admittedly not the personal God of the Semitic religions, whose image is strictly prohibited in Judaism and Islam, but justified in Christianity. It is more akin to the non-personal Brahman or the Dao. Similarly, the transcendent dharma truth is made accessible and conceivable to finite minds via the enjoyment bodies depicted in the Buddha statues. Buddhists do not worship the statues but, as in Hinduism, Daoism and sections of Christianity, they are powerful sacramental representations of a higher principle that pervades the cosmos, providing intelligibility, meaning and liberation.

Summary

While all six religions share a fundamental belief in a transcendent dimension to reality, there are both similarities and differences concerning their understanding of its true nature and the ways in which it is appropriately envisaged and represented. This chapter has focused on the use or non-use of the sacred image as a means of investigating those similarities and differences.

One of the most striking features of the synagogue and the mosque is the obvious lack of statues, paintings and icons depicting divinity. While artistic energy tends to be expressed via abstract symbolism and calligraphic design, Judaism and Islam are both absolutely insistent that there is no place for the sacred image in the house of worship. Such strong iconoclastic practice is grounded in the Jewish and Muslim emphasis on the invisibility and otherness of God. The taboo on images reflects their common stress on the transcendent nature of Ultimate Being. The creator cannot be compared to or portrayed as anything within creation. Any attempt to do so is doomed to failure, since the infinite cannot be captured by the finite. Such an object would undermine the true nature of the deity and its use would be unavoidably idolatrous. Consequently, the condemnation of false images is deeply entrenched in both faiths. The rejection of idolatry constitutes the second of the Ten Commandments of Judaism, while shirk is considered to be one of the most serious sins in Islam.

Moreover, Judaism and Islam not only champion the invisibility of God but also God's indivisibility. Idolatry not only fails to appreciate the elusiveness and mystery that shrouds the divine face, but also undermines the monotheistic foundation of both religions. The second Jewish commandment implies that the God of Israel is the only true God and Islam's first pillar is the proud declaration that there is no God but God. Both Judaism and Islam are truly described as Abrahamic religions in that they are both heirs to the legacy of the biblical figure who is considered by many to be the first to embrace an explicit and uncompromising faith in the oneness of God.

There is no doubt that Christianity endorses the ten Jewish commandments including the profession of one God and the rejection of idolatry. But there are interesting differences with Judaism and Islam when it comes to the use of sacred images. In the tradition of the Jewish second commandment and the Islamic rejection of shirk, Protestant Christianity is also suspicious of physical icons and tends to keep such potential idols out of its churches. In contrast, Orthodox and Catholic Christianity warmly endorse such artworks and treat the statue, the painting and the mosaic as valid components of worship. On this point, these Christian traditions not only move away from the Jewish and Islamic practice but also reflect a distinctive element in Christian belief that is employed as a justification for the use of the sacred image. That belief is the central Christian claim that God has become incarnate in the person of Jesus. In Christian thinking, the infinite transcendent God has assumed finite human nature forever. God now has a human face and, thus, the image of the human Christ is not an idol but a window on divinity. If Jewish, Muslim and Protestant Christian avoidance of the sacred image reflects the genuine difference between creator and creature, the Orthodox and Catholic use of the sacred image stresses a basic similarity between the divine and the human, which renders the concept of incarnation paradoxical but conceivable.

The Christian belief that Jesus is the incarnate Son of God not only constitutes a key element in the argument about the use or non-use of sacred images, but also has profound consequences for Christian monotheism. The idea that one aspect of God has taken on human nature (Son) while a second distinct aspect of God remains beyond the human (Father) leads naturally to the idea of three "persons" in one God. The Incarnation is the basis for the Christian doctrine of the Trinity. Thus, although Christianity is described as the third sibling in the Abrahamic family of monotheistic religions, the concept of a triune God means that it is a nuanced monotheism: a unity-in-plurality.

In so far as Christianity professes a mix of singularity and plurality within transcendent being, claims that divinity has assumed human form via an incarnation and, at least in certain Christian traditions, endorses the use of sacred images, it resembles not so much its Abrahamic cousins as Hinduism. The sacred image or murti is an integral part of worship in most Hindu traditions. Fashioned according to ancient guidelines and consecrated via the infusion of sacred breath, the murti represents a tangible point of contact between the profane and the sacred. Reminiscent of the Christian position, the use of the murti in Hinduism is justified by the doctrine of nirguna/saguna which acknowledges that Ultimate Being is simultaneously dissimilar and similar to the visible world. This paradox is reflected in the combination of non-anthropomorphic and anthropomorphic features in most statues and paintings. Moreover, the similarity is further supported by the tradition of Vishnu's avatars (incarnations). Although there are 10 traditional incarnations rather than one, and some of these are animal, nevertheless Hindus share the belief with Christians that the ontological gulf between divine and human is not so unbridgeable that the divine cannot assume human form.

The multiplicity of different figures represented by murtis also reflects the vastness of the Hindu pantheon, traditionally placed at 300 million gods. Such a staggering number tends to reinforce the popular notion that Hinduism is polytheistic. However, nirguna is a reminder that the many Hindu deities are ultimately particular manifestations of Ultimate Being itself (Brahman). Moreover, most Hindus tend to devote themselves to one particular form (ishta devata) of Brahman such as Vishnu, Shiva or the Mother Goddess. Again, like Christianity, Hinduism sits easily with the notion that transcendent reality involves both the one and the many.

Similarly, the Daoist pantheon consists of a huge number of deities who are ranked in a hierarchy that mirrors the bureaucracy of imperial China. These gods can be approached and petitioned via statues and paintings that are awakened through a special consecration ritual. Although most Daoist images are anthropomorphic, they follow conventional iconographical guidelines, which highlight the special role of each deity within the hierarchy. Although there is a tradition in which Daode tianzun becomes incarnate at various times to teach the truth, there is also a strong tradition that many of the gods are deified human beings. In fact, all gods are temporary beings and are manifestations of an Absolute Reality that lies beyond all images – the Dao.

Thus, Daoism simultaneously resembles icon-centered Hindu polytheism with its many gods and aniconic Hindu monism with its focus on Brahman as Absolute Mystery.

Finally, Buddhism's agnosticism with regard to the existence of a personal God or Brahman sets it apart from the other five faiths and leads many to question whether it is in fact a religion at all. Nevertheless, everyday Buddhist practices are ostensibly religious, including the widespread use of the Buddha image for meditation and supplication. In this sense, Buddhism is the converse of Judaism and Islam. If the latter are religions with one God and no images, the former is a religion with images but no God. Yet even this is not the full picture since many Buddha images in Mahayana practice do not depict the historical founder but celestial beings (Pure Land Buddhas and bodhisattvas) who are committed to assisting struggling believers on earth. These transcendent beings are accessed by devotion through the tangible Buddha image with the purpose of gaining assistance on the journey to liberation. Furthermore, even the statues that depict the historical Buddha suggest that there is more here than meets the non-believing eye. Many of the superhuman features that are incorporated into the image reflect the doctrine of the Buddha's three bodies (Trikaya), implying that Buddha Gautama was more than merely a wise teacher from the past; in fact, he represents an historical personification of an eternal, transcendent truth.

The idea of an eternal, absolute truth that pervades the universe and is made manifest in time and space touches on a second principal way in which religious believers, especially in the iconoclastic religions of Judaism and Islam, access transcendent reality – not via the visual sacred image but via the words of a holy book.

Discussion Topics

1. What is the difference between monotheism, monism, henotheism and polytheism?
2. Are humans made in the "image of God" or is there an unbridgeable difference between humanity and divinity?
3. Why are images banned in Judaism and Islam? Are there exceptions?
4. What are Sufism and the **Kabbalah**? Why are they sometimes seen as undermining Islamic and Jewish monotheism?
5. Compare and contrast the iconography of Hindu and Daoist deities.
6. Compare and contrast the Christian, Hindu and Daoist Trinity.
7. Compare and contrast the notion of divine incarnations in Hinduism, Daoism and Christianity.
8. How have Christ and Buddha been portrayed in religious art throughout history?
9. Is it appropriate to depict divinity in feminine as well as masculine form?
10. Should Buddhism be called a religion if it does not profess faith in a Supreme Being?

Notes

1 The Ten Commandments are found in Exodus 20:1–17 and Deuteronomy 5:6–21.

2 Exodus 20:4–5.

3 Exodus 32:20. A similar theme is found in the story of God refusing to show the divine face to Moses; see Exodus 33:18–23.

4 Shulhan Aruch 141:4–7.

5 Pilgrims in Mecca reach out to touch the Black Stone (Al-hajar al-aswad), which is set into the exterior of the Ka'bah at one corner. The object predates Islam and is considered to be a symbol of the covenant between God and Abraham.
6 Rather than designate a proper name for the deity, Allah is the Arabic term for "the one God" and is used by Christian and Jewish Arabs as well as Muslims. Scholars believe that it is etymologically linked to the Hebrew word El, which appears as a divine name in the Jewish scriptures.
7 Qur'an 112:1–4.
8 Qur'an 4:48.
9 Qur'an 4:171.
10 Qur'an 21:98.
11 A more recent and radical example of the Islamic abhorrence for idolatrous images is the destruction of the ancient Buddha statues of Bamyan, Afghanistan, in May 2001 by the extremist Taliban regime.
12 It is known as the Second Council of Nicea. The Catholic Church counts another 14 subsequent councils as "ecumenical" (representative of the entire Church) but these are not recognized as such by Orthodox and Protestant Christians.
13 The formal statement of Christian faith issued by the First **Council of Nicea** (325) and revised at the following Council of Constantinople (381). The majority of Christian churches today are in fundamental agreement on its content. The creed is recited during Sunday services in many churches including the Catholic, Orthodox and Anglican traditions.
14 Orthodox Christians touch their right then left shoulder, while Catholics begin with the left shoulder.
15 See the Council of Moscow in 1666.
16 For example, see Calvin's *Institutes of the Christian Religion*, book 1, ch. 12.
17 There are exceptions such as the Arya Samaj movement which banned the use of the sacred image in favor of the ancient Vedic fire ritual.
18 For example, Vishnu is usually recognizable by blue skin and the four symbols he carries: a conch, a mace, a discus, and a lotus. On the other hand, Shiva is usually depicted with white skin, a crescent moon in his hair, carrying a trident and a drum.
19 An early reference to the One is found in the Rg Veda 1.164.46.
20 Bhagavad Gita 4:8.
21 See Komjathy 251.
22 They are also known as the Three Divine Teachers, the Three Clarities or the Three Worthies.
23 Daode jing, ch. 42. See also Zhuangzi, chs. 2 and 4; Huainanzi, ch. 3.
24 Daode jing, ch. 1.
25 A similar pattern is found in the taegeuk: the horizontally divided, blue-red image at the centre of the South Korean flag.
26 Amitabha is known as Amida in Japan and O-Mi-To-Fu in China.
27 For example, the medieval Japanese schools founded by Shinran and Nichiren stressed devotion to Amitabha and Buddha Gautama respectively.

Further Reading

Bhaskarananda, Swami (2002). *The Essentials of Hinduism*. 2nd ed. Seattle: Viveka, chs. 8, 16.
Cohn-Sherbok, Dan (2003). *Judaism: History, Belief and Practice*. London: Routledge, pp. 343–56.
Eck, Diana (1998). *Darsan: Seeing the Image in India*. 3rd ed. New York: Columbia University Press.
Fine, Lawrence (ed.) (2001). *Judaism in Practice: From the Middle Ages through the Early Modern Period*. Princeton, NJ: Princeton University Press, chs. 21, 23.
Gordon, Matthew S. (2002). *Understanding Islam*. London: Duncan Baird, pp. 22–35.
Grimes, John (2004). "Darshana" in Sushil Mittal (ed.). *The Hindu World*. Abingdon: Routledge, ch. 23.
Harvey, Peter (2012). *An Introduction to Buddhism: Teaching, History and Practices*. 2nd ed. Cambridge: Cambridge University Press, ch. 8.
Knott, Kim (2000). *Hinduism: A Very Short Introduction*. Oxford: Oxford University Press, pp. 50–9.
Komjathy, Louis (2013). *The Daoist Tradition*. London: Bloomsbury, chs. 6, 13, 15.
Morgan, David (2005). *The Sacred Gaze: Religious Visual Culture in Theory and Practice*. Berkeley: University of California Press.
Reynolds, Frank E. & Carbine, Jason A. (eds.) (2000). *The Life of Buddhism*. Berkeley: University of California Press, ch. 2.
Swearer, Donald K. (2004). *Becoming the Buddha: The Ritual of Image Consecration in Thailand*. Princeton, NJ: Princeton University Press, chs. 1–2.
Wong, Eva (2011). *Taoism. An Essential Guide*. Boston: Shambhala, ch. 9.

2

Book

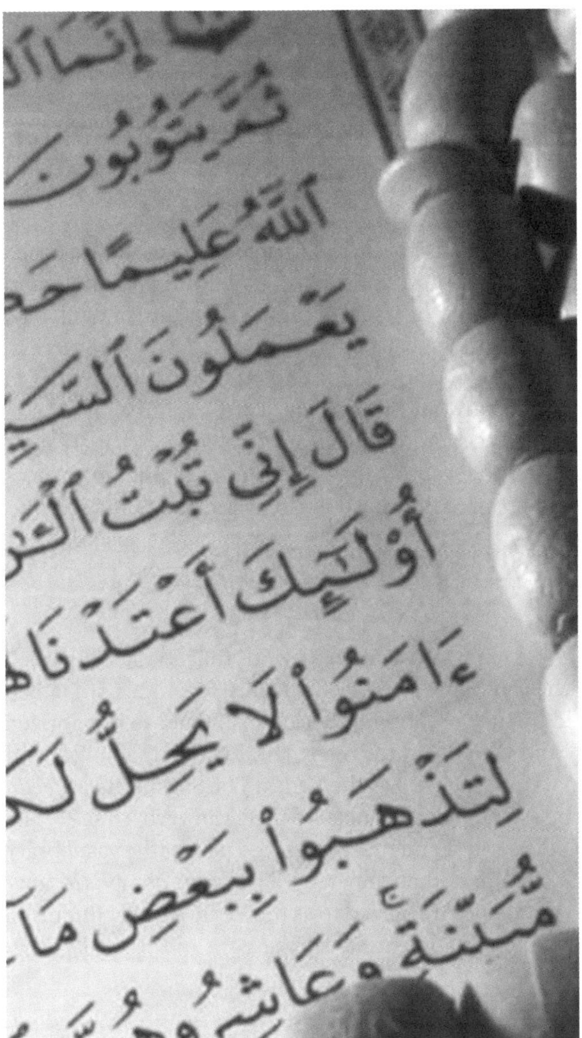

World Religions in Practice: A Comparative Introduction, Second Edition. Paul Gwynne.

CONTENTS

2.1 Introduction

Whether a religion supports or condemns the use of sacred images, each of the six major religions possesses a set of written texts that are considered to be uniquely holy and authoritative. If not all faiths accept the validity of visual access to the transcendent via a painting or an icon, there is a greater willingness to accept the legitimacy of verbal access. Religions may disagree as to whether the divine face can be depicted, but there is a broad consensus that the divine voice can be heard and the divine word captured in human language. In this chapter we shall explore the sacred books of each religion. What are their form and contents? What is the basis of their authority? Who were the human authors involved? Who may read the texts and how are they used in ritual and daily practice?

2.2 Shruti and Smriti

In Hindu worship, the gesture of offering food and drink to the gods must be accompanied by the sound of the sacred words if the ceremony is to be efficacious. Sign is accompanied by word; the visual is complemented by the verbal. The special texts that are memorized and chanted by the priest are many and varied, but for many Hindu sects the holiest and most authoritative books are a set of writings known as the Vedas. The Sanskrit term *Veda* literally means knowledge and may be etymologically linked to the Latin verb "to see".[1] The Vedas are generally considered to be the earliest and most esteemed part of the vast library of Hindu religious writings. Scholars estimate that they may have been composed anywhere between 1500 and 500 BCE, a period often referred to as the Vedic Age of Hinduism.

The Vedas comprise four works written in ancient Sanskrit:

Rg Veda (The Veda of Verses)
Sama Veda (The Veda of Chants)
Yajur Veda (The Veda of Sacrificial Prayers)
Atharva Veda (The Veda of the Fire Priests).

The oldest and most important is the **Rg Veda**, which is a collection of over 1,000 hymns to early Hindu deities such as Indra (god of war), Varuna (god of law) and **Agni** (god of fire). Later classical gods such as Shiva and Vishnu appear only briefly and as minor characters at this stage of development.[2] The Sama Veda is an anthology of mantras drawn from the Rg Veda and rearranged for musical recital at formal ceremonies, while the Yajur Veda gathers together formulas used at sacrifices. Finally, the Atharva Veda is somewhat different from the other three in that it contains magic spells and incantations that have little to do with the sacrificial system and are more typical of popular folk religion.

Each Veda contains not only a core collection of hymns (samhita) but also attachments known as brahmanas and aranyakas. These are essentially rubrics and instructions that ensure the ritual is carried out in the proper manner. Thus, the first three layers of the Vedic texts form an extensive hymnbook and manual for Hindu ritual. However, the brahmanas and aranyakas are not the only texts attached to the hymnodies. Each Veda also has appendixes known as Upanishads ("Sitting at the Feet"). As the term implies, these are works that were composed not in connection with official village ceremonies, but rather in the quiet refuge of the forest where the student sat at the feet of a spiritual master and learnt wisdom beyond mere ritual orthodoxy (Box 2.1).

The Upanishads contain philosophical musings set in dialogue form that explore classical themes such as the meaning of human existence, the identity of the self, and its relation to the Absolute. In fact, it is in the Upanishads that we find, for the first time, serious speculation about post-death existence and the emerging notion of reincarnation. The Hindu theological tradition that draws inspiration from the Upanishads is known as Vedanta: the "end" of the Vedas in the sense of fulfillment rather than mere termination. In this tradition, the Upanishads are understood as the completion of the Vedas, bringing them to their ultimate purpose. Rather than being interpreted literally as songs addressed to personified natural forces and processes, the Vedas are seen as metaphors of the soul's quest for ultimate union with Brahman.

Box 2.1 The Principal Upanishads (and Corresponding Vedas)

1	Aitareya	Rg
2	Kausitaki	Rg
3	Chandogya	Sama
4	Kena	Sama
5	Maitrayani	Sama
6	Brhadaranyaka	Yajur
7	Isa	Yajur
8	Katha	Yajur
9	Shvetashvatara	Yajur
10	Taittiriya	Yajur
11	Mandukya	Atharva
12	Mundhaka	Atharva
13	Prashna	Atharva

This fascinating combination of devotional hymns, **liturgical** guidelines and existential musings has enjoyed a traditional pre-eminence in Hindu religious literature. Consequently, the contents of these texts are described as shruti. The term literally means "that which is heard," implying that the ultimate source of the ideas encapsulated in these books lies beyond the human. "That which is heard" is from above, from the heavens. They are divine, not human, words. According to Hindu tradition, the Vedas were revealed to sages in an ancient era, a distant mythical past. These privileged ones, known as **rishis**, received the divine knowledge while in an advanced state of meditation, the product of years of dedication and study. The Rg Veda implies that this state of mind exists on another plane of mental awareness, in the world of the gods: "the rishis abide in the immutable supreme ether where are seated all the gods."[3] This inspired knowledge was translated into Sanskrit, considered to be the most perfect of human languages, and handed on for the benefit of posterity.

What is striking about classical Hinduism is that this holiest stratum of scripture is not for everyone's eyes or ears. According to the ancient Hindu legal code, the Laws of Manu, only adult males from the highest three classes (see Chapter 3) are considered worthy to read or chant the Vedas.[4] Those who belong to this privileged social group are known as the **twice-born**, because they participate in an initiation ceremony at the end of childhood that is analogical to a second, spiritual birth. The Vedas become their second mother, metaphorically. The underlying presumption is that only the twice-born possess the spiritual maturity necessary to appreciate and appropriate the wisdom found in the shruti writings.

Thus, it is considered inappropriate for women and children, as well as male members of the lower classes, to access these works. This means that the majority of believers do not have direct access to the holiest set of religious writings. How does Hinduism justify such disenfranchisement from the very source of wisdom needed for ultimate liberation? The traditional response is that, in the Hindu worldview, the twice-born are considered to be at a more advanced stage on the spiritual journey and are thus more capable of appreciating the profundity of these texts. Moreover, this advancement is the result of the build-up of good karma over many previous lives. That they are male members of the higher classes at this point in their journey is a consequence of the law of karma, which states that the extent to which a person fulfills the duties of this particular life determines the form in which they will be reincarnated in the next. The Vedas are for those who are nearing the end of that epic journey.

However, the ban does not imply that those who are not twice-born have no spiritual resources whatsoever to draw on. As mentioned earlier, the size and extent of the full corpus of Hindu religious writings is quite staggering. The shruti texts themselves constitute many bound volumes, but there are hundreds of other writings that are worthy of study and are also used in private and public worship. This is the vast category of smriti writings, a term that means "remembered." In contrast to shruti literature, which is divine wisdom "heard" by the sages during deep meditation and subsequently handed on, smriti literature is a mix of both divine inspiration and human composition. Thus, smriti is considered to be less authoritative than shruti. Nevertheless, because smriti is not restricted to the twice-born, it is actually more familiar to the average Hindu. Some of the most important smriti texts include poetic tales of the classical gods Shiva and Vishnu, known as the Puranas and the two great epics, the Ramayana and the Mahabharata.

Deep in the heart of the Mahabharata lies arguably the most popular and influential religious text in India today – the **Bhagavad Gita** ("Song of the Lord").[5] The Gita is a 700-verse poem that depicts a conversation between Arjuna, one of the heroes of the

Figure 2.1 The setting of the Bhagavad Gita: Krishna and Arjuna in dialogue. (Reproduced with kind permission of iStock.)

Mahabharata, and Krishna, an avatar of Vishnu, who is disguised as his charioteer (Figure 2.1). The scene takes place on the eve of a great battle during which Krishna advises Arjuna on the importance of both duty and devotion, subsequently revealing himself in his divine glory. Although it is technically part of the smriti literature, the Gita has acquired the status of shruti in most Hindu sects. Indeed its dialogue style and its profound musings on the meaning of life are reminiscent of the Upanishads. For many, its contents are an abiding synthesis of the various theological traditions within Hinduism, especially its teaching of the four ways to liberation: meditation (raja yoga), wisdom (jnana yoga), selfless action (karma yoga) and loving devotion (bhakti yoga).

The lack of a historical founder, a plethora of sacred writings, anonymous divinely inspired authors and diversity of opinion between schools as to which writings are the most important are some of the salient features of Hinduism. Such features are also characteristic of the vast library of sacred books that guide and inspire followers of the Dao.

2.3 Daozang

One of the main symbols of religious authority that is formally bestowed upon a newly ordained Daoist priest is the handing over of sacred texts. These precious calligraphic manuscripts, traditionally copied by hand, represent the wisdom and truth of past masters that are now being entrusted to a new generation of disciples for safekeeping. So central is the written word in the Daoist tradition that the scriptures are listed, along with the Dao and religious teachers, as the **Three External Treasures** (Wai sanbao). The technical term for the Daoist scriptures is **Daojing** ("Classics of the Dao"). The term *jing* implies a certain canonical status and, indeed, works that are officially included in this category are thought to provide authoritative definition and guidance for religious thought and practice.

Many works have been canonized throughout Daoist history and their literary type varies from poetry and narratives to commentaries, precepts and instructions. Moreover, different Daoist schools and communities will give priority to different writings. For example, although the Zhengyi (Orthodox Unity) and the Quanzhen (Complete Perfection) movements both acknowledge the central importance of the Daode jing (see below), each adds its own complementary works.[6] In contrast, the Taiqing (Great Clarity) school warned against overemphasizing the Daode jing and preferred its own scriptures.[7] In most communities the transmission of scripture is a key aspect of membership and identity, but the actual writings being handed on can vary considerably in each case.

There is a collection of principal Daoist scriptures that contains most of the key texts used across the various schools. Entitled the Daozang ("Treasury of the Dao"), it constitutes the primary textual source for the academic study of Daoism. This is the closest that we get to a Daoist **canon**. The first editions possibly go back to the fifth century CE but the current Ming version dates from about 1445 CE. The Daozang comprises over 1400 scrolls, divided into three "caverns" (dong):

True Cavern (Dongzhen) concerning meditation
Mystery Cavern (Dongxuan) concerning rituals
Spirit Cavern (Dongshen) concerning exorcisms.

The threefold division was probably inspired by the Three Baskets of Buddhism (see next section). It is tailored to the level of the initiate with the Spirit Cavern as the most basic and the True Cavern as the most advanced. Each cavern is subsequently divided into 12 sections as follows: main texts; talismans; commentaries; diagrams; histories; precepts; ceremonies; rituals; practices; biographies; hymns; and memorials. Around 500 CE four supplements were added, essentially drawing on older texts.[8]

Every major Daoist scripture is written in classical Chinese and, apart from the older classics like the Daode jing, few have been translated into English. The authors of these works are usually anonymous and, in most cases, it is presumed that they were gods or, at least, inspired by gods. Thus, Daoist scripture is not the mere product of human ingenuity but the result of divine revelation. The texts contain insights into and access to a transcendent reality. In some Daoist traditions, it is believed that an original edition of these works existed in ethereal form in a heavenly realm and, in time, they were expressed in human language for our benefit.[9]

The many texts of the Daozang remind us that there is no concise collection of canonical writings that all Daoist schools recognize as authoritative. Nevertheless, there are two relatively early texts that enjoy broad acceptance across the religion's many schools. These have been widely translated and popularized, and have had a profound impact on Chinese literature and culture in general, including Confucianism and Chinese Buddhism. These are the Daode jing and the Zhuangzi.

The title Daode jing can be translated in various ways but usually it is rendered as "The Classic of the Way and Virtue." There is still considerable debate among scholars concerning the date of authorship but many believe that it was written somewhere between 600 and 400 BCE, making it a very early Daoist work. The oldest versions yet discovered are written on bamboo tablets dating to the late fourth century BCE. Although current opinion is that there are several layers within the work, each authored by a different person, the Daoist tradition ascribes the book to a quasi-historical figure known as Laozi ("Old Master"; Figure 2.2). Laozi is often described as the "founder" of Daoism but such a claim is problematic because very little is known about him; most scholars think that he is probably a composite character. The main source of biographical information can be found in a second century BCE work entitled the **Shiji** (Grand Records of the Historian). According to the Shiji, Laozi was an archivist in the Zhou imperial court and a contemporary of Kongfuzi (Confucius), who lived in the late sixth and early fifth centuries BCE. It is said that when they met, Kongfuzi was so overwhelmed by Laozi's wisdom that he compared him to a dragon, because it is not known how such a creature "rides the wind and clouds and ascends into the heavens."[10] The composition of the Daode jing is briefly narrated thus:

> Laozi cultivated the Dao and inner power. He taught that one should efface oneself and be without fame in the world. After he had lived in Zhou for a long time, he saw that the Zhou was in decline. Then he departed. When he reached the pass, the keeper of the pass Yin Xi, said "We will see no more of you. I request that you write a book for us". Laozi then wrote a book in two parts, discussing the Dao and inner power in 5,000 words. Thereupon he departed. No-one knows where he ended his life.

Figure 2.2 Laozi.
(Reproduced with kind permission of Getty.)

As the story indicates, the Daode jing is a brief work of only 5,000 Chinese characters, traditionally arranged into 81 chapters and divided into two sections. The first 37 chapters constitute the Daojing (Classic of the Way) and the remaining chapters form the Dejing (Classic of Virtue). The literary style is poetic and rhetorical. There are many short statements that can easily be memorized as well as intentional contradictions that force the reader to ponder the paradoxes that we find in the natural world. The chapters are not thematically organized and the contents range from practical wisdom for ordinary folk to political advice for rulers. The overarching concern is to encourage the reader to observe, to understand and to harmonize with the Dao that pervades all things (Box 2.2).

Unlike other Daoist writings, the Daode jing has been translated many times and scholars are concerned that popular Western versions too easily misconstrue the original meaning. Part of the problem is that there are no punctuation marks and so it is difficult to know when a sentence begins and ends. Moreover, much of the language is deliberately vague and ambiguous, opening up a broad range of possible interpretations. The Daode jing occupies an important place within the Daoist canon and is studied in most Daoist schools. However, it is not proper to think of it as the written testimony of the founder, occupying a unique, elevated status above other canonical works, as in other religions.

The second important work that is widely used across Daoist schools is the **Nanhua zhenjing**. It is also known as Zhuangzi – "the work of Master Zhuang" – who is probably a historical figure from the late fourth century BCE.[11] The Zhuangzi consists of 33 chapters divided into three sections: Inner Chapters, Outer Chapters and Miscellaneous Chapters. Most scholars agree that the first section was written by Zhuangzi himself, whereas there is debate as to how much of the other two sections were penned by him or later authors. The Zhuangzi is a fascinating mix of allegories, fables, parables, anecdotes and dialogues but its main theme is aligning oneself with the Dao of the natural

Box 2.2 The Opening Chapter of the Daode jing

The Dao that can be told
Is not the eternal Dao.
The name that can be named
Is not the eternal name.
The nameless is the origin of heaven and earth;
The named is the mother of the myriad beings.
Always remain free from desires —
And you can see its wonder.
Always cherish desires —
And you can only observe its outcome.
Both these develop together
But have different names;
They are part of the mystery.
Mysterious and more mysterious —
The gate of all that is wondrous.

(translation by Livia Kohn)

world. Its tone is often humorous and irreverent, advocating spontaneous, free action and simple lifestyle rather than rational planning, social conformity and the quest for fortune and fame.

The concept of three treasures, a tripartite canon, the linking of writings to the founder figure, the ongoing canonization of and preference for additional writings, and difference of opinion as to the relative importance of the sacred word are not only features of the Daoist tradition. They are also evident in the daughter movement of Hinduism that abandoned its mother's sacred texts.

2.4 The Three Baskets

Soon after the death of Buddha Gautama around 480 BCE, about 500 of his disciples gathered at the Saptaparni caves near Rajagaha in northern India. One of the principal aims of this First Buddhist Council was to identify and accurately record the master's teachings for posterity (Figure 2.3). According to tradition, the Council turned to two monks renowned for their amazing powers of memory. **Ananda**, the Buddha's cousin and personal assistant, had traveled extensively with the founder and witnessed many of the sermons and discourses to various audiences over the years. It is said that Ananda recited the entirety of the Buddha's teachings for the Council, prefacing each sermon with the declaration: "Thus have I heard on one occasion." A second monk named Upali,

Figure 2.3 Buddha preaching to the first five disciples at Sarnath. (Reproduced with kind permission of iStock.)

who was famous for his diligent commitment to the way of the Buddha, summarized the rules of monastic life.

Although the historical Buddha had passed from this world and was no longer physically present to his community, his doctrinal vision and his practical guidelines for living had been captured and recorded for generations to follow. Monks would memorize the words and teach them diligently to their novices, establishing an unbroken chain of oral transmission. About 100 years later, historians note that a third collection of teachings appeared in which the Buddha's ideas were more logically analyzed and fashioned into a philosophical system. Thus, a threefold form of the Buddha's teachings emerged: a collection of Buddha Gautama's sayings; an extensive list of his prescriptions for community life; and a systematic analysis of reality as seen through Buddhist eyes. The oral tradition was eventually committed to writing in Sri Lanka around the year 30 CE under the command of King Vattagamani, and so appears the first official written anthology of Buddhist religious texts – a Buddhist canon.

The dominant school of Buddhism in Sri Lanka at the time was the Theravada and its scribes used **Pali**, an ancient western Indian language. Consequently, the collection is often referred to as the Pali Canon but, because of its tripartite form, it is also commonly called Tipitaka ("The Three Baskets").[12]

The imagery of baskets has several theoretical explanations. Some scholars focus on the ancient method of storage, arguing that the scriptures were originally written on long narrow palm leaves, stitched together at the edges and literally kept in three separate baskets, one for each part of the total collection. Others point to the metaphor of construction workers passing baskets along lines at building sites, thus stressing how the tradition is handed on from generation to generation. Whatever the origin of the analogy, the threefold arrangement is the most salient feature. So what exactly is in each of the baskets?

In the traditional ordering, the first basket is called the **Vinaya Pitaka** ("Basket of Discipline"). It is the smallest of the three and, as its title implies, it consists essentially of lists of disciplinary rules for monastic life. This is the collection that can be traced back to Upali's recitation at the First Council. In total there are 227 regulations for monks (**bhikkhus**) and 311 for nuns (**bhikkhunis**). The rules are designed to ensure that monks and nuns live according to the ideals of material simplicity, celibacy and inoffensiveness. Punishments vary from immediate expulsion for serious offenses to simple acts of penance and confession for relatively minor transgressions.

The second basket is the **Sutta Pitaka** ("Basket of Threads"). The Pali term **sutta** (**sutra** in Sanskrit) means a thread, and in both Hinduism and Buddhism it refers to authoritative teachings that were literally sewn together in written collections. Such teachings "sew" together the apparently disparate and disconnected aspects of human existence, investing life with purpose and meaning. In the Pali Canon, this second basket is the largest of the three, containing over 10,000 sayings attributed to the historical Buddha and memorized by Ananda. The Sutta Pitaka is usually divided into five sections or nikaya: (1) long discourses; (2) medium length discourses; (3) grouped discourses; (4) enumerated discourses, which are arranged according to themes or topics; and (5) minor discourses (Box 2.3).

In one sense, the Sutta Pitaka constitutes the heart of the Pali Canon. Its sayings are considered by Theravada Buddhists to be Buddhavacana, the actual words of Buddha Gautama. Typically each teaching is prefaced by Ananda's phrase "Thus have I heard,"

Box 2.3 The Three Baskets of Buddhism (Tipitaka)

Vinaya Pitaka: The Basket of Discipline
- Suttavibhanga (basic rules)
- Khandhaka (rules and sayings)
- Parivara (summaries)

Sutta Pitaka: The Basket of Threads
- Digha Nikaya (Long Discourses)
- Majjhima Nikaya (Medium Discourses)
- Samyutta Nikaya (Grouped Discourses)
- Anguttara Nikaya (Enumerated Discourses)
- Khuddaka Nikaya (Minor Discourses)

Abhidhamma Pitaka: The Basket of Higher Teaching
- Dhammasangani (phenomena)
- Vibhanga (treatises)
- Dhatukatha (elements)
- Puggalapannatti (individuals)
- Kathavatthu (points of controversy)
- Yamaka (pairs)
- Patthana (relations)

and the place and occasion of the discourse is provided. As each sermon concludes, the text tells us that the listeners were overjoyed at the wisdom that had been imparted to them. Two of the most beloved and widely read sections of the Sutta Pitaka are the Dhammapada and the **Jataka Tales**. The Dhammapada ("Verses on the Truth") is an anthology of over 400 short ethical maxims ascribed to the historical Buddha. It plays an important role in the life of monastic and lay Buddhists and has enjoyed extensive popularity in the West, not unlike the Bhagavad Gita. Its key themes are characteristic of the Buddhist worldview such as the quest for inner peace, tolerance toward others, and firm advocacy of non-violence. The Jataka Tales are stories concerning the Buddha's former lives. Although only the oldest poetic sections are considered canonical, the later prose additions recount the gradual spiritual development of the person who was destined to be eventually reincarnated as the Enlightened One for our epoch.

The third basket is the Abhidhamma Pitaka, or Basket of Higher Teaching. Scholars generally agree that this is a later addition to the original two collections that emerged from the First Council. Its contents represent subsequent reflection on, and a more philosophical elaboration of, earlier doctrine. The familiar world of humans, animals, plants, and matter is redefined in terms of fleeting abstract phenomena. Its esoteric themes and its dense, demanding style mean that the Abhidhamma is not widely read except in monasteries and by those who wish to probe Buddhism in a more scholarly fashion. Even Buddhist myth acknowledges that these are not words that were spoken by Buddha Gautama during his earthly life, although some say that he taught them privately to his outstanding disciple Sariputra. The Abhidhamma is considered to be a pure and highly advanced form of the Buddha's teaching that was revealed from the heavenly realms only after his death.

The idea that there are revealed truths that may not actually have been uttered by Buddha Gautama during his lifetime is a key aspect in the other major school of Buddhism: the Mahayana. If the Theravada school looks to the Three Baskets for its most authoritative texts based on the presumption that these are the words of Buddha Gautama, then the Mahayana school looks to other writings as well, but with the same justification for their authority – somehow these works also contain the teaching of the Buddha. While recognizing the authenticity and authority of the Three Baskets, Mahayana Buddhism adds a series of other writings that express typical Mahayana concepts such as the figure of the bodhisattva and liberation via the devotional path. One of the most prominent examples is the Lotus Sutra (Saddharmapundarika Sutra), which probably dates from the first century CE. In fact, most of the additional writings are also described as sutras – threads of truth as in the case of the Sutta Pitaka. These are works that were composed much later in the story of Buddhism, as it was gradually exported to new cultural contexts such as China, Japan, and Tibet. However, the general belief is that they contain sermons that Buddha Gautama preached to assemblies of bodhisattvas and other celestial figures in a transhistorical plane of reality. Eventually, these truths have been revealed to us in time and space either by Buddha Gautama himself or by celestial Buddhas and other beings. Sometimes Ananda's phrase "Thus have I heard" is affixed to the texts to indicate a connection with the Buddha, thus underpinning their canonical authority. There are also Buddhist traditions that bypass the written texts altogether, such as the **Zen** school which professes an oral transmission of sublime truths from generation to generation outside of the scriptures.

The doctrine of the Three Bodies (discussed in Chapter 1) expresses the idea that the historical Buddha Gautama is ultimately a particular manifestation in time and space of an eternal principle of truth – the dharma. This absolute cosmic principle has been expressed in human language via the words of Buddha Gautama, memorized by Ananda and Upali, and recorded in the Three Baskets. Even the later texts of the Mahayana schools are seen as authoritative articulations of that same eternal dharma, which has been revealed to the wise by the Buddhas and bodhisattvas of their visions. The belief that a timeless truth has become incarnate in a historical founder, and that the official record of that person's words and deeds carries enormous importance for the believing community, is applicable not only to the followers of the Enlightened One but also to the followers of the Anointed One.

2.5 New Testament

In the year 367 CE Athanasius, bishop of Alexandria, wrote an **Easter** letter to his congregation nominating 27 literary works as inspired by God and, thus, authoritative for Christians. This was the list of what was to become the Christian section of the canon. It may seem surprising that it took three centuries for the Church to sort out precisely which books were worthy of inclusion in its Bible, but the process involved more than just the official endorsement of ecclesiastical leaders. Prior to this, the books had to be composed in the first place, as well as widely used and accepted at the grass roots among Christian communities. Even in Athanasius's day, there were still concerns in some parts of the Church regarding one or two of the books,[13] but eventually the list was accepted as definitive by mainstream Christianity and came to be known as the New Testament (Box 2.4).

Box 2.4 The Books of the New Testament

Matthew	1 Timothy
Mark	2 Timothy
Luke	Titus
John	Philemon
Acts of the Apostles	Hebrews
Romans	James
1 Corinthians	1 Peter
2 Corinthians	2 Peter
Galatians	1 John
Ephesians	2 John
Philippians	3 John
Colossians	Jude
1 Thessalonians	Revelation
2 Thessalonians	

Although there are 27 books in the New Testament, it is not an enormous work, constituting a rather slim publication on a bookshelf. Moreover, none of the books were actually written by the founder himself, Jesus of Nazareth. In fact, the New Testament is a modest-sized anthology of writings composed by a generation of Christian authors during the mid to late first century CE. Upon opening a copy, the reader will immediately notice that the two main literary forms are gospel and letter: four gospels and 21 letters, to be precise.[14]

Traditionally the order of contents begins with the gospels. Assigning them pride of place is no coincidence, for these four works immediately take the reader to the very heart of the Christian religion. A **gospel** is essentially a partial biography of the founder; and, for the Christian, it is a life of enormous significance. The English term gospel is derived from the old English word *godspell*, itself a translation of the Greek *evangelion*, which means "good news." Christians see these four books as a way of encountering the message and the deeds of someone who is the epitome of good news for humankind.

The question arises as to why there are four versions of that one crucial life. Several attempts were made to harmonize the four into one single synthesis, the most notable being the Diatessaron of Tatian. However, the Church favored the retention of the four distinct accounts as the will of God, each contributing something valuable to the overall portrait of Jesus.[15] But it was not only a question of whether there should be one gospel or four. The burning issue was also whether there should be more than four, given that dozens of other gospels had been produced in the early centuries of the Christian era. In the end, the four traditional gospels alone prevailed, their canonicity being based on claims of more orthodox teaching, more reliable apostolic authorship and more widespread use by major Christian communities. The rejected versions became known as **apocryphal** gospels and, although they did not make the grade, scholars today point out that they contain a treasure trove of valuable information about Christianity in its infancy.

The authors of the four canonical gospels are named by tradition as Matthew, Mark, Luke and John,[16] although none of the gospels themselves explicitly identifies its author by name.[17] Scholars tend to agree that the gospels are the final written product of a decades-long process of oral transmission, traceable back to the original eyewitnesses and ultimately to Jesus himself. Each of the final editors – Matthew, Mark, Luke, and John – has selected, arranged and molded the material to generate his own distinctive portrait of the founder tailored for his particular audience. It is the same Jesus, but seen through different eyes and presented to a different readership.

Although it is usually listed second in the order, scholars tend to agree that Mark, the shortest gospel, is also the earliest, probably being finalized before the fall of Jerusalem in 70 CE. Mark's gospel is replete with stories about Jesus's miraculous healings but there is not a great deal of his teachings. Mark's original version is a non-stop narrative from Jesus's baptism in the river Jordan to his eventual arrest and execution in Jerusalem, with only minimal reference to the most significant claim of all: Jesus's **resurrection** from the dead.

The gospels of Luke and Matthew, which were written a decade or two later, reproduce Mark's stories in basically the same order but with two interesting additions. First, in contrast to Mark, both gospel writers include blocks of Jesus's teachings that are essentially the same. This curious fact (i.e., material common to Matthew and Luke but not found in Mark) led experts to posit the existence of a written collection of Jesus's sayings that was employed by both Matthew and Luke independently. The hypothetical work was called "Q" by nineteenth-century scholars after the German word *quelle* meaning "source." Moreover, because the first three gospels are so closely related in terms of general layout and borrowed contents, they are referred to as the **synoptic gospels**.

Second, again in contrast to Mark, both Matthew and Luke commence their gospel with the conception and birth of Jesus. The well-known Christmas motifs find their origin in the infancy stories at the beginning of these two gospels. There is a common kernel that includes Jesus's miraculous conception without a human father, the names of his parents, his birth in Bethlehem and his home in Nazareth. But there are also differences. Only Matthew mentions the three magi, the star and the escape of the family to Egypt. On the other hand, only Luke refers to the shepherds in the fields and the appearance of the angel to Mary. The subtle differences continue throughout the two gospels and suggest that each has been composed for very different groups of early Christians. Constant references to the Jewish scriptures, a genealogy of Jesus that starts with Abraham and the Sermon on the Mount, which portrays Jesus as a new Moses on a new Sinai dispensing a new Law, all suggest that Matthew's audience were Jewish converts. In contrast, Luke's references to pagans who are attracted to Jesus's message, a genealogy of Jesus that extends back to Adam (the first human being), and an opening sentence revealing that the gospel is written for "Your Excellency Theophilus" all suggest a non-Jewish audience. Matthew and Luke remind us that the early Church was a mixture of Jew and **gentile**, and that the Christian "good news" was intended not only for the people of Israel but for the entire human family.

The fourth gospel stands on its own as very different from the first three. For example, in contrast to the dozens of miracles recorded in the synoptic gospels, John mentions just seven – a number that signifies perfection in the Jewish tradition. Moreover, after each miracle Jesus delivers an extensive discourse about his true identity. It is clear that the fourth gospel is a result of a much longer process of reflection about the significance of Jesus. Consequently, it is usually dated to the end of the first century CE. Most significantly, it does not begin at the Jordan with an adult Jesus as in Mark, nor at the conception and birth of Jesus as in Matthew and Luke. The opening phrase of John's gospel takes the reader back to a moment before creation itself, echoing the book of Genesis: "In the beginning was the Word, and the Word was with God, and the Word was God."[18] "Word" here is a translation of the Greek term *Logos*, from which is derived the common English suffix of academic disciplines such as geology, biology and psychology. In Greek philosophy, Logos is the all-pervading intelligibility of the universe, which makes it possible for the inquiring human mind to investigate and make sense of the world around us. It is the difference between cosmos and chaos, and thus is the basis of all scientific inquiry. A few verses later, the fourth gospel goes on to state the most profound of Christian beliefs: "And the Word became flesh and lived among us."[19] What is implicit in the synoptic gospels becomes explicit in the fourth gospel. Jesus is not merely a prophet, or a royal child miraculously conceived, or an amazing miracle worker, but an **incarnation** of the eternal Logos.

It is not really surprising that the four gospels have pride of place in the Christian canon. The four biographies are the official record of the teachings and actions of the one whom Christians regard as the human incarnation of transcendent truth and intelligibility. Their status is borne out in ceremonial practice. For mainstream Christian churches, the gospel is traditionally the last in any series of biblical readings; the congregation is often invited to stand as the Book of Gospels is carried aloft to the pulpit; and only certain persons ordained for the purpose (deacons) may proclaim a gospel.

The second main literary type is the epistle (or letter). There are 21 epistles in the New Testament, each a piece of correspondence that provides a window into the beliefs and practices of the early Christians. Like the gospels, the epistles bear apostolic names that are meant to establish a link to Jesus himself via those who were closest to him during his life: Peter, James, John, Jude. It is difficult to say whether the Aramaic-speaking apostles actually wrote these Greek epistles, which deal with a range of issues and circumstances in the earliest communities. It is possible that the original apostle's authority stands behind the actual epistle writer in some sense. What is striking is that the majority of the epistles do not bear the name of any of the 12 disciples of Jesus. Rather, their author is a convert from Judaism who probably never met Jesus during his life but turned out to be one of the most indefatigable missionaries ever: Saint Paul. The titles of most of Paul's letters reflect the extent of his journeys aimed at establishing nascent Christian communities in towns and regions across the Roman Empire: Corinth, Thessalonica, Philippi, Galatia, Ephesus, Colossus, and Rome. Moreover, with 13 letters in the official canon, Paul's theological influence on Christianity is as undeniable as it is enormous. The letters of Paul and the other New Testament authors may be one degree removed from the figure of Jesus but they are still considered inspired writings that channel divinely sanctioned ideas and commands to the Christian believer.

The New Testament constitutes only about a quarter of the Christian Bible. The other three-quarters are equally considered to be divinely inspired. In the second century a Christian named Marcion enthusiastically proposed that, although Christianity had begun as a movement within Judaism, the Father of Jesus Christ was not the same as the God of Israel. Christianity had to sever ties with its mother religion in every respect. For Marcion this also meant expunging from the emerging Christian canon anything that looked remotely Jewish, including the gospel of Matthew, and rejecting the validity of all existing Jewish scriptures. Had Marcion prevailed, the Christian Bible would have been much slimmer: essentially the gospel of Luke and Paul's letters. However, the Christian leadership decided against his insistence on the radical novelty of the new Israel (the Church) and the obsolescence of the old Israel. Instead it acknowledged Christianity's Jewish heritage and accepted the authenticity of the Jewish holy books as God's preparation for the coming of his Messiah. As a result, Christian Bibles contain not only the 27 Christian writings known collectively as the New Testament but also a slightly rearranged version of the great religious corpus of Judaism, known to Christians as the Old Testament but referred to by Jews in its original format as Tanach.

2.6 Tanach

In mid to late October each year, at the end of the week-long feast of Sukkoth, Jews celebrate what is known as Simhat Torah ("Rejoicing with the Law"). On this day, the solemn mood of a synagogue service is transformed. All scrolls are removed from the holy ark, accompanied by vigorous dancing and singing. As the buoyant procession moves about the synagogue, participants jump up and down shouting "Moses is true and his Torah is true!" The high-spirited behavior marks the day on which the annual cycle of readings comes to an end. During the morning service, the last chapters of the book of Deuteronomy are proclaimed and are followed immediately by the first chapters of the book of Genesis; thus the cycle begins anew. The festival reveals the depth of emotion and respect with which Jews regard the most sacred part of their scriptures – the Torah.

The Hebrew word *Torah* can be translated in various ways including "teaching," "instruction" and, most commonly, "law." Although the term can mean the entire contents of Jewish law, more specifically it refers to the first five books of the Jewish Bible. In Hebrew the names of the books are taken from the first words in each: Bereishit, Shemot, Vayikra, Bamidbar and Devarim. In English they are usually referred to as **Genesis, Exodus, Leviticus, Numbers** and **Deuteronomy**.

These five writings constitute the oldest and most sacred stratum of the Jewish scriptures, and their contents are an interesting mix of narrative and commandment – lore and law. The books of Genesis, Exodus and Numbers contain the classical biblical stories of the creation of the world, Adam and Eve, Noah and the Flood, Abraham and his family, the escape from Egypt under Moses, the 40 years of wandering in the desert and the eventual arrival at the borders of the promised land. In contrast, the books of Leviticus and Deuteronomy (Greek for "second law") are essentially a collection of divine laws that are binding on Israel. These are the rules and regulations that constitute the holy covenant between God and his people.

The narrative books also contain prescriptions and proscriptions, including the famous Ten Commandments which are listed in Exodus as well as Deuteronomy. Torah is, thus, an apposite title given the pervasive presence of legal injunctions throughout. So great was the concern to know precisely what God requires that the rabbinic tradition undertook the task of identifying and enumerating each specific divine command in the Torah. The result is the traditional list of 613 **mitzvot** (commandments).[20] Some **rabbis** sought a symbolic meaning in the number. For example, Rabbi Simlai believed that the 365 negative commandments correspond to the number of days in the year, and the 248 positive commandments to the number of bones and joints in the human body.[21]

The Torah is also known as the Five Books of Moses, which hints at the traditional belief that Moses himself was its author, or to be more specific, that God revealed these words to the people through Moses. Modern biblical scholarship argues that the Torah actually consists of four distinct literary strata reflecting the hand of different editorial schools over time: the Yahwist and Elohist editors dating back to about 1000 BCE and differentiated by the name for God preferred by each (YHWH or Elohim); the Deuteronomic editor in the sixth century BCE; and finally the Priestly editor from the period after the return from **Babylonian exile** (537 BCE). However, most Orthodox Jews do not accept such theories and still insist on the Mosaic authorship of the total contents of all five books. Behind Moses stands the supreme authority of God. Thus, the Torah is not a man-made literary construct, but divine thought expressed in human language. It may have been revealed in time and space but it had always existed in the mind of the Creator before creation itself.

The annual cycle of Torah readings that begins and ends on Simhat Torah is part of the regular synagogue service on sabbath (Saturday) morning, when participants are invited to read a section of the day's text for the congregation. The act of "going up" to read the Torah is called **aliyah** – a biblical term that referred to a pilgrim making the journey up to Jerusalem for a festival.[22] It now signifies the migration of Jews to reside in modern Israel. In other words, the honor of stepping up to read from Judaism's most revered text is likened to an exile's long-awaited return to his or her homeland, or the pilgrim's joyous and relieved arrival at the gates of the holy city after an arduous journey. In one sense, the reader is on holy ground when standing before the word of God and uttering the sacred sounds for fellow worshipers.

The significance of the Torah is further highlighted by other practices and customs that surround it. For the synagogue readings, a Torah scroll (sefer Torah) is used rather than a bound book. Over 300,000 characters are meticulously copied with a quill and ink by an expert scribe onto a scroll of special parchment called gevil, according to very strict standards. A single error can render the scroll unworthy of use in official ritual. As a result, the entire process can take more than a year and be extremely costly.[23] The scroll is usually adorned with beautiful fabric and ornamental breast-plates, and reserved in an ornate container at the end of the synagogue called the holy ark. The **Pentateuch**, an alternative term for Torah often used in biblical scholarship, means "the five containers" and refers to the traditional manner of keeping Torah scrolls in special cases. During the reading, a small wooden or metal pointer called a yad is used not only to protect the parchment from contact with the skin but also to symbolize the respectful distance that should be kept in the presence of God's holy word (Figure 2.4).

Fundamental and authoritative as they are, the five books of the Torah are not the only literature that constitutes the Jewish canon of scriptures. The Hebrew Bible actually consists of 24 books grouped into three sections (Box 2.5): the 5 books of the Law (Torah); the 8 books of the Prophets (Neviyim); and the 11 books of the Writings (Ketuvim). Although these latter books do not carry the same authority as the Torah, they are nevertheless considered to be divinely inspired and, thus, have their proper place in synagogue worship, devotional piety and theological study.[24] The formal word for the entire collection of 24 canonical books is Mikra ("Readings"), but the more common term is an acronym formed from the first syllables of the Hebrew names of the three sections: Tanach.

Figure 2.4 A Jewish boy reads from a Torah scroll using a yad.
(Reproduced with kind permission of iStock.)

Box 2.5 The 24 Books of the Jewish Scriptures (Tanach)

The Law (Torah)
- Genesis
- Exodus
- Leviticus
- Numbers
- Deuteronomy

The Prophets (Neviyim)
- Joshua
- Judges
- Samuel
- Kings
- Isaiah
- Jeremiah
- Ezekiel
- The 12 minor prophets

The Writings (Ketuvim)
- Psalms
- Proverbs
- Job
- Song of Songs
- Ruth
- Lamentations
- Qoheleth
- Esther
- Daniel
- Ezra–Nehemiah
- Chronicles

When was the Jewish canon fixed? The scholarly consensus is that the books of the Torah were considered to be divinely inspired from the earliest times and that the books of the Prophets achieved canonical status soon after their composition, the latest of which dates to the period after the Babylonian Exile (586–537 BCE). There is less clarity about when the third section of Tanach, the Writings, was admitted to the canon. For many Jews, Tanach was closed soon after the construction of the Second Temple in the late sixth century BCE. For others, the process took longer. The historical evidence suggests that by the second century CE, the full collection of 24 Jewish writings was recognized as divinely authored, thus demanding the highest level of reverence and obedience. God had spoken his irrevocable word through the prophets, the greatest of whom was Moses. As the age of the prophets passed, so the inspired books ceased to be written and the canon was closed. From then on, it was a matter of sifting through the pages of Tanach in order to quarry its immense riches and spell out in more and more precise ways what the 613 mitzvot required. That enormous challenge was taken up by the rabbis and, in time, led to the composition of Judaism's classical and complex application of biblical commandments to everyday life: Talmud. Meanwhile the revelatory nature of Tanach was recognized not only by Christianity, which renamed it the Old Testament, but also by a new religion whose founder saw himself as the final prophet in that same long line.

2.7 Qur'an

One night during the month of Ramadan in the year 610 CE, a middle-aged Arabian merchant was meditating in a cave on Mount Hira, just outside the town of Mecca. According to tradition, he was suddenly overwhelmed by the presence of another being whose voice commanded him:

> Read in the name of your Lord Who created.
> He created man from a clot.
> Read and your Lord is Most Honorable,
> Who taught (to write) with the pen
> Taught man what he knew not.[25]

The events of that evening would prove to be a turning point not only for Muhammad but for religious history. The encounter was to be the first in a series of such experiences that would last until his death 22 years later. The messages that he received each time would eventually be collected into a single volume, constituting the holiest text in Islam – the Qur'an (Figure 2.5).

The term Qur'an (or Koran) refers to the collection of recitations that came about as a result of iq'ra, which literally means to read or to recite – the very command that Muhammad received in his first revelatory experience. As with any prophet, Muhammad's role was to recite a divine message in human language for his hearers. Given that the revelations were experienced from time to time over a long period, the fragmentary nature of the Qur'an is not surprising. Far from a systematic treatise of Islamic belief, it consists of poetic utterances of varying length whose meaning may or may not be immediately apparent to the reader. The Qur'an is traditionally divided into

Figure 2.5 Qur'an with prayer beads.
(Reproduced with kind permission of iStock.)

114 chapters (**surahs**) that are more or less organized in descending order according to their size – other than the first which is a short surah in the form of an introductory prayer. It is not clear why such an arrangement was originally chosen but it has persisted. Paradoxically, the effect is that the chronological order of chapters is often reversed, because the shorter chapters, which are more likely to be located later in the Qur'an, are considered by many scholars to contain earlier utterances of Muhammad. Furthermore, in most printed versions, each surah is prefaced by a phrase indicating whether it stems from the period during which Muhammad lived in Mecca (610–22) or the period during which he resided in Medina (622–32).

Each surah opens with the phrase "Bismillah ir-Rahman ir-Rahim" ("In the name of Allah, the Beneficent, the Merciful"), reminding the readers that the sacred words they are about to encounter are a result of divine favor.[26] Moreover, each surah also carries a traditional name that is derived from a striking word or particular incident described in the chapter itself and functions as a popular reference system. Some examples are "The Opening" (surah 1), "Women" (surah 4) and "The Clot" (surah 96).

The Qur'an contains over 6,000 verses or ayats – a term that literally means a divine sign or miracle. It is a significant word because, unlike Buddha Gautama and Jesus, there is no early tradition of miracle-working by Muhammad. When challenged to explain this apparent lack of evidence for his divine calling, Muslims point to the one miracle that authenticates their founder. For them, the Qur'an itself is the undeniable proof since it would have been impossible for an illiterate Muhammad to have produced such an exquisite literary masterpiece without divine involvement.[27] In fact, the Qur'an was one of the first written works in Arabic and, like Luther's German translation of the Christian Bible, had a considerable impact on the language itself. The Qur'anic language is a poetic form of Arabic that uses rhyme without regular meter. Moreover, scholars notice a shift from the succinct, vivid style in the earlier passages to a more prosaic, doctrinal style in the later.

As with Buddha Gautama and Jesus, Muhammad was not the actual writer of the holy book that bears the founder's stamp. Muhammad "recited" the divine words that came to him in his revelatory experiences, while his followers memorized them and eventually noted them down on materials such as parchment, stone, palm leaves and papyrus. There is some debate as to the precise historical process that led to a written Qur'an, but scholarly opinion tends to agree that an official version was commissioned around the year 650 during the reign of Uthman, the third caliph. The Qur'an today is essentially Uthman's edition in terms of content and layout.

Unlike Buddha Gautama and Jesus, Muhammad is not considered by Islamic faith to be the original author of the words. Muslims often stress that Muhammad is merely the conduit through which God transmitted a divine message. The tradition relates that Muhammad entered a trance-like state, during which he would often fall to the ground, sweat profusely and become oblivious to his surroundings. When he regained normal consciousness, he would speak the words that he had heard in this altered state to those present. The Qur'an itself describes the actual revelatory experience as occurring "by suggestion, or from behind a veil, or by sending a messenger to suggest what he pleases."[28] The implication is that Muhammad did not see God or even hear God's voice. God remains transcendent even as he communicates with humanity in the process of revelation. The Prophet was given insight into the divine mind only indirectly ("behind a veil") or via the mediation of a "messenger" or angel. In Islam, the voice that Muhammad actually heard was that of the angel Gabriel (Jibreel).[29] In Jewish tradition, Gabriel is the archangel who appeared to the prophet Daniel and explained the hidden meaning of his mysterious visions.[30] In Christianity, it is Gabriel who informs Mary that she is pregnant with the Christ-child.[31] In the **Abrahamic religions**, Gabriel and his fellow angelic beings bridge the gap between the infinite God and finite humans, assisting in the process of divine communication.

Gabriel is not the only Jewish or Christian figure that appears in the pages of the Qur'an. Prominent persons who are explicitly mentioned include Noah, Abraham, Moses, David and Jesus.[32] Although the Islamic creed, the shahadah, succinctly declares that Muhammad is *the* Prophet of God, this is always understood to mean the final prophet in a long series. The message of the prophets of Israel, especially their insistence on themes such as monotheism and social justice, is acknowledged by Islam to be divinely inspired. Jews and Christians are described as **People of the Book** – the book being that same history of divine revelation that comes to a close with the Seal of the Prophets and finds its ultimate expression in the words of the Qur'an.

In the end, Gabriel and Muhammad are but intermediaries. The true author of the Qur'an is God himself and the fundamental belief in its divine origin underpins the Islamic attitude toward this holiest of books. Moreover, there is a tradition that the Arabic Qur'an, dictated to Muhammad by Gabriel, is an earthly copy of a heavenly original. This is very close to the Jewish idea of a pre-existing Torah that was always with God, even before creation itself. Several Qur'anic verses support the notion of an uncreated Qur'an:

> I swear by the Book that makes things clear: Surely we have made it an Arabic Qur'an that you may understand. And surely it is in the original of the Book with Us, truly elevated, full of wisdom.[33]

Box 2.6 Al-Fatiha: The Opening Chapter of the Qur'an

In the name of Allah, the Beneficent, the Merciful.
All praise is due to Allah, the Lord of the Worlds.
The Beneficent, the Merciful.
Master of the Day of Judgment.
Thee do we serve and Thee do we beseech for help.
Keep us on the right path.
The path of those upon whom Thou hast bestowed favors. Not the path of those upon whom Thy wrath is brought down, nor of those who go astray.

The idea has its opponents within Islam who fear that an uncreated Qur'an, somehow distinct from God himself, too closely resembles the Christian idea of a pre-existing Word distinct from the Father, and thus verges on polytheism (shirk). Others justify the idea by insisting that the eternal book is God's speech, a quality of the one God, similar to his willing and knowing.

Because of the belief in its divine authorship, Muslims are generally reluctant to promote translations of the Qur'an. The old adage "Every translation limps" is particularly pertinent when dealing with the word of God. Published translations often have the Arabic and the vernacular juxtaposed. Arabic is always used in official worship and public ceremonies even though the majority of Muslims are not arabophone. The believers may not speak Arabic, but they are familiar with the Qur'anic text in its original form. There are also many believers around the world who have memorized all 80,000 words of the Qur'an and, as a result, are highly respected members of their local faith community. Such a person is called a hafiz (literally "guardian").

The Qur'an is intricately woven into Islamic life and practice. In place of sacred images, verses from the Qur'an adorn mosques and public buildings with full calligraphic flourish. The book itself is treated with the utmost respect, and ablutions have to be performed before handling it if one is not in a state of religious purity. Desecrating a Qur'an is considered a very serious and offensive form of blasphemy. Its verses are recited on a daily basis by millions of believers around the globe. Apart from the traditional 114 surahs, the text is also divided into equal sections (juz) for daily recitation during the month of Ramadan. Moreover, its opening surah, Al-Fatiha (Box 2.6), and other select Qur'anic passages, are an integral part of official daily prayers and rites of passage.

Summary

The existence of an authoritative collection of writings that shapes belief and practice is a common feature in all six religions. Such texts are held in the highest esteem by believers, who see them as priceless repositories of eternal truth and wisdom: divine thought captured in human language for posterity. Consequently, these texts play a vital role in religious study, meditation and ritual. They are diligently perused by those who seek a higher form of knowledge and reverently recited in formal public worship and private prayer. Although some of these religions reject the use of the holy image as tantamount to idolatry, all accept the notion that Ultimate Being can be effectively accessed through the words of holy books – a verbal gateway to the transcendent. But apart from this basic level of intersection, what similarities and differences exist between the religions in terms of the form, content and use of the sacred text?

Hinduism is characterized by the vast number of holy books and its peculiar lack of a universally accepted canon – a testimony to the utter diversity within Hinduism. However, many Hindu traditions recognize the unique religious status of an ancient stratum of writings categorized as shruti. The term is often translated as "heard," suggesting that these works are the product of a direct process of illumination experienced by seers in profound states of meditation long ago. At the core of the shruti literature are the four Vedas – anthologies of hymns and ritual instructions that have been used throughout the centuries for ceremony and worship. Attached to these ritual-centered documents are the Upanishads, with their contrasting emphasis on philosophical speculation and the individual's quest for truth concerning the self and the world. Shruti is a fascinating mixture of texts that pertain to public ritual and private spirituality. Moreover, Hinduism is also unique among the religions in that access to its most sacred writings is dependent on age, class and gender. Traditionally, only the twice-born males of the highest three classes were deemed worthy of reading the Vedas. The holiest of texts were meant only for the eyes of the advanced on the journey to final liberation. This limitation of access has led to widespread use of the other category of Hindu texts known as smriti, which includes such diverse forms of writing as the law code of Manu, the poetic Puranas and the two great epics known as the Ramayana and the Mahabharata. In particular, a work set deep within the Mahabharata is arguably the most beloved and influential text among the general Hindu populace today: the Bhagavad Gita.

The Daoist classics (jing) are counted as one of the Three External Treasures of that religious tradition, reflecting the importance given to the sacred texts. These writings are studied in private meditation, recited in public ritual and handed on in manuscript form to each new generation. They are not merely human compositions but the work of divine beings, providing insight into and access to transcendent reality itself. In some schools, it is taught that these writings existed in heavenly realms before being translated into human language (classical Chinese script) for our benefit. As in Hinduism, the holy texts that are canonized as jing are many and diverse. Furthermore, different schools give priority to different works, reminding us of the diversity within both religions. Two of the earliest and most influential are the Daode jing and the Nanhue zhenjing. The former is linked to the legendary figure of Laozi, misleadingly described as the founder of Daoism, while the latter is the work of a later figure, Master Zhuang, and his associates. Both are foundational in that they emphasize the importance of seeking the all-pervading Dao and aligning one's life with it. The many texts of Daoism have been collected into a threefold anthology known as the Daozang – a pattern that was probably inspired by Buddhist tradition.

Many sects within Hinduism did not accept the classical Vedic tradition and, thus, developed their own specific texts for study, meditation and ceremony. One such sect eventually blossomed into a major world religion. Although it retained many Hindu concepts drawn from the Upanishads, Buddhism rejected the Vedas and the practice of restricted access, replacing them with its own collection of authoritative texts known as the Three Baskets, which are available to all who seek enlightenment. What is different here is that the authority of these writings is grounded not in mystical knowledge revealed to sages in a distant past but in the credible eyewitness accounts of the teachings and actions of the historical Buddha as provided by his closest companions. The justification for the elevation of these writings to canonical status lies in their connection to the founder himself who is regarded as the supreme channel of transcendent truth for our epoch. Even in Mahayana schools of Buddhism, where later texts were subsequently added to and even surpassed the importance of the Three Baskets, the tendency is to understand these writings as further elaborations presented by the Buddha from a transcendent sphere of reality.

This emphasis on the teaching and example of the founder as the source of the holy book's authority is also characteristic of Christianity, which regards Jesus as the incarnation of eternal truth, the "Word made Flesh." Thus, the record of his words and deeds is of supreme importance to Christians. Like the historical Buddha, Jesus did not actually write a book but his sayings and actions were eventually recorded by those who claimed access to eyewitness accounts from within the circle of the first disciples. From the dozens of biographies that emerged over the subsequent decades of the early Church, four were chosen as official and placed at the head of the Christian canon. Not only do the works of Matthew, Mark, Luke and John enjoy primacy in the order of the New Testament books, but they are also typically given pride of place in Christian ritual and worship. Like the Three Baskets in Buddhism, the Four Gospels in Christianity provide access to the founder through whom transcendent truth and meaning are revealed to humankind. The remainder of the New Testament is primarily a collection of epistles whose inclusion in the canon was based not only on the orthodoxy of their content but also on their purported apostolic authorship, or at least their link to an apostle who is supposed to have enjoyed a personal knowledge of the founder.

What is unique about the Christian Bible is that it not only contains the 27 Christian writings collectively known as the New Testament but also a much longer section that acts as a preamble and is entitled the Old Testament. This preamble is in fact the entire canon of the Jewish faith, known in that tradition as Tanach – surely one of the most significant intersections between any of the six religions under consideration. Its inclusion in the Christian Bible reflects the self-understanding of Christianity as the new Israel, bringing to completion, but not totally abrogating, all that went before in the religious experience of the ancient people of God.

The acronym Tanach refers to the threefold subdivision of the Jewish Bible into the Law, the Prophets and the Writings. Unlike Christianity and Buddhism, the Jewish canon is not primarily centered on the life of a founder who is seen as an incarnation of divine truth. The Jewish scriptures were gradually composed over a period of 1,000 years and were definitively closed at about the same time as the Christians finalized their Bible. The first and most fundamental section of the Jewish canon is the Law (Torah). Its contents are deemed to have existed in the mind of God before creation itself. In this sense the Torah is eternal, but it has come down to earth in Hebrew form via the mediation of the greatest of all prophets, Moses. While the figure of Moses towers above all other spokespersons for God in the Jewish tradition and stands as the key human authority behind the Torah, nevertheless he is not considered the founder of Judaism or the personification of transcendent truth, as with Buddha Gautama or Jesus. It is the Torah, rather than Moses, that represents the most sublime yet tangible locus where divine truth is directly encountered. Jewish practice reflects the highest honor and respect for such holy texts in its insistence on impeccably transcribed Torah scrolls, which are stored in the most sacred place in the synagogue, carried in solemn procession during worship and buried with dignity when damaged.

On the one hand, Islam is unique among the religions in that its canon consists of only one book associated with just one prophet. On the other hand, it is similar to Christianity in that it sees itself as the true fulfillment of the Jewish prophetic line. Although Islam does not include Tanach in its canon, the Qur'an frequently refers back to significant religious figures of Israel and indeed to Jesus himself. Moreover, there are strong resonances with the Jewish understanding of sacred scripture. The rejection of visual images of God is a feature of both Judaism and Islam, and it is not surprising to find the same strong emphasis placed on the holy book by Muslims as well as by Jews. In one sense, the lack of the visual is compensated by the highlighting of the verbal. Thus, like the Torah, the Qur'an is also considered to be a pre-existing reality in the mind of God that became incarnate in time and space via the mediation of the last of the prophets, Muhammad. As in Judaism, the Prophet is not an incarnation of divine truth but a mouthpiece through which the thoughts of God are revealed in human language. Thus, it is in the sacred book itself, containing the very words of God, where the Muslim can most closely approach the divine on earth. Consequently, the Qur'an is regarded with extreme reverence by Muslims, many of whom memorize its entire contents in the hope of appropriating its essence.

The sacred writings of each religion provide an important verbal access to the divine. Although there are important differences in their extent, content and significance in each religion, these texts constitute a vital point of contact with transcendent reality. But the sacred texts also constitute an enduring litmus test for orthodox belief and a guide for practice. They shape not only the creeds but also moral and ritual life. The holy book, which reveals so much about that which lies beyond time and space, also significantly determines how believers are to live their lives within time and space. It is to such themes that we turn in the next part of the book.

Discussion Topics

1 Discuss the relative importance of written scriptures in each major religion.
2 Compare Daoist and Buddhist schools that downplay the importance of the written word.
3 Examine the idea of a pre-existing heavenly book in Daoism, Judaism and Islam.
4 Why are the Vedas and Upanishads not accepted by all Hindu traditions? Explore the alternative holy writings of those schools.
5 Identify the main scriptures of the Mahayana and Tibetan Buddhist traditions. What is the status of the Tipitaka in these traditions?
6 How and why do Catholic, Orthodox and Protestant Bibles differ?
7 How do Jews and Christians differ in the way they interpret Tanach or the Old Testament?
8 Compare the revelatory experiences of Muhammad with Jewish prophets such as Moses, Isaiah, Jeremiah or Ezekiel.
9 What are the Talmud and the Hadith? How do they complement Tanach and the Qur'an respectively?

Notes

1 Video literally means "I see" in Latin.
2 For example, certain traits of Shiva are recognizable in the earlier Vedic deity Rudra.
3 Rg Veda 1.164.39.
4 Laws of Manu IV.99.
5 Mahabharata, Bhishma Parva, chs. 23–40.
6 The Zhengyi movement also recognized the importance of the Xiang'er commentary on the Daode jing. The Quanzhen movement gave priority to the Yinfu jing (Scripture on the Hidden Talisman) and Qingjing jing (Scripture on Clarity and Stillness).
7 Preferred scriptures for the Taiqing movement include the Taiqing jing (Scripture on Great Clarity), Jiudan jing (Scripture on Nine Elixirs) and Jinye jing (Scripture on Gold Liquid).
8 The four supplements are the Taixuan (Great Mystery), Taiping (Great Peace), Taiqing (Great Purity) and Zhengyi (Orthodox Unity).
9 See Duren jing 1, 4.25b.
10 Shiji ch. 63.
11 See also Shiji ch. 63.
12 The Sanskrit form is Tripitaka.
13 For example, the Eastern Church was reluctant to canonize the book of Revelation due to its enigmatic language, while the Western Church admitted the Letter of James only belatedly because of doubts about its apostolic authorship. The canonical status of the latter was again called into question by Luther on the basis of its claim that faith cannot save without accompanying works.
14 The remaining two works are the Acts of the Apostles (an account of the early Church by Luke) and the book of Revelation (an apocalyptic work that portrays the final cosmic battle between good and evil in heavily symbolic language).
15 Irenaeus of Lyons argued that a fourfold gospel made sense given that there are four corners of the earth and four winds. See *Adversus Haereses,* 1.11.8.
16 The four gospel writers are often symbolized in Christian art by the four animals mentioned in the book of Revelation: a man, a lion, a bull and an eagle. See Revelation 4:6–7.
17 The author of the fourth gospel is described as "the beloved disciple" but his identification as John is not explicit. See John 13:23–5; 21:20–5.
18 John 1:1.
19 John 1:14.
20 Talmud Yoma 80a.
21 Talmud Makkoth 23b–24a.
22 See Genesis 50:14; Numbers 32:11; Ezra 2:1.
23 The gevil parchment consists of animal hide treated with salt, flour and special resin. See Maimonides, *Hilkoth Tefillin* 1:8, 14.
24 The Five Scrolls (Hamesh Megillot) from the Ketuvim are feature readings at important Jewish festivals throughout the year: Song of Songs at Passover; Ruth at Shavuot; Lamentations at Ninth of Av; Qoheleth at Sukkoth; and Esther at Purim.
25 Qur'an 96:1–5.
26 The one exception is Surah 9, which scholars think may originally have belonged to Surah 8.

27 The verse from Surah 96 that refers to "teaching man the use of the pen" is often quoted in this context. See also Qur'an 10:38 which challenges the skeptic to find a comparable work: "Let them come then with a surah like it."
28 Qur'an 42:50–2.
29 Qur'an 2:97.
30 Daniel 8:15–17; 9:20–4.
31 Luke 1:19.
32 Qur'an 6:83–90.
33 Qur'an 43:3. See also Qur'an 85:21–2 which speaks of a well-preserved "tablet."

Further Reading

Bhaskarananda, Swami (2002). *The Essentials of Hinduism*. 2nd ed. Seattle: Viveka, ch. 3.

Brown, Daniel (2009). *A New Introduction to Islam*. 2nd ed. Oxford: Blackwell, ch. 5.

Brown, Raymond (1997). *An Introduction to the New Testament*. New York: Doubleday, part 1.

Cook, Michael (2000). *The Koran: A Very Short Introduction*. Oxford: Oxford University Press.

De Lange, Nicholas (2003). *Introduction to Judaism*. 2nd ed. Cambridge: Cambridge University Press, ch. 3.

Gordon, Matthew S. (2002). *Understanding Islam*. London: Duncan Baird, pp. 36–45.

Hauer, Christian E. & Young, William A. (2011). *An Introduction to the Bible: A Journey into Three Worlds*. 8th ed. Upper Saddle River, NJ: Prentice Hall.

Komjathy, Louis (2013). *The Daoist Tradition*. London: Bloomsbury, ch. 12.

McGrath, Alister E. (2015). *An Introduction to Christianity*. 3rd ed. Oxford: Blackwell, ch. 2.

Michaels, Axel (2003). *Hinduism: Past and Present*. Princeton, NJ: Princeton University Press, pp. 47–66.

Miller, James (2003). *Daoism*. Oxford: Oneworld, ch.7.

Mittal, Sushil (ed.) (2004). *The Hindu World*. Abingdon: Routledge, chs. 2–5.

Pratt, Douglas (2005). *The Challenge of Islam: Encounters in Interfaith Dialogue*. Aldershot: Ashgate, ch. 3.

Part II

Within Time and Space

3

Ethics

World Religions in Practice: A Comparative Introduction, Second Edition. Paul Gwynne.

CONTENTS

3.1 Introduction

Religion not only concerns the nature of transcendent reality and its connection with our world, but also constitutes a comprehensive socio-cultural framework that provides members with ultimate meaning and purpose. In this respect, religion makes sense of human existence within time and space, casting a transcendent hue on the most ordinary aspects of life such as food and clothing, birth and death. In the following chapters we shall explore such themes, commencing here with the sense of ethical duty found in all cultures. How is the human experience of the "moral ought" expressed in the six religions? How does each religion understand the basic nature and purpose of moral life? How does morality relate to transcendent reality? What are the main sources of moral teaching? Do the religions share any fundamental moral principles?

3.2 Dharma

The Bhagavad Gita is indisputably one of the most popular and influential texts in Hinduism. Set on the eve of a great battle between good and evil, its 18 chapters relate the conversation between the hero-prince Arjuna and his charioteer, who is revealed as none other than Lord Krishna himself. Arjuna is troubled by the prospect of fighting his own cousins but Krishna advises him to ignore such fears for several reasons. For one thing, the body may be destroyed but the atman (spiritual essence) survives. Moreover, he will be considered a coward if he does not fight. But the most telling argument advanced by the divine counselor is that Arjuna is bound as a warrior to fight, even if the enemy is kin.[1] Put simply, he must do his duty. The need to fulfill one's obligations is a constantly recurring theme in the Bhagavad Gita, reflecting the importance of duty for Hindus in general. Like Arjuna, every Hindu experiences an all-embracing sense of religious, moral and social duty that is best encapsulated in the term dharma.

Dharma is a rich and complex term that can be translated into English in a variety of ways: duty, obligation, law, virtue and ethic. In fact, the term is broader than these, for it touches on not only the rules and regulations that pertain to human society but also the very fabric of the material world itself. The origins of dharma lie in the ancient Vedic idea of r'ta, which refers to the harmony, regularity and order of the physical universe. The early Hindu deity Varuna was its caretaker, ensuring that the planets kept to their proper paths and the seasons progressed on time.[2] It is the cosmic principle that holds all things together and enables them to run their course. Contemporary science knows it as "the laws of nature" such as the fundamental forces of gravity, electromagnetism and nuclear attraction. In Hindu thinking, the dharma of the sun is to rise in the east; the dharma of water is to flow downstream; and the dharma of a flower is to blossom in spring.

Apart from the regular processes of nature, dharma also refers to the laws that govern human activity. Hinduism sees a vital connection between the two, for the failure of humans to live by their dharma can have a deleterious effect on the physical world itself. When people ignore their duties, the cosmic order is threatened and the universe slides toward chaos and disintegration. In Hindu thinking, proper behavior literally keeps the world from falling apart. But what sort of behavior does human dharma involve? Traditional Hindu thought differentiates between two main types of dharma: vishesha dharma, which pertains to one's particular situation in life; and sadharana dharma, which consists of universal moral norms.

Vishesha dharma concerns the socio-religious obligations that are primarily determined by factors such as one's gender, caste and age. Such obligations differ for men and women, high and low castes, young and old. The classical Brahmanic formulation of such duties is summed up in the term *varna ashrama dharma*, where **varna** stands for the five traditional social classes (castes) and **ashrama** the four traditional life stages (Box 3.1). It is varna dharma that Krishna refers to in the Bhagavad Gita when he urges Arjuna to do his duty as a member of the warrior class. Vishesha dharma underpins a worldview in which each member of society contributes something valuable to the whole. Thus, it is the dharma of the priest to teach, of the warrior to defend, of the merchant to generate commerce, and of the servant to serve. Ideally it is the dharma of a high-caste boy to study the Vedas, of a young man to marry and beget children, and of an aging person to retire to the forest as a celibate mystic. Desiring the station of another

Box 3.1 Traditional Hindu Classes (Varna) and Life Stages (Ashrama)

Varna	
brahmin	the priestly class
kshatria	the warrior class
vaishya	the merchant class
shudra	the servant class
(dalit	the untouchable class)
Ashrama	
brahmacarin	the student
grihasthin	the householder
vanaprasthin	the forest-dweller
sannyasin	the ascetic

is a serious threat to the social harmony generated in such a system and, not surprisingly, Krishna insists several times in the Gita:

> Better one's own dharma, even if ineffective, than the dharma of another, practiced well. Better death in one's own dharma. The dharma of another only brings on fear.[3]

At this level, dharma is relative to the particular situation of the individual concerned and, thus, it is difficult to speak in terms of absolutes. The taking of life is permissible, even obligatory, for the **kshatria** in certain circumstances, while the duty of the ascetic is non-violent resistance and even martyrdom.

However, there is another form of dharma, beyond the contingencies of gender, class and age. Apart from vishesha dharma, Hindu thought also acknowledges the existence of general moral norms that are considered applicable to all human beings irrespective of religious affiliation or historical–cultural conditioning. The sadharana dharma is literally "universal" in its relevance as a guide for human behavior. This type of dharma is the ethical bedrock of Hinduism, which finds resonance in many other great religious traditions. But what precisely does the sadharana dharma prescribe?

For many, the most fundamental principle on which a superstructure of more explicit moral rules can be erected is the Golden Rule: treat others as you would have them treat you. The idea is not absent from Hinduism and can be found in a number of places in the Hindu holy writings, for example in the Mahabharata: "One should not behave toward others in a way which is disagreeable to oneself. This is the essence of morality. All other activities are due to selfish desire."[4] But how is that essential notion spelled out in more detail? There are many lists of moral prescriptions and proscriptions throughout the extensive volumes of Hindu sacred literature. One of the most convenient catalogues of the key ethical principles appears among the eight "limbs" of classical yoga in Patanjali's Yoga Sutra. Before the practitioner commences with the well-known bodily positions and breathing techniques associated with yoga, the first two "limbs" consist of the five yamas ("restraints") and the five niyamas ("relaxations"). As the term implies, the yamas restrain or control immoral behavior by identifying activities that should be avoided. According to Patanjali, these are:

1) the avoidance of violent thought and action;
2) the avoidance of dishonesty and betrayal;
3) the avoidance of theft and covetousness;
4) the avoidance of lust and drunkenness;
5) the avoidance of greed and desire.[5]

Whereas the negatively phrased yamas represent vices to be rejected, the positively phrased niyamas represent virtues to be cultivated or values to be unleashed. According to Patanjali, the five niyamas are:

1) purity in body, mind and speech;
2) contentment with one's possessions;
3) endurance and perseverance;
4) scriptural study and the quest for wisdom;
5) devotion, worship and meditation.[6]

Together, the yamas and the niyamas form two sides of the moral coin. One set proscribes while the other prescribes; one set reins in destructive activity while the other releases goodness.

As with all forms of dharma, these ethical principles are not decreed by an external creator god who imposes them as moral laws and judges according to the degree to which they have been obeyed. Although it is a type of "law," dharma is a natural law that is intrinsic to the universe. Even the Hindu gods are subject to dharma rather than being its source or author. Similarly, humans do not create the rules of moral and socio-religious life. The dharma is discovered rather than invented, discerned rather than devised. So important is this all-pervasive, multilayered reality that many Hindus prefer to call their religion sanatana dharma (the eternal and universal law). Moreover, living according to the dharma is listed as the first of the Five Constant Duties that define Hindu religious life: dharma (virtuous living); upasana (daily worship); utsava (festivals); tirthayatrai (pilgrimage); and samskaras (life-cycle rituals). The rich and varied ways in which Hindus practice their religion includes a fundamental commitment to the moral life. Religious practice is hollow without an ethical dimension, while the ethical dimension is taken up and given new meaning by religious faith.

The need to know and live out the dharma is important not simply because it constitutes a vital aspect of moral, social and religious life. The extent to which such obligations are fulfilled has significant long-term consequences beyond death itself. In the reincarnational worldview of Hindu faith, the form in which a deceased person is reborn into this world is directly affected by the extent to which he or she conformed to the dharma during their lifetime. This causal link between actions and their effects is known as karma. Those who heed Krishna's advice to Arjuna and complete their dharmic duties build up good karma and are, thus, likely to be reborn into more auspicious circumstances on earth or at a higher level in the cosmic hierarchy. Those who fail to do so generate bad karma and may find themselves reborn into a lower social class or even a lower form of life. Hindus may not live in fear of divine judgment at the end of their days, but the element of accountability is very real. The moral imperative may not be driven by apprehension about meeting one's maker, but concerns for a better rebirth and, ultimately, liberation from the wheel of reincarnation itself are powerful incentives for Hindus to take their dharmic responsibilities seriously.

Of course, the conviction that moral duty plays an important part in religious life and carries transcendent significance in the process is not limited to Hinduism. The belief that fulfilling one's ethical and religious duties greatly determines one's progress on the wheel of reincarnation is also a salient feature of its daughter religion. Moreover, the same recognition of the fundamental value of life, property, honest communication, sexual propriety and control of desire can be found in Buddhism's famous list of five basic moral principles.

3.3 Pancasila

Seven weeks after Prince Siddhartha Gautama achieved complete Enlightenment and became the Buddha for our epoch, he met up with his five former ascetical companions at a deer park at Sarnath. There, he delivered his First Sermon, sharing the profound wisdom he had received under the tree at Bodhgaya. The contents of that initial

Box 3.2 The Four Noble Truths

1) Suffering: Now this, monks, is the noble truth of suffering: Birth is suffering, ageing is suffering, sickness is suffering, death is suffering; union with what is displeasing is suffering; separation from what is pleasing is suffering; not to get what one wants is suffering; in brief, the five aggregates subject to clinging are suffering.
2) The Source of Suffering: Now this, monks, is the noble truth of the origin of suffering: It is this craving which leads to renewed existence, accompanied by delight and lust, seeking delight here and there; that is, craving for sensual pleasures, craving for existence, craving for extermination.
3) The Cessation of Suffering: Now this, monks, is the noble truth of the cessation of suffering: It is the remainder-less fading away and cessation of that same craving, the giving up and relinquishing of it, freedom from it, and non-reliance on it.
4) The Way to the Cessation of Suffering: Now this, monks, is the noble truth of the way leading to the cessation of suffering: It is this Noble Eightfold Path: that is, right view, right intention, right speech, right action, right livelihood, right effort, right mindfulness and right concentration.

discourse are known as the Four Noble Truths, which represent the very essence of Buddhist belief (Box 3.2).

Briefly, the First Noble Truth notes that human existence is full of suffering (dukha) at every level of our being: physical pain and debilitation; emotional troubles and anxieties; and a chronic existential unease resulting from the pointless cycle of birth, death and rebirth. The Second Noble Truth identifies the cause of all suffering as the misplaced desire for transient realities that can never fully satisfy the human mind or heart. It is this that binds us to the wheel of reincarnation. The Third Noble Truth holds up the hope of ultimate liberation (nirvana) from the apparently endless cycle and the cessation of all pathological cravings that shackle us to it. The Fourth Noble Truth outlines eight strategies that should be undertaken to make progress toward nirvana:

> Now this, monks, is the noble truth of the way leading to the cessation of suffering: It is this Noble Eightfold Path: that is, right view, right intention, right speech, right action, right livelihood, right effort, right mindfulness and right concentration.[7]

The Buddhist understanding of existence is very similar to that of Hinduism, which also sees the ultimate goal of the human person as liberation from the wheel of reincarnation. For the Hindu, the key to making progress toward final liberation is adherence to the dharma as both universal moral norms and particular obligations linked to caste, gender and age. It is at this point that Buddhism differs from its parent religion in its rejection of the relevance of the varna ashrama dharma. For Buddhists, dharma is not about adherence to caste laws and life-cycle rituals. Rather, dharma refers to the sublime truth that was rediscovered by Prince Siddhartha on the night of his Enlightenment and imparted to the earliest followers in the First Sermon. The essence of the dharma is the Four Noble Truths – the key that unlocks the dilemma of human existence and leads to ultimate liberation. Thus, the dharma (the teaching) combined with the Buddha (the teacher) and the **sangha** (the community that is taught) make up the **Three Jewels** of Buddhism.

Commentators often divide the eight aspects of the last Noble Truth into three subcategories. The first two paths – right view and right intention – are categorized as wisdom (panna) since these involve intellectual acceptance of the Buddha's teaching and volitional commitment to his way. The last three paths – right effort, right mindfulness and right concentration – are usually regarded as key elements of meditation that lead to awareness (**samadhi**), which is a necessary means to liberation. The middle three paths – right speech, right action and right livelihood – are classified as virtue (sila) since all three involve moral choices pertaining to relationships with others. Right speech demands that one's words are not deceitful, abusive or divisive. Right action is a general call to live with uprightness in all aspects of morality. Right livelihood acknowledges that certain occupations may be morally unacceptable and, thus, should be avoided.[8] In other words, three of the eight fundamental ways that the Buddha presents as being crucial to attaining final liberation touch on the ethical dimension of life.

Like Hinduism, the Buddhist understanding of morality is not based on commandments issued by a transcendent deity. In such a system, God defines what is good and evil, and it is the moral duty of the believer to obey divine law without question. Without clear belief in a personal Supreme Being, Buddhism grounds morality in the degree to which thoughts and actions either advance or impede progress toward final liberation. For this reason, Buddhists prefer to speak of actions as "skillful" (kausalya) or "unskillful" (akausalya), rather than as right or wrong. It is not a question of whether or not a certain act is in accordance with the will of a divine being. It is more a question of whether a certain act will contribute to eventual emancipation from the enslaving wheel of reincarnation.

There is no shortage of material in Buddhist literature when it comes to specific moral principles that provide practical guidance for people in their everyday lives. The life of Buddha Gautama himself is presented as a model that Buddhists should emulate on their journey toward nirvana. Most Buddhist schools uphold the belief that Gautama, like all Buddhas throughout the ages, was devoid of any moral fault and, therefore, constitutes a paragon of goodness and virtue. This is certainly true of his final reincarnation, but his earlier lives, narrated in the Jataka Tales, are also considered to be invaluable sources of moral inspiration and direction. In terms of teachings, the Golden Rule of ethics can also be found in the pages of Buddhist holy writings: "Comparing oneself to others in such terms as 'Just as I am so are they, just as they are so am I', he should neither kill nor cause others to kill."[9] But beyond that one general principle, the Buddhist heritage also contains a number of useful lists that sum up the main aspects of sila. The most prominent is known simply as "the five precepts" or Pancasila (Box 3.3).

Box 3.3 The Buddhist Pancasila

I refrain from destroying living creatures
I refrain from taking that which is not given
I refrain from sexual misconduct
I refrain from false speech
I refrain from intoxicants which lead to carelessness.

The Pancasila is considered to be the basic moral code for all believers, not just monks, and it plays a prominent role in Buddhist practice. Lay persons often explicitly recommit themselves to the five fundamental principles on the Buddhist monthly holy day known as uposatha. The Pancasila is an important part of the chanted recitations by monks at crucial moments such as birth, marriage and death, and is frequently the topic of sermons to visitors at monasteries. The laity themselves often recite the Pancasila on a daily basis as a constant reminder of their moral obligations.

The five precepts are phrased in negative terms: "I refrain from" a certain action. Like the Hindu yamas, the Pancasila identifies actions that are to be avoided because they impede progress toward nirvana. These ideas represent a minimum threshold beneath which one should not venture. But Buddhists often point out that each precept also contains a positive value that complements the negative language and urges the believer to strive for a higher ideal. It is not just a matter of conforming to the precepts; it is about using them as a springboard in order to reach greater ethical heights. Thus, the first precept requires the Buddhist to refrain from harming living beings, which is understood to include not only human but also sentient animal life. This makes sense in the Hindu–Buddhist world where individuals may be reincarnated as other life forms, thus blurring the sharper boundaries that normally apply in Western thinking. On the positive side, one finds values such as kindness, compassion and generosity. These ideals are manifest in the Mahayana concept of the bodhisattva, who defers nirvana and remains present in this world in order to save all beings. The first precept also lies behind the widespread Buddhist practice of vegetarianism, as well as playing a key role in Buddhist ethical debates concerning more controversial issues such as abortion, euthanasia and capital punishment.

The second precept concerns theft in its many forms, including obsession with material goods, which can lead to stealing. The positive virtue implied here is generosity, not only in terms of money but also in terms of time and talent. Alms-giving is an important aspect of Buddhist life, especially material support of the monastic community by the laity. Similarly, the monks' renunciation of physical possessions and comforts is a radical expression of detachment from what are seen as false treasures. The third precept recognizes that sexual desire is one of the most powerful and, potentially, one of the most dangerous drives in the human person. Buddhism acknowledges the existence of a sexual ethic involving both actions and thoughts, and built on integrity, fidelity and concern for the other. Although sexual activity is not considered unskillful or immoral per se, it is generally assumed that final progress toward nirvana eventually requires the adoption of the celibate way of life.

The fourth precept specifies that lying and deceit are unacceptable and that all communication should be not only honest, but also sensitive and constructive. Truth is an indispensable element on the path to ultimate liberation. Finally, the fifth precept focuses on the need for mental clarity which is a critical part of the Buddhist quest for wisdom via study and meditation. Consequently, all forms of alcohol, drugs and other intoxicating substances, which have the potential to cloud the mind and undermine responsibility, are considered unskillful. This can also include shallow and addictive forms of entertainment. This precept, which is targeted against the deleterious effects of alcohol, goes further than its Hindu counterpart. Rather than merely warn against drunkenness, the Buddhist ideal is to avoid alcohol and mind-numbing drugs altogether. It is not simply a matter of excess drinking; it is better not to drink at all.

Violence, dishonesty, theft, greed, lust and intoxication, in their manifold forms, are identified in Hinduism and Buddhism as morally unacceptable. Respect for life, property, truthfulness, sexual propriety and sobriety are recognized in both traditions as the very heart of ethical behavior. In the same vein, a third great Oriental tradition would explicitly adopt the Five Precepts of Buddhism as a central guide for conduct within its own ethical system.

3.4 Inner Power

As we saw in Chapter 2, one of the most influential texts in the Daoist tradition is the Daode jing. It is no coincidence that the term **de** ("virtue") has its place alongside the absolutely central notion of dao ("way") in its title. From the earliest times, Daoism has been keenly aware of the importance of moral thoughts and actions within the religious life. Practices such as meditation and ritual play major roles but these are considered fruitless without a solid ethical foundation. Consequently, Daoism has developed theories on what constitutes virtue and vice, as well as producing a range of practical moral guidelines for its adherents to follow.

De is commonly translated as virtue but this can be misleading given that this word carries with it significant linguistic baggage from different religious and philosophical systems. Perhaps more helpful is its common alternative translation as "inner power." Indeed, virtue in Daoism is not about following the externally imposed dictates of a Divine Judge as in the Abrahamic tradition. Rather, in the style of Hinduism and Buddhism, it is about becoming aware of and aligning oneself with the natural patterns within all things. Like the Hindu concept of dharma, the Daoist concept of de involves living in harmony with the Dao that is woven into the very fabric of the cosmos. The extent to which individuals achieve such accord renders them ethical beings; the extent to which they ignore or oppose the Dao renders them unethical. Furthermore, like the Hindu dharma, traditional Daoism teaches that there are real physical repercussions when humans fail to live by the Dao, both at the level of the environment and within our own bodies. Natural disasters such as floods, hurricanes, droughts and fires are seen as reflections of disharmony within human society.[10] Similarly, poor health and a shortened lifespan are symptoms that persons have not achieved a high level of harmony with the Dao. Unethical behavior dilutes the capacity to resist illness and exposes one to malevolent forces. Indeed, the sick were traditionally sent to "pure chambers" where they were asked to meditate on their mistakes, make acts of atonement and vow to be more ethical in future.

Given that Daoism sees the key to moral life as alignment with an inner natural power, it is not surprising to discover that, in early Daoism, there is a corresponding suspicion of ethical systems that impose moral rectitude from above or outside. This not only includes commandments from a creator God but also the imposition of social and familial duties upon individuals. In stark contrast to the Confucian emphasis on social order and duty, both the Daode jing and the Zhuangzi are highly critical of a conformity that restricts the individual freedom and suffocates the Dao. One passage from the Daode jing sums up this concern:

> After the great Dao was abandoned
> Humaneness and righteousness appeared.

After knowledge and cleverness arose
Great hypocrisy appeared.
After the six relationships lost harmony
Filial piety and familial kindness appeared.
After the state fell into chaos and disorder
Loyal ministers appeared.[11]

Moreover, virtue should be pursued with a maximum of personal freedom and not to gain reward or to avoid punishment. The practice of de should be in secret, without the need for praise or status.[12]

This fundamental idea of virtue as natural, innate and free rather than artificial, external and restrictive is reflected in two other key notions in Daoism: wuwei and ziran. **Wuwei** literally means "without deliberate action" but it is a tricky term and can be easily mistranslated. It certainly does not mean "inaction" in the sense of apathy or total non-involvement. It does not mean acting without thinking in the sense of spontaneous, self-centered behavior based on primal desires. And it does not mean "anything goes" in the sense of a laissez-faire attitude to all moral issues. A more accurate translation would be "effortlessness" in the sense of working with, rather than against, nature and, thus, allowing the Dao to take its course. Understandably, the most popular metaphor for wuwei is water, which exhibits characteristics such as receptivity, adaptability, flexibility, lowliness, fluidity and simplicity.[13] The second term, **ziran** (literally "self such") is often translated as spontaneity and naturalness. The main metaphor for ziran is an uncarved block of wood, ready to be molded into any shape. This is the pure state of passive potential that our minds should be in if we wish to be virtuous. Only by being like the uncarved wood and flowing water can one be truly in alignment with the Dao, and not succumb to the false values that arise from society and culture. As the Daode jing states:

The highest virtue manifests through non-action
And through this is free from effortful activity.
The lowest virtue acts upon things
And through this is filled with effortful activity.[14]

There are many traditional models of virtue that invite followers to consider and emulate. For instance, the Zhuangzi recounts stories of past masters and sages, highlighting their virtuous characters and personalities. Examples include: Master Zhuang himself; Changwuzi who could tuck the universe under his arm; and Cook Ding who could cut apart an ox with total effortlessness.[15] But there are not only human exemplars. The Zhuangzi also describes animals that embody the Dao and display the wuwei and ziran necessary for virtuous living. These creatures include the great Peng bird that wanders carefree above the world; fish and sea turtles that swim at ease in the oceans; magpies and wasps that undergo transformative processes; and tortoises that drag their tails in the mud.[16]

Paradoxically, despite the clear theoretical concern about external constraint and enforced conformity, there are, in practice, lists of specific virtues that followers are expected to manifest in their lives as confirmation that they are living in harmony with the Dao. There are many such lists, especially after the first century CE when organized Daoism emerged. However, even the Daode jing contains an example:

I have Three Treasures that I cherish and protect.
The first is compassion,
The second is frugality
And the third is not daring to be first.
Through compassion, one can be brave,
Through frugality, one can be expansive,
Through humility, one can become a vessel-elder.[17]

Thus, the three most precious ethical values nominated above are compassion that leads to courage, simplicity of lifestyle that leads to generosity, and humility that enables one to gather the Dao like water in a vessel.

A more widely utilized list of conduct guidelines was borrowed directly from a new religion that entered China from India. After the fourth century CE, when Buddhism was taking hold in Chinese culture, Daoism began to adapt central Buddhist ideas including its Pancasila. The order of the precepts varies slightly from the original Buddhist version, but the contents are the same. What is distinctive is that Daoism links each of the five moral precepts to aspects of its cosmological and physiological systems (Table 3.1). In other words, violation of these basic moral norms leads to health problems with the relevant organ of the body.[18]

Despite its initial rejection of ethical systems that are externally imposed and that are driven by rewards and punishments, later Daoist theology also developed the idea of the **Three Bureaus**. These are three celestial beings (gods) who abide in Heaven, Earth and the Water. Their responsibility is to administer morality in human society and they achieve this by keeping a precise record of each person's moral behavior, adding or subtracting time from our life expectancy accordingly. In one version, they take the form of **Three Worms** that reside in the head, torso and abdomen of each person, monitoring every thought and act. Once every 60 days (on gengshen day) they ascend to heaven and report on us. One traditional strategy to avoid a negative report was to stay awake on gengshen night to prevent them from submitting the report. Another method was to send formal petitions to the Three Bureaus via a ritual that involved placing a document on a mountain, burying a second in the ground and submerging the third in water.

The notion of virtue (de) as alignment with an innate, natural power and its link with the cosmic and physiological order is clearly reminiscent of Hindu dharma. Yet, despite early concerns about externally imposed moral systems and the restriction of individual

Table 3.1 The Daoist adaption of the Buddhist Pancasila.

Moral vice	Direction	Phase	Organ
Killing	East	Wood	Liver
Stealing	North	Water	Kidney
Sexual misconduct	West	Metal	Lungs
Intoxicants	South	Fire	Heart
Lying	Centre	Earth	Spleen

freedom, the Daoist tradition eventually established conduct guidelines including an explicit adaption of the Buddhist Pancasila. Moreover, its theoretical rejection of reward–punishment ethics is countered by the popular idea of the Three Bureaus who increase or decrease one's longevity according to one's moral conduct. This combination of an inner, natural, moral order and an external set of specific conduct guidelines with serious repercussions for non-compliance can also be found in the religions of Abraham.

3.5 The Ten Words

The Jewish biblical book named after the eighth-century BCE prophet Amos contains a startling passage:

> I hate, I despise your festivals, and I take no delight in your solemn assemblies. Even though you offer me your burnt-offerings and grain-offerings, I will not accept them; and the offerings of well-being of your fatted animals I will not look upon. Take away from me the noise of your songs; I will not listen to the melody of your harps. But let justice roll down like waters, and righteousness like an ever-flowing stream.[19]

It is an impassioned outburst from the God of Israel via his human mouthpiece, vehemently condemning any form of pious ritualism devoid of moral righteousness. While the sacrificial cult was considered a central part of official worship and a key expression of religious faith, what God ultimately wants is, according to Amos, not external religious formalities but ethical integrity in both thought and action. There is no point worshiping in the Temple while exploitation, oppression and perversion of justice prevail outside. It is an instructive passage because it is not unique to Amos. The strident call to justice and ethical behavior is a common theme in the message of most of Israel's prophets.[20] No wonder these inspired spokespersons have often been described as the conscience of Israel since "learn to do good" is their constant refrain.[21] While the prophetic books emphasize the importance of the social dimension, individual morality is stressed in other biblical books such as Proverbs and Psalms. The person who is truly pleasing to God is not only wise but also righteous.

The moral principles of the biblical prophets and the post-biblical rabbis are grounded in the first five books of the Jewish scriptures known collectively as the Torah. Its dramatic stories of the creation, the **patriarchs** and the escape from Egypt are filled with disturbing cases of disobedience, murder, treachery, deceit and corruption, as well as edifying examples of trust, courage, generosity, hospitality and forgiveness. But it is in the Torah's extensive legal codes that the foundation of Jewish moral teaching is to be found. As with most religions, the duty to be ethical in one's thoughts and actions is an integral part of Jewish religious life and its moral principles are ultimately derived from the 613 commandments that were distilled from the Torah by the rabbinic tradition. This means that moral duty for a Jew is different from a purely secular system based on human freedom, the voice of conscience or a set of philosophically derived values. While these aspects of moral life are generally accepted by Jewish thinking as valid, belief in a supreme creator God adds a completely new dimension. Right and wrong are defined not only in terms of human relationships but also in terms of the will of the creator who designed the world in the first place. Jewish morality is ultimately about faithful obedience to that divine will. Moreover, the final fate of every individual is determined by the divine judge who holds each individual morally accountable for their actions during life.

On this point, Judaism admits the existence of general moral norms available to all human beings outside the Jewish tradition. According to the Talmud, God gave to Noah seven fundamental laws that were to be the moral basis for future humanity. Thus, long before the Torah was revealed to Moses, the Noahide Laws were already available to all persons of goodwill. The seven laws are prohibitions against false gods, murder, theft, sexual immorality, blasphemy, cruelty to animals and corruption of the justice system.[22]

On one hand, Judaism is different from Hinduism, Buddhism and Daoism, none of which finds the ultimate source of morality in an external God who seeks obedience from his subjects. On the other hand, the divine will in Judaism is not some extraneous law imposed unjustly upon humankind. On the contrary, Judaism sees the divine commandments as reliable guideposts on the way to humankind's true destiny of eternal communion with God beyond death. Thus Judaism agrees with the Hindu, Buddhist and Daoist conviction that leading a moral life is a sure path to wellbeing and definitive fulfillment. The commandments of the Lord may seem restrictive and limiting at first but, like the dharma, they are in the best interests of the human subject in the end. It is as if the external moral law, which comes as a divine edict, finds an echo in the inner nature of the human person who has been designed for communion with his or her maker. There is a further dimension to the Jewish understanding of morality. The moral life is not only about obeying divine laws designed for the benefit of the human person in the first place. It is also about emulating the law-giver and creator-designer. Jewish faith holds that, although infinite and utterly beyond our imagination, nevertheless God is a personal being with traits similar to those found in humans, only perfect.[23] Thus the rabbinic tradition sees morality as an imitation of God, in whose image we are created.[24]

So what does God demand in terms of moral behavior? Is it possible to summarize the biblical commandments in terms of a few basic principles or norms? The rabbis often searched for a kelal or summary statement of the entire Torah.[25] One of the most outstanding examples comes from the first-century BCE teacher Hillel:

> A certain heathen came before Shammai and said to him, "Make me a proselyte, on condition that you teach me the whole Torah while I stand on one foot." Thereupon he repulsed him with the builder's cubit which was in his hand. When he went before Hillel, he said to him, "What is hateful to you, do not to your neighbour: that is the whole Torah, while the rest is the commentary thereof; go and learn it."[26]

Hillel draws on the Jewish version of the Golden Rule in Leviticus 19:18 which succinctly declares: "Love your neighbor as yourself." But the classical summary of the Jewish moral law is the list said to have been engraved by God himself on two stone tablets and given to Moses on the holy mountain Sinai for all posterity. Although popularly known as the Ten Commandments, the biblical term *aseret ha d'vareem* is better translated as "Ten Words," hence the commonly used Greek term **Decalogue**.[27]

Considered by many to be the quintessence of the Torah, the Decalogue can be described as a list of broad obligations into which all of the other commandments can be conveniently placed. Consequently, the number ten has come to symbolize completeness and totality in the Jewish tradition. There was a time when the Ten Words were recited as part of official daily prayers, although the rabbis discontinued the practice out of a concern that believers would mistakenly think that there were only ten commandments and, thus, neglect the other 603.[28] Nevertheless, the Ten Words still play a vital part in Jewish moral education and their revelation is the major theme of the festival of Shavuot. In the synagogue the congregation traditionally stands when the biblical passages containing the Ten Words are read, and the image of the two stone tablets is a popular theme in synagogue art.

The Ten Words are listed in two places in the Hebrew scriptures: once in Exodus and a slightly longer version in Deuteronomy.[29] In abbreviated form, the traditional Jewish order is:

1) I am the Lord your God who brought you out of the land of slavery.
2) You shall have no other gods before me; you shall not make for yourselves an idol.
3) You shall not misuse the name of the Lord your God.
4) Remember the Sabbath day and keep it holy.
5) Honor your father and mother.
6) You shall not murder.
7) You shall not commit adultery.
8) You shall not steal.
9) You shall not bear false witness against your neighbor.
10) You shall not covet.

Such an arrangement allows for a neat division into two groups of five commandments, reflecting the use of two tablets in the biblical story. The first tablet concerns the vertical relationship with God. Thus, the first commandment, which is in indicative rather than imperative form, is interpreted as requiring belief in the existence of God. The second emphasizes the oneness of God and the dangers of any form of idolatry; the third reflects the Jewish concern for the divine name; and the fourth sets aside one holy day of rest each week. The fifth commandment, which concerns respect for parents, may seem more appropriately listed on the second tablet, but Jewish tradition sees the parent–child relationship as a mirror of the relationship between God and humankind.

The second tablet lists the basic moral norms that underpin most human cultures and societies. As with almost all of the Ten Words, the last five are phrased as negative imperatives identifying certain activities as inherently immoral: murder, adultery, theft, lying and covetousness. The list is strikingly reminiscent of the fundamental ethical principles concerning relations between humans outlined in the Hindu yamas and the Buddhist Pancasila. Like the yamas and the Pancasila, the Ten Words are only general moral norms, from which more specific positions on a range of ethical issues are derived, such as abortion, euthanasia, genetic engineering, war, contraception and sexual orientation. These positions and teachings can vary significantly within Judaism, depending on the particular tradition such as Reform, Conservative or Orthodox. Yet, despite diverse positions in particular cases, all agree that the broad principles enunciated in the Ten Words are a key part of the moral argument and cannot be overlooked.

The complementary relationship between the vertical and the horizontal axes, symbolized by the two tablets, is a vital aspect of Jewish moral understanding. In fact, traditional teaching suggests that if there is a conflict between duty toward God and duty toward neighbor, it is the latter that should take precedence. The point is well made in a story from the book of Genesis where Abraham interrupts his prayer to offer hospitality to three strangers.[30] Paradoxically, the strangers turn out to be God in disguise. This is precisely Amos's concern (quoted at the start of this section): worship of God in heaven is futile if not accompanied by justice and peace on earth. The same concern to marry the two tablets was a key motif in the life of another Jewish prophet who is portrayed by his followers as the new Moses who taught a new law for a new Israel.

3.6 A New Commandment

> One of the scribes came near and heard them disputing with one another, and seeing that he answered them well, he asked him, "Which commandment is the first of all?" Jesus answered, "The first is, 'Hear, O Israel: the Lord our God, the Lord is one; you shall love the Lord your God with all your heart, and with all your soul, and with all your mind, and with all your strength.' The second is this, 'You shall love your neighbor as yourself.' There is no other commandment greater than these."[31]

The above incident from the gospel of Mark tells of the occasion when Jesus was invited, like many rabbis, to present his kelal or summary statement of the Torah. In response, he quotes two of the 613 commandments, treating them as if they were one commandment, but the greatest of them all. The obligation for all Jews to love God first and foremost with all of their being is found in Deuteronomy[32] while the imperative to love one's neighbor as oneself is taken directly from Leviticus.[33] There is nothing new or unique in either of the individual commandments cited or even the combination. Jesus is basically reiterating the fundamental link between the vertical and horizontal axes of religious life symbolized by the two tablets of the Decalogue. What it does reinforce is the fact that Christian moral teaching is utterly grounded in the Jewish tradition, although the daughter religion sees itself somehow moving beyond what it calls the "Old Testament."

Christian thinking agrees with the Jewish idea that the world is the work of a benevolent and wise God who has created humans with a specific destiny in mind: namely, eternal communion with God. An essential aspect of the path to that destiny is moral behavior, since it is one of the main criteria against which each individual will be held accountable by the divine judge on the last day. As in other religions, Christianity admits that fundamental moral norms are potentially available to all human beings, irrespective of whether they have religious faith or not. Saint Paul refers to this innate sense of morality in his letter to the Romans:

> When Gentiles, who do not possess the law, do instinctively what the law requires, these, though not having the law, are a law to themselves. They show that what the law requires is written on their hearts, to which their own conscience also bears witness.[34]

Christian churches disagree over the extent to which this natural sense of right and wrong is distorted by human sinfulness, thus rendering it unreliable. Protestant and Orthodox Christians tend to treat non-religious sources of ethics with a certain suspicion, while the Catholic tradition in general has been more accepting of the validity of secular moral reasoning and traditionally included "natural law" in its treatises on moral theology. Yet all Christians agree that the revealed word of God, recorded in the pages of the scriptures, provides a clearer guide to moral life. The Jewish scriptures, referred to as the Old Testament by Christians, are an essential first step.

Although many ancient Jewish customs and practices – such as circumcision, **kosher** and sabbath laws – were eventually abandoned by the early Church, the moral core of the biblical tradition was retained. When asked what is needed to achieve eternal life, Jesus refers to the Decalogue,[35] which has subsequently become the most widely used framework for Christian moral teaching throughout the ages. In his famous Sermon on the Mount, Jesus confirms the perennial validity of the Decalogue: "Do not think that I have come to abolish the law and the prophets; I have come not to abolish but to fulfill."[36] But he then proceeds to push its application well beyond the letter of the law:

> You have heard that it was said to those of ancient times, "You shall not murder"; and "whoever murders shall be liable to judgment." But I say to you that if you are angry with a brother or sister, you will be liable to judgment; and if you insult a brother or sister, you will be liable to the council; and if you say, "You fool," you will be liable to the hell of fire...
>
> You have heard that it was said, "You shall not commit adultery." But I say to you that everyone who looks at a woman with lust has already committed adultery with her in his heart......
>
> You have heard that it was said, "An eye for an eye and a tooth for a tooth." But I say to you, do not resist an evildoer. But if anyone strikes you on the right cheek, turn the other also...
>
> You have heard that it was said, "You shall love your neighbor and hate your enemy." But I say to you, Love your enemies and pray for those who persecute you.[37]

This corresponds to the call for moral excellence found in most religious traditions. Just as Hindus, Buddhists, Daoists and Jews are encouraged to transcend the minimum standards of the yamas, the Pancasila and the Decalogue, so too Christians are invited to embrace virtue enthusiastically rather than to avoid vice perfunctorily.

So the Ten Commandments represent an extremely important point of intersection between the Jewish and Christian traditions. Closer inspection reveals that the Christian listing varies slightly from the Jewish tradition (Table 3.2). Moreover, the version used by the Orthodox churches and most Protestant groups is different again from the Catholic and Lutheran version. The first difference is that the indicative statement of God's existence, which functions as the first commandment in the Jewish version, is considered a preamble in both Christian versions. Thus, the first Christian commandment concerns the oneness of God and the rejection of polytheism. The second variation is that the Orthodox and Protestant version separates out the ban on graven images as a commandment distinct from the general prohibition against other gods. Highlighting the dangers of images in this way makes sense given the general Protestant aversion to statues and icons, although it is unusual for the Orthodox Church which has championed the use of the sacred image for most of its history.[38] The effect of these two subtle differences early in the list is that the traditional numbering

Table 3.2 The Ten Commandments in its different forms.

	Jewish	Catholic and Lutheran	Orthodox and Protestant
1	*I am the Lord your God who brought you out of the house of slavery.*	I am the Lord your God and you shall have no other gods before me.	I am the Lord your god and you shall have no other gods before me.
2	You shall have no other gods besides me.	You shall not misuse the name of the Lord your God.	*You shall not make for yourself any graven image.*
3	You shall not misuse the name of the Lord your God.	Remember to keep holy the Lord's Day.	You shall not misuse the name of the Lord your God.
4	Remember the Sabbath day and keep it holy.	Honor your father and mother.	Remember to keep holy the Lord's Day.
5	Honor your father and mother.	You shall not kill.	Honor your father and mother.
6	You shall not murder.	You shall not commit adultery.	You shall not kill.
7	You shall not commit adultery.	You shall not steal.	You shall not commit adultery.
8	You shall not steal.	You shall not bear false witness against your neighbor.	You shall not steal.
9	You shall not bear false witness against your neighbor.	*You shall not covet your neighbor's wife.*	You shall not bear false witness against your neighbor.
10	You shall not covet anything that belongs to your neighbor.	You shall not covet your neighbor's goods.	You shall not covet anything that belongs to your neighbor.

Note: Italic denotes variation in the list.

of the following commandments is the same for Jews, Orthodox and Protestant Christians but slightly different for Catholics and Lutherans. The latter make up the number ten by dividing the ban on covetousness into separate commandments concerning the neighbor's wife and his goods. For many the Catholic–Lutheran version, which can be traced back to Saint Augustine, has the advantage of acknowledging the wife as a human person, clearly distinct from the neighbor's material possessions.[39] At the same time, the effect is to place greater emphasis on sexual transgressions since two commandments now touch on this aspect of morality: the sixth covering sexual acts and the ninth covering sexual thoughts.[40]

Important as the Ten Commandments are as a practical list of moral norms, there is a strong element in Christian thinking that these guidelines are insufficient in themselves. Stemming from the writings of Saint Paul, the Law of Moses, which is summarized in the Decalogue, is seen as good and holy but somehow imperfect. It supplies the essential information necessary for the moral life but lacks the motivating force needed to carry it out. In Paul's thinking, what is needed is a "new law," which not only provides the content but also the psychological drive to be virtuous. Part of that drive comes through faith in Jesus as the Savior of humankind. Thus, Jesus plays a central role in Christian morality. Like Siddhartha Gautama, Jesus's example provides an invaluable guidepost and a powerful source of inspiration for the faithful. Like the Buddha, the Christ is considered to be sinless and, thus, the perfect model for all to emulate.

However, Paul also argued that another force was needed to make Christians think and act in a righteous way: love. Of course, "love" can have many levels of meaning including romance, family relationships and friendship. But the New Testament uses the unusual Greek term *agape* to refer to a higher love than any of these.[41] Agape is God's love for humankind, made manifest in the life of his incarnate Son. This divine love constitutes the heart of an eleventh commandment which Jesus bequeaths to his followers: "I give you a new commandment, that you love one another. Just as I have loved you, you also should love one another."[42] The Jewish idea that morality is an imitation of the transcendent God of love and mercy evolves into the Christian idea of imitating that same God in human form. According to Paul, the discovery of that infinite love is the power and inspiration needed to awaken the human heart to love God and neighbor in return. Even the Golden Rule, explicitly endorsed by Jesus ("In everything do to others as you would have them do to you; for this is the law and the prophets")[43] is given a new interpretation. Now acts of kindness to others are also seen as acts toward the God-man himself: "Truly I tell you, just as you did it to one of the least of these who are members of my family, you did it to me."[44]

These are the general principles on which most forms of Christian moral teaching are based. Their application in specific ethical issues can vary considerably from church to church and within churches. For example, official Catholic morality is extensively shaped by the tradition of papal teaching, while Orthodox churches place great emphasis on Church Fathers,[45] and Protestant communities stress a close reading of the biblical text. However, for most branches of Christianity, the moral life is grounded in the divinely revealed commandments of the Old Testament, viewed in a new perspective in the context of the life and teaching of Jesus. A similar process can also be observed in Islam where the legacy of the Decalogue is absorbed and reinterpreted through the prism of the Qur'anic text and the example of the Prophet.

3.7 The Greater Jihad

There is a much quoted tradition in Islam that relates how Muhammad, upon returning from a battle, declared: "We now go from the lesser jihad to the greater jihad." The term **jihad**, commonly understood as "holy war," has become one of the most recognizable and notorious religious words today. Indeed, in the mainstream hadith tradition, jihad usually means a military encounter fought on behalf of the faith. However, the Arabic word literally means "struggle" and, apart from the possibility of a justified armed struggle (the lesser jihad), the saying indicates that there is a more important struggle that takes place within the soul of every individual (the greater jihad). Whereas the former is external, physical and occasional, the latter is internal, spiritual and constant. Some commentators further differentiate its various forms. The jihad of the soul refers to the fight against evil in the mind; the jihad of the pen is the struggle to gain greater knowledge of Islam through study; and the jihad of the hand is carried out via ethical behavior; the jihad of the tongue is waged by the spoken word, such as preaching. Whatever the differentiations, the idea is clear: the greater jihad is the everyday moral struggle against temptation that is an essential part of being a Muslim. As with other religions, Islam acknowledges the importance of the moral life and considers it inseparable from the life of faith. A Muslim's whole existence is permeated by ethical demands. But what are the guidelines for the Muslim who aspires to seek good and to avoid evil?

As with other major religions, Islam is aware of the Golden Rule. According to the hadith: "None of you truly believes until he loves for his brother what he loves for himself."[46] Moreover, like the Jewish Noahide Laws and the Christian natural law, Islam admits that a universal knowledge of the moral law is discernible by natural intelligence and forms a basis for the final judgment. One Qur'anic text hints at this innate sense of right and wrong:

> I swear by the Sun and its brilliance...And the soul and Him who made it perfect,
> Then He inspired it to understand what is right and wrong for it;
> He will indeed be successful who purifies it,
> And he will indeed fail who corrupts it.[47]

However, Muslims share the conviction with the other Abrahamic religions that natural knowledge of good and evil is unreliable and that only by special enlightenment or revelation can the human mind clearly and fully obtain truth including moral truth. Like its Jewish and Christian cousins, Islam holds that God has revealed his eternal will via a special line of prophets, thus rendering the content of the moral law more detailed and reliable. Moral duty is not just about establishing a society of justice and peace on earth. It is also about fulfilling the divine plan that destines humans for eternal communion with God. The word *Islam* literally means "submission," not in the sense of capitulation to an oppressive force but in the sense of trusting obedience to the creator who knows what is best for us.

Given that morality stems from the overarching divine plan for the world and its human inhabitants, the primary source of moral teaching for Muslims is the sacred book in which that divine plan for subsequent generations is stored. The Qur'an is the definitive measure of good and evil as stated in the opening of its twenty-fifth chapter, aptly named Al-Furqan ("Criterion"): "Blessed is He, Who sent down the Furqan upon His servant that he may be a warner to the nations."[48] As in Christianity, the Qur'an builds on truths already revealed through Muhammad's predecessors, the prophets of Israel. Thus, Islam approves of the moral teachings of the Jewish scriptures, including the Decalogue, although Muslims believe that the original texts have been corrupted over time. Consequently, the Decalogue does not appear as such in the Qur'an although one can find verses that support the main ideas of the Ten Words: the ban on idolatry (47:19) and swearing (2:224); the need to keep the holy day (62:9); respect for parents (17:23); and the prohibition of murder (5:32), adultery (17:32), theft (5:38–9), deceit (2:283) and covetousness (20:131).

One particular passage from the seventeenth chapter (The Children of Israel) is frequently described as the Islamic equivalent of the Decalogue. As with the Jewish text, the list of moral precepts can be divided in different ways. One possible combination is the following list of 10 basic principles:

1) Do not worship another god but God.
2) Be kind to your parents and care for them.
3) Give to your relatives what is their due.

4) Do not be miserly or extravagant with your possessions.
5) Do not abandon your children out of fear of poverty.
6) Do not fornicate.
7) Do not kill anyone whom God has forbidden except for a just cause.
8) Do not steal from orphans but deal with others honestly and justly.
9) Do not follow what you do not know.
10) Do not act with arrogance.[49]

Although the precepts do not coincide exactly with the Decalogue, there is considerable overlap, including the emphasis on monotheism, respect for parents and family, as well as the forbidding of unjustified killing, sexual impropriety, theft, injustice and an unhealthy preoccupation with material possessions.

The second main source of Islamic moral teaching is the Prophet himself. While the contents of the Qur'an are understood to be the literal words of God, Muhammad's own sayings and the example of his life complement the revealed truths found in the sacred text. It is as if Muhammad was a living commentary on the Qur'an, applying its ideals to his own words and deeds. As with Buddha Gautama and Jesus, Muhammad is held up as a model to be followed: "Certainly you have in the Apostle of Allah an excellent exemplar for him who hopes in Allah and the latter day and remembers Allah much."[50] Moreover, like Buddha Gautama and Jesus, Muhammad is considered to be morally impeccable and, thus, the most excellent of models. Hence, a profound knowledge and appreciation of the founder provides incalculable moral guidance and motivation to hundreds of millions of Muslims today. In contrast to Jesus, there is a considerable volume of biographical information about Muhammad, at least from the last two decades of his life, which has been passed down to posterity. This information, known as the hadith, contains the words and deeds of the Prophet that have been validated by reliable witnesses and organized into official collections.[51] Not only do believers have the wisdom and insight of the Qur'anic messages, but also the practical example of the Prophet's own sayings and actions.

Despite many relevant references in the Qur'an and the hadith, Islamic moral teaching is most explicitly enunciated in **shari'a** – the Islamic law. Shari'a lies at the very heart of Islamic practice including morality. For the Muslim believer, everyday ethical behavior is an integral part of one's religious life that is defined and shaped by the religious law. The eternal law of God is rendered accessible through the shari'a which encompasses the social and the individual, the civil and the criminal, the ritual and the ethical. Morality and legality coincide, and what is right and wrong is defined for the Muslim by the divine law. As the term shari'a suggests, this is the truest "path" to humanity's eternal destiny.

In a manner reminiscent of the twofold division of the Jewish Decalogue, shari'a is traditionally divided into two main sections: al-ibadat (our relationship with God), which deals with religious practices such as daily prayer, the sacred tax, fasting and pilgrimage; and al-mu'amalat (our relationships with others), which includes marriage and inheritance, business, crime and punishment and so forth. Both the vertical and horizontal axes of existence are an equally vital part of lived religious praxis. Within this twofold structure, all actions are placed into one of five fundamental categories: compulsory (fard); recommended (mandub); neutral (mubah); disapproved but permissible (makruh); and forbidden (**haram**).

Box 3.4 The Four Main Sunni Schools of Law

- The **Hanafi** school is the oldest and largest school, granting importance to human reason. It is predominant in Turkey, Syria, Egypt and Iraq, as well as central and south Asia.
- The **Shafi'i** school emphasizes precedents, especially those set by Muhammad and his companions. It is predominant in east Africa and southeast Asia.
- The **Maliki** school sees the early Medina community as an important source of law. It is predominant in north and west Africa.
- The **Hanbali** school stresses the primacy of the Qur'an and using analogy only with great caution. It is predominant in the Arabian peninsula.

All four schools recognize the Qur'an as the primary source of law, followed by the collected sayings and example of the Prophet (hadith), the consensus of the elders (ijma) and analogical reasoning (qiyas).

The development of shari'a since the time of Muhammad is as complex a subject as Christian canon law or Jewish Talmudic history and well beyond the scope of this work. However, it should be noted that while most Muslims are in broad agreement on matters of religious practice and morals, Shi'ite and Sunni Muslims have their own legal systems. Even within the Sunni world, there are at least four classical schools of jurisprudence (madhabs) named after prominent scholars who lived and wrote during the eighth and ninth centuries CE: the **Hanafi**, **Shafi'i**, **Maliki** and **Hanbali** schools (Box 3.4). Despite the plurality of schools, Sunnis accept all four as legitimate and often point out that the variations between them are usually minor. What the evolution of the four schools does indicate is that, while the Qur'an and the hadith represent fixed sources that do not change with time, Islamic legal reasoning also admits factors that allow for a degree of ongoing interpretation and application. The plurality of legal schools also reflects the fact that Islam, like other major religions, has no single central authority that speaks for all Muslims on matters of ethics, which makes it misleading to speak of "the" Islamic position on a particular issue. Nevertheless, the Qur'an, the hadith and shari'a constitute a solid threefold foundation on which Islamic moral teaching is based. The revealed word of God, the shining example of the Prophet and the detailed applications of the law provide the guidance and the orientation necessary for fulfilling one's moral duty.

Summary

The sense of moral duty, which is such a fundamental aspect of being human, constitutes an important practical dimension of all six major religions. Each in its own way incorporates the "ought" of conscience into the broader framework of a religious worldview and, thus, adds a special layer of significance to the basic duty of doing good and avoiding evil. Although not all decisions and actions are moral, those that are have their place firmly within the world of belief. Seen through the eyes of faith, the moral life is an integral part of religious life and moral obligations are often interwoven with other forms of religious obligation. For example, in Hinduism, the varna ashrama dharma embraces a complex range of social, cultural and ritual rules that vary according to personal circumstances. Yet, along with the more general sadharana dharma, these are still part of the all-encompassing cosmic law that must be fulfilled. Similarly, the 613 commandments of the Jewish Torah are a mixture of moral and ritual–cultic prescriptions, all of which are considered sacred and all of which must be obeyed with diligence and commitment.[52]

Once moral duty is placed within a religious context and given a religious interpretation, certain implications arise. The most obvious is the connection between moral behavior in this life and one's ultimate fate beyond death. This link and the powerful motivation it generates are features of all six religions. Doing the right thing now has serious consequences in the long term. Thus, in Hinduism, following the dharma and storing up good karma by way of ethical actions is one of the three traditional ways of obtaining ultimate liberation from the cycle of reincarnation. Similarly, three of the eight elements of the Buddha's Noble Eightfold Path that leads to nirvana highlight the need for ethical behavior. Virtue, as well as wisdom and meditation, is the key to final release. With its theory of the Three Bureaus, Daoism places more emphasis on the link between morality and the length of one's life rather than what follows death, but this still works as a powerful motivating mechanism. Although the Abrahamic religions in general do not embrace the Hindu–Buddhist notion of reincarnational existence, nevertheless moral actions in this present life have **eschatological** repercussions. Jews, Christians and Muslims all believe that individuals will be held accountable for their actions before the judgment seat of the creator and that moral character will be one of the most important criteria.

The connection between moral behavior and one's final destiny highlights an important difference between the oriental and the Abrahamic religions. In the latter, the ultimate source of moral right and wrong is the transcendent, personal creator God. Thus, moral duty takes the form of compliance with an eternal divine law that defines good and evil. Although there are other reasons for acting morally, not the least of which is respect for other beings, the Abrahamic religions profess that morality is also about trusting obedience. These religions claim that the divine law in question is not some oppressive, alien system of constraint imposed unfairly upon humankind. Rather, it is a guide offered by the one who designed humans with a particular end in mind: namely, eternal communion with God. In contrast, Hindu, Buddhist and Daoist worldviews see moral duty arising out of the cosmic order itself. The Hindu dharma is an eternal law but not the decree of a creator God. Rather, it is an intrinsic part of the universe itself that needs to be understood and followed for one's own benefit. Similarly, in Daoism, virtue (de) is inner power arising from alignment with the mysterious, impersonal Dao that abides in all things. Even the many gods of the Hindu and Daoist pantheons are subject to the dharma and the Dao respectively, although there are moments in the Bhagavad Gita when Krishna is presented as the loving source of the dharma in a similar way as God is the loving source of the moral law in the Abrahamic faiths.

Despite such differences, there is a considerable degree of agreement when it comes to the fundamental moral norms that underpin social and individual life. Each religion has its own list of core principles, whose contents are remarkably similar in essence. Admittedly there are differences of emphasis, such as the Buddhist concern to protect all forms of life (not just human) in contrast to the Jewish and Islamic understanding that not every form of killing is necessarily immoral. But the Hindu yamas, the Buddhist-Daoist Pancasila, the Jewish and Christian versions of the Decalogue and the seventeenth chapter of the Qur'an all identify murder, theft, sexual

Box 3.5 The Golden Rule of Ethics in Each Religion
One should not behave towards others in a way which is disagreeable to oneself. This is the essence of morality. All other activities are due to selfish desire. (Mahabharata)
Comparing oneself to others in such terms as "Just as I am so are they, just as they are so am I," he should neither kill nor cause others to kill. (Sutta Pitaka)
Regard your neighbor's gain as your own gain and your neighbor's loss as your own loss. (Taishang ganying pian)
What is hateful to you, do not to your neighbor: that is the whole Torah, while the rest is commentary; go and learn it. (Talmud)
In everything, do to others as you would have them do to you; for this is the law and the prophets. (Gospel of Matthew)
None of you truly believes until he loves for his brother what he loves for himself. (Hadith)

impropriety, dishonesty and greed as the most serious categories of immoral thought and action. Even the Golden Rule – treat others as you would have them treat you – can be identified within all six traditions (Box 3.5). Of course, these are broad principles and differences arise very quickly when one moves into more detailed ethical issues, not only between religions but also between the various subdivisions within them.

Finally, all traditions agree that such lists are only an indication of a minimum threshold of appropriate behavior. Ideally, the believer should seek to cultivate the positive values that constitute the reverse of the moral coin for each prohibition. One should maximize virtue rather than merely avoid vice. An important part of that quest is the example of religious figures from the past, especially the founder. In this respect, Buddha Gautama, Jesus and Muhammad all play a very important role in the moral life of Buddhists, Christians and Muslims. In each case, the founder is considered a sinless paragon of virtue to be emulated. Not only their teaching but the practical example of their lives provides inspiration and motivation for believers in the struggle to be good. But the practice of religion is not only a question of moral uprightness. Beyond ethical duty there lies a fascinating array of symbolic actions, customs, times and places that help to define religious identity, express religious faith and give transcendent meaning to the human journey from birth to death. It is to such themes that we turn in Chapters 4 to 11.

Discussion Topics

1 Do all religions agree on the fundamental moral norms for humanity?
2 How does each religion explain the origin of evil in the world?
3 Can there be a system of ethics that is not based on religious faith?
4 Do human persons have real freedom of choice or are we ultimately victims of fate? What do the world religions teach on this issue?
5 How does each religion explain why innocent persons suffer?
6 What is the position of each religion on contemporary moral "life" issues such as abortion, euthanasia, capital punishment and warfare?

7 Compare the Hindu–Buddhist belief in karma with the Daoist Three Bureaus and the Abrahamic religions' belief in divine judgment.
8 What are the arguments for and against belief in reincarnation?

Notes

1 Bhagavad Gita 2:30–3.
2 Rg Veda 1.15.1–21; 2.28.1–11.
3 Bhagavad Gita 3:35; see also 18:47.
4 Mahabharata, Anusasana Parva XIII.113.8.
5 Yoga Sutra, Sadhana Pada 2.35–9.
6 Yoga Sutra, Sadhana Pada 2.40–5.
7 Samyutta Nikaya 56.11.
8 Samyutta Nikaya 45.8.
9 Khuddaka Nikaya, Sutta Nipata 705; Samyutta Nikaya 5.353.
10 Chisongzi zhongjie jing; see Kohn 101.
11 Daode jing, ch. 18. See also chs. 46, 74, 75.
12 Similar ideas are found in Jesus's teaching. See Matthew 6:1-19.
13 See Daode jing chs. 8, 78; Zhuangzi ch. 17.
14 Daode jing ch. 38; Zhuangzi ch. 32.
15 Zhuangzi chs. 3, 17.
16 Zhuangzi chs. 1, 16, 17.
17 Daode jing ch. 67.
18 See Taishang laojun jiejing DZ 784. This is a sixth-century CE text associated with Louguan. See Komjathy 157. The Lingbao sect developed Ten Precepts, imitating the extra five Buddhist precepts for monks only. In the Daoist version, the extra five are: maintain harmony with ancestors and family; perform good deeds with joy; help unfortunate persons; do not think ill of those who wish to harm you; do not expect to attain the Dao as long as there are others who have not yet attained it.
19 Amos 5:21–4.
20 See Hosea 2:13; Isaiah 1:11; Micah 6:6–8; Jeremiah 6:20.
21 Isaiah 1:17.
22 Talmud Sanhedrin 56a–b.
23 Exodus 34:6–7.
24 Genesis 1:27.
25 For example, Rabbi Simlai noted various forms of kelal in Isaiah, Micah and Habakkuk. See Talmud Makkot 24a.
26 Talmud Shabbat 31a; see also Tobit 4:15.
27 The preferred rabbinic term is *Aseret ha-Dibrot,* which literally means "The Ten Sayings."
28 Talmud Berakoth 12a.
29 Exodus 20:1–17; Deuteronomy 5:6–21.
30 Genesis 18:1–5.
31 Mark 12:28–31.
32 Deuteronomy 6:4–5.
33 Leviticus 19:18.
34 Romans 2:14–15.
35 Mark 10:19.

36 Matthew 5:17.
37 Matthew 5:21–2, 27–8, 38–9, 43–4.
38 As noted in Chapter 1, Orthodox Christianity does ban images of God the Father.
39 The Exodus version lists the house first and the wife second, while the Deuteronomic version has the wife at the head of the list of the neighbor's possessions.
40 The other noteworthy difference between the Jewish and Christian versions of the Decalogue is the commandment concerning the taking of life. In the original Hebrew, what is prohibited is murder but the Christian tradition has translated the verb as kill, which is a broader category and not quite the same thing.
41 For example, see 1 Corinthians 13.
42 John 13:34.
43 Matthew 7:12.
44 Matthew 25:40.
45 Influential Christian theologians and writers from the period 100–800 CE.
46 The Forty Hadith of An-Nawawi, n.13.
47 Qur'an 91:1, 7–10.
48 Qur'an 25:1.
49 Qur'an 17:23–38; see also 6:151–3.
50 Qur'an 33:21, 33; 53:1-4. Yet 40:55 and 47:19 order Muhammad to seek protection for his "fault."
51 The six classical Sunni hadith collections are: Bukhari, Muslim, Abu Dawud, al-Tirmidhi, al-Sughra and Ibn Majah.
52 Technically, many of the 613 commandments no longer apply because they concern the ancient Temple-based sacrificial system. Some rabbis estimate that only about 369 commandments are still relevant today.

Further Reading

Bhaskarananda, Swami (2002). *The Essentials of Hinduism*. 2nd ed. Seattle: Viveka, ch. 12.

Burke, T. Patrick (2004). *The Major Religions: An Introduction with Texts*. 2nd ed. Oxford: Blackwell (see relevant sections on "ethics").

Cohn-Sherbok, Dan (2003). *Judaism: History, Belief and Practice*. London: Routledge, pp. 564–71.

Crook, Roger (2012). *Introduction to Christian Ethics*. 6th ed. Upper Saddle River, NJ: Prentice Hall, part 2.

Gordon, Matthew S. (2002). *Understanding Islam*. London: Duncan Baird, pp. 60–71.

Harvey, Peter (2012). *An Introduction to Buddhism: Teaching, History and Practices*. 2nd ed. Cambridge: Cambridge University Press, ch. 9.

Keown, Damien (2013). *Buddhism: A Very Short Introduction*. 2nd ed. Oxford: Oxford University Press, ch. 8.

Keown, Damien (2001). *The Nature of Buddhist Ethics*. Basingstoke: Palgrave Macmillan, chs. 1–2.

Kohn, Livia (2009). *Introducing Daoism*. London: Routledge, ch. 6.

Komjathy, Louis (2013). *The Daoist Tradition*. London: Bloomsbury, ch. 8.

Newman, Louis E. (2004). *An Introduction to Jewish Ethics*. Upper Saddle River, NJ: Prentice Hall, chs. 2–4.

Sherwin, Byron L. (2000). *Jewish Ethics for the Twenty-First Century: Living in the Image of God*. Syracuse, NY: Syracuse University Press.

4

Birth

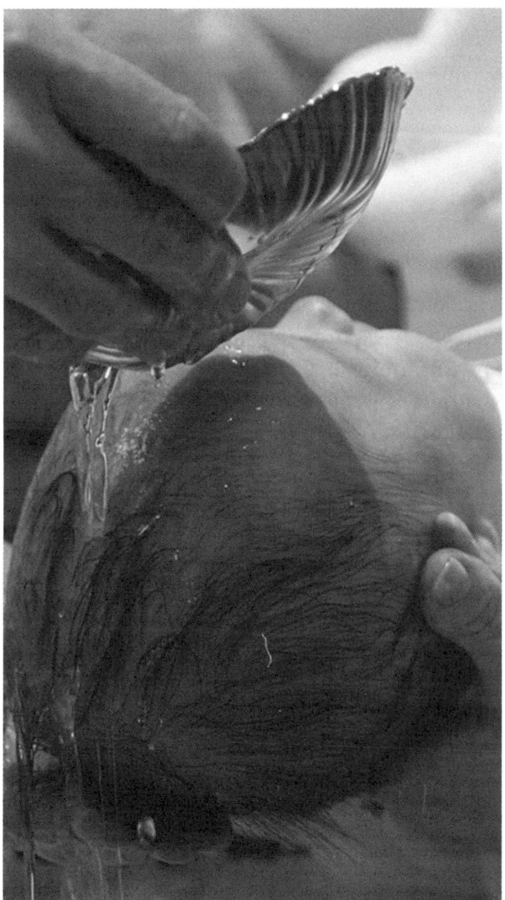

CONTENTS

4.1 Introduction

In addition to its ethical dimension, religion also sheds meaning on the journey of life, especially important milestones along the way such as birth, marriage and death. In Chapters 4 to 6 we will examine the life-cycle rituals associated with these three key moments, commencing in this chapter with the ways in which the six world religions celebrate and interpret the beginning of human life. What are the birth ceremonies in each of the six religions? What primary symbols and gestures are used and why? How do they convey notions of identity and membership of the faith community?

4.2 Baptism

All four gospels agree that the turning point in the life of Jesus occurred when he, along with many other Jews, was baptized in the Jordan River by the prophet John. Jesus experienced an epiphany that led him to enter the public arena as a religious figure.[1] Eventually Christians identified John as the precursor of the Messiah, and the symbolic action of washing in water was adopted by the Church as the definitive rite by which a person becomes a Christian (Figure 4.1). The term *baptism* literally means "to immerse" and John's use of water baptism was not without precedent in the Jewish world. The Torah prescribes a purifying bath (**mikveh**) for those who have become spiritually contaminated, for example women during menstruation or someone who has been in contact with a corpse.[2] Moreover, conversion to Judaism requires the mikveh, which symbolizes a total cleansing from past sinfulness and a new beginning as a member of the chosen people of God. However, the baptismal rite quickly became identified with initiation into Christianity. It seems to have been used as the gateway to the new faith from the very earliest generations. Initially baptism was celebrated for adult converts from either Jewish or pagan background but as Christianity eventually became the majority religion within the Roman Empire the ritual was increasingly performed for the newborn children of Christian families. Even today, while it is the official means to

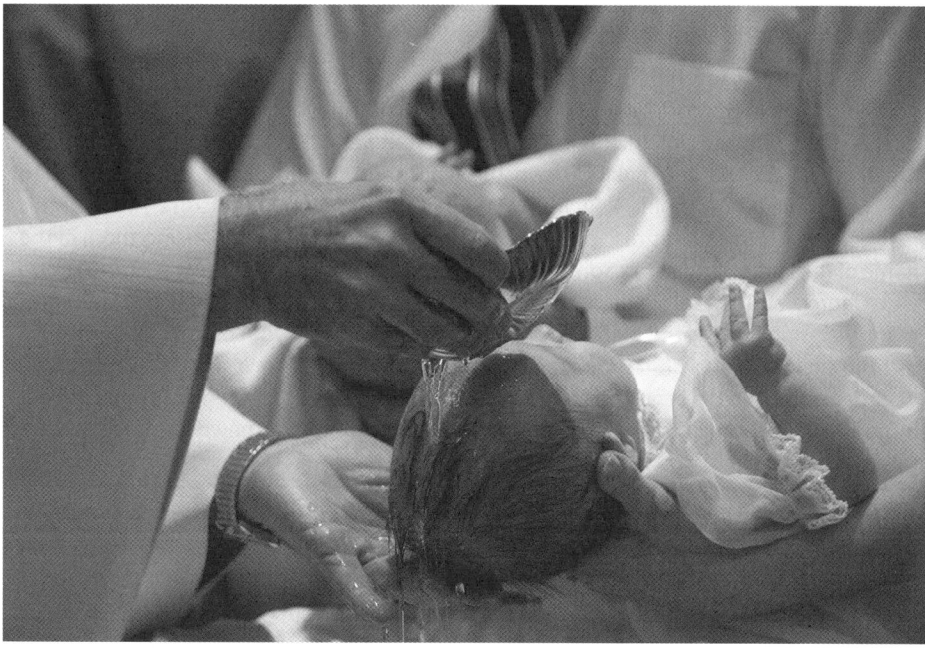

Figure 4.1 A priest pours holy water over a baby's head during a baptism. (Reproduced with kind permission of iStock.)

mark adult conversion into the Church, baptism is more commonly experienced in Christian societies as the ritual associated with human birth.

Not all Christian churches agree with the practice of infant baptism. For Baptists, Pentecostals, Seventh-Day Adventists, Jehovah's Witnesses and Mormons, the informed and conscious choice of the recipient is absolutely necessary for baptism. It is not as if these groups ignore the wonderful moment of childbirth, since most have a dedication service of some sort during which the congregation gives thanks for the birth of a new life and prays for the child. But in such churches, the appropriate age of baptism is when the person is aware of what is entailed and freely embraces the Christian faith. This can vary from 8 years among Mormons, who stress moral responsibility, to the threshold of adulthood in other communities. The fundamental birth imagery is carried forward because the person who is baptized at an older age is often described as being "born again."[3]

In contrast, infant baptism is common practice in the Orthodox, Catholic, Lutheran and Anglican Churches. There are several arguments proffered in justification. For some, especially the Catholic Church, a key motivation is the deep-seated concern for the fate of a baby who dies unbaptized, since only baptism can wash away original sin.[4] More prevalent today is the argument based on parental responsibility. Advocates point out that religious upbringing is one of many legitimate decisions taken by parents on behalf of a baby, along with food, clothing, shelter and education. Furthermore, the child is always free to ratify or reject the parents' choice when he or she reaches adulthood.[5]

Box 4.1 Prayer over the Baptismal Font (Catholic Rite)

Father, you give us grace through sacramental signs, which tell us of the wonders of your unseen power. In baptism we use your gift of water, which you have made a rich symbol of the grace you give us in this sacrament. At the very dawn of creation your Spirit breathed on the waters, making them the wellspring of all holiness. Your Son willed that water and blood should flow from his side as he hung upon the cross. And after his resurrection Christ told his disciples: "Go out and teach all nations, baptizing them in the name of the Father, and of the Son, and of the Holy Spirit." Father, look now with love upon your Church, and unseal for them the fountain of baptism. By the power of the Spirit give to the water of this font the grace of your Son. You created us in your own likeness: cleanse us from sin in a new birth to innocence by water and the Spirit. We ask you, Father, with your daughter/son, to send the Holy Spirit upon the water of this font. May all who are buried with Christ in the death of baptism, rise also with him to newness of life. We ask this through Christ our Lord. Amen.

So what happens during a baptism ceremony? Naturally, the central symbol is the water-bath, although the precise manner in which this occurs varies from full immersion to sprinkling or pouring of the water over the child's head. Most churches agree that immersion is a more powerful symbol, but many adopt the latter methods for convenience, particularly where tiny babies are involved. Baptisms may take place at rivers, lakes and other natural bodies of water, and even in the Jordan River itself. However, the majority of denominations perform baptisms inside the church building, usually over a special font or in a pool. The water itself is blessed, often with references to relevant biblical passages that stress the life-giving and saving powers of water: God's Spirit hovering over the waters of creation; Noah's ark with the kernel of a new human family surviving the Great Flood; and the miraculous crossing of the sea by Moses and the Israelites (Box 4.1).[6]

The action is always accompanied by words. Some churches prefer to baptize "in the name of Jesus," which may have been the original formula used in the early Church.[7] However, the traditional practice is to use the Trinitarian formula that appears at the conclusion of Matthew's gospel: "in the name of the Father and of the Son and of the Holy Spirit."[8] Sometimes the Trinitarian dimension is reinforced by a triple pouring or immersion.

Churches that advocate infant baptism agree that the ceremony must involve an expression of belief. Given that the baby is unable to speak for itself, the task of declaring the faith falls to the parents and godparents. In practice the latter are often close relatives or family friends but, in theory, they should also be models for the child's moral and religious upbringing. The profession of faith is usually based on ancient Christian creeds and commonly takes the form of question and answer. Often there is also specific renunciation of **Satan** or evil.

The baptismal ceremony is frequently called a christening, which today also carries the broader secular meaning of naming a person or object. Indeed, it is during baptism that a child is officially given his or her name, usually at the very moment of the water-bath itself. For generations in Western society, the individual "Christian" name along with the family surname designated social identity. Baptism is understood to "christen" the child, thus bestowing religious identity. Traditionally, the names of Christian saints or Old Testament figures were preferred, although secular influence, rather than religious piety, tends to determine the most popular names today.

The term christening is derived from the word Christ, which literally means "anointed one," and many churches actually include an anointing in the ceremony. The substance used is a scented form of olive oil called chrism, which is blessed by the local bishop at a special ceremony during Holy Week. The anointing itself symbolizes the gift of the Holy Spirit and is called chrismation in the Orthodox tradition. While Anglicans and Catholics anoint the baby during baptism, they also celebrate a second anointing ceremony later, when the person is mature enough to ratify the original decision of their parents to have their child baptized. The ceremony is appropriately named **Confirmation** and is the converse of the dedication ceremony for infants in churches that postpone baptism until a later age.

Thus, the fundamental meaning of baptism is initiation into the faith and the beginning of the Christian life. As the gateway into the Church, baptismal fonts are often located near the entrances of church buildings and baptism itself is understood as the first of the Christian life-cycle rituals known as sacraments (Box 4.2). Moreover, what this implies is that one is not automatically considered a Christian by virtue of being born into a Christian family. Christian identity is conferred by baptism, hence the traditional statement that Christians are "made, not born."

The use of water has several layers of meaning. As the most common cleansing agent on earth, it clearly evokes the idea of washing. The figurative dirt that is washed away in baptism is sin – past personal sins for adults and original sin for the newborn child. But Christians also see water as a symbol of the tomb – an idea that is much more effectively expressed when full immersion is practiced. As the person enters the pool and then emerges from it, they figuratively join Christ in his death and emerge with him to new life. The idea of union with the dying and rising Lord is also captured in other ritual elements such as making the sign of the cross on the child, the Orthodox practice of cutting a cross-shaped tonsure in the baby's hair, the giving of a candle (which represents the light of Christ), and clothing the baby in white to reflect its new dignity as a member of Christ's body, the Church.[9]

The decision of the early Church to use water baptism as its initiation rite was made against the backdrop of Christianity's gradual dissociation from its Jewish provenance. Although the process took several centuries, a key moment in the parting of the ways was the ruling that pagan male converts were not obliged to undergo the ancient ritual that, both spiritually and physically, indicated membership of God's chosen people: circumcision.[10]

Box 4.2 The Seven Sacraments

1) Baptism
2) Confirmation
3) Eucharist
4) Matrimony
5) Holy Orders
6) Reconciliation
7) Anointing of the sick

4.3 B'rit Milah

One week after the birth of a Jewish boy, family and friends gather together to celebrate one of Judaism's most ancient and distinctive rites: circumcision. On the night before the actual event, prayers are recited over the child to ward off evil spirits. A Tanach or other religious book may be placed under the pillow or mattress, symbolizing the hope that the baby will grow into a person of faith and wisdom. At this point the circumciser (**mohel**) examines the child to ascertain if there are any health risks involved (Figure 4.2). The next morning, the ceremony begins when the kvatter and kvatterin (a couple chosen for the occasion) bring the infant into the room while the guests stand. The baby is then placed on a highly ornate seat known as the Chair of Elijah, named after the prophet who is believed to be present at every circumcision ritual. The child is then placed in the lap of the sandek (godparent) and is given a formal Hebrew name. A prayer is offered expressing the community's hope for the child's future: "Just as he has been brought into the covenant, so may he enter Torah, the canopy of marriage, and the performance of good deeds." It is a great honor to be chosen as a sandek, and in Orthodox Jewish families the grandfather or a male relative fulfills this role, although Reform Judaism allows women.

The climax of the ritual is when the mohel performs the actual circumcision. He then places a few drops of wine on the lips of the child, which may originally have served as a mild form of anesthetic. Blood is removed from the wound and the infant is handed back to its mother, after which those present celebrate the occasion with a festive meal

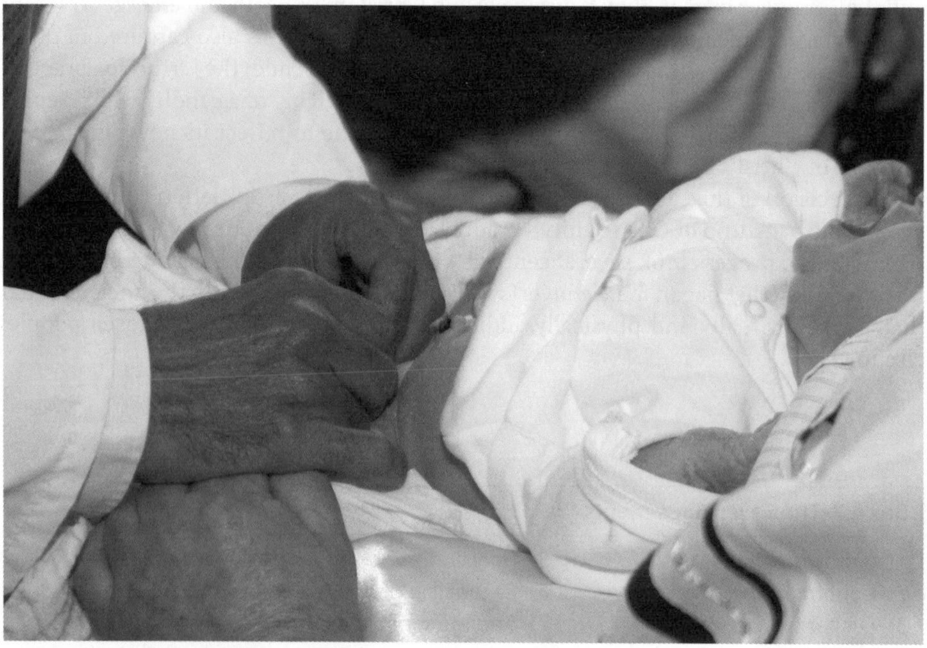

Figure 4.2 A mohel prepares a child for circumcision. (Reproduced with kind permission of iStock.)

(seudat mitzvah). The mohel is not necessarily a medical doctor, but he must have official certification indicating that he is capable of determining beforehand whether it is safe to proceed and, if so, that he is competent to perform the physical operation. Jews often stress that the circumcision ritual is essentially a religious event and not merely a medical procedure. Thus, a mohel is more than a physician; he must be a person of devout faith though not necessarily a rabbi.[11]

The practice of circumcision is far from unique to Judaism. Archeological evidence from artwork and tombs indicates that the Egyptians practiced circumcision as early as the Sixth Dynasty (c.2340–2180 BCE) and it seems to have been common among Semitic peoples by the first millennium BCE. However, it was so vehemently discouraged in the Greek and Roman Empires that it had essentially become associated with Jews and Jewish Christians by the beginning of the Common Era.[12] Circumcision is also found among certain African and Australasian indigenous peoples as well as throughout the Islamic world.

The purpose of the circumcision rite varies according to the socio-religious context. Reasons often cited for circumcising include its being an aid to hygiene, a means to suppress or enhance sexual desire, a sign of social status and a passage to adulthood.[13] In the case of Judaism, there are quite specific religious interpretations involved. Primarily, circumcision is an act of trusting obedience to the divine command. Jews circumcise their male children because it is God's will. Circumcision is one of the earliest of the 613 commandments of the Torah, appearing for the first time in Genesis where Abraham is told by God:

> This is my covenant, which you shall keep, between me and you and your offspring after you: Every male among you shall be circumcised. You shall circumcise the flesh of your foreskins, and it shall be a sign of the covenant between me and you. Throughout your generations every male among you shall be circumcised when he is eight days old.[14]

The text states that circumcision is a sign of the sacred pact between God and his people. Appositely, the Hebrew name of the ceremony, *b'rit milah*, means "covenant of circumcision."[15]

Circumcision does not make a newborn child Jewish in the way that baptism makes a child Christian. For one thing, that would disenfranchise half of the community since there is no female circumcision in Judaism. Jewish identity is conferred on both male and female by birth, not by ritual. Traditionally a child is considered Jewish if he or she is born of a Jewish woman, although there are some liberal groups today that regard those who have a Jewish father and a non-Jewish mother as Jewish. However, as the main Jewish ceremony associated with childbirth, circumcision powerfully expresses ideas of membership and belonging. The permanent mark left on the male body as a result of the act of circumcision carries strong connotations of identity. The circumcised look physically different from the uncircumcised, underlining the idea that the soul of Judaism, like the bodies of its male members, is unique.[16] Rabbinic commentators speak of the appropriateness of having the identifying sign on the male procreative organ since the sacred covenant is a priceless gift passed on from generation to generation. The theme of Jewish identity is further highlighted by the bestowing of a formal Hebrew name during b'rit milah (Box 4.3). Jewish naming customs vary but the most

Box 4.3 Prayer from a Jewish Circumcision Rite
Blessed are You, King of the universe, who sanctified your loved one from birth and established your law with his descendants giving them the sign of the holy covenant. By this merit our living God, you commanded to save your loved one from the abyss, because of the covenant made in the flesh. Blessed are You, the maker of the covenant. Our God and God of our fathers, let this child grow up with his parents, and let his name be called [name]. Let the father be happy with his progeny and the mother with her offspring.

popular sources are the names of relatives, prominent biblical and historical figures, and foreign names translated into Hebrew.[17]

Another theme associated with b'rit milah is the idea of completion. According to some commentators, the foreskin is an unnecessary addition and its removal symbolizes the complete formation of a new human being. In other words, one must cooperate with the creator in fashioning the whole person in both the physical and the spiritual sense. Circumcision is a reminder that one is not born perfect, and the cutting away of selfishness and sinfulness is a lifelong process that requires human intent as well as divine assistance.

Jewish law states that the child must be circumcised on the "eighth day" after birth, which corresponds to one week in the Western calendar. The rule applies even if that day falls on **Yom Kippur** or a sabbath when there are severe restrictions on what Jews can and cannot do. There are few Jewish institutions that take priority over the sabbath but b'rit milah is one of them, which is an indication of its extraordinary importance. The only justification for postponing b'rit milah is the health of the child, reaffirming the fundamental Jewish principle that human life has precedence over even the most binding ritual laws.[18] Although the Torah does not specify the exact hour, circumcisions are traditionally held in the morning, reflecting Abraham's enthusiasm to fulfill God's commandment.[19]

As mentioned above, female circumcision is not practiced in Judaism. Jewish girls usually receive their Hebrew name at synagogue on the first day of Torah-reading that the mother is able to attend after postnatal recovery. On that day, the girl's father is called forth to read the Torah, the cantor blesses the mother and baby, and the name is officially announced. The mother then says a prayer of thanksgiving in the presence of the congregation. Some have argued that women do not need to be circumcised since they carry within their ovaries the natural sign of the ongoing generative covenant. However, Reform Jewish groups, sensitive to the gender imbalance, have developed a ceremony akin in wording to male circumcision called b'rit hahayyim ("covenant of life"). The ritual contains the basic language of b'rit milah with its stress on covenant and membership, but there is no surgical procedure.

There are two other minor childhood rituals in Judaism, neither of which compares with the extensive practice and pre-eminent religious significance of circumcision. On the thirtieth day after birth, Orthodox and Conservative Jews celebrate pidyon ha ben ("redemption of the firstborn"). This rite recalls the miraculous deliverance from the tenth plague of the Exodus, which claimed the lives of all firstborn males in Egypt except those of the Israelites. According to Tanach, the spared sons were to be set aside as priests, but they joined in the idolatrous worship of the golden calf in the wilderness and were replaced by levites.[20] Consequently, every firstborn male child is in need of redemption, which is provided through the pidyon ha ben ceremony. Basically, the father of the child gives the equivalent of five silver shekels to a **cohen** (a descendant of the ancient priestly tribe of Israel).[21] The child is thus ransomed, but one duty remains for the rest of his life: to fast on the eve of the annual feast of **Passover** in memory of the Egyptian sons who perished in the plague – a touching gesture of compassion for an ancient foe.[22]

In another ceremony at 3 years of age, Orthodox Jews celebrate upsherenish ("cutting off") during which the child's hair is cut and weighed, and the equivalent value is given to the poor.[23] Often the child is invited to lick Torah letters made of honey, symbolizing the sweetness of God's word and the beginning of their Jewish education. Along with the key ritual of b'rit milah, these two secondary ceremonies enrich the way in which Jewish faith marks the birth of children. They also create strong resonances with another Abrahamic religion. Like Judaism, Islam also believes in membership by birth and marks the beginning of human life with circumcision, an official naming, a gesture of redemption, sweet food, the cutting of hair and its weight value donated to the needy.

4.4 Aqiqah

The Qur'an has no specific instructions on how to celebrate the birth of a newborn child. Nevertheless, the official collections of Muhammad's teachings and actions (the hadith) provide the basis for a series of traditional Islamic birth rituals. There is some debate between Islamic legal schools as to whether each of these rituals is obligatory or merely recommended, and there are variations on some of the details concerning the timing, the procedure and other aspects. Nevertheless, it is possible to identify three distinct moments in early infancy to which several ceremonies are linked.

The first moment occurs immediately after the birth of the child and consists of two simple symbolic actions. It is a widely held Islamic custom that the initial and final sounds that every human person should hear in this world are those of the **adhan** – the brief call to prayer that is broadcast from minarets five times each day (Box 4.4). Before the fragile child is exposed to the cacophonous din of the world and even before its mind is able to comprehend the meaning of the sounds, its tiny ears will hear the pristine truth that lies at the heart of Islam: there is no god but God and Muhammad is his Prophet. According to tradition, Muhammad recited the adhan at the birth of his grandsons, Hasan and Hussain, and today it is usually recited by one of the parents or a respected member of the community. The words are gently whispered so that the baby is not alarmed and it is often accompanied by the recitation of several verses from the Qur'an. Traditionally the adhan is spoken just once into the right ear of the child, but some Muslims also recite a similar phrase known as the iqamah into the left ear as well.[24]

The other ritual performed immediately after the birth is known as tahnik, in which the father or a person of good standing places a date in the baby's mouth. Substitutes such as honey or some other sweet foodstuff can be used if dates are not available. The idea behind the action is that goodness and virtue will be transmitted from the adult to the child. Again, the gesture harks back to a custom of Muhammad who would chew a date and place it into the mouth of the newborn to convey a special blessing.[25]

Box 4.4 The Adhan (Islamic Call to Prayer)
God is most great. I testify that there is no god except God. I testify that Muhammad is the Messenger of God. Come to prayer. Come to salvation. Prayer is better than sleep [*recited only at morning prayer*]. Come to the best of work *[added by Shi'ites]*. God is most great. There is no god except God.

The second moment comes approximately seven days after the birth when a series of rituals collectively known as aqiqah is celebrated. The precise timing of aqiqah is flexible, in contrast to Judaism's strict insistence that b'rit milah occur on the eighth day irrespective of sabbath or festival. There are three basic elements involved, although the exact order can vary. The term *aqiqah* literally means "to cut" or "to break" and, appropriately, the first element involves the cutting or shaving of the baby's hair. The shaving of scalp hair that has grown in the womb serves a hygienic purpose but, at another level, it symbolizes a new phase of life or a new state, similar to the haircut during the pilgrimage to Mecca. As in Judaism, the hair is weighed and the value of an equivalent quantity of precious metal is donated to charity. Once again, the ritual is grounded in the example of Muhammad who shaved the heads of his two grandsons and ordered that the hair be weighed and the equivalent in silver be given to the poor.[26]

The second element of aqiqah is the formal naming of the child, which is a common thread in birth ceremonies in the religions discussed thus far. Traditionally, the parents decide on the name, although they may invite another to do so in imitation of the companions of the Prophet who occasionally requested that Muhammad confer a name on their children. The hadith enjoins Muslims to choose wisely since each person will be called by their name on the day of resurrection.[27] The Prophet recommended religious names such as Abdullah ("servant of God") or the names of other prophets, but the name Muhammad itself is one of the most popular names for Muslim boys today.

The third element of aqiqah is the sacrifice of an animal, usually a goat, a sheep or a camel. The tradition does not specify the animal's gender but requires that the animal be at least one year old and without blemish.[28] The meat should be distributed in the same way as on the Feast of the Sacrifice (see Chapter 11): one-third for the family; one-third for neighbors; and one-third for the poor. The purpose of the animal sacrifice is ostensibly a form of redemption, not unlike the pidyon ha ben ceremony of Judaism, although the form of payment is different: the life of an animal rather than an amount of money. The idea of ransoming the newborn stems from a saying of Muhammad that neatly sums up the three elements of aqiqah: "A boy is ransomed by his aqiqah. Sacrifice should be made for him on the seventh day. He should be given a name and his head should be shaved."[29] Islamic scholars have offered a number of interpretations regarding the nature of the ransom but the most common is an act of thanksgiving. As with Jewish circumcision, aqiqah is not an initiation ritual because membership of the Islamic community is conferred by birth. Unlike Judaism, this passes through the line of the father rather than the mother.

The third and final moment associated with birth in the Islamic tradition is male circumcision, which constitutes an important area of overlap with Judaism. However, there are significant differences. While the Jewish age is firmly set, the timing of Islamic circumcision can vary enormously. Some Muslims circumcise soon after birth while others wait until the child is old enough to recite the Qur'an or even until the threshold of adolescence. Thus in Islam, circumcision is a birth ritual for some groups and a rite of passage to adulthood for others. Moreover, in contrast to the strong biblical basis for Jewish b'rit milah, Islamic circumcision is not mentioned in the Qur'an and legal opinion differs as to its importance and necessity. The Shafi'i school considers circumcision obligatory while the Maliki and Hanafi schools categorize it as a recommended but not mandatory practice. In Islamic thinking, the main purpose of circumcision seems to be hygienic and its origin has more to do with a pre-Islamic Arabian custom than with the Jewish religious rite. In one hadith, it is compared to other forms of personal grooming such as trimming the moustache, cutting the nails and cleaning the teeth.[30] For some, circumcision is necessary to ensure purity during daily prayer, since there is less danger of clothes becoming contaminated from small amounts of urine trapped in the foreskin. A more controversial issue is the question of female circumcision. The World Health Organization differentiates four degrees of what it calls female genital mutilation, which is mainly practiced in North African societies where it appears to be rooted in local pre-Islamic culture. Islamic opinion is divided on the issue. Female circumcision is not mentioned in the Qur'an and appears in only two weak hadith.[31] The Shafi'i school considers it to be compulsory but the practice has been condemned in recent times by other Islamic scholars.[32]

In summary, Islamic celebration of human birth is characterized by rites that are grounded in the example of the founder rather than obliged by law. Both Muslims and Jews officially name the child, perform a redemption ceremony, cut the hair and weigh it for alms, and circumcise male children. Yet in so far as Muslims also utter sacred words into the ear of the newborn child and offer it food, Islam resembles Hinduism with its elaborate series of sacramental rites stretching from the prenatal period into the first years of infancy.

4.5 Birth Samskaras

With over 40 ceremonies listed in its traditional manuals, Hinduism has one of the most extensive systems of life-cycle rituals among the religions that we are considering. These sacred rites of passage mark key moments in the human journey from conception to death and are collectively known as samskaras. In practice the full number was rarely celebrated and an abbreviated list of 16 ceremonies is most commonly cited (Box 4.5). Today even these are not always observed and there is considerable variation depending on sect, region, caste and gender. Yet the tradition of the samskaras is widely acknowledged as part of a common Hindu heritage and many life-cycle rituals today draw on their basic symbolism and form.

Although several samskaras mark important moments later in life such as adult initiation, marriage and death, 9 of the 16 rites concern birth and infancy, indicating a

Box 4.5 The Traditional Hindu Samskaras

Prenatal
- Garbhadhana: conception
- Pumsavana: consecrating a male child in the womb
- Simantonnayana: parting the hair of a pregnant woman

Childhood
- Jatakarma: birth ceremony
- Namakarana: naming ceremony
- Niskramana: first outing
- Annaprasana: first solid meal
- Cudakarana: first tonsure
- Karnavedha: piercing of the ear lobes

Adolescence
- Upanayana and Vedarambha: thread ceremony and commencement of Vedic study
- Keshanta: first shaving of the beard
- Samavartana: end of studies and return home

Adulthood
- Vivaha: marriage
- Vanaprasthin: forest-dweller
- Sannyasin: ascetic
- Antyesti: funeral rites

heightened interest in the earliest years of human existence. The first samskara is aptly named garbhadhana (conception) since its primary purpose is to facilitate the fertility of the couple. Conceiving children is considered a sacred duty for a Hindu, the value of which stems not only from religious belief but also from a historical period when having large numbers of offspring provided economic security in old age. The ceremony itself consists of a simple offering of food to the gods and the chanting of appropriate mantras that speak of the creative energy unleashed by the conjunction of male and female forces.[33]

The second samskara is pumsavana (prayers for a male child) during which the couple express their preference for a boy. The ceremony was traditionally carried out between the second and fourth months of pregnancy, just before the fetus begins to move in the womb. According to popular belief, the moment of quickening is when the gender is finally determined. Although seldom celebrated today, pumsavana reflects the strong traditional Hindu preference for male children which is still prevalent in many parts of India. This bias is partially based on the often prohibitive cost of a daughter's wedding as well as the concern to continue the family line, as daughters will eventually become members of their future husband's household.

The third and final prenatal samskara is simantonnayana (hair-parting) which is celebrated between the fifth and eighth month of the pregnancy. As the name implies, the husband parts his wife's hair three times from front to back using a special comb. The ritual symbolizes the hope that the child will have a quick and incisive mind. The

Figure 4.3 The Hindu sacred sound *aum*. (Reproduced with kind permission of iStock.)

mantras contain themes such as the ripening of fruit and protection from evil spirits. From now on, the mother must adapt her lifestyle with her unborn child in mind. This usually means an appropriate diet, restricted physical activity and the need to retain a calm and positive demeanor. Likewise, the husband should refrain from certain actions such as haircuts, coitus and pilgrimage.

The fourth samskara is performed immediately after the birth of the child and is known as jatakarma. Reminiscent of the Islamic practice of reciting the adhan and offering some sweet food, the father writes the sacred Sanskrit syllable **aum** (or om) on the baby's lips or tongue with a spoon dipped in honey, curds and ghee.[34] The syllable *aum* (Figure 4.3) is considered by Hindus to be the fundamental sound of the universe and often prefaces sacred chanting. In written form it is used as the identifying symbol for Hinduism in much the same way as the **Star of David** stands for Judaism and the cross for Christianity. The action marks the child as a new member of the Hindu world and also expresses the family's hope that it will use its organ of speech to express truth and wisdom. Just as Muslim babies enter the world to the sound of Islam's holy creed, the first sound heard by the Hindu infant is a sacred word that identifies him or her as part of the divine absolute itself.

After a 10 to 12-day period of ritual impurity has passed, the namakarana (naming) ceremony is performed.[35] The child is bathed, dressed in clean clothes and handed to the father who sits before a sacred fire – a common feature in Hindu life ceremonies and worship. The child's head should face north, since the realm of the dead is considered to lie in the south. Oblations of ghee are poured into the fire while appropriate mantras are chanted, during which the name is whispered into the child's ear. There are various customs concerning the choice of Hindu names such as the most auspicious letter or syllable. Astrological factors also play a role and a personal horoscope is usually drawn up and consulted for this purpose.

The final infancy samskaras mark various key moments in the early development of the child. At 3 to 4 months, the child is officially brought out of the house in a ceremony known as niskramana – the first encounter with the sun and moon.[36] Soon after dawn, the infant is bathed, dressed and taken out into the sunlight, once again in front of a sacred fire, with the baby's head facing north and an appropriate mantra being recited. A similar ritual is performed in moonlight on the evening of the same day. The annaprasana is usually celebrated at approximately 6 months of age at the time of the child's first solid meal. The themes of the mantras emphasize good digestive powers, robust health, wholesome thoughts and useful talents.[37]

Between 1 and 3 years of age, Hindus celebrate the eighth samskara, cudakarana (cutting of hair; Figure 4.4).[38] As in the case of Judaism and Islam, the literal cutting of

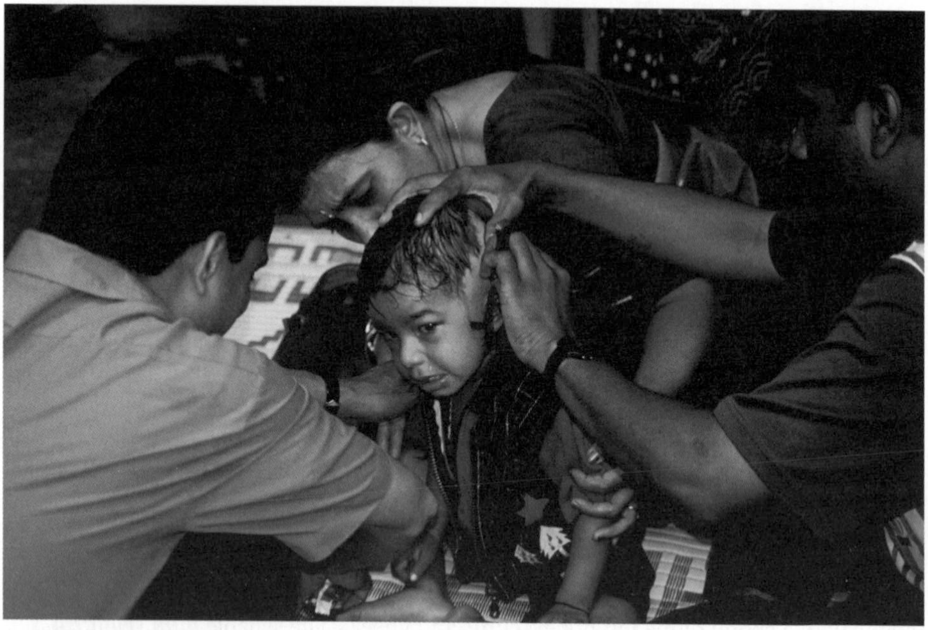

Figure 4.4 A Hindu child receives his first haircut in the cudakarana ceremony. (Reproduced with kind permission of Alamy.)

the child's hair stands for a figurative cutting off from impurity and evil. The shaven head denotes spiritual cleanliness and selflessness, helping to mitigate the negative karma that may have built up in the previous life. A barber shaves the child's head and the father rubs in some butter or other soothing substance, after which the child is bathed. Soon after the cutting of the hair ceremony, the final infancy samskara, karnavedha (ear-piercing), is performed.[39] Traditionally, the physician begins with the right ear for a boy and the left ear for a girl. Karnavedha is not only about beauty and personal adornment, but also represents the opening of the child's ears and mind to spiritual truth.

The term *samskara* itself is rich in meaning and can be translated in a number of ways that help to unpack its religious significance. First, it can denote "purification" or "refinement." Indeed, many of the above rituals are concerned with cleansing the child from impurities carried over from its previous existence or from physical birth itself which, like death, is considered to be particularly contaminating. Celebrating the samskaras for a child at the appropriate time helps to shape and refine the person, just as cutting and polishing a rough stone transforms it into a precious gem. Second, samskara can mean "construction" in the sense of the construction of the self within a particular socio-religious environment. The samskaras help to construct the spiritual setting in which the young person will grow and develop as an integrated member of Hindu society. Finally, samskara can also mean an "imprint" in the sense of psychological impressions that shape the person's moral, emotional and intellectual character from the earliest age. At this level, the Hindu samskaras function somewhat like Christian baptism, which is said to leave an invisible mark on the soul. As life progresses, the remaining samskaras continue to mold and orient the person at key milestones on the journey such as adulthood, marriage, worldly renunciation and finally death.

4.6 The Buddhist Exception

In stark contrast to the elaborate Hindu system, Buddhism is remarkably devoid of life-cycle ceremonies. Neither the historical Buddha nor the fundamental scriptural texts set down any explicit guidelines in this regard. Buddhist religious life is not particularly characterized by rites of passage or sacraments, being more focused on themes such as personal enlightenment, ethical integrity and liberation from undue attachment. Consequently, there is simply no universal Buddhist ceremony to mark the birth of a new child as in other major religions, making Buddhism an exception to the rule.

When seen in the context of Buddhism's cyclic view of human existence, birth can be interpreted as an unfortunate reminder that the person is still tied to the wheel of reincarnation and has not yet achieved complete liberation. Birth, understood as rebirth, is precisely what is not hoped for, signifying a delay in achieving one's ultimate purpose. Thus, the moments of conception and birth are both listed among the 12 stages of life as outlined in the theory of paticca samuppada ("dependent origination"). In this theory, each stage or moment is the cause of the next, therefore setting up a vicious circle of birth, suffering, death and rebirth (Box 4.6).

This is not to say that Buddhists fail to commemorate the crucial moment of childbirth altogether. They do. However, what one finds across the Buddhist world is an astounding variety in the ways birth is celebrated. Local custom plays a decisive factor in the form and content of such ceremonies. Moreover, in many Asian societies where Buddhism is the predominant religious belief, the rituals linked to the birth of a new child are often borrowed and adapted from Hindu practice. For example, in Sri Lanka, the Singhalese celebrate a series of birth rituals almost identical to the Hindu samskaras: the placing of milk on the lips of the baby; the first solid meal; the first outing; the cutting of hair; and the piercing of the ears.

Similarly, in Tibet there are a series of prenatal rites reminiscent of Hinduism such as ceremonies to help a woman conceive or to ensure a safe pregnancy. These usually involve repetition of sacred Buddhist mantras, as well as **circumambulation** of and

Box 4.6 The 12 Stages of Dependent Origination and Their Traditional Symbols (Buddhism)

1) Ignorance (blind person)
2) Intentional acts (potter's wheel)
3) Consciousness (monkey in tree)
4) Body and mind (passenger in vehicle)
5) The senses (house with windows)
6) Sense impressions (couple)
7) Feelings (arrow in eye)
8) Craving (sweet drink)
9) Clinging (gathering fruit)
10) Becoming (copulation)
11) Rebirth (childbirth)
12) Old age and death (corpse)

prostration before Buddha images. At birth, the sacred syllable *dhih*, symbolizing the bodhisattva Manjusri, is painted on the baby's tongue in saffron powder or butter in the hope that the child will grow up to be wise. The child is then taken to the local monastery to receive a name. The father prostrates before the lama and makes a small offering of money wrapped in a special scarf. The lama accepts the gift, blesses the scarf, and returns it to the family. Then, sitting in an upright position and concentrating on the baby, he cups his hands together and blows into a knotted cord that symbolizes protection for the child. The lama then bestows a name upon the baby and hands the cord to the father. A month later, on an auspicious day, the baby is taken outside for the first time, its nose blackened with ash to ward off demons.

In Thailand, the naming ceremony usually involves the local monks, either at the parents' home or at the monastery. The monks are invited to chant the Pancasila – the five elemental moral principles of Buddhism – and other popular texts from Buddhist literature such as the Mangala Sutta, the Ratana Sutta or the Metta Sutta. The child is then officially named by either the father or the head monk. After the monks leave the house, a festive meal is celebrated. In Hindu fashion, Thai Buddhists also perform a head-shaving ceremony one month after the birth.

Amid the wide variety of practices generated by local custom, there is one common feature in Buddhist birth rituals that is of particular interest – the involvement of the monks. Buddhist monks are not primarily priests who preside at a range of sacramental rites such as in Christianity or Hinduism. Hence, the monks do not necessarily play a leading role in life-cycle ceremonies. However, their presence at such events is keenly desired. The reason lies in the monk's fundamental vocation to meditate on and apply the Buddha's teachings in a radical manner. In this way they build up a surplus of positive karma, which not only facilitates their own personal advancement toward ultimate liberation but also constitutes a reservoir from which the laity might draw. On vital occasions such as childbirth, weddings or funerals, it is positive karma that is in great demand. Basically, the monks provide the laity with the spiritual benefits of their stored karma, while the laity in turn provide the monks with material needs such as food and clothing.

This exchange of tangible support for intangible karma constitutes the fundamental covenant between the two main subdivisions of Buddhist society and underpins most Buddhist life-cycle ceremonies including birth rituals. Typically people will either bring their newborn child to the monastery temple or invite the monks to their home. As with other religions, the monks chant appropriate scriptural passages and other mantras aimed at bringing protection, health and future success to the child. In return the family makes an offering to the monks. Significantly, the most common ritual action performed by the monks at birth ceremonies, as well as other life-cycle ceremonies, involves the pouring of water from one vessel to another. In one sense, the use of water takes us back to Christian baptism, discussed at the start of the chapter. But while water represents the washing away of sin for the Christian, in the Buddhist rituals flowing water symbolizes the transfer of positive karma from the holy monk to the layperson whether they are a newborn infant, a bridal couple or a deceased person lying on the bier.

Concern about misplaced emphasis on rituals per se and the lack of explicit birth ceremonies are not only features of Buddhism. Daoism is also characterized by a general wariness regarding ritualism, the absence of a universally accepted rite of passage to mark the birth of a baby and considerable overlap in practice with Buddhist, Confucian and folk traditions.

4.7 Chinese Customs

The key idea that persons should spontaneously align themselves with the mysterious Dao, rather than conform to social restrictions, tends to generate a natural suspicion regarding rituals in Daoism. As in the Buddhist tradition, preoccupation with religious ceremonies can easily distract one from what really matters and actually work against one's best interests. Despite this, Daoist religious practice has found a place for a rich spectrum of rituals, the most noteworthy of which are purification, ordination and funeral ceremonies.[40] Typically, such rites are aimed at establishing balance between yin and yang forces; they are designed to connect heaven with earth and create harmony between the **Five Elements**: water, wood, fire, metal and earth. What about birth rituals? Daoism does not ignore the religious significance of pregnancy and birth, but what is striking is that Daoist birth customs are not well defined or universally practiced. What happens in Chinese families when a child is born is usually fashioned by elements in the broader culture, especially popular folk religion.

The traditional Chinese attitude to birth is ambivalent. On one hand, birth is a messy biological process that involves blood and other bodily fluids. As in Hinduism, it is a dangerous time of physical and spiritual pollution, requiring various forms of cleansing and purification. On the other hand, the family is the primary unit in Chinese society and the continuation of the family line via descendants is a very high priority. Thus, children are seen as a blessing that guarantees the survival of the family throughout the generations. In other words, the birth of a baby is wonderful news. It is an event to be celebrated in the context of family gatherings and it is a gift for which the gods and ancestors must be thanked.

When a woman falls pregnant, prayers and offerings are made in the home and in temples as an expression of gratitude. Petitions are also submitted to the gods for the protection of the mother and fetus during the period of pregnancy. Many families pray to Guanyin (Goddess of Mercy) who is the Chinese version of the bodhisattva Avalokiteshvara in Buddhism. The other popular recipient of prayers is Jinhua Furen (Golden Flower Lady), who watches over pregnant mothers and protects them from illness and malignant forces. A common Chinese practice is to visit a temple where the mother burns incense, places offerings before the altar and makes a private vow in order to receive divine blessing and protection. On the practical side, expectant mothers are advised to avoid physical actions that might harm the baby and to avoid words that might offend the gods. Diet is also an important factor and certain foods may be recommended or avoided for reasons steeped in folk medicine.

Immediately after the birth of a child, the mother begins a one month period of confinement known as Zuo yuezi. The woman will literally sit out one month with her newborn baby in a bedroom or some limited space in the home, often under the care of her mother-in-law. Zuo yuezi serves two purposes. First, it provides an extensive interval of time during which the mother can recuperate from the birth. Second, it protects other members of the family and the gods from physical and spiritual impurities associated with the birth, especially blood and other bodily fluids. Often the windows are shut to keep the room dark and the mother is encouraged to cover her body, including her hands, feet and head. She should not bathe or even wash her hair, and she will be served a traditional Chinese diet that is meant to protect her from sickness and help her regain strength. Zuo yuezi ends on the thirtieth day after the birth, which is called Man yue (literally "full moon"). For many families, this milestone is as important as the baby's first birthday, and today it is often the occasion when family members gather to celebrate the "baby shower." Gifts are presented to the child such as precious garments and jewelry. Auspicious foods are also provided such as red colored eggs, pickled ginger, pork, chicken and sweet cakes.[41] On a more religious level, incense is burned and offerings are made to the gods in thanksgiving. To her relief, the mother may finally bathe and wash her hair, while it is common practice to shave the baby's hair at this point. Horoscopes may also be cast and the child will be given a formal name in a simple ceremony conducted by a Daoist, Confucian or Buddhist ritual master.

Some Chinese families have a special celebration for the firstborn son, reflecting a general preference for males over females in the culture – something that is echoed in other religious and cultural traditions. There are also celebrations at certain auspicious moments such as 100 days and four lunar months after the birth. One common symbol used on such occasions is the offering of peach cakes on the family or temple altars. The peach cakes are also consumed by children and guests. In Chinese mythology, the goddess Xiwangmu (the Queen Mother of the West) lives on Mount Kunlun in her Western paradise, where she keeps an orchard of the peaches of immortality. Every thousand years or so, fortunate guests are invited to share in a banquet and, by consuming this precious fruit, become immortal. Thus, the eating of peaches from the very start of one's life is meant to symbolize the quest for long life and immortality beyond physical death – a theme that we turn to in Chapter 5.

Summary

If one of religion's main functions is to provide ultimate meaning for existence, then the life-cycle rituals of the various faiths are prominent examples. Key moments of the human journey are given transcendent meaning via symbolic actions and words. This chapter has focused on the birth rituals of the six religions with an eye to the points of intersection.

The Christian ritual primarily associated with birth is baptism, although the Baptist tradition within Christianity defers the ritual until the person is old enough to make a free and informed decision for themselves. However, in the majority of churches, infant baptism is practiced on the understanding that adults responsible for the child's upbringing – parents and godparents – may legitimately speak for him or her in terms of faith. Essentially, the baptismal ritual involves a water-bath, symbolizing for some the washing away of original sin. More universally, it represents accompanying Christ into the tomb and beyond to risen life. As the gateway through which the child passes into Christianity, baptism is about initiation and religious membership. As the ceremony at which an official name is conferred on the child ("christening"), baptism is also about religious identity.

The baptismal rite was practiced from the very earliest stages of Christianity, its inspiration and imagery drawn from the memory of Jesus's own baptism in the river Jordan at the hands of the prophetic figure known as John the Baptist. John's choice of immersion in water to symbolize repentance and a new beginning was based on the Jewish ritual bath known as mikveh, which is still required of converts today. Despite its Jewish provenance, baptism is a symbol of the divergence of Christianity and Judaism, for the Jewish ceremony associated with birth is not a water-bath but circumcision of newborn males – a rite abandoned by the early Christians.

The physical operation of circumcision is not unique to Judaism, and is found in many cultures, both ancient and contemporary. However, in the Jewish religious context it carries a specific and profound meaning – a sign of the covenant between God and Israel. As one of the positive commandments of the Torah, circumcision on the eighth day after birth carries the highest priority, taking precedence even over important institutions such as the sabbath and Yom Kippur. The only valid reason for postponement is concern for the child's health. As in the case of Christian baptism, adults such as the parents and godparents act on behalf of the infant during the ritual. However, unlike Christian baptism, circumcision does not make a child Jewish since the ritual is only performed on male children. In Judaism, religious membership traditionally comes via birth from a Jewish woman.

Themes of identity and change are also important aspects of circumcision as is the case in baptism. Like the Christian ritual, circumcision also involves the conferral of a name. Yet, unlike a water-bath, circumcision leaves a very permanent, physical mark on the body, powerfully symbolizing the real and ongoing nature of religious identity. In terms of change, the waters of baptism represent the washing away of the old life and the commencement of a new life as a child of God. Similarly, the rabbinic tradition sees the cutting away of the foreskin as a symbol of the need to complete the birth process and shape the human person according to the divine will.

Judaism is not the only religion of the six to practice circumcision. There is a threefold intersection between Jews and Muslims when it comes to birth rituals. Both religions circumcise male children but they also have a redemption ceremony as well as the practice of cutting and weighing the child's hair, and donating an equivalent amount to the poor. Islamic birth rituals are somewhat more elaborate, based not so much on Qur'anic prescriptions but on the example of the Prophet. Immediately after birth, the child is given a sweet substance such as dates, and the Islamic call to prayer is whispered in its ear – food for both body and soul from the very first moment of life.

Approximately one week after birth the three aqiqah rituals are performed. A name is given according to traditional Islamic norms, the hair is cut and weighed and a donation given to the needy, and an animal is slaughtered as a gesture of redemption or thanksgiving. There are echoes here of the Jewish ritual of pidyon ha ben in which the firstborn male child is redeemed, although the symbolic ransom in the Jewish version involves the gift of coins to a priest rather than the gift of an animal to God. Finally, circumcision is performed but, unlike Judaism, the timing ranges from infancy to adolescence. Moreover, Islamic circumcision is not Qur'anic and is more associated with purity and hygiene, whereas in Judaism it is a sign of the divine–human covenant.

Islamic birth rituals not only intersect with Jewish practice but display a surprising similarity to classical Hindu ceremonies. Hinduism has arguably the most elaborate and extensive series of life-cycle rituals among the six religions and a significant number of these are prenatal, birth, and infancy rites, suggesting a particular concern for purity and propriety in childhood. Although there is considerable variation in practice depending on geography, caste and gender, the infancy samskaras are widely adapted across the myriad of Hindu sects. Prenatal rituals include simple ceremonies for various blessings at natural moments: prayers for fertility prior to conception; prayers for a male child at the quickening in the womb; and prayers for a healthy birth toward the end of the pregnancy. Similarities with other religions become apparent in the postnatal rituals such as the writing of the sacred sound aum on the newborn's tongue with honey, which resembles the Islamic custom of whispering the adhan. In both religions, the first forms of nourishment that the baby should receive are the most sacred sounds of all. Similarly, the Jewish idea that circumcision symbolizes the cutting and shaping of the raw soul is also reflected in the Hindu term samskara, which suggests a spiritual imprint, a refinement of the person or the construction of the true self.

The fact that Buddhism and Daoism have no specific birth ritual sets them apart from the other four faiths and serves as a reminder that the practical themes of this book are not necessarily relevant to all religions to the same degree. The religions have their own special character and cannot be forced into neat *a priori* categories. In one sense, Buddhism's lack of a common birth ritual reflects its understanding of human birth as the unfortunate return of a deceased spirit on the wheel of reincarnation. Birth is actually rebirth and the aim of Buddhism is to help people avoid being reborn into this world of enslaving desires. In contrast, Chinese culture sees the birth of a child as a blessing and a guarantee that the family line will continue. But Daoist ritual focus is later in life where diet, exercise and meditation are woven together to ensure health, long life and, ultimately, immortality. Despite less theological interest in birth as such, both traditions mark the event by borrowing from other sources. In the case of Buddhism, the source of inspiration is often Hindu customs such as nourishment for the newborn, the first solid food and the first excursion outside the house. In the case of Chinese families, birth customs are derived from the popular culture rather than Daoism as such. There is also resonance between Chinese practice and other faiths, especially Hinduism, in its concern for protection of mother and child during pregnancy, confinement after birth for purity reasons, the child's first haircut and gifts of symbolic food such as red eggs and peaches.

Initiation and membership, naming and identity, purifying and redeeming – these are some of the key themes that resonate across the birth rituals of the six religions. Furthermore, the notion of birth as unfortunate rebirth, which is shared by both Buddhism and Hinduism, leads naturally to life-cycle rituals that deal with the opposite end of life. The religious meaning of birth is inescapably tied up with the religious meaning of death.

Discussion Topics

1. Are people born Hindu, Jewish, Islamic, Christian, Buddhist or Daoist?
2. Explore the religious significance of naming a child in each religious tradition.
3. Examine the historical and religious reasons behind the practice of circumcision in Judaism and Islam.
4. Does Islam require female circumcision? Where is female circumcision practiced today and why?
5. Examine the arguments for and against infant baptism.
6. Compare the Jewish and Christian "confirmation" rituals.

7 To what extent are the traditional samskaras celebrated today? What alternative rituals are used?
8 Examine the variety of Buddhist and Chinese birth rituals in different communities within each religion.

Notes

1 Mark 1:9; Matthew 3:16; Luke 3:21–2; John 1:32.
2 See Leviticus 12:2; Numbers 19:11.
3 See John 3:1–8.
4 Christian theologians describe original sin in many different ways but essentially it is a state of guilt and sinfulness associated with Adam's first sin which is inherited by every human being at conception.
5 Orthodox Christianity cites Matthew 19:14 as justification: "Let the little children come to me, and do not stop them; for it is to such as these that the kingdom of heaven belongs."
6 Genesis 1:1; 7:11–8:22; Exodus 14:21–30.
7 Acts 2:38; 8:16; 10:48; 19:5.
8 The gospel ends with the Great Commission: "Go therefore and make disciples of all nations, baptizing them in the name of the Father and of the Son and of the Holy Spirit, and teaching them to obey everything that I have commanded you" (Matthew 28:19–20).
9 Colossians 3:10; Revelation 7:9.
10 Acts 15:1–29. Paul argued that Christian baptism replaced circumcision: Colossians 2:11–12; 1 Corinthians 7:19; Galatians 6:11–13; Philippians 3:2–3.
11 Shulhan Aruch, Yoreh Deah 264:1. If a male mohel is not available, then a female may perform the circumcision based on the precedent of Moses's wife Zipporah who circumcised their son. See Exodus 4:25.
12 Some Christian groups still circumcise today, such as the Copts and the Ethiopian Orthodox.
13 Jewish authors Philo and Maimonides argued that Jewish circumcision was intended to reduce the sexual urge; for example see Maimonides's *Guide for the Perplexed*, part III, ch. 49.
14 Genesis 17:10–12a; see also Leviticus 12:3.
15 B'rit milah is the Sephardic term while Ashkenazi Jews use the term Bris milah.
16 "Uncircumcised" is often used in Tanach as a metaphor for the gentile nations outside the covenant; see 1 Samuel 14:6, 31:4; 2 Samuel 1:20; Isaiah 52:1. It also refers to the unrepentant within Israel itself: see Jeremiah 9:25; Ezekiel 44:7, 9.
17 In general, Ashkenazi Jews tend to name their children after deceased relatives while Sephardic Jews prefer to choose names from living relatives.
18 Shulhan Aruch, Yoreh Deah 262:2; 263:1.
19 Genesis 17:23–7.
20 See Exodus 13:12–15; 22:29; 34:20; Numbers 3:45; 8:17; 18:16; Leviticus 12:2, 4.
21 Numbers 3:47.
22 If a boy's father fails to perform pidyon ha ben, then he is obliged to redeem himself before his coming of age. If the father is a cohen himself, he is exempt from the redemption rite.
23 Some see a link with the biblical law that the fruit of a tree cannot be picked until the third year. See Leviticus 19:23.

24 The iqamah is a second call, which signals to the congregation that prayers are about to commence. It is almost identical to the adhan in content.
25 Sahih Bukhari 7.66.378; 2.24.578; Sahih Muslim 25.5340.
26 Muwatta of Malik 26.1.2; 26.1.3.
27 Sunan Abu Dawud 4297.
28 Sunan Abu Dawud 2829; Muwatta of Malik 26.2.7.
29 Sunan al-Tirmidhi 1522; Sunan Abu Dawud 2838.
30 Sahih Bukhari 7.72.779: "I heard the Prophet saying: Five practices are characteristic of the Fitra: circumcision, shaving the pubic hair, cutting the moustaches short, clipping the nails and depilating the hair of the armpits."
31 Sunan Abu Dawud 5251, 5271.
32 See the 2006 fatwa issued by the Al Azhar University, Cairo.
33 See Rg Veda 10.85; Brhadaranyaka Upanishad 6.4.20; Chandogya Upanishad 1.6.
34 See Laws of Manu II.29; Brhadaranyaka Upanishad 6.4.24–28; Paraskara Grhyasutra 1.16.18; Asvalayana Grhyasutra 1.15.1–3.
35 See Laws of Manu II.30; Paraskara Grhyasutra 1.17.
36 See Laws of Manu II.34; Gobhila Grhyasutra 2.8.1; Paraskara Grhyasutra 1.17.
37 See Asvalayana Grhyasutra 1.16.1–5; Paraskara Grhyasutra 1.19.
38 See Laws of Manu II.35; Paraskara Grhyasutra 2.1; Gobhila Grhyasutra 2.8.10.
39 See Katyayana Grhyasutra 1.2; Rg Veda 1.89.8.
40 See Komjathy 248-9.
41 In Cantonese communities, pickled ginger is used because the word for sour has the same pronunciation as the word for grandson.

Further Reading

Cohn-Sherbok, Dan (2003). *Judaism: History, Belief and Practice.* London: Routledge, pp. 534–6.

Dessing, Nathal M. (2001). *Rituals of Birth, Circumcision, Marriage and Death among Muslims in the Netherlands.* Leuven: Peeters, chs. 2–3.

Fine, Lawrence (ed.) (2001). *Judaism in Practice: From the Middle Ages through the Early Modern Period.* Princeton, NJ: Princeton University Press, chs. 6, 7.

Hoffman, Lawrence A. (1996). *Covenant of Blood: Circumcision and Gender in Rabbinic Judaism.* Chicago: University of Chicago Press.

Holm, Jean. (ed.) (1994). *Rites of Passage.* New York: Pinter, passim.

Johnson, Maxwell E. (2007). *The Rites of Christian Initiation: Their Evolution and Interpretation.* 2nd ed. Collegeville, MN: Liturgical Press, ch. 1.

McGee, Mary (2004). "Samskara" in Sushil Mittal (ed.). *The Hindu World.* Abingdon: Routledge, ch. 15.

Michaels, Axel (2003). *Hinduism: Past and Present.* Princeton, NJ: Princeton University Press, pp. 71–89.

Segler, Franklin M. & Bradley, Randall (2006). *Christian Worship: Its Theology and Practice.* 3rd ed. Nashville: B & H Publishing Group, pp. 173–81.

White, James F. (2001). *Introduction to Christian Worship.* 3rd ed. Nashville: Abingdon Press, ch. 8.

5

Death

World Religions in Practice: A Comparative Introduction, Second Edition. Paul Gwynne.

CONTENTS

5.1 Introduction

A key element in religion's claim to provide an answer to the riddle of life is its insight into the meaning of death. The religious belief that a form of afterlife lies beyond the grave casts human existence in a completely new light. For believers, it opens up the possibility for definitive justice in a world where all too frequently the innocent suffer and die while the guilty go unrepentant and unpunished. It grounds the hope that love will not end and that dear ones may be seen again. It suggests that the desire to live forever, which is so deeply ingrained in the human spirit, is not in vain. But how does each of the six religions envisage the next world? What is the ultimate destiny of human beings? What is the significance of the physical body? What do the funeral rites of each religion tell us of these things?

5.2 The Wheel of Rebirth

One of the most common images in Mahayana Buddhist art is an elaborate six-spoked wheel held by the jaws, hands and feet of a fearsome beast representing death. The six sections created by the spokes correspond to the six divisions of the universe: the realms of gods, titans, humans, hungry ghosts, animals and hell. According to Mahayana belief, each time someone dies their spirit is reborn into one of these realms. At the top of the hierarchy, the realm of the gods (devas) is a place of peace and happiness beyond the many distractions of this world. Technically, it is further subdivided into many levels, some of which lie beyond the danger of rebirth. The realm of the titans (asuras) is inhabited by beings consumed with jealousy for the gods above, which deprives them of lasting joy. The human realm is our familiar world of sorrow and joy, pain and pleasure. The world of hungry ghosts **(pretas)** is considered lower again on the cosmic hierarchy where these spirits are constantly frustrated by the combination of small mouths and large appetites. The animal world is also considered inferior because such creatures do not have the level of intelligence, awareness and freedom enjoyed by humans. Finally, as one would expect, hell (neraka) is a state where inhabitants suffer a terrifying array of

Figure 5.1 Central section of the Buddhist wheel of life.
(Reproduced with kind permission of Alamy.)

tortures, but only until bad karma is purged and the spirit is able to be reborn into one of the higher realms. In the center of the wheel, a pig, a rooster and a snake chase each other in a tight loop, biting the tail of the preceding animal (Figure 5.1). The three creatures respectively symbolize ignorance, greed and hatred, which together form a vicious circle that binds beings to the cycle of rebirth. Around the hub, white and black paths indicate the concurrent upward and downward movement of spirits through the various realms.[1]

The entire schema is not only a fascinating item of Buddhist art, but also a compact theological statement on life and death. For the Buddhist, human existence is essentially cyclic. Birth leads to death, which in turn leads to rebirth, and so on. Each lifetime is merely one stage in the epic journey of the individual involving hundreds or even thousands of rebirths. This process is commonly described in English as reincarnation, or transmigration of the soul. In both the Hindu and Buddhist traditions, it is known as samsara and constitutes one of their most distinctive features. In the samsaric worldview, the main reason why certain people are more fortunate than others in this life is because of a quality that has been carried over from their previous life. That quality is karma, which determines the particular cosmic realm into which one will be reborn after each death. For Buddhists, karma is measured by the extent to which one overcomes or fails to overcome the enslaving vices of ignorance, greed and hatred. It is the force that drives the wheel of rebirth. For those who are advanced in the way of the Buddha, such as monks and nuns, there is a strong possibility that their good karma at death will elevate them into the realms of the gods or even enable them to attain final liberation. However, for the majority of laypersons who are not as wise or virtuous, the general expectation is rebirth into the world in some new form or some other realm.

Box 5.1 Buddhist Bardo Prayer (for the Dead)

O Buddhas and Bodhisattvas abiding in all directions,
endowed with great compassion, foreknowledge and love,
affording protection to sentient beings,
come forth through the power of your great compassion,
please accept these offerings, those actually presented and those mentally created.
O Compassionate Ones, you who possess the wisdom of understanding,
the love of compassion, the power of doing divine deeds and protecting in incomprehensible measure,
[Name of deceased] is passing from this world to the next.
He/she is taking a great leap and the light of this world has faded.
He/she has entered solitude with karmic forces and has gone into a vast silence.
He/she is carried away by the great ocean of birth and death.
O Compassionate Ones, protect those who are defenseless.
Be to him/her like a mother and father.
O Compassionate Ones, let not the force of your compassion be weak, but aid him/her.
Let him/her not go into the miserable states of existence.
Forget not your ancient vows.

Given the samsaric understanding of life and death, one can appreciate that each element of a Buddhist funeral is aimed at facilitating the journey of the deceased through the perilous process of death and rebirth. One way of providing the best passage for them is to ensure the presence of those who have an abundance of good karma: the monks. As a result, Buddhist monks tend to be more involved in funerals than in any other life-cycle ritual. Prior to death, monks are often invited to the home to chant or recite mantras so that the final thoughts of the dying person are wholesome. Similarly, monks return to the house after the person has passed away to continue the chanting and recitation of appropriate sacred texts (Box 5.1). They may also be invited to deliver a short talk on Buddhist teachings or to lead a session of meditation. In return for their spiritual service, families offer the monks food and clothing in the expectation that the merit gained through this gesture of generosity will benefit the deceased.[2] As at birth rituals, this is often accompanied by the act of pouring water from one vessel to another, symbolizing the transfer of good karma. In some cultures, family members even become a monk or a nun for a short period in order to contribute to the provision of good karma.

The corpse is bathed and dressed in preparation for the funeral, which in Buddhist tradition does not have to take place immediately. A delay of several days is permitted, especially if it allows time for relatives and friends who reside at some distance to attend the ceremony. On the day of the funeral it is customary in many places to carry the body out of the home via a special door. Monks are invited to join the funeral procession and traditionally precede the coffin. In Thailand, they carry broad ribbons (bhusa yong) that extend to the coffin itself, again indicating the hope that good karma will pass into the spirit of the deceased at this critical moment of transition between worlds. The procession is often accompanied by cheerful, rather than doleful, music aimed at consoling the bereaved so that more good karma can be generated.

It is a common practice in Buddhist cultures to cremate the body although there are exceptions. For instance, burial is common in Sri Lanka while Tibetan Buddhists, partly because of the scarcity of wood, practice "sky burials," where the corpse is cut up and left for the vultures. The prevalence of cremation elsewhere in the Buddhist world is partly due to hygienic reasons in warm climates as well as the enduring influence of Hinduism. But another significant factor is that the historical Buddha himself requested that his body be cremated and stored in a monument. In order to avoid jealous squabbling over the location of such a holy site, the ashes were divided and stored in eight **stupas** in different kingdoms.

In one sense it is understandable that Buddhists felt the need to retain some tangible link with the historical founder and other holy figures via access to their mortal remains. Similarly, the ashes of ordinary folk are usually collected after cremation, placed in an urn, and stored in special urns within temple complexes or Buddhist cemeteries. Yet in another sense, the physical body carries no lasting significance in the samsaric worldview. Given that this life is but one in a long series of births and rebirths in different forms and in different realms, the reduction of the corpse to ash via cremation makes theological sense: there is no further need of the body. But what happens to the part of the person that survives physical death and is reincarnated back onto the wheel of life?

Buddhists differ in their beliefs about the time between death and the next reincarnation. In the Theravada tradition it is almost immediate but Mahayana mourning rituals imply an interval of days or even weeks. During this time, the living make offerings in order to earn good karma, which is then transferred to the deceased in order to facilitate their next reincarnation.[3] A classical text on this intermediate period is the Tibetan Book of the Dead, which describes how the deceased moves through three stages or bardos[4] (Box 5.2). In the first stage, the person is not aware that they have passed away and a brilliant light appears to which they may have two possible reactions. Either they will be drawn toward it, indicating final liberation, or they will flee from it, indicating that they must be reborn. In the second bardo, the person is aware that they are dead and they experience a review of life with its karmic consequences. At this point they begin to yearn for a new body. In the third bardo, their karma leads them to the appropriate realm in which they are conceived again in new form.

Exactly which part of the person survives death and undergoes reincarnation is an elusive notion and the subject of much debate. Metaphors such as a flame that passes from one candle to the next are commonly cited but, in the end, Buddhism acknowledges the enigma that enshrouds not only death but also the concept of the self. Such humble agnosticism also flows over into Buddhist descriptions of nirvana. The term literally means "to

Box 5.2 The Six Bardos of Tibetan Buddhism

1) Bardo between birth and death: waking existence
2) Bardo of dreaming: sleep
3) Bardo of meditative stability: advanced state of meditation (samadhi)
4) Bardo of suffering: post-death unconsciousness
5) Bardo of becoming: reawakened consciousness
6) Bardo of gestation: consciousness unites with new embryo

extinguish" the fires of ignorance, greed and hatred that bind us to the process of rebirth. However, it is unclear whether this means purifying the self from egocentric desire so that it may enter an eternal state of perfect bliss or, more radically, its ultimate dissolution. In the end, the Buddha recommended respectful silence before the greatest of life's mysteries, his preferred explanation being that the self neither exists nor does not exist.

In so far as Buddhism sees the ultimate goal of human existence as final liberation from the cycle of reincarnation, it bears an unmistakable resemblance to its mother faith. Similarly, the theological appropriateness of cremation as a means of bodily disposal and facilitation of a safe passage for the deceased spirit is a salient feature of Hinduism, whose life-cycle rituals typically mark milestones in the human journey with the powerful symbol of fire.

ॐ 5.3 The Last Sacrifice

Travelers in India experience a myriad of fascinating and memorable images. One of the more unsettling scenes they might encounter is the sight of a human corpse lying on a wooden pyre beside the waters of a river, slowly being consumed by flames as mourners watch in sadness (Figure 5.2). The exposed nature of the public cremation process forces upon the onlooker the starkness and finality of death. The physical body is revealed in all its impermanence and fragility, while the atman (spiritual essence), with the assistance of Agni (the god of fire), is released for the next stage in life's journey.

Figure 5.2 Lighting a Hindu funeral pyre on the banks of a river. (Reproduced with kind permission of iStock.)

The Hindu funeral is the last of many life-cycle ceremonies (samskaras) that mark milestones along the way. As with other samskaras, the details of the funeral rites vary considerably depending on region, caste and gender. However, certain common elements can be identified across the Hindu world.

When a Hindu dies it is customary to hold the funeral as quickly as possible. The corpse is placed on a bier adorned with flowers including roses, jasmine and especially marigolds. The eldest son is considered the chief mourner and plays a crucial role in the following rituals for the happy release of the deceased, which is one of the main factors contributing to the intense socio-religious pressure on Hindu couples to have a boy. The body is carried feet first through a back or side door and then through the village or town along a special route symbolizing the unusual nature of this last journey. The bier is borne at the head of the procession, sometimes on a cart or a vehicle. Family and friends follow, traditionally with the oldest first.

Cremation is the most common means of bodily disposal in Hinduism, although there are some notable exceptions. Babies and children under the age of reason are often buried on the basis that they are still innocent and, thus, do not require the purifying effect of the flames. Similarly, radical ascetics (**sannyasins**) are not cremated because they are considered to be already dead in the sense of being utterly detached from enslaving material desires. Such persons are so spiritually advanced that they are effectively already enjoying final liberation before their physical death.[4] Even the post-funeral rituals are not deemed necessary in such cases. Depending on their particular sect, a sannyasin may undergo a water burial or a ground burial. Burial is also common among low caste Hindus in southern India.

However, for the majority of Hindus who are neither children nor saints, cremation is considered the best way of reducing ritual impurity and facilitating the passage of the atman to the next phase of existence since it is believed that the spirit will linger as long as the physical body remains. The place of cremation is first purified by formulas designed to drive away demons and the pyre is stacked with wood by a low caste member. The corpse is laid on the pyre with the feet facing south, toward the abode of Yama, the god of death. The cremation ground is usually located on the south side of villages and towns for the same reason. It is the duty of the eldest son to light the pyre with a torch. In doing so he walks around the body in a counter-clockwise direction – the opposite of normal clockwise circumambulation of sacred images designed to ensure that the impure left side of the body is facing away.[5] Similarly, he wears his sacred thread over the right shoulder rather than the usual left, once again symbolizing the contrary nature of death. It is also his duty to sprinkle water onto the burning remains to ease the pain of the deceased.[6]

The cremation fire serves several religious purposes. First, it acts as a purifying agent, burning away the decaying cadaver, which is a source of both hygienic and spiritual impurity. Second, fire is the common element in Hinduism's life-cycle rituals and daily worship. From the infancy and initiation samksaras to the wedding ceremony, offerings of food and drink are placed into the sacred fire for consumption by the gods. Now, at the end of life, the body itself is surrendered as a gift. Thus, cremation is rightly called antyesti – the final sacrifice. Third, the reduction of the physical body to a small mound of ashes is a powerful symbol of its transient nature. Only when the physical vessel is utterly destroyed by fire can the deceased begin to seek a new body and progress to the next plane of existence. In order to emphasize the need for the atman to depart from this temporary body, the eldest son performs the kapal kriya, in which a hole is made in the skull with a bamboo rod.[7] The aim is to release the atman through the fontanel, which is known as the brahmarandhra ("door of Brahma"). Alternatively, a large clay pot full of water is broken to symbolize the crucial transition.

It is also customary for Hindus to restrain their grief because they believe that the tears of the living cause distress for the deceased.[8] Consequently, the mourners return home in procession without looking back, this time led by the youngest family members. After several days the chief mourner will return to the cremation site to collect the bones and ashes. Generally Hindus prefer to scatter the mortal remains in a river or lake rather than store them in an urn, again highlighting the transitory nature of the physical body and the avoidance of anything that may inhibit the passage of the atman to the next phase. For this reason Hindu cremation sites are often located on steps beside a river (ghats). Some of the most famous cremation ghats in India are found in pilgrimage cities along the Ganges River, such as Hardwar, Allahabad and **Varanasi**. Those fortunate enough to have their ashes cast into sacred rivers are believed to pass directly into final liberation and escape from the wheel of rebirth.

While the cremation fire removes the impurities of the dead body itself, death has a spiritually polluting impact on members of the family, effectively cutting them off from ordinary life for a specific period of time. Typically the time of defilement lasts between 10 and 13 days depending on circumstances such as caste and local custom.[9] During this time all religious images are removed from the house and the sacred Vedas should not be read. Family members do not comb their hair, cut their beards or clip their nails until the period has passed, after which they shave their head. They should sleep on the floor and cook their food on a separate fire. It is as if they too are dead until the deceased has moved to the next stage.

That vital transition is effected by a series of post-funeral food offerings. In Hindu theology, the deceased person continues to exist as a preta (hungry ghost). As in the Buddhist scheme, pretas have thumb-sized spiritual bodies with large stomachs and tiny mouths, meaning that their basic desire for food and drink is constantly frustrated. Their only hope is that loved ones provide them with a fully developed spiritual body that will transform them from preta to pitri (ancestral spirit) and enable them to progress to the abode of the dead. Hence, the ritual involves offerings of special rice balls known as pindas. A series of 16 pindas are offered over the span of 10 days. Six rice balls are placed in strategic places associated with the death: where the person died; where the corpse was laid; the first crossing during the procession; where the bier stopped; where the cremation occurred; and where the ashes were scattered.[10] A pinda is also offered on each of 10 consecutive days in order to gradually create a new body for the deceased. According to Hindu tradition, the head is formed on the first day; the ears, nose and eyes on the second day; the neck, shoulder, arms and breasts on the third day; and so on until the new body is complete.[11] On the tenth day, the chief mourner shaves, has a bath and receives a new sacred thread. The deceased has now become a pitri and the long period of ritual defilement is ended.

The Hindu funeral rites described above are based on an ancient three-stage concept of the afterlife found in the Vedas. The purpose of the cremation and the post-funeral food offerings is to dispose completely of the old body as a source of pollution and to provide the preta with a new spiritual body, thus facilitating its transformation into a pitri. The deceased remains a pitri for three generations, after which it joins the anonymous ranks of all ancestral spirits who abide in the mysterious realm of the dead. Many commentators have noted that this view is not fully consistent with the later idea of the wheel of reincarnation that first appeared in the Upanishads and developed into one of the most striking elements of the Hindu worldview. There are some links to the samsaric worldview in the traditional funeral rites, such as the practice of not cremating holy ascetics who have already achieved final liberation, and the popular belief that scattering the ashes of the deceased in holy rivers will guarantee release from the cycle of rebirth. There are also occasional references in the funeral prayers to ultimate liberation, but the central paradigm is reaching the land of the ancestors.

In one sense, Hinduism and Buddhism share a cyclic view of human existence based on the hope of ultimate liberation from the wheel of reincarnation and the unimportance of the physical body, which is thus cremated each time. In another sense, the Vedic-based Hindu funeral rites reflect a more corporeal, linear understanding of the afterlife where the deceased needs a new form of embodiment before it can become an ancestral spirit and, after a number of generations, reach the land of the forefathers from which it is not expected to return to the world. These are themes that are variously found in Daoism and the Abrahamic religions.

5.4 Hun and Po

There is an ancient Chinese custom that, when a person dies, members of the family assemble on the roof of the house and, facing north, call out the deceased's name. The ritual is called *zhao hun* (literally "calling back the soul") and its aim is to beckon the departing spirit to return to the corpse lying inside the house. Sometimes the clothes of the deceased are taken to the roof in the belief that the spirit will re-enter them first. Chinese Buddhist families perform the same ritual but prefer to face west where the Buddha Amida resides. In the Daoist tradition, north is appropriate because, in the northern hemisphere at least, that is the shadow side of a hill: the direction of yin and death.

The fact that there is a Buddhist variation of zhao hun is a reminder that Chinese religious practice is often a complex mix of Daoist, Confucian, Buddhist and folk elements, and it is no different when it comes to funerals and models of the afterlife. In theory, the Hindu–Buddhist notion of reincarnation can often be found intermingled with Daoist ideas about what constitutes the self and post-mortem existence.[12] In practice, funeral services are often a mix of different religious elements, and the same funeral might even be officiated over by both a Buddhist and a Daoist monk. For example, one often encounters the semi-Buddhist idea that the deceased is reborn into a type of hell (neraka) where it is judged by the king (or ten kings) of that domain, then punished, purified and released for the next reincarnation.

In contrast, Daoism does not embrace a reincarnational view of the self but, rather, sees each human life as a one-off experience within a much grander cosmic process. On one level, Daoism stresses the fundamental impermanence of every human life. A person comes into being when cosmic energies converge; and they cease to be when those energies dissipate. In this view, the self is a transitory event: here one day and gone the next. The stuff that constitutes our being returns to the universe where it is recycled into new beings. Each individual can be thought of as part of a "vast compost system"[13] – an image that resembles the Hindu belief that all beings will eventually be absorbed back into Brahman. As stated in the Zhuangzi:

> Life between the heavens and earth resembles the passing of a white colt glimpsed through a crack in the wall – whoosh and then it's gone. Overflowing, starting forth, there is nothing that does not come out; gliding away, slipping into the silence, there is nothing that does not go back in. Having been transformed, things find themselves alive; another transformation and they are dead.[14]

In this model, there is no post-mortem existence because the self evaporates once the body ceases to be alive. For this reason, early Daoist practice was more concerned with this present life rather than worrying about the next. Based on ideas in the Daode jing, the aim was to discover practices that enhanced health and increased one's lifespan here and now. Even today, much Daoist literature is dedicated to the range of spiritual and physical exercises, collectively known as alchemy, which are designed to prolong life and postpone death. Over time, the purpose of alchemy was extended beyond longevity to immortality. In other words, the hope was now to generate a spiritual body that would survive the dissolution of the physical body, at least for a period of time. The soul was not naturally immortal but, with hard work and dedication, one could create something that lasted well beyond the grave.

The quest for immortality in the Daoist sense is allied with a more nuanced notion of the self known as the hun–po model.[15] In this model, **hun** is literally the "cloud soul" that is associated with yang, and **po** is literally the "white soul" that is associated with yin. At death, the hun ascends to heavenly realms and the po decomposes into the earth with the body. It is the departing hun that is addressed by the bereaved family members standing on the rooftop and crying for the return of their loved one. If the hun does not return to the body, which means that the person has truly died, then the next duty of the family is to ensure that the hun's new existence as an ancestral spirit is a pleasant one. Similar to the preta–pitri model discussed earlier in Hinduism, the living should remember and venerate the dead for a certain period of time. In Daoism, this is traditionally seven or eight generations, after which it is natural to forget the long-deceased spirit. Also, as in Hindu and Buddhist traditions, the po of a neglected ancestor can become a hungry ghost who wanders the world and can cause injury to the living if not appeased.

The hun–po theology of the afterlife is reflected in a rich variety of mourning and funeral practices. As in other religions, the body is treated with great respect. It is cleaned and dressed in the finest clothes, usually white, black or blue but never red, which is associated with joy and, thus, is avoided during the funeral process. Mourners typically dress in similar colors, depending on the person's relationship to the deceased. Meanwhile, the deceased's face may be covered with a white or yellow cloth. Statues in the home are also covered and a white cloth is sometimes placed over the main door. Mirrors are removed since it is an old Chinese belief that if anyone sees a reflection of the coffin in a mirror then death will strike the family again soon. The sex of the deceased may be symbolized by placing objects, such as a gong on the left side of the door for women and the right side for men.

An altar is usually set up near the coffin with incense and a lit candle. Mourners may burn spirit money as a sign of support for the dead person.[16] A Daoist priest or monk chants from the scriptures and makes offerings on behalf of the deceased and the family.[17] Mourners are encouraged to lament loudly in order to express their grief and this is often accompanied by the sound of gongs, flutes, trumpets and other musical instruments. The traditional Chinese coffin has three bumps to support the neck, back and legs but, today, Western style coffins are increasingly being used. There is a general taboo on looking at the coffin at key moments such as when it is being closed and when it is being lowered into the ground. Valuable items may be placed inside the coffin and spirit money is sometimes burned or scattered at the head of the funeral procession as payment to evil spirits who may be blocking the way. Relatives sometimes carry sticks that represent the roots and branches of the family tree.

Full ground burial, and not cremation, is the traditional Daoist means of bodily disposal. This reflects the fact that Daoism is a body-affirming religion, but the preference for burial is not because Daoism teaches that the body will be raised up at some future date. The main reason is to settle the po into the earth and to provide time for the hun to ascend to the heavenly realms. Whereas Hinduism and Buddhism hold that the spirit can only move forward when the physical remains are destroyed, or at least reduced to ash, Daoism claims that preservation of the body in a tomb or grave prolongs the afterlife of the hun. Chinese cemeteries are usually located on a hillside according to the principles of **feng shui**, which are based on the harmonious interplay of the Five Elements and their corresponding direction (Table 3.1).

After the funeral, family members take home a specially blessed tablet, which is placed on the family shrine for future veneration. Several tablets may be distributed but usually it is presumed that the hun resides in the one held by the eldest son.[18] As with its theology of death, many Daoist mourning customs have been influenced by Buddhist thinking. For example, the traditional mourning period is 49 days, with prayers occurring every seven days. During this time, haircuts are avoided as are weddings, parties and other happy occasions. Litanies are conducted by priests so that the deceased's shortcomings and failures will be forgiven by the gods and he or she will be released from hell quickly and allowed to ascend to the higher heavens. Similarly, lanterns are lit and placed on rivers and lakes in order to help the deceased navigate his or her passage to the next world. Also, there are Daoist deliverance rituals that are designed to help the dead, especially those who have become hungry ghosts. These prayers and symbolic actions help to open the throat of the ghost so that its suffering is relieved and it can ascend to the higher realms with greater ease.

In summary, the Daoist tradition is characterized by a linear, rather than reincarnational, view of human existence, an avoidance of cremation in favor of ground burial and a defined mourning period that involves taboos, prayers for the dead and the symbolic use of color and clothing. Similar features can be found in Judaism but with one significant difference: the addition of a very distinctive theory about the ultimate fate of the corpse.

5.5 Resurrection of the Body

A common feature of many Jewish communities around the world is an organization of men and women dedicated to assisting fellow believers during the distressing time of death. The primary purpose of the hevra kadisha ("holy society") is to ensure that the bodies of deceased Jews are prepared for burial in a manner that accords with Jewish law. The corpse is firstly cleansed and then dressed in the tahrihim, or Jewish burial shrouds. These shrouds are a series of simple, white garments identical for all Jews, stressing the equality of all persons before God.[19] The pants have no pockets, emphasizing the total severance from the material world that is a consequence of death. Perhaps the most significant piece of tahrihim apparel is a white jacket known as the kittel, which some Jewish men wear for the first time on their wedding day and thereafter at New Year and Yom Kippur. On each of these occasions, as at death, the white kittel represents humble contrition for sin and the fervent hope of God's mercy.[20] The body is then wrapped in the tallit (prayer shawl) with one of its tassels cut to further symbolize the loss of life.

The casket is then sealed, although not hermetically because it is Jewish belief that the body should have some contact with the earth in order to facilitate the natural process of decay. To this end, Jewish coffins are typically made of wood and sometimes holes are bored into the sides. In Israel itself, coffins are avoided; the corpse is wrapped in thick shrouds and is buried directly in the earth. There is usually no viewing of the body, or wake, although members of the hevra kadisha may act as shomrin ("watchers"). As in Hinduism, it is the Jewish custom to bury the person as quickly as possible, which provides psychological closure for the family.[21] However, the haste to bury is counterbalanced by the practice of having the funeral procession stop seven times on the way to the gravesite, acknowledging the natural unwillingness to lose a loved one.[22] At some stage before the actual burial, the official mourners will perform kriah, where a piece of garment or a substitute ribbon is torn, symbolizing the emotional rendering caused by death.[23]

In contrast to the Hindu–Buddhist tradition of cremation, traditional Judaism has always insisted on burial. Admittedly, Reform Jews have permitted cremation as an option since the nineteenth century and some Orthodox Jews allow the ashes of Jews who have been cremated to be placed in a Jewish cemetery. But in the eyes of Orthodoxy, cremation is strictly forbidden by God's law. For Jews, burial is an ancient custom dating back to the earliest biblical period, whereas burning is associated with capital punishment for serious sins.[24] Behind the weight of the divine imperative and age-old tradition, there are other reasons for the emphasis on burial. Some argue that natural decomposition is preferable to the artificial destruction of the body by fire, while others claim that burial is a more reverent way of disposing of a sacred object, citing as example the Jewish practice of burying damaged Torah scrolls or prayer shawls. Cremation also has sinister connotations because many Jews were burned to death during the medieval Inquisition and in Russian pogroms. Moreover, the corpses of millions of Jews were incinerated in the death ovens of the Holocaust. But Jewish belief concerning the ultimate fate of the corpse is also an important factor. Unlike the Hindu–Buddhist worldview of reincarnation and spiritual liberation, the main streams of Jewish theology see human existence beyond death involving not only an immortal soul but also a resurrected body.

The term **resurrection** has become so strongly associated with Christianity that it is surprising for many to discover that it was actually a pre-existing Jewish concept. The term can be interpreted in various ways, including resuscitating a dead person back to earthly life. Technically, however, it refers to the revitalization of the corpse after physical death – usually at the end of the world – with the result that the new transfigured body will never die again. At the time of Christianity's birth, there was disagreement among Jewish schools over the veracity of the concept. The Sadducee party maintained that it could not be a part of Jewish belief because resurrection is not explicitly mentioned in the Torah.[25] Their opponents, the Pharisees, accepted the notion on the basis of other biblical references, especially Daniel 12:2, which speaks of the last days: "Many of those who sleep in the dust of the earth shall awake, some to everlasting life, and some to shame and everlasting contempt."[26]

Scholars generally agree that the book of Daniel was written during the Maccabean wars (167–164 BCE). The non-canonical books of the Maccabees, dating from the same period, also explicitly mention the notion of God raising the bodies of the dead on the last day in order to reward the martyrs of the campaign and punish their murderers. In these works, bodily resurrection is connected to the final judgment. For this reason, it is thought that the concept originated in Persian **Zoroastrianism**, which makes the same strong connection. Given that the innocent often die and the guilty go unpunished in this life, ultimate justice is possible only beyond death in the court of the divine judge. Moreover, the authors of these books presume that human existence is bodily, whether in this life or in the next. The underlying anthropology so stresses the psychosomatic union of the human person that existence in the afterlife must involve some sort of body. In Jewish thinking, the human person is understood as an animated body rather than the embodied spirit of the Hindu–Buddhist worldview.[27]

After the destruction of the Temple in 70 CE, the Pharisaic school prevailed and became the fountainhead for the new rabbinic form of Judaism. Thus, most classical and medieval Jewish rabbis accepted the notion of bodily resurrection. For example, the Mishnah states: "All Jews have a portion in the world-to-come ...But these do not have a portion in the world-to-come: one who says that resurrection of the dead is not from the Torah."[28] The last of Maimonides's famous Thirteen Principles includes the resurrection of the dead as a fundamental Jewish belief. Moreover, the second blessing of the Amidah (Eighteen Benedictions), one of the most important prayers in the thrice-daily synagogue service, praises God as one who "revives the dead." Consequently, Orthodox Judaism emphasizes the need to preserve the body for the final resurrection – or at least one part of the body, which the rabbis identified as the coccyx bone at the base of the spine. Today, Orthodox Jews disapprove of processes that compromise the integrity of the corpse such as cremation and even organ donation.[29] The practice of burial follows naturally from the doctrine of resurrection. However, not all Jews accept the belief nor do they insist on the practice. The Reform movement rejects a literal understanding of bodily resurrection and, thus, has revised the second blessing prayer and now permits cremation.

Jewish mourning is divided into three distinct stages, reflecting a gradual movement from intense sorrow to full resumption of a normal lifestyle, similar to Hindu post-mortem practice. Immediate family members are considered to be "official" mourners and carry special duties during this time.[30] The first stage is known as aninut and lasts from death to the burial, which is usually the same day. The mourners are exempt from religious duties such as daily prayer, but are obliged to abstain from meat, wine and sexual activity. After the funeral is complete, the second phase commences and lasts until seven days after the death, hence the name *shiv'ah*, meaning seven.[31] Upon returning home from the funeral, the hands are washed as a gesture of purification and a simple meal of consolation is served (seudat havra'ah). A range of normal activities are prohibited for the official mourners during this time: pleasurable bathing and anointing; washing garments; cutting hair; wearing leather shoes; sexual intercourse; reading the Torah; and work in general. Forms of entertainment and parties should also be avoided and, in some Jewish cultures, all mirrors in the house are covered as a further reminder that personal vanity is totally inappropriate at this time.[32] The common phrase "sitting shiv'ah" refers to the custom of family members sitting on low benches or even on the floor to express the depth of their sorrow and to accept condolence visits.

The third stage is called *sheloshim* ("thirty") and, as the name implies, lasts until the thirtieth day after the death, except for the children of a deceased parent, in which case it continues for one year. During sheloshim the official mourners may return to work and other normal activities, but they should still refrain from attending parties and functions with live music such as bar mitzvahs and weddings. Sheloshim is also the period during which mourners recite the Kaddish prayer for the deceased, although those who have lost a parent continue the practice for 11 months (Box 5.3). On the first anniversary of death it is customary to light a candle for 24 hours and recite Kaddish at synagogue services. A headstone is sometimes consecrated at this time as a mark of respect. The Jewish practice of placing stones on the grave is interpreted as a contribution to the construction of the headstone as well as a sign that the family has visited the cemetery (Figure 5.3).

Box 5.3 Jewish Kaddish Prayer

May His great Name grow exalted and sanctified in the world that He created as He willed.

May He give reign to His kingship in your lifetimes and in your days, and in the lifetimes of the entire family of Israel, swiftly and soon. Amen.

May His great Name be blessed forever and ever.

Blessed, praised, glorified, exalted, extolled, upraised and lauded be the Name of the Holy One. Blessed is He beyond any blessing and song, praise and consolation that are uttered in the world. Amen.

May there be abundant peace from Heaven and life upon us and upon all Israel. Amen.

May He, who makes peace in His heights, make peace upon us and upon all Israel. Amen.

Figure 5.3 Memory stones on a Jewish grave.
(Reproduced with kind permission of iStock.)

The recitation of the Kaddish for a certain time after the funeral reflects the Jewish belief that the efforts of the living can benefit the dead. Although some liberal Jews think that the concept of an afterlife is unbiblical and unfounded, mainstream Jewish thinking holds that human life continues beyond death and that the final destiny of the human person is the olam haba, or the world to come. Olam haba is a state of spiritual perfection beyond human imagination, like the joy of sabbath multiplied a million times. At times it is described as Gan Eden ("Garden of Eden"), for the rabbis believed that it is modeled on the pristine state of humanity. However, only the holiest of persons reach Gan Eden immediately after death. For most, the prerequisite is a purifying process that the soul undergoes in a place known as Gehinnom. The term is derived from the name of a rubbish tip outside the walls of ancient Jerusalem where fires burned incessantly. It is said that pagans sacrificed children to their gods in the same valley, adding to its opprobrium. Gehinnom is the origin of the Christian concept of hell, but the Jewish place is not eternal. In most cases, the fiery purification of Gehinnom should take no longer than 12 months. However, some rabbis believe that the most wicked persons will either remain in Gehinnom forever or be annihilated.[33]

Gehinnom functions within Judaism in much the same way as the cycle of samsara does in Hinduism and Buddhism. Both address the fact that most humans are spiritually and morally imperfect at the time of their death. Consequently, both traditions agree that further refinement is necessary before the person is capable of attaining complete communion with the Absolute. In the samsaric worldview, the residual bad karma is gradually erased over a series of reincarnations until final liberation is achieved. It should be noted that a similar notion exists in some streams of **Hasidic** Judaism that believe in gilgul – a reincarnation of the soul in various bodies over time until the required repentance is complete. However, in the predominant Jewish worldview, the person lives and dies just once, with purification taking place at some point after death. Jews are not alone in such a linear eschatology. The equivalent of Gehinnom and the garden of Eden can be found in Islam, along with the typically Abrahamic insistence on burial and its theological corollary, the resurrection of the body.

5.6 Salat al-Janazah

According to Islamic belief, death ushers in the next stage of existence known as barzakh, or life in the grave. The immortal soul separates from the body and is interrogated by two angels, Nakir and Munkar, who ask three questions: who is your God? who is your prophet? and what is your religion?[34] The answers to the angelic questions are of the utmost importance because they will determine both the person's ultimate destiny at the end of the world and the sort of experience the soul will have during barzakh. As the deceased souls await the last days, they experience the pressure of the grave pressing in on them, in proportion to the weight of their sins. Thus, it is a common custom among Muslims to prepare the dying person for their encounter with the angels by whispering the shahadah (the single-sentence testimony of faith) into their ear. The last words heard by the deceased on earth will provide the answers sought by the heavenly messengers: there is one God, Allah; Muhammad is his Prophet; and Islam is the true religion. In addition, a Qur'an is sometimes placed under the pillow of the deceased so that God's word is near them at the end.

The Qur'an does not contain many instructions for Islamic funeral rites, but this lack of detail is compensated by the example of the Prophet and the manuals of law. According to that tradition, the body is first washed and clothed in simple, white burial shrouds. The one exception is the case of martyrs who are buried in the clothing in which they died as a graphic testimony to the blood they shed for the faith. Modesty requires that those performing the bathing and shrouding are of the same gender as the deceased, except in the case of a child or spouse. In accordance with Islamic dietary law, no alcohol is allowed in the scenting process and any form of embalming is strictly prohibited. Many Muslims use three sheets for a male, for the tradition states that the Prophet himself was buried in this manner.[35] Five sheets are commonly used for a woman – the extra two sheets consisting of a waist cloth and a head veil, reminiscent of the hijab that covered her hair in public during life.

Prayers for the dead person are offered either in the home of the deceased, in a mosque or even in an open courtyard, which was the common practice in Muhammad's time (Box 5.4).[36] The official prayer for the dead (salat al-janazah) has the same basic structure as the standard salat (the five daily prayers). The service is led by an imam who stands beside the corpse with everyone facing Mecca.[37] However, there are differences that highlight the special nature of this particular service. For example, most of the formulas are said silently rather than aloud, and the usual bows and prostrations are omitted. The salat al-janazah is said for all Muslims who have passed away, including infants who have died at birth.

Muhammad once declared, "Hasten the funeral rites," out of respect for the deceased and, thus, Muslims share with Hindus and Jews the preference for a quick funeral.[38] Islamic funerals are characterized by moderation, simplicity and a concern to avoid idolatry of any kind. Extravagant expenditure on the funeral service itself and ostentatious structures over the grave are frowned upon,[39] even though the temptation is not always resisted. The placing of flowers, plants, food, drink, candles or money around the grave is strongly discouraged because it is believed that such gifts are of no benefit to the dead.[40] Instead, the money should be spent on a worthy charity or used to pay any outstanding debts incurred by the deceased.

The emphasis on moderation also extends to mourning customs, for the Prophet explicitly forbade the excessive forms that were typical in the Arabian culture of his day, such as prolonged wailing and shrieking, tearing the hair and clothing, slapping the face, beating the chest and breaking objects. All of this only increases the pain of the

Box 5.4 A Muslim Funeral Prayer

Glory be to You, O Allah and praise. Blessed is Your name and You are exalted. Your praise is glorified, and there is no god other than You.

O Allah! Have mercy on Muhammad and on those related to him, just as You have mercy and You send peace and blessings and have Compassion on Abraham and on those related to Abraham. Surely You are Praiseworthy, the Great!

O Allah! Forgive those of us who are still living and those who are dead; those of us who are present and those who are absent; our minors and our elders. O Allah! Let the one whom You keep alive from among us, live his life according to Islam, and let the one You cause to die from among us, die as a believer. Peace be upon you and Allah's mercy.

deceased soul. According to Muhammad: "Truly the dead are punished in their graves by the wailing of their family over them."[41] Several hadith recommend only a brief mourning period of three days, unlike the more defined and extensive Jewish tradition.[42]

The means of bodily disposal in Islam is ground burial (Figure 5.4). As in Orthodox Judaism, there is a strict ban on cremation, although when a corpse is burned it does not preclude the soul from attaining Paradise. There are several reasons for this aversion to cremation. First, it is a popular belief that the dead person can feel the pain of the flames, just as they can be distressed by excessive wailing of the mourners. Second, Islam considers incinerating the corpse, or leaving it to be devoured by animals, to be an act of sacrilege. This is because the body is seen as an integral part of the human person and not merely as a temporary or dispensable component. Such a corporeal anthropology is not unlike the Jewish conviction that the human person is a psychosomatic unity not just during earthly life but also in its post-mortem form. Although both religions embrace the notion of an immortal soul that survives physical death, they also sense

Figure 5.4 Muslim women visiting a cemetery. (Reproduced with kind permission of iStock.)

that a disembodied person is somehow incomplete. Consequently, Islam also professes belief in the resurrection of the body at the end of time, when the complete person is restored, body and soul. As was noted with Judaism, such a belief is consistent with the practice of burial, through which the body is at least partly preserved, even if long-term decay and decomposition leave only the bones.

As the body of a deceased Muslim is lowered into the grave, supplication is offered reflecting the hope of eventual resurrection. The corpse is laid on its right side, with the head facing toward Mecca. For the entire duration of the barzakh, the Muslim will be oriented toward the holy city, as in official prayer. As the mourners sprinkle handfuls of dirt into the grave, appropriate verses from the Qur'an may be recited such as the following from Surah 36:

> And the trumpet shall be blown when, lo, from their graves they shall hasten on to their Lord. They shall say: O woe to us! who has raised us up from our sleeping-place? This is what the Beneficent God promised and the apostles told the truth. There would be naught but a single cry when lo! they shall all be brought before Us. So this day no soul shall be dealt with unjustly in the least, and you shall not be rewarded aught but that which you did.[43]

As noted above, the Qur'an may not contain much explicit material on funeral rites per se, but there is no shortage of verses pertaining to what Muslims call the Yawm al-Qiyamah (The Day of Resurrection).[44] Eschatology is a key theme in Muhammad's message and it is considered to be one of the most important doctrinal principles of Islam. On the last day, the dead will be raised from their graves and will gather for final judgment by God. Unlike Jewish eschatology, two ultimate possibilities await each human person.

Those who have rejected the authentic revelation of the prophets such as Moses, Jesus or Muhammad, or converted from Islam to another religion, or lived wicked lives, will be condemned to Jahannam (hell). The term is derived from the Hebrew Gehinnom and is described in highly figurative language as an abyss of fire into which evil-doers fall as they attempt to cross the narrow bridge (the Sirat) that leads to eternal happiness. According to the Qur'an there are several levels in Jahannam, the lowest of which contains the bitter tree Zaqqum and a cauldron of fire and pitch.[45] The gravity of one's sin determines the level into which one is condemned. The Qur'an implies that although the most iniquitous souls are doomed to remain in Jahannam for eternity, others will be released after a time of purification, as with the Jewish Gehinnom.[46]

In contrast, the righteous are able to cross the bridge with consummate ease and enter Jannah (heaven). Once again the religious language used to describe the pleasures of Jannah is highly figurative and grounded in earthly experience. Jannah is described as well-shaded, luxuriant gardens whose inhabitants enjoy sumptuous food, drink and an endless supply of obedient servants and pure companions (houri).[47] Muslims, along with virtuous members of the **People of the Book** (Jews and Christians), are expected to reach Jannah. However, one of the most popular Islamic names for Allah is "The Merciful One" and Muslims are convinced that the Prophet himself will intercede for all humankind on the day of resurrection. Moreover, the family of each deceased soul is able to pray for their loved one in the hope that God will exercise clemency.[48]

All in all, Islamic and Jewish eschatology share remarkable similarities: a preference for ground burial linked to the notion of the resurrection of the body; a linear view of human existence with one post-mortem judgment based on a single lifetime; and a temporary post-mortem punishment that prepares the person for final communion with God. The third Abrahamic faith also shares these elements, but with one important difference: the claim that a single case of resurrection has already occurred, within history rather than at the end of time.

5.7 First Fruits

In no other world religion is so much theological weight placed on the ultimate fate of the founder as in Christianity. According to the New Testament, Jesus was crucified on a Friday afternoon and died after a few hours on the cross. His body was hastily buried before sundown in order to avoid breaking the rules of the sabbath. After respecting the day of rest, several female followers visited the tomb early on the Sunday morning only to discover that it was open and empty. The initial reaction of shock and consternation was soon transformed into a new religious faith when various groups of disciples claimed that Jesus had appeared to them in a partially recognizable bodily form. Given the Jewish background of the disciples, the inescapable conclusion was that the resurrection of the dead had begun and the world was about to end.[49] As time passed, Christian faith had to adjust to the obvious fact that the last days were not upon them, recasting the single resurrection of Jesus into a unique event within human history and not at its close.

The implications for Jesus's identity were enormous, eventually leading to the acceptance of his divine status. But it also had a considerable impact on the Christian understanding of death and the afterlife. Jesus's resurrection is seen as tangible proof of the veracity of the Pharisaic belief in the resurrection of the body – an item of faith that was incorporated into the earliest Christian creeds.[50] Moreover, Jesus's resurrection was a foretaste of what was to come in the distant future: the "first fruits" of a harvest that would one day include all of humankind.[51] Given the centrality of the resurrection, it is to be expected that Christian funeral rites are dominated by the theme of Jesus's victory over death and the promise it holds for those who die with faith in him.

Spiritual care for the dying Christian varies from church to church but often involves prayers of comfort and appropriate scriptural readings. In the Catholic tradition, the priest performs a threefold ritual known as the "last rites" which comprises confession of sins, anointing with oil and consumption of the sacred bread known as viaticum, or food for the final journey. In all traditions the emphasis is on consolation and hope grounded in faith in the risen Lord who has conquered death and the fear associated with it.

Once death has occurred, there is no concern to bury quickly as in Judaism and Islam. In many cases the funeral is held after three or so days, reflecting the length of time that Jesus spent in the tomb.[52] During this period many Christian groups hold a simple vigil at which the mourners pray beside the coffin of the deceased either in a church or a funeral parlor. There is no prohibition in Christianity on viewing the body, and often the coffin is open for this purpose. Some Orthodox Christian churches have a continuous three-day vigil that symbolizes the unceasing praise of God by the angels and saints in heaven.[53] The recitation of the rosary is a common Catholic practice in this context.

The funeral service itself is usually conducted in a church or cemetery chapel and presided over by a priest or minister. Occasionally, a plain-colored cloth known as a pall is placed over the coffin to signify the separation brought about by death.[54] The cross or crucifix is a common feature on coffins and graves, linking the deceased to the saving death of the founder. The service typically consists of readings from the Christian Bible, especially narratives of Jesus's resurrection and his teachings on eternal life.[55] The sermon expands on these themes, offering consolation and hope for the mourners. In Orthodox churches a small bowl of boiled wheat mixed with honey, sugar and dried fruits (kolivo) is placed on a stand and mourners are invited to take some in remembrance of the words of Jesus: "Very truly, I tell you, unless a grain of wheat falls into the earth and dies, it remains just a single grain; but if it dies, it bears much fruit."[56] It is common practice in Orthodox churches to open the coffin for a final time before burial and to place an icon of Christ in the hands of the deceased and a wreath on the forehead. Other denominations place wreaths of flowers on the coffin itself, symbolizing Jesus's victory over death and the crown of life that he shares with his own followers.[57]

Gestures and objects associated with the baptismal ceremony often reappear as part of the funeral service, forming a sacramental link between birth and death. The sprinkling of holy water over the coffin reminds mourners of the waters of baptism through which the deceased passed, entering the tomb with the crucified Christ in the hope of exiting the tomb with the risen Christ. The large Easter candle, which is used at baptisms, is kindled again at the funeral in the hope that the soul of the deceased now dwells in the brilliant light of God's presence. The use of incense is a sign of reverence for the physical body, which is considered to be a temple of the Holy Spirit who dwells in the baptized person.

Given Christianity's Jewish provenance and its traditional belief in the resurrection of the body, for most of Christian history burial has been the preferred form of disposal. Even today, the Orthodox churches are adamantly opposed to cremation, which is seen as a denial of both the lasting significance of the body and the reality of resurrection. Moreover, burial is considered to be a more faithful imitation of Jesus's own experience. However, Catholic and Protestant churches have allowed their members the option of cremation in recent times.[58] In their thinking, the burning of the corpse no longer implies an attack on the notion of resurrection.

Although all Christian churches agree that the hope of everlasting life springs from belief in Jesus's resurrection, there is debate as to whether the prayers of the living can benefit the dead in any way. The question is linked to the nature of the afterlife itself, especially what is known as the intermediate state between an individual's death and the general resurrection at the end of time. According to the Catholic tradition, most virtuous souls still require further cleansing before they are worthy of living in the presence of God. The post-death process in which the remnants of sin are purged away is aptly known as purgatory.[59] Although the most common metaphor for purgatory is a painful but purifying fire, its flames are often confused with hell, the state of eternal damnation. Purgatory is actually good news, for it is a temporary process that guarantees eventual access to heaven. There is always a tendency to apply spatio-temporal language literally when discussing the afterlife and purgatory is a prime example. In popular Catholic imagination, purgatory was understood to be a place where souls spent a certain number of days, months or years depending on the degree of purification required. The principle that prayers of the living could aid the dead was thus often expressed in terms of shortening their stay. Catholic theology found "scriptural" backing in the second book of Maccabees where prayers and sacrifice are offered on behalf of the dead so that their sins might be forgiven.[60] Hence, Catholics are encouraged to offer masses and rosaries for the souls in purgatory. Moreover, the second day in November each year (All Souls' Day) is set aside for the purpose of praying for deceased souls in order to expedite their passage to heaven.[61]

It is also common practice in Christian Orthodox churches to pray for the dead, especially on days of special significance such as the fortieth day after burial, drawing on the belief that Jesus ascended to heaven 40 days after his resurrection. Apart from the anniversary of death for each individual, Orthodox Christians also set aside the eve of Pentecost to remember all the faithful departed. Yet despite such practices, the Orthodox churches do not profess a doctrine of purgatory and the dominant metaphor for the intermediate state is "sleeping in the Lord" – an image reminiscent of Islamic barzakh. In fact, the term *cemetery* is derived from a Greek word meaning a place to sleep (Figure 5.5). The deceased, good and evil, are envisaged resting in their graves as they

Figure 5.5 Cross and flowers on a Christian grave. (Reproduced with kind permission of iStock.)

await the general resurrection and judgment. This analogy is also present in the Catholic tradition where a requiem mass literally means prayers offered so that the deceased may "rest in peace."

Protestant Christianity is even less enthusiastic about praying for the dead and generally rejects the concept of purgatory for a number of reasons. Martin Luther's initial protest against Rome was triggered by his outrage that indulgences, which guaranteed the shortening of a soul's term in purgatory, were being sold to raise ecclesiastical funds. Apart from the simony attached to the practice, there are two more profound theological reasons for his position. First, the Protestant tradition does not recognize the books of the Maccabees as part of their Bible since they are not part of the Jewish Tanach.[62] Consequently, Protestant churches argue that there is no scriptural foundation for the Catholic practice of praying for the dead.[63] Second, and more importantly, Protestant theology considers that praying for the dead implies that Jesus's sacrifice on the cross is insufficient to save souls and requires the supplementation of human works. Protestant Christians agree that most souls need further cleansing before they are able to enter heaven, but the intermediate state is usually understood to be a painful yet instantaneous purification wrought by God's grace and not by human prayers.

What awaits virtuous souls after their period of purification is an eternal existence in the presence of the creator in a state known as heaven. Numerous metaphors from biblical and traditional sources are employed to describe the wonders of the Christian heaven. These include: the festive wedding banquet of Jesus's parables; the garden of Eden (or Paradise), echoing Jewish and Islamic themes; the heavenly Jerusalem illuminated solely by the light of God; and the beatific vision in which the creature gazes in ecstatic wonder at the divine countenance. In stark contrast, mainstream Christianity also admits a terrible alternative fate for unrepentant perpetrators of evil – hell. The dominant image of hell that emerges from the gospels is an underworld of darkness and unquenchable fires where there is "weeping and gnashing of teeth."[64] Unlike the Jewish Gehinnom, the Christian hell is a state of total and eternal alienation from God. As in Dante's epic, *The Divine Comedy,* the sign over the gates of this dreaded place sums up the horror of its never-ending nature: "Abandon all hope ye who enter here."[65] Not surprisingly, the fear of unending damnation has served as a powerful motivation in Christian preaching over the centuries. Moreover, the torments of hell have been graphically depicted in sermon, book and art. Despite its horrific and frightening nature, Christian churches are reluctant to declare officially that any particular person is in hell, even the most despicable figures of human history. In contrast, there is a long-standing Catholic tradition of confident formal declarations that outstanding examples of virtue and faith populate heaven: the saints.

Summary

If religion is about recasting key moments of human life in the light of belief in transcendent being, there is perhaps no more pertinent moment than physical death. The religious claim that there is a dimension of reality beyond time and space becomes immensely relevant as the person passes away. Each of the six major religions has developed funeral and mourning practices that not only provide pastoral support for the believer but also reveal each religion's fundamental beliefs about the mystery of death. What emerges from a comparative study of the funeral rituals is a reinforcement of the classical division between the Hindu–Buddhist tradition on the one hand and the three Abrahamic religions on the other, with Daoism sharing elements from both.

The Hindu–Buddhist worldview considers human existence to be fundamentally cyclic. Birth leads to death, which is followed by rebirth into this world, and so forth. This particular life is only one in a long series of reincarnations, aptly symbolized by the image of the wheel. The universe itself is hierarchical and the spiritual essence of the individual re-enters it at a different level each time, depending on the amount of good or bad karma that has been accumulated in each reincarnation. In both Buddhist and Hindu thinking, good karma is generated by behavior in accordance with specific ethical, social and religious norms. In this sense, the wheel of reincarnation and the law of karma function as a compelling moral incentive as well as an explanation for the apparent inequalities in the world. One's actions in this life determine one's reincarnated form in the next.

In contrast, the Abrahamic religions display a more linear view of human existence, which entails being born and dying just once before judgment that determines one's eternal fate. There is no wheel of reincarnation – just a line from birth through death to everlasting life. However, it must be acknowledged that this division between the cyclic Oriental worldview and the linear Semitic worldview is broad and far from absolute. The Hindu post-funeral ritual, which is aimed at providing a new body for the deceased who can then proceed directly to the land of the ancestors, suggests a more linear, corporeal notion of the afterlife. Conversely, the Jewish gilgul tradition, which envisages a series of reincarnations until the soul is purified, echoes the Hindu–Buddhist wheel of samsara.

Although profoundly affected by Buddhism in its theory and practice, strictly speaking, Daoism embraces a linear view of the human existence in that there is no ongoing cycle of rebirth across many lives. Instead, each person is a unique combination of energies that exists for a period of time until those same energies dissipate. The end point resembles the Hindu and Buddhist idea that all beings will eventually be reabsorbed back into Ultimate Reality. However, Daoism also teaches the notion of the hun, or ancestral spirit, that survives death for a certain number of generations and, during that time, relies on the memory and veneration of the living for its ongoing existence and benefit.

Perhaps the most salient feature of funeral rituals that reflects the contrast between the cyclic and linear worldviews is the means of bodily disposal. One consequence of the Hindu and Buddhist samsaric understanding is that the physical body has only limited importance since it is merely one particular form in a long series of lives. Moreover, none of the physical forms will play any part in final liberation. Thus, the general custom of cremation among Hindus and Buddhists makes theological sense. The situation is quite different in the Abrahamic religions where the physical body carries much more significance. The absence of a cycle of reincarnation means that each person only ever has one body which constitutes an integral part of their identity. This is true not only during earthly life but also beyond the grave. Embodiment of some sort or other is understood as an essential aspect of being human. The classical doctrine of the afterlife that expresses such strong psychosomatic anthropology is that of the resurrection of the body. The central idea is that the remains of the person will be raised up at the end of time and transformed into a new, spiritual body for all eternity. The notion first appears explicitly in the Maccabean period of Jewish history and may have its origins in Persian Zoroastrianism. Eventually, it became a part of classical Jewish, Christian and Islamic faith, although there are differences of opinion today as to whether it should be taken literally or metaphorically.

The importance of the physical body in the Abrahamic religions is reflected in their traditional preference for ground burial as a means of bodily disposal, although cremation has been permitted in sections of Judaism and Christianity in recent times. What sets Christianity apart from Judaism and Islam, therefore, is not belief in the resurrection of the body but the claim that one resurrection has already occurred within history, which carries immense implications for the identity of the one who was raised. Daoism's psychosomatic view of the human person also implies that the body is not some unnecessary adjunct, but a vital part of being human, thus underpinning its preference for ground burial. Moreover, although it does not envisage a final resurrection of the body, a dignified burial helps to settle the po and release the hun into the next phase of existence as an ancestral spirit.

All six religions teach that the final destiny of the human person lies in a transcendent world beyond death, although earlier forms of Daoism and Judaism focused primarily on this life and gave little thought to the next. In Hinduism and Buddhism, this destiny is best described as liberation. Both religions agree that the wheel of reincarnation is a source of frustration and suffering. The physical world is an attractive and seductive place, which causes its inhabitants to desire transient things that cannot bring ultimate satisfaction. The final goal of all beings is to escape from the wheel once and for all, as indicated by both the Hindu concept of moksha and the Buddhist concept of nirvana. Both traditions also agree that liberation can take a considerable amount of time and that most human deaths will lead to rebirth. Only those who are extremely advanced in the ways of spiritual progress can hope to find liberation when they pass away. For the rest, the general hope is reincarnation at a higher level on the hierarchy. However, there is a considerable degree of debate and ambiguity as to the precise nature of liberation and the final fate of the self in both religions. Some Hindu schools speak of absorption of the self back into the all-embracing Brahman, while others envisage a continuing purified self in perfect harmony with Brahman. Buddhism, following the lead of its founder, is reluctant to describe nirvana in positive terms, preferring to stress that it is the extinguishing of suffering and desire, but leaving the fate of the self in some doubt. Early Daoist thought also stressed the temporary nature of the self and focused on health and longevity in this life. However, Daoism borrowed from Confucianism the notion of an ancestral spirit surviving death, at least for a number of generations, during which time it could be purged of its failures and sins via the dutiful devotion of living members of the family. After seven or eight generations most spirits would be forgotten, at which point they presumably fade back into the Dao from which they originally came.

In contrast, the three Abrahamic religions link the ultimate fate of the person to a post-death judgment in which they are held accountable for their earthly actions. One possible outcome in Christian and Islamic traditions is a state of eternal damnation and punishment for the most evil individuals. However, all three religions also teach a post-death process of purification after which the person is capable and worthy of living forever in the divine presence. This process acknowledges that most persons are not perfect at death. In this sense, it parallels the function of the Hindu–Buddhist cycle of reincarnation, which also aims at the eventual purification of the individual prior to ultimate fulfillment. What takes many reincarnations in Hinduism and Buddhism or several generations in Daoism, occurs during an intermediate period after death in the Jewish, Christian and Islamic worldviews. Moreover, these religions have less ambiguity about the survival of the self than Hinduism and Buddhism. For Judaism, Christianity and Islam, the final destiny of the individual soul is not absorption or extinction but ongoing communion with a personal God and other virtuous beings in a state of supreme happiness. Although the exact nature of Jewish Gan Eden, Islamic Jannah and Christian heaven is beyond human imagination, a prevalent image is that of a luxurious garden, echoing the pristine environment of newly created humankind in the Jewish book of Genesis.

The post-death process of purification also has ramifications for those who remain on earth. The mourning rituals not only provide an outlet for emotional grief but also reflect a common feature that cuts across all six religions: the idea that the actions of the living can bring some benefit to the dead. The ten days of Hindu post-mortem food offerings contribute to the construction of a new body for the deceased person. Gifts to Buddhist monks generate good karma that can be transferred to the dead who seek rebirth in an appropriate form. In Daoism, the 49 days of self-restraint and the ongoing remembrance via the sacred tablet help to prolong the existence of the ancestral spirit. The Jewish recitation of Kaddish for 11 months after death coincides with the period during which the soul is purified in Gehinnom, without implying the person needs the full 12 months. The Islamic salat al-janazah and private prayers include petitions to God for mercy toward the deceased. Catholic Christian prayers for the souls in purgatory are said to help the soul move more swiftly through the fires of purification and into heaven. Despite the significant differences concerning cyclic and linear worldviews, reincarnation and resurrection, cremation and burial, all religions offer their followers hope and meaning beyond the grave. They also provide opportunities for the bereaved to express grief in their loss and to assist the deceased in the next stage of their spiritual journey.

Discussion Topics

1. Compare how the living can assist the dead according to each religious tradition.
2. How does each religion offer consolation for mourners who have lost loved ones?
3. Is Hindu moksha the same as Buddhist nirvana?
4. Does the resurrection of the body make sense? What problems are associated with the concept?
5. Examine the extent to which Buddhism and Confucianism have influenced Daoist theories about the afterlife and Daoist practice regarding funerals.
6. Compare Jewish, Christian and Islamic ideas about whether the soul is judged immediately after death or at the general resurrection.
7. Compare Jewish, Christian and Islamic images of heaven. How should such language be interpreted?
8. What are the arguments for and against the Islamic and Christian belief that some people deserve to remain in hell for eternity?
9. Explore the origins and significance of the Jewish tradition of reincarnation (gilgul). How does it relate to mainstream Jewish beliefs about death?

Notes

1 The wheel is a common motif in Buddhist art and architecture. An eight-spoked wheel represents the Eightfold Path to enlightenment and liberation.
2 For example, in Thailand the mataka-bhatta and mataka-vastra-puja are offerings of food and clothing respectively for the benefit of the deceased (mataka).
3 The period varies from three days to several years, although 49 days is widely practiced.
4 Sannyasins often burn an effigy of themselves signifying their death to the material world and its pleasures.
5 The left hand is associated with impure bodily functions such as going to the toilet. The prejudice against the left side of the body is not absent from the Western tradition: consider, for example the negative connotations of the Latin word for left: *sinister*.
6 Garuda Purana Uttarakhanda 24.12.
7 Garuda Purana Sarodhara 1.33.
8 For example, in the classical Hindu epic the Mahabharata, the hero Yudhisthira is reprimanded by the holy teacher Vyasa for grieving his nephew's death.
9 According to tradition, the defilement period differs according to class: 10 days for a brahmin, 12 days for a kshatria; 15 days for a vaishya; and one month for a shudra. The death of a child causes little pollution and the period of impurity is only a few nights.
10 Garuda Purana Sarodhara 10.9 ff.; 12.57–9.
11 Garuda Purana Sarodhara 1.50–4.
12 For example, Lingbao Daoism (Numinous Treasure), which was eventually absorbed into the Zhengyi movement, incorporated many Buddhist ideas about the afterlife including the notion of transferring karma to the deceased.
13 Komjathy 128.
14 Zhuangzi ch. 22, ch. 6; Daode jing ch. 42.
15 Daode jing ch. 10; Zhuangzi ch. 22.
16 Also known as joss paper, spirit money traditionally consisted of sheets of gold or silver paper meant to symbolize money or other gifts for the deceased. In modern times, these are made to resemble actual banknotes.
17 For example, the Book of Salvation, the Book of the Jade Emperor and the Book of the Three Officials are often recited at funerals.
18 The tradition of the spirit tablet is usually attributed to the Confucian tradition, in particular the Family Rituals of Zhu Xi.
19 A similar stress on this democracy in death is reflected in the traditions of avoiding ornate decorations on coffins, and the preference for charitable donations rather than money spent on lavish flower arrangements.
20 The white of the kittel also symbolizes cleansing from sin as expressed in the text from Isaiah 1:18: "Though your sins are like scarlet, they shall be like snow." The kittel is also worn by the head of the family at the Passover meal.
21 Deuteronomy 21:23 states that the corpse of an executed criminal must be buried on the same day and this is usually extended to all deceased persons. As a result, Jewish tradition disapproves of autopsies and other processes that delay the burial.
22 Traditionally psalms of consolation, such as Psalm 91, are read at these pauses.
23 Tearing of clothing is a common sign of grief in the Jewish Bible. For example, see Genesis 37:34 where Jacob mourns for Joseph whom he thinks is dead.

24 The patriarchs of Israel and their wives were buried in the ground or in caves; see Genesis 25:9; 35:8; 47:29–30; 48:7; 49:29–31; 50:5. Perpetrators of incest, priests' daughters who commit prostitution and persons in possession of certain banned objects are to be burnt to death according to Leviticus 20:14, 21:9, and Joshua 7:15.

25 According to most of the Tanach, the souls of the dead go to a shadowy subterranean world known as *sheol*, not unlike the Greek Hades. See Genesis 37:35; 42:38; 1 Samuel 2:6; Psalm 6:5; Proverbs 1:12; 7:27; and Job 7:9.

26 Other biblical verses that are sometimes interpreted to refer to bodily resurrection include 1 Samuel 2:6; Job 19:26; Isaiah 26:19; Ezekiel 37:12.

27 A similar contrast can be seen between the anthropologies of the Greek philosophers, Aristotle and Plato respectively.

28 Talmud Sanhedrin 90a.

29 Some rabbis allow organ donation because it not only saves lives but it does not involve the bones, which are considered essential for resurrection.

30 Jewish law specifies the following categories as official mourners: father, mother, son, daughter, brother, sister and spouse. See Leviticus 21:2–4.

31 There are several explanations for the origins of the seven-day mourning period. According to the Talmud, seven days of mourning were observed even before the Flood (see Talmud Sanhedrin 108b). Others claim that it is a reversal of the seven days of celebration during the Passover and Sukkoth festivals, citing Amos 8:10: "I will turn your feasts into mourning." There are also specific rules on how to count the seven days if a sabbath or festival falls within the period.

32 Some traditions suggest that the mirrors are covered so that the spirit of the deceased does not see itself and become traumatized.

33 Talmud Rosh Hashanah 17a. The Kaddish prayer is recited for 11 rather than 12 months because the latter would imply that the deceased was in need of maximum purification and thus reflect poorly on their moral character.

34 See Qur'an 79:1–2.

35 According to the hadith, the Prophet was shrouded in three white sheets from Yemen: Sahih Bukhari 2.23.354.

36 Sahih Bukhari 2.23.337; Sahih Muslim 4.2077.

37 Sunan Abu Dawud 3188.

38 Sahih Bukhari 2.23.401; Sahih Muslim 4.2059.

39 Sahih Muslim 4.2116.

40 The hadith records one exceptional occasion when Muhammad placed a palm leaf on a grave: Sahih Bukhari 2.23.443.

41 Sahih Bukhari 2.23.379; Sahih Muslim 4.2015.

42 Sahih Bukhari 7.63.254; Sahih Muslim 9.3552; Sunan Abu Dawud 4180.

43 Qur'an 36:51–4.

44 Qur'anic references to the day of resurrection are numerous. Surah 75 of the Qur'an is even entitled Al-Qiyamah (The Resurrection).

45 Qur'an 44:43–6.

46 Qur'an 6:128.

47 Qur'an 3:185; 4:57; 9:72; 64:9.

48 Qur'an 59:10; Sahih Muslim 35.6590.

49 Paul's earliest letters reflect the overriding sense that time was short and that Christ would return very soon to usher in the final judgment of humankind. See 1 Thessalonians 4:135:7; 2

Thessalonians 2:1–12; 1 Corinthians 7:25–31. The gospel of Matthew hints at the general resurrection when it describes how the tombs of many holy men and women were opened on the day Jesus died, and their occupants were subsequently seen in the holy city (Matthew 27:51–3).

50 For example, the final segment of the Apostles' Creed, which dates from the second century, states: "I believe in the communion of saints, the forgiveness of sins, the resurrection of the body and life everlasting."

51 Paul uses this metaphor in 1 Corinthians 15:20–3.

52 The statement that Jesus was raised "on the third day" is found in the earliest Christian creeds and picks up a recurrent theme in the Jewish Tanach: the day on which God acts in a decisive manner. In the case of Jesus it is linked to the discovery of the empty tomb on the Sunday morning – the first day of the week in the Jewish calendar but the third day after his death if one follows the ancient custom and counts Friday as the first day.

53 See Revelation 4:8.

54 Hence the ones who carry the coffin are called pallbearers.

55 For example John 11:24–27; 14:1–4. Another popular biblical text is Psalm 23, which commences with the well-known verse "The Lord is my shepherd."

56 John 12:24.

57 See 1 Corinthians 9:24–6; Revelation 2:10.

58 The Vatican lifted the ban on cremation for Catholics in 1963. In 1997 it allowed Catholics to hold a prayer service with the cremated remains of the deceased.

59 The term first appears in the eleventh century CE but the concept of post-death cleansing is evident in the works of Church Fathers such as Tertullian, Cyprian and Origen.

60 See 2 Maccabees 12:41–5.

61 It follows immediately after All Saints' Day (All Hallows) on November 1 when Catholics recognize the vast number of anonymous holy men and women down through the ages who have not been officially declared saints by the Church. The date was probably chosen on the basis of a pre-Christian Celtic festival on October 31 known as Samhain (Summer's End) which honored the dead. Under Christianity the name was changed to Halloween (All Hallows Eve).

62 The Protestant Old Testament coincides with the Jewish Tanach but Catholic and Orthodox Bibles also include a number of Greek texts that were part of the ancient Greek version of Tanach known as the Septuagint. Thus, these works are called apocryphal by Protestant Christians and deutero-canonical by Catholic and Orthodox Christians. They consist of 1 and 2 Maccabees, Judith, Tobit, Ecclesiasticus (or Ben Sirach), The Wisdom of Solomon, Baruch and parts of Daniel. The Orthodox churches also add 1 Esdras, 3 and 4 Maccabees and Psalm 151.

63 See Martin Luther, Small Catechism (expanded), question 211; The Thirty-Nine Articles, article 22.

64 See Matthew 5:22, 29–30; 8:12; 22:13; 25:41–6; Luke 16:19–28.

65 Dante Alighieri, *The Divine Comedy,* Inferno, canto III.

Further Reading

Bhaskarananda, Swami (2002). *The Essentials of Hinduism.* 2nd ed. Seattle: Viveka, pp. 92–6.

Coward, Harold & Knitter, Paul (eds.) (2005). *Life after Death in World Religions.* Maryknoll, NY: Orbis.
Davies, Douglas James (2003). *Death, Ritual and Belief: The Rhetoric of Funeral Rites.* London: Continuum.
Dessing, Nathal M. (2001). *Rituals of Birth, Circumcision, Marriage and Death among Muslims in the Netherlands.* Leuven: Peeters, ch. 5.
Garces-Foley (2005). *Death and Religion in a Changing World.* London: Routledge, Part 1.
Gordon, Matthew S. (2002). *Understanding Islam.* London: Duncan Baird, pp. 90–7.
Holm, Jean. ed. (1994). *Rites of Passage.* New York: Pinter, passim.
Keown, Damien (2013). *Buddhism: A Very Short Introduction.* 2nd ed. Oxford: Oxford University Press, ch. 3.
Komjathy, Louis (2013). *The Daoist Tradition.* London: Bloomsbury, chs. 7, 10, 13.
Marcus, Ivan G. (2004). *The Jewish Life Cycle: Rites of Passage from Biblical to Modern Times.* Seattle: University of Washington Press, ch. 4.
Michaels, Axel (2003). *Hinduism: Past and Present.* Princeton, NJ: Princeton University Press, pp. 131–58.
Obayashi, Hiroshi (1991). *Death and Afterlife: Perspectives of World Religions.* New York: Praeger.
Reynolds, Frank E. & Carbine, Jason A. (eds.) (2000). *The Life of Buddhism.* Berkeley and Los Angeles: University of California Press, chs. 9, 14.

6

Marriage

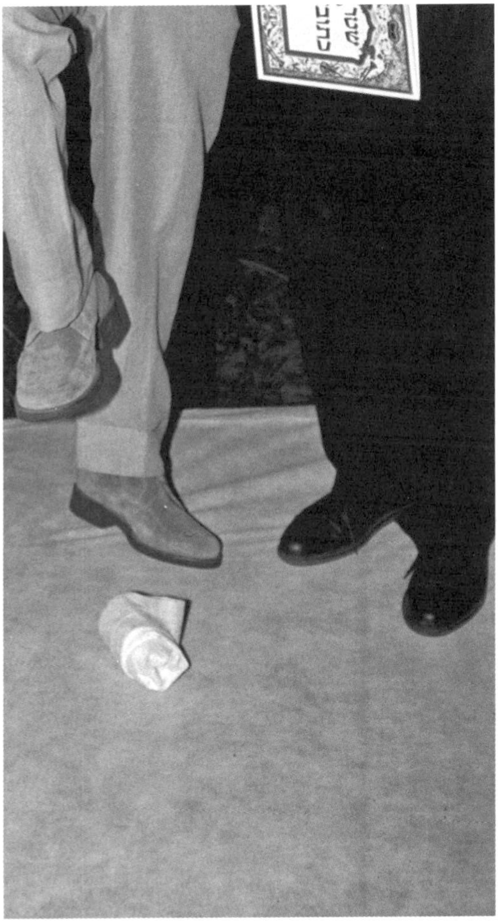

CONTENTS

6.1 Introduction

Alongside birth and death, the third rite of passage that is commonly invested with religious meaning and celebrated with religious ritual is marriage. For many faiths, the formal union of husband and wife is not merely a vital social institution in which children are conceived but also a serious religious duty, a means of worship and an earthly symbol of a transcendent reality. How does each of the six world religions understand the meaning of marriage? What are its primary ends? How does this understanding affect practical issues such as interfaith marriages, the number of partners and the conditions of divorce and remarriage? How is this meaning expressed in the symbolism of the wedding ceremony? What is the attitude of each religion to celibacy as an alternative lifestyle? What impact has the example of the founder had on belief and practice?

6.2 Nikah

When Muhammad was approximately 25 years of age he married a woman named **Khadijah** who was his employer and about 15 years his senior. Khadijah bore Muhammad four daughters[1] and was one of the first believers in his prophetic claim. Her constant support as loving wife and faithful disciple was a crucial factor during the difficult early years of Muhammad's preaching in Mecca. So respected and valued was Khadijah that the year of her death in 619 CE is described as the "year of sorrow."[2] Muhammad eventually married another 11 women before his own death in 632 CE, including two from Jewish and Christian backgrounds respectively. For Muslims, the wives of Muhammad are affectionately known as the "mothers of the faithful" (Box 6.1). Moreover, the example and teaching of the Prophet, who was both husband and father, is a key element in the Islamic understanding of marriage.

Marriage is considered to be of the utmost importance in Islam and there is extensive material in both the Qur'an and the hadith on the vital role it plays in the life of faith. It is often described as having both a vertical and a horizontal dimension. On the vertical plane, marriage is understood as an act of worship in that it is pleasing to Allah and

Box 6.1 The Wives of Muhammad

Khadijah	Widow and Muhammad's employer who bore him four daughters
Sawda	Widow and early convert to Islam
Aisha	Daughter of Abu Bakr
Hafsa	Widowed daughter of Umar
Zainab bint Khuzayama	Widow from the battle of Badr
Umm Salama Hind	Widow from the battle of Uhud
Zainab bint Jahsh	Widow who married then divorced Muhammad's adopted son, Zaid
Juwairiya	Daughter of the leader of the Mustaliq tribe
Ramalah	Widowed daughter of Abu Sufyan, leader of the Quraish tribe in Mecca
Safiyah	Daughter of the leader of the Jewish Nadir tribe
Maymunah	Widow from a leading Quraish family
Maria al-Qibtiyah	Coptic Christian sent as a slave to Muhammad

fulfills the divine plan. According to tradition, Muhammad declared that no institution is more loved by Allah. Moreover, when a person marries, he or she has completed "half of his religious obligations."[3] On the horizontal plane, marriage is a legal contract between two individuals. In this sense, it requires the usual elements of any contract: mutual consent between the parties, specified conditions and public witness.

As in many cultures, Islamic marriages have been arranged for much of history and this is still common practice today. The involvement of parents and family in the selection of a suitable partner is based on the principle that marital success cannot be founded on romantic love alone. Long-term compatibility is an essential factor that includes considerations such as moral character and religious faith. Marriage is seen as not only the union of two individuals but also the joining of two families and, thus, broader interests must be taken into account. However, an arranged marriage is not a forced marriage and Islamic law stipulates that the free consent of both parties is necessary for its validity, even if the bride acts through her official guardian (wali).[4]

The Islamic marriage contract specifies certain conditions as binding on both parties. In terms of financial responsibility, it is the husband's duty to provide for his wife and children irrespective of her personal wealth, which she is entitled to retain for her own purposes. Moreover, a dowry, or mahr, must be paid to the wife in order for the marriage to be valid. The mahr can be in the form of money or some other asset. The mahr becomes part of the wife's personal property and she may use it as she wishes. In practice many women use the mahr to support their families but the law does not oblige them to do so.[5] Often only part of the mahr is paid at the time of the wedding on the understanding that the remainder is due in the event of divorce – a deterrent to a husband who may be considering a divorce without good reason. It is relatively simple for a husband to obtain an Islamic divorce because all that is required is that he must inform his wife of his intentions on three separate occasions, with a period of one month between each declaration. Conversely, a woman usually needs to establish grounds for divorce but one possible option for her is to return her mahr and obtain a "no fault" divorce.

Islamic weddings vary considerably according to local culture but typically there are two stages. The first is the signing of the marriage contract, or nikah – the common term for marriage in Islam which suggests that commitment to the marriage covenant is the heart of the matter. It is often a simple ceremony involving the two parties and official witnesses. There is no special religious ritual as such, although nikah is performed in the presence of an Islamic religious official (imam) with appropriate readings from the Qur'an and a short sermon. The second stage of the ceremony is the walima, or wedding banquet, during which the couple and their families and friends celebrate the joyous event. The walima serves to express the public dimension of the marriage, although its actual timing can vary from immediately after the signing of the contract to some time after the consummation of the relationship.

One of the more striking features of Islamic marriage is the existence of a limited form of **polygyny** based on the Qur'anic text:

> And if you fear that you cannot act equitably towards orphans, then marry such women as seem good to you, two and three and four; but if you fear that you will not do justice (between them), then (marry) only one or what your right hands possess.[6]

This verse has traditionally been understood as granting permission for Muslim men to take up to four wives concurrently.[7] The revelation should be considered in the original context of pre-Islamic Arabia where there was no limit to the number of wives a man could have at the same time. As with many Qur'anic teachings regarding marriage, the intent is to improve the lot of women. This underlying principle is further evident in the strict condition that applies to Islamic polygyny. The Muslim husband must be able to support all of his wives and treat them with equality. This means parity not only in terms of material support, but also in all aspects of the marriage including emotional and sexual relationships. Basically, the husband cannot indulge in favoritism. Some Muslims argue that the Qur'an itself implies that this is extremely difficult and, thus, its spirit is one of discouragement rather than encouragement:

> And you have it not in your power to do justice between wives, even though you may wish (it), but be not disinclined (from one) with total disinclination, so that you leave her as it were in suspense.[8]

The implication is that polygyny is really only appropriate in exceptional circumstances such as a severe scarcity of males in time of war.[9] Indeed this was the situation during Muhammad's lifetime when many of his own wives, and those of his companions, were women who had lost their husbands in the series of battles between Mecca and Medina.[10] In reality, polygyny is relatively rare in the Muslim world today, and is more or less restricted to wealthy men in countries whose civil law codes allow the practice. Moreover, marriage contracts sometimes include a clause requiring the husband to obtain permission from the first wife before he is able to marry a second.

There is a strong expectation in Islam that both partners are Muslim. Marrying a non-believer is explicitly prohibited by the Qur'an unless he or she converts.[11] An exception is made in theory for Muslim men who may marry women "of the Book": in other words, Jewish and Christian women who share with Islam the revealed truth of God's oneness.[12] However, in practice it is often restricted to men living under Islamic law. The rule is designed to ensure that the children are raised as Muslims, based on the patrilineal principle that faith is passed on via the father, not the mother. Islamic marriage is understood to have two primary objectives. The first is the mutual support and companionship of the spouses. When referring to marriage the Qur'an often uses the term *zawj*, which means partner or friend. It is part of Allah's design that a husband and wife find joy and comfort in each other's company: "And one of His signs is that He created mates for you from yourselves that you may find rest in them, and He put between you love and compassion."[13] The second objective of marriage is procreation. The intimate sexual union of man and woman not only powerfully expresses their conjugal relationship but also has the potential to generate new life. In the divine plan, marriage is the sacred context in which children are conceived.[14] The Qur'an describes marriage as a "fortress" of chastity where the powerful sexual drive can be safely channeled and controlled for the good of the offspring and society in general. Extramarital sex is considered to be a serious breach of the marriage covenant and a grave sin.[15] Yet sexual activity in itself is understood as part of God's good creation and an essential element of the conjugal relationship.

Although there are set times for abstaining from sexual intercourse such as during the Ramadan fast and menstruation,[16] Islam does not perceive voluntary celibacy as a means of spiritual advancement or a higher form of religious life. There are cases of celibacy among the mystical **Sufis** but these are exceptional.[17] Islamic law places marriage in the category of what is recommended, even obligatory, for those with a strong sexual drive. Muhammad himself is reported to have declared that "there is no celibacy in Islam" and his own example, as well as that of the prophets of old, testifies to the idea that marriage is the divine preference.[18] The same emphatic insistence on marriage as a fundamental part of God's plan and a binding religious duty, the example of the prophets and a general suspicion of celibacy can also be found in Judaism.

6.3 Under the Huppah

The first book of the Jewish scriptures opens with two accounts of the creation of the world. In the first chapter of Genesis, God shapes the cosmos over six working days and rests on the seventh. At the climax of the process, God creates male and female human beings "in his image" and immediately instructs them: "Be fruitful and multiply, and fill the earth and subdue it."[19] The very first explicit divine commandment in the Torah is the duty to procreate. In the second chapter of Genesis an older version of creation describes how God first fashions a man (adam) from clay (adamah) and places him in a garden as cultivator and keeper. The creator acknowledges that it is not good that man should be alone and so he creates the animals as potential companions. But none of these satisfy the fundamental yearning of the solitary man for an equal, complementary partner. Thus, while the man sleeps at night, God takes one of his ribs and fashions woman. Upon seeing the new creature Adam joyously exclaims that "this at last is bone of my bones and flesh of my flesh."[20] Only when both male and female are joined together is the human person complete. The biblical author then adds a reference to marriage at the conclusion of the story: "Therefore a man leaves his father and his mother and clings to his wife, and they become one flesh."[21]

The two creation narratives powerfully highlight the twofold purpose of marriage in Judaism: companionship and procreation. Marriage is a divinely ordained partnership that fulfills the deep human need for intimacy and flows over into the generation of new human life. In Jewish theology, the relationship between husband and wife is described as kiddushin – a means of sanctifying each other in an exclusive and faithful bond of love in accordance with the will of God. This notion of the God-given partner who fills the gap in an individual's life is reflected in the long-standing Jewish tradition of seeking one's bashert ("soul mate"). Moreover, the prophetic tradition, especially the book of Hosea, added a third layer of meaning to marriage. The conjugal love between the groom and the bride is seen as a symbol of the transcendent love of God for Israel. In one sense, God is "married" to his people.[22]

Such language presupposes monogamy as the ideal form of marriage and this is reflected in contemporary Jewish law, although this was not always the case. Many prominent biblical characters such as Abraham, Jacob, Moses, David and Solomon practiced polygyny and the Talmud allowed a Jewish man to have up to four wives concurrently. The ban on polygyny is usually traced to the Ashkenazi Rabbi Gershom of Mainz (d. 1028 CE) who taught that a Jewish man should have only one wife, possibly as a result of pressure from the surrounding Christian culture. In contrast, Sephardic Jews living in Islamic lands were allowed to have more than one wife in accordance with Muslim law.[23]

Clearly, Judaism places much emphasis on marriage as a divinely ordained institution and the rich imagery of the traditional Jewish wedding ceremony expresses the depth of its religious significance. Timing is an important issue for Jews and there are certain days and dates on which a wedding is inappropriate. These are the sabbath, a day of fasting or during the 50 days between Passover and Shavuot, known as the Counting of the Omer, with the exception of the thirty-third day, which is a popular choice for nuptials.[24] Tuesday is a considered to be an auspicious day since the first Genesis creation story twice declares "it was good" on the third day (Tuesday).

The themes of purification and a new start find practical expression as the bride and groom attend the mikveh or ritual bath on the eve of their wedding. On the day itself, the couple fast prior to the ceremony and confess their sins as all Jews do annually on Yom Kippur (Day of Atonement). Seated on a throne, the bride receives her guests while, in a separate room, the groom is expected to deliver a discourse on the Torah despite his family and friends continually interrupting in good humor. The groom is then taken to his bride for the bedeken, or veiling ritual, which is a remnant of the ancient year-long period of betrothal.

A formal legal contract known as a ketubah is signed by the bride, groom and two valid witnesses. The ketubah states the conditions of the marriage, especially the rights of the wife and the responsibilities of the husband. It usually specifies the amount to be paid to the wife in the event of divorce as well as the obligation of the husband to provide her with food, shelter, clothing and sexual satisfaction.[25] As with the Islamic mahr, the primary purpose of the ketubah is to dissuade the husband from divorcing his wife without good reason.[26] Ketubah texts are often artistically rendered and adorn the homes of married couples.

The wedding ceremony is celebrated under an embroidered cloth canopy supported by four poles known as the huppah – a term that has become synonymous with "wedding." The huppah represents the new home that the couple will create out of their mutual love. Like Abraham's tent, which was visited by God disguised as a traveler, it is open on four sides as a sign of hospitality to all.[27] When the bride reaches the huppah, she circles the groom seven times. There are many explanations for this practice, including the staking out of a claim, in a similar way to how land was staked out in ancient times, or alternatively implying that her life now revolves around her husband.[28]

The wedding consists of two stages, the first of which is known as kiddushin ("sanctification"). As a sign of their union, the couple drinks from a cup of wine – a common element in Jewish life-cycle rituals – which is blessed by the officiating rabbi. The rabbi recites a blessing that praises God for the gift of marriage and the groom places a ring on the bride's right forefinger.[29] Many Jewish weddings now include a double ring ceremony. The traditional Jewish wedding band is plain gold with no jewels or decorations except for engraving on the inside. The groom declares, "Behold, you are consecrated to me with this ring in accordance with the laws of Moses and Israel," after which the signed ketubah is read aloud.

The second stage is called nesuin ("elevation") and consists of the sheva brachot, or the seven wedding blessings. This litany of prayers expresses sincere gratitude for such gifts as life, wine and married love, and asks that God grant joy and peace to the couple as well as to all of Israel's children (Box 6.2). The symbolic number seven, frequently used in both ritual and calendar, is linked to the seven days of the Jewish week and the seven days of creation, signifying completeness and newness.

The couple drinks from the cup of wine for a second time and the groom breaks a glass with his foot – a gesture that carries a number of meanings (Figure 6.1). According to the Talmud, it signifies the need for decorum and sobriety even in the most joyous of moments.[30] For many, it is a reminder that marriage involves not only happiness but also sacrifice. The shattered glass also recalls the destruction of the First and Second Temples.[31] The couple is then escorted to a private room for a short period known as the yihud, during which they end their pre-nuptial fast with a brief meal and share their first moments alone together as husband and wife. Traditionally, this was understood as an opportunity for the new couple to consummate their marriage. Finally they rejoin their family and friends for the seudat mitzvah – a festive meal that marks the fulfillment of a divine commandment such as a circumcision, a bar mitzvah or a wedding.

Given the significance of marriage in Judaism, the choice of a partner is a serious consideration not only in terms of social and economic issues but also in terms of religion. Traditionally, a shadchan (matchmaker) would identify a prospective spouse and

Box 6.2 The Seven Jewish Wedding Blessings

Blessed are you, our God, Ruler of the universe, Creator of the fruit of the vine.

Blessed are you, our God, Ruler of the universe, Creator of all things for Your glory.

Blessed are you, our God, Ruler of the universe, Creator of man and woman.

Blessed are you, our God, Ruler of the universe, who creates us to share with You in life's everlasting renewal.

Blessed are you, our God, Ruler of the universe, who causes Zion to rejoice in her children's happy return.

Blessed are you, our God, Ruler of the universe, who causes loving companions to rejoice. May these loving companions rejoice as have Your creatures since the days of Creation.

Blessed are you, our God, Ruler of the universe, Creator of joy and gladness, friends and lovers, love and kinship, peace and friendship. O God, may there always be heard in the cities of Israel and in the streets of Jerusalem the sounds of joy and happiness, the voice of loving couples, the shouts of young people celebrating and the songs of children at play. Blessed are you, our God, who causes lovers to rejoice together.

Figure 6.1 Traditional breaking of the glass at a Jewish wedding. (Reproduced with kind permission of Alamy.)

arrange a series of meetings to ascertain whether the couple was compatible. The shadchan might be a family member, a rabbi or even a professional hired for the purpose. As in Islam, arranged marriages still require the free consent of both partners and Judaism insists that a couple must at least have seen each other before the wedding. Also as in Islam, Orthodox Judaism insists that the married couple share the same Jewish faith in accordance with the explicit biblical prohibition on marriage to certain gentile nations.[32] In this view, the kiddushin ceremony has little meaning if one of the partners is non-Jewish and such a marriage does not enjoy religious legitimacy. Nevertheless, the frequency of interfaith marriages today is steadily growing among Jews in the Western world. Reform rabbis will often allow such a marriage provided the children are educated in the Jewish faith.

Despite its lofty ideals, Judaism has acknowledged from earliest times that marriages can fail and, thus, has allowed for divorce and remarriage. The religious document of divorce is known as a get, without which neither party can marry again in the eyes of

Jewish law. However, according to the Torah, only the husband can issue a get, making it difficult for a wife who seeks divorce but whose husband refuses.[33] Women in such a position, as well as those whose husband's death cannot be incontrovertibly established, are effectively blocked from remarrying in a Jewish ceremony and are known as agunot ("anchored"). A common solution to this dilemma is to include a clause in the ketubah that requires the husband to attend a religious court or pay an exorbitant amount of money if he refuses to cooperate.[34]

As one of the first positive biblical commandments, marriage is seen as a fundamental duty for all Jews. In a sense, an unmarried person is considered incomplete. As with the Muslim worldview, religious celibacy has had little relevance in Jewish belief and practice. Traditionally, leadership positions in the Jewish community were expected to be occupied by married persons. Talmudic literature frequently endorses marriage and raises questions about celibacy.[35] Exceptions to the general rule exist such as the prophet Jeremiah who was commanded by God not to marry, but scholars point out that this was because of the impending doom that threatened Jerusalem as a result of the invasion of the Babylonian army.[36] Somewhat surprisingly, the sacred canopy, circling movements and a sevenfold blessing are also features of Hindu wedding ceremonies. Moreover, the Jewish and Islamic understanding of marriage and procreation as a fundamental sacred duty is also a salient feature of the Vedic tradition within Hinduism. However, the life stage of the married Hindu householder is complemented by other life stages where celibate renunciation takes on a more positive value than for Jews and Muslims.

6.4 Householder and Forest-Dweller

Most Hindu life-cycle rituals are sensuous events but perhaps none more so than a wedding with its exuberant atmosphere, stunning imagery and rich symbolism. As with the Hindu religion itself, there is an enormous variety of wedding traditions across the subcontinent. Nevertheless, common elements can be identified, many of which are drawn from the classical Hindu literature.

The physical appearance of bride and groom is vitally important because on this special day they represent incarnations of Vishnu and his consort **Lakshmi**. On the morning of the wedding, bride and groom bathe and anoint their bodies with substances associated with fertility such as turmeric, sandalwood paste and oil. One of the most distinctive customs associated with Indian weddings is mehendi, or the painting of intricate patterns on the bride's hands and feet with red and brown henna.[37] The term *mehendi* is often used as a synonym for marriage in much the same way as *huppah* in Judaism and *nikah* in Islam. The bride's dress is customarily a shade of red or pink, which is considered an auspicious color. She also wears as much jewelry as possible, such as necklaces, earrings, bangles, rings, nose-ring, anklets and toe-rings, in the same way as statues of Hindu goddesses are lavishly adorned out of respect and honor.

The traditional venue is the home of the bride although today weddings can be held in parks, hotels and special halls. When the bride arrives she is escorted to the center of the hall where a mandap has been constructed. Like the Jewish huppah, the mandap is a canopy of cloth with four poles draped in flowers, symbolizing the protection of

Figure 6.2 A Hindu wedding with canopy (mandap) and sacred fire.
(Reproduced with kind permission of Alamy.)

the gods and the new household about to be created. As with most Hindu life-cycle ceremonies, the central rites of marriage are performed before a fire which symbolizes Agni, the god of fire and chief witness to the proceedings (Figure 6.2). After offering some rice or other food to Agni, the couple walks around the fire seven times during which they declare their wedding vows.[38] The groom then ties a piece of their clothing together in a knot and the bound couple take seven steps (saptapadi) together, each of which symbolizes a particular blessing: food, strength, prosperity, happiness, progeny, longevity and friendship. According to Indian civil law, the marriage is finalized at the end of the seventh step.[39] The bride's married status is usually symbolized by a garland or necklace known as mangalsutra that is placed around her neck. Also a line of vermilion sindoor powder is drawn along the parting of her hair by the groom.

The stars play an important part in the planning of all important events for Hindus and weddings are no exception. The couple's horoscopes are initially consulted in order to fix the most auspicious date for the wedding, and the heavens also figure in the traditional ceremony itself. If the wedding occurs in the evening, the couple will be invited by the priest to step outside and turn their eyes toward the Pole Star. This star remains perfectly stationary as the night sky revolves around it, symbolizing the steadfastness and trust that will be the axis of the couple's new life together. If the wedding occurs during the day, the couple faces the sun and meditates on it as the utterly reliable source of life and warmth.[40] The ideals of fidelity are also expressed in the Shila Arohan (Ascending the Stone). The bride steps onto a stone slab as a symbol of steadfast faithfulness to her husband. The bride and groom worship for the first time as a couple by placing food offerings in the sacred fire. After seeking blessings from their parents they leave the mandap and the grand wedding feast begins.

The wedding ceremony marks the passage from the first to the second life stage (see Box 3.1), that of the **grihasthin** (householder). In many ways this is the most important of the stages since it supports the others, and the wedding ceremony that ushers it in is the most intensely celebrated of the many samskaras. In the Vedic worldview, it is a holy duty to marry once a person reaches a certain age. Marriage is a part of the cosmic dharma that is incumbent upon all who are physically and mentally capable. Although polygamy is condoned in the ancient Laws of Manu, most contemporary Hindu sects see monogamy as the ideal form of marriage. Wedlock is often compared to the union of primal complementary forces that give rise to the cosmos. Moreover, marriage is a mirror of the transcendent. The human love of bride and groom reflects the love between divine couples such as Vishnu and Lakshmi, Shiva and Parvati, Rama and Sita. Marriage reflects the mysterious unity of the male and female within the ultimate mystery itself. In this sense, the householder life stage is a holy reality and within its sacred context spouses are free to savor the pleasures (kama) of married life including sexual enjoyment.[41] Indeed, the obligation to beget children, especially sons, is very strong. Not only do male children carry on the family name but a son is essential for the proper performance of the funeral rites.

The stress on the union of the couple has been so emphatic, especially among high-caste Hindus, that remarriage has been almost impossible for widows, who are expected to remain faithful to their husband even after death. The extreme case of such ongoing devotion is the practice of **sati**, which involves the widow lying on her husband's funeral pyre and being cremated with him. There is some debate as to the actual frequency of sati in times past, but it occurs only rarely today. It was definitively outlawed by the British in 1829 as a result of persistent efforts to ban it by the prominent nineteenth-century reformer Ram Mohan Roy.[42] The ideal of eternal marriage that reflects a divine reality leaves little room for divorce. Indian civil law allows for divorce based on a range of legitimate grounds but many devout couples, especially among the higher castes, will not take such a step for fear of public humiliation and social disapproval.

As with Judaism and Islam, Hindu marriages have traditionally been arranged by the parents, with the consent of the young persons (at least theoretically). Key considerations in partner selection include caste, family background, financial status, appearance and character. Although secular Indian law allows marriages across castes and religious affiliations, there are still powerful socio-religious forces in place that mean ostracism and even injury or death when couples defy conventions. An important aspect of the premarital arrangements is the question of the dowry, which is an amount of money given by the family of the bride to the family of the groom. The gift is intended as compensation for the cost of the groom's education necessary to secure his future earnings. Sadly, abuse of the dowry system by unscrupulous in-laws has sometimes resulted in extortion, violence and even the murder of the bride for monetary gain. Consequently, Indian law banned dowry in 1961, but the practice still occurs.[43]

Not surprisingly, most Hindus fulfill the householder life-stage duties by marrying and having a family. In this respect, Hinduism shares with Judaism and Islam the belief that the married state is sanctioned by divine law and, thus, constitutes a serious duty that should not be ignored. In the ashrama system it is an important step on the way to ultimate liberation. However, where Hinduism begins to depart from the Abrahamic religions is the existence of two more life stages, beyond that of the householder, in which celibacy is seen as the higher way. The third life stage is known as **vanaprasthin** (forest-dweller). According to the Laws of Manu, when a householder sees "his skin wrinkled, his hair white and the sons of his sons"[44] he should leave behind the familiar world of society and assume the lifestyle of the religious ascetic. Now that his duties as householder are complete, in that his sons have married and he has seen the birth of his grandchildren, he should abandon the material world for the world of the spirit. His dwelling place is no longer in the family home but in the solitude of the forest. According to tradition, his wife was permitted to accompany him during the third ashrama, but the expectation was that their relationship would be celibate. In Hindu spirituality, sexual abstinence is seen as a means to facilitate meditation. Sexual energy is rechanneled up through the spine and into the mind where it activates higher levels of consciousness. In practice, very few Hindus progress to this demanding ashrama since most remain in the householder stage as husbands, fathers and grandfathers.

Those who do undertake the arduous lifestyle of the forest-dweller are essentially preparing themselves for the fourth and final ashrama: the sannyasin (ascetic). There is really only a difference of degree between the third and fourth ashramas. The forest-dweller is permitted to maintain some contact with society. He may continue to use fire to cook his meals and may enjoy the company of his wife, albeit in a platonic relationship. However, the fourth stage requires absolute renunciation. A sannyasin no longer uses fire for cooking but must rely entirely on natural food or begging. Setting aside his name and family, a sannyasin will often burn an effigy of himself to symbolize the utter severance of all ties with his past and the material world. Such persons are considered to be already liberated from the wheel of reincarnation. They have died to the world and have achieved moksha (liberation), even though they still live. They are considered so holy that when they die their corpses are not cremated but simply placed in a river or lake.

Thus, for Hinduism, there is an appropriate time for marriage and sexual activity (the householder stage), and a time for celibacy (the forest-dweller and ascetic stages). At a certain age, there is a divine duty to marry and have children, and at another age the spiritually advanced should move beyond material concerns and earthly passions to embrace the life of abstinence and renunciation. The ideal that the same adult person should adopt both states of life at different phases of the journey is unique among the six world religions. However, the acknowledgment that both marriage and celibacy serve a purpose and possess genuine value is similar to the other Abrahamic religion that considers matrimony to be part of the divine plan and a symbol of a heavenly reality, but whose founder never married.

6.5 Bride of Christ

According to the gospel of John, Jesus's first miracle was performed at a wedding feast in the village of Cana, where he turned six large jars of water into wine. Moreover, one of most common images in his parables is the wedding banquet which functions as a familiar symbol for the more abstract notion of the Kingdom of God.[45] The choice of a wedding as the venue for his first public sign and as a prominent pedagogical theme in his teaching is an apt one given that the preacher and his audience were Jewish. Jesus and his listeners would have appreciated the high-spirited joy of wedding celebrations and would have shared the Jewish understanding of marriage as an integral part of God's plan. The Christian theology of marriage has inherited much from the Jewish tradition, including the classical expression of its threefold purpose found in the books of Genesis and Hosea.

Christian churches frequently teach that the first purpose of marriage is lifelong partnership between two persons, as expressed in Genesis chapter 2. The human individual is essentially a relational being and the most intensive, intimate form of relationship is the unique love that finds its fulfillment in wedlock. Thus, Christianity stresses the exclusivity of such love and views adultery as a grave offense against one's partner and God. The second purpose of married life is the generation of children, which flows naturally from the conjugal love of husband and wife. In the spirit of Genesis chapter 1, fertility is a gift from God who invites humans to cooperate with him in the ongoing creation of the world. Thus, churches often insist that married couples explicitly declare their willingness to have children before the marriage can be blessed. As in other religions, Christians share the belief that marriage is the ideal social institution in which children should be conceived and raised. Marriage channels the powerful sexual drive and safeguards against sexual sins.[46]

The third purpose of marriage takes up the theme, expressed by the Jewish prophet Hosea, that God is married to the people of Israel. However, in the Christian version it is applied to the relationship between Christ and the Christian community.[47] In other words, Christian marriage not only formalizes the exclusive, fruitful love between two human persons, but also mirrors a more profound transcendent reality, namely, the love of Christ for his bride, the Church. For this reason the Orthodox and Catholic traditions include matrimony as one of the seven sacraments (see Box 4.2) – official ecclesiastic rituals that mark specific moments in Christian life and confer God's special grace. For Christians, marriage is seen as part of God's design and as a means of sanctification.

As in other religious traditions, the rich theology of marriage is manifest in the wedding ceremony itself. As a public declaration of love, Christian weddings are usually conducted in a place of worship, in the presence of the Church's representative (the minister), official witnesses (groomsmen and bridesmaids) and the believing community itself (Figure 6.3). The ceremony can vary considerably depending on denomination and culture but usually there is a selection of pertinent scriptural readings such as references to prominent Old Testament couples (Box 6.3), the gospel story of Cana, a parable of the wedding feast or well-known passages from the writings of Saint Paul. The minister may then deliver a sermon on the joys and duties of marriage. The central part of the rite involves the wedding vows, which are solemn public promises by the bride and groom that they will love and honor each other for the remainder of their days. Rings are blessed

Figure 6.3 A Christian bride and groom take their vows before the altar. (Reproduced with kind permission of iStock.)

Box 6.3 Prayer from an Eastern Orthodox Wedding Rite

O Lord our God, who did accompany the servant of the patriarch Abraham into Mesopotamia, when he was sent to seek a wife for his lord Isaac, and who, by means of the drawing of water, did reveal to him that he should betroth Rebecca: Do Thou, the same Lord, bless also the betrothal of these thy servants, [*names*], and confirm the word which they have spoken. Establish them in the holy union which is from Thee. For Thou, in the beginning, did make them male and female, and by Thee is woman joined to the man as a helpmate, and for the procreation of the human race. Wherefore, O Lord our God, who has sent forth Thy truth upon Thine inheritance, and Thy covenant to Thy servants our fathers, even Thine elect, from generation to generation: Look Thou upon Thy servant [*name*], and upon Thy handmaid [*name*], and establish and make stable their betrothal in faith, and in oneness of mind, in truth and in love.

and exchanged, and the couple is declared husband and wife. The register is signed, the bride and groom are blessed, and the new union is celebrated by family and friends at the wedding reception. Today, many churches symbolize the union of the two groups of kin by having the couple light a single candle from two family candles. In the Orthodox tradition, the priest places a crown (stephana) on the head of the bride and groom, signifying the new "royal" household that will be established by the couple. The stephana also evokes the image of the martyr's victory, indicating that a successful marriage will require self-sacrifice by both parties.[48]

There are also gestures that are reminiscent of Jewish and Hindu practices that express the union of the couple. In Orthodox Christianity, the bride and groom encircle the wedding table several times while the priest holds a Bible indicating that the word of God is their guide and that their love is endless like the circle in which they walk.[49] In many denominations the wedding ceremony also includes the consumption of consecrated bread and wine as a sign of their communion with each other and with Christ. In a similar vein, the priest or minister will sometimes wrap the hands of the bride and groom in his own vestments as a symbol of how their lives are now interwoven as one.

Traditionally Christians have been encouraged to marry other baptized persons, in many cases members of the same denomination. Although interdenominational and interfaith marriages are now very common in Western society, Catholic canon law still officially describes such a situation as an "impediment" that requires the permission of the local bishop (usually given as a matter of course). Moreover, a marriage between a Christian and a non-Christian, while valid, is not considered a sacrament and the Catholic partner must promise to do all that is reasonable to ensure that the children are raised in the Catholic faith. Statistically, marriage has been a source of many conversions to Catholicism by the non-Catholic partner. The Orthodox tradition is even stricter on such matters. While a church wedding is possible for an Orthodox Christian who marries another baptized Christian, it is not permitted for marriage with a non-Christian.

The Christian ideal is that marriage is a permanent relationship and that divorce is contrary to the divine will, based on the explicit teaching of Jesus:

> Some Pharisees came to him, and to test him they asked, "Is it lawful for a man to divorce his wife for any cause?" He answered, "Have you not read that the one who made them at the beginning 'made them male and female', and said, 'For this reason a man shall leave his father and mother and be joined to his wife, and the two shall become one flesh?' So they are no longer two, but one flesh. Therefore what God has joined together, let no one separate." They said to him, "Why then did Moses command us to give a certificate of dismissal and to divorce her?" He said to them, "It was because you were so hard-hearted that Moses allowed you to divorce your wives, but at the beginning it was not so. And I say to you, whoever divorces his wife, except for unchastity, and marries another commits adultery."[50]

Despite the firm teaching of the founder, most Christian churches accept the reality of marriage breakdown and allow divorce and remarriage for pastoral reasons. The Orthodox tradition permits marriage a second, and even a third time, but it is no longer considered a sacrament and the tenor of the ceremony is more restrained. The Protestant tradition likewise stresses the ideal of permanence but allows for divorce and remarriage within the Church. Even the Catholic Church, which is strictest in its interpretation of the permanence of marriage, has developed a process of annulment whereby a Catholic may remarry within the Church if it can be established that an element was lacking in the original marriage that prevented it from being considered a sacrament: for example, psychological maturity or the willingness to have children. Otherwise, Catholics who remarry outside the Church may not participate in Holy **Communion** until the situation is rectified.[51]

Most Christian churches believe that marriage lasts "until death do us part" and, thus, a person is free to remarry if their spouse dies. The key basis for this position is Jesus's response to a question regarding the true husband of a widow who remarries several times. His answer is instructive because it not only implies that marriage is restricted to this world, but it also alludes to the classical alternative to the married state and the reason why Jesus himself never married: "For in the resurrection they neither marry nor are given in marriage, but are like angels in heaven."[52] In other words, while married love is divinely ordained and a sacrament of the love of Christ for his bride, the Church, there is an even higher form of love that is an anticipation of the life of heaven itself: celibacy.

Given the Jewish view of marriage as a divine commandment, it would have been quite unusual for someone like Jesus to be still unmarried in his thirties. One gospel passage hints at the possibility that he may even have been ridiculed as a eunuch by his opponents, but it also reveals that his choice of the celibate life was a result of his absolute commitment to his vocation:

> For there are eunuchs who have been so from birth, and there are eunuchs who have been made eunuchs by others, and there are eunuchs who have made themselves eunuchs for the sake of the kingdom of heaven. Let anyone accept this who can.[53]

The term "eunuch for the kingdom" refers to the free choice of celibacy for a higher purpose, classically expressed in the Christian monastic life. In the Catholic and Orthodox traditions, celibacy is seen as a more radical imitation of the founder, a sign of the world to come and a practical lifestyle that frees the person from the duties of family life for apostolic service to the Church and community. In this respect the nuptial image was applied to nuns who were known as "brides of Christ" and whose vows ceremony was modeled on a wedding in which they "married" the Lord. Monks and nuns, who renounced marriage and family, were traditionally seen to have chosen "the better way,"[54] although the Protestant Reformation vigorously challenged this bias. Recent Catholic theology has also adopted a more balanced approach and acknowledges the intrinsic value of both states of life.

Compulsory celibacy has also been a condition of the clerical state in certain churches. Catholic priests are still required to be celibate by canon law although some exceptions exist.[55] Orthodox priests are allowed to be married, but the marriage must have taken place before ordination. However, Orthodox bishops are usually chosen from among the celibate monks or they must assume a celibate life if they are a married priest. The Anglican Church has no restrictions on the marriage of bishops and priests and most Protestant churches encourage their ministers to marry and raise a family.[56]

Thus Christianity shares with Judaism, Islam and Hinduism a positive understanding of marriage as part of the divine dispensation. However, the unmarried state of Jesus and the traditional Catholic and Orthodox leaning toward celibacy as a higher path not only resembles the Hindu forest-dweller tradition but also finds strong resonance in Buddhism where the founder was a husband and father who renounced married life for a more advanced path to liberation.

6.6 The Renunciation

When Siddhartha Gautama was about 16 years of age, he was married to a cousin named Yasodhara, who eventually gave birth to a son, Rahula. As the years went by it seemed that Siddhartha's career would be a political one in accordance with his father's strategic plans. However, something happened one day that changed everything – it was the crucial turning point in his life, akin to the baptism of Jesus in the Jordan and Muhammad's first encounter with Gabriel in the Meccan hills. Despite his privileged existence, Prince Siddhartha was constantly troubled by a deep unease and curiosity. On that fateful day he asked his charioteer to take him outside the palace walls for a short excursion. Along the way he saw what Buddhists call the Four Sights: a sick person; an aged person; a corpse being carried in a funeral procession; and a celibate ascetic (sannyasin). Disturbed by his first experience of illness, old age and death, Siddhartha eventually made the most important decision of his career. He would leave his comfortable, privileged existence and embark on a spiritual quest for the ultimate meaning of life. It was a quest that ended one night under a tree at Bodhgaya when the prince gained supreme enlightenment and became the Buddha. The moment of his departure from the palace is known in Buddhist tradition as the Renunciation, symbolized by the image of Siddhartha cutting his hair. To this day, Buddhist monks still shave their heads as a sign of complete detachment from ordinary married life (Figure 6.4).

As we have already seen, the life and example of the founder has a profound influence on the way in which a religion understands the place of marriage and celibacy. Like Muhammad, and unlike Jesus, Siddhartha experienced marriage and parenthood first-hand. However, unlike Muhammad, and like Jesus, Siddhartha renounced the life of the householder for a higher path. The Renunciation of the Buddha definitively sets up monastic celibacy as the more advanced road to liberation in Buddhism. It is interesting to note that the name of Buddha's son, Rahula, is usually translated as "fetter" or "chain" – an implication that family responsibility was an obstacle to his true destiny. This is not to say that Buddhism condones abandonment of marital and parental responsibilities. The decision of the Buddha to leave behind his spouse and son is a very special circumstance, taken for the good of humankind.

Given the example set by Buddha Gautama, where does marriage fit into the Buddhist worldview? Certainly there is no suggestion in Buddhism that married life is an evil to be avoided at all costs. The vast majority of Buddhists in the world are married with families, and Siddhartha's own treatment of his wife and child during the years of his

Figure 6.4 A new Buddhist novice with shaven head and robes.
(Reproduced with kind permission of Alamy.)

marriage is considered to be exemplary in terms of loving kindness. The Buddha's teachings contain a legacy of practical advice for spouses on the values and virtues needed to live happy and fulfilling married lives.[57] Marital fidelity is also implied by the third of the five fundamental Buddhist moral precepts, the Pancasila, which states that all Buddhists, not just monks, should refrain from improper sexual activity such as adultery and fornication.

However, in comparison to other world religions, Buddhism is less concerned with marriage in theory and less engaged with marriage in practice. Marriage is not understood by Buddhists to be an earthly symbol or sacrament of a divine–human relationship, neither is it seen as a sacred duty incumbent upon humans. There is no specific set of instructions from the Buddha or the tradition with regard to issues such as interfaith marriage, polygamy, divorce and remarriage. Neither is there any Buddhist wedding ceremony as such. In fact, the involvement of the monks is minimal. In many Buddhist cultures, it was considered inauspicious to have monks attend a wedding ceremony, partly because it was thought that their vow of celibacy could cause infertility, and partly because monks are primarily associated with the funeral service. According to the Theravada tradition, the Vinaya Pitaka prohibits a monk from being involved in any activity that might lead to a romantic relationship or marriage:

> Should any bhikkhu engage in conveying a man's intentions to a woman or a woman's intentions to a man, proposing marriage or paramourage – even if only for a momentary liaison – it entails initial and subsequent meetings of the Community.[58]

In practice, many Buddhist couples seek the blessing of monks at some stage before or after the wedding by visiting a Buddhist temple or inviting monks to the family home. This visit usually involves revering Buddha images, the recitation of mantras and a short sermon by a monk. As on other occasions in life, material gifts such as food and clothing are offered to the monks in return for the transfer of good karma. Sometimes this is symbolized in some tangible way, such as the pouring of water or the Thai custom of a ribbon connecting the couple to the monks, much the same as in funeral services. Monks are also consulted for astrological advice as to the most auspicious date for a wedding. However, the wedding ceremony itself is usually a purely civil affair or is celebrated with non-Buddhist elements from the local culture. For example, in China, the wedding of a Buddhist couple is often performed with Confucian features, while in Japan the ceremony is usually carried out in a **Shinto** temple. In recent times, especially in Mahayana Buddhism, the traditional taboo on monastic involvement has been relaxed and weddings are now sometimes held in Buddhist temples with the blessing of the monks who are also able to issue the legal marriage certificate.[59]

Underpinning this general lack of involvement, even deliberate distancing, of monks from weddings is the fundamental principle expressed by the Buddha's own renunciation, namely that celibacy is the more advanced spiritual path that brings one closer to nirvana. Although not inherently evil, the sexual desires and activity that constitute such a significant part of married life are seen as transient cravings that can impede our progress toward ultimate liberation.[60] To reinforce the point, marital scenes are sometimes depicted on artistic renditions of the wheel of life, indicating that marriage can bind us to the cycle of reincarnation and postpone our final goal. Detachment from all sensual desires is the necessary means by which true inner peace can be found.[61] The preference for sexual abstinence is also reflected in the common belief that only a celibate is really capable of becoming an **arhat**, someone who is so spiritually advanced that they will reach nirvana after death. The best that the married lay person can realistically hope for is that they are reincarnated as a monk or a nun in their next life.

For those who are ordained, celibacy is a serious matter. The classical scriptural text that outlines the rules for monastic life, the Vinaya Pitaka, is replete with material aimed at protecting the vow of celibacy. Engaging in sexual intercourse is one of the most serious infringements possible and an offending member is instantly expelled from the community. However, the Vinaya explicitly identifies and warns against a host of other situations that could cause a monk's thoughts or actions to be sexually compromised. For example, a monk should not travel alone with a woman or allow a woman to sew him special robes or have physical contact with a woman.[62]

It should be stressed that although monastic celibacy involves a substantial degree of self-control, it is a lifestyle that should be undertaken freely and without compulsion. Celibacy should flow naturally from the perspicacious mind that understands the illusory nature of the self and the unsatisfying nature of sensual pleasure. Furthermore, those who become Buddhist monks or nuns are not usually bound by lifelong vows and are free to leave at any stage. In some cultures, such as in Thailand, many young men join a monastic community for a short period of time, especially during the wet season. Even a brief period of such radical detachment earns good karma for the young man and his family. In Laos and Myanmar, men occasionally return to the monastery for a temporary period after being married, provided that they obtain their wives' permission.

There are also exceptions to the general rule of celibacy for Buddhist monks and nuns such as the Nying-ma (Red Hat) sect in Tibet and certain groups in Korea. But perhaps the most striking example is Japanese Buddhism where the majority of monks are married with families. As long ago as the thirteenth century, the Japanese Buddhist reformer Shinran (d. 1262), founder of the Jodo-Shin school, radically advocated the marriage of monks. Shinran himself was married and had children. In his view celibacy implied a lack of faith in the Buddha Amitabha and unnecessarily alienated the monk from the experience of the ordinary layperson. Several centuries later, in the nineteenth century, the Meiji government strongly encouraged monks to marry. However, these are exceptions that prove the rule. Celibacy is still the norm in most Buddhist monastic traditions where the idea of a married monk is a contradiction in terms and a sign of the fading of the dharma as predicted by the Buddha.

Minimal theological interest in marriage as a sacred institution, lack of a distinctive wedding ceremony and the preference for celibate leadership are not only features of the Buddhist tradition. Similar traits can be observed in the Daoist tradition where at least one main branch has adopted the Buddhist model of monastic celibacy, wedding rituals are often a mix of various Chinese cultural symbols and the main focus of theological discussion is not the wedding chapel but the bedroom.

6.7 Arts of the Bedchamber

The topics of marriage and weddings are rarely discussed in books on Daoism, where the focus is usually on practices concerning meditation, alchemy, longevity and visualization. As in Buddhism, the reason for this absence is that Daoism has little theological interest in marriage as such and, consequently, no clearly defined wedding ceremony as in other

Figure 6.5 Tea ceremony at a Chinese wedding. (Reproduced with kind permission of iStock.)

religious traditions. While it is a good thing, marriage is not seen as a reflection of divine–human love as in the Abrahamic religions or an imitation of divine couples as in Hinduism. Most Chinese marry and have children, which is consistent with the value that Chinese society in general places on the family unit and the importance of continuing the family line. As in many cultures, marriages were arranged affairs between families, often brought about through the efforts of matchmakers. Indeed, Chinese tradition speaks of a marriage god, the Old Man of the Moon, who stands behind all conjugal unions. Moreover, as we saw in Chapter 4, it was hoped that such unions, with the help of the gods, would result in many children, ensuring that one will be cared for in old age and that the funeral rites will be carried out properly.

As noted, it is misleading to speak of a Daoist wedding ceremony in the sense of a defined ritual with universally accepted words and actions. In most cases, Chinese weddings are shaped by a variety of factors drawn from the broader cultural tradition and often mixed with Daoist, Confucian, Buddhist and folk elements. For example, the traditional "Three Prayers" – for deceased ancestors, the family elders and the couple themselves – are a feature of most Chinese weddings, but these may be performed before images of Daoist gods whose blessings are sought on the day. Similarly, a wedding may incorporate the Chinese tea ceremony, during which sweet tea is offered by the bride and groom to members of both families in a designated order (Figure 6.5). There are also features reminiscent of the Hindu tradition. The preference for red as the color of joy is reflected in the dress of the bride and the wrapping used for the wedding gifts. Similarly, astrological information is taken into consideration to ensure that the bride and groom are compatible and that the date of the wedding is auspicious.

One distinctive symbol, often used at Chinese weddings, does highlight the principal theological meaning of marriage in Daoism: the creative union of yin and yang.

The **Bagua** ("eight symbols") is an octagon containing the eight trigrams of Chinese cosmology arranged in a particular order around a central taijitu (Figure 6.6). A trigram consists of three horizontal lines, each of which is either broken (yin) or unbroken (yang), thus creating eight possible combinations.[63] These symbolize the eight fundamental aspects of nature: fire (li), earth (kun), lake (dui), heaven (qian), water (kan), mountain (gen), thunder (zhen) and wind (xun). The Bagua is used in many contexts, but for a Daoist wedding it is usually painted on the floor with the chairs for the bride and groom placed on it in opposite corners. The groom sits over the symbol of fire with an urn of fire at his side; the bride sits over the symbol of water with an urn of water at her side. Eight lit candles are also placed over each symbol, forming a circle that encloses the couple. At the appropriate moment, they bring their urns to the centre of the Bagua and the water is poured over the fire. The result, of course, is steam, which symbolizes not just the powerful, dynamic relationship between husband and wife but, on a grander cosmic scale, the harmonious union of yin and yang.

Figure 6.6 The Bagua (Later Heaven version). (Reproduced with kind permission of iStock.)

Although Daoist literature has little to say about the theological significance of marriage, there is plenty of interest in what is generally called the "Arts of the Bedchamber." As early as the second century BCE, Daoism has taught that there is a fundamental link between sex and spiritual wellbeing.[64] Over time, a set of ideas and practices developed that outlined how one could gain better health, longer life and even immortality if one engaged in certain sexual practices. The context for this is the Daoist tradition known as **internal alchemy**, which understands the physical body as a crucible in which elements can be combined and transformed into new substances. According to Daoism, the physical body contains a vital substance known as jing, without which it would die. Jing is found primarily in bodily fluids, especially in semen. The generation of semen via sexual arousal increases the amount of jing and increases vitality. However, loss of the semen would mean a loss of jing, which results in fatigue, illness and premature ageing. In other words, the ideal is to retain the semen by avoiding ejaculation. More accurately, the intention is to redirect the semen, which carries the jing, upwards to the brain where it brings beneficial effects.

In order to achieve this end, one could practice permanent or temporary celibacy, as in the case of the Hindu forest-dweller who rechannels conserved sexual energy into the mind in order to enhance meditation. Alternatively, one could engage in sexual acts but avoid ejaculation, as in the tantric traditions of Hinduism and Buddhism.[65] In the Daoist context, the aim of non-ejaculatory intercourse is neither procreation nor erotic pleasure but, rather, to improve health and lengthen life. The texts mainly speak about retaining semen and, thus, focus on the benefits of these practices for the male. The issue of the woman's role is more contentious. On one hand, some commentators note that the man should ensure that his sexual partner is also aroused and that there seems to be no loss of jing if the woman reaches orgasm. On the other hand, there are texts that seem to treat the woman as a mere instrument in the man's quest for vigor and longevity.[66]

Mention of the Hindu forest-dweller tradition raises the question of the status of permanent celibacy in Daoism. The earliest legends speak of hermits who followed an austere lifestyle in the mountains or the forests, dedicating their lives to seeking the Dao.[67] However, it is likely that these persons did not completely abandon their family or their property, and that their stay in the wilderness probably only lasted several years. Today, the two main branches of Daoism reflect the tension between the traditional Chinese commitment to family and the imported Buddhist notion of renunciation. Although they are very similar in matters of philosophy and practice, the Zhengyi (Orthodox Unity) and the Quanzhen (Complete Perfection) branches can be differentiated by their contrasting attitude to priestly celibacy. In the Zhengyi branch, which is predominantly found in southern China and Taiwan, the priest (**daoshi**) is usually married and lives in his own home with his family. Often, their priestly work is a part-time occupation. In contrast, the Quanzhen branch, which is predominant in northern China, was more open to Buddhist influence from its beginnings in the twelfth century CE. Quanzhen clergy are expected to take vows of celibacy and live in monastic communities, patterned on the lifestyle of the Buddhist monks. A classical example of the celibate priest-monk is the twelfth-century figure of Liu Biangong, who left home as a 15-year-old and lived a life of silence, vegetarianism and celibacy. Over the centuries, the Quanzhen branch has been the form of Daoism preferred by Chinese rulers, who supported a clear distinction, even segregation, between married laity and celibate clergy. It is also the branch of Daoism that has been given custodianship of most Daoist temples and pilgrimage sites in mainland China by the Communist government. One of the oldest and most famous communities of celibate Daoist priest-monks is Louguan in northern China, where, according to legend, Laozi gave the Daode jing to the Guardian of the Pass.

Summary

As a prominent rite of passage and a fundamental social institution in most cultures, marriage often constitutes an important element of religious practice. With the exception of Buddhism and Daoism, the major religions have developed extensive theological interpretations of marriage in general and have profoundly shaped the wedding ceremony in particular. A comparison of the main elements across the religions reveals not only distinguishing differences in belief and practice, but also considerable overlap in terms of the meaning, purpose and symbolism of marriage.

In their own way, each of the religions acknowledges that marriage is the formalization of a special union between two persons. Much of the symbolism associated with the wedding ceremony is about binding the couple and their families into a new relationship of mutual support and companionship. The exchange of promises, rings, wine, crowns or garlands, or the mixing of fire and water, symbolizes the coming together of two individuals and the establishment of a unique, permanent and potentially fruitful relationship. The Judeo-Christian tradition draws on the biblical image of man and woman being essentially one flesh, while Hinduism and Daoism tend to depict the conjugal bond as a reflection of complementary cosmic forces. The idea that marriage involves the creation of a new home is physically signified by the traditions of the Jewish huppah, the Hindu mandap and the Orthodox Christian crowns.

The legal dimension of marriage is highlighted by some religious traditions more than others. The Islamic wedding ceremony (nikah) is usually quite simple, focusing on the signing of the contract which implies rights and duties for both parties. A similar stress on the contractual aspect of marriage is reflected in the Jewish ketubah, which is solemnly read at the wedding and proudly displayed in the home. The public nature of the marriage contract is reflected in the roles of the official witnesses such as the best man and chief bridesmaid at Christian weddings. In the Hindu tradition the fire itself symbolizes the silent divine witness that blesses and validates the ceremony.

If the first purpose of marriage is spousal companionship, the second is procreation. Most religions welcome the birth of children and traditionally teach that the proper place for their conception is within the parameters of married life. Thus, premarital and extramarital sexual intercourse are considered to be serious infringements of the social and moral order. The duty to procreate is perhaps most strongly experienced in Judaism, Hinduism and Daoism, which is consistent with the fact that these are non-missionary faiths and, thus, greater pressure is placed on the need to grow membership from within. For Jews, the first positive commandment in Tanach is to increase the human family, and Daoism upholds the classical Chinese concern to preserve the family tree and to care for the elderly. Similarly, classical Hinduism sees the conception of children, especially sons, as a sacred duty for a young man in the householder stage of life.

Apart from its twofold purpose on the horizontal plane, marriage is also given religious significance on the vertical plane. Muslims see marriage as an act of obedience to God and, thus, as a genuine form of worship. Judaism and Christianity also see marriage as an earthly symbol of the mystical relationship between the divine and the human. God is Israel's faithful spouse, and the Church is the bride of Christ. Hinduism also acknowledges a transcendent dimension to marriage in that the couple is seen as a mirror of the love between divine partners such as Vishnu and Lakshmi, or Shiva and Parvati, as symbolized by the lavishness of Hindu wedding attire and bodily adornment.

The idea that marriage reflects the pure, exclusive love of the divine tends to lend itself more naturally to monogamy as the ideal form. Indeed, this is the case in the majority of the six religions today although various forms of polygamy were practiced in past periods such as biblical and Vedic times. The obvious exception is Islam where a conditional form of polygyny is allowed – a tradition that stems from a social context in which widowhood was tantamount to penury and unmarried women faced a precarious existence. Islamic law limits the number of concurrent wives to four and the Qur'an insists that all wives must be treated fairly and equally.

All of the religions consider marriage to be permanent, ideally, but also acknowledge that the ideal is often not achieved in reality. Jewish and Islamic law allow for religious divorce and remarriage. Despite the explicit teaching of Jesus against divorce, most Christian churches also have processes in place to enable divorced believers to remarry in a religious ceremony. Arguably Hinduism sets the highest expectations in this regard, especially for high-caste women where remarriage after the death of the husband was traditionally frowned upon and the practice of sati was an extreme expression of such unconditional fidelity and companionship.

The religious affiliation of the spouse has also been an important consideration in most traditions where marriage to a non-believer has been either discouraged or even prohibited. Muslim men are permitted to marry Jewish and Christian women on the basis that the People of the Book share with Muslims a fundamental belief in monotheism. The converse is not allowed on the presumption that the faith of the children is determined by the father. Similarly, Jews and Christians have traditionally been expected to marry within the faith, or even within one's specific denomination. Such limitations have now been eroded by contemporary social forces in most Christian and more liberal Jewish communities. However, the choice of partner is still a serious matter within the Hindu world, not only in terms of religious belief but also in terms of caste, family background and financial status. Similarly, Daoism takes heed of astrological factors when testing a couple's compatibility.

Finally, attitudes to celibacy vis-à-vis marriage differ quite sharply across the six religions and, understandably, the example of the historical founder has considerable impact. At one end of the spectrum, Judaism and Islam concur that marriage is an integral part of God's plan for humankind and a basic duty for all believers. Consequently, voluntary celibacy is seen as a failure to fulfill the divine command to marry and procreate. Muhammad's own life is a resounding endorsement of marriage – a long, monogamous relationship with his first wife, Khadijah, and subsequent marriage to 11 other women, many of whom were widows and all of whom are highly respected "mothers of the faithful." The prophets of Jewish tradition were also married men, and a rabbi is generally expected to have a spouse and raise a family in order to gain full respect and authority.

Hinduism is more nuanced on the celibacy issue in that its classical system of four ashramas (life stages) allows for both lifestyles at different times. In the householder stage of young adulthood to middle age, there is a strong obligation on the Hindu believer to marry and have children. However, in later years, the ideal is a turning to the celibate life as forest-dweller, where ordinary existence is abandoned and sexual energy channeled into spiritual enlightenment. Although few Hindus actually take such a radical step, those who do so are regarded as holy persons on the verge of final liberation from the cycle of rebirth. The Daoist tradition also values the idea of channeling sexual energy to the mind, but it is primarily for the sake of health and long life.

Christianity is similarly nuanced, although not in the Hindu sense of different lifestyles for different phases of life. Although Christianity sprang from a Jewish context, Jesus embraced a celibate life and, thus, set an abiding example that tilted the scales away from marriage for much of Christian history. Marriage is still a holy sacrament that was sanctioned by God and considered to be the appropriate lifestyle for most Christians. But the radical imitation of Christ undertaken by the celibate monk and nun has been traditionally seen as the higher way, at least in Catholic and Orthodox traditions. Along with its suspicion of divine images, the Protestant downplaying of monastic celibacy places it closer to the Jewish and Islamic positions.

Vindication of the celibate life is even more powerfully epitomized in the life of Buddha Gautama who left his wife and child for a more advanced spiritual path. That crucial moment, known as the Renunciation, established monastic celibacy as the nobler pathway to nirvana, and much of the Vinaya Pitaka is devoted to protecting the monk and the nun from situations in which their vows might be compromised. Consequently, of the six religions Buddhism is the strongest endorser of celibacy and the least interested in marriage. As with birth rituals, there is no Buddhist wedding ceremony as such, and the involvement of the monks has traditionally been discouraged. Buddhism's primary focus on liberation from distracting earthly desires has meant the avoidance of anything that might bind one to the wheel of reincarnation, including the sexual desire that lies at the heart of the conjugal relationship. Although the Buddha left a legacy of wise advice on what is required for a successful marriage, his own example and the thrust of his philosophy point to the higher path of sexual abstinence. Similarly, Daoism has not developed a theology of marriage and lacks a distinctive wedding ceremony. Moreover, while the Zhengyi branch is characterized by married priests, in line with traditional Chinese values, the Quanzhen clergy have embraced the Buddhist model of monastic celibacy, which brings them closer to the Dao. Thus ends our consideration of the ways in which religion understands and ritualizes the three major life-cycle moments: birth, death and marriage. In Chapters 7 and 8 we discover how the religions understand and sanctify the most basic of human needs: food and clothing.

Discussion Topics

1 Is celibacy a more spiritual lifestyle than marriage? What are the advantages and disadvantages of religious celibacy?
2 Why does the Catholic Church still insist on a celibate priesthood?
3 Compare the lifestyle and role of Daoist, Buddhist and Christian nuns.
4 Compare the Jewish Song of Songs and the Hindu Krishna-Radha stories. Is it appropriate to apply sexual or erotic imagery to the divine?
5 Why do feminists criticize traditional religious views about the roles of husband and wife? How far does this critique apply to each religion?
6 What does each religion teach about sexual activity outside of marriage?
7 What does each religion teach about contraception?
8 What does each religion teach about homosexuality?
9 Why does Islam allow polygamy? What are the arguments for and against the practice?
10 Is it easy or difficult to obtain a divorce in each religion?

Notes

1 Zainab, Ruqayyah, Umm Kulthum and Fatima. Shi'ite Muslims claim that only Fatima was Muhammad's daughter, the other three being children of Khadijah from an earlier marriage or her nieces. Khadijah also gave birth to two sons who died in infancy.
2 Muhammad's uncle, Abu Talib, who had effectively raised him and whose social and political influence provided much-needed protection, also died in the same year.
3 Wasa'il al-Shiah, vol. 5.
4 The wali is usually the girl's father or a close male relative. Most law schools (except the Hanafi) require a young woman to obtain her wali's permission in order to marry.
5 Qur'an 4:4: "And give women their dowries as a free gift, but if they of themselves be pleased to give up to you a portion of it, then eat it with enjoyment and with wholesome result."

6 Qur'an 4:3.
7 Muhammad is considered to be an exception on the basis of his unique role as God's final Prophet who was allowed to set an example of the different types of marriage, such as protection for widows and tribal alliances. Others claim that he had already married his wives before the revelation and was allowed to keep them but not add any more. Moreover his wives were forbidden to marry another man; see Qur'an 33:53.
8 Qur'an 4:129.
9 For example, in 2006 the government of Chechnya considered changing marriage laws to allow Muslim men to take more than one wife as a response to the serious lack of men due to the war in that country.
10 Nine of Muhammad's wives were widows: Khadijah, Sawda, Hafsa, Zainab bint Khuzayama, Umm Salama Hind, Zainab bint Jahsh, Ramalah, Safiya and Maymunah.
11 Qur'an 2:221.
12 Qur'an 5:5.
13 Qur'an 30:21.
14 Qur'an 16:72.
15 See Qur'an 17:32; 24:1–3.
16 See Qur'an 2:187, 222.
17 There are rare cases of Muslim mystics living as celibates such as Rabi'a of Basra (d. 801) and Lalla Zaynab (d. 1904).
18 See Qur'an 13:38: "And certainly We sent apostles before you and gave them wives and children."
19 Genesis 1:28.
20 Genesis 2:23.
21 Genesis 2:24.
22 See Hosea 2:14–16; Song of Songs, *passim.*
23 Even today many elderly Yemenite and Ethiopian Jews are polygamous and those who migrated to Israel in the 1940s and 1950s were allowed to retain their wives under a special dispensation.
24 Fast days include Tishri 3 (the Fast of Gedaliah), Tevet 10, Tammuz 17, Av 9 and Adar 13 (the Fast of Esther).
25 Exodus 21:10; Talmud Ketubot 61b.
26 Talmud Yevamot 89a.
27 See Genesis 18:1–8. The theme of hospitality is also prominent at the Passover meal where a cup is set aside for the unexpected visitor who may turn out to be the prophet Elijah.
28 Some interpret this custom in terms of Joshua and the Israelite army circling the walls of Jericho seven times before they miraculously collapsed. In the case of marriage, the walls that divide the couple will fall and their souls be united. In more progressive communities, the groom also circles the bride.
29 The right forefinger is considered the most important finger and some sources note that it is also the seventh finger from the left.
30 Talmud Berakhot 31a.
31 See Psalm 137:5. Kabbalist Judaism sees the breaking of the glass as a symbol of the broken fragments of creation which is in need of spiritual repair.
32 Deuteronomy 7:3. Some have described the increasing rates of marriage to non-Jews as the "silent holocaust." See also Ezra 9:10–15.
33 Deuteronomy 24:1.

34 This is known as the Lieberman clause in Conservative Judaism.
35 Talmud Yevamot 62b, 63a. Marriage was so important that if finances were at stake, one should sell a Torah scroll in order to marry (see Talmud Megillah 27a). According to the Shulhan Aruch, only one who is married should lead the congregation in worship, just as the High Priest was required to be married in biblical times (Shulhan Aruch, Orach Hayim 581:1).
36 Jeremiah 16:1–4. There were also celibate members of the Essene sect and the Therapeutae community near Alexandria.
37 Henna is a tropical shrub whose leaves, when dried and ground into a paste, give out a rusty-red pigment. It possesses a cooling property and has no side effects on the skin.
38 The circumambulation of the fire is known by various names throughout India, including Pratigna-Karan, Parikrama, Pradakshina, Mangal Fera and Pheras.
39 See Section 7(2) of the Hindu Marriage Act 1955.
40 See Rg Veda 10.173.4; 7.66.16.
41 This is the context for the famous Hindu text on the art of sexual love, the Kama Sutra.
42 Some of the socio-religious factors that contributed to sati include: the belief that a widow could expect little of life after her husband's death, especially if she was childless; the halo of respect associated with the sacrifice; the sense that a widow was a drain on the family's resources; and the taboos associated with a widow as a source of impurity and misfortune.
43 The converse practice of a bride-price or payment by the groom to the family of the bride is more common in lower castes. The reason for the inversion is that low-caste women are expected to engage in manual wage-earning work and, thus, contribute to the family income whereas the high-caste wife is often seen as a non-income-earning financial burden.
44 Laws of Manu VI.2.
45 For example see Matthew 9:15–16; 22:1–15; 25:1–13; Luke 14:8–14.
46 See 1 Corinthians 7:9.
47 Ephesians 5:28–32.
48 The first Christian martyr was Stephen whose name is derived from the Greek term for crown. See Acts 7:55–60.
49 The gesture is called the Dance of Isaiah. See Isaiah 61:10.
50 Matthew 19:3–9.
51 See Catechism of the Catholic Church 1665.
52 Matthew 22:30.
53 Matthew 19:12.
54 A reference to the gospel episode where Jesus visits the home of two sisters, Mary and Martha. Jesus remarks that Mary has chosen the better part by sitting and listening to him, rather than her sister Martha who is busy preparing the food. Christian tradition has seen the two women as symbols of the monastic and married life respectively. See Luke 10:39–42; Matthew 19:29.
55 For example, Anglican priests who converted to Catholicism and were ordained have been allowed to remain married. Also certain Eastern Catholic rites, such as the Lebanese Maronite rite, have married priests.
56 The Protestant Reformers felt that the oath of celibacy undermined the holiness of marriage and was a key reason for widespread sexual misconduct by the clergy at the time. See Calvin, *Institutes of the Christian Religion*, IV.12.23–8.
57 See Anguttara Nikaya 8.54.
58 Suttavibhanga, Sanghadisesa 5.117.

59 The Mahayana tradition tends to interpret the Vinaya rule cited above in a different manner, namely, as a prohibition on a monk facilitating an immoral sexual relationship between two persons. Thus, Mahayana monks are more likely to be registered as marriage celebrants and to perform the wedding ceremony in a temple.
60 Anguttara Nikaya 4.159.
61 Anguttara Nikaya 3.34.
62 See Suttavibhanga, Sandhadisesa 1.90; 2.100; 4.115; Suttavibhanga, Parajika 1.45; Suttavibhanga, Nissaggiya Pacittiya 4.182; 17.214; Suttavibhanga, Pacittiya 7.280; 22.323; 27.329.
63 There are two versions of the Bagua, known as Early Heaven and Later Heaven. The former stands for the original configuration of the universe while the latter represents a new configuration as a result of time and change. The former is often used for burials while the latter is used at weddings.
64 One of the earliest texts on this topic is the "Uniting Yin and Yang" from the Mawangdui tomb excavations (c. 168 BCE).
65 The two main methods were "coitus conservatus" and applying pressure to the perineum in order to retain semen.
66 For example see the Ming Dynasty texts: "Mental Images of the Mysteries and Subtleties of Sexual Techniques" by Zhao Liangpi; and "Instructions in the Physiological Alchemy" by Zhang Sanfeng.
67 See Zhuangzi chs. 23, 28.

Further Reading

Bhaskarananda, Swami (2002). *The Essentials of Hinduism*. 2nd ed. Seattle: Viveka, pp. 35–46.

Browning, Don S., Green, M. Christian, & Witte, John Jr. (eds.) (2006). *Sex, Marriage and Family in World Religions*. New York: Columbia University Press.

De Lange, Nicholas (2003). *Introduction to Judaism*. 2nd ed. Cambridge: Cambridge University Press, ch. 5.

Dessing, Nathal M. (2001). *Rituals of Birth, Circumcision, Marriage and Death among Muslims in the Netherlands*. Leuven: Peeters, ch. 4.

Fine, Lawrence (ed.) (2001). *Judaism in Practice: From the Middle Ages through the Early Modern Period*. Princeton, NJ: Princeton University Press, ch. 4.

Kaelber, Walter O. (2004). "Ashrama" in Sushil Mittal (ed.). *The Hindu World*. Abingdon: Routledge, ch. 17.

Komjathy, Louis (2013). *The Daoist Tradition*. London: Bloomsbury, ch. 4.

Madan, T. N. (2003). "The Householder Tradition in Hindu Society" in Gavin Flood (ed.). *The Blackwell Companion to Hinduism*. Oxford: Blackwell, ch. 13.

Marcus, Ivan G. (2004). *The Jewish Life Cycle: Rites of Passage from Biblical to Modern Times*. Seattle: University of Washington Press, ch. 3.

Michaels, Axel (2003). *Hinduism: Past and Present*. Princeton, NJ: Princeton University Press, pp. 111–30.

Miller, James (2003). *Daoism*. Oxford: Oneworld, pp. 84–7.

Neusner, Jacob et al. (eds.) (2000). *Judaism and Islam in Practice*. London: Routledge, part II.

Olivelle, Patrick (2003). "The Renouncer Tradition" in Gavin Flood (ed.). *The Blackwell Companion to Hinduism*. Oxford: Blackwell, ch. 12.
Ramon, Einat (2001). "Tradition and Innovation in the Marriage Ceremony" in Harvey E. Goldberg (ed.). *The Life of Judaism*. Berkeley: University of California Press, ch. 8.
Segler, Franklin M. & Bradley, Randall (2006). *Christian Worship: Its Theology and Practice*. 3rd ed. Nashville: B & H Publishing Group, pp. 246–52.
White, James F. (2001). *Introduction to Christian Worship*. 3rd ed. Nashville: Abingdon Press, pp. 276–95.
Wijayaratna, Mohan (1990). *Buddhist Monastic Life: According to the Texts of the Theravada Tradition*. Cambridge: Cambridge University Press, ch. 6.

7

Food

World Religions in Practice: A Comparative Introduction, Second Edition. Paul Gwynne.

CONTENTS

7.1 Introduction

It is generally acknowledged that the two most basic physical necessities of human existence are food and clothing. As corporeal beings in time and space, our bodies need inner nourishment and external protection. These two ordinary aspects of daily life also constitute an important part of religious practice and are invested with extraordinary meaning. In this chapter we focus on religious practices involving food, drink and meals. What types of food does faith favor or forbid? What principles lie behind traditional food taboos? How does food reflect the relationship between fellow believers, and between the believer and divine reality? What role does food play in worship and the quest for salvation or liberation?

7.2 Cuisines of Immortality

There is an enigmatic verse in the Daode jing that reads: "The five colors make one blind in the eyes; the five sounds make one deaf in the ears; the five flavors make one tasteless in the mouth."[1] Commentators have interpreted the verse in various ways over the centuries but one implication seems to be that preoccupation with culinary pleasures is a vain exercise. The one who seeks exotic combinations of tastes will only find tastelessness in the end. Epicurean delights are not a priority in this religion, which stresses the natural over the artificial. In fact, the verse may originally have been directed at those who attended elaborate banquets where expensive, rare foods were served and social convention was a priority. Simplicity and moderation are more important for Daoism, which acknowledges the value of a balanced diet not only for the physical health of the body but also the spiritual health of the mind.

There is a considerable variety of diets across different Daoist movements and many have incorporated traditional Chinese customs such as honoring one's ancestors before all meals, eating a more substantial meal in the morning (the time of the stomach), taking a walk afterwards to facilitate digestion and having only a light snack in the evening. One widely accepted custom involves a Daoist application of the old Chinese concept of five flavors, which is mentioned in the above quote. The traditional five flavors are sour, bitter,

Table 7.1 The Five Elements of Daoism.

Element	**Wood**	**Fire**	**Earth**	**Metal**	**Water**
Direction	East	South	Center	West	North
Season	Spring	Summer	Late Summer	Autumn	Winter
Color	Green	Red	Yellow	White	Blue
Organ	Liver	Heart	Spleen	Lungs	Kidneys
Taste	Sour	Bitter	Sweet	Spicy	Salty

sweet, spicy and salty. Of course, a similar list can be found in many culinary cultures, but Daoism has adapted them into a broader cosmological schema that is used to determine what types of food should be eaten or avoided at certain times. The schema is based on the Five Elements (or Five Phases), which constitute the very structure of the cosmos itself. Each of these elements – wood, fire, earth, metal and water – is associated with a particular direction, season, color, organ and flavor (Table 7.1). Thus, a Daoist diet is not simply a matter of eating and drinking whatever we feel like on a particular day. Rather, it is a question of being in harmony with factors such as the time of year and the condition of one's vital organs. Sour foods benefit the liver and are best consumed in spring; bitter foods benefit the heart and are best consumed in summer; sweet foods benefit the spleen and are best consumed in late summer; spicy foods benefit the lungs and are best consumed in autumn; and salty foods benefit the kidneys and are best consumed in winter. It is also worth noting that it is not only food and drink but also sleeping patterns that should be determined by the natural ebb and flow of the seasons. Traditionally, one should sleep more in the winter months (when yin dominates over yang) and less in summer months (when yang dominates over yin). Moreover, it is thought that the more one becomes attuned with the Dao, the less food and sleep is required. Ideally, one should reach a stage of advancement when all that is required is the vital energy known as qi. For example, an eighth-century CE text, known as the Scripture on Prohibitions and Precepts for Ceremonial Eating, promotes the idea of gradually moving through a hierarchy of food types – vegetables, grains, herbs – until one is able to live solely on qi.

Apart from the general principles suggested by the Five Elements schema, there are a number of other Daoist dietary practices aimed at improving one's health, prolonging one's life and, ultimately, enabling one to survive death and attain a state of immortality. In particular, four examples are worth noting: the avoidance of grains; external alchemy; swallowing saliva; and ingesting qi.

The practice of avoiding grains (bigu) involves exactly what the name suggests, namely the complete elimination of grains from the diet. However, the term *bigu* can also refer to other forms of abstinence and fasting, which are linked to breathing exercises aimed at generating higher levels of qi in the body. There are various lists of what constitutes "grains" (wugu), but they typically include wheat, barley, rice, soybean, millet, corn and sesame. Instead of grain, one should eat wild foods such as berries, nuts, seeds and the products of uncultivated plants.[2] Some scholars think that the avoidance of grains reflects the fundamental Daoist preference for natural over artificial processes. It represents a return to the beginning of history when humankind had not yet developed agriculture, living a simpler and purer lifestyle.[3] Indeed, some authors see farmed crops as the primary cause of the human population explosion and the concomitant destruction of the environment.[4] In addition, bigu is primarily aimed at eliminating the **Three Death Bringers** (sanshi) that inhabit the body and bring about premature death. Also known as the Three Worms (sanchong), they are spiritual parasites that reside in the head, the heart and the lower abdomen.[5] It is believed that they live off cereals and grains, so cutting off their supply of nourishment results in their expulsion. According to medieval writers, abstaining from grains for 100 days was sufficient to rid oneself of them. More recent writers have reinterpreted the Three Death Bringers as negative psychological states. For example, the head Death Bringer represents gluttonous cravings, the heart Death Bringer represents greed and anger, and the lower abdomen Death Bringer symbolizes sexual lust and drunkenness.

The second example mentioned above is Daoist alchemical practice, or more explicitly what is called **external alchemy**. The English word alchemy refers to the refinement and transformation of ordinary elements into something much more precious, such as turning lead into gold. In Daoism, alchemy has two forms: external and internal. External alchemy (waidan), which effectively ended in the ninth century CE, involved the creation and consumption of elixirs made from special herbal and mineral ingredients. The aim, as always, was to improve health and extend life, both in this world and into the next. Hence, the elixirs were often called "pills of immortality," although the resultant mix was sometimes highly toxic and the person who consumed it became seriously ill or died of accidental poisoning.[6] The elixirs were often prepared in a special chamber with a furnace or stove set on a three-tiered altar. It was believed that the elixirs would expel parasites from the body and increase the clarity of mind and consciousness. In contrast, internal alchemy (neidan) was a reaction to the external alchemy tradition characterized by a shift in focus. Instead of imbibing substances that are created outside of the body to bring health and immortality, internal alchemy endeavors to channel substances already present within the body. Exercise techniques that fall under this broad category include meditation, visualization, breathing and bodily posture. All of these were intended to preserve the life essence within the body and improve its flow throughout the body. Two internal alchemy practices that are relevant for this chapter are swallowing saliva and ingesting qi, which are our third and fourth examples.

The third example is swallowing saliva. According to Daoist belief, saliva, like semen, is a vital bodily fluid that contains large amounts of qi. The practice of generating and retaining semen via sexual arousal and non-ejaculation, discussed in Chapter 6, is reflected in the tradition of saliva swallowing. The aim is the same in both cases: producing and directing an important fluid into appropriate parts of the body, including the brain, in order to enhance health and lengthen life. The practitioner usually learns the art of creating saliva through formal training. The tongue (Crimson Dragon) is used to gather the saliva in the mouth, the teeth are tapped, and the saliva is swallowed in three portions while the person meditates on the process of it going down the throat and into the stomach. In Daoism, saliva is not merely the spittle that naturally forms in the mouth and is swallowed or spat out. Rather, saliva refers to clear and pure fluids generated by specialized training. Hence, it is associated with natural elements such as mist, dew and wind. As a result, saliva is often given honorific names such as gold fluid, jade nectar, mysterious pearl, snow flower, spirit water and sweet dew.[7]

The fourth and final example is a similar practice known as qi ingestion or "nourishing on light." There are many forms but one well-known example is the Method of Mist

Absorption, which is described in Shangqing and Lingbao texts of the Zhengyi branch of Daoism. At dawn, the person stands and faces each of the five directions in turn, usually starting with the east. Saliva is swallowed and the person meditates on the symbolic color of each direction. Then they imagine a mist appearing, which slowly concentrates into a small pill of light that can be consumed. The person meditates on how the light will pass to the organ associated with each direction, as outlined in Table 7.1.

All of the above– the five flavors, the avoidance of grain, alchemy elixirs, swallowing saliva and ingesting qi – are aimed at living healthier and living longer, including the notion of a post-mortem state of existence. In that sense, the Daoist dietary practices are sometimes described as "cuisines of immortality."[8] Certain substances are avoided or ingested in order to increase one's longevity in the first place, and to assist one to survive death in a spiritual form.

There is one final element in Daoist food practices that should be acknowledged: the ascetical influence. Unlike the Zhengyi branch, which adheres more closely to traditional Chinese dietary practices, the Quanzhen branch of Daoism has embraced monastic life, and with that comes specific dietary practices. Traditionally, Quanzhen monks gathered together for a meal in a communal hall at breakfast and lunch, after which they fasted until the next morning. Although this practice is not as extensive as in the past, it reflects the ideal of balancing detachment and health. One should not be attached to food but one should not neglect the body's need for nourishment either. Similarly, Quanzhen monks often practice vegetarianism, although there are exceptions and those who do eat meat do so on the understanding that the animal has been killed with minimal pain. Behind this is the belief that fear and suffering experienced by the animal will pass into the spirit of the one consuming the meat. Quanzhen monks also avoid strong smelling vegetables such as onion, garlic and leek since it is believed that these kindle sexual desire, which is a dangerous force for celibates. Finally, Quanzhen monks generally abstain from intoxicants and prefer tea instead. It is believed that alcohol injures the organs and disrupts the flow of qi within the body. In contrast, tea enhances consciousness and alertness. In other words, the Quanzhen monastic tradition is characterized by dietary practices that are aimed at controlling physical appetite, minimizing animal suffering, defusing sexual desire and avoiding mental dullness. These features are not typical of Chinese culture but, rather, were adapted from the Indian religion that was brought to China by its wandering missionaries: Buddhism.

7.3 Ahimsa and Samadhi

Some time after the young Siddhartha Gautama renounced the comfortable, protected life of the palace in search of a higher spiritual truth, he joined a small group of wandering ascetics. For several years he adopted their radical lifestyle of utter detachment from material pleasures including a severe regime of fasting and self-discipline. Although such extreme measures were meant to liberate the spirit from the enslaving passions of the body, Siddhartha eventually came to the realization that these practices led to emaciation rather than emancipation. He was simply becoming seriously ill. Thus, one day, to the utter consternation of his companions, he decided to break the strict fast and take a meal. It was to be a prelude to the fateful moment when, now strengthened by the nourishment, Siddhartha spent an entire night under the bodhi tree in meditation and became the Buddha. It is for this reason that Buddhism often describes itself as "the middle way." For the Buddha, truth lies between two extremes, and this applies also to the most basic of human needs – food. Neither indulgent hedonism nor excessive mortification benefits the mind's search for enlightenment and liberation. The body should be neither pampered nor neglected. Hence, Buddhist monks and nuns have always eaten responsibly, but they also fast on a daily basis by not taking any food after the midday meal.

Apart from the daily monastic fast, are there other customs regarding what Buddhists should or should not eat? Does Buddhism have any food laws? The answer lies in the set of fundamental moral principles known as the Pancasila, or Five Precepts (see Box 3.3). In particular, the first and fifth of these basic ethical norms have repercussions for the Buddhist diet, especially in terms of meat and alcohol.

The first precept of the Pancasila states that the believer must refrain from taking life. The intrinsic value of innocent human life is a common feature in most religious and moral systems, but the first precept is not limited to human beings in its application. Its scope is broader and neatly summed up by the term **ahimsa**, or unwillingness to harm. Ideally, all forms of life should be respected and violence in any form is to be avoided. In Buddhist thinking, violence begets violence and ultimately brings negative karmic consequences on the perpetrators themselves. The principle of ahimsa, which was eventually incorporated into Hinduism, was originally championed by the two influential religious movements of the fifth century BCE: **Jainism** and Buddhism. While Jains avoid the destruction of both plants and animals, Buddhists interpret ahimsa in terms of sentient creatures, namely animal life. Thus, the question arises whether the first precept of the Pancasila requires that a Buddhist refrain from eating meat.

There is some disagreement within Buddhism on this issue. Buddhists who profess strict vegetarianism naturally base their argument on the principle of ahimsa. The eating of meat necessarily involves the slaying of animals in contravention of the first precept. Not only is there suffering on the part of the slaughtered beast, but its spirit is forced to recommence the painful process of rebirth. Although there is little scriptural support for strict vegetarianism in the Theravada Pali Canon, a number of later Mahayana writings explicitly condemn the consumption of meat.[9] One prominent example is the Mahaparinirvana Sutra. On the eve of his death, the Buddha orders his followers to abstain from meat on the basis that it undermines the compassion expected of a bodhisattva. The text also declares that monks should not consume meat even if it is given to them during the alms round (Figure 7.1 and Box 7.1).[10]

However, according to the Tipitaka, the Buddha was not an absolutely strict vegetarian himself and his teaching on the issue is nuanced. In Buddhaghosa's account, the Buddha's last meal was tainted pork which purportedly caused his death, although Mahayana versions claim it was truffles.[11] The Pali Canon suggests that there were occasions when he ate meat and even recommended certain types as a cure for particular illnesses. The incident most often quoted in this regard is the story of the conversion of General Siha who prepared a meal for the Buddha and his companions at which meat was served.[12] In this context the Buddha revealed his threefold guideline for monks: "Do not eat meat knowing that it has been killed specially for your use. I allow the use of fish and meat blameless in three ways, unseen, unheard and unsuspected."[13] Later, toward the end of Siddhartha's life, the monk Devadatta requested that he revise the rules concerning monastic diet and impose a total ban on meat-eating. The Buddha refused and reiterated the threefold rule.[14]

Figure 7.1 Buddhist monks carrying bowls on their daily alms round.
(Reproduced with kind permission of iStock.)

Box 7.1 The Buddha's Teaching on Eating Meat (Mahayana version)

"This indeed is how the Bodhisattvas, custodians of my doctrine, should understand. Son of my lineage, even those who keep close company with me, must not eat meat. Even if, in a gesture of faith, almsgivers provide them with meat, they must shrink from it as they would shrink from the flesh of their own children." Then the Bodhisattva Kashyapa asked the Buddha, "But why indeed, O Lord and Tathagata, do you forbid the consumption of meat?" "Son of my lineage!" the Lord replied. "Eating meat destroys the attitude of great compassion." "But in the past, O Lord," asked Kashyapa, "did you not allow the eating of meat found suitable after it has been examined in three ways?" "Yes," the Buddha said. "I allowed the eating of meat found suitable after threefold examination, in order to assist those who were striving to overcome their habit of eating meat." (Mahaparinirvana Sutra)

Thus, Theravada Buddhism distinguishes between two kinds of meat: blameful and blameless. Only the latter may be consumed by monks in good conscience, but what constitutes "blameless" meat? The Buddha refers to three criteria: that the monk has not actually witnessed the killing of the animal; that the monk has not been told that the meat had been prepared specially for him; and that the monk does not suspect that such a meal was being prepared. This position acknowledges that there can be degrees of involvement in the killing of the animal. Direct involvement brings negative karma and hence the meat trade is listed among occupations that are inappropriate for Buddhists: "Business in weapons, business in human beings, business in meat, business in intoxicants and business in poison."[15] But less direct involvement opens up the possibility that other factors be taken into account such as courtesy toward a host or donor who offers food. Thus, the principle of ahimsa is not necessarily violated provided the monk is adequately distanced from the negative karma associated with the animal's death. This is achieved by ensuring that the meal has not been prepared specifically for him. Although the teaching is addressed to monks and nuns, it is often understood as an ideal toward which the laity should also strive.

Some argue that the threefold guideline applies only to monks who receive food on their alms round and, therefore, have no say over what they are given. However, if monks purchase food from the marketplace then, like the slaughterer and the vendor, they too must accept the karmic implications. The stricter vegetarian position of the later Mahayana texts may reflect the fact that many Mahayana monasteries owned their own cultivated fields, which enabled them to avoid reliance on donated food. In contrast, there has always been a stress in Theravada Buddhism on the alms round and the humble acceptance of whatever is placed in the bowl including meat or even rotten food. The practice has been part of the daily routine of the Buddhist monk since the earliest times, although not all communities still practice it today.

The fifth precept of the Pancasila also impacts on Buddhist dietary practices. Whereas the first precept condemns violence and, thus, implies vegetarianism, the fifth condemns the use of any intoxicating substance and, thus, implies abstinence from alcohol and other mind-transforming drugs. Such a position is understandable given that the Buddhist Eightfold Path to nirvana is based on clear-minded wisdom and responsible moral action. The Buddha's last words stress the importance of awareness: "Behold, O monks, this is my last advice to you. All component things in the world are changeable. They are not lasting. Strive with clarity of mind to gain your liberation." According to the Buddha's final injunction, the quest for liberation requires a heightened awareness that results from meditation (samadhi). While alcohol and drugs can alter one's mental state, Buddhism traditionally sees their effects as negative and in direct opposition to samadhi. Although most Buddhist cultures have not prohibited alcoholic drinks, monks and nuns are expected to embrace total abstinence.

A well-known Mongolian folk story makes the point. A Buddhist lama was on a journey among the nomadic tribes who gave him food and accommodation in exchange for his advice and good karma. One night he was offered lodging by a young single woman on condition that he would do one of three things: sacrifice a goat, sleep with the woman or drink alcohol. After pondering his dilemma, the monk decided that the third option was the least harmful. However, after several hours he became drunk. In his intoxicated state, the sound of the goat annoyed him so much that he killed it, and when he woke up the next morning he found that he had slept with his hostess.

The fifth precept does not imply that alcohol in itself is evil but, rather, warns against its inebriating effects, which cloud judgment, reduce self-control and undermine the other four precepts. Similarly, the first precept does not imply that meat in itself is evil but, rather, that the process by which meat is obtained involves the violent death of animals and, thus, undermines the principle of ahimsa. Buddhist dietary practice suggests that it is moral attitude and action that render one impure rather than the food or drink that one consumes.[16] Buddhist concerns about meat and alcohol are not focused on the substances themselves but on their potential to bind one to the wheel of samsara and, thus, postpone nirvana. This intrinsic link between food and liberation from samsara is also a strong theme in Hinduism where diet affects spiritual purity and devotees eat the blessed leftovers of food offerings to the gods.

7.4 Blessed Leftovers

Hinduism places such great emphasis on the role of food that it has been appositely called "the kitchen religion." The regular social greeting "Have you eaten?" carries the same meaning as "How are you?" in Western cultures, hinting not only at the importance of physical nourishment but its socio-religious significance as well. As with most things Hindu, there is enormous diversity. Many culinary customs stem from the ancient **dharmashastras** but vary from region to region, depending on factors such as climate, geography and culture. However, the link between food and spiritual purity is a common feature across the many sects and general patterns can be identified.

Like Buddhism, Hinduism sees a fundamental connection between the food that is consumed and the quest for liberation from the cycle of reincarnation. Eating and drinking are relevant to the atman's search for moksha, since these fundamental human activities have the potential to generate significant amounts of good or bad karma, thus facilitating or impeding its progress. Whereas Buddhist restrictions regarding meat and alcohol are essentially based on the principles of non-violence (ahimsa) and clarity of mind (samadhi) respectively, the more extensive Hindu food taboos are primarily aimed at protecting the believer from spiritual pollution. Ensuring that one eats the correct food types that have been prepared in the correct manner and consumed in the correct company is a lifelong concern for devout Hindus.

There are many factors that directly affect the purity of a meal, including how the food is prepared, who prepares it, and with whom one dines. In terms of preparation, it is vital that the cooking is performed in an unpolluted environment. Although it may come as a surprise to Western ears, the kitchen should be the purest room in the house, so much so that Hindus often keep household images (murti) there. The person preparing the food must also be unpolluted because it is widely believed that the consciousness of the cook enters the food and influences the mind of the consumer. Cooked food in particular is vulnerable to the essence of the person preparing it. Thus, the caste of the cook is an important consideration and high-caste cooks and waiters, if they are available, have traditionally been in demand in restaurants and temples, although such customs are gradually being eroded in contemporary urban life. Conversely, members of the higher castes endeavor not to accept food cooked or offered to them by members of lower castes.

Purity is also contingent upon those with whom one eats. Sharing a meal is not simply a question of eating and drinking at the same time and in the same place. Dining with another person carries rich layers of social implications in all human cultures. In Hinduism, where food itself is particularly sensitive to pollution, there is heightened concern for purity at mealtimes. Caste laws generally require that a person dines only with members of the same caste or those just above or below. Thus, Hindus are careful about whom they invite to dinner and are cautious about taking food communally.

Food and purity are linked in terms not only of caste distinction but also of individual spiritual advancement. In the Hindu worldview, the food that one consumes has a profound influence on the spirit as well as the body.[17] We are what we eat in more than just the physical sense and, thus, a proper diet is essential for progress on the path to moksha. Such a diet would include food types that purify and exclude those which pollute. An entire section of the Laws of Manu is dedicated to this topic,[18] although in practice there is considerable variation from place to place. Many food customs are based on elements such as whether the food is raw or cooked, boiled or fried, grown above ground or below, prepared at home or elsewhere. Many Hindus also abstain from alcohol although there is no explicit ban on intoxicants as in Buddhism.[19] Some foods are innately pure such as the products of the cow, including milk, yoghurt and ghee. Moreover, food that is fried in ghee is considered purer and safer than food that is prepared in water, which is more susceptible to polluting influences. Thus, fried foods are categorized as pukka (literally "cooked" or authentic), and can be eaten outside of the home and even across caste boundaries to some extent. In contrast, boiled foods are described as katcha (literally "raw" or poor quality), and must be prepared in the purity of one's own kitchen.[20]

Of the various Hindu sects, Vaishnavism possesses a developed theology of food that places edibles into three categories based on the **gunas**, or fundamental qualities that shape the universe and all beings within it.[21] The first and highest guna is sattva, which refers to superior qualities such as wisdom, compassion, tranquility and nobility. According to the Bhagavad Gita, sattvic food is "smooth, firm and pleasant."[22] It is purifying to the mind and healthy for the body. It facilitates meditation and generates energy and vitality. Sattvic foods include vegetables, fruits, nuts and dairy products. The second guna is rajas, which describes personal qualities such as courage, decisiveness, passion and strength. The Gita tells us that rajasic foods are "hot, salty and sour."[23] Such food excites the emotions and generates actions and passions, but it also distracts the mind from higher spiritual things. Rajasic foods include meat, fish, eggs, spices, onions, tea, coffee and tobacco. The third guna is tamas, which refers to negative qualities such as lethargy, dullness, ignorance and inertia. Thus, tamasic foods are stale, tasteless, juiceless and impure such as leftovers, half-cooked or overcooked foods.[24]

Meat is sometimes listed as a tamasic food and is, hence, something to be avoided. Indeed, there is a strong tradition of vegetarianism in Hinduism, especially among members of the **brahmin** class, which is associated with sattvic qualities and carries higher expectations than in other classes. Even for those who eat meat, beef is usually forbidden and pork often restricted. As with Buddhism, the principal motivation behind Hindu vegetarianism is ahimsa or non-violence. The Laws of Manu warn of the karmic consequences of eating meat: "Meat can never be obtained without injury to living creatures, and injury to sentient beings is detrimental to the attainment of heavenly bliss; let him shun the use of meat."[25] However, the specific ban on beef is linked to the special status given to the cow in Hinduism as a result of several factors. First, the cow was traditionally a vital asset on the farm and it made economic sense to use its produce rather than slaughter it for meat. Second, leaders like Dayananda Saraswati and Mahatma Gandhi promoted the cow as the symbol of Indian independence and the Hindu faith during the years of British colonial occupation. Converts to Islam and Christianity were often given a meal of beef to signify their complete abjuration of the Hindu faith. Third, the cow is seen by Hindus as a supreme example of generosity because it provides so many beneficial products and asks nothing in return except a grassy paddock. Not surprisingly, dairy products are considered to be inherently auspicious and capable of purifying other foods as well.

There is a further important link between food and faith in Hinduism that involves the consumption of food offered to the gods. During the standard form of daily worship (**puja**), a range of foodstuffs are set before the image. It is believed that the divine guest consumes the invisible essence of the food. What remains are merely the physical leftovers known as **prasad** – a term that literally means compassion or generosity.[26] Unlike Buddhists, who tend to distribute the leftovers from worship to beggars and animals, prasad is in great demand among Hindu believers because it is no longer ordinary food – it has become blessed leftovers.

As a key element of Hindu worship, prasad is rich in religious meaning. First, it reminds Hindus of the need to purify any meal by first offering it to the gods at the domestic shrine.[27] Second, leftovers from temple worship are usually distributed to all believers irrespective of caste or gender. Paradoxically, prasad reflects the fundamental equality of all Hindus, rather than reinforcing hierarchical and caste differences as meals usually do. Third, if prasad conveys equality among believers on the horizontal plane, then it is because all believers are utterly subordinate to the deity on the vertical plane. Just as the wife ate after her husband and sons in the traditional Hindu home, so the believer dines on leftovers only after the deity has been satisfied.

Finally, prasad has passed the lips of the gods and is now sanctified. Although these are leftovers, they are from the divine table and consumption of them brings the believer closer to the deity in a very physical sense. Thus, a fourth level of meaning arises for prasad: communion between the believer and their Lord. The dual potential of Hindu prasad to symbolize not only the fundamental unity among believers on the horizontal plane but also intimate union between the divine and the human on the vertical plane, finds a strong resonance in Christianity where the central ritual involves a meal of bread and wine that is understood as a holy communion.

7.5 Bread and Wine

One of the most important features in many Christian churches is a piece of furniture that usually occupies central position either in the very middle or at the far end of the congregational seating. Variously described as an altar or a table, it is the place at which the principal Christian ritual is performed – the Eucharist. Over the centuries, the Eucharist has evolved into a variety of forms, ranging from casual gatherings to grandiose ceremonies. It has been interpreted in differing ways that have provoked some of the deepest divisions among Christians. But despite the many layers of **liturgical** accretions and theological controversies, it remains in essence a meal of bread and wine (Figure 7.2). As in Hinduism, at the heart of Christian worship one finds food and drink.

One of the earliest names for the Eucharist was the "breaking of the bread" and it was already common practice among the very first generation of Christians.[28] According to the New Testament, the ritual originated in certain words and actions of the founder during his final meal with his followers. We are told that, at his Last Supper, Jesus took some bread, broke it, and handed it to those present, declaring "Take and eat; this is my body." Similarly, he passed around a cup of wine with the words, "Drink from it, all of you; for this is my blood." Finally he ordered his followers: "Do this in memory of me."[29] The stories state that the occasion was the Jewish Passover meal, which would have included unleavened bread and wine among other symbolic foods. But his unforgettable gesture was understood by the first Christians as the institution of a new rite.

As noted above, the manner in which the Eucharist is celebrated today varies considerably across Christian denominations, but in each case it is essentially a re-enactment of the Last Supper. Catholic and Orthodox Churches insist that the Eucharistic

Figure 7.2 Bread and wine used in a Christian Eucharist.
(Reproduced with kind permission of iStock.)

president must be an ordained male priest because they take on the role of Jesus. Other Christian denominations allow women to preside because they do not consider maleness to be essential for the part. The Eucharist typically involves readings from the Christian Bible accompanied by a sermon and other prayers including petitions for a variety of needs. Many churches organize the biblical readings around annual cycles so that a selection of holy text is proclaimed and pedagogically expounded over a specific period of time. For many Christians, especially in the Protestant tradition, this is considered at least as important as the meal that follows in terms of spiritual nourishment.

The bread and wine are prepared beforehand on the altar/table or, in some churches, brought to it in a formal procession. The president prays over the bread and wine, using a formula that incorporates the words of Jesus from the Last Supper (Box 7.2). At the sound of those words, Christians believe that the Holy Spirit descends upon the food and consecrates it. After further prayers, the sanctified bread and wine are then distributed to the congregation for consumption, although in some churches, especially in the Catholic tradition, only the bread is given for practical reasons. Many churches use a form of unleavened bread on the presumption that this is what would have been used at the Last Supper if it was a Passover meal. However, Orthodox churches and some Protestant Christians prefer to use leavened bread. Similarly, most churches use alcoholic wine as in the Jewish tradition, although many Protestant congregations prefer non-alcoholic grape juice because of their commitment to temperance.

There are also differences between churches concerning the preferred name of the ritual, its frequency and the appropriate age of reception. Orthodox Christians refer to it as "the Divine Liturgy," Catholics speak of "the Mass," while Protestant communities often use terms such as "communion service," "the Lord's Supper" and "breaking of the bread." The frequency of celebration varies from a daily event in Catholic churches to occasional or even annual celebrations in certain Protestant traditions. The age at which children are allowed to start receiving Eucharist also varies from infancy in Orthodox churches to "first communion" at the age of reason in Anglican and Catholic traditions.

Box 7.2 Prayer from an Anglican Rite of the Eucharist

CELEBRANT: On the night he was handed over to suffering and death, Our Lord Jesus Christ took bread; and when he had given thanks to you, he broke it, and gave it to his disciples, and said, "Take, eat: This is my Body, which is given for you. Do this for the remembrance of me." After supper he took the cup of wine; and when he had given thanks, he gave it to them, and said, "Drink this, all of you: This is my Blood of the new Covenant, which is shed for you and for many for the forgiveness of sins. Whenever you drink it, do this for the remembrance of me." ...We celebrate the memorial of our redemption, O Father, in this sacrifice of praise and thanksgiving. Recalling his death, resurrection, and ascension, we offer you these gifts. Sanctify them by your Holy Spirit to be for your people the Body and Blood of your Son, the holy food and drink of new and unending life in him. Sanctify us also that we may faithfully receive this holy Sacrament, and serve you in unity, constancy, and peace; and at the last day bring us with all your saints into the joy of your eternal kingdom. (Rite Two of the US Book of Common Prayer, 1979)

Given its strong links with Jesus's last explicit wish and its pride of place in Christian practice, it is not surprising that the Eucharist carries a rich array of theological meanings. The term *Eucharist* was in use by the end of the first century and literally means "thanksgiving."[30] It possibly stems from the Jewish practice of giving thanks to God at meals for daily nourishment, but the gratitude expressed by Christians is for more than the gift of ordinary food and drink. As mentioned above, the central piece of furniture is described not only as a table, around which the sacred meal is consumed, but also as an altar on which a sacrifice is commemorated. The language of "body and blood" naturally evokes images of death, and clearly the dramatic words and actions of Jesus at the Last Supper were intended to shed light on the events of the following day. For Christians, his bloody crucifixion on Good Friday can only be properly understood in the light of Holy Thursday – not as a tragic death but as the unique and supreme self-sacrifice that brings definitive nourishment to a hungry world and renders all other forms of sacrifice (animal or otherwise) redundant.[31]

The "body" language of the Eucharist also evokes the important theme of communion. On the vertical plane, communion refers to the spiritual union established between the individual and Christ via the act of consuming the sacred bread and wine that are now understood to be somehow his body and blood. In this sense, the Eucharist has a strong hint of theophagy (the eating of one's God) which echoes to some extent the Hindu idea that food is Brahman and Brahman is food. Theophagy was characteristic of the mystery religions of the Roman Empire at the time that Christianity emerged. Thus, some have speculated that this is the source of the Christian Eucharist since it seems unlikely that Jesus, as a Jew, would have commanded others to drink blood even in a symbolic sense. Christians understand that the consumption of the consecrated bread and wine establishes an extraordinary and intimate communion between the believer and Christ. The physical appropriation of the man-God makes the Christian more godlike. As in Hinduism, we become what we eat.

Communion also operates on the horizontal plane between Christians themselves. The "body of Christ" refers not only to the consecrated bread used during the rite, but can also mean the body of believers, the Church.[32] The act of breaking a single loaf of bread and sharing a single chalice of wine signifies the fellowship among believers gathered around the table of the Lord.[33] Sadly, this communion has been broken by acrimonious theological disputes and shattering ecclesiastical divisions. Ironically, the great sacrament of Christian fellowship is actually a stumbling block to Christian unity today. For instance, although most churches welcome members of other Christian denominations at their Eucharistic celebrations, not all churches feel free to offer the sacred bread and wine to their guests. For example, Catholic and Orthodox Churches believe that the sacred bread and wine can only be shared with other Christians once the theological differences have been resolved and unity has been restored.

One significant cause of these divisions is the conflicting ideas about what actually happens to the bread and wine during Eucharist. Most Christians accept the notion of a "real presence" of Christ in the sanctified bread and wine. However, Catholic and Orthodox theology have traditionally understood Jesus's phrase "this is my body" in a literal and permanent sense. In other words, for them the bread and wine actually become the body and blood of Christ, even though there is no change in their outward appearance. The classical theological formulation of this position is the medieval doctrine of transubstantiation, which borrows the Aristotelian philosophical categories of "substance" and "accident" to explain the religious mystery. What is visible to the senses (accidents) does not change. What "stands beneath" these and constitutes the reality of a thing (substance) is miraculously transformed. It is ultimately a question of faith since nothing empirical could ever be observed or proven. But in the eye of the believer, what is consumed is no longer bread or wine but the real flesh and blood of the Savior.[34] High Anglican and Lutheran traditions profess a more nuanced approach in which the consecrated host is simultaneously bread and Christ's body.[35] The further one moves along the Protestant spectrum, the less literal and more symbolic the interpretation becomes.[36]

A direct consequence of the belief in transubstantiation is the practice of "reserving" remaining bread after the ceremony. In Catholic, Orthodox and High Anglican churches, the consecrated breads (called hosts) are placed in a receptacle known as a tabernacle. A lit candle burning beside the tabernacle indicates the presence of the sacred bread inside. In the Catholic tradition, a host is occasionally brought out and placed in an ornate container for viewing and prayerful adoration by believers. Processions of the host are often held on the Catholic feast of Corpus Christi (Body of Christ), which was established precisely to reinforce belief in the real presence.[37] While most Protestant Christians do not reserve the sacred bread after the Eucharist has ended, many Christians agree that it may be set aside for those unable to attend the communion service due to sickness.[38]

Apart from the significant role that food plays in its central ritual, Christianity does not have the sort of dietary restrictions that typify Buddhism and Hinduism. Christians fast and abstain from certain foodstuffs such as meat or sweets during the season of Lent (see Chapter 9), and some churches promote the total avoidance of alcohol in a manner akin to the fifth precept of Buddhism. But otherwise there are few, if any, specifically Christian food laws. The reason for this lies in both the teaching of the founder himself and a key decision taken by the early Christian community. Mark's gospel reports Jesus's attitude to existing food customs: "'Do you not see that whatever goes into a person from outside cannot defile, since it enters, not the heart but the stomach, and goes out into the sewer?' Thus he declared all foods clean".[39] Furthermore, the Acts of the Apostles describes a vision experienced by Peter in which God declares all foods fit for consumption.[40] The context of both texts is the increasing admission of non-Jewish converts into the nascent community and the question of what precisely should be required of them. Just as Christianity no longer insisted on circumcision for its new members from a pagan background, so too it further differentiated itself from its mother religion by abandoning the extensive system of Jewish food laws.

7.6 Kosher

If Hinduism is sometimes called the "kitchen religion" because of its strong links between food and spiritual liberation, then Judaism could equally qualify for such a title given the considerable impact of its food laws on the dietary habits of its members. The generic term that gathers together the complex network of Jewish food rules and regulations is *kashrut,* from which the common term *kosher* (fitting or proper) is derived. In the broad sense, kosher can apply to a range of religious objects and processes, but in its narrow sense it refers to food that is fit for consumption according to Jewish law. In contrast, forbidden food is designated as treifah, which literally means torn.[41] The basis on which foods are categorized as kosher or treifah is the will of God, expressed in the Torah, elaborated in the Talmud and codified in classics such as the Shulhan Aruch ("The Well-Set Table"). So which foods are kosher and which are treifah? Before delving into the intricacies of kashrut, it is important to note that food is not rendered kosher by blessing prayers, even though the recitation of prayer at mealtimes is a vital part of Jewish practice and an expression of profound gratitude to the creator. Similarly, although restaurants sometimes advertise "kosher-style" cooking, the manner of preparation is not relevant as it is in Hinduism where fried foods are traditionally preferred over boiled foods. The definition of kosher food can be summed up in seven fundamental principles.

First, animal type is vitally important. The popular image that Jews cannot eat pork is true but its prominence is based on the fact that pork was popular in Europe and an important source of protein. There are many other meats that are also banned by kashrut. According to the Torah, the only land animals that may be eaten are those that have a divided hoof and chew the cud. Thus, meat from sheep, cattle, goats and deer is kosher whereas meat from pigs, rabbits, horses and camels is treifah.[42] The prohibition also extends to the organs, eggs, milk and fat of forbidden animals. The Torah further specifies that the only marine animals that may be consumed are those with fins and scales.[43] Thus, shark, eel, shellfish, lobster, oyster and crab, among others, are forbidden.[44] The Torah also provides a list of unclean birds from which the rabbinic tradition inferred that all predatory and scavenger birds are treifah, whereas domestic fowl such as chickens, geese, turkeys and ducks are kosher.[45]

Second, the manner of death is relevant, at least for land animals. Animals that die of natural causes or are killed by other animals or as part of hunting sports are treifah.[46] The animal is kosher only if it has been slaughtered according to the proper method, or shehitah. This involves a qualified ritual slaughterer (shohet)[47] making a swift cut across the throat with a perfectly sharp knife. Kosher laws specify that the blade of the knife must have no burrs or nicks, that there must not be any hesitation or delay while drawing the knife, and that there not be any chopping, burrowing or tearing motion. The principle behind such detailed requirements is the minimization of the animal's distress and pain. In other words, although the method may sound archaic and brutal to modern ears, the point of the entire operation is to reduce suffering on the part of the animal by rendering it unconscious as quickly as possible.[48]

Third, the Torah expressly forbids the consumption of blood, which is regarded as a creature's life source and, thus, properly belongs to the creator. For this reason, the next step in the slaughtering process is to hang the carcass so that as much blood as possible can be drained.[49] Other methods are also utilized such as soaking, salting and grilling. Eggs with spots of blood are avoided for the same reason. Fourth, certain parts of the animal are prohibited, in particular the hind quarters that surround the sciatic nerve, and fat around vital organs such as the kidney and spleen.[50] The ban on meat from the hind quarters stems from the biblical story of Jacob who wrestled with an angel of God one night. The angel struck him on the sciatic nerve to gain the ascendancy but the injured Jacob was rewarded for his resilience and was renamed Israel.[51]

The fifth principle originates from an enigmatic Torah passage that states: "Do not boil a kid in its mother's milk."[52] The command probably refers to an ancient pagan custom that Israel is warned to avoid. However, the rabbinic tradition has interpreted it to mean that the kosher meat of land animals and birds must never be consumed at the same time as dairy products.[53] For some, the separation of the two food types symbolizes the fundamental distinction between life (dairy) and death (meat). Kosher laws specify that three to six hours should transpire after the consumption of meat before one should take dairy food since particles can remain in the mouth for a considerable time. The reverse order usually requires only rinsing the mouth and eating some neutral food such as bread. Because of the need for constant vigilance in this regard, many Jews have adopted vegetarianism as a convenient way of compliance with the meat–dairy rule, taking inspiration from the biblical creation account, which portrays God's original plan for humankind as vegetarian.[54] Jewish advocates of vegetarianism also argue that abstinence from meat helps to usher in the messianic age, in which the world will revert to the pristine state of Eden. However, there is also a strong Jewish tradition that meat should be eaten on the sabbath and major festivals as a sign of celebration and joy.

The sixth kosher principle is a direct consequence of the fifth principle in that the separation of meat and dairy also applies to the kitchenware used to cook both food types. Ideally, a separate set of utensils, dishes, towels and tablecloths should be used for meat and dairy foodstuffs. Thus, Jews who follow kosher laws strictly often have two entire sets of utensils and even two kitchens if they can afford it. The seventh and final principle is the ban on wine or grape juice that has been produced by non-Jewish sources. This idea stems from the biblical concern that the pagans often used wine and other forms of alcohol in their religious rituals. The aim was once again to distinguish Israel from its polytheistic neighbors and their idolatrous practices. Consequently, a kosher certificate is normally required for such products.

There are a number of theological explanations for kosher laws. The biblical texts do not always provide a clear-cut explanation, and so rabbinic commentators have argued that the true purpose is hidden in the mystery of God's unfathomable wisdom. They are hukkim commandments, meaning that this requires trusting obedience from the believer. However, others maintain that God always has a reason for his commandments. For instance, kosher laws reinforce the difference between Israel and other peoples. The people of God are a holy nation in an unholy world, and the food laws emphasize their unique status and calling, setting them apart from the rest. Just as Hindu food laws often serve to reinforce the internal boundaries between castes, Jewish food laws serve to reinforce the external boundary between Israel itself and the world.

Jewish commentators also point out that the kosher laws challenge the believer to exercise the virtues of discipline and self-control. They strengthen one's ability to make difficult moral choices, curb dangerous appetites and help the mind to channel desire in correct directions.[55] In this sense they are part of the call to moral goodness. Others point out that many of the ancient kosher laws reflect a historical concern to avoid what were perceived as dangerous or unhealthy dietary practices at the time. In other words, hygiene and health are the real issue. Examples include: the separation of meat from dairy in order to minimize cross-contamination; the inspection of the lungs of the slaughtered animal for various diseases; the ban on eating carrion or animals that have died of natural causes; the avoidance of shellfish and other animals that feed on the seabed; and the prohibition of pork, which is a common source of trichinosis when not properly cooked. It could be argued that religious dietary law has been built on ancient dietary prudence.

The level of adherence to the food laws varies considerably across Judaism. Orthodox and Conservative Jews are more likely to practice kosher meticulously, while more liberal Jews tend to see it as less relevant. But there are other food customs that mark Jewish practice, in particular the association of certain foods with various festivals on the religious calendar, giving each a distinctive flavor. Jewish New Year is marked by honey and apples, which symbolize the sweetness of a new beginning.[56] The feast of Hanukkah, which commemorates the miracle of the Temple oil that lasted eight days, is appositely characterized by fried foods such as potato pancakes and doughnuts. At Purim, copious amounts of wine are drunk to the point of inebriation.[57] At Shavuot (Pentecost), dairy foods, such as ice cream and cheesecake, are served, based on the description of the Torah as "milk and honey" under one's tongue.[58]

Arguably the most concentrated use of symbolic foods occurs during **Pesah** (Passover), which celebrates the escape of the Hebrew slaves from Egypt. As a symbol of the haste with which the refugees fled, only unleavened bread (matzah) is eaten.[59] At the Passover meal a range of foodstuffs are placed on the table, each signifying an aspect of the Exodus experience (Figure 7.3): horseradish (maror) and bitter herbs (hazeret) for the bitterness of slavery; salt water for tears of sorrow; a mixture of nuts, apples and wine (haroset) representing the mortar used by the Hebrews as slave laborers; the shankbone of a lamb (zeroah) symbolizing God's outstretched arm, which signaled to the angel of death to "pass over" the Hebrew homes; a green vegetable (karpas) such as celery or parsley for the new life of spring; a burnt egg (beitzah) representing the temple sacrifice; and four cups of wine symbolizing the stages toward liberation.

As noted above, there is a strong possibility that Jesus's Last Supper was a Passover meal. With Christianity's decision to abandon the elaborate kosher laws of Judaism, the historical and symbolic link between the Jewish Passover and the Christian Eucharist became the principal intersection between these two religions concerning food. In contrast, the third Abrahamic faith adopted many Jewish kosher laws with some modifications and one striking exception.

Figure 7.3 Jewish Passover plate with symbolic foods. (Reproduced with kind permission of iStock.)

7.7 Halal

One of the most common signs posted on the front of butcher shops in cities and towns around the globe is the word **halal** (Figure 7.4). For over 1 billion Muslims, the term indicates that the meat sold in these shops is in accordance with Islamic law as expressed in the Qur'an, the hadith and the legal tradition. As with kosher, the term *halal* can have both a general and a particular sense. Its broad meaning refers to a range of items or activities that are appropriate such as certain behavior, speech or dress. Its more technical meaning pertains to the food laws of Islam. But it is not only the terms that are similar. There is an unmistakable resemblance between Islamic halal and Jewish kosher. Both are based on the conviction that certain foods have been prohibited by God and that obeying these laws is a vital aspect of religious practice. Moreover, many of the details of the two systems have much in common, although there are also important differences.

Islam divides food into three basic categories: halal (fitting); mushbooh (uncertain); and haram (forbidden). The basic presumption is that all foods are halal except for those that are explicitly identified otherwise. The Qur'an declares: "O you who believe, eat of the good things that We have provided you with, and give thanks to Allah if Him it is that you serve."[60] For Muslims, the plants and animals of the earth are part of the bountiful providence of the creator. So which foods in particular are considered haram?

As in Judaism, there is a strong focus on meat in Islamic food laws. With regard to marine life, Islam teaches that all sea creatures are halal provided that they live in the water all the time: "Lawful to you is the game of the sea and its food, a provision for you and for the travelers."[61] Thus, the Muslim diet is less restrictive than Judaism when it comes to seafood, although some Muslims avoid crustaceans such as lobsters, oysters and prawns.[62] Amphibious animals that do not fit neatly into either aquatic or terrestrial

Figure 7.4 An Islamic butcher shop in England.
(Reproduced with kind permission of Alamy.)

categories are considered haram. A similar pattern can be seen with land animals. The Islamic position is once again more liberal than the Jewish because there is no equivalent of the kosher requirement that the animal has cloven hooves and chews the cud. Unlike Jews, Muslims are not banned from eating camel, horse and rabbit. However, there are some limitations that are stated in a key Qur'anic text from the second surah (The Cow): "He has only forbidden you what dies of itself, and blood, and flesh of swine, and that over which any other name than Allah has been invoked."[63] The hadith adds animals with fangs, birds of prey, pests and poisonous animals to the list[64] but the Qur'anic focus is on the three main items of pork, blood and carrion – all of which are also features of kosher law.

It is well known that Muslims, like Jews, are not permitted to consume pork, ham, bacon and other related products. Many foods are categorized as mushbooh precisely because it is suspected that they contain derivatives of pork such as emulsifiers, gelatine and certain enzymes. Like the Torah, the Qur'an does not provide an explicit reason for the need to avoid pig flesh, suggesting that the divine reason is hidden from our minds and, ultimately, is not as important as trusting obedience. Some Muslim writers appeal to hygiene as the underlying purpose, pointing out that porcine flesh is more liable to disease than other types of meat. Moreover, pigs are considered filthy animals in popular Islamic culture and many believe that eating pork contributes to moral laxness. As in Hinduism and Christianity, we become what we eat.

The ban on consuming blood also echoes both Jewish practice and the Jewish justification. The blood of an animal is its life source, which belongs exclusively to Allah, the ultimate source of all life. Consequently, animal carcasses must be thoroughly drained and hung before being prepared for sale. But the parallel with Judaism continues in the Islamic concern with the manner of the death as well. According to the Qur'an, carrion is also taboo. Animals that have died of natural causes or that have been killed by other animals are haram. The animal must be slaughtered in the proper way to be halal. Just as Judaism prescribes shehitah, so the proper Islamic method of slaughter is known as zabihah, which applies to land animals and birds but not seafood.

Zabihah requires that the slaughterer be a mature, committed Muslim who understands the method and is approved by the religious authorities. As in Judaism, there is a general concern to minimize the animal's suffering. It should be given some water to drink beforehand in order to quench its thirst. Moreover it is forbidden to sharpen the knife in front of the animal, which only increases its distress. The knife itself must be non-serrated and perfectly sharp. A single swift stroke should be made across the throat in order to render the animal unconscious as quickly and painlessly as possible.[65] A blessing such as Bismillah Allah-u-Akbar ("In the name of God, God is Great"), or at least the name of Allah, must be uttered before or during the slaughtering as an acknowledgment that the creator is the one who gives life and takes it back: "Therefore, eat of that on which Allah's name has been mentioned if you are believers...And do not eat of that on which Allah's name has not been mentioned."[66] The interval between the recitation of the divine name and the slaughtering must not be excessive.

The significant similarity between Jewish and Islamic food laws raises the issue of whether Muslims may eat kosher meat, especially when halal meat is not available. Some note that the Qur'an implies an affirmative answer when it states: "This day, all the good things are allowed to you; and the food of those who have been given the Book is lawful for you and your food is lawful for them."[67] Others disagree, claiming that a Jewish slaughterer would not satisfy the requirement that the name of Allah be uttered over the animal as expressly stated in the quotation from the Qur'an in the previous paragraph.

If Judaism is more restrictive than Islam when it comes to meat taboos, the converse is the case with regard to alcohol. As noted above, wine is a common feature of Jewish ritual and a much treasured gift from the creator. In contrast, a noticeable aspect of Islamic practice is the total ban on alcohol and any other form of intoxicant. There is evidence in the Qur'an that Muhammad and his young community only gradually came to such a belief. Initially, the Qur'an simply states the fact that certain plants are the source of both fruit and intoxicating drink: "And of the fruits of the palms and the grapes – you obtain from them intoxication and goodly provision; most surely there is a sign in this for a people who ponder."[68] At a subsequent point the Qur'an warns that alcohol can lead to intoxication, which has the potential to undermine daily prayer: "O you who believe! Do not go near prayer when you are intoxicated until you know well what you say."[69] Alcohol is also linked to gambling and, thus, is seen as a possible source of vice: "They ask you about intoxicants and games of chance. Say: In both of them there is a great sin and means of profit for men, and their sin is greater than their profit."[70] The point is made even more strongly in another Qur'anic verse where alcohol and gambling are described as "Satan's works," which must be shunned totally.[71] Muslims understand this evolution of thought as part of God's educative process, whereby he patiently reveals the true nature of alcohol and steadily weans the community off a long-established pre-Islamic habit.

The ban extends to all intoxicating substances, foodstuffs that contain alcohol and commercial transactions involving it. For some Muslims even medicines and mouthwashes that contain small amounts of alcohol are haram, especially if non-alcoholic alternatives can be found. It is not alcohol per se but the deleterious effects of intoxication that are the problem, including immorality and the neglect of daily prayer. Thus, the Islamic vision of heaven includes an abundance of wine but it does not muddle the mind.[72] If there is significant common ground between Islam and Judaism on the question of meat, Islam clearly moves away from its Abrahamic cousin on the question of alcohol. In fact, it has much more in common with Buddhism and the Quanzhen branch of Daoism that it inspired. Islam's concern that abuse of alcohol undermines mental clarity, moral responsibility and spiritual health brings us full circle, resonating with the sentiments expressed in the fifth precept of the Buddhist Pancasila.

Summary

As the most basic of human needs, food plays an important role in religious ritual and practice. The ordinary reality of eating and drinking is taken up and given a new, extraordinary significance through the eyes of faith. A meal can provide access to ultimate reality and become a channel of transcendent meaning. Food is linked to spiritual purity and holiness, religious identity and membership. For a range of reasons, certain foods are prescribed while others are proscribed. Each major religion uses food in a rich variety of ways that reflect both the distinctiveness of each tradition and the fascinating intersections between them.

Many of the food customs of the six religions concern the consumption of meat. Vegetarianism is widely considered to be mandatory for Buddhists, or at least Buddhist monks, given the fundamental importance of the principle of non-violence (ahimsa). The first principle of the Pancasila prohibits the taking of animal life. However, the historical Buddha's own example and teaching admit that there may be exceptional circumstances when strict vegetarianism is not possible, such as when meat is offered during the alms rounds. The general principle in Theravada Buddhism has been that a monk may consume meat when offered, provided it was not prepared specifically for him. The link between the monk and the actual act of slaughter must be minimal. Ahimsa is also a principle highly valued in the Hindu tradition where the higher the caste the greater the expectations. High-caste Hindus have traditionally practiced vegetarianism for this reason. Quanzhen Daoist monks also follow the Buddhist custom and avoid meat as much as possible, but Zhengyi Daoists are more concerned with avoiding grains, which are seen as unnatural foods that generate disharmony with the Dao and foster spiritual parasites in the body. Although vegetarianism is not as pronounced in Judaism and Islam, the required method of slaughter in both Abrahamic traditions reflects a concern to reduce the suffering of the animal in the spirit of ahimsa. Shehitah and zabihah both require that the animal be killed by a swift cut to the throat so that unconsciousness is instantaneous and pain is minimized.

Jewish and Islamic food laws are also quite specific about the type of meat that the believer may eat. Jewish kosher law allows only marine animals with scales and fins, and terrestrial animals that have cloven hoof and chew the cud. This means that many types of foods are prohibited for Jews including crustaceans as well as common meats such as horse, rabbit and pork. Islam is less restrictive in that it singles out pork as the main form of prohibited meat and allows most seafood. Both Abrahamic traditions prohibit the consumption of blood and carrion. Blood symbolizes the life force in all animals, and its avoidance is an expression of respect for the creator's dominion over life. The ban on carrion reflects a concern for the manner of the animal's death that is related to the rules of slaughter. Jews and Muslims accept this set of restrictions as part of the divine will, although both religions admit that hygienic reasons may also be part of the overall rationale. Pork is particularly prone to contamination; carrion is likely to be diseased or flawed; and crustaceans are filter-feeders that live on the muddy seabed and are considered impure. If kosher and halal laws partly reflect this fundamental link between diet and bodily health, then the food customs of Hinduism are also based on the same premise: we are what we eat, both spiritually and physically. Thus, the traditional Hindu classification of foods into pukka and katcha, or into the three gunas in the Vaishnavite tradition, rests on the notion that certain types of food are more spiritually uplifting than others. Daoism shares the same idea and many of its food practices – such as seasonal diets, external alchemy and saliva swallowing – are aimed at generating and channeling spiritual energy (qi) for the benefit of both mind and body, even to the point of attaining a form of immortality.

Alcohol is also given prominence in religious food customs, albeit in quite contrasting ways. The fifth precept of the Buddhist Pancasila specifies that the believer should refrain from taking anything that reduces the capacity to think and behave responsibly. Clarity of mind (samadhi) is considered essential for concentrated meditation and moral propriety. Thus, the devout Buddhist will avoid not only alcoholic drink but any form of intoxicant or drug that compromises this standard. As with vegetarianism, Quanzhen Daoism follows the Buddhist practice and shuns alcohol as a substance that dulls the mind. Among the other major religions, it is Islam that most prominently shares this stress on the negative effects of alcohol and drugs. The Qur'an reflects a gradual educative process whereby Allah slowly brings the young Islamic community to the point of abjuring existing customs and accepting a total ban on alcoholic beverages. In contrast, Judaism and Christianity not only allow the responsible consumption of alcohol but have incorporated wine into their holy ritual. The central Christian rite of the Eucharist is essentially a sacred meal of bread and wine that originated in Jesus's Last Supper. For many, the Last Supper was probably a Jewish Passover meal during which wine is drunk to symbolize salvation and blessing. Although some Protestant Christian churches use non-alcoholic grape juice at the Eucharist and preach total abstinence from alcohol, mainstream Catholic, Orthodox, Anglican and Lutheran Christians share a positive attitude toward wine that is more typical of Judaism. Indeed, Jewish life-cycle ceremonies such as circumcision, bar mitzvah and weddings use wine as a symbol of human happiness and abundant divine blessing. Wine is also an important part of many Jewish festivals, including Purim when the rabbinic tradition actually encourages the believer to become inebriated for the sheer joy of God's liberating power.

Food laws are also linked to notions of membership and identity. In Hinduism, where fulfillment of caste duties is a means to ultimate liberation, meals function as a reinforcement of caste boundaries in much the same way as marriage. Hindu caste expectations not only determine whom one can marry but also with whom one should eat. In this way, purity is maintained and liberation from the wheel of reincarnation is a step closer. Even the well-known ban on eating beef became a proud badge of Hindu identity under British rule. Jewish kosher laws also function in a similar way. Unlike Hinduism where the differentiation is internal and between castes, Jewish food customs set Israel apart from the other nations and ground its special call to holiness in an unholy world. The Christian Eucharistic meal is also understood as a symbol of unity among fellow believers who gather around the table of the Lord and celebrate their fellowship as the "body" of Christ. Sadly, the great rite of Christian unity has actually become a focal point of Christian division. Catholic and Orthodox churches believe that, until theological differences are resolved, there can be no meaningful sharing of the bread and wine with members of other Christian denominations.

Finally, religious food customs also represent communion with the transcendent. The Christian Eucharist not only symbolizes a horizontal union among fellow believers but also a vertical union with the incarnate God who offers himself as nourishment to the communicant. Although there is debate among Christian churches over whether the focus should be on the bread and wine itself or the act of eating and drinking, all Christians acknowledge a "real presence" of Christ in the Eucharist in some sense. Whether the words are taken literally or metaphorically, somehow the bread and wine become the body and blood of Christ, which are real nourishment for body and soul. On this point, there is a discernible intersection with the Hindu practice of prasad in which the believer and the deity share a meal. In Hindu worship, where the deity is symbolized in physical terms by the murti and treated like a royal guest, food offerings naturally play a vital role. The divine visitor eats the essence of the food and the human host consumes the leftovers that not only symbolize subordination but also a loving communion that is the goal of the bhakti tradition of Hindu devotion. Such are the food customs of the six religions. In the next chapter, we turn to that other fundamental human need: clothing.

Discussion Topics

1. Is alcohol inherently good or evil? Compare attitudes to alcohol in the six religions.
2. Compare the Daoist avoidance of grains with Jewish and Islamic avoidance of pork.
3. For what religious reasons do some people espouse vegetarianism?
4. Compare Jewish, Islamic and Christian attitudes to the consumption of blood.
5. Why are Jewish and Islamic food laws so similar? Are they essentially a question of hygiene?
6. Compare the Hindu prasad and the Christian Eucharist.
7. Examine how Jewish Passover themes are applied to the Christian Eucharist.
8. Explore the practice of fasting in each religion.

Notes

1 Daode jing, ch.12.
2 Popular items include pine nuts, berries, black sesame seeds and ginger.
3 Kohn, Livia (1993). *The Taoist Experience*, 149.
4 Schipper, Kristofer (1993). *The Taoist Body*, 170.

5 See Komjathy, 130; Zhengtong daozang 87, 7a-8a.
6 Classical texts on external alchemy include Baopuzi neipian (Inner Chapters of Master Embracing Simplicity) by Ge Hong and Shennong bencao jing (The Divine Farmer's Classic of Herbology) by Tao Hongjing.
7 Zhuangzi, ch. 1.
8 Komjathy, 174.
9 Shurangama Sutra 6.20–3; Brahma Net Sutra 6.3; Lankavatara Sutra 8.
10 Shurangama Sutra 6.
11 The Buddha's final meal was "suukaramaddava," which can be translated as pig's flesh (pork) or pig's delight (truffles).
12 Khandhaka, Mahavagga 6.31–2.
13 Khandhaka, Mahavagga 6.233.
14 The Vinaya Pitaka lists 10 types of flesh that should not be consumed by monks: human, elephant, horse, dog, snake, lion, tiger, leopard, bear and hyena. The implication may be that other meats are permissible (Suttavibhanga, Pacittiya 8.4).
15 Anguttara Nikaya 5.177.
16 Khuddaka Nikaya, Sutta Nipata 245: "The Buddha said: Anger, arrogance, inflexibility, hostility, deception, envy, pride, conceit, bad company, these are impure foods, not meat."
17 Chandogya Upanishad 6.6.1–2.
18 See Laws of Manu, ch. V.
19 In fact the Vedas make frequent reference to a ritual drink known as soma whose intoxicating effects induced altered states of mind.
20 In contemporary India, inferior housing is categorized as katcha (constructed from mud and leaves) or pukka (constructed from burnt bricks or other superior forms of building materials).
21 The three gunas are features of the Samkhya philosophical school in Hinduism. In contrast to the Vaishnavite tradition, Shaivite Hindus observe fewer dietary restrictions and Shakta followers of the Mother Goddess are more inclined to eat meat, which is traditionally obtained from animal sacrifice.
22 Bhagavad Gita 17:7–8.
23 Bhagavad Gita 17:9.
24 Bhagavad Gita 17:10.
25 Laws of Manu V.48. A few verses later Manu acknowledges that meat-eating, along with alcohol and sexual intercourse, are natural activities, albeit ones that should be minimized as far as possible: "There is no sin in eating meat, in (drinking) spirituous liquor, and in carnal intercourse, for that is the natural way of created beings, but abstention brings great rewards" (Laws of Manu V.56).
26 In Vedic literature, prasad also means a mental state experienced by gods, sages and other powerful beings marked by spontaneous generosity. Later texts, such as the Shiva Purana, begin to apply the term to the material food offered to the deity in worship and subsequently consumed by the believer.
27 Bhagavad Gita 3:13; see also 9:27.
28 See Acts 2:42, 46; 20:7.
29 See Matthew 26:26–8; Mark 14:22–4; Luke 22:17–20; 1 Corinthians 11:23–5.
30 See Didache 9; Ignatius, *Letter to the Philadelphians,* 4.
31 WCC Faith and Order Paper 111: Baptism, Eucharist, Ministry: Eucharist, E8.
32 See 1 Corinthians 12:12–27; Ephesians 5:23–32.

33 1 Corinthians 10:16–17.
34 Council of Trent (1551), DS 1642; see Catechism of the Catholic Church (1992), 1376.
35 Augsburg Confession, article 10.
36 Calvinism accepts the notion of Christ's "real presence" but emphasizes the believer's faith rather than any real change in the bread and wine. See Westminster Confession of Faith, ch. 19. Baptist and other Protestant Christian groups follow Zwingli who stressed the symbolic nature of the meal and rejected any miraculous change in the bread and wine.
37 Corpus Christi is traditionally celebrated on the second Sunday after Pentecost.
38 WCC Faith and Order Paper 111: Baptism, Eucharist, Ministry: Eucharist, E32.
39 Mark 7:18–19.
40 Acts 10:1–17.
41 The term is derived from the biblical ban on eating animals that have been killed ("torn") by other beasts. See Exodus 22:31.
42 Leviticus 11:3–4; Deuteronomy 14:4–8.
43 Leviticus 11:9–10; Deuteronomy 14:9–10.
44 The swordfish is an interesting case in point since it has scales when young but sheds these in adulthood.
45 Leviticus 11:13–19; Deuteronomy 14:11–18. The Leviticus text goes on to forbid rodents, reptiles, amphibians and most insects.
46 Exodus 22:31; Deuteronomy 12:21.
47 The shohet is not merely a butcher but must also be a person of faith, familiar with kashrut and officially authorized by a recognized rabbinic authority.
48 Modern methods such as reversible stunning (electric shock), irreversible stunning (bolt) and anaesthesia are usually rejected since the traditional law demands that the animal must be conscious when killed so that the slaughterer and consumer are aware that life is being taken. Contemporary animal rights groups have criticized Jewish and Islamic slaughtering methods as cruel but traditional religious authorities usually respond by insisting on the effectiveness of the method when properly implemented. A related law disallows the killing of the offspring and parent on the same day out of compassion. See Leviticus 22:28.
49 Leviticus 7:26; 17:10–14; Genesis 9:4. The ban on blood does not apply to marine animals.
50 Leviticus 7:23–5.
51 Genesis 32:22–32.
52 Exodus 23:19; 34:26; Deuteronomy 14:21.
53 Talmud Hullin 8.1–3.
54 Genesis 1:29.
55 See Maimonides, *Guide for the Perplexed,* 3.48.
56 The circular shaped hallah bread signifies the cycle of the seasons.
57 Talmud Megilla 7b. Traditionally a Jew is encouraged to drink wine on Purim until he can no longer distinguish between the phrases *arur Haman* ("cursed is Haman") and *baruch Mordechai* ("blessed is Mordechai"). See also Shulhan Aruch, Orach Hayim 695.
58 Song of Songs 4:11. Another explanation states that the gift of the Torah meant that kosher rules came into effect. Because the Israelites had not slaughtered their meat legally on that first day of the new law, they ate dairy foods instead.
59 Exodus 12:15–20; 13:7. The "hametz (leaven) hunt" is usually held on the night before the festival starts.
60 Qur'an 2:172.

61 Qur'an 5:96.
62 Shi'ites as well as Sunnis from the Hanafi and Shafi'i schools avoid crustaceans.
63 Qur'an 2:173. See also 16:115; 5:3.
64 Sahih Bukhari 7.67.438.
65 Sahih Muslim 21.4810. Islam also agrees with Judaism that it must be killed while still conscious and so anaesthesia or stunning are disallowed.
66 Qur'an 6:118, 121.
67 Qur'an 5:5.
68 Qur'an 16:67.
69 Qur'an 4:43.
70 Qur'an 2:219.
71 Qur'an 5:91–2. See also Sahih Bukhari 7.69.481–543.
72 Qur'an 56:18–21.

Further Reading

Bhaskarananda, Swami (2002). *The Essentials of Hinduism*. 2nd ed. Seattle, WA: Viveka, ch. 7.
Cohn-Sherbok, Dan (2003). *Judaism: History, Belief and Practice*. London: Routledge, pp. 554–8.
Cooper, John (1994). *Eat and Be Satisfied: A Social History of Jewish Food*. Lanham, MD: Jason Aronson.
Komjathy, Louis (2013). *The Daoist Tradition*. London: Bloomsbury, ch. 9.
Michaels, Axel (2003). *Hinduism: Past and Present*. Princeton, NJ: Princeton University Press, pp. 175–85.
Miller, James (2003). *Daoism*. Oxford: Oneworld, ch. 6.
Saeed, Abdullah (2003). *Islam in Australia*. St Leonards, NSW: Allen & Unwin, ch. 10.
Segler, Franklin M., & Bradley, Randall (2006). *Christian Worship: Its Theology and Practice*. 3rd ed. Nashville, TN: B & H Publishing Group, pp. 173–86.
Vajda, Georges (2006) "Fasting in Islam and Judaism" in G. R. Hawting (ed.), *The Development of Islamic Ritual*. Aldershot: Ashgate, ch. 8.
White, James F. (2001). *Introduction to Christian Worship*. 3rd ed. Nashville, TN: Abingdon Press, ch. 9.

8

Clothing

CONTENTS

8.1 Introduction

Along with food, clothing is one of the most fundamental of human physical needs. Apart from the basic function of providing protection for the body from the elements, the clothes that we wear also carry an array of social meanings. Different styles of apparel can be used to maintain levels of modesty, indicate particular occupations and roles, and signify membership of socio-cultural groups. In some respects, the old adage has a point: "Clothes maketh the man." Religious practice is also characterized by the inherent potential in ordinary clothing to convey deeper theological values. This chapter will explore the most prominent forms of religious attire in each of the six religions. In what specifically religious ways do believers dress and fashion their appearance? Do such customs apply to all believers or only certain members of the faith? Are they linked to daily life or special circumstances? Most importantly, what religious meanings do they signify?

8.2 The Veil of Modesty

In late 1989, three female Muslim students were suspended from a secondary school in Creil, France, for refusing to remove their veils in the classroom. At stake was the secular nature of the French public school system versus the right of all citizens to freedom of religious expression. Then, in 2011, France banned covering one's face in public on security grounds as well as the importance of facial recognition and expression in social communication. One of the main targets of the ban was the Islamic burqa, which was seen as symptomatic of the suppression of women. Given such events, there is little doubt that the veil is currently the most striking and controversial aspect of clothing in Islam.

The requirement that women cover the whole or certain parts of their bodies in public is not unique to Islam. Women have been expected to wear veils in cultures as diverse as ancient Greek, Byzantine, Persian and Indian societies. Moreover, in ancient times the veil was usually a sign of elevated social status rather than subjugation. The Qur'an does not have much to say on the matter but there are two relevant texts:

> And say to the believing women that they cast down their looks and guard their private parts and do not display their beauty except what appears thereof, and let them wear their head-coverings (khimars) over their bosoms, and not display their beauty except to their husbands or their fathers, or the fathers of their husbands, or their sons, or the sons of their husbands, or their brothers, or their brothers' sons, or their sisters' sons, or their women, or those whom their right hands possess, or the male servants not having need of women, or the children who have not attained knowledge of what is hidden of women; and let them not strike their feet so that what they hide of their beauty may be known; and turn to Allah all of you, O believers, so that you may be successful.[1]

> Prophet! Say to your wives and your daughters and the women of the believers that they let down upon them their over-garments (jilbabs); this will be more proper, that they may be known, and thus they will not be given trouble; and Allah is Forgiving, Merciful.[2]

The two passages clearly call for women to behave and dress modestly in public but it should be noted that the Qur'an makes the same basic demand upon men: "Say to the believing men that they cast down their looks and guard their private parts; that is purer for them; surely Allah is aware of what they do."[3] The central issue for both genders is what Islamic scholars call the awrah: those parts of the body that should be concealed in public. The main legal schools agree that the awrah for men extends from the navel to below the knees, although the Maliki school allows for the knees to be uncovered. Moreover, men are traditionally prohibited from wearing silk clothing and gold or silver ornaments because such items are associated with worldly splendor and ostentation.[4]

In contrast, women are allowed to adorn themselves in fine clothes and jewelry in order to enhance their physical beauty, provided this is not done with the intention of stimulating sexual desire in men other than their husbands. Indeed, it is precisely the concern to control sexual arousal that constitutes the rationale for the more rigorous dress requirements that apply to women. Thus, the dress code does not come into effect until the age of puberty when sexuality becomes a factor. Furthermore, it does not apply when a woman is in the company of her husband, young boys, close male relatives with whom marriage is forbidden, or other women. In general, Islamic tradition prescribes that female clothing should be sufficiently loose and thick to hide the shape of the body and the color of the skin. Nevertheless, the garments should be sufficiently different from male apparel so as to reflect her femininity.

What this means in practice varies since there is considerable difference of opinion within Islam as to the precise extent of the awrah for women. The Qur'anic text itself is somewhat ambiguous in that it speaks of drawing a head-covering over the bosom and not displaying beauty "except what appears thereof." This enigmatic phrase has consequently given rise to different interpretations, which in turn give rise to different degrees of sartorial concealment (Figure 8.1). Most positions agree that the arms, legs and hair must be covered, but not necessarily the face. According to one relevant hadith, the Prophet himself specified:

> Asma, daughter of Abu Bakr, entered upon the Apostle of Allah (peace be upon him) wearing thin clothes. The Apostle of Allah (peace be upon him) turned his attention from her. He said: "O Asma, when a woman reaches the age of menstruation, it does not suit her that she displays her parts of the body except this and this" and he pointed to her face and hands.[5]

Figure 8.1 Islamic women in the veil. (Reproduced with kind permission of iStock.)

Thus, many Muslim women believe that by wearing a veil they are fulfilling the divine commandment. The term *hijab* literally means a partition or barrier, but in the context of religious clothing it refers to a simple scarf that covers the hair and neck but leaves the face visible. A more formal variation of the hijab is the khimar, a semi-circular flare of fabric with an opening for the face, somewhat resembling the wimple of a Catholic nun. However, there are Islamic leaders who adopt a stricter interpretation of the awrah and insist that not even the face should be exposed in public.[6] This theological position is reflected in forms of dress that are more concealing than the hijab. The niqab covers the lower part of the face from the nose to the chin. The burqa covers the entire body, including all of the face, with a thinner fabric over the eyes so that the woman can see.

As mentioned earlier, many Western critics see the female dress code as indicative of an allegedly oppressive attitude toward women in Islamic societies. Religiously sanctioned restrictions on a woman's ability to participate in public life and the underlying presumption that a woman's God-given role is limited to the domestic sphere are serious issues that affect all religions founded in ancient patriarchal societies. Critics also add that women are being blamed for men not being able to control their sexual thoughts and desires. Yet Islamic voices, many of them female, point to the positive meanings signified by the veil. First, the Qur'an makes it clear that the dress code is basically an assertion of the importance of sexual modesty. In fact, many Muslim women argue that their Western sisters are the ones who are really enslaved by the pressures of a superficial popular culture in which a woman's value is essentially based on her physical attractiveness. The veil is a silent protest against the exploitation of women via the cult of beauty.[7] Second, many Muslim women point out that, paradoxically, the dress code actually allows them to leave their homes and participate in social, economic and political life protected from sexual harassment and abuse to a greater degree than in the West. Finally, Islamic dress, especially when worn in multicultural Western societies, is an unambiguous statement about religious identity. A woman who wears the hijab, niqab or burqa is making a declaration not only about modesty and the need to see beyond physical beauty but also about her Islamic faith. She is proudly declaring that she is Muslim by the very apparel in which she is clothed.

The status of the veil as arguably the most recognizable form of Muslim religious dress is highlighted by the fact that no special attire is required for official communal worship. Shoes must be removed before entering a mosque so as not to defile the sacred space and in some cases men are encouraged to wear a head-covering such as a cap or turban. Women would naturally wear a veil since the prayers are in the public arena. One hadith confirms the connection between covering the head and prayer: "The Prophet (peace be upon him) said: Allah does not accept the prayer of a woman who has reached puberty unless she wears a veil."[8]

The prominence of the everyday veil is further reinforced by the fact that Islam has no priesthood and thus no special garb to differentiate the cleric from the layperson. The imams who lead Islamic prayer services in mosques do not customarily dress any differently from the congregation although in some traditions a colored turban indicates such a role. Shi'ite religious leaders prefer to wear black as a sign of mourning for Ali, the cousin and son-in-law of Muhammad. A black turban may also indicate that the wearer is a sayyid or sharif: a descendant of the Prophet through his daughter Fatima and her husband Ali. Where one does find special symbolic apparel is among the mystical brotherhoods whose garments reflect their individual spirituality. The term *Sufi*, which refers to Islamic mystical sects whose members traditionally wore a simple robe of white wool, is derived from the Arabic word for "wool." Sometimes the habit of the brotherhood has a deeper meaning. For example, the Turkish Mawlawiyah order, better known as the "whirling dervishes," wear somber black garments and tall hats symbolic of the grave and headstone. However, when they commence their famous twirling dance of meditation, they remove their doleful outer layers to reveal stunning white garments, symbolic of the resurrection.

Perhaps the best example of a special Islamic dress associated with a particular religious practice is the garment worn by pilgrims to Mecca. Upon arrival in the holy city, the visitor dons a simple, two-piece white garment known as the ihram. Irrespective of their social or financial status, all pilgrims wear the same uniform and stand before Allah as equals. Muslims also interpret the ihram as the dress of the beggar who comes humble, empty-handed and utterly dependent before the Almighty. Many pilgrims retain their ihram and some request that they be buried in the garment, which symbolizes a state of purity and consecration. While male pilgrims must, out of respect, keep their heads bare during the pilgrimage, women wear a simple white dress or their own native costume, with the ever-important veil.

Apart from the Qur'anic emphasis on clothing (especially female clothing) as a means to ensure modesty of thought and action between the sexes in social settings, Muslim women also use their attire as a statement of true feminine worth and religious affiliation. The function of clothing as a badge of identity and differentiation can also be found in the religion of Moses where, at least for men, the covering of the head with a small skullcap is both an act of reverence before God and an unambiguous public profession of Jewish belief.

8.3 Kippah, Tefillin and Tallit

At some stage during the first millennium CE, a tradition emerged in Judaism that drew its inspiration from the head-covering that the priests in ancient Israel always wore while serving in the Temple.[9] In the treatise on the sabbath, the Talmud commands the believer: "Cover your head in order that the fear of heaven may be upon you."[10] Elsewhere, the Talmud relates how Rabbi Huna never walked more than four cubits (about two yards) with his head uncovered as a sign of his faith that the divine presence was always over him.[11] Thus began the custom of men wearing the distinctive kippah, which has become one of the most recognizable signs of Jewish identity today.

The kippah is typically a thin, slightly rounded cloth skullcap that is worn on the crown of the head. Rabbinic commentators teach that it should be large enough to be called a head-covering and visible from all sides, but it has evolved into a small, lightweight cap, probably as a result of practical convenience. The color and style of the kippah can also be indicative of religious or political persuasion within Judaism. For example, a blue or brown crocheted kippah is often associated with **Zionism** and a black velvet kippah is popular among Orthodox Jews.

According to Maimonides, the kippah should be worn by Jewish men during prayer times[12] and, thus, many Jews don their kippah when attending synagogue, praying privately, studying the Torah, performing a ritual, and during meals because these are accompanied by blessings. However, Orthodox Jews usually abide by the Shulhan Aruch, which teaches that it should be worn always on the basis of Rabbi Huna's example quoted above. The kippah may be removed if etiquette requires, such as in courtrooms, or when it is impractical to wear, such as while swimming or bathing.

As expressed in the Talmud, the primary meaning of the kippah is that the believer stands under the authority and power of the Almighty. The Hebrew term kippah literally means "dome" and the one who wears this dome acknowledges the constant divine presence that covers them. The **Yiddish** term for the skullcap, *yarmulke*, connotes the same idea because it derives from an **Aramaic** phrase that means "in awe of the King." Thus, wearing the kippah is first and foremost an act of humility and an affirmation of the sovereignty of God in all aspects of life. Like the Temple priests of old, the believer covers the crown of the head, the highest point on the human body, in reverence and submission before a higher being.[13] The kippah is also an aid to concentration during prayer, especially when it is not worn at other times and, thus, it accentuates the sacred nature of the exercise. For the Jewish men who wear the kippah at all times, it functions as a public statement of religious identity just as the veil is a badge of faith for Islamic women.

But what of Jewish women? Traditionally the kippah was restricted to male Jews, although some Reform Jewish women now wear it. In Orthodox circles, married Jewish women wear a scarf, hat or snood to synagogue and there is also a general expectation that a woman will cover her hair in the presence of men other than her husband for modesty's sake. Some ultra-orthodox wives fulfill the requirements of a head-covering without actually wearing one by using a wig, although some rabbis argue that this is against the spirit of the law. In this case, the aim of the head-covering has shifted from signifying reverence before God to concealment for the sake of modesty, as in Islam. In some Hasidic and Sephardic communities, the wig is not sufficient and women are required to wear some other covering as well.

Hair is also an issue for Jewish men. The book of Leviticus states: "You shall not round off the hair on your temples or mar the edges of your beard."[14] The rabbinic tradition has interpreted this commandment to mean that Jews are not to use a razor to shave their beard or their sideburns.[15] For those who prefer to be clean-shaven, scissors, electric razors – which are deemed to operate like scissors rather than a razor blade – and depilatory powder are permitted. However, many Jews grow a small beard that they keep trimmed. Hasidic Jews often allow their beards and sideburns (peyot) to grow long in obedience to the commandment, curling the sideburns or tucking them behind the ears or into the kippah. The Torah does not specify the reason for the prohibition on the use of the razor although some suggest that shaving in this way was a practice among pagan priests and, thus, the Jewish ban is a statement against polytheism.[16]

If the kippah, the wig, the beard and the peyot are aspects of everyday Jewish appearance and attire, there are also clothing traditions that are associated with explicitly religious activity. As with Islam, there is little emphasis in Judaism on distinctive garments for the leaders of official prayer ceremonies. The rabbi and the cantor in a synagogue service do not function as a cultic priesthood presiding over a sacrificial ritual. Simple gowns similar to those used in the Protestant Christian tradition tend to be the norm. However, there is one traditional piece of apparel worn by Jewish laymen that links sacred moments across an entire lifespan: the simple white robe known as the kittel. A man will wear the kittel for the first time at his wedding and for the last time as his grave clothes. In between those two crucial moments, it is donned each year by the leader of the Passover meal and by married men in attendance. The kittel is also worn for the two High Holy Days (New Year and Yom Kippur) at which penitence is a major theme. The kittel's white hue symbolizes the purity that results from the forgiveness of sin.[17]

There are two other prominent Jewish dress customs that are directly based on the Torah and provide rich layers of meaning for the act of prayer. The first is the tefillin, which are two small black boxes made of kosher animal skin with straps attached. Each box contains four texts from the Torah inscribed on special parchment.[18] In each of these texts there is a commandment to "bind" these words on the forehead and the hand as a reminder of the liberating acts of God in Israel's history. Thus, the tefillin are a literal fulfillment of that command. One tefilla is strapped around the head so that the box sits in the middle of the forehead. The second tefilla is strapped around the left arm so that the container rests on the inside of the bicep, near the heart (Figure 8.2).[19] The strap is wrapped around the arm seven times and symbolically knotted around the hand and fingers. The process of donning the tefillin is accompanied by the recitation of special prayers (Box 8.1). The tefillin are sacred objects and the user normally stands when removing them, kissing them as he does so. They are worn by adult Jews, especially of the Orthodox tradition, during weekday morning prayer services, but not on sabbath or festivals since it is felt there is less distraction to spiritual concentration on

Figure 8.2 Jewish boy wearing kippah, tallit and tefillin.
(Reproduced with kind permission of iStock.)

Box 8.1 Prayers on Donning the Tefillin
[*As the hand tefilla is placed on the left arm*] Blessed are you, Lord, our God, sovereign of the universe, Who has sanctified us with Your commandments and commanded us to put on tefillin. [*As the head tefilla is fitted*] Blessed are you, Lord, our God, sovereign of the universe Who has sanctified us with Your commandments and commanded us about the mitzvah of tefillin. Blessed be the Name of Your glorious kingdom forever and ever. [*As the strap is wrapped around the hand*] I will betroth you to me forever; I will betroth you to me in righteousness and in justice and in kindness and in mercy; I will betroth you to me in faithfulness and you will know the Lord.

such occasions. Jewish law does not require women to wear the tefillin but there is debate as to whether this implies that women may wear them.

The second important item of Jewish apparel associated with official prayer is the tallit, or prayer shawl. The term literally means "cloak" and it is probable that the tallit evolved from a garment originally used during outdoor prayers. The relevant biblical text is found in the book of Numbers:

> Speak to the Israelites, and tell them to make fringes on the corners of their garments throughout their generations and to put a blue cord on the fringe at each corner. You have the fringe so that, when you see it, you will remember all the commandments of the Lord and do them, and not follow the lust of your own heart and your own eyes. So you shall remember and do all my commandments, and you shall be holy to your God.[20]

Given that most garments in the ancient world were rectangular in shape, the intention of the original commandment was that everyday clothes were to have fringes added to the corners as a reminder of the divine law. As fashion evolved and four-cornered garments became less common, the commandment was deemed to be fulfilled by wearing the specially designed shawl. Thus, a tallit is a rectangular piece of cloth large enough to cover the shoulders as well as the neck so that it qualifies as a garment. Twisted strings are inserted into a hole at each corner and then twirled and knotted in intricate patterns to form the tassel. The tallit may be made of any material provided it is not a combination of wool and linen, which is forbidden by the Torah.[21] In general practice, wool is the most common choice.

The background color is traditionally white but the Numbers text states that a "blue cord" should be attached to each tassel. In time, blue parallel stripes were added along the sides of the shawl in place of the blue cords, creating the well-known pattern reflected in the design of the Israeli flag. The tallit is worn over the shoulders during morning prayer services including sabbath and holy days. Along with the kittel, the tallit is also linked to key moments in the journey of life. A Sephardic boy usually receives his tallit at bar mitzvah when he comes of age and, therefore, is obliged to fulfill the commandments as an adult. Ashkenazi Jews often commence wearing the tallit when they are married. Indeed, the garment is often worn by the groom on his wedding day. Furthermore, a deceased Jew is often clothed in the kittel and the tallit with one of the tassels cut off as a symbol of loss. In other words, the person enters the shadow of the grave with the great symbols of their prayer life draped about them.

Like the tefillin, the obligation to wear the tallit applies only to male Jews but many rabbinic authorities through the ages, including Rashi and Maimonides, have taught that there is no legal impediment to women wearing it. Consequently liberal Jewish communities now permit women to use the shawl but the practice is still discouraged in Orthodox Judaism.[22] Today, Jewish women's movements often use the tallit (and tefillin) as a symbol of their struggle for religious equality.

At one level, the kippah, the tefillin and the tallit all function as reminders of the fundamental covenantal relationship between God and the believer. The covering of the crown of the head, the words strapped to the forehead and the arm, and the shawl worn over the shoulder with its intricate tassels and distinctive blue stripes are all designed to keep in mind the faith and its obligations. In Judaism, religious clothing is designed to prompt memory and recall basic truths. Attire is about remembering the commandments, but there are also other layers of significance at work. As in Islam, the wearing of the skullcap in public is a declaration of faith and a badge of identity. Moreover, the prayer shawl, first received at bar mitzvah and ultimately taken by the believer to the grave itself, is also associated with initiation into adult faith life with its greater obligations and its ultimate goal of communion with the divine. Such connections can also be seen in other major religions, including Hinduism, where marks on the forehead serve as a public statement of religious affiliation and a special thread worn over the shoulder is given when one comes of age spiritually.

8.4 The Thread and the Mark

One of the most important of the many Hindu life-cycle rituals is the **Upanayana** ceremony – a term that literally means to bring someone into sight of the truth. It is an apposite title, for the ritual marks the end of childhood and the beginning of the first of the four ashramas: the **brahmacarin** (student) phase. At the heart of the ceremony, the young man is presented with an item of clothing that will serve as a permanent sign of his Hindu faith, his caste, and his newly acquired adult status. So important is the symbolic piece of apparel that the alternative name for the entire ritual is derived from it: the sacred thread ceremony.

The Upanayana is essentially a clothing ceremony with each item carrying particular religious meaning. The traditional deerskin loincloth is replaced today by a yellow cotton garment with some deerskin threads attached. It symbolizes the detached and pure lifestyle of the student who seeks life-giving wisdom. A simple girdle holds the loincloth in place and represents how the sacred Vedas will encircle the boy's understanding and outlook. A wooden staff evokes the image of support on life's journey that the Vedas will provide. But the most important sartorial symbol is the upavita,[23] or sacred thread, that constitutes the climax of the ritual (Figure 8.3). The guru places the thread over the left shoulder and under the right armpit so that it wraps diagonally around the body. The thread is a permanent item of clothing, never to be removed, even when bathing or going to the toilet. In this sense, it becomes part of the person. During inauspicious ceremonies such as funerals, its position is reversed so that it sits on the right shoulder, reflecting the contrary nature of the event. Threads are usually changed each year at a specific time, often linked to the festival of Raksha Bandhan in July or August. Even then, the new thread is put on before the old one is removed.

The thread itself is highly symbolic, consisting of three strands folded three times over each other and knotted in a particular manner.[24] The three strands have many numerological interpretations: the **Trimurti**, or three chief deities (**Brahma**, Vishnu and Shiva); the three primal forces (gunas) of the universe (sattva, rajas and tamas); the threefold debt to one's ancestors, the ancient sages and the gods; or the three syllables

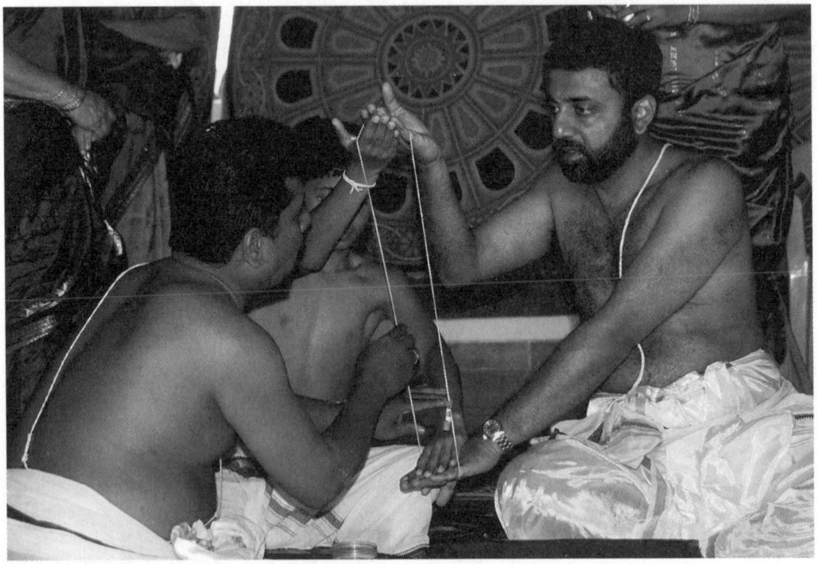

Figure 8.3 A young man receives the sacred thread during an Upanayana ceremony. (Reproduced with kind permission of Alamy.)

of the sacred sound aum. The physical intertwining of three strands into one thread captures the common Hindu theme of the interplay between the one and the many within the created universe and within Ultimate Being itself.

According to the Laws of Manu, the Upanayana ceremony was performed only for male children of the upper three classes: the brahmin (priestly class), the kshatria (warrior class) and the vaishya (merchant class). The ceremony rendered the person twice-born in the sense that a new stage of the spiritual journey had begun. The boy received a new religious name and looked upon his teacher as his new father and the Gayatri Mantra as his new mother. The Gayatri Mantra, arguably the most popular in Hinduism, is recited by high-caste Hindus on a daily basis: "Almighty Supreme Sun, enlighten us with your divine brilliance so we may attain a noble understanding of reality."[25]

The Laws of Manu specify the ideal ages at which high-caste boys should receive their sacred thread: 8 years for brahmins; 11 years for kshatrias; and 12 years for vaishyas (Box 8.2).[26] However, in contemporary Hinduism, the Upanayana has become almost exclusively associated with the brahmin class. Moreover, most thread ceremonies are something of a formality, performed in a perfunctory manner just prior to a young man's wedding, when it is considered to be the last opportunity to carry out the ancient rite. However, the thread continues to be worn by many Hindus today and remains a highly treasured symbol of religious faith.

As with the Jewish tallit and tefillin, which are also traditionally restricted to male believers, the sacred thread has attracted criticism on the basis of its implied gender and class discrimination. Advocates of women's religious rights point out that girls received the thread during Vedic times but were subsequently excluded from the mainstream life-cycle rituals by the Laws of Manu. Their initiation into spiritual adulthood is marked either at the commencement of menstruation or at their wedding. Thus, the thread is often symbolic of the debate between conservative and liberal forces within Hinduism. Many reform movements, such as the Arya Samaj, teach that both genders and all classes should be allowed to receive the sacred thread as a public sign of spiritual maturity.

Apart from the sacred thread for the twice-born, there are few items of clothing that are specifically Hindu. Paradoxically, one of the most striking examples of Hindu religious dress is precisely a lack of dress. When a person reaches the final ashrama and

Box 8.2 The Upanayana Ceremony

In the eighth year after conception, one should perform the initiation of a Brahmin, in the eleventh year after conception that of a Kshatria, but in the twelfth year that of a Vaishya. Let students, according to the order of their castes, wear (as upper garments) the skins of black antelopes, spotted deer, and he-goats, and lower garments made of hemp, flax or wool. The sacrificial string of a Brahmin shall be made of cotton, twisted to the right and consisting of three threads; that of a Kshatria of hempen threads; and that of a Vaishya of woolen threads. A Brahmin shall carry, according to the sacred law, a staff of Bilwa or Palasa; a Kshatriya, of Vata or Khadira; and a Vaisya, of Pilu or Udumbara. Having taken a staff according to his choice, having worshipped the sun and walked round the fire, turning his right hand towards it, the pupil should beg alms according to the prescribed rule. (Laws of Manu, chapter II) embraces the ascetical life of the sannyasin, they have no further regard for the physical body and its appearance. Thus, the sannyasin is usually seen with unkempt, matted hair and dressed in the barest of rags or even naked ("sky-clad").

There is another important sign that is "worn" by the Hindu and which carries a range of theological meanings, even though it is not a piece of clothing as such. The tradition of marking the forehead with a colored paste can be traced back to Vedic times and has become an important element in most Hindu ceremonies. The most common mark is a single tiny dot in the center of the forehead known as a bindi. Various substances can be used to create the paste, including sandalwood, ashes, clay and sindoor powder, all of which are reputed to have a cooling effect on both the body and the spirit. In contemporary India, many people, including non-Hindus, wear a bindi purely as a form of decoration with no explicitly religious intention. Nevertheless, for many who do have the sacred dot applied to their body, it is a profoundly religious sign.

Traditionally, the bindi is a shade of red or yellow, which is understood as a symbol of the sun, the source of illumination and life. This is close to the more common interpretation of the bindi as the "third eye" and sometimes it is actually painted in the shape of an eye. Just as the two natural eyes are the organs of physical sight so, in Hindu theology, the third eye is the means of seeing on the spiritual plane. Like the Jewish kippah, tefillin and tallit, the bindi is also a constant reminder of the holy other.

A second highly significant bodily mark is the red line traced along the parting in the hair of a married woman. The name *sindoor* derives from the type of powder commonly used. The sindoor functions as a sign of a woman's married state in much the same way as the wedding ring does in the West. The groom applies the sindoor for the first time during the actual wedding ceremony and, thereafter, it is a part of her daily routine of adornment. The sindoor is removed when a woman is widowed.

Finally, the tilak is a symbol painted on the forehead to indicate association with a particular tradition within Hinduism. Shaivites usually mark their foreheads with three parallel horizontal lines, representing the same range of spiritual notions that are also linked to the triple-stranded sacred thread. Vaishnavites draw two vertical lines on the forehead roughly in the shape of a U or a V, while followers of Shakti use a single vertical line.

As in Islam and Judaism, Hindu clothing can function as a badge of religious identity. The thread and mark are both quite visible to the public eye and, thus, constitute unmistakable statements that the wearer is an adherent of the sanatana dharma. The bindi, which symbolizes the third eye, is a declaration that the religious vision provides a more profound and penetrating perception of existence than is otherwise possible. Other forms of head markings can indicate marital status or association with a particular Hindu deity such as Shiva or Vishnu. The sacred thread itself is traditionally worn only by the twice-born males of the highest three classes, who are considered closest to ultimate liberation from the wheel of reincarnation. On this level, the links to a second spiritual birth and a privileged male class pertain not only to Hindu but also to certain Christian clothing customs.

8.5 Vestments and Habits

During a Catholic ordination ceremony, immediately after they have been consecrated by the bishop, the new priests are vested in garments indicative of their sacerdotal role. The clothing of the candidates at the high point of the ritual marks their special status in the Christian community. It also calls to mind the initiation of their faith life many years earlier when, as infants, they were baptized in holy water and clothed in white garments as a sign of their Christian dignity. In both ceremonies, the act of putting on physical garments carries the deeper symbolic meaning of clothing oneself in Christ – a metaphor used on several occasions in the writings of Saint Paul.[27] The clothing dimension of both rituals powerfully captures the notion that the baptized baby and the ordained adult are somehow wrapped up in a new relationship with Christ.

In practice, the special garments of baptism are worn only on that day. Few Christian churches require their members, children or adults, to wear anything distinctive in public or even at worship, such as the Jewish skullcap or the Hindu bindi. If there is a mark of baptism it is an invisible one on the soul, rather than something visible on the body. The common sartorial phrase "Sunday best" refers to a time when Christians dressed up for the weekly service and it was considered improper for a woman not to wear a hat or head scarf when inside a church.[28] But many of these customs have been relaxed or discarded in recent decades. Even a cross hanging from a necklace today is often a secular item of fashion rather than a sign of Christian faith. This is not to say that Christianity has no clothing customs. It does, but they pertain more to special positions within the Christian community– in particular, the cleric and the monk – than to the ordinary lay member.

Historical records suggest that Christian clergy did not use a distinctive form of clothing in the early centuries of the Church. However, after the collapse of the Roman Empire in the sixth century CE, priests and bishops began to dress differently from the laity. By the time of the Middle Ages, a tradition of clerical dress was well established and even sanctioned by canon law in both the Eastern and Western Churches. Despite changes in fashion over time and variations based on local culture, many denominations are still characterized by a form of attire that sets the ordained minister apart from the rest. Black has been the traditional color of the general clergy across the Christian spectrum, although more colorful styles have appeared since the late twentieth century. Color has an important hierarchical significance in this context. In the Western Church, purple usually denotes the rank of bishop and red the rank of cardinal, while white is reserved for the Pope. A similar colored skullcap (zucchetto), which is a derivation of the Jewish kippah, is also used by higher-ranking ecclesiastics.

However, it is during official ceremonies that the symbolism of sacred clothing reaches its fullest potential, especially in denominations that stress the sacramental, ritual dimension of Christianity such as the Orthodox, Catholic, and Anglican Churches. During prayer services, especially the Eucharist, the priest dresses in an elaborate set of garments known as vestments with designs based on the standard fashion of late antiquity.

The most common liturgical undergarment is a long robe held around the waist with a girdle. In Western Christianity it is called an alb, from the Latin for white, while in the Eastern Churches it is known as the sticharion. For both traditions it represents the garment worn at baptism, which is the commencement of Christian life and the foundation for all other spiritual developments. Just as this hidden vestment sits underneath the other more elaborate and visible items, so too baptism underpins the dignity of the priestly vocation.

Over the alb the priest wears a number of garments, the most important of which are presented to them on the day of their ordination. The first is a long, narrow strip of colored cloth that is draped around the neck and hung down the front of the body or crossed over the chest. Variously called the stole in Western Christianity and the epitrachelion in Eastern Christianity,[29] it is the primary symbol of the Christian priesthood. The imagery is taken from a well-known saying of Jesus:

> Come to me, all you that are weary and are carrying heavy burdens, and I will give you rest. Take my yoke upon you, and learn from me; for I am gentle and humble in heart, and you will find rest for your souls; for my yoke is easy, and my burden is light.[30]

A yoke is a bar of wood or metal placed across the back of a farm animal, such as an ox or cow, so that it can easily be controlled and steered for plowing and other chores. In the context of spirituality, the term is both etymologically and metaphorically linked to the great Hindu tradition of yoga, which is essentially about yoking or disciplining the body and mind in order to attain sublime levels of meditation. In the Christian tradition, the "yoke of the Kingdom" is the burden that any follower of Christ must shoulder, but the priestly stole reminds its wearer that they carry the special responsibility of Christian leadership in both prayer and life.

The other important vestment worn by the Christian priest when he presides at the Eucharist is a colored sleeveless outer garment known as the chasuble in the West and the phelonion in the East.[31] The chasuble is a large round or rectangular piece of cloth with a hole in the center through which the head passes. Thus, it sits over all other vestments like a poncho or a small house (casula), from which its Western name derives. Its meaning is usually taken from Paul's statement: "Above all, clothe yourselves with love, which binds everything together in perfect harmony."[32]

The color of the chasuble and stole symbolizes the liturgical season. Purple, the somber color of penitence and self-denial, is worn during the seasons of Advent and Lent. In contrast, white, the color of joy and purity, is used for the seasons of Christmas and Easter. Red, the color of blood, is worn on Good Friday and the feasts of martyrs who sacrificed their lives for the faith. For ordinary days outside of the main seasons, vestments are traditionally green in Western churches and gold in Eastern churches. The use of symbolic colored vestments for church ceremonies is not widely practiced in the Protestant tradition where the stress is more on the verbal than the visual. In fact, the appropriateness of liturgical garb was the central issue in the Vestments Controversy which broke out in England during the reigns of Edward VI and Elizabeth I. Consistent with the emphasis on preaching rather than sacramental rites, the attire of most Protestant ministers tends to be either normal dress or a style of academic garb featuring gown, scarf and hood.

Like everyday clerical dress, liturgical vestments also reflect ecclesiastical rank. While bishops in the Western tradition wear the skullcap for everyday affairs, they don a more elaborate head-dress known as a miter during sacramental ceremonies. The Western miter, a tall, pointed, two-sided folding cap, evolved from hats worn by Byzantine court officials. Eastern bishops also wear a miter but their version is more rounded, reminiscent of the imperial crown itself. The implication is clear. The miter symbolizes the privileged status and authority of the bishop as teacher and leader of the believing community. This pedagogical dimension of the bishop's role is complemented by a more pastoral symbol that is carried during ceremonies. The crosier is shaped like a shepherd's staff and stands for the guidance and protection offered by one who stands in the place of Christ, the Good Shepherd (Figure 8.4).

Figure 8.4 Image of St Patrick in episcopal dress with miter and crozier. (Reproduced with kind permission of iStock.)

In striking contrast to the ceremonial vestments are the robes of the Christian monk and nun. The traditional monastic dress consists of a gown, a girdle and a hood.[33] The girdle traditionally has three knots representing the religious vows of poverty, chastity and obedience. These garments signify a radically different lifestyle and a special place in the Christian world, but they also serve to differentiate different monastic orders, often by their color. This has given rise to three well-known monastic synonyms: "Whitefriars" for the Carmelites; "Blackfriars" for the Dominicans; and "Greyfriars" for the Franciscans. Until recently most nuns' habits were very similar, with a wimple and head-veil in place of the hood, although many orders have relaxed their dress codes since **Vatican II**. Black is a common color for monks in the Eastern churches whose garments also reflect grade or seniority.

While the liturgical vestments are colorful and ornate, depicting the beauty and splendor of ceremonial Christianity, the monastic habit is traditionally sober and modest, depicting a life of humble service and material simplicity. Where one type of garb is reminiscent of the prince, the other is evocative of the pauper. Just as the new priest receives the stole and chasuble on the day of ordination, the novice monk or nun enters the community by means of an investiture ceremony. The newly professed cast away their old apparel and dress themselves in a different set of clothes to symbolize their passage from secular daily life to the spiritual world of the monastery. A traditional part of that passage was the tonsure, or shaving of some hair from the crown of the head to signify severance from the past life. Moreover, it is no coincidence that the monastic uniform is called a habit, for the person is expected to adopt a new mindset and a new style of behavior, literally becoming what their clothing signifies.

Christian liturgical dress customs have echoes in the other religions discussed above, even if they are faint at times. In the sense that the Christian stole is worn over the shoulders and signifies initiation into the priestly class, it is reminiscent of the Hindu sacred thread which is also worn over the shoulder and promotes a young man into the adult echelons of the higher classes. In some cases within both religions, the rites of passage, with their clothing symbolism that was once the monopoly of the male, are now being extended to female members. Similarly, the donning of special clothing to symbolize entry into the sacred time of official prayer is reflected in both the Christian priestly garb and the Jewish tallit and tefillin customs, although in one case it is the prayer leader alone while in the other it applies to all worshipers. In addition, both Christian and Hindu clothing traditions point to the radical lifestyle of the ascetic. In Hinduism the sannyasin dresses in rags or even discards all clothing and allows the hair to grow wildly as a sign of utter renunciation.

The double clothing tradition of priestly vestment and monastic habit found in Christianity is also a feature of another religion where colorful, symbolic robes mark the heavenly role of priest, and a simple robe and hair topknot indicate an advanced commitment to seeking the Mystery that enfolds us like a garment.

8.6 Garments of the Gods

One of the most common forms of attire for Chinese men is popularly known as the dao pao (literally "Daoist robe"). Dating back to at least the Ming period, it is a wide-sleeved, full-length robe with side slits from below the waist. Despite the name, the dao pao does not imply that its wearer has some formal affiliation with Daoism per se. In fact, it is not meaningful to speak of lay Daoist clothing customs because it is not meaningful to speak of lay Daoists as such. As we have noted, Daoism is one of the Three Teachings (along with Confucianism and Buddhism) that influence Chinese religion and culture in general. However, as in Christianity, there is a rich sartorial tradition connected to the Daoist priests and monks, especially when they are leading formal rituals.

According to Daoist tradition, ritual dress originated long ago with the legendary **Yellow Emperor** who is believed to be the ancestor of the Chinese people, ruling over China for many years in the third millennium BCE.[34] It is said that, one day, the Yellow Emperor saw a god dressed with a golden crown and a golden robe adorned with colorful clouds. Thanking the god for protecting the world, the Yellow Emperor then proceeded to design the Daoist ritual dress based on the divine model standing before him. He reasoned that heavenly clothing styles would be the most appropriate dress to wear when one approaches heaven in prayer. In other words, when a Daoist priest dresses for ritual, he is putting on the garments of the gods (Figure 8.5). Historically speaking, Daoist ritual dress is inspired by pre-modern Chinese fashion in the same way that Christian clerical dress is essentially patterned on earlier Roman styles. While the laity in both religions dress in today's contemporary styles, their clergies wear forms of apparel that set them apart, thus reflecting their special status within the community and their privileged access to the gods.

As in Christianity, there are some basic denominational differences in clerical fashion within Daoism, which act as an identification badge. In the Zhengyi branch, laity and priests tend to wear Western dress in their daily lives but the priests don special vestments for formal ritual occasions. Regarding headwear, Zhengyi priests prefer what is known as the "nine-fold scarf" (jiuliang jin). This is usually black and has a flat top that conspicuously slants forward like the leaning roof of a house. It has nine folds,

Figure 8.5 Daoist priests in ritual vestments.
(Reproduced with kind permission of iStock.)

resembling the shape of a piece of corrugated iron, as well as silk folds hanging like bamboo tablets at the back. For large-scale rituals, especially those involving petitions to the gods, Zhengyi priests often wear a scarlet robe (jiangpao) with long, wide sleeves and embroidered golden symbols. When the priest extends his arms, it creates the effect of a square that represents the four corners of the earth. As the priest performs the movements associated with the ritual, such as pacing out the pattern of the Big Dipper constellation, the impression is created that he is gliding between heaven and earth. Special footwear, known as "cloud shoes" because of the cloud shapes that are painted or embroidered on them, are also worn for such ceremonies. The persons designated to chant the scriptures during rituals also dress for the occasion, albeit in a less elaborate style. For example, bright red is commonly used for Golden Register Rituals that are designed for village or temple renewals, and yellow garments are worn for Yellow Register Rituals, used for burials.

In contrast to the Zhengyi school, the Quanzhen priest-monks wear traditional, uniform robes during their daily lives. These garments are very precious items and are treated with great respect and care. The standard robe, called dao yi (robe of the Dao), is traditionally made of cotton or hemp and has a diagonally folding design based on Chinese imperial dress. The right portion folds across the body to the left, and the left portion folds over the right. The dao yi has long, wide sleeves aptly described as "cloud sleeves" since they appear to flow and billow as the monk goes about his daily routine. The entire garment is believed to be an imitation of the dress worn by the gods and other beings who have achieved immortality. The collar often has three sections, reflecting the importance and widespread use of the number three in Daoism, as with the Hindu sacred thread.

The threefold division has many possible meanings: the Three Essentials; the Three Treasures; the Three Pure Ones; the Three Heavens and so on. Although monks sometimes wear white robes in summer to avoid the heat, the traditional color of the Quanzhen robe is dark blue or indigo, evoking the darkness and obscurity surrounding the Dao itself. As the Daode jing states: "Mysterious and again more mysterious, the gateway to all that is wondrous."[35] The symbolism is clear. As the Daoist priest dons his robe, he effectively clothes himself in the Dao, wrapping his body in the colorless color of the great Mystery that enfolds all things. The garment conveys the priest-monk's special standing within his community, as one who participates in and communicates with the heavenly realms at an advanced level. Monks also may possess a less formal robe that allows greater freedom of movement and is aptly called the "convenient garment" (bianfu). It is a more appropriate dress when going on a pilgrimage or seeking the Dao by walking in the mountains – a practice called "cloud wandering."

Quanzhen priest-monks also wear distinctive headwear but, unlike the Zhengyi ninefold scarf, Quanzhen clerics prefer what is known as the Hat of Primal Chaos (hunyuan jin). This is a black, round, flat-topped hat with a hole in the centre for the topknot, which involves the elaborate binding of their long hair and fixing it with a hairpin. The pattern of the topknot varies from monastery to monastery since it is usually a private custom passed on from teacher to pupil. Hairpins are typically made of wood rather than bone or horn, which probably reflects the Quanzhen commitment to vegetarianism and not harming animals. Popular shapes for the decorative hairpin include lotus pods, lotus blossoms, dragons, phoenixes and especially the flaming pearl, which symbolizes the Dao as origin and end.

Like their Zhengyi counterparts, Quanzhen priest-monks also lead formal ceremonies and, in order to emphasize the sacred nature of the occasion, they don special ritual vestments. Usually a red robe with black borders is worn by cantors and assistants for daily chanting. The robe worn by the ritual leader himself is more ornate, and its primary color can vary significantly. Common colors are red, yellow, purple, turquoise and orange. The robe is also characterized by symbols including the Bagua (Eight Trigrams), the Three Pure Ones, clouds, mountains, sun, moon and animals that represent immortality such as the dragon and the crane. Some commentators have noted the horizontal and vertical dimensions of the robe's symbolism.[36] The horizontal plane is linked to the Bagua, which not only appears on the robes but, as in the wedding ceremony, is also often drawn on the carpet or floor where the ritual is performed. The Trigram depicts the eight possible combinations of yin and yang that constitute our world that has emanated from the original Dao. As the priest moves about the altar area, the robe and the carpet together delineate a horizontal sacred space in which the priest's ritual power takes effect. On the vertical plane, the robe often has an image of a heavenly realm depicted on the back. A common theme is the abode of the Jade Emperor (Luotian). As noted in Chapter 1, the Jade Emperor rules over the cosmos in a manner similar to the terrestrial emperor's rule over China. Thus, the pattern on the back of the robe gives hope to worshippers, who stand inside the horizontal circle of ritual influence, that their needs will be carried vertically upward by the priest's intercession to the highest heavenly office.

The sumptuous robes and vestments worn by the Zhengyi and Quanzhen priests are among some of the most visually stunning works of Daoist art. Their spectacular colors and images are not merely decorative, but are designed to transform the setting of the ritual from a mundane earthly place into a celestial court. The garments themselves are understood to be copies of the clothes worn by the gods. The symbols drawn on them create a horizontal sphere of influence for those present and a vertical access to the gods above. Moreover, the indigo robe worn by the Quanzhen monks on a daily basis marks them as persons who are dedicated to seeking harmony with the all-embracing cosmic order and clothing themselves in the Dao. These broad themes are echoed in the priestly vestment tradition and monastic habit tradition of Christianity, but the latter also finds resonance in our sixth religion where a detached lifestyle is symbolized not by an elaborate topknot and hairpin, but by the cutting of one's hair and investiture in beggar's robes.

8.7 The Three Robes

A few weeks after the end of the wet season, Buddhist communities around Asia celebrate a ceremony known as Kathina. The term comes from an ancient Pali word meaning a wooden frame for sewing clothes. As the name suggests, Kathina concerns the gift of clothing by the lay community to members of the local monastery. On the day of the festival, visitors arrive at the monastery and enjoy a meal together. On behalf of the entire sangha, two monks are chosen to receive the gift of new cloth from the lay community. The ceremony reflects the mutual dependence of monastics and laity. While the former offer an abundance of good karma, the latter provide material necessities, especially food and clothing. The Buddhist scriptures relate how the laity were delighted when the Buddha gave monks permission to receive robes because they realized that their gifts would bring karmic benefits.[37] While there are many occasions during the year when such an exchange takes place – such as naming ceremonies, weddings and funerals – Kathina is a formal annual acknowledgment of its importance. Moreover, it is also indicative of the important symbolic value placed on the clothing worn by the monks.

Although there is no particular dress or marking worn by lay Buddhists to indicate their religious affiliation, one of the most striking features of the Buddhist monk is their distinctive robe. The robe is one of just five items that a monk was traditionally allowed to possess, the other four being a bowl, a water-strainer, a razor and a needle. Today, monks have access to a range of basic commodities beyond these rudimentary objects. Nevertheless, the principle enshrined in the ideal is absolute detachment, which is the key to ultimate liberation. A monk will rely on others for his food; he will strain small creatures from his drink out of respect for life; he will shave his head regularly as an ongoing sign of renunciation; he will mend his own clothes; and his entire wardrobe will consist of a single set of robes that are still based on the pattern set by the Buddha.[38]

The Vinaya Pitaka (Basket of Discipline), which contains the rules of Buddhist monastic life, dedicates a number of sections to the question of the monk's clothing. The traditional monastic habit is known as the tricivara and consists of three basic garments: an inner robe, a thick waistband and an outer garment or mantle that can be worn over the shoulders. When a monk leaves the monastery, he should ensure that he is wearing all three robes and that the mantle covers both shoulders.[39] However, while inside the monastery he should leave the right shoulder uncovered (Figure 8.6). Many statues of the Buddha depict him dressed in the tricivara with his right shoulder bare as prescribed in the rule.

Figure 8.6 Thai Buddhist monks in their traditional robes. (Reproduced with kind permission of iStock.)

The religious symbolism of the tricivara is essentially one of simplicity. For the monk, there is little inherent value in the material things of life and the robes themselves should convey this ideal of complete indifference to physical comfort and pleasure. Thus, the very cloth from which the robes are made is symbolic. Apart from fabric that is donated by the laity, monks were instructed to obtain cloth by collecting rags from the local rubbish heap and cemeteries: "I allow householder robe-cloth. Whoever wishes, may be a rag-robe man. Whoever wishes may consent to householder robe-cloth. And I commend contentment with whatever is readily available."[40] The rags were then stitched together in a rough patchwork style reminiscent of Asia's paddy fields. According to the tradition, the Buddha asked his close companion, Ananda, to create a design for the outer garment. Looking out over the countryside, he noticed the chessboard appearance of the rice fields and proposed this as the pattern, which was accepted. It is also the individual monk's duty to ensure that his robes are mended when necessary – hence the needle, which is one of the monk's basic possessions.

When people today think of the robes of a Buddhist monk, they often imagine the saffron-colored garments widely used throughout southeast Asia. Although the bright orange of saffron may suggest royalty and opulence, the intention is actually the very opposite. The choice of saffron originated in the desire to ensure that all monks' robes were uniform in color, thus denoting a fundamental equality beyond caste. Monks simply dyed the rags and cloths in the cheapest and most readily available substances such as turmeric and ochre. The result was a bland brownish-yellow hue that was meant to be unpretentious rather than ostentatious. Some see a deeper symbolism in the autumnal colors. Just as the red, yellow and brown leaves drop from trees during autumn, so too the monk must avoid clinging to the things of this earth that bind one to the wheel of reincarnation. As Buddhism expanded to the north along the Silk Road, and eventually west again into Tibet, the standard colors of the robes evolved as cultural influences set in. Dark red is a common inexpensive dye color in Tibet and, thus, Tibetan robes are often maroon or crimson. In the Far East, dull blue, gray and black are more common, in compliance with the principle to avoid strong primary colors.

As in Christianity, the entry into Buddhist monastic life is symbolized by an investiture ceremony in which the candidates receive a form of tonsure and replace their ordinary clothes with the new garments of holiness and self-discipline. While the tonsure for Christian monks involved cutting a portion of the hair on the crown of the head, Buddhist monks have their entire scalp and eyebrows shaved. The gesture echoes the decisive moment in the life of Buddha Gautama when he left the palace for a higher path, marking the moment by cutting off his long, princely hair. Today, Buddhist monks and nuns have their heads shaved on a regular basis as a sign of their religious commitment. After the shaving, the newly professed Buddhist monks, like their Christian counterparts, put on the garments of their new state.

The presentation of the cloths to the monks at the Kathina ceremony each year draws on a rich array of history and symbolism. At a general level, the robes function as badges of religious identity like garments in other religions. To be seen in public with shaven head and dyed robes is an unambiguous statement of one's Buddhist faith. But not all Buddhists are monks and, thus, the robes also symbolize a special type of believer within the tradition – one who has taken an extra step and embraced a community lifestyle of radical renunciation. The fundamental equality of the members of the sangha is symbolized in the uniform shape and color of the robes. But ultimately the most powerful message conveyed by the tricivara is detachment from the material world. The shaved head, rag-like cloth, rough sewing patterns and subdued color all speak of frugality and austerity. Ultimately, the three robes worn by the Buddhist monk symbolize in graphic manner the core of Buddha Gautama's teaching that clinging to a transient world cannot bring ultimate satisfaction or freedom.

Summary

Each of the six religions has its various forms of clothing traditions and, although these are undeniably unique to each faith, nevertheless interesting points of connection are discernible. One of the most basic functions of clothing is to ensure appropriate levels of modesty in society, although this can vary enormously across human cultures due to variable factors such as geography and climate. In general, each of the six religions endorses respect for the human body and appropriate covering in public with a view to controlling sexual arousal. The most striking example of this principle among the six religions is the Islamic veil. Although the Qur'an requires modest dress for both male and female, women's clothing has been the subject of more extensive theological and legal interpretation over time. The veil is not worn by all Islamic women, but when it is, the custom varies from a simple hijab covering the hair to the full burqa concealing the entire face and the eyes. On one hand, many in the West see the veil as symptomatic of an entrenched prejudice against women which limits their role to domestic duties. On the other hand, the veil is interpreted by many Muslim women as a protest against a demeaning attitude to women in Western fashion, which implies that they are ultimately sexual objects whose worth is primarily grounded in physical attractiveness.

However, most forms of religious clothing customs are more concerned with identity than modesty. The veil itself is not only a means of safeguarding respectability in public but is also an unambiguous statement of a woman's Islamic faith. In this sense religious garments can function as a badge of membership. The Jewish kippah and the Hindu bindi are similar examples. Moreover, the style and appearance of these items can further signify the type of membership within Islam, Judaism and Hinduism. The grades of veil from the hijab to the full burqa reflect different ways in which Muslims apply Qur'anic principles. The size, stitch and color of the Jewish kippah can imply liberal or conservative stances. In Hinduism, a V-shaped marking on the forehead indicates a follower of Vishnu, while three horizontal lines are the sign of a devotee of Shiva. The nine-fold scarf and the hat of Primal Chaos reflect membership of the Zhengyi and Quanzhen branches of Daoism respectively.

Clothes are also used to symbolize a special stage or position within a religious tradition, especially via official investiture ceremonies. The sacred thread ceremony of Hinduism is one of the most important of the classical life-cycle rituals, celebrating adult initiation for males of the upper three classes, although today it is mainly confined to Brahmins just prior to marriage. The thread itself, which is worn every day of one's life, signifies the harmony of the one and the many at various levels within the cosmos. It renders the recipient twice-born. There are echoes in the Jewish bar mitzvah ceremony, which marks the coming of age of a young Jew. Although bar mitzvah is essentially about reading the Torah in synagogue for the first time, it is often the occasion on which a young man receives his tallit or prayer shawl. The tallit and the tefillin are worn at certain prayer services in fulfillment of the biblical injunction. Like the thread for the Hindu twice-born, the shawl and the black boxes remind the Jew of their covenantal relationship with God, which is the key to their identity.

Baptismal rites often include special garments, symbolizing the "second birth" of a Christian child or adult, although these are not worn every day or even at prayer as in the case of Hinduism and Judaism. In many churches, greater emphasis is placed on the link between investiture and the role of the cleric or the monk. Many Christian clerics dress in distinctive garb in everyday life as a sign of their special ministry. Clothing also indicates the various ranks within the clergy, mainly by the specific colors associated with priests, bishops, cardinals and popes. But it is in the role of the president of official ritual that Christian clothing customs find their most elaborate expression. The liturgical vestments are based on the fashion of late antiquity and are typically ornate in style, reflecting the importance of the occasion. The two most prominent items worn by Eucharistic presidents in Catholic, Anglican and Orthodox traditions – the stole/epitrachelion and the chasuble/phelonion – signify the yoke of obedience and the mantle of love respectively. The colors of these garments also follow the cycle of Christian liturgical seasons. In many Protestant churches, where the verbal nature of the ceremony and the didactic role of the ministry are emphasized, the president's garb is more reminiscent of academic dress. The clothing tradition that sets apart the priestly class is also a feature of Daoism where pre-modern styles of robes are worn by ritual masters during the sacred ceremonies. It is thought that these are inspired by the garments of the gods themselves, and represent the priest's privileged access to higher realms.

In contrast, the Quanzhen priest-monks wear a traditional robe, distinctive headpiece, elaborate topknots and hairpins in their daily lives as a sign of their monastic lifestyle. The robe's indigo color represents the dark, mysterious Dao in which the monk literally wraps himself each day. On a similar note, the Christian monastic habit is somber in color and design, symbolizing renunciation of the material world. The phrase "taking the habit" not only means the clothing ceremony at the commencement of one's monastic life, but also the very lifestyle itself characterized by poverty, chastity and obedience. This is the most obvious point of contact with Buddhism, given its central stress on radical detachment from worldly pleasures personified by the monk or nun. The traditional three-fold monastic robes of the Buddhist monk are traceable to Buddha Gautama's own example and instructions. The robes themselves were traditionally made from rags, sewn roughly together and dyed in a simple, uniform color. Moreover, the cutting of hair in both Christian and Buddhist monastic traditions adds to the symbolism of severance from the norm. Conversely, the radical world-renouncers of Hinduism allow their hair to grow long and unkempt, but the same principle is at stake: letting go of that which hinders spiritual progress. In its most radical form, the sannyasin transcends clothing altogether and goes about "sky-clad."

Chapters 7 and 8 have considered the ways in which food and clothing are used symbolically across the religions; Chapters 9 to 11 turn to the themes of time and space, with a particular focus on the annual calendar, the sacred building and holy pilgrimage.

Discussion Topics

1. List the different types of Islamic female dress. Do they represent suppression or liberation for Islamic women?
2. Should believers be allowed to wear religious dress in public schools?
3. Compare the meaning attached to growing, knotting or shaving hair in different religions.
4. Examine the use and meaning of the sacred thread for Hindus today.
5. Why do Hindus paint markings on their bodies?
6. Why do some Jews wear the tallit, kippah and tefillin while others do not?
7. How and why do Hasidic Jews dress in a distinctive manner?
8. Compare the symbolism of ritual ecclesiastical vestments in Daoism and Christianity.
9. Compare the design and symbolism of monastic robes in Daoism, Buddhism, Christianity and other religious traditions.

Notes

1 Qur'an 24:31.
2 Qur'an 33:59.
3 Qur'an 24:30.
4 The Qur'an is silent but there are many hadith on this issue, e.g. Sahih Bukhari 7.69.536–9.
5 Sunan Abu Dawud 4092.
6 An often quoted hadith that supports this view is Sahih Bukhari 6.60.282: Aisha used to say: "When the Verse about the veil was revealed, the ladies cut their waist sheets at the edges and covered their faces with the cut pieces."

7 Aisha is quoted as saying that she wore the veil so that she might be valued for what she was rather than what she looked like.
8 Sunan Abu Dawud 641.
9 Exodus 28:4.
10 Talmud Shabbat 156b.
11 See Talmud Shabbat 199b; Talmud Kiddushin 31a.
12 Mishneh Torah, Ahavah, Hilkhot Tefillah 5:5.
13 Shulhan Aruch, Orach Hayim 2:6.
14 Leviticus 19:27.
15 Shulhan Aruch, Yoreh Deah 181:10.
16 Leviticus 19:9. Others point to a connection with a verse in the same section of Leviticus that commands farmers not to harvest the corners of their fields but to leave these for "the poor and the stranger."
17 See Isaiah 1:18.
18 Deuteronomy 6:4–9; 11:13–21; Exodus 13:1–10; 13:11–16.
19 The hand tefilla has one compartment, which contains the four texts written upon a single piece of parchment in four parallel columns. The head tefilla has four compartments, each of which contains one piece of parchment. See Talmud Berachot 13b; Talmud Eruvin 95b; Talmud Kiddushin 36a.
20 Numbers 15:38–9. See also Deuteronomy 22:12.
21 Leviticus 19:19; Deuteronomy 22:9–11.
22 See Shulhan Aruch, Orach Hayim 17:2.
23 The thread is also referred to as yajnopavita.
24 The Laws of Manu specify that a different fabric be used for the different castes: cotton for brahmins; hemp for kshatrias; wool for vaishyas. See Laws of Manu II.44. Similarly the recommended season varies for each caste: brahmins in spring, representing moderation; kshatrias in summer, indicating fervor; and Vaishyas in autumn, when commerce recommences after the wet season. See Shatpath Brahmana 2.13.5.
25 See Rg Veda 3.62.10.
26 Laws of Manu II.36.
27 See Galatians 3:27–9; Romans 13:14; Ephesians 6:10–17.
28 See 1 Corinthians 11:3–10.
29 There are three types of stole in Eastern Christianity: the orarion for deacons; the epitrachelion for priests; and the omophorion for bishops.
30 Matthew 11:28–30.
31 Eastern bishops usually wear a sakkos or tunic with half-sleeves and a distinctive pattern.
32 Colossians 3:12–14.
33 The Italian term for hood is *cappuccio*, from which is derived the term *cappuccino* – literally "hooded" coffee.
34 The Yellow Emperor (Huang di) is credited with having introduced Chinese medicine, technological inventions and many religious practices.
35 Daode jing, ch. 1.
36 Komjathy, 293.
37 Khandhaka, Mahavagga 8.1.35.
38 For rules concerning an extra robe see Khandhaka, Mahavagga 8.13.6–8.
39 Khandhaka, Mahavagga 8.23.1.
40 Khandhaka, Mahavagga 8.1.34.

Further Reading

Corrigan, John et al. (1997). *Jews, Christians, Muslims: A Comparative Introduction to Monotheistic Religions.* Upper Saddle River, NJ: Prentice Hall, pp. 341–418.
El Guindi, Fadwa (2003). *Veil: Modesty, Privacy and Resistance.* Oxford: Berg.
Esposito, John (2011). *What Everyone Needs to Know about Islam.* Oxford: Oxford University Press, pp. 105–111.
Göle, Nilüfa (1997). *The Forbidden Modern: Civilization and Veiling.* Ann Arbor, MI: University of Michigan Press.
Komjathy, Louis (2013). *The Daoist Tradition.* London: Bloomsbury, pp. 290–293.
Kuhns, Elizabeth (2003). *The Habit: A History of the Clothing of Catholic Nuns.* New York: Doubleday.
Michaels, Axel (2003). *Hinduism: Past and Present.* Princeton, NJ: Princeton University Press, pp. 92–107.
Shirazi, Faegheh (2003). *The Veil Unveiled: The Hijab in Modern Culture.* Gainesville, FL: University Press of Florida.
Tarlo, Emma (1996). *Clothing Matters: Dress and Identity in India.* Chicago, IL: University of Chicago Press.
Wijayaratna, Mohan (1990). *Buddhist Monastic Life: According to the Texts of the Theravada Tradition.* Cambridge: Cambridge University Press, ch. 3.

Part III

Time and Space

9

Year

CONTENTS

9.1 Introduction

Human existence is played out in a four-dimensional cosmos, shaped by the fundamental categories of time and space. The very fabric of our being and all aspects of our world are intrinsically spatio-temporal by nature. Even religion, which points beyond time and space toward transcendent reality, is rooted in this world of now and then, here and there. As with other aspects of daily life, these basic categories are taken up and transformed by religious understanding. Time and space are recast through the eyes of faith and given a more profound, holy meaning. This chapter focuses on the temporal aspect of reality, in particular the annual calendars of the six religions. What is its basic structure? How are the years counted? When do major festivals occur? What practices and meanings are associated with them? Are there specific periods or seasons inserted into the year and what do these signify?

9.2 Four Seasons

An observer attending Catholic, Anglican or Orthodox services would notice that the vestments worn by the priest vary according to the four Christian seasons. These are not the natural seasons of spring, summer, autumn and winter. Rather, they are liturgical seasons that hinge on the two most important feasts: Christmas Day and Easter Sunday. In each case, the feast is preceded by a time of preparation and followed by a time of celebration. Thus, many Christians prepare for the birth of Christ during the season of Advent and celebrate the joyous occasion during the season of Christmas. Similarly, they prepare for the death of Christ during the season of Lent and celebrate his triumphant resurrection during the season of Easter (Table 9.1).

In the Western Church, the season of Advent (Latin for "coming") commences four Sundays prior to Christmas Day and is traditionally regarded as the beginning of the Christian year. In contrast, the Eastern Church year commences in September, but Orthodox Christians have a preparatory season for Christmas that is known as Winter Lent. As with the main season of Lent, this pre-Christmas period is traditionally a time

Table 9.1 The Western Christian calendar.

Season	Holy day	Time of year
Advent begins	First Sunday of Advent	Four Sundays before Christmas
Christmas begins	Christmas Day	25 December
	Epiphany	6 January
Lent begins	Ash Wednesday	40 days prior to Easter Sunday (omitting Sundays)
	Palm Sunday	Sunday before Easter Sunday
	Holy Thursday	Thursday before Easter Sunday
	Good Friday	Friday before Easter Sunday
Easter begins	Easter Sunday	Sunday following the first full moon after the March equinox
Easter ends	Pentecost Sunday	Seven weeks after Easter Sunday

of fasting and lasts for 40 days. The link with Lent is also visible in the Western tradition where the color of both seasons is purple, symbolizing sobriety and penance. The themes of Advent focus on keeping vigil for the coming of the Messiah. For Christians, this can have two meanings, past and future. First, it refers to Israel's long wait for the promised savior-king, which, for Christians, was fulfilled in the historical birth of Christ at Bethlehem. Second, it refers to the present-day waiting for the second coming of Christ at the end of time.[1] In some traditions, the motif of waiting is symbolized by the Advent wreath, which is placed in the sanctuary of the church with four candles attached. As each week of the season passes and Christmas draws ever closer, another candle is lit. Advent concludes with the first of the great Christian festivals: Christmas Day.

Both Western and Eastern Christians agree that the date of Christmas is December 25, but the celebrations are actually held on different days because the two traditions use different calendars. The Western churches follow the Gregorian calendar, named after Pope Gregory XIII who, in 1582, authorized a revision of the existing calendar to account for a 10-day lag that had arisen since its adoption under Julius Caesar.[2] However, many Eastern Churches continue to use the older Julian calendar to determine religious dates. Today, the difference between the calendars has increased to 13 days and thus December 25 in the Julian calendar actually falls on January 7 according to the Gregorian calendar.

The date of Christmas is itself an interesting historical tale given that the gospels do not provide any information regarding the precise timing of Christ's birth.[3] The most popular explanation is that Christmas represents the adaption of an existing pagan feast associated with the northern winter solstice (December 21). In 274 CE, the emperor Aurelian chose December 25, a few days after the actual solstice, as the festival of Sol Invictus ("Unconquered Sun").[4] After the conversion of **Constantine**, the fourth-century Church was able to celebrate its festivals without fear of persecution, and it seemed a natural choice to transform Aurelian's solstice festival into the Christian feast of the Savior's birth.

The birth of Christ was also to become the key marker from which all Christian time would be measured. A monk named Dionysius Exiguus developed the new system in the sixth century by converting the old Roman year number to the new Christian designation Anno Domini ("in the year of the Lord").[5] For the sake of convenience, this numbering system has been almost universally adopted by international organizations today, although the preferred phrase is "Common Era" out of deference to non-Christians.[6] However, the original Christian system expresses the profound theological point that all cosmic time is divided into two great eras on either side of the momentous event of the Incarnation. The focus on the birth of the Son of God is also reflected in traditions such as the nativity scene which adorns churches, homes, public squares and even department stores in many societies (Figure 9.1).

Christmas is a popular time for gift-giving, a tradition that has now overflowed into post-Christian secular society. The biblical inspiration is Matthew's description of the mysterious magi ("wise men") who follow a star from the East and discover the child Jesus at Bethlehem. There they present him with gifts of gold, frankincense and myrrh.[7] The historical inspiration is Saint Nicholas, a fourth-century bishop from the southern Turkish town of Myra, who gave gifts to poor children at Christmastide. Dutch settlers in New York brought with them the tradition of Sinterklass ("Saint Nicholas") who was eventually refashioned by twentieth-century cartoonists and commercial advertisers into the contemporary myth of Santa Claus. The actual day of gift-giving can vary from culture to culture. In some places, it is Saint Nicholas's Day (December 6); in others, it is December 25 itself; in others still, it is January 6, the feast of the Epiphany which marks

Figure 9.1 Christmas nativity scene.
(Reproduced with kind permission of iStock.)

the arrival of the wise men in Bethlehem and sets up the traditional 12 days of Christmas (following Christmas Day). In Western Christianity, the Christmas season lasts until one week after the Epiphany and the joyful color white is used in churches. However, Eastern Christians set aside 40 days to celebrate the birthday of the Savior, taking the season to February 2 – the Purification of Mary,[8] or Candlemas when priests traditionally bless all candles for the coming year.

The second great annual Christian feast is Easter, which is preceded by a period of preparation known as Lent (from the German for "springtime"). The more somber mood of Lent is signified by the liturgical color purple. Lent is the principal season of penitence and self-denial, a time when Christians are encouraged to seek forgiveness for sin and to subdue physical desires by fasting, abstinence and more intensive spiritual activity. Forty days are set aside for Lent on the basis that Jesus fasted in the wilderness for that length of time at the commencement of his public ministry.[9] However, the method of calculating the 40 days varies. In Eastern Christianity, the days are counted back from Palm Sunday (a week before Easter), which means that the season begins on what is called Clean Monday. In contrast, the Western Church counts back from Easter Sunday but does not include Sundays, which are considered to be days of celebration rather than self-denial. Consequently, the Western Lent begins on Ash Wednesday, so named because ashes are placed on the foreheads of believers as a reminder of their mortality and need for continual repentance.

Most Christians practice some form of fasting or abstinence during Lent. For example, in Orthodox Christianity, the Sunday before Clean Monday is Cheesefare Sunday, which is the last day to consume dairy foods until Easter. Similarly, the Sunday before this is Meatfare Sunday, on which the last meat meals are eaten. The equivalent in the Western tradition is Mardi Gras ("Greasy Tuesday") – the day before Ash Wednesday and, thus, the final opportunity to enjoy food, drink and other sensual pleasures before the austerities of Lent commence.[10] Given its connection with the death of Christ, Friday is the preferred day for acts of self-denial in Western Christianity. But Lent is not only about giving up enjoyment. Many churches encourage believers to undertake positive actions such as spending more time in personal prayer and giving practical help to the poor via Lenten donation programs.

The final week of Lent is commonly referred to as Holy Week. It commences with Palm Sunday, which commemorates Jesus's final entry into Jerusalem, accompanied by his followers who enthusiastically waved palm branches in recognition of his messianic status. The season reaches its climax on the final three days: Holy Thursday (Jesus's Last Supper); Good Friday (Jesus's death); and Holy Saturday (Jesus's body lies in the tomb). Re-enactments of the Last Supper are a common feature of Holy Thursday ceremonies, including Jesus's gesture of washing his disciples' feet at the meal as a sign of leadership via service. Good Friday liturgies vary from denomination to denomination but the common theme is the death of Christ. The gospel description of his arrest, torture and crucifixion (the Passion), is usually read in some form and many Christian groups perform the Stations of the Cross, a re-enactment of his final walk from Pontius Pilate's court to the hill of Calvary, interspersed with prayerful pauses ("stations") with particular themes linked to his suffering and death.

As the sun sets on Holy Saturday, the sorrowful, penitential mood of Lent gives way to the exuberant joy of the Easter season, which celebrates Christ's resurrection from the dead. The term Easter is derived from *Eostre*, the Old English word for April and possibly linked to a pre-Christian goddess of springtime. However, in the majority of European languages the name of the season is clearly derived from the Hebrew *Pesah* (Passover). This is significant because Christians consider Jesus's resurrection from the dead to be an even greater "passover" than the miracle that saved the Israelite nation from Egyptian slavery (see section 9.6). Thus, Easter is the "paschal" season. The connection was considered so important that parts of the early Church insisted on celebrating Easter on the same day as the Jewish Passover, which, as a full moon feast, could be any day of the week. However, other parts of the Church, including Rome, preferred the Sunday following the Passover moon. In 325 CE, the Council of Nicea adjudicated in favor of Sunday, in keeping with the emerging Christian tradition of setting aside that weekday as a sacred time of rest and prayer. The use of the Julian calendar by Orthodox Christians means that their Easter is usually later than the West.[11]

Following the Jewish tradition of considering sunset as the start of the day, Easter ceremonies commence on the evening of Holy Saturday. Fire and light are the key elements used to express the theme of glory and triumph. A prominent symbol is the large paschal candle on which is inscribed the first and last letters of the Greek alphabet (alpha and omega) as well as the year number. The paschal candle stands in the sanctuary as a constant reminder to believers that the risen Christ is not only the Light of the World but also the Lord of Time.[12] The joyful atmosphere is also reflected in the change from purple to white vestments. The popular Easter egg is a religious symbol of Christ breaking free from the tomb. The season of Easter lasts for seven weeks and a day, ending on Pentecost Sunday when Christians commemorate the descent of the Holy Spirit on the apostles and the beginning of the Church's missionary outreach.

The remainder of the year, between Pentecost and the following Advent, is considered to be "ordinary time," during which the traditional color is green in the West and gold in the East. This period is sprinkled with a range of other feasts such as All Saints' Day (Halloween), which is another example of a pre-existing pagan ritual being redefined and subsumed into the new religion's calendar. There is also a myriad of saints' anniversaries, but the overarching theme that shapes the entire Christian year is clearly the person of Christ. The calendar essentially traces his career from birth through adult ministry to death and resurrection. In none of the other five major religions is such extensive and overwhelming attention given to the founder in the cycle of festivals that mark the religious year. However, a similar focus on the key events in the life of the founder is evident in Buddhism where Buddha Gautama, like Jesus, is considered to be the personification of eternal wisdom and the key figure of the age.

9.3 Full Moons and Monsoons

If a certain degree of diversity among churches typifies the Christian year, this is even more the case in Buddhism where no universally recognized calendar exists. For some Buddhists, a preoccupation with festivals may be an unhelpful distraction because every day of the year should be dedicated to the dharma. Nevertheless, Buddhist cultures have developed annual cycles of celebrations. These can vary enormously because quite often they have incorporated local pre-Buddhist customs, but they also share a core of common festivals that celebrate key moments in the life of Buddha Gautama. The beginning of the year itself varies across Buddhism. In the Theravada tradition, it is

Table 9.2 The Theravada Buddhist calendar.

Holy day	Date
New Year	Full moon (March–April)
Vesak	Full moon (April–May)
Asalha Puja	Full moon (June–July)
	Three-month Vassa period begins
Pavarana	Vassa ends
Kathina	Within one month of Vassa
Abhidhamma Day	Full moon (Sept–Oct)
Magha Puja	Full moon (Jan–Feb)

linked to the sun entering the constellation Aries, marking the beginning of a new solar year. The April full moon is commonly chosen to mark the event. In Thailand, the New Year festival is known as Songkran,[13] which is characterized by the cleaning of houses and the playful throwing of perfumed water over each other. In the Mahayana tradition, New Year is usually determined by the January new moon (following the winter solstice).

The more important festivals from a religious perspective are connected to events in the life of the founder. In the Theravada tradition, three in particular are noteworthy, each of which occurs on a full moon and takes its title from the Hindu name of the lunar month in which it occurs (Table 9.2). In one sense, these three festivals also correspond to the Three Jewels of Buddhism: the teacher (Buddha); the teaching (dharma); and the community (sangha).

The first festival occurs on the full moon of the month of Vaishakha (April–May) and, thus, is commonly known as Vesak or Buddha Day. Vesak is the most important of all holy days because it commemorates three critical events in the life of Buddha Gautama: his birth, Enlightenment and death – all of which were said to have occurred under a tree on the full moon of Vaishakha. Any one of these three would have given Vesak the same significance as Christmas or Easter in Christianity. In fact, these three events are often separated in Mahayana calendars such as in the Japanese Buddhist tradition.[14] In Theravada Buddhism, however, the threefold celebration on the one day concentrates an enormous amount of religious significance into Vesak. Practices vary according to local culture but often the laity flock to temples and monasteries to join the monks in honoring the Enlightened One by mantras, readings, sermons, meditation and alms-giving. Customs include circumambulation of the temple or monastery three times to symbolize the Three Jewels, avoiding activities that may cause harm to small creatures, releasing caged birds as a sign of relinquishing anxiety, lighting lamps to signify the Buddha's illumination, and abstaining from meat for those who are not strictly vegetarian.

The second festival is celebrated two months later on the full moon of the Hindu month of Ashadha (June–July), from which its name is derived: Asalha Puja Day. It marks the other crucial event in the life of Buddha Gautama not included in Vesak – the Buddha's First Sermon to his five companions at Sarnath. It was this discourse that began the imparting of eternal truth once again. Thus, Asalha Puja Day is also known as Dharma Day and resembles Pentecost Sunday in Christianity, which celebrates the formation of the first believing community and the beginning of missionary outreach. Tibetan Buddhists mark Dharma Day (known in Tibet as Chokhor) by carrying scriptures on long rectangular wooden blocks in procession as a symbol of the spread of the Buddha's teachings.

The third festival falls on the full moon of the lunar month Magha (January–February) and is, thus, named Magha Puja Day. Its other title is Sangha Day, which is appropriate given that it commemorates a gathering of monks just prior to the Buddha's death. On this occasion, the Buddha provided them with a summary of the monastic rule. It is also called Fourfold Gathering Day, because it is said that four miracles were involved: the assembly was spontaneous; all of the monks were arhats; all of them had been ordained by Buddha Gautama; and it was a full moon. As in Christianity, there are other festivals that mark various events taken from the Buddha's life on earth. One such commemoration is Abhidhamma Day in the Theravada tradition. It recalls Buddha Gautama's return to earth from one of the heavenly realms where he met his mother and preached the Four Noble Truths to her. Akin to Dharma Day, it is also a statement that the transmission of truth should have no bounds. In the Pure Land Mahayana tradition, where the stress on the celestial bodhisattva Guanyin is greater than on Buddha Gautama, the key festivals commemorate her birth, enlightenment and death.

Just as the main Buddhist feasts parallel those of Christianity by focusing on key events in the life of the founder, the Buddhist calendar also contains a Lent-like period during which believers should withdraw from everyday concerns and renew spiritual energy. Immediately after Asalha Puja Day, the Vassa period, or Rains Retreat, commences and, as the name suggests, lasts until the end of the wet season. Buddha Gautama and the early generations of monks practiced itinerant preaching but, during the monsoon period, travel was difficult as rivers swelled and roads became muddy. Moreover, their health could easily be undermined if they spent too much time outdoors in the rain. Thus the Buddha instructed monks to remain in one sheltered place for the duration of the season. A spiritual meaning subsequently arose from this practical necessity. It became a period of retreat spent in study and meditation. The rains also mean that fewer visitors come to the monasteries, enabling the monks to focus on such activities.[15]

The intensive spiritual activity of Vassa is not restricted to the monk or the nun. Lay persons often join a monastic community for part or all of the season and are sometimes appositely called "rain monks." In some Buddhist societies, such as Thailand and Myanmar, there is a strong expectation that a young man will become a temporary monk at some stage during his adolescence (Figure 9.2). For those who do not actually join a monastery, there are other ways of observing Vassa, such as adopting monastic vows privately, giving alms to the monks more frequently, abstaining from meat, alcohol or tobacco, and practicing regular daily chants. In some cultures, families avoid planning weddings during this period. Many Buddhist communities hold special celebrations with meals to mark the end of the Vassa retreat on Pavarana Day. For some, it is also a time when their son returns home after his term in the monastery.

Within a month of the termination of the Vassa retreat, many communities hold a special ceremony during which the laity offer new robes to the monks. The Kathina ritual takes its name from the traditional wooden frame used for sewing clothes. The laity present the monastery with fabric that is used by the monks to cut and sew a set of robes. These are then presented by the lay community to nominated monks who have

Figure 9.2 Young Buddhists often join a monastery during the wet season (Vassa). (Reproduced with kind permission of iStock.)

just completed the Vassa retreat. Kathina ceremonies can attract large crowds and constitute an important opportunity for monasteries to raise funds as well.

Another major event on the Buddhist calendar, especially in the Mahayana tradition, is Ulambana, or the Festival of the Hungry Ghosts. One of the realms on the Buddhist wheel of life, into which the dead can be reincarnated, is that of the **hungry ghosts**. According to popular Buddhist belief, the ghosts are released for 15 days at this time of year and allowed to wander the earth in search of food offerings. For many families, it is possible that some of their deceased relatives may be among the hungry ghosts and so it is imperative that action be taken to alleviate their suffering and help them along the road to liberation. Ulambana is a particularly appropriate time for Buddhists to pay their respects to the dead by visiting cemeteries and stupas, and making small offerings of food as in the Hindu tradition. In Japan, the festival is known as Obon and is characterized by paper lanterns displayed in front of homes and in cemeteries so that the wandering ghosts are able to find their resting place at the end of the period. Sometimes lanterns and candles are floated down rivers or out to sea to symbolize the return of the spirits to their proper abode. The festival of hungry ghosts reflects a fundamental belief in Buddhism that the actions of the living can, in some way, benefit the dead. It is a similar idea to that which underpins the Christian holy days dedicated to assisting the deceased such as All Souls' Day in the Catholic tradition and the eve of Pentecost in the Orthodox Church.

A myriad of other feast days populate Buddhist calendars, many of them culturally specific such as the Festival of the Tooth in Sri Lanka, the Elephant Festival in Thailand, and Guru Rimpoche's birthday in Tibet. However, Buddhist calendars in general are characterized by an emphasis on the key moments in the life of Buddha Gautama in the Theravada tradition or of Guanyin in the Mahayana tradition, as well as the insertion of a special season of spiritual renewal. In this respect, the Buddhist year resembles the Christian year which is heavily structured on the life of the founder and includes the Lenten season as a time of self-denial and replenishment. Even the numbering of the years is similar to the Christian system, although it is the death of Buddha Gautama (traditionally 544 BCE), rather than his birth, that is considered Year One of the Buddhist Era. Furthermore, although Buddhism does not have a dedicated holy weekday such as the Christian Sunday, monks do hold special spiritual activities on Uposatha days, which fall on the new moon and the full moon of each lunar month.

However, the Buddhist concept of cosmic time is radically different from that of Christianity and the other Abrahamic religions. For Buddhists, the universe comes into being and dissolves again in an eternal series of cycles. Each cycle spans billions of years and is further subdivided into eons. The progression from one eon to the next is generally characterized by a gradual decline in wisdom and virtue. Buddha Gautama himself predicted that, as the years went by, his teaching would eventually be forgotten and the next Buddha in the long series, **Maitreya**, would come to restore the lost truth.[16] Such a sweeping cyclic cosmology was inherited from its mother religion, Hinduism, which is the source of several notable features of the Buddhist calendar including festival dates determined by the lunar phases, the names of the months, and special religious significance attached to the wet season.

9.4 Day of Brahma

It is said that Hinduism has a longer list of festivals than any other religious tradition, with a celebration of some sort on almost every day of the year. Part of the reason for such a proliferation of feasts is the enormous regional and cultic diversity within Hinduism itself. For example, at the time of independence, the Indian government identified over 30 different religious calendars in operation. However, amid the bewildering variety there are some common traits, especially across the two calendars most widely used in India for religious purposes: the Vikram calendar in the north and the Shalivahana calendar in the south.

As with many religions, Hinduism defines its months by the phases of the moon. Thus, in the Shalivahana system, the month always begins with a new moon and is always divided into a bright half while the moon waxes (shukla paksha) and a dark half while the moon wanes (krishna paksha). Conversely, in the Vikram system the month commences with the full moon. In both systems, 12 lunar months equate to only 354 days and, thus, an extra month (adhik mas) is added every two or three years to maintain synchronicity with the solar cycle.[17] The two calendars also differ in the way they reckon the beginning of the year. In the north, New Year is celebrated on the full moon of Kartika (October–November) while in the south it is the new moon of Chaitra (March–April). In both traditions, not only the New Year but the creation of the universe itself is commemorated since it is said to have occurred on this day. In many parts of India, houses are cleaned and decorated, greetings and sweets are exchanged, and people visit temples to hear a reading of the new almanac with its predictions for the coming year in terms of personal and public life.

Table 9.3 The southern Hindu calendar.

Season	Hindu month	Western months	Date	Holy day
Spring	Chaitra	March–April	new moon	New Year
Summer	Vaishakha	April–May		
	Jyaistha	May–June		
Rains	Ashadha	June–July	11th of bright fortnight	Sleep of Vishnu commences
	Shravana	July–August	full moon	Raksha Bandhan
Autumn	Bhadra	August–Sept	14 days of dark fortnight	Ancestors' Fortnight
	Ashvina	Sept–Oct	10 days following new moon	Navaratri-Dussehra
Winter	Kartika	Oct–Nov	new moon 11th of bright fortnight	Divali Sleep of Vishnu ends
	Agrahayana	Nov–Dec		
Cool	Pausha	Dec–Jan		
	Magha	Jan–Feb		
Spring	Phalguna	Feb–March	new moon full moon	Mahashivaratri Holi

The Hindu year is traditionally divided into six seasons: spring, summer, rains, autumn, winter and cool season (Table 9.3). Each season has its own particular themes and rituals, the most prominent of which are those in the rains and autumn seasons. While Buddhism sets aside the wet season as a time of retreat, the Vaishnavite tradition sees the period of monsoon rains as a dangerous and inauspicious time. On the eleventh day of the bright fortnight of Ashadha, it is said that Vishnu retires below the ocean for four months of deep sleep. Caution and care are needed for the world is without its Lord and, thus, subject to malevolent forces. Hence, Hindus avoid weddings and abstain from a certain food each month, such as spinach, yoghurt, milk and lentils.

Despite the sense of dread, some of Hinduism's most important feast days are held during the Sleep of Vishnu, partly as a means of countering the spiritual danger. The first of these is Raksha Bandhan, which occurs on the full moon of Shravana (July–August). The term literally means "a band of protection" which points to the central symbolic act. On this day, sisters tie a band (rakhi) around the wrist of their brothers. Hindus believe that the band will bring protection and security to the wearer. Conversely, the tying of the band also signifies the duty incumbent on the brother to care for the woman he loves as a sibling. Raksha Bandhan is thus a time to renew the mutual bonds of family love. Rakhis are often made of colored silk and are highly decorated. The rakhi is placed on a plate along with other objects such as a small lamp, water, rice, sweets and vermilion powder. As the rakhi is tied, a bindi is applied to the forehead and the sweets are eaten. In some places, Raksha Bandhan is also the occasion on which high-caste Hindus replace their sacred thread.

One month later, at the very heart of Vishnu's sleep, Hindus dedicate the dark fortnight of Bhadra to the dead. Prayers and offerings for deceased family members are a feature of every new moon, but the Ancestors' Fortnight is a special time to assist those who have passed away. Akin to the Buddhist Festival of the Hungry Ghosts and the Christian All Souls' Day, Ancestors' Fortnight is characterized by food offerings for hungry ghosts (pretas) as well as acts of charity for which good karma is generated and diverted for the benefit of the dead.

As the new moon of Ashvina brings the Ancestors' Fortnight to a close, it simultaneously ushers in the nine-day festival of Navaratri ("Nine Nights") followed by a tenth day known as Dussehra. The main focus of Navaratri is the Mother Goddess. There are many ways in which Navaratri is commemorated, one of which is to dedicate three sets of three days to each of the main personifications of the Mother Goddess: **Saraswati** (goddess of the arts and learning); Lakshmi (goddess of wealth and prosperity); and Durga (goddess of strength and fortitude). In some parts of India, a statue of Durga is taken to the local riverbank or seashore and immersed as a symbol of the purging of accumulated bad karma.[18] Navaratri is an auspicious time to commence new projects and often people bring along items from their work such as tools or equipment to be blessed. On the tenth night, Dussehra, the main theme shifts from prayers for prosperity to the victory of Rama over the demon Ravanna as told in the Hindu epic the Ramayana. Huge paper and wooden effigies of Ravanna are burned on this night, symbolizing the destruction of evil.

The next new moon, in the month of Kartika, is arguably the most popular and widely celebrated festival on the Hindu calendar: Divali. The name means "a row of lamps" and, indeed, light is the dominant symbol of the holy day, which is linked to the New Year in the northern calendar. Under a dark moonless sky, the Indian landscape becomes ablaze with millions of lights emanating from sources that range from oil lamps to electric globes (Figure 9.3). Houses are cleaned and decorated with beautiful rangoli patterns on the floor; lamps are placed on window sills and porches, and brilliant fireworks are set off during the night. The theme of illumination is given various meanings, of which two are prominent. First, Divali commemorates the safe return to India of Rama and his rescued bride, Sita. According to the Ramayana, people lit the way home by placing lamps along the path in the darkness. Second, Divali is the time when Lakshmi, the goddess of prosperity, visits the earth bringing fortune and success to those she blesses. Thus the washing, decorating and illuminating of homes are all intended to attract her attention and benevolence. Lakshmi's image is usually portrayed with coins falling from her hands, and many businesses prefer to commence their new financial year at this time. As with Christmas, Divali is not only an occasion for giving gifts and exchanging cards but also a powerful stimulus to the Indian economy.

The time following Divali is quieter, but two key festivals highlight the final month of the year according to the southern calendar system. The new moon of Phalguna constitutes the important Shaivite holy day, Mahashivaratri ("Great Night of Shiva"). Unlike Divali and Navaratri, this is a time of self-discipline in the spirit of Shiva himself, who is considered to be the supreme model of worldly renunciation. Followers observe strict fasting and abstinence. Often meat, curry and cereals are avoided, and in some cases only water is taken. The mood is solemn rather than joyful. Believers visit temples and spend the entire night in vigil, chanting hymns, making food offerings, and bathing images of Shiva in foodstuffs such as milk, curds, ghee, sugar and

Figure 9.3 Hindu girls lighting lamps on the feast of Divali.
(Reproduced with kind permission from World Religions Photo Library/Gapper.)

honey. The holy day has various meanings. One version claims that on this night Shiva performs the Tandava dance through which the universe was created and continues to be sustained. One of the most recognizable forms of Shiva in statues and paintings is Nataraja, the many-armed Lord of the Dance, surrounded by the fiery circle of the ever-changing physical world. A second theme associated with the Great Night is Shiva, not as the detached ascetic, but as the ideal husband who weds his consort Parvati. The night is considered especially auspicious for women. Young unmarried girls petition the god for a future groom, while wives pray for the wellbeing of their husbands.

In striking contrast to the ascetical mood of Mahashivaratri is the raucous, licentious festival Holi, which falls on the full moon of the same month. Holi is an abbreviation of Holika, sister of the demon king Hiranyakasyapu. According to the myth, Holika had the power to walk through fire unharmed and was asked by the king to kill his son, Prahlad, who refused to worship him. However, when she sat with the boy on a burning pyre, it was Holika who was burned to death while Prahlad survived. The moral of the story is the triumph of good over evil. The myth is recalled every year via the burning of images representing Holika and Prahlad in huge bonfires at dusk. Usually the Holika figure is constructed of flammable materials, while the Prahlad figure is non-combustible in order to achieve the appropriate effect. People participate by throwing branches and pieces of wood onto the fire. Coconuts and coins are tossed in and people circumambulate the flames a number of times for good karma. The following morning, believers gather the ashes, which are considered to be holy and auspicious, smearing them on their bodies.

There is a second aspect to Holi for which it is more widely known. Alcohol and meat are more liberally consumed; verbal exchanges are less restrained and even ribald; wives may disagree with their husbands; lower caste members may taunt higher caste members; and general deportment becomes more riotous and merry. In a religion where caste and gender rules impinge heavily on social behavior, Holi, like the Christian Mardi Gras, is an occasion when these restrictions can be shifted if not altogether removed. The abiding image of Holi is of people indiscriminately throwing colored water or powder over each other in an atmosphere of gay abandonment. The result is that persons of all ages and classes and both sexes look the same color – usually a shade of pink or purple. For one day in the year, the color of one's class (varna) is irrelevant, suggesting a fundamental equality beneath the socio-religious superstructure. Thus, it is not surprising that Holi is one of the most loved festivals in India, especially among the lower classes.

The Hindu calendar is also dotted with numerous birthdays of gods and heroes: Rama, Hanuman, Krishna and Ganesha to name a few. While most key festivals are held on a new moon or a full moon, Hindus also celebrate the sankranti: the day on which the sun moves into a new zodiacal constellation. Two of these have particular significance. The Aries sankranti (Mesh Sankranti) represents the commencement of a new solar year when Hindus often begin wedding preparations for their sons and daughters. The Capricorn sankranti (Makar Sankranti) is associated with the winter solstice and, like Christmas, represents the return of the sun to the northern hemisphere and the gradual lengthening of the days.

The Hindu year number is traditionally calculated from the death of Krishna, which is said to have occurred in 3012 BCE. This event ushered in the final phase of the fourfold cycle of Hindu cosmic time. Each phase (yuga) becomes progressively shorter and is characterized by a gradual decline in spiritual knowledge and morality. The current phase is the Kali yuga which will last for 432,000 years. The entire cycle consists of four such yugas and endures for over 4 million years (Box 9.1). As in Buddhism, the vastness of Hindu time scales becomes even more apparent when it is realized that the lifespan of the current universe is said to be 1,000 of these cycles, or over 4 billion years. This is known as one Day of Brahma after which he will sleep for a 4-billion-year-long night and the current universe will cease to be.

The cyclic view of time, the counting of the years from a legendary past figure, the preference for lunar months, the addition of an intercalary month to retain synchronization with the seasons, the tracking of the sun's movement across the zodiac and a time to remember and assist deceased relatives are all features of the Hindu calendar that find an echo in the Chinese tradition.

Box 9.1 The Four Yugas (Ages) of the Hindu Time Scale

1) Satya Yuga: 1,728,000 years (age of perfect spiritual knowledge)
2) Treta Yuga: 1,296,000 years (age of advanced mental powers)
3) Dvapara Yuga: 864,000 years (age of rational thought)
4) Kali Yuga: 432,000 years (age of materialism)

9.5 The 78th Cycle

According to traditional accounts, Chinese civilization was founded long ago by a legendary figure known as the Yellow Emperor (Huangdi). It is said that he lived during the third millennium BCE and, through his brilliance, profoundly improved the conditions of his world. He taught his people how to build permanent homes, domesticate animals and grow the five cereals. He is also reputed to have invented the wheel, boats, weapons, clothing, mathematics, astronomy and the Chinese calendar. In memory of his unparalleled contributions to science and technology at the dawn of history, Chinese culture today marks the passage of time from 2636 BCE, which, it is said, is when the calendar was implemented. However, unlike other religions that simply count the number of years since the designated starting point (such as the birth of Christ, the death of the Buddha or the death of Krishna), the Chinese system uses a 60-year cycle. Thus, in 1984 we entered the 78th cycle, which will end in 2043. The first year of each cycle is known as a jiazi year, which is commemorated with an enormous festival involving rituals, parades, banquets, shows and other community activities.

The 60-year cycle comes from a combination of two elements: the 10 Celestial Stems and the 12 Terrestrial Branches. The Celestial Stems result from the pairing of each of the Five Elements (Wood, Fire, Earth, Metal and Water) with Yang and Yin respectively. The list starts with Yang Wood, Yin Wood, Yang Fire and so forth, ending with Yin Water. The Terrestrial Branches are the well-known list of twelve animals: rat, ox, tiger, hare, dragon, snake, horse, sheep, monkey, rooster, dog and pig.[19] The last Year of the Rat was 2008 and so it is easy to calculate which animal is associated with one's birth year. When the two lists are juxtaposed and paired, the result is a 60-year cycle, commencing with Yang Wood Rat and ending with Yin Water Pig. For example, 2016 is a Yang Fire Monkey year (the 33rd year of the 78th cycle).

The Chinese calendar is even more complicated because it divides the year in two ways (Table 9.4). The first way follows the Hindu–Buddhist tradition of using lunar months. Thus, some festivals are determined by the new moon (the first day of the month) or the full moon (the 15th day of the month). Also, following the Hindu–Buddhist model, the Chinese calendar adds an extra (13th) lunar month every now and then to keep dates synchronized with the sun and the seasons.[20] Fasting or

Table 9.4 The Chinese calendar.

Solar date	Lunar date	Holy day
Late January/ early February	New moon nearest Feb 4	New Year
February	Full moon after New Year	Lantern Festival
April 5		Tomb Sweeping Day
June	5th day of 5th lunar month	Dragon Boat Festival
August	Full moon of 7th lunar month	Hungry Ghost Festival
September	Full moon of 8th lunar month	Mid-Autumn Festival
October	9th day of 9th lunar month	Double Ninth Day

vegetarianism may be practiced on certain days of the lunar month including the new moon, the full moon and the half moons. The second way in which the year is subdivided is determined by the movement of the sun. The 365-day solar year is broken up into 24 "solar terms" (or "nodes"), each of which is approximately 15 days long.[21] The two **equinoxes** (21 March and 23 September) and the two **solstices** (21 June and 21 December) are among the 24 nodes, which are important reminders of the eternal dance of yin and yang. The equinoxes are the two dates when day and night are of equal length everywhere on earth, symbolizing the balance of yin and yang. The solstices are the longest and shortest days of the year, when yin or yang dominates over the other for a brief moment before the cycle moves on. Somewhat surprisingly, the first solar term does not correspond to any of these, but rather is linked to a node known as the "Start of Spring" in early February.[22] The religious attention given to the sun's annual journey across the heavens echoes the Hindu sankranti tradition. In Daoism, the 24 nodes are a time to practice "daoyin". This involves taking up a bodily posture, such as sitting, standing or kneeling, and repeating certain designated exercises. The aim is to achieve alignment with the flow of the Dao and improve one's health and longevity.[23]

Sprinkled across the solar terms and lunar months are a myriad of festivals and, for space reasons, we will look at six of the most popular ones. Many of these are shared by Daoist, Confucian and Buddhist traditions. Specifically Daoist celebrations of these moments often involve an elaborate mix of purification rituals, food offerings, invocations, hymns, dances and formal pacing by Daoist priests. We start our exploration with the New Year. This occurs on the new moon closest to the Start of Spring node (February 4), which means that it is a movable feast that can fall on any date between January 21 and February 21 each year. Two weeks are set aside for festivities, in which time people call on gods, such as the Jade Emperor, to bless them in the coming year. The general atmosphere is one of excitement and joy, as families come together to exchange gifts, traditionally wrapped in auspicious red paper. New statues of gods are placed in the kitchen to bless all food prepared there, while divine images and good luck proverbs are installed in doorways to protect the house from evil forces. Parades are held in the streets where musicians and dancers process in colorful costumes, accompanied by the sound of firecrackers and whistles.

The celebrations end on the Lantern Festival, which marks the first full moon of the year. This day commemorates the birthday of the Heavenly Official (Tianguan) – the first of the Three Officials who oversee Heaven, Earth and Water. Tianguan is responsible for the allocation of good fortune throughout the world. As implied by the name, the main theme of the Lantern Festival is light. Thousands of lanterns, large and small, are carried about by people or sent up into the sky on balloons with prayers for good luck, prosperity and health. A traditional food eaten during the New Year season is tangyuan – a rice dumpling rolled into a ball and filled with sweet foodstuffs. The stickiness of the tangyuan symbolizes the cohesive forces of love and respect that bind families together.

When the sun enters the fifth solar term (April 5) each year, the Chinese commemorate Qingming or Tomb Sweeping Day. Other names for this holy day include the Clear Bright Festival, Ancestors' Day and Chinese Memorial Day. There are two themes associated with Tomb Sweeping Day. The first is a celebration of the season of spring when planting occurs. People are encouraged to spend time outside and appreciate the rebirth of the natural world. Activities include flying kites and breaking open colored eggs that symbolize new life, as at Christian Easter. The second theme is remembering deceased relatives. As implied by the name, families literally sweep the graves of their beloved departed, as well as laying out food and drink offerings. Bamboo or rice paper is cut into squares to resemble banknotes and this "spirit money" is burned at the graveside in the belief that it will reappear in the spirit world and benefit the deceased.

In addition to Tomb Sweeping Day, there is another occasion on the calendar when the living can assist the dead: the Hungry Ghosts Festival (Zhongyuan). Unlike Tomb Sweeping Day, the timing of this second festival for the dead is determined by the full moon of the seventh lunar month, thus placing it in August. Appropriately nicknamed "Chinese Halloween" and "Chinese All Souls Day", it coincides with the Mahayana Buddhism festival known as Ulambana. As in Buddhism, Daoism holds that the spirits of the dead are free to wander the earth for a period of time during the seventh lunar month. These are hungry, troubled and disoriented ghosts and they have the potential to harm the living if we do not attend to them. The most appropriate action is to offer them nourishment and directions. Thus, food and drink are given but, unlike Tomb Sweeping Day, these gifts are placed in front of homes or in the street. Sometimes an extra place is prepared at the dinner table as an invitation for the ghost to dine with the family. Paper boats and lanterns are released on rivers and lakes as a way of directing the ghosts to their proper resting place. During this dangerous time, people often avoid swimming, camping trips and outdoor activities.

One of the most popular events on the Chinese calendar is the Dragon Boat Festival, which is held on the fifth day of the fifth lunar month (June), hence its alternative name of "Double Fifth" Day. At the heart of the festivities are the dragon-boat races in which competing teams row their elaborately decorated vessels to a loud drumbeat (Figure 9.4).

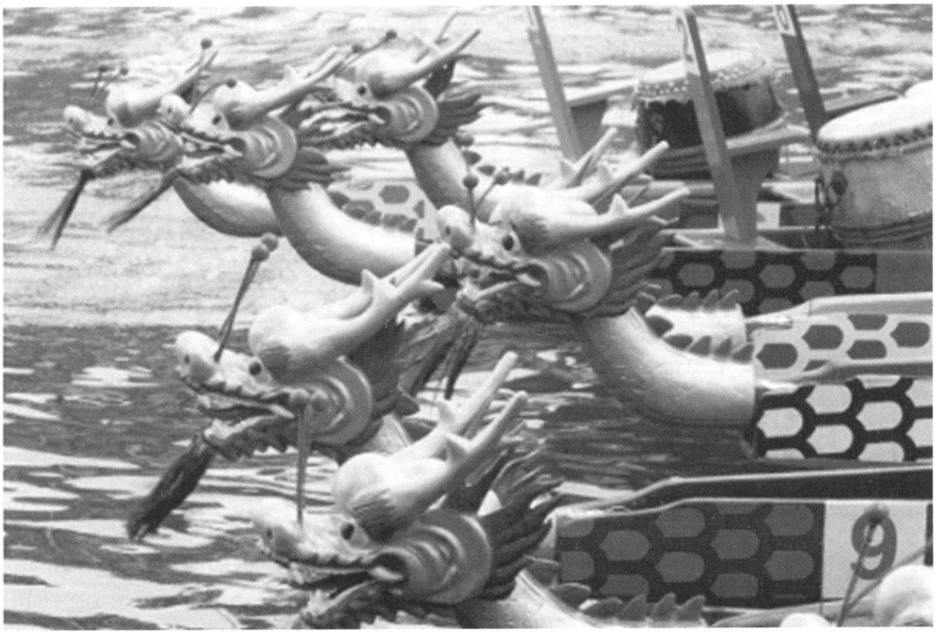

Figure 9.4 Chinese Dragon Boat Racing.
(Reproduced with kind permission of iStock.)

The festival commemorates the attempts by local fishermen to save an honest minister who drowned himself because of government corruption on this date in the third century BCE. The traditional dish at this festival is zongzi, which is a rice-ball filled with a variety of foodstuffs, wrapped in bamboo leaves or corn husks and steamed.[24] Special rice wine is also consumed to ward off evil spirits and it is customary to stand an egg on its end at noon for good luck.

In addition to "Double Fifth Day," there is also a festival known as "Double Ninth Day," which as the name suggests, falls on the ninth day of the ninth lunar month (mid-October). Nine is a prominent yang number and it is believed that yang energy is doubled on this date. A popular activity is to go hiking in the mountains and high places, not only in search of fresh air and quiet, but also to gain clarity of spiritual perspective. Double Ninth Day is a time to eat a special rice-cake known as gao, which sounds like the Chinese word for height. The cakes resemble blooming flowers and often contain chestnuts, ginkgo seeds and pine nuts, all of which are thought to improve health. Chrysanthemum wine is drunk and dogwood sprigs are carried in order to enhance physical and spiritual wellbeing.

Balancing the earlier focus on spring, the mid-Autumn Festival (or Moon Festival) is held on the full moon of the eighth lunar month (usually September). Just as the planting time was marked at Qingming, this festival focuses on the harvest season and, for some, its importance is second only to New Year. Its distinctive dish is the mooncake, which resembles a fruitcake or plum pudding and comes in many varieties. Mid-Autumn Festival is also called the Festival of Reunion because it is a time when families gather for a common meal. Indeed, the circular shape of the full moon is interpreted to represent the circle of love that binds blood kin together.

There are many other events on the calendar including birthdays of gods and early figures such as Laozi, but the six festivals described above are the major events that are celebrated. The mix of lunar and solar calendars, the importance of the cycle of the natural seasons, the focus on agricultural fertility and harvests, a new year period defined by two key days, the importance of an annual family meal and the use of distinctive foods to characterize the tone of each holy day or season are not only features of the Chinese calendar. These elements can also be found in the way that sacred time is counted and commemorated in the Jewish tradition.

9.6 Harvests, History and High Holy Days

For two days in September or early October each year, Jews gather in large numbers in synagogue for a long and solemn service. The usual colored cloths covering the Ark are replaced by white, the color of purity. At various points during the prayers, the sound of a ram's horn (shofar) pierces the air, announcing that the Books of Life and Death have been opened in heaven and a new religious year has begun. The festival is known by various names such as the Day of the Horn Blowing, the Day of Judgment and the Day of Remembrance. However, its most popular title is Rosh Hashanah ("Head of the Year"). Rosh Hashanah falls on the new moon that marks the first day of Tishri (Table 9.5). This is the month in which it is traditionally believed that God created the world in 3760 BCE, the basis for the calculation of the Jewish year number. Thus, the year 5777 on the Jewish calendar began in 2016. Unlike the New Year tradition in many

Table 9.5 The Jewish calendar.

Hebrew month	Western month	Hebrew date	Holy day
Tishri	Sept–Oct	1 10	Rosh Hashanah Yom Kippur
		15–21	Sukkoth
		22	Simhat Torah
Heshvan	Oct–Nov		
Kislev	Nov–Dec	25	Hanukkah
Tevet	Dec–Jan		
Shevat	Jan–Feb		
Adar (second Adar added in leap year)	Feb–March	14	Purim
Nisan	March–April	14–21	Pesah (Passover)
Iyar	April–May		
Sivan	May–June	6	Shavuot
Tamuz	June–July		
Av	July–August	9	Tisha B'Av
Elul	August–Sept		

other cultures and religions, the Jewish year begins in an atmosphere of soul-searching and penitence rather than exuberant joy and revelry. Rosh Hashanah, the first of the **High Holy Days** of Judaism, ushers in a 10-day period known as the yamim noraim ("days of awe").[25] During that brief time, each person strives to ensure that their name is written in the Book of Life by honest self-examination and a sincere request for forgiveness from God and neighbor. Similar to the Hindu custom at Dussehra, Ashkenazi Jews perform tashlikh, in which they visit a riverbank or the seashore and throw away breadcrumbs from their pockets, symbolically casting off sins that have attached to their person during the previous year.[26] But Rosh Hashanah is not only about acknowledgment of guilt and purification: Jews also thank God for the sweet gift of another year, signified by dipping bread and apple in honey.

The ten days end with Yom Kippur, the second High Holy Day and arguably the most important day in the entire Jewish calendar. Sometimes described as the "sabbath of sabbaths," it is a time when almost all activity in Israel shuts down.[27] Like Christmas in Christianity, Yom Kippur is the one day of the year when non- practicing Jews are most likely to attend synagogue. In many ways it is as much about Jewish identity as about religious devotion. There are five synagogue services that run almost continuously from evening to evening and some devout Jews remain in the synagogue for almost the whole night and day.

The term *Yom Kippur* literally means Day of Atonement, and forgiveness of sin is indeed the key theme. On the previous day, Orthodox Jews perform the kapparot ritual.

Based on the biblical scapegoat ceremony, kapparot involves holding a rooster (for a man) or a hen (for a woman) over one's head and swinging it in a circle three times while reciting a prayer that transfers guilt onto the animal.[28] Alternatively, the animal is replaced by a small bag of coins. Some Jewish men also take a ritual bath (mikveh) in preparation. During the service, a litany of sins is then read out on behalf of believers who acknowledge their collective guilt and ask God for pardon. As with Rosh Hashanah, white is used for synagogue adornments as a symbol of the purity that comes from divine forgiveness. Many Ashkenazi Jews also wear the traditional white tunic known as the kittel.

Yom Kippur is perhaps best known for its strict 25-hour fast, which, it is said, brings one closer to the angels, who do not require food. The fast is also one of the five innuyim (forbidden activities) that represent the ascetical dimension of Yom Kippur. Apart from avoiding food and drink, Jews also abstain from anointing with oil, sexual intercourse, pleasurable baths and wearing leather shoes. The final service is aptly named Ne'ilah, or the "closing of the gates." As the shofar sounds for the last time, the 10 days of awe come to an end, the heavenly books are closed, and the opportunity for formal reconciliation passes for another year.

There are several other fast days on the Jewish calendar, but only one that lasts the full 25 hours and involves the five innuyim as on Yom Kippur. Tisha B'Av (Av 9) commemorates the tragic destruction of the First and Second Temples, which is believed to have occurred on the same date. The colors of the synagogue are changed to dark blue, marking one of the saddest days on the calendar. Tisha B'Av is also one of the holy days on which one of the Five Scrolls (**Megillot**) is read (Box 9.2). In this case it is the book of Lamentations, which narrates the devastation of Jerusalem under the Babylonian armies. Four other days during the year involve a simple dawn-to-dusk fast.[29]

The Jewish year is not restricted to days of fasting and penitence. There are also great feasts of cheerful celebration. While white symbolizes an atmosphere of penitence and forgiveness, the synagogue is adorned in green for three prominent annual religious festivals that acknowledge nature's bounty and God's gracious intervention in Israel's history. Together, they are known as the pilgrim festivals because male believers in biblical times were required by law to make their way to Jerusalem as pilgrims and offer the first fruits of the harvest to the Temple priests. The first pilgrim festival is Sukkoth which commences on the full moon of the first month Tishri, just five days after Yom Kippur. Sukkoth lasts for seven or eight days and coincides with the autumn fruit harvest. The term *sukkoth* means "booths" or "tents," and the festival commemorates the 40 years that the freed Hebrew slaves spent in the wilderness as tent-dwelling nomads prior to settling in the land of Israel.[30] Thus, the key theme is divine protection. For the

Box 9.2 The Five Scrolls and Their Corresponding Holy Days

Scroll	Holy day
Song of Songs	Passover
Ruth	Shavuot
Lamentations	Tisha B'Av
Qoheleth	Sukkoth
Esther	Purim

duration of the festival, Jews build a simple booth in their backyards with a partially open roof so that the stars can be seen at night.[31] In solidarity with the Israelites of old, believers take their meals inside the booth, and some even sleep in it.[32] The other important symbolic action at Sukkoth is the four species. At morning synagogue services during the festival, Jews go in procession carrying a citron (lemon-like fruit) in the left hand and branches of palm, myrtle and willow in the right. These items are waved in all directions, acknowledging the omnipresence of God and in fulfillment of the commandment to rejoice before the Lord.[33] The Megillah for Sukkoth is the book of Qoheleth. Its pessimistic tone is sometimes associated with the transition from summer to winter which is said to occur on Shemini Atzeret, the last day of the festival. The following day is known as Simhat Torah, on which the annual cycle of synagogue Torah readings ends and immediately recommences.

The second pilgrim festival is Pesah, or Passover. One of the best known of Jewish festivals, it commences on the full moon of Nisan, following the March 21 equinox. In terms of agricultural significance, Passover is associated with the spring barley harvest. In terms of historical significance, it commemorates the most important event in Israel's past: the miraculous escape from Egypt.[34] The term *passover* actually refers to the moment when the angel of death passed over the homes of the Hebrew slaves during the final plague because they had marked their doorposts with the blood of a lamb.[35] Naturally, the key theme of the festival is liberation from all forms of slavery.

As with many Jewish festivals, food is given a special religious meaning. One of the key symbols is the use of unleavened bread (matzah) for the entire week. On the eve of the full moon, houses are emptied of all leaven (hametz) in a sort of spring-clean.[36] Matzah symbolizes the haste with which the Israelite slaves were forced to leave Egypt. Some also see in its flattened shape the rejection of "puffed up" vanity and pride. Unleavened bread is only one of the highly symbolic foodstuffs that are placed on the table during the evening Passover meal (seder). Each food type represents an aspect of the Exodus experience: either the harshness of slavery or the sweetness of the escape (see Chapter 7). As with most Jewish ceremonies, wine symbolizes the goodness of God, and four cups are drunk at Passover, while a fifth is kept in case Elijah appears unexpectedly. Dress is usually formal and in Ashkenazi families the head of the household wears the kittel, which also functions as a wedding gown, a burial shroud and a garment for Yom Kippur. Passover is essentially a family affair, celebrated with happiness and gratitude around the domestic table, during which the youngest child asks four ritual questions designed to explain the meaning of the Exodus. The Megillah for Passover services is the joyous Song of Songs.

The third pilgrim festival comes seven weeks after Passover and thus is suitably named Shavuot ("weeks"), or Pentecost ("fifty" in Greek). A one- or two-day festival in May or June, Shavuot celebrates the summer wheat harvest but it also commemorates the revelation of the Torah to Moses on Mount Sinai. Hence the key theme is the gift of knowledge and learning. There are no specific rituals such as the Passover meal, but it is customary to decorate homes and synagogues with flowers and plants, symbolizing the height of the harvest season. Dairy products such as cheesecakes and pancakes are commonly served, based on the belief that the first Israelite community had no time to prepare a kosher meat dish on the day the Torah was revealed and thus ate dairy foods to avoid breaking the law. The special scroll for Shavuot is the book of Ruth, possibly because of its agricultural setting. The period between Pesah and Shavuot is known as the Counting of the Omer (Sheaf), and many families use a special board for this purpose, based on the biblical commandment to count the days between the two harvests.[37] Jews also see it as a reminder that the Exodus was not complete until the Torah was given. Freedom needs to be complemented with truth and purpose. The 50-day interval from Passover to Shavuot is mirrored in the 50 days from Easter Sunday to Pentecost Sunday on the Christian calendar.

There are many other festivals scattered throughout the Jewish year, two of which deserve special mention. The feast of Purim occurs on the full moon of Adar in March. It is appropriate that the Megillah that is read is the book of Esther, for Purim commemorates the courage of the story's heroine who saves her people from destruction under the wicked Haman. Purim literally means "lots," and refers to the casting of lots to determine the date for the planned massacre.[38] The Megillah is proclaimed publicly at evening and morning services, evoking noisy banging and shouting from the congregation as the enemy's name is read out. Although Judaism does not condone intoxication, the rabbinic tradition encourages the celebratory drinking of alcohol at Purim until one can no longer distinguish the phrases "Cursed be Haman" and "Blessed be Mordecai" (Esther's uncle).[39] Masks and costumes add to the carefree, carnival-like atmosphere of Purim, which is reminiscent of Hindu Holi and Christian Mardi Gras.

While scholars have doubts as to the historicity of the Esther story, there is no uncertainty about the events behind the other prominent Jewish festival that celebrates victory over Israel's enemies. Hanukkah commences on the 25 Kislev (November–December) and commemorates the recapturing of the Temple in 165 BCE from Hellenistic overlords by a small group of Jewish freedom fighters.[40] The term *Hanukkah* literally means "rededication" and refers to the fact that the Jews had to purify their holiest shrine after it had been desecrated by pagan practices. The festival lasts for eight days in memory of the miracle of the oil. According to the Talmud, the only uncontaminated oil found in the Temple was a small cruse that should have been exhausted after one day but amazingly lasted eight days.[41] Thus, foods cooked in oil – such as potato pancakes, doughnuts and fritters – are popular at Hanukkah. Jews also play a game involving the spinning of a top (dreidel) with four Hebrew characters that stand for "a great miracle happened here." As in the Hindu Divali, the predominant symbol is light. In place of the usual seven-branched **menorah** (candelabra), a special eight-branched version, known as a hanukkiyah, is used (Figure 9.5). Each evening after sunset, an extra candle is lit, building up to eight by the end of the feast. Of course, the candle is lit before sunset on the Friday to avoid contravening the sabbath law. The Talmud encourages Jews to place their candles in doorways and windows to proclaim God's miraculous intervention.[42]

The Jewish year is also punctuated by the regular holy weekday known as Sabbath. The tradition is grounded in the creation story in the first chapter of Genesis, where God spends six days fashioning the cosmos and then rests on the seventh.[43] Sabbath commences at sunset on Friday when the woman of the house lights two candles. It is closed at the following sunset via the havdalah ritual, which involves prayers over a cup of wine, a box of spices and a multi-wick candle.[44] Sabbath is meant to be a time of greater spiritual activity and there are seven Torah readings at synagogue services, based on an annual cycle that recommences every Simhat Torah. But it is also about resting from work and Jews are required to observe a set of 39 prohibitions, which, when interpreted strictly, severely limit one's activities on the day (Box 9.3).

Figure 9.5 Eight-branched menorah (with central lighting candle) used at Hanukkah. (Reproduced with kind permission of iStock.)

Box 9.3 The 39 Prohibited Activities on the Jewish Sabbath

1) sowing
2) plowing
3) reaping
4) binding sheaves
5) threshing
6) winnowing
7) selecting
8) grinding
9) sifting
10) kneading
11) baking
12) shearing wool
13) washing wool
14) beating wool
15) dyeing wool
16) spinning
17) weaving
18) making two loops
19) weaving two threads
20) separating two threads
21) tying
22) untying
23) sewing two stitches
24) tearing
25) trapping
26) slaughtering
27) flaying
28) salting meat
29) curing hide
30) scraping hide
31) cutting hide up
32) writing two letters
33) erasing two letters
34) building
35) tearing down a building
36) extinguishing a fire
37) kindling a fire
38) hitting with a hammer
39) taking an object from a private to a public domain, or transporting an object in the public domain

The Jewish calendar reflects the vicissitudes of Israel's experience in a fascinating blend of joy and sorrow, pleasure and austerity, feasting and fasting. At one level its key feasts express gratitude for the God of nature who ensures the earth's fertility year after year via the harvests. At another level they also commemorate the saving intervention of the God of history at crucial moments in the past. As in Hinduism, Buddhism and Daoism, the cycles of the moon and the seasons are used as a natural background against which to celebrate holy days of particular significance. This is possible because all four religions combine the lunar month with the solar year. Christianity, in contrast, adopted the Roman solar calendar in which the months have no connection to the moon. Conversely, the religion of the crescent moon and the star embraced a purely lunar year and, thus, disconnected its festivals from the natural cycle of the seasons. Moreover, Islam's calendar is not primarily constructed around the life of the founder as in the case of Christianity and Buddhism. In contrast, its focal points lie elsewhere.

9.7 Lunar Year

In September 622 CE, the fledgling Muslim community emigrated from the town of Mecca to the town of Yathrib, some 250 miles to the north. After a decade of hostility and persecution, the epic relocation would bring security and consolidation. Yathrib was aptly renamed Al-Medina al-Nabi ("Town of the Prophet"), which was shortened to Medina. From this new base, Muhammad would prove to be not only an authoritative spokesman for God but also a successful leader of men. Later, when the caliph Umar decided to number the years according to a new Islamic calendar, it was that journey, known as the Hijra, that was chosen as Year One.[45] Hence, Islamic years are traditionally followed by AH (Anno Hegirae, or "in the year of the Hijra") in the same way as the Christian system uses AD (Anno Domini, or "in the year of the Lord").

However, when one considers that 2015 CE was 1435 AH, it becomes apparent that the difference between the two systems is currently 580 years and not the expected 622. The reason is that the Islamic year is shorter than the Western year by 11 days and, thus, is slowly catching up. This is because the Muslim calendar uses a lunar year or 12 lunar months, each lasting only 29 or 30 days (Table 9.6). The Qur'an unambiguously states that the new religious community is to avoid the Arabian and Jewish practice of inserting an intercalary month.[46] The consequence is that all annual Islamic festivals, which are set to lunar dates, drift through the seasons on a 33-year cycle.

The Islamic year begins on the first day of the month of Muharram but there is only limited religious significance attached to the date. In some cultures, cards are exchanged and the New Year is ushered in with thanksgiving and joy. However, for Shi'ite Muslims it is the beginning of 10 days of preparation for one of their most significant holy days. On the tenth day of Muharram, they commemorate the death of Muhammad's grandson, Hussain, at the Battle of Karbala in 680 CE.[47] Popularly known as Ashura (tenth), it is a day of intense sorrow, akin to Tisha B'Av for Jews and Good Friday for Christians. Men gather in public for ceremonial chest-beating known as matam (Figure 9.6). The climax of the event is a passion play re-enacting Hussain's death, much like the Christian Stations of the Cross. Emotions run high because Shi'ites consider Hussain to have been the rightful successor to the Prophet via his father, Ali.

Table 9.6 The Islamic calendar.

Month	Date	Holy day
Muharram	1 10	New Year Ashura
Safar		
Rabi' al-awwal	12 or 17	Birthday of Muhammad
Rabi' al-thani		
Jumada al-awwal		
Jumada al-thani		
Rajab	27	Night Journey
Sha'aban	15	Birthday of the Mahdi or Night of Forgiveness
Ramadan (month of fasting)	23 or 27	Night of Power
Shawwal	1–3	Id al-Fitr
Dhu al-Qi'dah		
Dhu al-Hijjah	10	Id al-Adha

Figure 9.6 Shi'ite Muslims beating their chests during Ashura. (Reproduced with kind permission of Alamy.)

In contrast, Ashura is when Sunnis commemorate the escape of the Hebrews from slavery. Some Sunnis also fast on this day in imitation of Muhammad who was inspired by the Jews of Medina keeping the fast of Yom Kippur, which is ten days after New Year.[48] However, the most important fast on the calendar is sawm – the fourth pillar of Islam. It is held during the ninth month, Ramadan, ostensibly because the first Qur'anic revelation occurred in that month, although the precise date is unknown.[49] Described by the Qur'an as Lailat al-Qadr ("Night of Power"),[50] it falls by tradition on an odd-numbered date toward the end of Ramadan. Sunnis commemorate it on Ramadan 27, while Shi'ites prefer Ramadan 23.

Among the six religions under consideration, there is no fasting regime as strict or as extensive as Ramadan. For the entire month, from dawn to dusk, Muslims abstain from all food, drink, smoking and sexual intercourse. The fact that Ramadan, like all events on the Islamic calendar, drifts through the seasons is often taken to be a sign of God's mercy because it will not always be in the long hot days of summer.[51] Those exempted from all, or part, of the demanding fast include children, the elderly, the sick, pregnant women, young mothers, menstruating women, soldiers in battle and travelers. There is a general expectation that if the condition is temporary, then the number of days lost should be made up at a later date, prior to the next Ramadan.

Given the rigors of the daily fast, the evening meal (iftar) and the pre-dawn meal (suhoor) carry special significance during Ramadan, and are often the occasion for community gathering. The physical act of fasting is accompanied by a range of spiritual activities that make Ramadan a particularly sacred time. Muslims not only give up eating and drinking during daylight hours, but they also endeavor to avoid other vices. The mastery of the stomach reflects a deeper mastery of the soul. Hence, Ramadan is also a time for extra prayer and reflection. Many Muslims attend tarawih at mosque each night, during which one-thirtieth of the Qur'an is read so that the entire holy book is completed by the end of the month. Devout believers make a special retreat, known as i'tikaf, by spending the last 10 days of Ramadan inside a mosque in prayerful reflection and study, "seeking" the Night of Power. Ramadan ends with Id al-Fitr (Feast of the Fast-Breaking), which occurs on the first three days of the subsequent month, Shawwal. Faith communities often gather for a common celebratory meal, with gifts for children and accompanied with the greeting "Id mubarak" ("Happy Feast").

The second Id occurs during the twelfth month of the year and is associated with the fifth pillar of Islam: the pilgrimage to Mecca (see Chapter 11). Id al-Adha (Feast of the Sacrifice) is celebrated not only by those present in Mecca at the time but by all Muslims worldwide. While Ramadan is grounded in the revelation of the Qur'an, the pilgrimage focuses on events in the life of Abraham, the father of monotheism. The feast itself, which falls on the tenth day of Dhu al-Hijjah, recalls Abraham's willingness to sacrifice his son out of obedience to the one God.[52] In Jewish, Christian and Islamic theological traditions, his decision is considered to be the outstanding paradigm of trusting faith. According to the story, God substituted a ram for the boy after the depth of Abraham's faith was proven. In commemoration, Muslims slaughter an animal for the main meal on the day of the feast. According to custom, one-third of the meat is for the family, one-third for neighbors and one-third for the poor.

It is noteworthy that neither of the two great Islamic festivals directly concerns the life of the Prophet per se, in contrast to Buddhism and Christianity where the birth and death of the founders constitute major holy days. It is as if the Islamic calendar deliberately downplays the importance of Muhammad for fear of idolatrous deification – a position consistent with the decision to date the Islamic year from the Hijra. Muhammad's birthday (Mawlid an-Nabi) is celebrated in a modest manner by Sunnis on Rabi al-awwal 12 and by Shi'ites on the 17th of the same month. However, the Wahhabi school of Saudi Arabia rejects the day altogether as a later medieval innovation. Tradition also holds that Muhammad died on his birthday but his death does not carry anything like the theological weight of Good Friday, Vesak or even Ashura. The priority given to Ramadan on the calendar suggests that it is not the life of the Prophet that is crucial but the revelation of the eternal truth of the Qur'an through him – more akin to the Buddha's Enlightenment, the Christian Epiphany and the Jewish Shavuot.

One important birthday that is commemorated by Shi'ite Muslims on the fifteenth of Sha'aban is that of the twelfth imam, Muhammad al-Mahdi (born 868 CE). In Islamic theology, the **Mahdi** is an eschatological figure who will appear at the end of time with the prophet Jesus and usher in a final age of justice and peace during which Islam will become the global religion. Twelver Shi'ites identify this future figure with the twelfth imam who is said to have disappeared at five years of age and is in "occultation" until the designated hour of his reappearance. Sunni Muslims accept the notion of a final Mahdi but do not identify him as the twelfth imam. Nevertheless, they celebrate mid-Sha'aban as Lailat al-Barah, or the Night of Forgiveness. It is believed that on this night God shakes the heavenly tree to determine who shall die in the coming year.[53] With one's immediate fate being determined on this night, believers seek divine forgiveness, in much the same way as Jews do during the days of awe when the heavenly books are temporarily open. The Night of Forgiveness is also a time when Muslims visit the graves of relatives and pray for the dead.

One outstanding event in Muhammad's life that is celebrated is his mystical Night Journey on the winged creature Buraq from Mecca to Jerusalem (Isra) and from there to heaven (Mi'raj). The journey is said to have occurred in 621 CE, just prior to the Hijra. The relevant verse in the Qur'an states: "Glory be to Him Who made His servant to go on a night from the Sacred Mosque to the remote mosque of which We have blessed the precincts, so that We may show to him some of Our signs."[54] On the night of Rajab 27, Muslims offer extra prayers in memory of the journey on which it is believed Muhammad received the command to pray the five daily prayers. Muslims mark the night with optional prayers and sometimes light up mosques and homes in celebration.

Just as Jews and Christians set aside Saturday and Sunday respectively as a holy day, Islam also has a regular weekday gathering of believers for spiritual purposes. Salat, the second pillar of Islam, involves a short series of official prayers that must be said by all adult Muslims at five designated times each day (Box 9.4). Salat may be prayed anywhere provided the person faces the qibla. However, men are required to attend mosque

Box 9.4 Salat Prayer Times

fajr (dawn)	From dawn to the first moment of sunrise
zuhr (midday)	After the sun has passed the zenith until mid-afternoon
asr (afternoon)	From mid-afternoon to sunset
maghrib (evening)	From sunset until dusk
isha (night)	From dusk to dawn

for the Friday noon prayers each week. The Friday tradition in Islam is not primarily a day of rest as in the case of the Jewish Sabbath. The main reason is to ensure that believers receive a weekly sermon to nourish their faith and understanding, reminding them that their religion is both personal and communal.

Summary

Each major religion sanctifies the year in its own distinctive way with a unique mixture of seasons, feasts and fasts. No two religious calendars look the same and there is considerable variation within each tradition as well. However, there are also important connections and parallels worthy of note. In terms of basic structure, five of the six religions use the lunar month. The consequence is that many major religious festivals are held on a new moon or a full moon, with its consequent natural symbolism. Christianity is the exception with its purely solar year, but the dating of its great feast of Easter is still linked to the timing of the full moon of the Jewish Passover. Hinduism, Buddhism, Daoism and Judaism maintain a basic synchronicity with the sun by occasionally inserting an extra month, but Islam stands alone among the religions with its shorter lunar year and the result that its holy days drift through the seasons.

It is probably not surprising to find that the key to the Buddhist and Christian calendars is the founder. Significant events in the life of the Buddha and the Christ constitute the major festivals in both traditions, reflecting the elevated status that each founder holds in their respective faiths. The entire Christian calendar hinges on two focal points that celebrate the birth and the death–resurrection of Jesus, while the most important festivals in Buddhism celebrate the Buddha's birth, Enlightenment, First Sermon and death. Moreover, the year number in both systems is based on the founder's birth or death. One might expect a parallel pattern in Islam but there is a noticeable moderation in the way the Muslim calendar commemorates its founder, grounded in the conviction that Muhammad was the greatest of the prophets but not a divine incarnation. Daoism does not count time from the life of its quasi-founder, Laozi, instead adopting the Chinese custom of starting with the founder of Chinese culture: the legendary Yellow Emperor. There has always been some ambiguity as to the "founder" of Judaism and, thus, the focus of its calendar is the story of Israel itself as God's covenantal partner. Similarly, that Hinduism also has no single historical founder is reflected in its calendar which features the births and outstanding achievements of its pantheon of deities and their incarnations. Significantly it counts the years from the death of Krishna, the eighth avatar of Vishnu.

If the Islamic calendar avoids placing the Prophet in the spotlight, what it does focus on is the eternal truth of monotheism. Thus, the main motif of the pilgrimage month and its climactic Feast of the Sacrifice is the faith of Abraham. Similarly, the month of Ramadan, with its mysterious Night of Power, commemorates the first revelation of the Qur'an to Muhammad. The celebration of transcendent truth made manifest in time is celebrated in other traditions such as the Christian Epiphany, the Jewish Shavuot, and the Buddhist Vesak and Asalha Puja. Of course, there are many similar themes that can be traced across the six calendars. For example, the foundation of the believing community itself is a key theme in Jewish Passover, Christian Pentecost, Buddhist Asalha Puja and the Islamic Hijra, which functions as the basis for the numbering of Islamic years. Another example is the theme of victory over evil that is a central aspect of Hindu Dussehra, Christian Easter and the Jewish feasts of Passover, Hanukkah and Purim. A third example is the special day or period set aside to pay respects to and to assist the dead such as the Hindu Ancestors' Fortnight, the Buddhist and Daoist Festivals of the Hungry Ghosts, the Daoist Tomb Sweeping Day, Christian All Souls' Day and Pentecost Eve, and Islamic mid-Sha'aban. There are even moments during the year when the tradition appears to acknowledge the need for psychological release from the constraints of the faith and followers are allowed, or even encouraged, to indulge themselves such as on Hindu Holi, Jewish Purim and Christian Mardi Gras.

The consecration of the year is not only about joyous celebration of divine truth, protection and blessing. There are also times when the mood is more somber and austere, reflecting the need for self-denial, penitence and spiritual replenishment. In their own individual ways, each of the six religions caters for this dimension of the religious experience. In Buddhism, the naturally restrictive impact of the wet season has given rise to the rains retreat when monks intensify their study and meditation, and the laity become monks, albeit temporarily. The same connection with the annual monsoons is seen in the Hindu idea of Vishnu's Sleep, during which more extensive fasting is undertaken and weddings are avoided. Similarly, Shaivite Hindus dedicate the Great Night of Shiva to rigorous fasting and prayer. In Daoism, fasting or abstaining from meat often occurs on key days during each lunar month. Weddings, parties and other social celebrations are taboo for Jews during the 50 days of the Counting of the Omer and the three weeks between the fast days of Tamuz and Av. However, the main Jewish period for penance and self-examination is the Ten Days of Awe at the very start of the Jewish year, culminating in Yom Kippur. Abstinence and penance are also the main features of Christian Lent, which is based on Jesus's own 40-day fast in the wilderness and which is fundamentally a preparation for the Easter festival. Arguably, the most demanding form of austerity and self-control for the ordinary believer is the Islamic month-long dawn-to-dusk fast of Ramadan.

The regular rhythm of the holy day and the annual cycle of the great feasts and fasts constitute a rich elaborate tapestry in which religious belief is symbolically and profoundly expressed. The ordinary units of day, week, month, season and year are all taken up and transformed into a vast temporal framework in which faith is lived out. Time itself is consecrated and given transcendent meaning. However, human existence is not only temporal; it is also set within a three-dimensional world. Consequently, the sanctification of time is complemented by the sanctification of space. Religions not only have their sacred moments but also their sacred places and sacred journeys.

Discussion Topics

1. Compare the various understandings of the creation of the world and time.
2. Compare how each religion sets aside time to commemorate and help the dead.
3. How do Buddhist, Christian and Muslim calendars commemorate the life of their founders?
4. Identify common features between the sacred periods Ramadan, Lent, Vassa and the Ten Days of Awe.
5. How do feasts like Holi, Mardi Gras and Purim involve the relaxation of laws?

6 How is the theme of light used in festivals such as Divali, the Lantern Festival, Hanukkah and Easter?
7 Which religious festivals celebrate fertility of the land?
8 Identify other themes that can be traced across the religious calendars.

Notes

1 Christian churches that stress the imminent nature of Christ's second coming are often described as "Adventist" churches.
2 The Julian calendar was slightly too long, causing the equinox to drift slowly backwards. The solution was to remove three leap years every 400 years on the century year. Thus 1700, 1800 and 1900 were not leap years but 2000 was. Ten days were also removed from the calendar from October 4 to 15, 1582, although Britain and its colonies did not accept the revision until 1752. Today the difference between the Gregorian and Julian calendars is 13 days.
3 The date of December 25 first appears in the third century CE and may be a consequence of the belief among some Christians that Jesus was conceived and died on the same date, 25 March. One of the earliest references to December 25 as Jesus's birthday is Sextus Julius Africanus in his *Chronographiai* (c.221 CE). The third-century Christian writer Origen condemned the idea of celebrating Christ's birthday on the basis that such a practice was only appropriate for human kings.
4 The link with the winter solstice is also evident in Germanic culture where Yuletide denotes the shortest day or the lowest point of the wheel (yule). Christmas symbols such as mistletoe, holly and ivy originate here.
5 The Anglo-Saxon chronicler Bede used the Anno Domini system in his *Ecclesiastical History of the English People* (731 CE) which was subsequently adopted by Alcuin during the ninth-century Carolingian renaissance under Charlemagne.
6 Ironically, scholars point out that Dionysius made a small error in his calculations and it is likely that Jesus of Nazareth was actually born in the year 5 or 6 BCE.
7 See Matthew 2:1–12.
8 Leviticus 12:2–8. The feast is also called the Presentation of the Lord in the Temple (see Luke 2:22–39).
9 Mark 1:12–13; Matthew 4:1–11; Luke 4:1–13.
10 Another name for this time is Carnival, which literally means "farewell to meat."
11 The Passover moon is the first full moon following the vernal equinox (taken as March 21). Thus, Easter Sunday can fall anywhere between late March and late April.
12 John 1:3–5; Colossians 1:16.
13 Songkran is derived from the Hindu term *sankranti* – the movement of the sun from one zodiacal constellation to the next.
14 In Japanese Buddhism, the Buddha's birth is celebrated on April 8, his Enlightenment on December 8, and his passing into nirvana on February 15.
15 Khandhaka, Mahavagga 3.5.4ff.
16 Samyutta Nikaya 16.13.
17 The month is added when two new moons occur while the sun is in the same zodiacal constellation.

18 The same action is performed with images of Ganesha on his birthday – the fourth day of the bright fortnight of Bhadra.
19 Scholars think that the 12-year cycle was probably derived from the planet Jupiter, which takes 12 years to orbit the sun and, thus, spends approximately one year in each zodiacal constellation.
20 This is called an intercalary month and it needs to be added 7 times out of 19 years.
21 Technically, the solar terms change when the sun moves 15 degrees along the ecliptic (the path of the sun in the sky that passes through the zodiacal constellations).
22 At this point the sun is at 315 degrees longitude on the ecliptic.
23 See Komjathy, 202.
24 The filling can include egg, beans, fruits, walnuts, dates, sweet potato, mushrooms and meat.
25 Some Jews consider the days of awe to include the 30 days of the previous month, Elul. These 40 days correspond to the time Moses spent on Mount Sinai before descending with the Decalogue (see Exodus 34:27–8).
26 Micah 7:19.
27 Leviticus 23:32. See Talmud Yoma for laws pertaining to Yom Kippur.
28 Leviticus 16:5–22.
29 Tishri 3 (the assassination of Gedaliah, governor of Israel, during the Babylonian invasion); Tevet 10 (the beginning of the siege of Jerusalem by the Babylonians); Adar 13 (the fast of Esther); Tamuz 17 (the breaching of the city walls by the Romans).
30 Leviticus 23:42–3.
31 For details see Talmud Sukkah 1a.
32 In the Kabbalist tradition, an invisible guest visits the booth on each evening: Abraham, Isaac, Jacob, Joseph, Moses, Aaron and David.
33 Leviticus 23:40.
34 Exodus 14:10–31.
35 Exodus 12:21–7.
36 Exodus 12:15–20. This is also called the hametz hunt.
37 Leviticus 23:15–16. Jews refrain from weddings, parties, dances and haircuts except on the thirty-third day (Lag B'Omer), when an ancient plague lifted. A similar period of restriction is observed between the two fast days of Tamuz 17 and Ab 9, around July each year.
38 Esther 3:7.
39 Talmud Megillah 7b.
40 1 Maccabees 4:56.
41 Talmud Shabbat 21b. According to 2 Maccabees, the eight days of celebrations were based on the fact that Sukkoth lasts for eight days.
42 Talmud Shabbat 23b.
43 Genesis 2:1–3.
44 The wine symbolises joy, the spices ease the pain of another Sabbath ending, and the candle symbolises the return to work.
45 The Hijra is celebrated annually on 8 Rabi' al-awwal.
46 Qur'an 9:36–7.
47 Karbala is located about 60 miles southwest of Baghdad in present-day Iraq.
48 Sahih Bukhari 3.31.222.
49 Qur'an 2:185.
50 Qur'an 97:1–5.

51 The word Ramadan is derived from the Arabic term for "scorching heat."
52 The Jewish and Christian traditions identify the boy as Isaac, Abraham's son by his wife, Sarah. However, Islamic tradition understands him to be Ishmael, Abraham's older son by his slave-girl (and wife) Hagar.
53 The tree mentioned in Qur'an 53:14 is considered to be the boundary of the seventh heaven, beyond which no creature can pass. The names of all living individuals are said to be written on its leaves.
54 Qur'an 17:1.

Further Reading

Cohn-Sherbok, Dan (2003). *Judaism: History, Belief and Practice.* London: Routledge, pp. 474–82; 507–32.

De Lange, Nicholas (2000). *Introduction to Judaism.* Cambridge: Cambridge University Press, pp. 91–104; 127–142.

Goitein, S. D. (2006). "Ramadan, the Muslim Month of Fasting" in G. R. Hawting (ed.). *The Development of Islamic Ritual.* Aldershot: Ashgate, ch. 9.

Gordon, Matthew S. (2002). *Understanding Islam.* London: Duncan Baird, pp. 80–9.

Hickman, Hoyt, et al. (1992). *The New Handbook of the Christian Year.* Nashville, TN: Abingdon Press.

Knott, Kim (2000). *Hinduism: A Very Short Introduction.* Oxford: Oxford University Press, pp. 56–63.

Lazarus-Yafeh, Hava (2006). "Muslim Festivals," in G. R. Hawting (ed.). *The Development of Islamic Ritual.* Aldershot: Ashgate, ch. 17.

McGrath, Alister E. (2015). *An Introduction to Christianity.* 3rd ed. Oxford: Blackwell, pp. 236–50.

Michaels, Axel (2003). *Hinduism: Past and Present.* Princeton, NJ: Princeton University Press, pp. 295–314.

Schauss, Hayyim (1996). *The Jewish Festivals: A Guide to their History and Observance.* New York: Schocken.

Segler, Franklin M., & Bradley, Randall (2006). *Christian Worship: Its Theology and Practice.* 3rd ed. Nashville, TN: B & H Publishing Group, pp. 219–34.

Solomon, Norman (1996). *Judaism: A Very Short Introduction.* New York: Oxford University Press, ch. 4.

White, James F. (2001). *Introduction to Christian Worship.* 3rd ed. Nashville, TN: Abingdon Press, ch. 2.

Wong, Eva (2011). *Taoism. An Essential Guide.* London: Shambhal, pp. 131–3.

10

Building

CONTENTS

10.1 Introduction

Religion not only casts a transcendent light on time but it also sanctifies the three-dimensional space that characterizes our world. Although most religions believe that the Absolute is ubiquitous, they also identify particular places where it can be more tangibly and powerfully experienced. In Chapters 10 and 11 we shall explore two ways in which ordinary space is given extraordinary meaning: via religious buildings and sacred journeys. This chapter will focus on the physical edifices that serve as places of communal prayer and devotion. What is the religious building of each major faith? What primary and secondary functions does it serve? What are its salient architectural features? What religious beliefs are expressed by the details of its exterior and interior design?

10.2 Mosque

Soon after Muhammad arrived in Medina in 622 CE, the year of the Hijra, he built a residence for himself and his two wives, Sawda and Aisha. According to one tradition, he chose the very place where his camel stopped after the long and perilous journey, purchasing the plot from two local orphans. It was a modest four-sided construction made of mud bricks, with his private chambers at the eastern end of a large courtyard.[1] For the next 10 years, until his death in 632 CE, the building functioned not only as his private domicile but also as a place to settle disputes, receive official visitors, delegate administrative tasks, distribute aid, attend the sick, plan military action, preach and lead community prayer. It was the political and religious center of the new faith and it came to be known as the Masjid al-Nabawi (Mosque of the Prophet).[2] Today, it is considered the second holiest place in Islam, containing the tombs of Muhammad and the first two caliphs, Abu Bakr and Umar.

Despite its early origins, the Masjid al-Nabawi is not considered to be the first Islamic mosque. That honor is usually bestowed upon the Quba mosque located just outside Medina. It is said that Muhammad laid its foundation stones as he approached the town during the last stage of the Hijra.[3] Alternatively, some prefer to think of the Ka'bah in

Mecca as the first mosque in the sense that Muhammad and his followers prayed there during the years prior to the Hijra.[3] The Qur'an records how, at one stage, local authorities prohibited the young community from the area around the Ka'bah, thus forcing them to recite their prayers in private homes or even in the streets of the town.[4] After Muhammad's triumphant return to Mecca in 630 CE, the Ka'bah was converted into an Islamic symbol. Today it stands in the center of the magnificent Masjid al-Haram (The Sacred Mosque), which is Islam's holiest site, the universal focus of daily prayer and the destination of the annual pilgrimage.[5]

Of the three buildings, it was the Masjid al-Nabawi that became the model for all subsequent Islamic places of worship due to its key role in the early community during the crucial years of consolidation in Medina. As was the case with the prophet's mosque-residence, mosques today can still have a range of different purposes, both secular and sacred. A mosque and its surrounding complex can serve as a function hall, library, classroom, kitchen, infirmary, bazaar and place of temporary lodging. But its primary purpose is reflected in the Arabic term from which the English word mosque is derived. A *masjid* literally means "a place of prostration." [6] In other words, a mosque is first and foremost a venue for communal prayer – a sacred space in which the religious community physically comes together in official worship.[7] Although the five daily prayers may be recited alone and in any place, men are obliged to pray in a mosque at Friday noon as a reminder of the public and collective aspect of religion. On this point, the hadith suggests that, although not mandatory, it is many times more meritorious to pray salat in the company of others.[8]

From the beginning, the mosque has been a vital aspect of Islamic practice and a natural means of expressing religious belief in architectural form. As with many religions, the shape and design of Islam's holy building varies considerably depending on the period and the culture. Yet it is possible to identify the main features of a typical mosque and to explore what these tell us about the ways in which Islam sanctifies space.

The exterior of major mosques is often characterized by a number of important features, in particular the dome, the minaret and the place of ablutions. The earliest mosques, such as the Masjid al-Nabawi in Medina, were typically flat-roofed, rectangular buildings with a covered area for prayer and an enclosed courtyard. However, since the Ottoman era, mosques generally have had a domed roof above the main prayer hall, which has subsequently become a trademark feature.[9] Although an external feature, the effect of the dome is really felt inside the building because it represents the vault of the sky, reminding the worshiper of the splendor of the creator, who reigns over the heavens and the earth.

The second visible external feature of a mosque is the tall, graceful tower known as a minaret (Figure 10.1). Appearing for the first time during the **Umayyad** period (seventh century CE), the minaret was probably an adaptation of the spire on Christian churches that had been converted into mosques. Functionally, the minaret was the place from which the muezzin chanted the call to prayer five times per day. Prior to the introduction of the minaret, the call was proclaimed from nearby rooftops but the height of the minaret naturally facilitated the audibility of the summons. Even today, the call is usually broadcast via loudspeakers set high on the minaret. Larger mosques usually have more than one minaret, reflecting their importance and prestige.[9] Quite often a crescent moon and star adorn the very top of the dome or minaret. The image is recognized universally as a symbol of Islam and appears in many settings including the national

Figure 10.1 A mosque with two minarets in Azerbaijan.
(Reproduced with kind permission of iStock.)

flags of predominantly Muslim countries such as Algeria, Tunisia, Libya, Turkey, Azerbaijan, Pakistan and Malaysia. In fact, the crescent and star is only a relatively recent badge of Islamic identity. It was originally the symbol of Constantinople and was adopted throughout the Ottoman Empire after the Muslim conquest of that city in 1453 CE.[10]

The third important exterior feature is the taps and wells for the ablutions that are necessary before daily prayer. If the worshiper is in a minor state of impurity, they must perform wudu, which comprises washing the face, arms, hands and feet. Such a state is brought about by falling asleep, breaking wind, going to the toilet or touching the skin of a person of the opposite gender who is of marriageable age. In the case of major impurity, which results from sexual intercourse or ejaculation, a full bath (ghusl) is required. Sometimes larger mosque complexes provide facilities for this purpose. Apart from the actual ablutions, the theme of cleanliness and purity applies in other ways to the mosque. For example, shoes should be removed before entering a mosque. Purity is also the reason for the argument that women should refrain from spending time in a mosque during their menstrual period.[11]

The interior of a mosque is characterized by a striking lack of furniture. A mosque is essentially a prayer hall, and even the largest structures are devoid of any seating (unlike Jewish synagogues and Christian churches). Such uncluttered space facilitates the performance of Islamic prayer, which involves a series of bodily movements including prostration – the etymological basis for the term masjid, as we saw earlier. Instead of benches and pews, the floor of the mosque is usually covered with carpets to ensure that the ground on which the official prayers are uttered is clean. Many Muslims use their own private prayer mat when reciting salat outside of a mosque, as Muhammad himself did.[12] Another striking feature of mosques is the lack of statues, paintings and icons of any sort. As was noted in Chapter 1, Islam considers any attempt to depict Allah in a finite worldly manner as idolatry, the greatest of all sins. Thus, it vigorously opposes sacred images. In the majority of Islamic schools, the ban extends not only to Muhammad and other prophets, but also to all human and animal figures, since such "creations" are seen as usurping the role of the Creator.[13] Instead, the walls and ceilings of mosques are often adorned with more abstract designs such as geometric shapes or the images of plants. Calligraphy is also a popular means of decorating mosques, especially as the flowing Arabic script lends itself to decoration. Thus, the names of Allah and Muhammad, as well as verses from the Qur'an, are used to enhance the aesthetic dimension of worship and to reinforce the religious nature of the space.

From the time of Muhammad, the believer has been obliged to face in a particular direction, known as the qibla, when reciting the five daily prayers. The original qibla was Jerusalem but soon after Muhammad arrived in Medina it was changed to the Ka'bah. Muslims may recite their prayers anywhere (except for men at Friday noon) but they must ensure that they are physically orientated toward the holiest point on earth in a global symbol of religious community. This fundamental aspect of official prayer is reflected in the most important internal feature of the mosque – the mihrab. The mihrab is a niche in the wall that faces Mecca (aptly known as the qibla wall). It is usually designed in the shape of an archway and is often highly decorated to emphasize its role as the focal point for prayer.

The other important interior feature is the *minbar* – a term derived from the Arabic word for "high." The minbar is essentially the equivalent of a Christian pulpit from which a sermon is delivered to the congregation. Muhammad himself used to preach standing on a three-stepped platform at the end of the Masjid al-Nabawi so that he might be easily visible.[14] The minbar became a standard feature of all mosques and is usually located against the qibla wall near the mihrab. It is often richly adorned and shaped like a small tower with stairs, highlighting the importance of the spoken word in Islamic worship. The limitation of the visual image places greater weight on verbal expression – prayers recited from the mosque floor and faith preached from the elevated minbar.

Most mosques also have a separate space reserved for women. It may be defined by a partition, railing or even a separate room adjacent to the prayer hall. While women are not barred from attending mosque prayers, they are not under the same obligation as men to attend at Friday noon.[15] Thus, men usually outnumber women at communal prayers. Moreover, the law requires that women stand behind men during salat for modesty's sake because official prayer involves bowing and prostrating. With regard to access, the Qur'an implies that the mosque is not an appropriate place for "idolaters" but most Islamic law schools allow non-Muslims to enter mosques.[16]

From the humble house of the Prophet in Medina to the stupendous wonders of Islamic architecture, the "place of prostration" has been the sacred space within Islam where communal prayer is offered, wisdom imparted, and faith expressed by the design and contents of the building itself. The ban on idolatrous images, the emphasis on the word symbolized by the minbar, the segregation of the sexes and the importance of the physical direction of prayer are all salient features of the Islamic mosque but they are also characteristic of sacred space within Judaism.

10.3 Synagogue

In the year 586 BCE, the army of Nebuchadnezzar conquered the city of Jerusalem, destroyed the Temple and forced its king, its aristocracy, and a great number of other citizens into exile in Babylon.[17] The Temple had been constructed by King Solomon 400 years earlier and was the heart and soul of Israelite religious life. Faced with the prospect of existence without temple, priesthood or sacrificial system, the exiled Jews began to create an alternative forum for worship in private homes where believers would come together to read the holy texts, listen to sermons and pray as a community.[18] After the return to Israel in 537 BCE, and despite the rebuilding of the Temple in Jerusalem thereafter, the tradition developed into one of the most important of all Jewish institutions: the synagogue. For many, it was the more "portable" form of synagogue-based Judaism that enabled the faith to survive the destruction of the Second Temple by the Romans in 70 CE and the subsequent dispersal of the Jewish people throughout the empire and beyond. In time, the synagogue became the sacred space where communal, intellectual and religious life was grounded.

The word synagogue is derived from the Greek for "gathering," but there are other terms used for the Jewish place of communal worship. The Hebrew *beit k'nesset* ("house of assembly") conveys the same notion of a place where believers come together for a common purpose. As in Islam, a synagogue complex can be a venue for a range of cultural–religious events such as circumcisions, bar mitzvahs and weddings, as well as social welfare or organizational meetings. The Yiddish term *schul*, commonly used among Orthodox Jews, and the alternative Hebrew term *beit ha-midrash* ("house of study"), both reflect the role of the synagogue in Jewish education. Often a synagogue will have a library and some classrooms where religious lessons for adults and children are conducted. A more debated word is "Temple," which reflects different views among the Jewish community regarding the ongoing role of the Jerusalem Temple. For Reform Jews, who use "Temple" to refer to their local synagogue, the period of the Jerusalem Temple with its priesthood and sacrifices has passed. However, for Orthodox Jews, who hope that the Jerusalem Temple will one day be rebuilt, it is an inappropriate term for one's local synagogue.

Even more than Islam, Judaism is a congregational religion that expects its adherents to express their faith not only as individuals but also as members of a community. Certain prayers are ideally said at specified times in the company of fellow believers, and the traditional quorum (**minyan**) required for certain official prayers is 10 adult men. Most synagogues hold prayer services on a regular thrice-daily basis: evening, morning and afternoon. So what are the key physical features of a synagogue and how do they reflect elements of the Jewish faith?

The external appearance of synagogues varies considerably from culture to culture. In times past, Judaism's minority position in Christian or Islamic society was evident in that synagogues were often deliberately designed to be inconspicuous. It was forbidden that a synagogue be taller or more splendid in appearance than neighboring churches or mosques. After the Enlightenment, Western synagogues tended to become grander and more attractive as Jews emerged from the ghetto and found confidence to express their faith architecturally in the public sphere. Classical styles were often chosen and adapted. However, unlike the mosque with its dome and minaret, synagogues are not possessed of specific universally distinctive external features. The unique identifying elements tend to be found inside the sacred space.

In contrast to mosques, synagogues tend to be fully furnished, with seating for the congregation whose bodily movements during services involve sitting, standing and bowing. In some synagogues, special boxes are located beneath seats where members may store their prayer shawls and books because Jewish law restricts what may be carried on a sabbath. As in mosques, the direction in which the congregation is orientated during communal prayer is highly pertinent. In the case of Judaism, the synagogue itself and the congregation gathered within it both face toward Jerusalem. When a synagogue is not able to be orientated in this direction for some reason, the congregation will turn toward Jerusalem at certain moments such as during the recitation of the Amidah.[19]

Similarly, just as the mihrab marks the qibla inside the mosque, the most important item in a Jewish synagogue is the **aron ha kodesh** ("holy ark"), which is usually located on the wall pointing in the direction of Jerusalem.[20] As the name suggests, the holy ark is a sacred cabinet that holds the Torah scrolls (Figure 10.2). It is either set into or mounted on the wall, and covered by a thick curtain known as the parokhet, reminiscent of the curtain in the Temple sanctuary that screened the Holy of Holies.[21] The congregation normally stands whenever the doors of the ark are opened and a Torah scroll is brought out for the readings. It is considered an honor to be the one chosen to open or close the ark doors and curtain. The ark is usually the most lavishly adorned object in the synagogue, reflecting the precious nature of its contents. Sometimes it is embellished with an appropriate image, such as the Star of David or an apt Hebrew phrase such as "Know before whom you stand." Nearby, the ner tamid ("eternal flame") burns constantly, indicating the ongoing presence of God in this sacred space.[22] The ner tamid may be a specially designed electric light or a more traditional oil lamp, but it reminds Jews of the altar of incense that burned day and night in the Temple. As a source of light in a holy place, the ner tamid is often compared to the golden seven-branched candelabrum, or menorah, that stood in the sanctuary of the Temple. Tradition suggests that the shape of the menorah symbolizes the burning bush from which God first called Moses to his prophetic mission. The menorah has become one of the most widely recognized symbols of Judaism and features prominently in Jewish art and decoration.

A central feature of a Jewish worship service is a series of readings from the holy texts through which it is believed God still addresses his people. On Monday and Thursday mornings and on Saturday mornings and afternoons, the Torah scrolls are removed from the ark and respectfully carried in procession to a lectern on a raised platform

Figure 10.2 Torah scrolls inside the holy ark in a synagogue. (Reproduced with kind permission of iStock.)

known as the bimah.[23] The location and orientation of the bimah varies within Judaism. The traditional approach, still used by Orthodox Jews, is to place the bimah in the very center of the synagogue facing the ark. Symbolically, this arrangement recaptures the moment when the people of Israel stood around Mount Sinai while the Torah was revealed to Moses. In contrast, nineteenth-century Reform Judaism shifted the position of the bimah to the front of the synagogue, directly before the ark and facing the congregation. The physical change resulted in a synagogue layout that resembled the plan of Christian churches and that reflected Reform Judaism's desire to assimilate itself into, rather than differentiate itself from, surrounding society. Similarly, Reform synagogues also introduced the use of organ music, choirs and vestments for prayer leaders.

The other important architectural innovation introduced by the Reform movement was the removal of the mehitza, the dividing barrier between the male and female seating areas. As in Islam, gender segregation during worship is still considered important in Orthodox Judaism in order to avoid distractions and focus the mind on spiritual matters. The mehitza may take the form of a curtain or a lattice. Alternatively, it can be a designated seating section at the side or back of the synagogue, or even an upstairs balcony. Despite these differences, Orthodox and Reform synagogues both share one characteristic that is also typical of mosques: the noticeable absence of any attempt to depict the deity in the form of a statue or icon. Three-dimensional sculptures of living creatures are also considered to constitute a form of idolatry and, thus, are banned. However, synagogues are not without aesthetic quality and many are beautifully decorated with symbolic imagery such as the Star of David, the menorah, the Tablets of the Law and apposite quotes from the Hebrew scriptures.

The architectural changes brought about by Reform Judaism already hint at a certain basic similarity between the Jewish synagogue and the Christian church. In so far as both religions stress congregational worship, their respective places of gathering naturally play an important role in the practice of the faith. On the one hand, the centrality of an elevated place from which the holy text is read to the listening congregation and the avoidance of idolatrous images resonate strongly with Protestant Christian practice. On the other hand, the central focus on the receptacle of a sacred object and the use of a lamp to mark the divine presence have similarities with Catholic and Orthodox places of worship.

10.4 Church

The contemporary English word church is a derivation from the Old English *cirice*, which in turn was based on the Greek *kyriakon* ("of the Lord"). It reflects the notion that the building, in which believers gather to worship, belongs to God. It is sacred Christian space. Of course, the first Christians were originally Jews and there are ample references in the New Testament to prayers that were held in both the Jerusalem Temple and synagogues throughout Israel and Asia Minor.[24] However, as Christianity gradually drew away from its mother religion, Christians began to worship in their own private dwellings.[25] By the second century CE, they were constructing their own edifices specifically designed for public congregational prayer.

As with the Islamic mosque and the Jewish synagogue, the history of church architecture is long and varied. In Western Christianity, styles range from the early basilicas,[26] which were adaptations of Roman public buildings, through the classical forms of Romanesque, Gothic and Baroque to more modern styles (Figure 10.3). Despite the enormous variety, it is possible to identify some of the enduring salient features of a church, which reflect key aspects of Christian belief and practice.

Two of the most common external features on a church, and those which set it apart as a religious building, are the steeple and spire. The steeple was originally adapted from military watch-towers and incorporated into church design as a bell-tower. As noted earlier, it was probably the historical inspiration for the Islamic minaret. Like its Islamic equivalent, the steeple traditionally served as the point from which the call to prayer was broadcast via the ringing of the church bells. The spire is a conically pointed structure erected either as a continuation of the steeple or in its place. The term comes from the Anglo-Saxon for "spear," giving the impression of strength, but also suggestive of prayer rising inexorably upwards.

Like the crescent moon and star on mosques, a cross – the unambiguous badge of Christianity – is usually placed at the very highest point of the spire, as well as on many other parts of the building. Moreover, in many traditional churches, the building itself has a cruciform shape. In this scheme, the main axis consists of the nave and sanctuary while the shorter axis comprises the two transepts. Sometimes a dome was constructed directly over the intersection point, under which the main altar was located. As in Islam, the dome depicts the heavens over which the creator rules and under which believers worship. In classical Christian architecture, the entire structure ideally faced east, toward the rising sun, as a statement of faith in Jesus's resurrection, although in practice many churches are not orientated in any particular direction.

Figure 10.3 Notre Dame Cathedral, Paris.
(Reproduced with kind permission of iStock.)

The interior of a church is designed fundamentally to provide space for the congregation at prayer. As in Jewish synagogues, Christian churches usually have seating that is orientated toward the focal point of the building. However, the physical focal point varies across denominations, reflecting a different liturgical emphasis. In traditions that stress the importance of the Eucharistic meal, like Orthodox, Catholic, and some Anglican churches, the architectural focus is on the altar (or table). The altar is often covered with a special cloth and adorned with candles and flowers to highlight its central role. The area around the altar/table is considered particularly holy and is known as the sanctuary or chancel. Usually, access to the sanctuary during a service is restricted to the clergy and those with special roles. The sanctuary is often slightly elevated with steps and delineated by a low railing. In Orthodox churches, the boundary is marked by the iconostasis, a tall, highly decorated stand across the church on which icons of Christ and the saints are hung.[27]

Churches that prefer the term "altar" stress the idea that the communion ritual is essentially a memorial of Christ's sacrificial death, which brings salvation to the world. The theme of sacrifice is also discernible in the Catholic practice of placing the relic of a saint in the altar-stone itself. Similarly in Orthodox churches, the bread and wine are placed on a small piece of cloth known as the antimension, which is decorated with motifs of Christ's burial and in which a relic is sewn. In contrast, churches that prefer the term "table" place more emphasis on the Eucharist as a communion meal modeled on Jesus's Last Supper.

In most churches, the altar is separate from the wall so that the priest or minister stands behind it, facing the congregation. However, in pre-Vatican II Catholic churches, the altar was set against the back wall, which meant that the priest faced the same way as the worshipers during the most sacred parts of the service, as in Islam. The decision by the Second Vatican Council in 1965 to move the altar away from the wall and reverse the direction of the priest's orientation was similar to the Reform Jewish initiative to move the bimah to the front of the synagogue so that it faced the people. In both cases, the change in physical configuration reflected a radical rethinking of the theology of worship and divine presence. In one system, the leader and the congregation face outwards together, toward a transcendent deity beyond the group. In the other, the leader and congregation face each other, forming a closed circle in which an immanent deity resides.

The other distinctive architectural feature associated with the sanctuary is the receptacle for the sacred bread that is reserved for the sick. Its common designation *tabernacle* comes from the Latin word for "tent," which draws on the image of the Tent of Dwelling used by the Israelites to house the Ark of the Covenant during their wanderings in the Sinai wilderness. In Orthodox churches, the tabernacle is usually located on the altar, whereas in the Catholic tradition it is placed in a separate part of the sanctuary or even in its own chapel. In a similar manner to the Jewish ner tamid, a lamp burning near the tabernacle indicates that there is consecrated bread inside.[28]

Thus far, the internal features described have been linked to the central act of blessing the bread and wine at the altar or communion table, and distributing them to the congregation for consumption. However, the first part of the Christian Eucharist involves a figurative feeding of the people via the word of God. In all Christian churches, scriptural readings and an accompanying sermon are considered essential nourishment for the spiritually hungry. Analogous to the Islamic minbar and the Jewish bimah, the Christian *pulpit* ("elevated platform" in Latin) is the point from which the spiritual leader proclaims the holy writings and their interpretation. In churches that emphasize the communion meal – such as Orthodox, Catholic and Anglican denominations – the pulpit is usually located on the left side of the sanctuary as seen by the congregation. In Protestant churches, which give priority to the proclaimed word over sacramental ritual, the pulpit is aptly located in a prominent central position with the communion table, if there is one, less conspicuous. Pulpits can vary from simple stands to highly ornate structures with staircase and canopy.

The contrast between altar-centered and pulpit-centered churches flows over into the question of images. In general, Orthodox and Catholic churches are characterized by a liberal use of statues, paintings and icons, which can be found on any part of the building including ceilings, walls, doors and windows. One example in Catholic churches is the 14 stations of the cross, which commemorate Jesus's final journey from his trial to his burial. In contrast, Protestant churches prefer to minimize the use of such imagery for fear of idolatry and superstition, in much the same manner as Jews and Muslims. Even crucifixes (crosses which include the corpus of Christ) are avoided and the empty cross is preferred – a practice based on fulfillment of the second commandment but also intended to stress Jesus's resurrection.

Churches also contain secondary features, which pertain to rituals other than the celebration of the communion meal or the Service of the Word. For example, a baptismal pool is often located behind the central pulpit in a Baptist church, while a baptismal font might be situated in the sanctuary or near the main doorway of an Orthodox,

Catholic or Anglican church. Catholic churches also have small fonts at all entrances so that the faithful may "bless" themselves as they enter by dipping their hand into the holy water and making a sign of the cross. The gesture not only calls to mind the waters of baptism but also suggests the need for purification as one enters holy space, not unlike the Islamic wudu.

While Christian churches have several features in common with the mosques and synagogues of the other Abrahamic religions, there are also interesting parallels with the sacred buildings of the sanatana dharma. The tower that reaches to the skies, the inner sanctuary at the heart of the edifice, statues and images that evoke a sense of the divine presence, the use of candlelight, flowers and incense, the purifying water fonts at entrances and the offering of blessed food are aspects of not only the altar-centered Christian church but also the Hindu temple.

10.5 Mandir

Unlike the Abrahamic religions, Hinduism is not primarily a congregational faith that expects attendance at a communal service on a regular basis. Devotional worship is first and foremost a domestic affair. However, Hindu practice is not without its communitarian dimension, and groups of believers often gather on festivals and other key occasions in a Hindu temple or *mandir*, which literally means a "house of god."[29] As the term implies, a mandir is a place where the deity "resides" in the sense that the worshiper is able to experience the divine presence in a more powerful and tangible manner. As was noted in Chapter 1, such an encounter often takes the form of a "seeing" (darshana) of the deity represented in physical form by the sacred image (murti).

The site for a mandir is traditionally chosen with care and an eye for a range of factors including the soil color, which can determine the caste. An ankura-arpana ritual is often performed, in which a seed is planted to symbolize the impregnation of mother earth and to test the level of fertility. If the plant germinates satisfactorily then the site is accepted.[30] The ground is leveled and the Vastu Purusha mandala is used to devise the floor plan.[31] This mandala is essentially a sacred grid in which the human figure of Vastu Purusha (the god of buildings) lies with his head in the northeast corner, his feet in the southwest corner and his elbows and knees in the opposite corners (Figure 10.4). The very center of the grid lies precisely over the figure's navel, symbolizing fertility. The mandala is usually divided into squares, each of which carries a special religious and architectural significance. As with the cruciform Christian church, the shape of the temple as seen from above reveals a holy pattern.

Two other natural images are the key to the structure of the mandir as seen at ground level. The first image is the cave. As dark, quiet places removed from the dazzle and noise of society, caves have been used as places of spiritual retreat in many religious traditions.[32] Hinduism is no exception and the cave is associated with the radical self-renunciation of those who have reached the final life stage of the sannyasin.[33] The deep, dark recesses of the cave are also linked symbolically to the womb from which human life springs. Thus, it is not surprising that the Hindu mandir is designed to represent a journey into the depths of a sacred womb-cave, an inward pathway toward immanent holiness.[34] At the same time it is also a reflection of the individual's journey through various states of meditation toward ultimate awareness and liberation.

Figure 10.4 The Vastu Purusha Mandala.

As believers approach the exterior of the mandir, they are greeted by hordes of sculpted figures covering almost every surface of the structure representing the infinity of being. Many of the scenes are explicitly erotic and violent, typical of the lowest level of spiritual life engrossed in the transient features of the physical world. Inside the temple, classical scenes from Hindu mythology begin to elevate the worshipers' minds to a plane beyond mundane reality. As the devotees move inward toward the center of the structure, decorations become less and less elaborate until finally they reach the inner sanctum directly above the center of the sacred mandala: the navel of Vastu Purusha. This sacred space is known as the **garbhagrha** (womb-house) because it contains the most important object in the entire temple: the murti of the main deity. There are no windows or lavish sculptures in the garbhagrha, only the stark simplicity and darkness of the cave, which directs the observer toward the primary focus of their devotion. Sometimes entry to the garbhagrha is restricted to the temple priests alone, in which case the worshipers sit in an anteroom. The main murti is usually fixed, but there are portable temple murtis that are brought out of the sanctum to be displayed or carried in procession on festivals.

The second natural image used in temple design is the mountain. As with caves, many religions regard mountain peaks as places where the sacred is more readily experienced. In the Hindu tradition, the mythical **Mount Meru** is the abode of the gods and the vertical axis that joins heaven to earth. Thus, it makes sense that the distinctive external shape of a Hindu temple is that of a holy mountain rising upwards toward the sky. If the womb-cave represents the journey inward toward immanent divinity at the heart of being, the mountain evokes the idea of reaching upwards toward transcendent reality, which presides over the cosmos.

Commentators speak of two major styles of temple architecture, based on the shape and position of the tower-mountain. The Dravidian style, typical of southern India, is characterized by the gopura or gateway tower. Gopuras typically have a stepped pyramidal shape with gradually receding levels divided by horizontal bands. Although not necessarily part of the temple itself, the gopura is usually the highest structure in the complex. The northern, or Nagara, style of temple design is typified by its tower which is known as a shikara, meaning "summit" or "peak." In contrast to the Dravidian model, the shikara usually has a semi-conical shape with curved edges and bulging sides, more suggestive of a row of mountains (Figure 10.5). Like the gopura in the south, the shikara is the highest part of the structure. Unlike the gopura, it is located directly above the garbhagrha, joining mountain and cave – the convergence of the immanent and the transcendent. Approaching the murti within the womb-house on the horizontal plane puts one directly on the vertical axis that joins heaven and earth.[35]

Because the mandir is considered a sacred place, purity and propriety are important issues for devotees and visitors. Shoes and sandals are not permitted and the soles of the feet must always point away from the sacred image. Modest clothing should be worn and many visitors cover their heads out of respect, especially women. Meat, alcohol and tobacco are avoided and, as in Islam, tradition requires that women not enter the mandir during menstruation. Near the altar there is often a bowl of water that is used to bathe the feet of the deity. In a manner reminiscent of Catholic Christians, devotees sip or sprinkle this holy water on their heads for blessing and purification.

The basic threefold imagery of body, cave and mountain provides the key to understanding the architectural patterns and the theological significance of the Hindu mandir. Worshipers stand on a holy mandala fashioned in the shape of a divine body. They journey inwards toward a visual encounter with the deity symbolized by the murti

Figure 10.5 Hindu mandir (temple) at Khajuraho, India.
(Reproduced with kind permission of iStock.)

located in the depths of the womb-cave. They gaze upwards toward the holy mountain in the hope of ultimate transcendence and liberation. Although Hinduism is not primarily a congregational faith, its places of communal gathering and worship are rich in spiritual symbolism and artistic beauty. The same is true of its daughter religion, which also stresses the importance of the visual image, the offering of food and incense, and the cosmic symbolism of the tower.

10.6 Temple Complex

One of the most popular and widely used mantras in Buddhism is known as the Three Jewels: "I go for refuge to the Buddha; I go for refuge to the Dharma; I go for refuge to the Sangha." The believer seeks haven in the teacher (Buddha), in the truth that he imparted (dharma) and in the community that he founded (sangha). The third jewel suggests that there is more to Buddhism than simply individual acceptance of the wisdom of Siddhartha Gautama. Although the way of the Buddha is essentially about one's own personal search for enlightenment, which cannot be delegated to another, the reference to the sangha suggests that there is also a communal dimension to the religion. Buddhism may not be a congregational faith to the same degree as the Abrahamic religions but the individual Buddhist is not alone. One can and should turn to the sangha for support. Thus, although a great deal of devotional worship is carried out before Buddha images in the privacy of an individual's own home, there are also special places that Buddhists may visit from time to time to worship alongside others, to gain counsel from the wise, to honor the memory of the dead or to be inspired by the example of past saints. Such a place is the Buddhist temple complex with its cluster of buildings, three of which are the most significant.

The first important building in a temple complex is hinted at by the word *sangha*. In the broad sense, sangha means the larger community of the Buddhist faithful, not only in one's own nation or culture but across the globe. In the narrow sense, it refers to the local community of Buddhist monks or nuns who live out the dharma in a radically dedicated manner. The third jewel not only means taking consolation in that one is a member of a worldwide family of fellow believers. It can also have the very practical meaning of visiting a nearby monastery. It is noteworthy that the Sri Lankan term *vihara* and the southeast Asian term *wat* are both commonly translated as "temple," but their primary meaning is a monastic residence or school. In cultures like Thailand, Cambodia and Laos, many temples are attached to monasteries and, thus, the two terms are virtually synonymous.

The earliest Buddhist monks were itinerant and often found hospitality in the homes of the laity. During the wet season they would stay in simple huts or natural abodes such as caves. As Buddhism expanded, permanent residences began to be erected under the sponsorship of wealthy patrons. Ideally, the monastery was located near enough to a town so that the daily alms round was possible, but secluded enough to provide a peaceful ambience for meditation and study. The architectural style of monasteries varies from culture to culture, and may be inspired by the design of an imperial palace, a military fortress or a rustic farmhouse. Monasteries are essentially residential and, thus, consist of individual cells with spartan conditions. A typical monastery also has a study hall, a library and a guest area where laity are able to attend talks, sermons and other forms of spiritual education. One of the holiest rooms, especially in Thai monasteries, is the bot, or ordination hall. Here monks convene on a regular basis for the recitation of the rule and on special occasions for the ordination of new monks. The bot is built on consecrated ground and is surrounded by eight stones (sima) that demarcate the sacred space and provide spiritual protection.

The second type of building that constitutes a vital part of any Buddhist temple complex is the main shrine hall. Usually the most central and publicly accessible section, the shrine hall contains the main Buddha images that are popular aids to meditation and devotion by resident monks and lay visitors.[36] The space is usually highly ornate with a selection of prominent figures organized in particular patterns. In the Theravada tradition, the historical Buddha Gautama may be depicted alone or flanked by his closest companions. In the Mahayana tradition, Gautama is often accompanied or even replaced by a variety of celestial Buddhas and bodhisattvas such as Amitabha, Avalokiteshvara, Maitreya, Manjusri and others. As in certain Hindu and Christian traditions, sumptuous offerings of flowers, candles, incense sticks and food are placed before the images by devotees seeking assistance from above. Placing gold leaf on a Buddha statue is also a common gesture intended to gain good karma. Near the entrance of the shrine hall there is usually an instrument such as a drum or a bell for announcing scheduled times for meditation and devotion. As in other religious cultures, such as Islam and Hinduism, visitors to Buddhist temples are asked to remove their footwear at the door and ensure that the soles of their feet never point to a Buddha image or a monk.

In Tibetan Buddhism, the walls of the shrine hall and other parts of the monastery are often adorned with special cloth paintings known as thangkas. These images depict episodes from the life of Buddha Gautama, scenes from the Jataka Tales, or icons of celestial Buddhas and bodhisattvas. The observer will also notice rows of prayer wheels of varying size around the complex. Small texts containing holy mantras are attached to the wheel, which is spun by the believer, symbolizing the multiple recitation of the mantra. A similar principle underlies the practice of Tibetan prayer flags, which are common features in monastic complexes, private homes and across the countryside. It is Buddhist belief that, as the wind blows through the colorful flags, the mantras written on them are carried upwards to the celestial Buddhas and bodhisattvas. In contrast, Japanese Zen Buddhist complexes are distinguished by the lack of such visual aids because of the emphasis on inner reflection. Hence, exquisitely manicured gardens of rocks, sand and trees are the main external aid to peaceful meditation.

The third important building type in the Buddhist temple complex is usually the most conspicuous structure because of its height. The feature is known by various names in different cultures: stupa in south Asia; dagoba in Sri Lanka; chedi in Thailand; chorten in Tibet and Bhutan; and pagoda in China and Vietnam. Outsiders frequently mistake its prominent size and shape to mean that it is the place where Buddhist devotional worship occurs. In fact, the stupa or pagoda is the part of the complex in which sacred relics and the ashes of the deceased are stored. After the death of Buddha Gautama, his ashes were distributed among eight kingdoms and placed in simple structures known as stupas. The bell-like shape of the stupa is based on Indian burial mounds and cairns that were used to cover the remains of cremated nobility (Figure 10.6). Relics and memorabilia of Buddha Gautama were later distributed to other sites and housed in stupas, as were the remains of other holy persons.[37] Consequently, the stupa emerged as the first type of Buddhist religious monument. Pilgrims came to pay their respects and meditate near the sacred relics, while monks and nuns established residences nearby to care for

Figure 10.6 Kuthodaw Buddhist Temple in Mandalay, Myanmar. (Reproduced with kind permission of iStock.)

the site. Thus, the stupa developed into the stupa–shrine and eventually into the stupa–shrine–monastery complex that is often described as a "temple" today.

Over time the design of the stupa became more complex and took on new religious meanings. Eventually, the typical stupa, especially in south Asia and Tibet, came to consist of five main layers, each of which stood for one of the five fundamental elements of the universe. The entire structure rests on a square base with four sides facing the cardinal points, symbolizing earth. Above this is the original hemispherical or bell-shaped dome that, in this new cosmic imagery, stands for water. It is here that relics and the ashes of the dead are usually housed. A stepped spire sits above the dome, representing fire. Above this lies a crescent moon or parasol which stands for the air. At the very apex of the stupa, a jewel or pointed finial signifies ether (Figure 10.7). As Buddhism expanded into eastern Asia, the stupa evolved into a more pyramidal design known as the pagoda. The term *pagoda* is probably a derivation of the Sanskrit dhatu garba, meaning a womb that contains something precious.

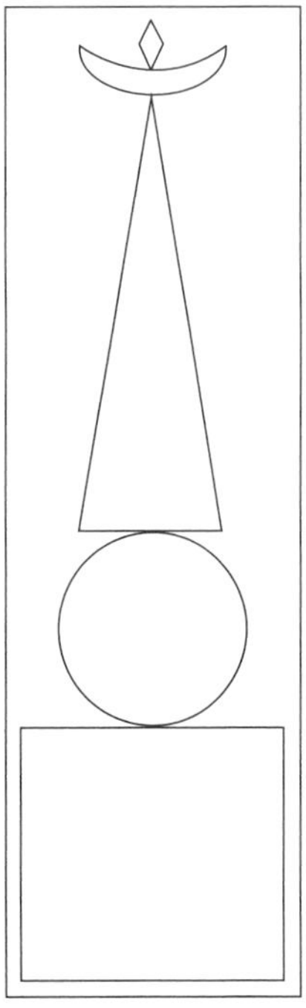

Figure 10.7 Basic geometric patterns of the stupa design. (Reproduced with kind permission of Sally Host.)

Similar to the function of the Vastu Purusha mandala in a Hindu mandir, Buddhist temple complexes are often designed to reflect the body of the meditating Buddha. Similarly, moving through the complex is sometimes interpreted as a symbolic journey from ignorance to enlightenment. Perhaps the best-known example of such symbolism is the great Buddhist temple at Borobudur in central Java. On the lowest levels, the sculptured reliefs feature events in the life of the historical Buddha and the Jataka Tales. As visitors move upwards, they pass images relating to more advanced Buddhist thinking such as the vocation of the bodhisattvas. Finally, at the summit, three concentric terraces house 72 stupas, symbolizing the attainment of nirvana. There are other buildings in the typical Buddhist temple complex but the mix of monastic residence, devotional shrine hall and reliquary tower constitutes the kernel of Buddhist sacred space. It is a practical expression of the third jewel's promise that the sangha will provide safe haven for the spiritual traveler.

A physical complex that comprises shrine halls with elaborate images and monastic residences, markers of sacred boundaries, colorful thangkas and flags, the sound of drums and bells, and the smell of food, flowers and incense are features not only of the Buddhist temple but also of the space in which Daoists gather for prayer and meditation.

10.7 Guan

There are many terms used to designate a Daoist sacred place and each highlights something special about the location. Words such as *an* ("hut") and *dong* ("cave") refer to hermitages or buildings where the residents seek seclusion and solitude. Words such as *ci* ("shrine") or *miao* ("temple") are more general and can equally apply to a Daoist or Buddhist temple.[38] The term *gong* ("palace") was a title granted exclusively by the emperor to the largest and most prestigious temples, which often benefited from imperial patronage. But the most common term used to designate a Daoist temple is **guan** – a word that can be variously translated as "hall," "hostel" or "observatory." As a hall it refers to the place where the local community gathers for festivals and rituals. As a hostel it refers to the residences in which priest-monks actually live. As an observatory it connotes the idea of watching the starry heavens in an astronomical sense but also looking for the Dao in a spiritual sense.

Like the buildings that we have explored in the other five religions, the Daoist guan has many aspects that reflect a range of purposes including halls for sacrifices, altars for petitions, rooms for chanting scriptures, monasteries for living, rooms for visitors and grounds for strolling in meditation. In general, Daoist guans have been designed according to traditional Chinese architectural styles. Buildings are normally constructed of timber or brick, supported by large columns and covered with sloping tiled roofs and overarching eaves (Figure 10.8). Stone is often used for elements such as steps, railings and arches. The fundamental principle is that of harmony between the human and the natural. The built environment of the guan should blend into the landscape and reflect the symmetry and balance of the Dao. There are many architectural styles utilized but commentators recognize two major ones.

The first is a traditional symmetrical layout with its main axis on a north–south orientation, following one of the most fundamental principles in feng shui.[39] Literally meaning "wind water," feng shui is an ancient Chinese system used to determine the most beneficial alignment of buildings. Adapted by Daoism, it provides guidance on how to maximize connection with the natural energy known as qi and ensure proper alignment with the mysterious Dao that is all around. Specifically, when feng shui is applied to Daoist architecture the result is that the front of the temple faces south (Vermillion Bird), its back faces north (Black Tortoise), its right faces west (White Tiger)

Figure 10.8 Qingyang Daoist Temple in Sichuan, China.
(Reproduced with kind permission of Alamy.)

and its left faces east (Azure Dragon).[40] This is not orientation towards a holy city, such as in Judaism or Islam, but it is reminiscent of those Christian churches built to face the rising sun that symbolizes the resurrection of Christ. Here, however, the primary orientation is south, which is the yang or sunny side of the hill (in the northern hemisphere). Indeed, the origins of feng shui were possibly associated with the practical quest to maximize light and warmth from the sun. Within the Daoist temple complex, the main altar halls are organized hierarchically along the north–south axis but, perhaps surprisingly, it is the lesser deities that are placed at the southern end and the higher deities, such as the Three Pure Ones, that are located at the northern end. The reason for this is that the Dao is considered to be mysterious and elusive, removed from our bustling, profane world. Thus, the north–south axis functions in a similar way to the inward journey of the Hindu cave temple. The lesser, local gods are found at the sunny, southern end but as one moves north, one moves up the divine hierarchy and further into the dark mystery of the Dao itself.

The second prominent architectural pattern often used for the layout of Daoist temples is the Bagua (Eight Trigrams). Similar to the arrangement of the wedding hall, all structures of the temple are organized according to the eight combinations of yin and yang that encircle a central point where perfect harmony is achieved. The center of the Bagua is often the location for the sacred furnace or stove in which the pills of immortality are made.

The guan usually provides open courtyards and grounds with pathways and seats so that residents and visitors may stroll or sit in peaceful meditation. Chinese Daoist temples are easily confused with Chinese Buddhist structures and, indeed, the basic architectural styles are very similar. Distinctive Daoist symbols to look for include images of a dragon and a tiger, representing the dynamic interaction of yang and yin respectively. This pair of powerful animals frequently features on the roof of the guan or as guardians at the main gate. Sometimes a phoenix replaces the tiger as the yin symbol.[41] In contrast, Buddhist temples tend to use the image of two giants guarding the principal entrance.

One noteworthy feature of a typical Daoist guan is the sill that is fixed to the ground across entrances and doorways. This structure is usually about one or two feet high and serves both a practical and spiritual purpose. Practically, it helps prevent rain and mud from entering the hall or yard. Spiritually, it marks a boundary between profane and sacred space. Moreover, Daoist mythology teaches that the sills also keep out small one-legged demons that are unable to hop over it. In other words, it wards off evil powers and provides protection for those inside. In contrast to the preference for the right side in other traditions such as Islam or Hinduism, the visitor crosses the sill by lifting the left foot first. The physical stepping over the sill boundary compels visitors to be aware of the sanctity of the area that they are entering.

Once inside, the visitor will notice many religious symbols adorning the space, especially in the areas where altars are located. As noted in Chapter 1, each Daoist altar usually has an array of objects that are used for formal rituals. These include images of the relevant deities, scrolls, paintings, incense burners and candles, as well as a drum (eastern side) and a bell (western side). Altars are usually decorated with flowers and fruit, especially peaches, which symbolize immortality. Bowing mats are placed in front for worshipers to honor the god concerned.

There are interesting similarities with Buddhist temples, such as shrine rooms in which statues and paintings of Daoist gods can be found throughout the guan. As noted earlier, their positioning and order is far from random and reflects the celestial hierarchy with the more important gods given places at the northern end of the guan. The images are usually three-dimensional statues but it is common to find two-dimensional paintings that bear the same name as their Buddhist equivalents: thangkas. As in Buddhism, the Daoist thangkas function as portable tools of worship and education for mobile monks and priests as well as adornments for the guan. Triangular or square flags featuring mystical writing and diagrams are flown around the guan providing protection from evil, guidance for ancestral spirits and blessings to the temple visitors – not unlike the prayer flags of a Buddhist temple. There are also connections with other religious architectural traditions. Reminiscent of the Islamic calligraphic tradition, Daoist poems and other verses are engraved on temple boards that are hung above entrances and walls. Chinese characters such as fu (blessing), shou (longevity) and ji (auspicious) appear on windows and doors to bring benefits to all who enter. Books and manuscripts are also housed in the guan in a fashion similar to the holy ark of the Jewish synagogue.

Distinctive symbols are used to decorate and sanctify the space within the guan. Similar to the cross in Christianity and the crescent moon and star of Islam, the taijitu (the yin and yang symbol) is frequently used around the guan as the badge of Daoism. Another common image is the seven stars of the Big Dipper.[42] One of the most prominent constellations in the northern sky, the Big Dipper is seen in Daoism as the place where the key celestial gods reside and, thus, it often features in Daoist spiritual practices. For example, one form of meditation involves imagining the stars of the Big Dipper resting above one's head. As concentration levels increase, the Three Pure Ones appear in the Dipper bowl and make their way to the handle from where they enter the practitioner's body. Many other symbols feature within the guan: celestial objects such as the sun, moon, stars and clouds that represent illumination; animals such as tortoises, deer, bats and fish that variously symbolize immortality, health and blessing. There are also weapons such as swords, which remind the Daoist of the constant struggle to remain in touch with the energy of nature and align oneself with the Dao itself.

The guan is a welcome haven for those seeking spiritual quiet, a gathering place for ritual worship and a residence for those advanced in the religion. Above all, it is a powerful, artistic statement in wood, brick and stone of some of the most fundamental theological notions in Daoism. The idea that the Dao can be effectively accessed and celebrated in the local guan flows over to the idea that it can also be powerfully experienced by the pilgrim in those places where the heavens come closest to the earth: the mountains.

Summary

As a fundamental aspect of human society, buildings are used for a vast array of activities including religious worship and devotion. Although religions teach that transcendent reality is literally everywhere, practice indicates that it is encountered in a special way within the sacred building where space itself is sanctified and earth meets heaven. All six major religions have such places where communities gather for congregational worship or individuals come for private devotion and inspired meditation. As with all buildings, the shape and design of the structure itself reflects not only the devotional practices that are carried out within it but also the religious beliefs that lie behind the practices. Although the designs, practices and beliefs are unique to each religion, it is also possible to identify some interesting points of similarity between the traditions.

In some cases the entire edifice itself is a statement of faith. Hindu and Buddhist temples are both fashioned on the shape of the human body, albeit in different ways. The Hindu mandir is traditionally erected on consecrated land according to the pattern of a sacred diagram. The classical mandala used as the floor plan for Hindu temples is the body of Vastu Purusha, the god of buildings and land. Similarly, Buddhist temples are often designed to imitate the shape of the meditating Buddha seated in the lotus position as seen from a lateral perspective. Traditional Christian churches often had a cruciform pattern so that, from above, the building itself formed the shape of the cross. Although Islamic places of worship do not necessarily have any such overall pattern, an external feature on almost all mosques (as well as many Christian churches) is the domed roof symbolizing the heavens in which God dwells and under which the worshiping community gathers. Historically, the capacity to express Jewish faith through the external appearance of the synagogue was limited as a result of restrictions imposed by the Muslim or Christian social majority. When greater freedom was granted in nineteenth-century Europe, the tendency was to borrow from classical and even Christian building styles, with the result that the truly distinctive nature of a synagogue is more apparent internally than externally.

The other external feature that is common to many sacred buildings is the tower that reaches upwards toward the sky. In Christianity, it takes the form of a steeple or spire. The steeple usually functioned as a bell-tower from which the call to prayer was tolled in traditional times. With or without a spire, the steeple also symbolizes prayers and human hope rising up to God. A cross is often placed at the very apex of the structure, thus stamping the building as a Christian place of worship. In an Islamic mosque, the tower feature takes the form of the minaret, which may originally have been an adaptation of the Christian steeple. In one sense the minaret serves the same purpose as the steeple since it is the elevated place from which the voice of the muezzin calls believers to prayer five times per day.

The tower feature of the Hindu mandir is a symbol of the holy mountain Meru where the gods abide, making it the counterpart to the dome of the mosque and the church. However, as the tallest feature of the mandir, it also represents the vertical axis connecting heaven and earth. In northern India, the tower is known as a shikara and is located directly over the central part of the mandir. In the south it is the gopura, which forms part of the gateway to the temple. In the Buddhist temple, the tower feature is known by a variety of names including stupa or pagoda. Although often mistaken for the main part of the complex, it is actually the place for housing relics and the cremated ashes of the deceased. The original bell shape of the stupa was based on the traditional Indian funeral mound. Over time it evolved into a multilayered symbol of the cosmos with each level representing one of the fundamental elements. In eastern Asia, the stupa evolved into the slender pyramidal shape of the pagoda. Just as the dome sits above mosque and church representing divinity's dominion over the cosmos, the stupa-pagoda rises above the temple complex symbolizing the cosmos itself in all of its levels through which the individual must journey toward ultimate liberation.

The interior of the sacred building is also replete with religious symbolism and meaning. The main issue is the focus of attention. The interior of a mosque is strikingly empty of seating, creating an open atmosphere but also reflecting the need for space given that much of Muslim prayer involves bodily prostration, as the etymology of the term mosque suggests. The key feature is the arch-shaped wall niche (mihrab) indicating the direction of Mecca (qibla) toward which every official prayer must be directed. Thus, every mosque physically orientates the believing community toward the symbol of Islamic unity. In fact, the original qibla was Jerusalem, which constitutes the direction of official Jewish prayer. Like mosques, synagogues indicate the direction of the holy city via the positioning of their most important interior feature, the holy ark. Christian churches were traditionally oriented to the east because the rising sun was considered a symbol of the resurrection. Similarly, Daoist guans are oriented on a north–south axis according to a feng shui principle aimed at alignment with natural flows of energy.

Apart from being a direction indicator, the holy ark is essentially a receptacle for the Torah scrolls, which are read during synagogue services on an annual cycle. A lamp burns alongside the ark, indicating the presence of the scrolls inside. That the holy writings occupy pride of place inside the sacred building attests to the unrivaled importance accorded to the inspired word in the Jewish tradition. In a similar manner, Protestant churches often give prominence to an enthroned Bible over the communion table. It is no coincidence that Judaism, Islam and Protestant Christianity all share a pronounced emphasis on the word, rather than the image, as the principal way to approach divinity. Thus, synagogues, mosques and Protestant churches are also notable for their lack of icons, statues and any other image that might be considered idolatrous. Moreover, a key feature in each of them is the platform from which the holy texts are recited and interpreted: the bimah, the minbar and the pulpit.

In contrast, the sacred image is an essential part of worship and devotion in other mainstream Christian churches, as well as in Hindu mandirs, Buddhist temples and Daoist guans. Although Catholic, Orthodox and Anglican churches have scriptural readings during their services, the pulpit is usually not in the center of the sanctuary but to one side. Central position is given to the altar or communion table on which the Eucharistic bread and wine are consecrated. Like the Jewish holy ark, these churches also have a receptacle, known as the tabernacle, with a lamp burning beside it. However, unlike the Jewish ark, the Christian tabernacle contains sacred bread rather than sacred texts. Moreover, these churches warmly endorse the use of icons, statues and other images in the sacred building. Often the faithful will pray before the image and light candles as a gesture of devotion. Similarly, the main focus within the Buddhist temple complex is the shrine hall, which houses images representing the historical Buddha or a selection of celestial Buddhas and bodhisattvas. Here the faithful meditate or make offerings of incense, flowers, lighted candles and food. Altars with images of various gods as well as candles, flowers and other symbols are key points of activity within the Daoist guan. The lesser gods are located at the sunny, south end of the temple complex while the higher gods are located at the darker north end, which is representative of the mysterious Dao.

In the same tradition, Hindu worship involves offerings of similar substances before the sacred image (murti) through which the devotee gains a vision (darshana) of the deity. As with Buddhism, much Hindu devotion occurs in the privacy of the domestic shrine, but the Hindu mandir is typically replete with images of Brahman's many manifestations. The central space inside a Hindu mandir is the inner sanctum in which the image of the main god is kept. As a small, cave-like space set deep within the structure, it is appropriately described as the garbhagrha (womb-house). The very act of entering a Hindu mandir – passing from the highly ornate and brightly lit exterior to the inner sanctum via the ever-narrowing passageway and finally encountering the garbhagrha – is a powerful metaphor for the spiritual journey. In northern Indian mandirs, the garbhagrha lies directly beneath the shikara tower and directly above the navel of the Vastu

Purusha, thus representing the convergence of transcendence, immanence and origin at this crucial point in space.

The sacred building has been a source of inspirational architectural design through the centuries and across the religions. At a practical level it functions as the forum for public worship. At a theological level, it stands as a statement of faith in stone, metal, wood and glass. In many ways mosques, synagogues, churches, mandirs, guans and temple complexes have their own unique characteristics that reinforce the distinctiveness of each religion. Yet beneath the visible differences there also lies a basement of commonality. Whether the emphasis is on congregational or individual devotion, the priority of the verbal or the visual, the heights of transcendence or the depths of immanence, in all cases the sacred building is the place where the sacred meets the profane, where heaven touches earth, and where ordinary space is given extraordinary meaning.

Discussion Topics

1. How do religious buildings use height and depth symbolically?
2. What does a sacred building tell us about that religion's concept of transcendent reality?
3. Explore how water, light and other symbolic substances are used in sacred buildings.
4. How is purity an issue in sacred buildings?
5. Is the Hindu home more important than the temple for worship?
6. How do Catholic, Orthodox and Protestant churches differ in their fundamental design features?
7. How do Muslims and Jews adorn their sacred buildings without falling into idolatry?
8. Compare the presentation of altars in Christianity, Daoism, Hinduism and Buddhism.

Notes

1. See Qur'an 49.4: "Those who call out to you from behind private chambers." Surah 49 is aptly named The Chambers.
2. See Sahih Muslim 4.1068–70.
3. Some see an oblique reference to the Quba mosque in Qur'an 9:108 which speaks of a mosque built on piety "from the first day."
4. Qur'an 2:217; 5:2; 8:34; 22:25.
5. The Masjid al-Haram's present structure was completed by Sultan Selim II in the late sixteenth century.
6. The Arabic term *masjid* is rendered as *masqid* in Egyptian and *mezquita* in Spanish. The Qur'an also uses masjid to refer to places of worship in general, including the pre-Islamic Ka'bah.
7. Qur'an 24:36. Because of its aptness, this verse is a popular calligraphic theme in mosques.
8. Sahih Bukhari 1.8.466.
9. The Masjid al-Haram in Mecca is distinguished by its seven minarets while the Blue Mosque in Istanbul has six minarets. The builder of the Blue Mosque, Sultan Ahmed I, was criticized for having the same number of minarets as the Masjid al-Haram at the time (c.1616). Consequently, he sponsored the seventh minaret for the Meccan mosque.

10 The star symbolised Mary, the mother of Jesus, and the crescent represented Diana, the Roman goddess of the moon. In Muhammad's time, a simple black flag with no symbolism was used.
11 Sunan Abu Dawud 1.232. Menstruating women may pass through a mosque but not remain in it.
12 Sahih Bukhari 1.8.376.
13 Other Islamic schools, especially the Shi'ite tradition, are less concerned about the artistic depiction of Muhammad and the prophets. Moreover, there are examples of Islamic artwork in which the Prophet is depicted either in full or with his face veiled.
14 Sahih Bukhari 1.8.374, 411, 466.
15 Sahih Muslim 4.884–96; Sahih Bukhari 2.13.23. These hadith indicate that women should not be prevented from attending mosque but they should not wear perfume.
16 Qur'an 9:17–18.
17 2 Kings 24:1–15; 25:9–12.
18 See Ezekiel 8:1; 14:1. Ezekiel 11:16 speaks of God becoming a "sanctuary" for the exiles which is often interpreted as the nascent synagogue.
19 Traditionally all seats face the holy ark in Ashkenazi synagogues while the seating in Sephardic synagogues tends to follow the perimeter of the sanctuary, although worshipers face the ark when they stand for prayer.
20 The term *aron ha kodesh* is used among Ashkenazi Jews. The Sephardic tradition prefers the term *heikhal*.
21 Exodus 26:31–7; 36:35–8.
22 See Exodus 27:20.
23 *Bimah* is the Ashkenazi term while the Sephardim prefer *tebah* or *taivah*.
24 Mark 1:21; 3:1; etc.; Acts 13:5; 14:1; 17:10, etc.
25 Acts 2:46; 12:12; 20:7.
26 Originally a basilica was a Roman public building, usually in the forum of a town, but eventually the word came to mean a large Christian church modeled on a similar design.
27 The iconostasis usually has three doors that are open or closed depending on the festival or ceremony.
28 Catholic Code of Canon Law, canons 938–40. Some Anglican parishes also use tabernacles that are located behind, above, or on the altar with a lamp nearby.
29 *Devalaya* and *devagrha* are also common terms for a Hindu temple and carry the same meaning, namely "dwelling of a god."
30 During construction, a gold or silver casket filled with auspicious items such as jewels, plants and soil is buried near the temple door.
31 The story of Vastu Purusha is told in the Matsya Purana. See also Brihat Samhita 53.1–3.
32 For example, the cave features in the spiritual experiences of Elijah, Saint Benedict and Muhammad in the Jewish, Christian and Islamic traditions respectively.
33 Svetashvatara Upanishad 2.10.
34 Some Hindu temples are constructed inside caves, for instance the classical fifth-century CE examples at Ellora in Maharashtra, India.
35 The equivalent of the shikara in southern temples is the vimanam, but it is not the most prominent part of the structure.
36 The shrine hall is called a kondo in Japan and vihara in Thailand.
37 Thai Buddhism distinguishes between various types of stupa, or chedi: those that contain relics of the historical Buddha or his companions (prathart chedi); those that

contain personal belongings of the Buddha and his companions (boriphoke chedi); and those that contain written records of his teachings (dhamma chedi).

38 Many temples of Chinese popular folk religion were incorrectly designated as "Daoist" because the term was associated with "superstition" in the nineteenth and early twentieth centuries.

39 Feng shui principles also apply to other buildings, including offices.

40 These mythological creatures correspond to four constellations in Chinese astronomy and represent the four cardinal directions. The Azure Dragon is formed by stars in Virgo and Scorpio; the Black Tortoise is formed by stars in Aquarius and Pegasus; the White Tiger is formed by stars in Aries, Taurus and Orion; and the Vermillion Bird is formed by stars in Gemini, Cancer and Hydra.

41 A flaming pearl, similar to the pattern used on priestly hairpins, may also be used to stamp the place as Daoist.

42 The Big Dipper is a popular name for the northern constellation officially known as Ursa Major (the Great Bear).

Further Reading

Bhaskarananda, Swami (2002). *The Essentials of Hinduism*. 2nd ed. Seattle, WA: Viveka, ch. 18.

Cohn-Sherbok, Dan (2003). *Judaism: History, Belief and Practice*. London: Routledge, pp. 483–7.

Davies, J. G. (1984). *Temples, Churches and Mosques*. Oxford: Blackwell.

De Lange, Nicholas (2000). *Introduction to Judaism*. Cambridge: Cambridge University Press, pp. 121–36.

Fisher, Robert E. (1993). *Buddhist Art and Architecture*. London: Thames & Hudson.

Frishman, Martin & Khan, Hasan-Uddin (2002). *The Mosque: History, Architectural Development and Regional Diversity*. London: Thames & Hudson.

Gordon, Matthew S. (2002). *Understanding Islam*. London: Duncan Baird, pp. 72–9.

Holm, Jean & Bowker, John (eds.) (2000). *Sacred Place*. London: Continuum.

Komjathy, Louis (2013). *The Daoist Tradition*. London: Bloomsbury, pp. 295–9.

Meek, Harold (1995). *The Synagogue*. London: Phaidon.

Michell, George (1988). *The Hindu Temple: An Introduction to its Meaning and Forms*. Chicago: University of Chicago Press.

Reynolds, Frank E. & Carbine, Jason A. (eds.) (2000). *The Life of Buddhism*. Berkeley: University of California Press, ch. 1.

Segler, Franklin M. & Bradley, Randall (2006). *Christian Worship: Its Theology and Practice*. 3rd ed. Nashville, TN: B & H Publishing Group, pp. 205–18.

White, James F. (2001). *Introduction to Christian Worship*. 3rd ed. Nashville, TN: Abingdon Press, ch. 3.

Wilkinson, John (2002). *From Synagogue to Church: The Traditional Design*. London: Routledge.

11

Journey

World Religions in Practice: A Comparative Introduction, Second Edition. Paul Gwynne.

CONTENTS

11.1 Introduction

Transcendent reality can be experienced in the special space within the house of worship, but it is also sought after in more distant places of exceptional significance. Such locations beckon the believer to visit them and to draw on their unique ethos, even if only once in a lifetime. Ordinary space is rendered extraordinary not only by the sacred building but also by the sacred journey. In this chapter we explore the sanctification of space via the experience of the pilgrim. What are the main pilgrimage destinations in each of the six religions? Why are these particular places so significant? What physical features mark the sacred location and what specific actions and rituals are performed there? What are the main motives for such journeys and what aspects of belief are highlighted and expressed?

11.2 The Sacred Ford

In the Forest Chapter of the great Hindu epic, the Mahabharata, the sage Pulastya describes a grand circuit encompassing all of India and taking in hundreds of interesting sites. The litany of mountains, rivers and cities is not only a revealing insight into ancient Indian geography but also one of the more explicit references in Hindu scripture to the concept of the religious journey. Although naturally disinclined to leave Mother India and travel across the contaminating "black waters" (kala pani) of her seas, Hindus have always felt a powerful urge to travel within her borders to places of outstanding religious significance. From ancient times to the modern day, pilgrimage has occupied an important place in Hindu belief and practice.

The traditional Hindu term for pilgrimage is *tirthayatra,* which literally means "a journey to the ford." It is an apt metaphor for the special threshold where the spiritual traveler is able to cross over a figurative river from the profane to the sacred. As with all pilgrim destinations, the tirtha (ford) is a liminal point – a place at the edge of the mundane where the transcendent is more powerfully experienced. In the Hindu imagination the sky is a river that separates earth and heaven but that is traversed by the gods who descend into our world. In pilgrimage, the movement is in the opposite direction as the human subject crosses over to the other side and ascends to a higher level of existence, even if for only a brief moment. So important is pilgrimage that it is often included as one of the five basic duties of all Hindus alongside daily worship, festivals, rites of passage and a virtuous lifestyle.[1] The development of modern forms of transport has served only to further stimulate the practice in contemporary India. Millions take advantage of train, bus and plane to visit sacred sites, which are scattered like jewels across the subcontinent.

The specific reasons why Hindus embark on pilgrimages are many and varied. Often the pilgrimage is a form of petitionary prayer in the sense that the effort invested may persuade the gods to answer a request such as conceiving a child, finding romance or succeeding in business. Conversely, some people undertake the journey as an expression of gratitude for a blessing already granted or to fulfill a vow made in perilous circumstances. Many believe that holy sites possess a special ethos and that devotions and sacrifices are naturally more efficacious offered there than elsewhere. For example, many Hindus journey to places where funeral offerings are thought to have a greater effect. Elderly pilgrims travel to hallowed places in the hope that dying there will guarantee them liberation from the wheel of reincarnation. For others pilgrimage is primarily about purification from bad karma, usually symbolized by bathing. The site may also be associated with incarnations of particular deities, for example their birthplace, childhood home, royal palace or last dwelling place on earth. Visiting such auspicious places brings the pilgrim into more tangible, intimate contact with the deity. Ultimately, the pilgrim has come to "see" the divine and be transformed in the process. They come to cross the ford.

The time and energy invested in traveling to a sacred site are an essential part of the overall experience and generate good karma along the way. Upon arrival, the Hindu pilgrim engages in a series of activities that express inner faith and symbolize the purpose of the journey. One of the first actions usually performed is bathing in the purifying waters of the river, lake or ocean. Thus, many popular pilgrimage sites are located on or near the banks of rivers, seven of which are considered to be particularly holy in the Hindu tradition: the Ganges, the Yamuna and the (underground) Sarasvati in northern India; the Narmada in central India; the Godavari and the Kaveri in the south; and the Indus in present-day Pakistan. In particular, the Ganges is considered to be the most sacred of all rivers. In Hindu mythology it flows from its celestial source (the Milky Way) down through the hair of Shiva and onto the earth where it brings life, fertility and purification. Many of India's great pilgrimage cities are located on its banks.

Most sacred sites have a temple or series of temples in which pilgrims are able to experience a "seeing" (darshana) of the deity. They may circumambulate the temple or the image within the temple in the usual clockwise direction, keeping their unclean left side away from the object of veneration. Offerings are made to the god whose powerful presence is mediated via the image. The pilgrim may make an offering to the temple priests, providing much appreciated practical support for those who maintain the site as well as generating good karma for the donor. Pilgrims will often listen to discourses or receive spiritual counsel from the local priests or gurus.

Traditionally, a tirthayatra involves a high degree of self-denial. In this way, the pilgrim, at least temporarily, emulates the radical detachment of the sannyasin who is described as a wanderer on the earth. Going on pilgrimage often means fasting or abstaining from certain foods and avoiding sexual activity. The journey to the ford is a time of austerity and discipline, during which the bodily passions are subdued and spiritual matters given priority. The metaphor of the ford is appropriate because, during this special journey, ordinary persons are invited to cross over to the other side and adopt the lifestyle of those who have attained the final stage of the ashramas.

There is also another sense in which tirthayatra involves crossing over: namely, the dilution of caste and gender boundaries. Commentators have noted how Hindu pilgrimage tends to highlight equality rather than hierarchy in that everyone and anyone is able to make the sacred journey. People who may be ordinarily separated by geographical, social and religious barriers converge on sacred sites and discover themselves to be fellow companions.

As the Mahabharata text above suggests, there are thousands of places of pilgrimage scattered across the landscape of India, making a detailed consideration impossible in the space available here. However, it is worthwhile taking a closer look at three prominent examples of tirtha in the Hindu world: the char dham, the Kumbha Mela and the city of Varanasi.

According to Indian tradition, the eminent eighth-century CE sage, Shankara, once made an epic journey around India, establishing shrines at the four cardinal points (Figure 11.1). The all-embracing route came to be known as char dham ("the four abodes") and is still looked upon as the archetypal Hindu pilgrimage. Few have had the time, the resources or the energy to emulate Shankara's extraordinary feat in a single journey, although many Hindus aspire to visit each of the four dhams at least once during their lifetime. Traditionally, the pilgrimage begins at the eastern dham situated in the coastal city of Puri, in the province of Orissa. The main temple houses three enormous statues of Jagganath (Krishna), his brother Balarama and his sister Subhadra. Each year, during the month of Ashadha (June–July), hundreds of thousands of pilgrims flock to the city to witness the grand procession through the town to the nearby Gundicha Temple. The statues are placed on huge chariots known as rathas, which are dragged through the streets by dozens of the faithful. At times the crowds have been so large that people have been injured in the crush, giving rise to the English term juggernaut, which signifies a massive unstoppable vessel.

The char dham follows a clockwise direction, imitating the normal circumambulation of a sacred image. From Puri, the sacred route takes the pilgrim to the southern shrine at Rameshvaram, in Tamil Nadu. As the name implies, Rameshvaram is considered to be the site where Rama prepared himself spiritually prior to his battle with the demon Ravanna in Sri Lanka. It is the same site where Rama built a shrine in thanksgiving after his victorious return. The extensive temple is located on a small island off the coast and is reputed to have over 1,000 stone pillars and more than a mile of corridors. Inside the complex are 22 special pools, each of which cleanses the pilgrim who bathes in them from a particular type of impurity. The temple is also believed to be one of the 12 locations scattered around India where Shiva manifested himself as a gigantic column of light (jyotirlinga).[2] Two sacred linga stones are housed in the temple, their phallic shape symbolizing the life-giving power of the deity.

The third dham is the city of Dwarka on the western coast of Gujarat, facing the Arabian Sea. According to Hindu legend, Krishna founded the city and reigned there as king until the end of his earthly life. Dwarka is also listed among the sapta pura, or seven holy cities of India that bring liberation from the wheel of reincarnation for those who

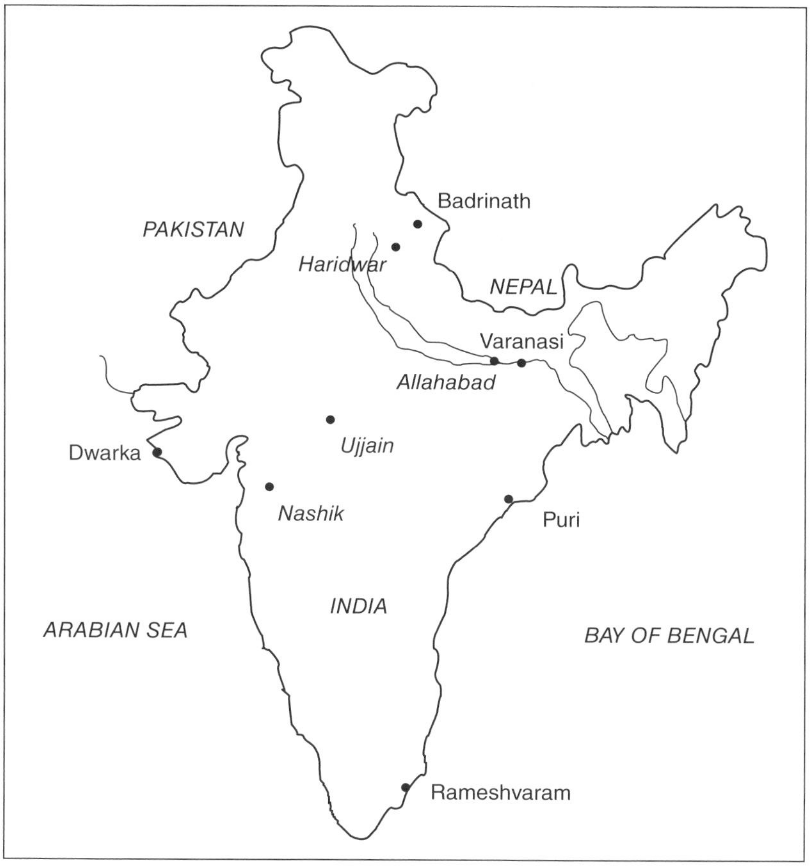

Figure 11.1 Major pilgrimage sites in Hinduism.

die within their borders.[3] A beautiful temple located between the town and the sea marks the actual pilgrimage site. The fourth and northern dham is Badrinath, nestled over 10,000 feet above sea level in the snowy peaks of the Himalayan Mountains. For many, Badrinath is the final and most important of the traditional dhams. So extreme is its altitude that the temple can only be opened to visitors during the summer months. The track to Badrinath is an arduous one, promising an abundance of good karma for those who make the effort to reach their destination. The name of the town is derived from a legend that narrates how the goddess Lakshmi turned herself into a badri tree to protect Vishnu, her partner. In place of the four classical dhams, a more local Himalayan version has evolved known as the chota ("little") char dham which attracts thousands of pilgrims each year. The spiritual journey begins in Yamunotri, source of the Yamuna River, and progresses to Gangotri at the headwaters of the Ganges. From here the pilgrim walks for several days to remote Kedarnath, another of the 12 Shaivite jyotir-linga sites. The circuit terminates in Badrinath, as it does in the case of the traditional char dham.

The second example of Hindu pilgrimage constitutes one of the largest gatherings of human beings on the planet: the Kumbha Mela. The term literally means a jar of nectar and refers to an episode in Hindu mythology in which the demons stole the pitcher of immortality from the gods. After a struggle, the gods retrieved the container but, as it was being transported back to the heavens, four drops of the precious nectar fell to earth. Four cities now stand where the drops landed: Prayag (Allahabad), Ujjain, Nashik and Haridwar. Every three years, a colossal religious festival is celebrated in each of the cities in turn, thus creating a 12-year cycle. The actual dates of the Kumbha Mela are determined astrologically by the position of the sun, moon and the planet Jupiter, which has a 12-year synodic period.[4] Although Hardwar and Ujjain are counted among the seven sacred Hindu cities, the largest gatherings in the cycle occur at Prayag where crowd estimates have ranged from 10 to 20 million. Activities include worshiping in temples, listening to the teachings of distinguished gurus, feeding the poor and especially bathing. Thousands of sadhus and sannyasins emerge from their reclusive lifestyles to attend the festival. Traditionally, they are given the honor of bathing before all others.

The third example is arguably the best-known pilgrimage site in all of India – a place whose image is virtually synonymous with being Hindu. Varanasi is situated on the Ganges River in Uttar Pradesh and it is believed that Shiva lived there as an ascetic. It is also one of the 12 jyotirlinga sites of Shaivism. The city is the premium destination for pilgrims from all Hindu sects and more than a million come each year to bathe at the famous ghats (steps) along its riverbanks (Figure 11.2).[5] There are over 1,000 temples in Varanasi where pilgrims offer puja to their personal deity. In traditional Hindu fashion, many visitors circumambulate the entire city by walking the Panchkosi Road and stopping at the many shrines along the way. The circuit is nearly 35 miles long and can take up to five days to complete on foot.

Figure 11.2 The holy city of Varanasi (Benares) on the Ganges. (Reproduced with kind permission of iStock.)

For most Hindus, the greatest motive for making the tirthayatra to Varanasi is to die there and have one's ashes scattered on the waters of the Ganges. Death in Varanasi, as in all seven holy Hindu cities, circumvents the cycle of samsara and offers the deceased instant access to ultimate liberation. Thus, many elderly Hindus migrate to Varanasi to live out their final days while those who pass away elsewhere have their corpses transported hundreds of miles to the sacred city for cremation. At places along the river, funeral pyres burn day and night, releasing deceased spirits from their mortal bodies for the most important of all journeys. As the holiest Hindu city on the banks of Mother Ganges, where death brings final release from the wheel of rebirth, Varanasi is the epitome of tirthayatra in the world of Hinduism.

Hindu pilgrimage is marked by a number of noteworthy features: a series of sites arranged according to the points of the compass and embracing the cultural homeland itself; a preference for natural settings where heaven and earth draw closer; and locations associated with foundational events of long ago. The same features can also be found in one of China's classical religious traditions where the main analogy for pilgrimage is not crossing a river but climbing a mountain.

11.3 Reverencing the Mountain

There is a story in the Zhuangzi that tells of a spirit whose strict diet and disciplined meditation enabled him to transcend physical limitations. As a result he is able to harness the natural forces that control human health and agricultural fertility.

> He does not eat the five grains, but sucks the wind, drinks the dew, climbs up on the clouds and mist, rides a flying dragon and wanders beyond the four seas. By concentrating his spirit, he protects creatures from sickness and plague and makes the harvest plentiful.[6]

It is not only his fasting and contemplation that make a difference. This spirit lives in the mountains and it is this lofty setting that plays a major part in his advancement. Up there, he is in the clouds and closer to Ultimate Reality. Indeed, high places have always been seen as locations where one can more effectively gain access to the Dao and tap into its infinite power and energy. From the earliest times, Daoist hermits abandoned the noise and distractions of human society, seeking peace and wisdom in the mountains. There they could collect immortal substances, seek mystical experiences and receive divine communications. It is easier to cultivate one's spiritual self on a mountain because this, of all places on earth, is where earth (yin) and heaven (yang) draw closest together. They are truly portals to the sacred and there are a number of Daoist terms that reflect this reverence for high places. *Rushan* not only means to enter the mountains but it also denotes the common practice of meditation as well as ascending to an altar during formal ritual. *Yunyou*, or "cloud wandering," refers to the practice of trekking into the hills for prayer and meditation in order to find the Dao. Finally, *chaosheng*, the term for pilgrimage, is actually an abbreviation of a Chinese expression that means "reverencing the holy mountain."

Although the Dao can potentially be experienced anywhere, there are many sites within China that carry special significance and these have been the destination of pilgrims across the centuries (Figure 11.3). These sites have been singled out for two

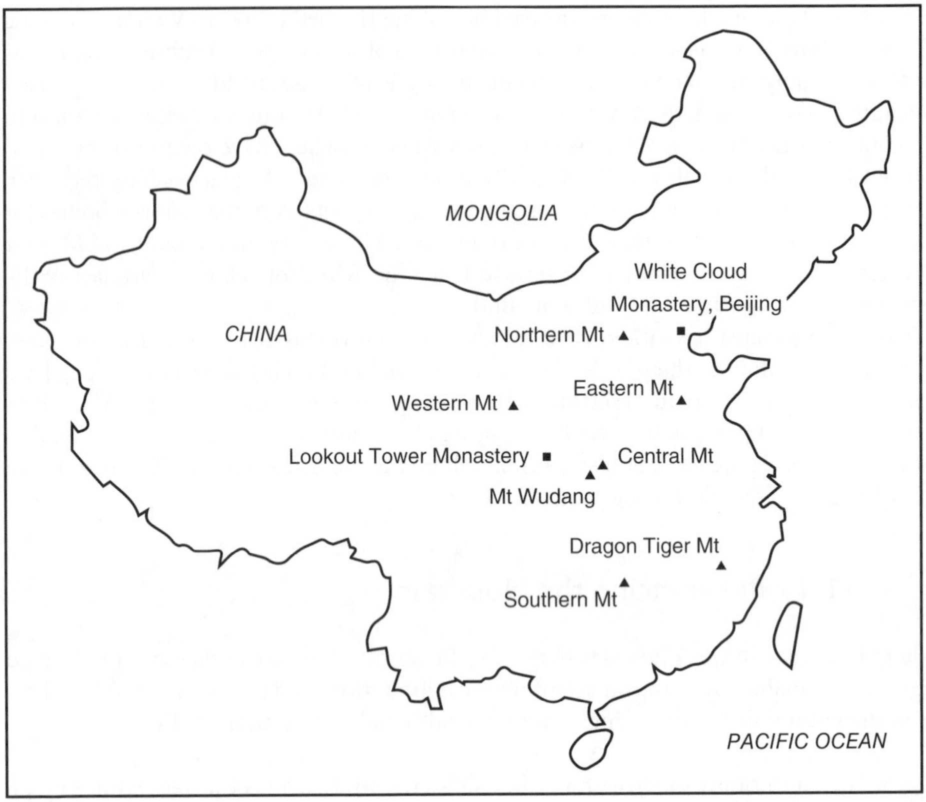

Figure 11.3 Major pilgrimage sites in Daoism.

reasons. First, they have some striking geographical characteristic. Indeed, in the majority of cases, they are located on a mountain with awe-inspiring surrounding scenery. Second, some important mythical or historical event is thought to have occurred there, such as a key revelation given to a founding figure or the establishment of an early religious community. Typically, there is a resident community of monks who tend to the shrines, temples and guesthouses for visitors. Today, most Daoist pilgrimage sites in China are under the care of Quanzhen monks, because it is this branch of Daoism that is formally linked to the Chinese Bureau of Religious Affairs.

A map of Daoist pilgrimage sites in China can seem very cluttered because of the sheer number of holy places available to visit. For example, the tradition speaks of 10 major and 36 minor "grotto heavens" (dongtian), which are mountain caves where hermits lived in times past.[7] There are also 72 auspicious sites (fudi) where the energy of the Dao can be tapped and channeled. However, for the sake of convenience, we will focus on a selection of the more popular locations on the Daoist pilgrimage itinerary. Our sample consists of the Five Mountains, **Mount Wudang** and key foundational sites in both the Zhengyi and Quanzhen traditions.

The Five Mountains (Wu yue) are arguably the most renowned mountains in Chinese culture and religion. Their importance dates back to the Han dynasty (approximately 200 BCE–200 CE) when emperors began to travel to them on pilgrimage and provide material support for their upkeep. Chinese Buddhism and Daoism both claim the Five Mountains as part of their religious heritage and there have been times in the past where the two traditions both competed and co-operated over their spiritual custodianship.[8] The Five Mountains are not a random set of peaks without any interrelationship. On the contrary, like the Hindu char dham sites, each mountain is associated with one of the five cardinal directions (North, South, East, West and Center) and together they form a gigantic cross over 1,000 miles in width, covering much of mainland China. Reminiscent of the Vastu Purusha story in Hinduism, Daoist mythology relates how the five mountains originated from the body of the first being, Pangu, who lay face-down on the earth with his head in the East, his feet in the West, his right arm to the South, his left arm to the North and his belly in the middle. The cross-shaped layout of the mountains is the inspiration for the widely used Daoist talisman (sacred diagram) that is used to ward off evil powers and provide guidance when on pilgrimage.

The Northern Mountain, Hengshan ("stable mountain"), is located in Shanxi province. It is the highest of the five and surrounded by dense forests and steep cliffs. The Southern Mountain, also called Hengshan ("balanced mountain"), is actually a range of peaks in Hunan province. The Eastern Mountain, Taishan ("tranquil mountain"), is arguably the most famous of the five. Situated in Shandong province, it is characterized by granite walls and a thousand-step stone pathway known as the Stairway to Heaven, which meanders to the temple at the summit (Figure 11.4). Taishan was added to the UNESCO World Heritage list in 1987. The Western Mountain, Huashan ("flower mountain"), is in Shaanxi province and is so named because its five peaks resemble a lotus flower. The pilgrimage route starts at the Temple of Jade Spring and ascends to the top where there are hermit caves, shrines, temples and guesthouses. Finally, the Central Mountain, Songshan ("lofty mountain"), is actually a chain of peaks in Henan province. Songshan is usually associated in the popular imagination with its Buddhist Shaolin temple and the gong fu (kung fu) tradition that its monks pioneered and mastered.[9]

The Daoist equivalent of the Buddhist Shaolin community and their commitment to the martial arts is found at another mountain, south of Songshan in northern Hubei province. Although not counted among the Five Mountains, Mount Wudang (Wudangshan) enjoys even greater popularity among pilgrims. Founded during the Tang Dynasty (approximately 600–900 CE), Mount Wudang developed into a major monastic–pilgrimage complex with over 70 temples and dozens of other buildings, including the famous Palace of the Purple Heavens. Here, monks gather several times each day, at the sound of the drum and bell, to recite Daoist texts and chant Daoist songs. Mount Wudang is also associated with the god Zhenwu, who is depicted as the perfect warrior and the mythical founder of Chinese martial arts (gong fu).[10] Visitors can see Wudang masters practicing their arts on rooftops, in courtyards and in the hills surrounding the complex.

There are also a number of important pilgrimage destinations associated with the Zhengyi and Quanzhen branches of Daoism. As noted above, many of these are linked to foundational events or centers of authority within each tradition. Three of the most important Zhengyi sites are Crane Cry Mountain, Azure Wall Mountain and Dragon Tiger Mountain. Crane Cry Mountain (Mount Heming) is located in Sichuan province. For some schools, it is here that the original revelation was given by a heavenly Laozi to the founder of the Zhengyi school, Zhang Daoling around 140 CE. Other Zhengyi schools disagree and locate that same revelation on another mountain in Sichuan province: Azure Wall Mountain (Mount Qingcheng). A third key Zhengyi pilgrimage site is

Figure 11.4 Stairway to Heaven, Taishan. (Reproduced with kind permission of Alamy.)

Dragon Tiger Mountain (Mount Longhu) in Jiangxi province in eastern China. For centuries, it served as the headquarters for the leader of the Zhengyi movement, the Celestial Master. In 1949, the 63rd Master was forced to flee to Taiwan after the Communist Party took power in mainland China.

The Quanzhen branch of Daoism also has pilgrimage locations based on key foundational events in its history. The first of these marks the place where it is believed Laozi gave the Daode jing to the Guardian of the Pass. According to the second-century BCE Shiji account, this happened at Hangu Pass, near Lingbao city in Hunan province.[11] However, in the fifth century CE, Daoists shifted the location to the Zhongnan Mountains in Shaanxi province. Consequently, Lookout Tower Monastery was built on the spot, which is considered to be the birthplace of Daoism. Lookout Tower was a refuge for southern Daoists fleeing persecution under Emperor Wu (464–549 CE) of the Liang dynasty. It received imperial patronage during the Tang dynasty (approximately 600–900 CE) partly because the Tang ruling family considered themselves to be descendants of Laozi. Miraculous events are said to have occurred here and some texts state that this was also where Laozi ascended to the heavens and reappeared as a god, bestowing more secrets on the Guardian of the Pass.[12] Today, there is a flourishing Quanzhen monastery and temple at Lookout Tower. Appropriately, the primary altar is dedicated to Laozi and two steles have the Daode jing engraved on them.

Also in Shaanxi province are two other key Quanzhen sites associated with the founder of Quanzhen Daoism, Wang Zhe (died 1170 CE). Paralleling Crane Cry Mountain in the Zhengyi tradition, the Palace of the Eight Immortals (Baxian gong) in Xi'an city commemorates the area where Wang Zhe converted to Daoism and received five revelations. The temple was restored by the Chinese government in the 1980s and consists of many halls and courtyards. Similarly, the Palace of Chongyang marks the place where Wang Zhe later joined a monastic community and effectively went into seclusion. At Chongyang today the pilgrim will find a small community of monks, a modest temple and the tomb of Wang Zhe. Although most of the important Quanzhen sites are in or near the city of Xi'an, in Shaanxi province, our final example takes us to the capital, Beijing. The White Cloud Monastery (Baiyun guan) was founded in the eighth century CE and, paralleling Dragon Tiger Mountain in the Zhengyi tradition, it became the headquarters for Quanzhen Daoists. It survived the purges of the Cultural Revolution (1966–1976) and is a flourishing monastic community and pilgrimage site today. It is also the seat of the Chinese Daoist Association.

The overlap of Daoist and Buddhist interest in the Five Mountains leads naturally to our next religion whose founder lived in India not China. The places where Daoist founders gave or received initial revelations, such as Lookout Tower, Crane Cry Mountain and the Palace of the Eight Immortals, have their Buddhist equivalent in the rediscovery of a long lost truth at Bodhgaya. Similarly, the locations where new communities were established, such as Dragon Tiger Mountain and Chongyang, find resonance where the First Sermon was delivered under a tree at Sarnath, on the outskirts of Varanasi.

11.4 Traces of Tathagata

According to Buddhist scripture, as Buddha Gautama approached the end of his life, his cousin and close companion, Ananda, asked how his followers would be able to pay their respects to the master after his death. In response the Buddha spoke of four places where the believer could go to experience his abiding influence.

> Bhikkhus, after my passing away, all sons and daughters who are of good family and are faithful should, as long as they live, go to the four holy places and remember: Here at Lumbini, the enlightened one was born; here at Bodhgaya he attained enlightenment; here at Sarnath he turned the wheel of Dharma; and there at Kusinagara he entered Parinirvana.[13]

The Tipitaka text goes on to describe how the Buddha predicted that believers would make their way to these sites and perform acts of devotion such as circumambulation and offerings. The visitors would be reminded of the Buddha truth and achieve advanced states of mental awareness via meditation. In effect, the Buddha was predicting the future emergence of a Buddhist pilgrimage tradition. Like Hinduism, Buddhism acknowledges the intrinsic value of the sacred journey and shares with its mother religion many related beliefs and practices. Pilgrimage is an act of faith requiring discipline but promising good karma in return. Pilgrimage involves the adoption of a simple lifestyle and many pilgrims donate gifts of food and clothing to the resident monks who maintain the sacred sites. Pilgrimage holds out the promise of rebirth in a higher realm of heavenly happiness for those who die on the way. As in other religions, the motivations behind Buddhist pilgrimage include the expression of devotional faith, the earning of karma by self-denial and the reaping of benefits prior and subsequent to death.

There are many holy places in the Buddhist world but the above text identifies the four principal sites and highlights the key that links them: the historical founder (Figure 11.5). Unlike Hinduism, which has no such figure and whose sacred places are primarily associated with mythological events or natural symbolism, the main destinations for the Buddhist pilgrim are locations where the devotee can draw closer to the Enlightened One. Buddha Gautama is often described as **Tathagata**, meaning "the one who has come and gone." In the physical sense he is no longer here because his body was cremated long ago. Yet Buddhist faith holds that he left "traces" in this world that

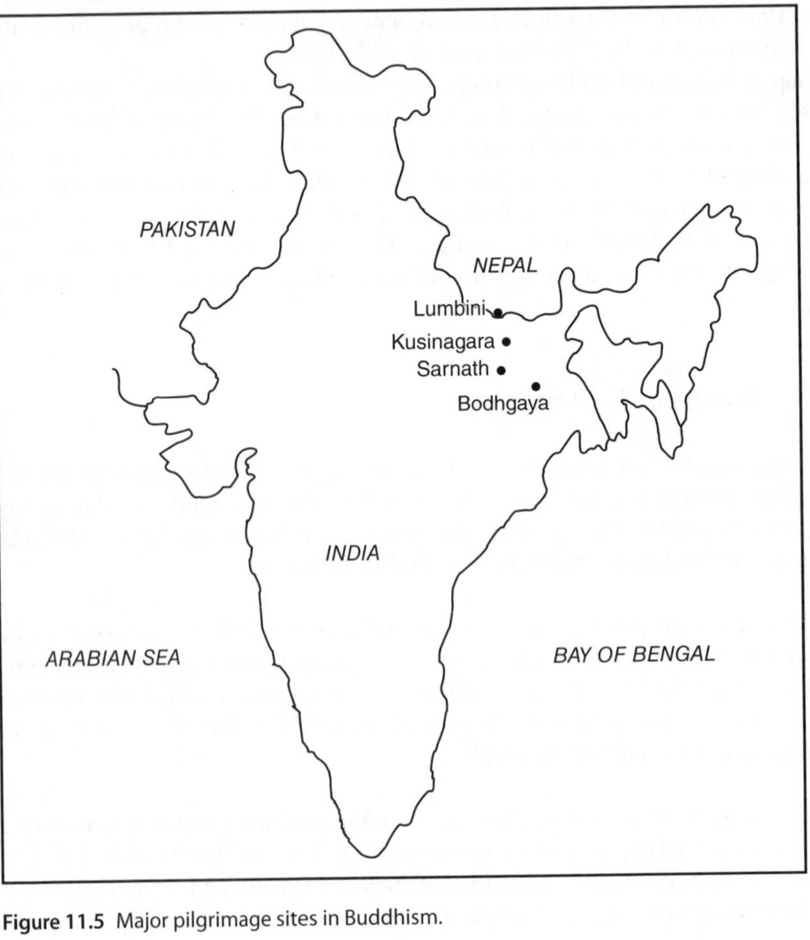

Figure 11.5 Major pilgrimage sites in Buddhism.

provide powerful and tangible links with his person. One obvious form of such traces is the relics and personal possessions of the Buddha that are stored in temples and shrines across Asia. But another type is a place where a significant event in his life occurred and there are no more significant events than the four enunciated above: his birth, Enlightenment, First Sermon and death.

The historical origins of Buddhist pilgrimage are obscure but it appears that believers began to make their way to places that figured in the life of Buddha Gautama at a relatively early stage. The most important impetus given to the practice of pilgrimage came from the Emperor Ashoka, a convert to Buddhism and one of its greatest political sponsors. In obedience to the sutta text, Ashoka set out on a dhammayatra ("journey of truth") in 249 BCE, visiting the four sites as well as others where the Buddha was reputed to have worked various miracles.[14] He erected a monument in each place and, despite the vicissitudes of history, the four main locations are once again on the itinerary of Buddhist pilgrimages and religious tours today.

Lumbini, the site of Buddha Gautama's birth, is located in the Rupandehi district of Nepal near the Indian border. Tradition has it that the Buddha's pregnant mother, Maha Devi, was on her way to her parents' home when she went into labor. She disembarked from the royal carriage and gave birth to her son while leaning against a tree in the grove. As with many other Buddhist holy places, Lumbini fell into neglect and ruin for centuries until it was rediscovered and restored by archaeologists in the late nineteenth century. It was declared a World Heritage Site by UNESCO in 1997. The visitor to Lumbini is first greeted by the remains of Ashoka's great stone pillar and a tree that is said to have supported the Buddha's mother during birth. Nearby is a commemorative stone that marks the precise spot where it is believed that the young Prince Siddhartha first saw the light of day. The new shrine contains a bas-relief depicting the birth scene and a pond where the mother bathed after the nativity.

Although Lumbini marks the beginning of the last reincarnation of the Buddha, greater prestige is bestowed upon the place where the prince became the Buddha. Bodhgaya lies approximately 120 miles east of the holy city of Varanasi. Like many Buddhist shrines, it was devastated by the Muslim invaders of the twelfth century CE and became a Hindu place of worship for many centuries. The renowned British archaeologist, Sir Alexander Cunningham, excavated the site in the 1880s and it was eventually returned to the Buddhist community in the twentieth century. Consequently, the pilgrimage tradition has been revived and Buddhist faithful from all over the globe visit the complex every year. The earliest buildings date from the time of Ashoka but the present Mahabodhi Temple was erected in the second century CE. It is thought that the relics stored in the stupa are those of Siddhartha Gautama himself. The interior is dominated by a giant golden statue depicting the Buddha sitting in a serene earth-touching posture, just as he would have sat under the bodhi tree on that fateful night. The gesture of reaching down to the earth symbolizes how the Buddha resisted the temptations of Mara during the process of Enlightenment. Pilgrims circumambulate this most holy place by following a marble walkway around the temple. In 2002, five years after Lumbini, the Mahabodhi Temple was also declared a World Heritage Site.

The two most venerated objects in all of Buddhism are located behind the temple: the bodhi tree (Figure 11.6) and the diamond throne. The tree under which Siddhartha Gautama became the Buddha is a type of fig tree (*Ficus religiosa*). Sadly, it has been destroyed, intentionally and unintentionally, on a number of occasions, but each time it

Figure 11.6 Buddhists meditating at the bodhi tree, Bodhgaya. (Reproduced with kind permission of Alamy.)

has been revived or replaced with cuttings from saplings connected to the original tree.[15] It is said that each Buddha attains enlightenment under a tree of their choice which becomes the bodhi tree for that epoch. According to tradition, the tree in Bodhgaya was chosen by Siddhartha because no other place on earth could support the weight of the dharma. In front of the tree are the remains of Ashoka's shrine known as the Vajrasana ("Diamond Throne"), which is thought to be the very place where Buddha Gautama sat in meditation. The precise spot is now marked by a red sandstone slab and considered by Buddhists to be the holiest place on earth. There are also markers indicating where the Buddha spent the next seven weeks after his Enlightenment absorbed in the bliss of nirvana on earth.[16]

After the seven weeks passed, Buddha Gautama left Bodhgaya in search of his five former companions whom he found in a deer park at Sarnath, just outside Varanasi.[17] It was there that he conveyed to them the Four Noble Truths in his First Sermon. Like other sites, Sarnath has experienced moments of destruction and protracted periods of neglect but, once again, it was nineteenth-century archaeological excavations that reclaimed the site for posterity.[18] The park itself still exists and the ancient Dhamek Stupa indicates the traditional place where the First Sermon was delivered. A short distance away, the pilgrim can visit the Dharmarajika Stupa which once held bodily relics of Buddha Gautama before they were inadvertently consigned to the Ganges by well-meaning Hindus in the late eighteenth century. The main ruins are thought to be the house where Buddha Gautama spent his first rains retreat.

The fourth sacred site is Kusinagara in Uttar Pradesh, about 60 miles south of Lumbini. It was here that the Buddha lay down in a grove of trees and passed into nirvana. The immediate cause of his death was tainted food that had been offered to him by a blacksmith in Pava. His body was cremated and the ashes distributed between eight local kingdoms. Pilgrims made their way to the site of his passing for centuries until it was left deserted after the twelfth-century Islamic conquests. Kusinagara was identified and restored as part of Cunningham's archaeological projects during the late nineteenth century. Today pilgrims visit the Mahaparinibbana Temple with its 20-foot-long statue of a reclining Buddha in the process of passing into nirvana. Within the same complex, the Makutabandhana Stupa is erected on the traditional place where Buddha Gautama's remains were cremated.

There are many other shrines, temples, monasteries and holy sites throughout the Buddhist world that attract pilgrims and religious visitors. Part of the attraction in many cases is that they contain relics of Buddha Gautama and other saintly figures from the past. Unlike Hinduism and Daoism, Buddhism's most important pilgrimage destinations, like its religious festivals, are strongly linked to the life of its founder. The pilgrim who visits the place of the Buddha's birth, Enlightenment, First Sermon or death is ultimately seeking the Buddha himself. The traces he left on earth in the form of relics and holy sites are a powerful, tangible point of spiritual contact for the believer. This quest for the founder via the actual locations in which he lived and died is a feature not only of Buddhism. Sacred sites such as Lumbini, Bodhgaya, Sarnath and Kusinagara have their Christian equivalents in places such as Bethlehem, Nazareth and Jerusalem.

11.5 The Quest of the Magi

In the second chapter of Matthew's gospel, the evangelist describes how "wise men" (magi) from the East saw a new star in the heavens and recognized it as a portent of some imminent and momentous event. Following the celestial sign, they eventually came to a stable in the village of Bethlehem where they discovered a newborn infant lying in a manger. In recognition of the holiness and royalty of the child, they offered gifts of gold, frankincense and myrrh, and then returned home without betraying the location to the jealous King Herod.[19] The story of the wise men, which has become a popular aspect of the celebration of Christmas, carries many layers of profound theological meaning for the Christian. One of them concerns the journey from a distant country to the scene of Christ's birth and back home again. For many Christians, the visit of the magi is the archetype of all sacred journeys made by the believer in search of the divine. In one sense, it is the scriptural basis and model for all Christian pilgrimages.

Like Hinduism and Buddhism, Christianity is also characterized by a long, esteemed history of pilgrimage. The journey undertaken in faith to a place of great religious significance has, if anything, become even more widely practiced in recent times with advances in the means of transport. Throughout history, Christians have traveled to an impressive range of holy sites. One of the earliest forms of pilgrimage was to visit living saints who dwelt at the edge of civilization, such as the deserts of Egypt and Syria. Even today, Orthodox Christians often travel to remote monasteries, such as Mount Athos in northern Greece, to seek spiritual counsel and blessings from the holy monks who reside there.

In time, a more common form of pilgrimage emerged that involved visiting not the home of a living saint but the grave of a deceased one. The tombs of the saints, especially martyrs, were considered to be exceptionally sacred places where faith could be reinvigorated, sins forgiven and blessings bestowed. Probably the best-known European example is the ancient imperial capital itself where Christian tradition holds that Saints Peter and Paul were executed and buried, although historical divisions within Christianity have meant that Rome is now associated primarily with Catholic pilgrimage. Since the fourteenth century, popes have declared special Jubilee Years during which Christians are encouraged to make their way to the Eternal City and pray in the two basilicas, which are said to have been constructed on the gravesites of the two apostles. The other prominent example of an apostolic tomb that has attracted great numbers of Christian pilgrims, since medieval times at least, is Santiago de Compostela in northwest Spain. According to legend, the remains of the apostle James (*Iago* in Spanish) are housed in the crypt of the cathedral.[20] Pilgrims would travel to Compostela by various routes that were described collectively as the Way of Saint James. Other later examples of popular saints include the tombs of Saint Thomas Becket at Canterbury (England), Saint Francis in Assisi (Italy) and Saint Theresa in Avila (Spain).

Another type of Christian pilgrimage has come to prominence in the Catholic tradition in recent centuries. Every year, crowds of the faithful flock to places such as Guadalupe (Mexico), Fatima (Portugal), Lourdes (France) and Medjugorje (Bosnia-Herzegovina) where it is claimed that miraculous apparitions of Mary, the mother of Jesus, have been seen. However, as in the case of Buddhism, the most important Christian pilgrimage destination throughout history and across denominations is the place where the founder himself lived and died. Although Christianity eventually spread across the Roman Empire and beyond, it never lost sight of its geographical origins. Mary and the saints are important figures in many churches, but there is no one more central to Christian belief than the incarnate Son of God who once walked the earth in the land of Israel.

Historical records indicate that small numbers of Christians were visiting the Holy Land as early as the second century CE. However, as in Buddhism, the most important impetus came from an imperial source. Just as Ashoka's tour of holy sites was responsible for the consolidation of Buddhist pilgrimage practice in northern India, it was Saint Helena, mother of the Roman Emperor Constantine, who turned Christian eyes and hearts irreversibly toward Israel. She visited Jerusalem in 326 CE, when she was in her eighties, and erected shrines at principal places associated with the life of Jesus. Tradition claims that she discovered the cross on which Jesus was crucified, buried beneath a pagan temple that had been erected on what is considered to be Calvary. Thus began a stream of visitors to the holy sites where churches, monasteries and various forms of lodgings were established as part of a supportive infrastructure for pilgrims.[21] The tradition continued even when the land fell under Muslim control, although one of the ostensible motives for the Crusades was to recapture the Holy Land from the Muslim "infidel" and secure a safe route for pilgrims. Military religious orders, such as the Knights Templar, were specifically founded to provide escorts for travelers. In the nineteenth and twentieth centuries, biblical scholars and archaeologists contributed to a more accurate historical appreciation of the Holy Land. Today, the tradition of returning to the place where it all began is as strong as ever.

Most Christian pilgrimages to the Holy Land take in the main places mentioned in the gospels, as well as other significant Old Testament sites (Figure 11.7). In Galilee, a typical pilgrim group would visit the Church of the Annunciation in Nazareth where it is believed the angel Gabriel announced to Mary that she would become pregnant with

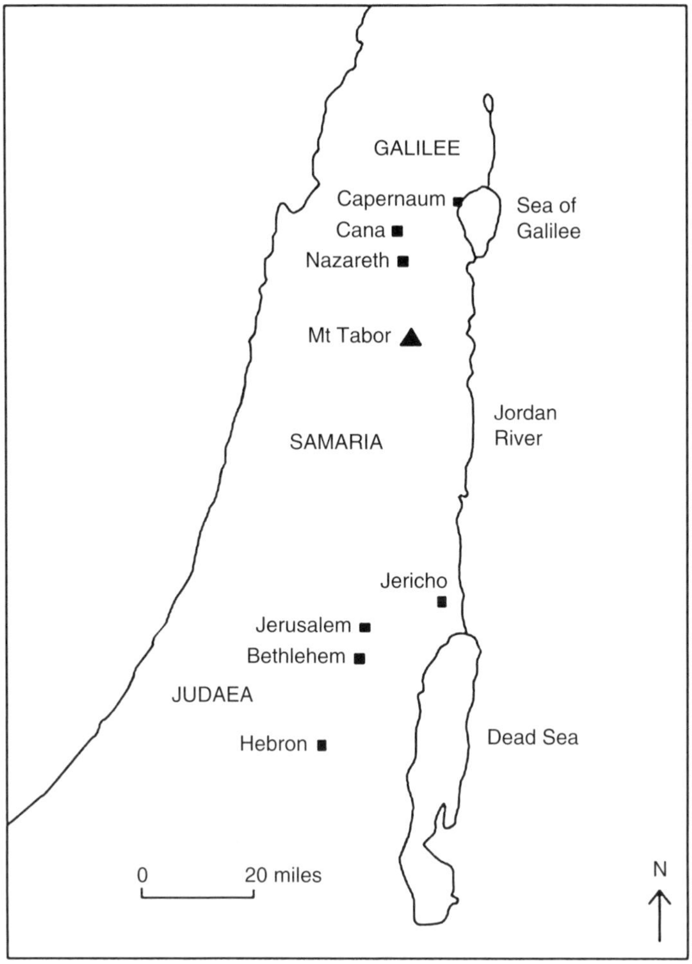

Figure 11.7 Major Christian pilgrimage sites in Israel.

the holy child. At nearby Cana, Christians recall Jesus's first miracle of turning water into wine at a wedding feast and many couples take the opportunity to renew their wedding vows. Similarly, Christian pilgrims either renew their baptismal vows or are actually baptized in the waters of the river Jordan. Other popular sites include Capernaum on the shores of the Sea of Galilee, where the synagogue ruins date to Jesus's time, and Mount Tabor, which is considered to be where Jesus was gloriously transfigured for a few brief moments in the presence of his closest disciples.

However, the climax of the pilgrimage is Jerusalem itself where the most sacred sites in Christianity are located (Figure 11.8). The Church of the Nativity in Bethlehem, about six miles south of the city, commemorates the birth of Jesus and the image of the magi's star, set in the floor before the main altar, marks the traditional spot. Just west of Jerusalem, pilgrims visit the Mount of Olives from where, it is believed, Jesus ascended to heaven. Nearby, the garden of Gethsemane still contains a grove of olive trees where Jesus experienced his "agony in the garden" on the night before his death. In the same

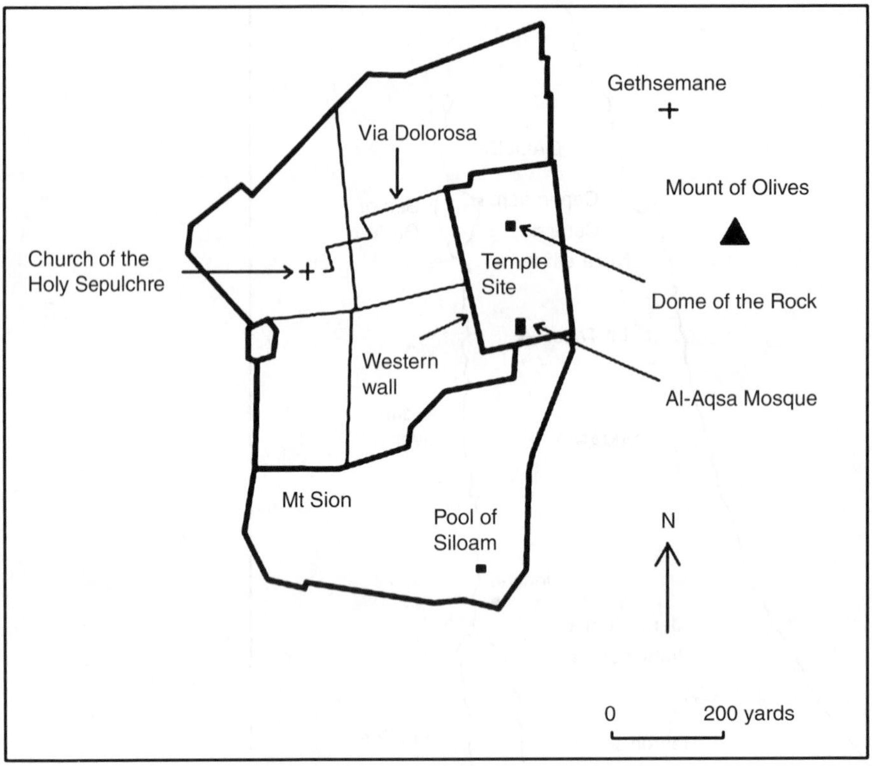

Figure 11.8 The old city of Jerusalem.

district, the medieval "Cenacle" church (from the Latin for "evening meal") contains an upper room that commemorates the Last Supper. Arguably, the most striking expression of Christian pilgrimage in Jerusalem is to walk the Via Dolorosa ("The Way of Suffering"), re-enacting the final journey of Jesus who was forced to carry his own cross to his death. The Via stretches from the Antonia Palace, where Jesus was probably tried by Pontius Pilate, through the ancient city streets to the most important shrine of all, the Holy Sepulchre Church (Figure 11.9). Here the pilgrimage reaches its apex. This edifice stands on what is believed to be Calvary, where Jesus was crucified and died. Of all the sites visited by the pilgrim, this is without rival. In this holiest of places, Christians believe that the most important event in human history took place: the Son of God died, was buried and rose again for the salvation of the world.

As with Hinduism, Daoism and Buddhism, the motives for embarking on Christian pilgrimage are multiple. Often the pilgrim hopes to obtain some spiritual or material blessing, such as forgiveness of sin or physical healing. In this respect Christian leaders have often pointed out the inherent dangers of superstition and a misplaced emphasis on shrines and relics. Protestant Christianity has been most vocal in expressing such concerns. For example the Augsburg Confession described pilgrimage as foolish and idolatrous.[22] Instead Protestantism has traditionally stressed the pilgrimage of the soul itself from birth to its final destination in heaven. The individual's exile in this world and its epic return to its true home with God is an element in New Testament theology but

Figure 11.9 Church of the Holy Sepulchre, Jerusalem.
(Reproduced with kind permission of iStock.)

its classical expression is John Bunyan's *Pilgrim's Progress* (1642).[23] In one sense, every Christian pilgrimage is a mirror of life itself. Even the common term *parish*, which denotes the basic organizational unit in many Christian denominations, is derived from the Greek word *paroikia*, which means "to live in exile." The Catholic Church took up the theme of the pilgrim church at the Second Vatican Council, stressing that not only individuals but the entire Christian community throughout the ages are on an epic journey toward God under the guidance of the Holy Spirit.[24]

In the main, Catholic and Orthodox churches admit the veracity of Protestant concerns and endeavor to guard against abuse and excess. Ideally, the journey to a tomb or shrine should not fuel superstition but enable the believer to be inspired by the legacy of the saint. The principle applies above all in the case of the founder himself. Just as visits to Lumbini, Bodhgaya, Sarnath or Kusinagara are ultimately about discovering traces of Buddha Gautama, so too a Christian pilgrimage to the Holy Land must ultimately be about drawing closer to the person of Jesus of Nazareth. Although pilgrimage is not an obligation for the Christian, experiencing first-hand the places where the founder lived and died has the potential to deepen personal faith in him. Like the magi of old, the Christian pilgrim comes to the land of the gospels to gain a glimpse of the Savior.

If Christian pilgrimage resembles Buddhist pilgrimage in that both involve traveling to places that were significant in the life of the founder and other holy figures from the past, it also shares a fundamental geographical intersection with its mother faith. As a Jew, Jesus himself would have visited Jerusalem three times each year, as John's gospel notes during his public life.[25] All the canonical gospels agree that it was during one of these visits, in the proximity of the Temple, that Jesus was arrested and executed. Eventually, Christians would describe Christ as the new Temple – a living holy of holies where divinity and humanity meet. But long before the advent of Christianity, the ancient Temple was the focus of national religious attention and the regular destination of Jewish citizens who were obliged by divine law to "go up" to the holy city as pilgrims.

11.6 Aliyah

Among the 150 sacred hymns that comprise the Book of Psalms in the Hebrew Bible, there are 15 that are prefaced with the phrase "Song of Ascent." Psalms 120 through to 134 are short joyful expressions of faith that dwell on a number of themes, including that of journeying to Jerusalem. As the preface to each psalm suggests, these were canticles sung by groups of religious travelers on their way to the holy city. In fact, Jerusalem is situated in the hill country of Judaea and a journey to the gates of the ancient capital would have meant a real physical ascent – one which appropriately symbolized the ascent of the mind and heart toward God. The Songs of Ascent reflect the most prominent example of pilgrimage in ancient Judaism – aliyah le regel ("going up for the festivals"). According to the Torah, every Jewish adult male was obliged to make his way to Jerusalem three times each year:

> Three times a year all your males shall appear before the Lord your God at the place that he will choose: at the festival of unleavened bread, at the festival of weeks and at the festival of booths. They shall not appear before the Lord empty-handed; all shall give as they are able, according to the blessing of the Lord your God that he has given you.[26]

The Deuteronomy text specifies the three occasions as the feasts of Passover, Shavuot and Sukkoth. These feasts still constitute three of the most important religious holidays on the Jewish calendar, commemorating key events in Israel's past: the escape from Egypt; the giving of the Torah on Sinai; and the wanderings in the desert before the settlement of the promised land. But the three feasts also marked key harvest times in the agricultural cycle. The feast of Passover is also known as the festival of spring. It is a week-long celebration commencing on the full moon of the Hebrew month of Nisan (March–April) and coincides with the barley harvest in the land of Israel. The feast of Shavuot, often called the feast of gathering, comes seven weeks after Passover and corresponds with the wheat harvest, the last grain harvest for the year. The third festival, Sukkoth, commences on the full moon of the month of Tishri (September–October). As an early autumn feast, Sukkoth celebrates the fruit harvest but is also a general thanksgiving for the entire harvest season.

According to the Torah, these three feasts had to be celebrated in the city of Jerusalem. Consequently Passover, Shavuot and Sukkoth are collectively known as shalosh regalim ("foot festivals"). In addition, the believer was obliged not only to go up to Jerusalem for the feasts but also to ensure that he did not arrive empty-handed. In other words, the pilgrim was required to make an offering of the first fruits to the Temple priests who would grant a special blessing in return. The offering of the first fruits is essentially an act of thanksgiving to the creator whose beneficence makes the harvest possible in the first place.[27] Furthermore, the most appropriate place to celebrate God's mighty actions in the past and to offer the fruits of the harvest as a gesture of gratitude was the Temple.

Jerusalem came to prominence as the religious center of the nation when King David captured it and established it as his new capital. His son, Solomon, subsequently constructed the First Temple on a hill within the city, known as **Mount Zion**. It is believed that this is the same place where Abraham was prepared to sacrifice his son, Isaac, to God in obedience.[28] The Temple was not only the primary place of worship but it also housed the Ark of the Covenant within its inner sanctum. Sadly, the Temple has had a turbulent history. It was first destroyed by the Babylonians in 586 BCE but was rebuilt after the return of the exiles 50 years later. It was desecrated by Hellenistic overlords in the middle of the second century BCE, an act that sparked the Maccabean revolt and the events commemorated at Hanukkah. The temple was expanded by Herod the Great at the turn of the epoch only to be destroyed a second time by Roman armies in 70 CE.

After the destruction of the Second Temple and the ban on Jews entering the holy city, the aliyah le regel lapsed. The three pilgrim festivals remained a very important part of the religious calendar, but the term *aliyah* eventually took on a new form and meaning: the return of the Jewish exiles to their homeland. With the loss of the Temple and its priesthood under the Romans, Jewish prayers began to include the hope that one day the Temple would be rebuilt and the nation gather again in the land of Israel. At daily synagogue service Jews would face toward the land of Israel and pray for a return. At the Passover meal and at the end of the Yom Kippur fast, Jewish prayers speak of gathering "next year in Jerusalem." At Jewish weddings, a glass is broken in commemoration of the destruction of the Temple and the seven blessings speak of the hope that one day the streets of Zion will be filled with her own children.

As the centuries went by, Jews gradually began to make their way back to the land of their fathers. Religious persecution in Europe and the expulsion of Jews from places such as England (1290), France (1391), Austria (1421) and Spain (1492) were interpreted by many as a sign of the end days, prompting large numbers to migrate to Israel. However, it was the Zionist movement in the late nineteenth century that led to the establishment of the modern Israeli state in 1948 and the mass return of Jewish exiles that followed. Today aliyah still means immigrating to Israel as an individual or as a group. Its converse, emigration from Israel, is considered to be "going down" (yeridah). The exiled Jews go up to their true home just as their forefathers also went up to Israel from Egyptian slavery and Babylonian captivity.[29] For many Jews, aliyah is considered to be a religious duty and those who do so are known as olim. The Law of Return guarantees assistance for any Jew who wishes to immigrate and automatic citizenship upon arrival. Today, the journey up to Jerusalem, which was once to celebrate the three festivals after which the pilgrims returned home, is for many a one-way journey to a religious homeland given to Abraham by God long ago.

Of course not all Jews make the modern aliyah and migrate permanently to Israel. The majority still live in other parts of the world and no longer consider themselves literally "in exile." However, many visit Israel for religious reasons, especially to see for themselves places associated with prominent figures from the past such as patriarchs, kings and holy persons. Examples of modern-day Jewish pilgrimage sites include the tombs of Abraham, Isaac and Jacob in Hebron; the tomb of King David in Jerusalem; and the graves of Rabbi Simeon Bar Yohai in Meron and Rabbi Meir Ba'al Na Nes in Tiberias. But the holiest space in the Jewish world and the main focus of all journeys to the land of Israel is the last visible remnant of the primary symbol of a nation's faith and the destination of its ancient pilgrimages: the **Western Wall** (Figure 11.10).

Figure 11.10 The Western Wall, Jerusalem.
(Reproduced with kind permission of iStock.)

When the Roman army destroyed the Second Temple in 70 CE, it left part of Herod's outer retaining walls still standing. Some say that it was deliberately spared by Titus as a constant reminder of Roman power. For Jews, however, it was seen as a divine sign providing a tangible link with the great building in which a nation once worshiped. For many Jews, the divine presence that occupied the Holy of Holies moved into the Western Wall, transforming it into a sacred place. Over the centuries Jews who made their way to Jerusalem would visit the Temple Mount and pray before the Wall. The sorrow they expressed at the destruction of Israel's most sacred building led non-Jewish observers to call it the "Wailing Wall," but the preferred term within the Jewish community is Western Wall (HaKotel).

The growth of the Jewish population in Israel from the nineteenth century saw an increase in the religious and political significance of the Western Wall. Jews were prevented from visiting the Wall when it came under Jordanian control in 1948. In June 1967, Israeli forces captured the city and the adjacent residential quarter was demolished. On the first day of Shavuot that year, a quarter of a million Jews converged at the Wall to celebrate the ancient pilgrim festival. Today, a wide paved plaza has been created in front of it for easier access. One of the most widely recognized images of Judaism is that of Jews praying before the Wall and placing petitionary prayers written on a small piece of paper (tzetel) into its crevices.

The Western Wall has also become a popular place for the bar mitzvah ceremony in which a young Jewish male is considered to enter spiritual adulthood. In one sense it is an appropriate location because at bar mitzvah the young man has the privilege of reading the Torah at synagogue for the first time. The term for approaching the bimah in order to read the sacred text is *aliyah la-Torah*. Hence, the physical movement of going up to the elevated platform that holds the word of God here takes on the special resonance of the ancient practice of going up to the Temple to celebrate the great pilgrim festivals. The movement may involve a few yards or thousands of miles, but in both cases it is an aliyah, a sacred journey upwards from the mundane into the presence of the divine.[30]

As we have seen, the old city of Jerusalem, in particular the Temple Mount, is a holy place of pilgrimage for both Christians and Jews. For Christians these are the streets where Jesus spent his last days on earth prior to his saving death and glorious resurrection. For Jews, it is David's city in which believers would gather three times each year to celebrate God's past intervention in their history and his ongoing blessing of their fields. But today, when visitors cast their eyes toward the site of the ancient Temple, what they see above the Western Wall is not a Jewish or Christian shrine but two Islamic buildings.

11.7 Hajj

Soon after he captured the city of Jerusalem in 637 CE, the caliph Umar erected a mosque next to the place where, according to Islamic belief, Muhammad had paused on his mystical Night Journey from Mecca to heaven. The building was named after the Qur'anic reference to "the furthest mosque" (al-Masjid al-Aqsa).[31] Several decades later, the caliph Abd al-Malik erected a shrine over the actual rock where Muhammad is said to have set foot, just to the north of Umar's mosque. It was aptly named the Dome of the Rock. These two buildings, which dominate the Temple Mount today, constitute what Muslims call the Holy Sanctuary. The nearby Western Wall is described as the al-Buraq Wall, after the creature that is said to have transported Muhammad on his nocturnal flight. Thus, Jerusalem is not only a sacred city of pilgrimage for Jews and Christians. It also figured prominently in Muhammad's religious vision from the earliest times. The original qibla, or direction of prayer, was toward Jerusalem, which is still considered to be the third holiest city in Islam and one of the few places Muslims are encouraged to visit as pilgrims. However, soon after the Hijra, the qibla was moved to Mecca, the hometown of the Prophet and the principal focus of Islamic pilgrimage.

Of the six major religions under consideration, the obligation to go on pilgrimage is strongest in Islam where it constitutes the last of the five pillars of faith for Sunnis and one of the ten branches of religion for Shi'ites.[32] The Qur'an declares that "pilgrimage to the House is incumbent upon men for the sake of Allah, upon everyone who is able to undertake the journey to it."[33] The "House" referred to is understood to be the Ka'bah in Mecca, which was already a center of Arabian pilgrimage before Muhammad (Figure 11.11). When the Prophet captured the town in 630 CE, he removed the Ka'bah's idols, converting it into a central symbol of Islamic unity and the destination for all Islamic pilgrimages. Although Muhammad continued to reside in Medina and was eventually buried there, he made several pilgrimages to Mecca in the last years of his life, thus consolidating the practice as an essential aspect of the new religion. The fifth pillar was named *hajj*, an Arabic term that means "to set out on a journey." The Muslim who completes a hajj is given the honorific title *haji*, which carries a degree of social status and has sometimes been handed down as a family name.

Figure 11.11 Muslim pilgrims at the Ka'bah, Mecca.
(Reproduced with kind permission of Alamy.)

The fifth pillar requires that all adults who are physically and financially capable make the pilgrimage to Mecca at least once in their lifetime. However, Islamic tradition acknowledges that this is not possible for everyone. In fact, only a small proportion of the world's Muslims are able to afford to make the journey, especially those who live at a considerable distance from Saudi Arabia. A Muslim should not go into debt to pay for the hajj, nor should he jeopardize the welfare of his family who are his primary responsibility. Moreover, money used for the hajj should be purified beforehand by the Islamic religious tax known as zakat.

Pilgrims traditionally travel with family or friends from the local mosque. In past times, many joined the main caravans from places such as Egypt, Syria and Iraq to ensure safety on what could be an arduous and perilous journey. Today, millions of pilgrims converge on the holy city by modern means of transport. Since Muhammad's final visit in 632 CE, only Muslims have been allowed to enter the exclusive inner precinct of Mecca. The holy city is a place of religious pilgrimage, not secular tourism, although there have been occasions when non-Muslims have entered clandestinely.[34]

The hajj proper commences when the pilgrim arrives at a miqat: a marker that indicates the boundary of the sacred space. Traditionally there are six miqats to serve pilgrims arriving from different directions.[35] Here, the pilgrim is required to bathe and don a special garment known as an ihram: a white, seamless, two-piece garment for men. There is no particular dress for women although many often wear a white gown with head-covering. The color white suggests purity while the uniform look indicates the fundamental equality of all pilgrims before God in a manner reminiscent of grave clothes. As with other religious traditions, pilgrimage involves purity and self-denial. Shaving, clipping hair and nails, wearing jewelry and perfume, eating meat and sexual activity are all prohibited.[36]

There are actually two types of pilgrimage in Islam. The "lesser hajj," or umra, may be performed at any time of the year and consists of two basic activities. The first is the tawaf, or sevenfold circumambulation of the Ka'bah. Unlike Hindu circumambulation, the tawaf is performed in an anti-clockwise direction so that the heart is closer to the sacred object. According to Islamic belief, the Ka'bah was originally built by Adam but, somewhat like the tree in Bodhgaya, it has been destroyed and reconstructed many times in its history. On one occasion it was Abraham and his son Ishmael who rebuilt the edifice. It is said to be located directly under the heavenly mosque used by the angels and is, thus, the spiritual axis of the world. As noted in Chapter 1, it originally housed the idols of the pre-Islamic Arabian religion before they were destroyed by Muhammad. Today it is an empty shrine with a simple unfurnished interior and lamps hanging from the ceiling. It is covered by a black cloth known as the kiswa, on which Qur'anic verses are embroidered in gold. The pilgrims are not required to enter the building but, as they circumambulate, they reach out their arms toward the Black Stone which is inserted in the eastern external corner. The Black Stone itself is not an object of worship and probably became part of hajj practice because Muhammad used to reverence it on his visits to Mecca.[37]

The second component of the umra is the Sa'y circuit. Pilgrims walk seven times back and forth between two small hills (Safa and Marwah) that are now housed at either end of a long corridor extending from the main courtyard of the Ka'bah. The walk is a re-enactment of the desperate search for water in the desert by Abraham's wife Hagar in order to save their son Ishmael from dying of thirst.[38] According to the biblical story, God provided her with a spring of water that saved their lives. Islamic tradition claims that the Well of Zamzam, located near the Sa'y walk, is the same spring. Like Catholics at Lourdes, Muslims drink from the well and take containers home as gifts for relatives and friends because it is believed that the water has miraculous healing power. At this point the pilgrim is allowed to shave or cut some hair to indicate the end of the sacred state and the completion of the umra.

In contrast to the umra, the "greater hajj" always occurs on three specific days during the twelfth month of the Islamic calendar, which is known as Dhu al-Hijjah. It is during these days that millions of pilgrims descend on Mecca every year to fulfill the obligations of the fifth pillar. On the eighth day of Dhu al-Hijjah, the pilgrims put on the ihram and travel to the village of Mina, about five miles east of Mecca (Figure 11.12). There they spend the remainder of the day reciting salat. On the morning of the ninth, they continue for another 10 miles to the Plain of Arafat. Here, from noon until sunset, millions of pilgrims engage in the wuquf ("standing") ceremony. As the name implies, the great sea of believers stands in silent meditation, reflecting on themes such as the Day of Judgment and Abraham's willingness to sacrifice his son Ishmael out of obedience to God, which is believed to have occurred nearby. Pilgrims believe that wuquf wipes away sin and enables them to make a fresh start in life.[39]

At the center of the plain is a small hill known as the Jabal al-Rahmah ("Mountain of Mercy"). It is said that Adam and Eve were separated for some time after their descent

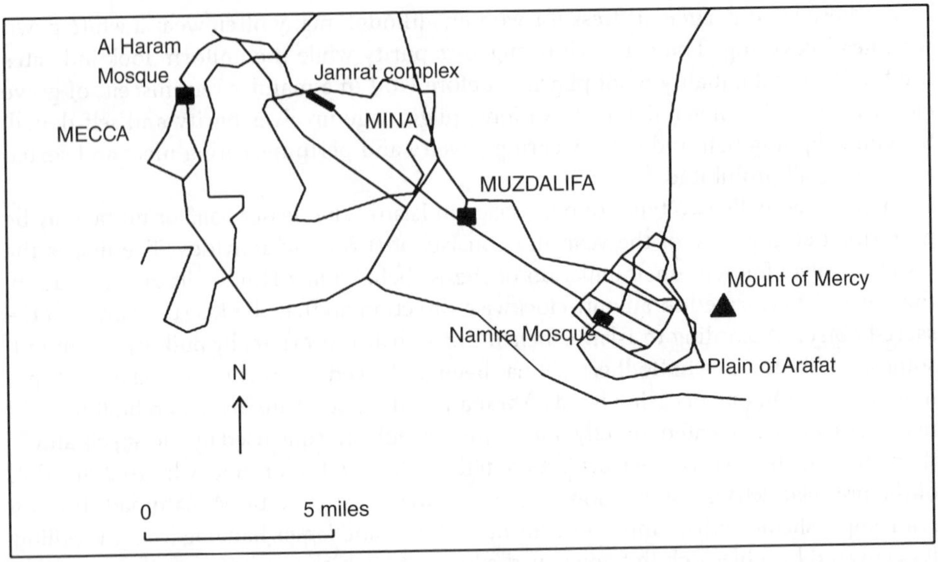

Figure 11.12 Sites of the Hajj.

from Paradise and found each other again here. It is also the location of Muhammad's Farewell Sermon in 632 CE to over 100,000 followers who had gathered for the hajj. Today, a sermon is still preached during hajj from the same place by the chief qadi (judge) of Mecca. On the evening of that same day, pilgrims set out for Muzdalifa where they collect some small pebbles. On the tenth of the month, the pilgrims return to Mina where they throw seven pebbles at a jamrah (originally a pillar but recently converted into a wall for safety reasons). The gesture recalls how Abraham resisted the temptation of Satan to disobey God and not proceed with the sacrifice of Ishmael. This day is also known as Id al-Adha, or the Feast of the Sacrifice. All Muslims around the world join the pilgrims in Mecca in sacrificing a sheep or goat in memory of the animal that God provided in place of Ishmael. Traditionally the meat of the animal is shared out: one-third for the family, one-third for neighbors and one-third for the poor. With this, the greater hajj comes to an end. Pilgrims make a final tawaf at Mecca, have a haircut and remove their ihram. Some visit Medina to see the tombs of Muhammad, Abu Bakr and Umar, but this is never done wearing the ihram because it is not part of the official hajj. Muslim authorities have always been concerned about possible deification of the Prophet at his final resting place. To this end, visitors are advised not to prostrate themselves or kiss or touch the grave as they do at the Ka'bah.

The annual hajj is one of the largest gatherings of human beings on earth, rivaling events such as the Hindu Kumbha Mela and Catholic Jubilee Year pilgrimages to Rome. Like pilgrimages in other religions, the hajj is also a powerful symbol of a worldwide faith community, a gathering of believers from different cultures and nationalities, dressed in simple, uniform garments. Surprisingly, the hajj does not emphasize links with the founder as Buddhist and Christian pilgrimages do. As noted, the tomb of Muhammad is not an official part of the hajj and there are deep concerns about any idolatry associated with it. Although Mecca is the birthplace of the Prophet and the place where his religious mission began, the symbolic acts of the hajj are more about

Abraham than Muhammad. The Ka'bah is a symbol of the Abrahamic covenant; the Sa'y circuit recalls the miraculous survival of Abraham's wife Hagar and his first son Ishmael; the wuquf ceremony at Arafat focuses on Abraham's obedience; the stoning of the jamrah commemorates Abraham's resistance of temptation; and the feasting on Id al-Adha recalls God's intervention in Abraham's sacrifice. It is as if Islam's great pilgrimage deliberately deflects attention away from the final Prophet and toward the first believer in the one God. In that sense it is a sacred journey back to the very origins of monotheism.

Summary

All six religions agree that transcendent reality is truly omnipresent and can be accessed in any place within the physical world. Yet each religion also acknowledges that there are special loci in which it is more readily experienced within time and space. These are the holy sites that attract religious visitors in large numbers from all parts of the global faith community. While the tradition of pilgrimage is quite ancient in each case, the popularity of pilgrimage today has been greatly facilitated by the advances in transport.

In some religions, the act of pilgrimage is an obligation. This is particularly so in Islam where the hajj constitutes the fifth pillar within the Sunni tradition and one of the ten branches of religion in Shi'ite Islam. The expectation, based on explicit Qur'anic verses, is that all adult Muslims visit Mecca at least once in their lifetime, with exemption for those who are not financially or physically capable. Thus, one should not go into debt or jeopardize the welfare of one's family in order to make the hajj. Pilgrimage was also a religious duty in the ancient Jewish tradition when adult males were obliged to "go up" to Jerusalem three times each year on the "foot festivals" of Passover, Shavuot and Sukkoth. These three pilgrimage festivals celebrated the saving intervention of God in Israel's history as well as the ongoing fertility of the land. With the destruction of the Temple, the obligation has lapsed, but the duty of "going up" to Jerusalem has taken a new form in some branches of Judaism as the migration of Jewish exiles to the land of Israel.

In other religions the act of pilgrimage may not be compulsory but it is keenly felt by believers as a worthy act of devotion. The reasons why individuals make a pilgrimage are multiple and varied. Many seek a material good such as healing from illness or success in a venture. For example, Muslims believe that the water from the well of Zamzam in Mecca has healing properties, just as Catholic Christians take home water from the shrine at Lourdes. Jewish pilgrims place tzetels into the cracks of the Western Wall, while Hindus who die on the banks of a holy river hope for immediate liberation from the wheel of reincarnation. But many also seek more spiritual benefits such as good karma, a deeper faith, the forgiveness of sins, longevity and health, or some blessing or grace. Ultimately, a pilgrimage is both an external expression of inner faith and a means to strengthen that same faith. Belief and commitment are deepened by the anticipation generated on the journey and the inspiration generated upon arrival in a place of enormous significance.

The source of the destination's significance varies somewhat across the religions. In Daoism, Buddhism and Christianity, holy pilgrimage sites are associated with founding figures. Pilgrims visit places where Laozi gave the Daode jing to the Guardian of the

Pass or where Zhang Daoling and Wang Zhe first received revelations and established their initial communities. According to Buddhist tradition, the four most important places to visit correspond to the most crucial events in Buddha Gautama's career: his birth, Enlightenment, First Sermon and passing to nirvana. Similarly, the main Christian shrines in the Holy Land are found at the location of Jesus's birth, miracles, sermons and his last days. In addition all three pilgrimage traditions were promoted and maintained by imperial support.

One might expect a similar pattern in Islam, yet the main focus of the hajj is not Muhammad. The place of pilgrimage, Mecca, is where the Prophet was born and the Qur'an was first revealed, yet the hajj is not explicitly concerned with either event. Its main theological focus is Abraham: the Ka'bah that he rebuilt; the Sa'y circuit of Hagar and Ishmael; the stoning of the jamrahs; the meditation themes at Arafat; and the animal sacrifice on Id al-Adha. Although the Islamic hajj was established by Muhammad during his lifetime, the center of attention is the person considered by Jews, Christians and Muslims to be the first believer in the one God.

An even greater overlap between the three Abrahamic religions is evident in the importance that each places on Jerusalem. Christian pilgrimages come to their climax in the city where Jesus spent his last days, with visits to the Cenacle, Gethsemane, the Via Dolorosa and the Church of the Holy Sepulchre. Muslims consider Jerusalem to be the third holiest city on earth. It was the original qibla and Muhammad is said to have paused on the hill of Zion during his mystical journey to heaven. Today, the Dome of the Rock and the al-Aqsa mosque testify to its significance in Islamic eyes. The overlap is also a source of considerable tension, for this is also the site of the ancient Jewish Temple. Although Jewish pilgrims visit the tombs of patriarchs, kings and rabbis, there is no single founder figure. Instead, the heart of religious life and the focus of pilgrimage in ancient Israel was the Temple. Today, the remains of that Temple have become the most sacred place in Judaism and the destination of pilgrims from other parts of Israel and the entire Jewish world. As Jews stand before the Western Wall in prayer, they express their sorrow at the tragic loss of their holiest shrine, but draw strength from its enduring stones that God has not abandoned his people.

While Hinduism has a highly developed pilgrimage tradition, unlike the other five religions its sacred journeys do not focus on historical or quasi-historical founders or a single unifying temple-shrine. In contrast, it has thousands of holy places dotted around the subcontinent like jewels in a tiara – locations linked to deities from Hindu mythology rather than historical memory. It shares the notion with Daoism that natural geographical settings are places where Ultimate Reality (Brahman or the Dao) can be encountered in unusually powerful ways. Hinduism's holiest cities lie on the banks of rivers where pilgrims bathe to rid themselves of bad karma and hope to die in order to obtain immediate moksha. Similarly, most Daoist pilgrimage sites are located on mountains where heaven and earth meet. In one sense, India itself is a holy shrine to be circumambulated via the four dhams located at the four compass points. Similarly, in Daoism, the Five Mountains form a gigantic geographical cross marking the cardinal directions within China. Finally, Hinduism, Daoism and Judaism all use a natural analogy to describe the act of pilgrimage. In Hinduism it is crossing the river; for Daoism and Judaism it is ascending the mountain. In the latter religions, the same analogy is applied to approaching the focal point within the sacred building (rushan and aliyah). Both images powerfully capture the ideal of all pilgrims whether they stand in Varanasi,

Mount Wudang, Bodhgaya, Mecca or Jerusalem. Pilgrimage is not merely a physical journey to a distant destination involving time, effort and risk. Pilgrimage is also a spiritual journey of the mind and heart seeking out the bedrock of religious belief. Pilgrimage is a mirror of the journey of human life from birth to death and beyond those shores to the other side. In the end, pilgrimage, like so many other aspects of religious practice, is crossing over from, or ascending above, the ordinary to the extraordinary.

Discussion Topics

1 How does a religious pilgrimage reflect the "journey of life"?
2 What are the main motives for embarking on a religious pilgrimage?
3 Why is Jerusalem so important to Jews, Christians and Muslims? What problems have arisen as a result?
4 What are the main events in the history of the Jewish Temple? Do all Jews believe that the Temple should be rebuilt?
5 What was the significance of the Ka'bah before Islam? Why is it so important to Muslims?
6 Why is the Ganges so significant in Hinduism? Are other rivers also considered holy?
7 What are the main Marian pilgrimage sites in Catholicism and why are they so popular?
8 Compare Buddhist and Daoist pilgrimage sites in China.
9 Compare pilgrimages associated with the tomb of a holy person in different religions.

Notes

1 The five fundamental duties are referred to as the panca kriya: upasana (worship); utsava (holy days); dharma (virtuous living); tirthayatra (pilgrimage); and samskara (rites of passage).
2 The 12 jyotirlinga temples are in Rameshwaram, Ujjain, Nashik, Varanasi, Kedarnath, Prabhas Patan, Srisailam, Omkareshwar, Bhimashankar, Dogarh, Hingoli and Verul.
3 The seven holy cities are Ayodhya, Mathura, Hardwar, Varanasi, Kanci, Ujjain and Dwarka.
4 The festival is held at Prayag when Jupiter is in Taurus; at Ujjain when Jupiter is in Leo; at Nashik when Jupiter is in Scorpio; and at Hardwar when Jupiter is in Aquarius.
5 A popular custom involves bathing at the five main ghats: Asi, Dashashwamedha, Adi Keshava, Panchganga and Manikarnika.
6 Zhuangzi, ch. 1.
7 The ten major grotto heavens are located on these mountains: Wangwu, Weiyu, Xichen, Xixuan, Qingcheng, Chicheng, Luofu, Gouqu, Linwu and Guacang.
8 Daoists began to claim jurisdiction over Five Mountains in the period of Disunion (220–589 CE).
9 It is said that the founder of Chan Buddhism, Bodhidharma, attained enlightenment at Songshan.

10 The 2000 film *Crouching Tiger, Hidden Dragon* featured the Wudang martial arts (gong fu) tradition.
11 Shiji, ch. 63.
12 See Xisheng jing: Scripture on Western Ascension DZ 666.
13 Maha Parinibbana Sutta 5.16–22.
14 Apart from the four main sites, Ashoka also visited Savatthi, Sankasia, Rajagaha and Vesali where the Buddha worked various miracles.
15 The present tree is over 100 years old and was taken from the former tree, which collapsed during a storm in 1876.
16 According to tradition, the Buddha spent a week in each of seven places near the original tree, meditating on the dharma.
17 The five companions became the first Buddhist monks: Kondanna, Vappa, Bhaddiya, Mahanama and Assaji.
18 It suffered under the sixth-century CE Hun invasion and again under the Islamic invasions in the late twelfth century CE.
19 Matthew 2:1–12.
20 Although Acts 12:1-2 states that James was executed in Jerusalem, the tradition claims that he had earlier preached in Spain and that his associates brought his body there after his death. The 1884 Bull of Pope Leo XIII accepted the authenticity of the relics but Catholic scholarship remains ambivalent.
21 The *Pilgrimage of Etheria* (c.400 CE), which records the journey of a Spanish nun to the Holy Land, speaks of a well-organized system of guides and lodgings for pilgrims.
22 Augsburg Confession 12.14; 21.16.
23 See Hebrews 11:13–16; 13:14; 1 Peter 1:17; 2:11.
24 See Second Vatican Council's Constitution on the Church (*Lumen Gentium)*, ch. VII, "The Pilgrim Church."
25 See John 2:13; 7:10; 11:55.
26 Deuteronomy 16:16–17. See also Exodus 23:17; 34:23.
27 See Talmud Moed, Treatise 12 (Hagigah) which deals with the pilgrimage festival offerings.
28 See Genesis 22:1–3.
29 See Genesis 13:1; 46:4; 50:14; Numbers 32:11; Ezra 1:3; 2:1.
30 The term *aliyah* also refers to the miraculous ascension to heaven of holy persons such as Enoch and Elijah. See Genesis 5:23–4; 2 Kings 2:11.
31 Qur'an 17:1: "Glory be to Him Who made His servant to go on a night from the Sacred Mosque to the remote mosque of which We have blessed the precincts."
32 Shi'ite Islam speaks of the five "roots" of religion (monotheism, justice, prophethood, leadership and the day of judgment) and the ten "branches" of religion (daily prayer, fasting, alms, tax, pilgrimage, struggle, goodness, avoidance of evil, loving the community and hating the enemies of the community).
33 Qur'an 3:97.
34 See Sir Richard Francis Burton, *Pilgrimage to Al Madina and Mecca* (1885).
35 The six traditional miqats are: Zu'l-Hulafa, near Medina, and Al-Johfa, near Jeddah, for those arriving from Egypt and Syria; Zat-i-'Irq, northeast of Mecca, for those coming from Iraq; Qarnu l-Manazil, east of Mecca; Yalamlam, south of Mecca, for those arriving from Yemen; and Taneem, situated in Mecca, for its citizens. Pilgrims arriving by the airport in Jedda are required to put on their ihram about one hour before landing.

36 Qur'an 2:197–8.
37 Muslims believe that the Black Stone symbolises the covenant between Allah and Abraham. It fell from heaven and turned black because of the sins of humanity.
38 Qur'an 2:158.
39 Qur'an 2:198–9.

Further Reading

Bhardwaj, Surinder M. & Lochtefeld, James G. (2004). "Tirtha" in Sushil Mittal (ed.), *The Hindu World*. Abingdon: Routledge, ch. 21.
Coleman, Simon, & Elsner, John (1997). *Pilgrimage: Past and Present in the World Religions*. Cambridge, MA: Harvard University Press.
Feldhaus, Anne (2003). *Connected Places: Region, Pilgrimage and Geographical Imagination in India*. Basingstoke: Palgrave Macmillan.
Forbes, Duncan (2010). *Buddhist Pilgrimage*. New Delhi: Motilal Banarsidass.
Fuller, C. (2004). *The Camphor Flame*. 2nd ed. Princeton, NJ: Princeton University Press.
Granoff, Phyllis, & Shinohara, Koichi (eds.) (2003). *Pilgrims, Patrons and Place: Localizing Sanctity in Asian Religions*. Vancouver: University of British Columbia Press.
Harpur, James (2002). *Sacred Tracks: Two Thousand Years of Christian Pilgrimage*. Berkeley, CA: University of California Press.
Holm, Jean, & Bowker, John (eds.) (2000). *Sacred Place*. London: Continuum.
Hurgronje, C. Snouck (2006) "The Meccan Feast," in G. R. Hawting (ed.), *The Development of Islamic Ritual*. Aldershot: Ashgate, ch. 14.
Komjathy, Louis (2013). *The Daoist Tradition*. London: Bloomsbury, ch. 14.
Levine, Lee I. (1999). *Jerusalem: Its Sanctity and Centrality to Judaism, Christianity and Islam*. London: Continuum.
Müller, Sven (2015) "Spaces of Rites and Locations of Risk: The Great Pilgrimage to Mecca" in Stanley Brunn (ed.) *The Changing World Religion Map. Sacred Places, Identities, Practices and Politics*. Lexington, KY: Springer, ch. 42.
Peters, F. E. (1996). *The Hajj*. Princeton, NJ: Princeton University Press.
Scott, Jamie, & Simpson-Housley, Paul (eds.) (1991). *Sacred Places and Profane Spaces*. London: Greenwood.
Shariati, Ali (2005). *Hajj: Reflection on its Rituals*. Houston, TX: Free Islamic Literatures.
Singh, Rana & Haigh, Martin (2015) "Hindu Pilgrimages: The Contemporary Scene" in Stanley Brunn (ed.). *The Changing World Religion Map. Sacred Places, Identities, Practices and Politics*. Lexington, KY: Springer, ch. 39.
Stoddard, Robert H. & Morinis, E. Alan (eds.) (1997). *Sacred Places, Sacred Spaces: The Geography of Pilgrimages*. Baton Rouge, LA: Geoscience Publications, Louisiana State University.
Storper Perez, Danielle & Goldberg, Harvey E. (2001). "Meanings of the Western Wall" in Harvey E. Goldberg (ed.), *The Life of Judaism*. Berkeley, CA: University of California Press, ch. 12.
Subhadra Sen Gupta (2003). *Chaar Dhaam: A Guide to the Hindu Pilgrimages*. New Delhi: Rupa.

Conclusion

At the end of our comparative tour of practice in six major religions, it is time to gather together and identify the salient features that have emerged. How similar or different are these six great traditions? What points of intersection can be seen from our juxtaposition of thematic cross-sections? The first general observation to be noted is that each religion is different from all of the others and, thus, is genuinely unique. The ever-present danger of the comparative approach is to force similarity at the expense of authentic difference. An overemphasis on the areas of common ground can easily neglect the fact that each religion has its own distinctive qualities that differentiate it from others and provide it with its identity. This is true in the broadest sense. Buddhism is really different from Hinduism and Daoism; Judaism is not the same as Islam or Christianity. It is also true in terms of particular practices. For example, although they can all be described as festivals of light, Hanukkah, Divali and Easter are very different in their meanings and their specific combination of symbols, words and actions. Similarly, although they are all holy texts, the Qur'an, the Daode jing and the Tipitaka are very different in content and context. Again, although they are all sacred buildings where believers occasionally gather, a synagogue is not a mosque, and a mandir is not a church.

The need to recall the differences between the religions is reinforced by the fact that each religious tradition is not monochrome but consists of a multicolored spectrum of subdivisions. There are not only real differences between the religions but also within each of them. Not only is Divali different from Hanukkah and Easter, but not all Hindus celebrate Divali and those who do approach it according to their particular Hindu sect. Theravada and Mahayana Buddhists interpret and use the Tipitaka in quite different ways. A church is very different from a synagogue but the shape, layout and use of a church can vary considerably for Orthodox, Catholic and Protestant Christians.

Yet it would be inaccurate to simply stop there and be satisfied with the statement that all religions are fundamentally unique. While it is important to acknowledge the variations within each religion as well as the real differences between them, it is also important to recognize that there is also a considerable degree of similarity. The glass is both half empty and half full. But in what sense are they similar? At the most basic level, the six are similar because they are all members of the category of "religion" even though, for some, Buddhism sits uneasily there. The fact that, in most cases, the 11 practical themes chosen for this book found resonance in each religious tradition confirms this fundamental level of commonality. All six religions profess that the ultimate meaning of human existence is found in reference to a transcendent reality that can be fully encountered only beyond physical death. All six religions believe that truths pertaining to this transcendent reality

World Religions in Practice: A Comparative Introduction, Second Edition. Paul Gwynne.

and its relevance for human existence have been mediated to us via a corpus of writings. These texts are consequently revered as holy and are, thus, determinative of belief and practice. All six religions are committed to the idea that part of the journey toward our ultimate destiny is the duty to live a moral life according to a shared core of fundamental norms. Each religion celebrates the key moments of that journey – such as birth, marriage and death – in ways that highlight their transcendent nature. Each religion takes up common aspects of human existence – such as food and clothing – and imparts to these a transcendent significance that gives expression to religious faith. Finally, all six religions consecrate the very fabric of our spatio-temporal world. Time itself is given transcendent meaning via the cycles of holy days, weeks, months and years, while space is sanctified via the architecture of the sacred building and the common tradition of pilgrimage to holy places. In other words, although the six religions are unique, they are also very similar, at least in the sense of possessing these practical features of a religion. There are real resemblances as well as differences.

However, simply pointing out that the six religions share these 11 aspects of practice is still very general. It has also been possible to identify more nuanced patterns of similarity and difference between them. These specific points of intersection are reflected in the order in which each religion is treated in each chapter. When the religions are set out beside each other on the table, where do the natural bridges appear? The most obvious pattern that emerges is not surprising because it reflects the historical mother–daughter connection between two pairs of religions: Hinduism–Buddhism and Judaism–Christianity. In both cases, the latter has sprung from the former and, although it eventually evolves into a distinctive religion in its own right, the daughter also naturally inherits and retains many of the elements of its mother.

Thus, Hinduism and Buddhism both share a quasi-cyclic reincarnational understanding of human existence as an extended series of births, deaths and rebirths, leading eventually to final liberation. The relative unimportance of the physical body is reflected in the common (but not universal) funeral practice of cremation, which facilitates advancement toward final emancipation. Progress toward liberation is also gained by the fulfillment of ethical–religious duties summed up in both traditions by the term *dharma*, understood as an intrinsic cosmic order or truth rather than a code of law given by an external creator God. In both Hinduism and Buddhism, the more advanced stages of the samsaric path are characterized by the renunciation of worldly pleasures and the adoption of the celibate lifestyle as in the ideal of the Buddhist monk and the Hindu sannyasin. Both traditions also profess that spiritual advancement involves a commitment to non-violence toward living creatures, which is reflected in the practice of vegetarianism in higher-caste Hinduism and Buddhist monastic life. The cyclic Hindu–Buddhist worldview is also symbolized in the religious calendar via an emphasis on the lunar cycle, especially in the calculation of regular holy days. Both traditions also give religious meaning to the annual monsoon season as a special time of spiritual retreat or caution while the gods sleep. Finally, Hindu and Buddhist sacred buildings commonly contain a special room housing sacred images that assist the believer in their encounter with transcendent reality, whether in the form of the many Hindu deities, the glorious body of Buddha Gautama or the celestial Buddhas and bodhisattvas of the Mahayana tradition.

Similarly, Judaism and Christianity share an extensive area of overlap based on their historical connection. Both are commonly referred to as monotheistic faiths given their explicit belief in a single personal God. Judaism's emphasis on the transcendent, invisible nature of God and the concomitant danger of idolatry is evident in the traditional lack of visual images in synagogues. This is most clearly reflected in Protestant Christianity's version of the Ten Commandments and its churches which are usually devoid of statues or icons. One very important point of intersection is the corpus of sacred writing known as Tanach for Jews and the Old Testament for Christians. Although interpreted in very different ways by each tradition, this common set of holy texts is read in both synagogue and church over annual cycles and constitutes a vital part of official worship, private devotion and theological study. Synagogues and churches are both places where the divine word is reverently stored, liturgically proclaimed and theologically interpreted for the gathered faithful. Embedded in that sacred corpus is the Decalogue which lists the principal religious and moral precepts for what is often referred to as the Judeo-Christian tradition.

In contrast to the Hindu–Buddhist reincarnational worldview, Judaism and Christianity generally adhere to a linear understanding of human existence in which an individual lives and dies just once. One's unique physical body carries much greater significance and is considered to be an essential part of one's being both now and beyond death. Thus, both religions traditionally profess a belief in the resurrection of the body and both have historically preferred burial over cremation. Jews and Christians understand marriage as part of the divine dispensation and see the love of husband and wife as an earthly symbol of the vertical relationship between the divine and the human. Christianity has also inherited and transformed other Jewish practices including the ritual use of bread and wine, the weekly day of rest and prayer, the 50-day season from Passover to Shavuot (Easter to Pentecost) and the recognition of the land of Israel, in particular the city of Jerusalem, as a place of unparalleled religious importance. But what of the other two religions with no direct mother–daughter relationship: Daoism and Islam?

Because Daoism and Buddhism – along with Confucianism – are the major religious traditions associated with Chinese culture, it is not surprising to find considerable intersection between the first two. Like the Three Baskets, the Daoist canon is a sizeable anthology of works traditionally divided into three "caverns." The quasi-historical founder of Daoism, Laozi, is credited as the author of the most foundational work in that canon, the Daode jing, but there is considerably less interest in tracing scriptural texts to his authority than in the case of Buddha Gautama. The five fundamental Daoist ethical principles are borrowed directly from the Pancasila and Daoist dietary customs include the avoidance of meat and alcohol. Like Buddhism, Daoism has a diminished interest in birth and wedding rituals, while Quanzhen monks adopt a celibate, communal lifestyle in imitation of their Buddhist counterparts. Finally, Chinese Daoist and Buddhist temples are often difficult to distinguish because of their similar architecture and shared features such as shrine halls, meditation grounds, flags, thangkas and the sound of the drum.

As a non-missionary religion inherently tied to a particular ethnic culture, Daoism also shares a number of features with Buddhism's mother religion. Daoism and Hinduism are both characterized by a hierarchical pantheon of gods whose many elaborate images adorn temples and homes. Prayer and supplication are performed before these sacred images, which are ritually consecrated and powerfully symbolize the presence of the deity. Yet, behind the many gods lies one inscrutable, infinite Mystery that constitutes the source and end of all things: Brahman and the Dao. Like Hinduism, the Daoist canon is a loose collection of many works composed over many centuries, with different schools preferring different works over others. Like the Vedic model of the afterlife, Daoism speaks of an ancestral spirit that survives physical death and needs help from the living for a number of generations. As in the Hindu forest-dweller tradition, the retention of semen is believed to enhance the mind and body and bestow longevity. The Chinese calendar also combines the solar and lunar year, with a heightened interest in the zodiac and the seasons. Time itself is cyclic and the passage of time in both religions is counted from a legendary event long ago: the death of Krishna for Hindus and the invention of the calendar by the Yellow Emperor for Chinese. Like the Vastu Purusha floor plan of the Hindu temple, the orientation of a Daoist temple is also important, although, in the latter case, it is feng shui that is paramount. And like the pathway to the inner womb-room in a mandir, physically moving northward through a guan complex takes you on a journey upward toward the Dao. Similar to the char dham circuit in India, the five holy mountains of China are associated with the cardinal directions and form a gigantic talisman covering central China itself. Moreover, pilgrimage sites in both traditions are typically striking settings where heaven and earth meet, although the geographical analogies differ: crossing the river in Hinduism and climbing a mountain in Daoism.

There are also a number of themes where Daoism resembles the Abrahamic tradition. Its linear view of human existence and the preference for burial is an obvious point although there is no belief in bodily resurrection. The use of colorful priestly vestments and monastic robes calls to mind Christian customs, and the importance of harvest, family meals and the symbolic use of food to mark different holy days is strongly reminiscent of the Jewish calendar.

Because Muhammad and the first Muslims were not Jews, Islam is not a daughter religion of the Jewish tradition in the same sense as Christianity. Nevertheless, it is properly included with its two monotheistic cousins under the label of the Abrahamic religions. In fact, a comparison of practices reveals an extensive range of similarities between the religions of the Qur'an and the Torah. Unlike Christianity, which is more nuanced on both issues, Islam shares with Judaism an uncompromising stress on the oneness of God and an absolute ban on divine images. Thus, the interiors of a mosque and a synagogue both display the same absence of icons and the same preference for adornment via abstract symbol or scriptural text. For both Jew and Muslim, the verbal has priority over the visual. Space also has its relevance for both traditions in that synagogues and mosques are physically orientated toward a particular location on earth: Jerusalem and Mecca respectively, although the original qibla was also Jerusalem.

Muslims hold to a linear view of existence and agree with Jews and Christians on the eternal relevance of the physical body. Islamic belief in the resurrection of the dead is, thus, accompanied by a strict prohibition on cremation. Along with Jews and Christians, Muslims also pray for the dead in the hope that divine judgment will be clement and merciful, although Islam agrees with Christianity, in contrast to Judaism, on the possibility of eternal damnation for the most wicked. Muslim and Jewish birth rituals both include circumcision, a ransom ceremony and the custom of weighing for alms-giving. Both traditions also see marriage and procreation as fundamental religious duties and thus share a distrust of religious celibacy. Finally, halal and kosher food laws are strikingly similar although the Islamic version is somewhat more lenient.

At points where Islam and Judaism converge, the third Semitic faith appears to shift toward the Hindu end of the spectrum. Whereas synagogues and mosques (and Protestant churches) are devoid of divine images, Catholic and Orthodox Christian churches are full of icons and statues, making them more similar to the Hindu mandir. The difference, of course, is that Christianity claims a single historical incarnation that underscores a fundamental likeness between the divine and the human and justifies the use of the sacred image. While this is anathema to Judaism and Islam, which stress God's transcendence and otherness, it is very close to the Hindu concept of the avatar and the prolific use of the murti as a bridge between heaven and earth. Similarly, the Christian understanding of God as Trinity is a more explicit acknowledgment of plurality within the one God, which echoes the Hindu notion of one Brahman manifest in a host of forms or deities, as well as the Daoist pantheon that emanates and returns to the eternal Dao. Moreover, the traditions of Christian Eucharist and Hindu prasad both utilize the symbol of a sacred meal to express tangible connection with transcendent yet immanent divinity. Finally, Christianity and Hinduism, in their own distinctive ways, accept the legitimate place of both marriage and celibacy, in contrast to the Islamic and Jewish caution with regard to the celibate life.

Similarly, there are times when Christian practice also shares significant similarities with Buddhism, even though the latter is at best ambiguous about the existence of both an external God and an inner soul, or atman. The crucial link is the role and impact of the founder in both cases, a feature reflected in that the names of both religions are based on their theological titles: the Buddha and the Christ. Similarly, the heart of the scriptural canon of both Buddhism and Christianity is grounded in the teachings and authority of the founder who is understood as the personification of eternal truth. The main festivals in the annual religious calendars are key moments in their respective lives including their birth and death, and the main places of pilgrimage are sites of those key moments. Finally, traditional priority is given to the monastic way of life, which is reinforced by both founders' option for celibacy.

This is not to say that there are no specific points of connection between Judaism and Islam on one side and Hinduism, Buddhism and Daoism on the other. For example, Jewish tradition acknowledges a form of reincarnation and there are many elements of the richly symbolic Jewish wedding ceremony that resonate with the Hindu equivalent, including the use of the canopy and the number seven. Similarly, certain aspects of Muslim birth rituals resemble Hindu practices and Islam shares with Buddhism and Daoism the same explicit concern for the compromising effects of alcohol and drugs. The Islamic calendar also marks the birthday and death of the Prophet as in Buddhism (and Christianity), but Islam downplays the importance of its founder in terms not only of its calendar but also of its pilgrimage tradition for fear of deifying God's greatest human messenger and descending into idolatry.

Such are the general patterns that emerge from a comparative look at the practical dimensions of the six major religions. As noted in the Introduction, Ninian Smart posited other dimensions – doctrine, narrative, spirituality, ethics and institution – and a similar comparison of these may turn up a very different set of patterns. The purpose of this exploration, with its practical–ritual focus, was to contribute a deeper appreciation of both the undeniable uniqueness of each of the six major religions as well as their rich interrelationship. Hopefully it has highlighted not only the points where each religion appears singular and distinctive, but also where it shares common ground with others. The poet John Donne's classical statement of the fundamental connectivity between human beings can perhaps be paraphrased and aptly applied here: "No religion is an island."

Glossary

Abraham (c.1800 BCE) patriarch of the Israelite people and recognized by Jews, Christians and Muslims as the first believer in the one God.
Abrahamic religions Judaism, Christianity and Islam.
Abu Bakr (c.573–634) one of the first converts to Islam, a close companion of Muhammad, and the first caliph.
adhan Islamic call to daily prayer chanted by the muezzin.
Agni Hindu god of fire.
ahimsa principle of non-violence.
alchemy, external (waidan) Daoist practice involving the creation and consumption of special elixirs.
alchemy, internal (neidan) Daoist practice aimed at channeling bodily substances to the mind in order to gain health and longevity.
Ali (c.599–661) cousin and son-in-law of Muhammad and husband of Fatima; regarded by Sunni Muslims as the fourth caliph but by Shi'ite Muslims as the true successor to Muhammad.
aliyah (going up) (1) return of Jewish emigrants to Israel; (2) going up to read from the Torah scrolls at synagogue; (3) making a pilgrimage to Jerusalem in ancient times.
Allah Arabic term for (the one) God.
Amitabha (or **Amida)** Buddha of the Western Pure Land.
Ananda cousin of Sakyamuni and one of his earliest disciples.
Anglican Church originally the Church of England, which separated from Rome in 1534 under Henry VIII; today it consists of an international communion of autonomous churches, known under various names such as the Episcopal Church in the USA.
aniconism the belief that divinity cannot be depicted in human or worldly form.
apocrypha books excluded from a sacred canon, especially in Judaism and Christianity.
Aramaic Semitic language written in Hebrew script and widely spoken in the period of the Second Temple.
arhat in Buddhism, someone so advanced in the spiritual life that they are assured of nirvana after physical death.
Ark of the Covenant (aron ha berith) container that held the stone tablets on which the Ten Commandments were written.
aron ha kodesh (holy ark) an adorned cabinet or receptacle in a synagogue where sacred scrolls are stored.
Arya Samaj Hindu reform movement founded in the late nineteenth century that rejected ritualism and caste discrimination.

World Religions in Practice: A Comparative Introduction, Second Edition. Paul Gwynne.

Ashkenazi form of Jewish culture associated with central and eastern European communities (see also **Sephardic**).

Ashoka third century BCE Mauryan ruler who converted to Buddhism and extensively promoted the religion throughout his empire.

ashrama the four traditional Hindu life stages according to the Laws of Manu: student (brahmacarin), householder (grihasthin), forest-dweller (vanaprasthin) and ascetic (sannyasin).

atman in Hinduism, the inner spiritual essence or true self that lies beneath the temporary features of each reincarnation.

aum (or **om**) in Hinduism, the fundamental sound of the universe and the source of all mantras.

Avalokiteshvara important bodhisattva in Mahayana Buddhism who personifies compassion; also known as Guanyin in China and Kwannon in Japan.

avatar an incarnation of a Hindu god (especially Vishnu) in human or animal form.

Babylonian Exile (586–537 BCE) period during which many Israelites were taken in captivity to Babylon after the fall of Jerusalem.

Bagua octagonal Chinese symbol containing the eight trigrams surrounding the taijitu.

baptism Christian initiation rite.

Baptist Christianity branch of Christianity that rejects infant baptism and teaches that baptism requires the personal faith of the recipient.

bar mitzvah (son of the commandment) Jewish ceremony that initiates a 13-year-old boy into religious adulthood.

Benares see **Varanasi**.

Bhagavad Gita (Song of the Lord) one of the most important texts in Hinduism; it is found in the sixth book of the Mahabharata and consists of a dialogue between Arjuna and Krishna.

bhakti in Hinduism, the path to liberation based on loving devotion.

bhikkhu/bhikkhuni a Buddhist monk/nun.

bodhisattva (being of enlightenment) in Mahayana Buddhism, a being who, out of compassion, delays nirvana to assist others.

Brahma one of the three main gods who form the Hindu trinity or Trimurti (with Vishnu and Shiva).

brahmacarin (student) the first life stage (ashrama) of Vedic Hinduism.

Brahman Hindu term for ultimate reality or the impersonal absolute beyond all attributes.

brahmin (or **brahman**) the priestly class – the highest of the four traditional classes in Hindu society (see **varna**).

Buddha (Enlightened One) (1) title given to the historical founder of Buddhism, Siddhartha Gautama; (2) any enlightened being, especially in Mahayana Buddhism.

caliph a successor to Muhammad.

Calvinist Christian churches whose theology and practice are inspired by the teachings of the key Protestant reformer John Calvin (1509–64).

canon set of authoritative religious texts, often considered to have been divinely inspired.

caste see **varna**.

Catholic Church (1) the "universal" Church; (2) the Roman Catholic Church whose organization and governance is centered on the bishop of Rome (the Pope).

Celestial Masters see Zhengyi.
Christ (Anointed One) title given to Jesus by Christians, who recognize him as the true Messiah.
circumambulation movement around a sacred object as an expression of devotion.
cohen (or **kohen)** member of the priestly line in Judaism.
commandments see **mitzvot**.
Communion, Holy see **Eucharist**.
confirmation Jewish or Christian adulthood initiation ceremony.
Conservative Judaism a branch of Judaism between Orthodox and Reform Judaism.
Constantine (c.280–337) the first Roman emperor to legalize Christianity.
Council of Nicea (325) early Christian council that defined Jesus as the incarnation of the divine Son of God.
Dalai Lama title given to the spiritual and political leader of Tibetan Buddhism.
Dao, The (The Way) in Daoism, the all-pervading divine presence and the absolute origin and destiny of all beings.
Daode jing one of the earliest and most important Daoist texts allegedly authored by Laozi.
Daojing (Classic of the Way) (1) general term for all Daoist scriptures; (2) first part of the Daode jing.
daoshi a Daoist priest.
Daozang (Treasury of the Dao) a threefold medieval collection of sacred Daoist scrolls.
David (c.1000 BCE) one of the earliest kings of Israel.
de Daoist term meaning virtue or power.
Decalogue (Ten Words) see **Ten Commandments.**
Deuteronomy (Second Law) the fifth book of the Jewish Torah.
dharma (1) in Hinduism, the fundamental order of the universe which holds all things in being and which is manifest in natural, ethical and socio-religious laws; (2) in Buddhism, the Buddha's teaching.
dharmashastras ancient Hindu writings on morality and law.
Durga warrior-like Hindu goddess of strength and fortitude, and consort of Shiva.
Easter Christian festival held in March–April celebrating Jesus's resurrection from the dead.
Eastern Christianity general term for the family of Orthodox churches in communion with the Patriarch of Constantinople.
ecumenical council an official gathering of bishops and leaders representing the entire Church. Most Christians recognize seven such councils between 325 and 787, but Catholics recognize another 14, the last of which was Vatican II.
Elijah Israelite prophet from ninth century BCE; in Judaism, Elijah will return to herald the coming of the Messiah.
Enlightenment, the night on which Siddhartha Gautama gained supreme insight and became the Buddha for our epoch.
equinoxes (21 March and 23 September) the two days of the year when day and night are equal length.
eschatology branch of theology that deals with death, the afterlife and the end of the world.
Eucharist (thanksgiving) the central Christian ritual modeled on Jesus's Last Supper.

Exodus (1) the second book of the Torah; (2) the miraculous escape of the Israelites from Egypt under the leadership of Moses.
Fatima daughter of Muhammad and wife of Ali.
feng shui ancient Chinese system used to determine the most beneficial alignment of buildings.
Five Elements the five fundamental elements in the Daoist universe: wood, fire, earth, metal and water.
Five Phases see **Five Elements.**
Four Noble Truths the four key principles of the historical Buddha's teachings.
garbhagrha (womb-house) the inner chamber of a Hindu temple that contains the main image.
Genesis the first book of the Jewish Torah.
gentiles traditional term for non-Jewish peoples.
gospel (good news) a faith-inspired biography of Jesus.
grihasthin (householder) the second life stage (ashrama) of traditional Hinduism during which it is obligatory to marry and have children, especially sons.
guan a Daoist temple.
Guanyin Chinese name for Avalokiteshvara.
gunas the three fundamental components of all things according to the Hindu Samkhya school: sattva (lightness), rajas (movement) and tamas (dullness).
hadith the authorized accounts of Muhammad's words and deeds that constitute an important complement to the Qur'an; the two most reliable collections are those of Al-Bukhari (810–70) and Muslim bin Al-Hajjaj (821–75).
hajj the fifth pillar of Islam: annual pilgrimage to Mecca.
halal Islamic term indicating that a certain act is permissible.
Hanafi one of the four main Sunni law schools, prevalent in Turkey, Syria, Egypt, Iraq, and central and south Asia.
Hanbali one of the four main Sunni law schools, prevalent in the Arabian peninsula.
haram Islamic term indicating that a certain act is forbidden.
Hasan (624–69) first son of Ali and Fatima and considered to be the second caliph by Shi'ite Muslims.
Hasidism form of Judaism that originated in eighteenth-century Europe and that stresses spiritual joy and constant communion with God; Hasidic Jews are often recognizable by their distinctive dress.
henotheism worship of one God while acknowledging the existence of other gods.
High Holy Days the two main Jewish festivals of New Year and the Day of Atonement.
Hijra emigration of Muhammad and the first Muslims from Mecca to Medina in 622.
hun in Daoism, the soul that ascends to heavenly realms at death. See also **po**.
hungry ghost see **preta**.
Hussain (626–80) second son of Ali and Fatima who was killed at Karbala and is honored as the greatest of martyrs by Shi'ite Islam.
iconoclasm the rejection of the use of icons and images for worship, especially in Christianity.
imam (1) a leader of Islamic congregational prayer; (2) according to Shi'ite Islam, one in the line of authentic successors to Muhammad.
incarnation (1) a divine being in human form; (2) in Christianity, the belief that the eternal Son of God took human form in Jesus of Nazareth.

Isaac son of Abraham and Sarah, and father of Jacob; in Judaism, Abraham is asked to sacrifice Isaac as a test of his faith.

Ishmael son of Abraham and Hagar; in Islam, it is Ishmael whom Abraham is asked to sacrifice.

Jacob son of Isaac and Rebecca, and grandson of Abraham; his 12 sons are the forefathers of the 12 tribes of Israel.

Jade Emperor the highest god of the Chinese pantheon and an important god in Daoism.

Jainism ancient Indian religious movement that teaches a radical form of asceticism and non-violence.

Jataka Tales stories of previous incarnations of the Buddha.

Jerusalem city in Judea originally conquered by David and established as the capital of Israel; it contains sites of outstanding religious importance to Jews, Christians and Muslims.

Jesus of Nazareth (c.6 BCE–30 CE) founder of Christianity; in Christian theology, Jesus is the long-awaited Messiah of Israel and the unique incarnation of the Son of God; in Islam, Jesus is one of the prophets in the line from Adam to Muhammad.

jihad (struggle) primary meaning is the moral struggle against evil but also refers to armed defense of the faith.

Ka'bah cube-shaped building in the center of the Great Mosque of Mecca toward which all Muslims are required to face during the five daily prayers; it is also an important part of Islamic pilgrimage customs.

Kabbalah Jewish mystical tradition that stresses intimate knowledge of God via contemplation and illumination.

karma the concept that good and bad actions carry corresponding consequences not only in this life but also in terms of the next reincarnation.

Khadijah (c.555–619) the first wife of Muhammad.

kosher in Judaism, something that is permissible, especially in relation to food laws.

Krishna eighth avatar of Vishnu.

kshatria the warrior class – the second of the four traditional classes in Vedic Hindu society (see **varna**).

Lakshmi consort of Vishnu and Hindu goddess of wealth and prosperity.

Laozi (Old Master) legendary sixth-century BCE founder of Daoism and supposed author of the Daode jing.

Laws of Manu the most influential of the ancient Hindu law codes known as dharmashastras and thought to date from about 200 BCE to 200 CE.

Leviticus the third book of the Jewish Torah.

linga phallic symbol common in Shiva worship.

liturgy official worship, especially in Christianity.

Lutheran Christian churches whose theology and practice are inspired by the teachings of the key Protestant reformer Martin Luther (1483–1546).

Mahabharata Hindu epic that narrates the battle between the five Pandava brothers and their evil cousins, the Kauravas; it contains the Bhagavad Gita.

Mahayana Buddhism (Greater Vehicle) major subdivision of Buddhism predominant in China, Vietnam, Japan, Korea, Mongolia and Tibet; it stresses the importance of compassion for other beings, typified in the concept of the bodhisattva (see also **Theravada Buddhism**).

Mahdi in Islam, a future figure who will appear at the end of the world; Twelver Shi'ites identify him as the twelfth imam who entered into "occultation" in 874.

Maimonides (1135–1204) distinguished Jewish philosopher and author, also known as Moses ben Maimon or Rambam.

Maitreya the future Buddha who is expected to come at the end of this age.

Maliki one of the four main Sunni law schools, prevalent in north and west Africa.

mandala in Buddhism and Hinduism, a sacred diagram usually of concentric design used during meditation and ritual.

mantra a sacred verse repeatedly chanted as part of worship or meditation.

Mecca place of Muhammad's birth and the center of the Islamic pilgrimage tradition.

Medina the town to which Muhammad and the first Muslims emigrated in 622 (see **Hijra**); it is also the location of Muhammad's tomb.

Megillot, Five (Five Scrolls) (sing. megillah) five biblical scrolls read at certain festivals during the Jewish year: Esther, Lamentations, Qoheleth, Ruth and Song of Songs.

menorah Jewish seven-branched candlestick.

Messiah (Anointed One) (1) in Judaism, a future descendant of King David who will usher in an era of justice and peace; (2) in Christianity and Islam, the title given to Jesus and rendered as "Christos" in Greek.

mikveh Jewish ritual bath.

minyan official quorum of 10 adult men for certain Jewish prayers and ceremonies.

mitzvot (commandments) (sing. mitzvah) religious duties incumbent upon Jews once they reach adulthood; the rabbinic tradition identified 613 commandments in the Torah.

mohel a ritual circumciser in Judaism.

moksha Hindu concept of final liberation from the cycle of reincarnation (see **nirvana**).

monism the philosophical belief that there is ultimately only one reality and that all forms of plurality or individuality are illusory.

monotheism belief in one God.

Moses (c.1250 BCE) leader of the Hebrews during the escape from Egypt and the period of wandering in the desert; Moses received the Law from God on Mount Sinai and is considered the greatest prophet in Judaism.

Mother Goddess see **Shakti**.

Mount Meru in Hinduism and Buddhism, the mythical mountain that forms the axis of the world and is the abode of the gods.

Mount Sinai mountain on which Moses received the Ten Commandments.

Mount Wudang (Wudangshan) sacred Daoist pilgrimage site in northern Hubei province, China.

Mount Zion (or **Sion**) traditional name for the hill on which the Jewish Temple was built.

mudra the position of the hands on a Buddha statue.

Muhammad (c.570–632) founder of Islam and considered by Muslims to be the last and greatest of the prophets.

murti Hindu sacred image.

Nanhua zhenjing see **Zhuangzi**.

New Testament the 27 Christian writings that constitute the second part of the Christian Bible.

Nicene Creed major Christian statement of faith issued at the Council of Nicea (325) and expanded at the Council of Constantinople (381).
nirvana Buddhist term for final liberation from the cycle of reincarnation (see **moksha**).
Numbers the fourth book of the Jewish Torah.
Old Testament Christian term for the Hebrew Scriptures that are included in the Christian Bible; Catholic and Orthodox Christians also include other Jewish writings known variously as apocryphal or deutero-canonical books.
om see **aum**.
Orthodox Churches family of autonomous (Eastern) Christian churches that recognize the Patriarch of Constantinople as a symbolic figurehead; they officially separated from Rome (see **Western Christianity**) in 1054.
Orthodox Judaism traditional forms of Judaism that stress fidelity to the oral and written law as handed down (see also **Reform Judaism**).
Pali Indo-Aryan language in which the Buddhist Tipitaka (Three Baskets) is written.
Pancasila (Five Virtues) (or **Five Precepts**) five fundamental ethical principles of Buddhism.
Panchen Lama Tibetan spiritual leader traditionally based in Tasilhunpo; the current Dalai Lama identified Gedhun Choekyi Nyima as the eighth Panchen Lama in 1995 but the Chinese government has produced its own candidate, Gyaltsen Norbu.
Parvati Hindu goddess and consort of Shiva.
Passover (Pesah) major Jewish festival commemorating the escape from Egypt as recounted in the book of Exodus.
Patriarchs, the Abraham, Isaac and Jacob.
Pentateuch see **Torah**.
People of the Book Islamic term for Jews and Christians that acknowledges their common monotheistic faith.
Pesah see **Passover**.
po in Daoism, the soul that decomposes into the earth with the body. See also **hun**.
polygyny marriage of a man to more than one wife.
polytheism belief in the existence of many gods.
prasad food offered to a Hindu deity that is subsequently distributed to believers for consumption.
preta (1) in Hinduism, the intermediate state of a deceased person between death and the land of the ancestors; (2) in Buddhism, an inhabitant of one of the six realms into which one can be reincarnated.
prophet in the Abrahamic religions, a person who speaks on behalf of God.
Protestant Christianity broad subdivision of Christianity comprising churches and communities that arose as a result of the sixteenth-century Reformation, including the Lutheran, Anglican, Calvinist and Baptist traditions.
puja Hindu devotional worship often involving the use of a murti (image).
Puranas ancient Hindu poems considered part of the smriti literature.
Pure Land Buddhism a form of Mahayana Buddhism that emphasizes devotion to a Buddha who dwells in a spiritual "pure land"; the aim of the devotee is to be reincarnated into the pure land from which attainment of nirvana is guaranteed.
qi (pronounced "chee") in Daoism, numinous cosmic energy.
qibla the direction of the Ka'bah, toward which all Muslims must face during official daily prayer.

Quanzhen (Complete Perfection) one of the two main branches of Daoism. It has been heavily influenced by Buddhism and emphasizes asceticism, mystical experience and self-preservation practices. See also **Zhengyi**.

Qur'an Islam's holiest book which consists of a collection of the divine revelations experienced by Muhammad during his lifetime.

rabbi leader of a Jewish community.

rabbinic Judaism main form of Judaism that arose as a result of the destruction of the Temple in 70 CE and the subsequent loss of the priesthood and sacrificial system.

Rama hero of the Ramayana and the seventh avatar of Vishnu.

Ramadan ninth month of the Islamic year during which Muslims fast from sunrise to sunset.

Ramayana Hindu epic that narrates the story of Rama and the rescue of his kidnapped wife with the help of an army of monkeys.

Reform Judaism a liberal form of Judaism that is more open to the adoption of contemporary ideas such as the use of vernacular language in worship and the rabbinic ordination of women.

reincarnation see **samsara.**

resurrection of Jesus the Christian belief that Jesus was raised bodily from the dead soon after his crucifixion.

resurrection of the body the idea that the body will be raised up and transformed into a new, glorious state beyond death, usually at the end of the world.

Rg Veda oldest and most sacred of the four Vedas.

rishis authors of the Vedas.

sabbath seventh day of the Jewish week on which no work is to be performed.

sacraments official Christian rituals that use visible objects and actions to symbolize invisible spiritual benefits; in the Catholic, Orthodox and Anglican traditions there are seven sacraments (see Box 4.2); in most Protestant churches only two are acknowledged as having scriptural basis (Baptism and the Eucharist).

sacred thread see **Upanayana**.

Sakyamuni (Sage of the Sakya People) common title for Siddhartha Gautama, the historical Buddha.

salat the second pillar of Islam: the five official daily prayers.

samadhi advanced state of mental awareness as a result of intense meditation.

samsara the belief that a deceased person is reborn into the world in a new bodily form (reincarnation) that is determined by the amount of good or bad karma generated during their life; the cyclic process of birth, death and rebirth continues until one achieves final liberation.

samskara traditional Hindu life-cycle ritual.

sangha Buddhist monastic community.

sannyasin (ascetic) the fourth and final life stage (ashrama), according to classical Hinduism, during which all ties with family and society are severed.

Sanqing see **Three Pure Ones**.

Saraswati Hindu goddess of the arts and learning, and consort of Brahma.

Satan the main enemy of God in Judaism, Christianity and Islam.

sati (or **suttee**) in Hinduism, self-immolation of a widow at her husband's cremation.

sawm the fourth pillar of Islam: the annual fast during the month of Ramadan.

Sephardic form of Jewish culture associated with communities from Spain, Portugal and northern Africa (see also **Ashkenazi**).

Shafi'i one of the four main Sunni law schools, prevalent in east Africa and south-east Asia.

shahadah the first pillar of Islam: a concise declaration of faith in the one God and his prophet, Muhammad.

Shaivite major Hindu tradition in which Shiva is the main object of worship.

Shakti Mother Goddess, often manifest as a consort of Shiva; sects devoted to the worship of Shakti constitute one of the main subdivisions of Hinduism.

Shankara (c.788–820) prominent Hindu thinker and proponent of the Advaita Vedanta school.

shari'a (path) Islamic law.

Shema key Jewish prayer derived from several Torah passages and recited at evening and morning synagogue services.

Shi'ite Islam minority subdivision of Islam which claims that the true successors to Muhammad were Ali and his descendants.

Shiji (Grand Records of the Historian) a second-century BCE Daoist text.

Shinto the indigenous religion of Japan.

shirk Islamic term for idolatry.

Shiva one of the three main gods of Hinduism along with Vishnu and Brahma; he is often depicted in art as Nataraja, Lord of the Dance.

shruti category of Hindu sacred writings considered to have been directly revealed by the gods, in particular the Vedas and the Upanishads (see also **smriti**).

shudra the servant class – the fourth and lowest of the traditional classes in Vedic Hindu society (see **varna**).

Shulhan Aruch code of Jewish law compiled by Joseph Caro (1488–1575) and widely used among Ashkenazi Jews.

Siddhartha Gautama (c.560–c.480 BCE) personal name of the historical Buddha.

smriti category of Hindu sacred writings, which are authoritative but secondary to shruti literature.

solstices 21 June and 21 December; the longest and shortest days of the year (reversed in the Northern and Southern hemispheres).

Star of David six-pointed star often used as a symbol for Judaism.

stupa bell-shaped construction widely used in Buddhism for storing relics and the ashes of the dead.

Sufi Islamic mystic.

Sunni Islam majority subdivision of Islam that accepts the legitimacy of the first four caliphs and their successors.

surah a chapter of the Qur'an.

sutra (or **sutta**) (thread) (1) in Hinduism, ancient manuals for various purposes; (2) in Buddhism, collections of the Buddha's teachings.

sutta see **sutra**.

Sutta Pitaka (Basket of Threads) the part of the Tipitaka that contains the sermons of the Buddha.

synagogue place for Jewish congregational worship and other communal activities.

synoptic gospels the gospels of Matthew, Mark and Luke which (unlike the gospel of John) are similar in structure and content and thus considered to be historically interrelated.

taijitu Chinese symbol depicting the interplay between yin and yang.

Talmud extensive body of written commentary on the Jewish scriptures composed by rabbinic experts during the centuries after the destruction of the Second Temple.

Tanach acronym for the Jewish Scriptures, derived from the three main subdivisions: Torah (Law), Neviyim (Prophets) and Ketuvim (Writings).

tantrism alternative stream within Hinduism and Buddhism that emphasizes the bipolar (masculine/feminine) nature of reality and the need to unite the two by a range of practices, some of which are considered unorthodox by the mainstream.

Tathagata (Thus Gone) the Buddha's preferred self-designation.

Temple, Jerusalem main focus of worship in biblical times, initially constructed by Solomon; it was destroyed by the Babylonians in 586 BCE, rebuilt under Ezra after the return from Exile, and destroyed a second time by the Romans in 70 CE.

Ten Commandments the fundamental moral–religious principles given by God to Moses on Mount Sinai in the form of two stone tablets.

Theravada Buddhism main form of Buddhism in south and southeast Asia which emphasizes the authority of the Pali Canon (see also **Mahayana Buddhism**).

Three Baskets see **Tipitaka**.

Three Bureaus in Daoism, three celestial beings who keep a precise record of each person's moral behavior.

Three Death Bringers (sanshi) in Daoism, they inhabit the body and bring about premature death.

Three External Treasures the Dao, the Teacher and the scriptures.

Three Jewels the three most precious items in Buddhism: the Buddha, the dharma (his teaching), and the sangha (the monastic community).

Three Pure Ones the three highest gods of the Daoist pantheon.

Three Worms (sanchong) see **Three Death Bringers**.

Tianshi (Celestial Masters) see **Zhengyi**.

Tipitaka (or **Tripitaka**) (Three Baskets) threefold collection of Buddhist canonical writings: the Vinaya Pitaka (monastic code), the Sutta Pitaka (the Buddha's teachings), and the Abhidhamma Pitaka (higher learning).

Torah first five books of the Jewish Bible, also known as the Law or the Pentateuch.

Trimurti the three main gods of Hinduism: Vishnu, Shiva and Brahma.

Trinity in Christianity, the concept that there is a threefold plurality (Father, Son and Holy Spirit) within the one God.

twice-born adult males of the upper three classes of Hindu society who receive the sacred thread and are thus given access to the Vedas.

Umar (or **Omar**; c.584–644) second caliph and key architect of the Islamic expansion following the death of Muhammad.

Umayyads (661–750) first hereditary dynasty of caliphs in Islam that began when Mu'awiyya prevailed over Ali during a period of civil war.

Upanayana the sacred-thread ceremony in Hinduism during which a young male of the upper three classes is initiated into spiritual adulthood (see also **twice-born**).

Upanishads collections of Hindu philosophical writings that are attached to the Vedas but move beyond their emphasis on ritual by seeking the meaning of human existence.

Uthman (c.580–656) the third caliph.

Vaishnavite major Hindu tradition in which Vishnu is the main object of worship.

vaishya the merchant class – the third of the four traditional classes in Hindu society (see **varna**).

vanaprasthin (forest-dweller) according to classical Hinduism, the third life stage (ashrama), during which one severs ties with family and society and lives as a celibate.
Varanasi (also **Benares** or **Kasi)** one of the holiest cities in Hinduism located on the Ganges.
varna (color) the five classes (major castes) of Hindu society.
Vatican II (1962–5) the most recent ecumenical council of the Catholic Church during which many significant reforms in theology and practice were implemented.
Vedas the four ancient texts that constitute the oldest and most sacred stratum of Hindu sacred writings: the Rg Veda, the Yajur Veda, the Sama Veda and the Atharva Veda.
Vinaya Pitaka (Basket of Discipline) the part of the Tipitaka that contains the rules for Buddhist monastic life.
Vishnu one of the three main gods of Hinduism along with Shiva and Brahma; often described as the preserver of the cosmos, Vishnu becomes incarnate during times of crisis (see **avatar**).
Wahhabi Islam conservative Islamic movement that is predominant in Saudi Arabia and follows the Hanbali school of law.
Western Christianity general term for churches in the Latin tradition, especially after the Great Schism of 1054; as a result of the sixteenth-century Reformation, Western Christianity was further divided into the Catholic and Protestant Churches.
Western Wall part of the remains of the Second Temple in Jerusalem, which was destroyed by the Romans in 70 CE.
White Cloud Monastery (Baiyun guan) Beijing headquarters for Quanzhen Daoists.
wuwei (effortlessness) working with, rather than against, nature and allowing the Dao to take its course.
Yellow Emperor (Huangdi) legendary ancestor of the Chinese people.
Yiddish a mixture of German, Hebrew and other languages used by Ashkenazi Jews.
yin and yang (shadow and sunny sides of a hill) opposite yet complementary forces found throughout nature.
Yom Kippur Jewish Day of Atonement.
Yuhuang dadi see **Jade Emperor**.
zakat the third pillar of Islam: a religious tax for the benefit of the poor and needy.
Zen form of Buddhism that derived from the Chinese "Chan" school and became widespread in Japan and Korea; it stresses inner meditation and the gaining of insight outside the scriptures.
Zhengyi (Orthodox Unity) one of the two main branches of Daoism (see also **Quanzhen**), characterized by a married priesthood and community rituals such as exorcisms and healings. Also known as Celestial Masters (Tianshi).
Zhuang, Master late fourth-century BCE author of the Zhuangzi.
Zhuangzi early Daoist text attributed to Master Zhuang.
Zionism Nineteenth-century political–religious movement aimed at establishing a homeland for the Jews.
ziran (self such) in Daoism, spontaneity and naturalness.
Zoroastrianism religion founded by the prophet Zoroaster (or Zarathustra) in the tenth century BCE; professing one good God (Ahura Mazda) and an opposing evil force (Angra Mainyu), it became the state religion of the Persian Empire during the sixth century BCE.

Select Bibliography

Badlani, Hiro (2008). *Hinduism. Path of Ancient Wisdom*. Bloomington, IN: iUniverse.
Bahadur, Om Lata (2000). *The Book of Hindu Festivals and Ceremonies*. 2nd ed. Delhi: UBS.
Bechert, Heinz & Gombrich, Richard (eds.) (1991). *The World of Buddhism*. London: Thames & Hudson.
Bell, Catherine (2009). *Ritual. Perspectives and Dimensions*. Oxford: Oxford University Press.
Berkwitz, Stephen & Korom, Frank (eds.) (2006). *Buddhism in World Cultures: Comparative Perspectives*. Santa Barbara, CA: ABC-CLIO.
Bhaskarananda, Swami (2002). *The Essentials of Hinduism*. 2nd ed. Seattle, WA: Viveka.
Binns, John (2002). *An Introduction to the Christian Orthodox Churches*. Cambridge: Cambridge University Press.
Bowden, John (ed.) (2006). *Christianity: The Complete Guide*. London: Continuum.
Bowen, John (2013). *Religions in Practice: An Approach to the Anthropology of Religion*. 6th ed. Boston: Allyn & Bacon.
Bowker, John (2006). *World Religions: The Great Faiths Explored and Explained*. Harlow: Dorling Kindersley.
Brown, Daniel (2009). *A New Introduction to Islam*. 2nd ed. Oxford: Blackwell.
Browning, Don S., Green, M. Christian, & Witte, John Jr. (eds.) (2006). *Sex, Marriage and Family in World Religions*. New York: Columbia University Press.
Brunn, Stanley (ed.) (2015). *The Changing World Religion Map. Sacred Places, Identities, Practices and Politics*. Lexington, KY: Springer.
Burke, T. Patrick (2004). *The Major Religions: An Introduction with Texts*. 2nd ed. Oxford: Blackwell.
Canon, Jon (2013). *The Secret Language of Sacred Spaces*. London: Watkins.
Charing, Douglas & Cole, W. Owen (eds.) (2004). *Six World Faiths*. London: Continuum.
Chilton, Bruce (2002). *Redeeming Time: The Wisdom of Ancient Jewish and Christian Festal Calendars*. Peabody, MA: Hendrickson.
Cleary, Thomas (1996). *Practical Taoism*. Boston, MA: Shambhala.
Clothey, Fred (2007). *Religion in India*. London: Routledge.
Cohn-Sherbok, Dan (2014). *The Illustrated Guide to Judaism*. 3rd ed. Dayton, OH: Lorenz.
Cohn-Sherbok, Dan (2003). *Judaism: History, Belief and Practice*. London: Routledge.
Coleman, Simon & Elsner, John (1997). *Pilgrimage: Past and Present in the World Religions*. Cambridge, MA: Harvard University Press.

World Religions in Practice: A Comparative Introduction, Second Edition. Paul Gwynne.

Conze, Edward et al. (eds.) (2006). *Buddhist Texts through the Ages*. Whitefish, MT: Kessinger.
Cook, Michael (2000). *The Koran: A Very Short Introduction*. Oxford: Oxford University Press.
Cooper, John (1994). *Eat and Be Satisfied: A Social History of Jewish Food*. Lanham, MD: Jason Aronson.
Corrigan, John et al. (2011). *Jews, Christians, Muslims: A Comparative Introduction to Monotheistic Religions*. 2nd ed. Upper Saddle River, NJ: Prentice Hall.
Coward, Harold & Knitter, Paul (eds.) (2005). *Life after Death in World Religions*. Maryknoll, NY: Orbis.
Cox, James (2013). *The Three Treasures of the Ancient Daoists*. Charleston, SC: Four Winds.
Cragg, Kenneth & Speight, R. Marston (2002). *The House of Islam*. 3rd ed. Belmont, CA: Wadsworth.
Crook, Roger (2012). *Introduction to Christian Ethics*. 6th ed. Upper Saddle River, NJ: Prentice Hall.
Das, Rasamandala (2014). *Hinduism Faith and Practice*. 3rd ed. Leicester: Southwater.
Davies, Douglas James (2003). *Death, Ritual and Belief: The Rhetoric of Funeral Rites*. London: Continuum.
Davies, J. G. (1984). *Temples, Churches and Mosques*. Oxford: Blackwell.
De Lange, Nicholas (2003). *Introduction to Judaism*. 2nd ed. Cambridge: Cambridge University Press.
Denny, Frederick Mathewson (2011). *An Introduction to Islam*. 4th ed. Upper Saddle River, NJ: Prentice Hall.
Dessing, Nathal M. (2001). *Rituals of Birth, Circumcision, Marriage and Death among Muslims in the Netherlands*. Leuven: Peeters.
Domnitch, Larry (2000). *The Jewish Holidays: A Journey through History*. Lanham, MD: Jason Aronson.
Doniger, Wendy (2014). *On Hinduism*. Oxford: Oxford University Press.
Dosick, Wayne (2010). *Living Judaism*. New York: HarperOne.
Eck, Diana (2012). *India. A Sacred Geography*. New York: Harmony.
Eck, Diana (1998). *Darsan: Seeing the Image in India*. 3rd ed. New York: Columbia University Press.
El Guindi, Fadwa (2003). *Veil: Modesty, Privacy and Resistance*. Oxford: Berg.
Ellwood, Robert S. & McGraw, Barbara A. (2013). *Many Peoples, Many Faiths: Women and Men in the World Religions*. 10th ed. Upper Saddle River, NJ: Prentice Hall.
Eskenazi, Tamara et al. (eds.) (1991). *The Sabbath in Jewish and Christian Traditions*. New York: Crossroad.
Esposito, John (2011). *What Everyone Needs to Know about Islam*. 2nd ed. New York: Oxford University Press.
Esposito, John (2010). *Islam: The Straight Path*. 4th ed. New York: Oxford University Press.
Esposito, John et al. (eds.) (2014). *World Religions Today*. 5th ed. New York: Oxford University Press.
Etzioni, Amitai & Bloom, Jared (eds.) (2004). *We are What We Celebrate: Understanding Holidays and Rituals*. New York: New York University Press.
Falk, Nancy (2005). *Living Hinduisms: An Explorer's Guide*. Belmont, CA: Wadsworth.
Faure, Bernard (2011). *Chan Buddhism in Ritual Context*. London: Routledge.

Feldhaus, Anne (2003). *Connected Places: Region, Pilgrimage and Geographical Imagination in India*. Basingstoke: Palgrave Macmillan.

Fine, Lawrence (ed.) (2001). *Judaism in Practice: From the Middle Ages through the Early Modern Period*. Princeton, NJ: Princeton University Press.

Fisher, Mary Pat (2013). *Living Religions*. 9th ed. Upper Saddle River, NJ: Prentice Hall.

Fisher, Robert E. (1993). *Buddhist Art and Architecture*. London: Thames & Hudson.

Flood, Gavin (ed.) (2003). *The Blackwell Companion to Hinduism*. Oxford: Blackwell.

Forbes, Duncan (2010). *Buddhist Pilgrimage*. New Delhi: Motilal Banarsidass.

Fowler, Jeaneane (2015). *Hinduism: Beliefs and Practices*. 2 vols. Brighton: Sussex Academic Press.

Frishman, Martin & Khan, Hasan-Uddin (2002). *The Mosque: History, Architectural Development and Regional Diversity*. London: Thames & Hudson.

Fuller, C. (2004). *The Camphor Flame*. 2nd ed. Princeton, NJ: Princeton University Press.

Garces-Foley (2005). *Death and Religion in a Changing World*. London: Routledge.

Geffen, Rela M. (ed.) (1993). *Celebration and Renewal: Rites of Passage in Judaism*. Philadelphia, PA: Jewish Publication Society of America.

Ghamidi, Javed (2012). *Islam. A Comprehensive Introduction*. Lahore: Al-Mawrid.

Goldberg, Harvey E. (2003). *Jewish Passages. Cycles of Jewish Life*. Oakland, CA: University of California Press.

Goldberg, Harvey E. (ed.) (2001). *The Life of Judaism*. Berkeley, CA: University of California Press.

Goldman, Ari L. (2007). *Being Jewish: The Spiritual and Cultural Practice of Judaism Today*. New York: Simon & Schuster.

Göle, Nilüfa (1997). *The Forbidden Modern: Civilization and Veiling*. Ann Arbor, MI: University of Michigan Press.

Goodman, Hananya (ed.) (1994). *Between Jerusalem and Benares: Comparative Studies in Judaism and Hinduism*. Albany, NY: SUNY Press.

Gordon, Matthew S. (2002). *Understanding Islam*. London: Duncan Baird.

Granoff, Phyllis & Shinohara, Koichi (eds.) (2003). *Pilgrims, Patrons and Place: Localizing Sanctity in Asian Religions*. Vancouver: University of British Columbia Press.

Harpur, James (2002). *Sacred Tracks: Two Thousand Years of Christian Pilgrimage*. Berkeley: University of California Press.

Harvey, Peter (2012). *An Introduction to Buddhism: Teaching, History and Practices*. 2nd ed. Cambridge: Cambridge University Press.

Hauer, Christian E. & Young, William A. (2011). *An Introduction to the Bible: A Journey into Three Worlds*. 8th ed. Upper Saddle River, NJ: Prentice Hall.

Hawley, John Stratton & Narayanan, Vasudha (eds.) (2006). *The Life of Hinduism*. Berkeley, CA: University of California Press.

Hawting, G. R. (ed.) (2006). *The Development of Islamic Ritual*. Aldershot: Ashgate.

Hawting, G. R. (2002). *The Idea of Idolatry and the Emergence of Islam: From Polemic to History*. Cambridge: Cambridge University Press.

Hedayetullah, Muhammad (2010). *Unity and Diversity in World's Living Religions*. Victoria, BC: Trafford.

Hedayetullah, Muhammad (2002). *Dynamics of Islam: An Exposition*. Victoria, BC: Trafford.

Heehs, Peter (ed.) (2002). *Indian Religions: A Historical Reader of Spiritual Expression and Experience*. London: Hurst.

Heilman, S. C. (1999). *Synagogue Life: Study in Symbolic Interaction*. Somerset, NJ: Transaction.
Herrou, Adeline (2013). *A World of Their Own: Daoist Monks and Their Community in Contemporary China*. Honolulu: Three Pines.
Hick, John & Hebblethwaite, Brian (eds.) (2001). *Christianity and Other Religions*. 2nd ed. Oxford: Oneworld.
Hickman, Hoyt et al. (1992). *The New Handbook of the Christian Year*. Nashville, TN: Abingdon Press.
Hillenbrand, Carole (2015). *Introduction to Islam. Beliefs and Practices in Historical Perspective*. London: Thames & Hudson.
Hinnells, John R. (ed.) (2010). *A Handbook of Living Religions*. 2nd ed. Ringwood, Vic.: Penguin.
Hoffman, Lawrence A. (1996). *Covenant of Blood: Circumcision and Gender in Rabbinic Judaism*. Chicago: University of Chicago Press.
Holm, Jean & Bowker, John (eds.) (2000). *Sacred Place*. London: Continuum.
Hopfe, Lewis M. & Woodward, Mark R. (2008). *Religions of the World*. 11th ed. Upper Saddle River, NJ: Prentice Hall.
Howard, Veena & Sherma, Rita (eds.) (2015). *Dharma: The Hindu, Buddhist, Jain and Sikh Traditions of India*. London: I.B. Tauris.
Isaacs, Ronald H. (2001). *Every Person's Guide to the High Holy Days*. Lanham, MD: Jason Aronson.
Johnson, Maxwell E. (2007). *The Rites of Christian Initiation: Their Evolution and Interpretation*. 2nd ed. Collegeville, MN: Liturgical Press.
Keene, Michael (2006). *World Religions*. Louisville, KY: Westminster John Knox Press.
Keown, Damien (2013). *Buddhism: A Very Short Introduction*. 2nd ed. Oxford: Oxford University Press.
Keown, Damien (2001). *The Nature of Buddhist Ethics*. Basingstoke: Palgrave Macmillan.
Klostermaier, Klaus (2007). *Hinduism. A Beginner's Guide*. Oxford: Oneworld.
Knapp, Stephen (2006). *The Power of the Dharma*. Lincoln, NE: iUniverse.
Knott, Kim (2000). *Hinduism: A Very Short Introduction*. Oxford: Oxford University Press.
Kohn, Livia (2009). *Introducing Daoism*. London: Routledge.
Kohn, Livia (2001). *Daoism and Chinese Culture*. 3rd ed. Honolulu: Three Pines.
Komjathy, Louis (2013). *The Daoist Tradition*. London: Bloomsbury.
Kraemer, David (1999). *The Meanings of Death in Rabbinic Judaism*. New York: Routledge.
Kuhns, Elizabeth (2005). *The Habit: A History of the Clothing of Catholic Nuns*. New York: Doubleday.
Lamm, Maurice (2012). *The Jewish Ways of Death and Mourning*. 2nd ed. Middle Village, NY: Jonathan David.
Levine, Lee (1999). *Jerusalem: Its Sanctity and Centrality to Judaism, Christianity, and Islam*. London: Continuum.
Lieber, Andrea (2012). *The Essential Guide to Jewish Prayer and Practices*. New York: Alpha.
Lipner, Julius (2010). *Hindus*. 2nd ed. London: Routledge.
Madan, T. N. (ed.) (2004). *India's Religions: Perspectives from Sociology and History*. New Delhi: Oxford University Press.
Marcus, Ivan G. (2004). *The Jewish Life Cycle: Rites of Passage from Biblical to Modern Times*. Seattle, WA: University of Washington Press.

Matthews, Warren (2012). *World Religions*. 7th ed. Belmont, CA: Wadsworth.
McArthur, Meher (2002). *Reading Buddhist Art*. London: Thames & Hudson.
McGrath, Alister E. (2015). *An Introduction to Christianity*. 3rd ed. Oxford: Blackwell.
Meek, Harold (1995). *The Synagogue*. London: Phaidon.
Michaels, Axel (2003). *Hinduism: Past and Present*. Princeton, NJ: Princeton University Press.
Michell, George (1988). *The Hindu Temple: An Introduction to its Meaning and Forms*. Chicago: University of Chicago Press.
Miller, James (2003). *Daoism*. Oxford: Oneworld.
Mittal, Sushil (ed.) (2004). *The Hindu World*. Abingdon: Routledge.
Mittal, Sushil & Thursby, Gene (eds.) (2006). *Religions of South Asia: An Introduction*. Abingdon: Routledge.
Møllgaard, Eske (2011). *An Introduction to Daoist Thought. Action, Language and Ethics in Zhuangzi*. London: Routledge.
Molloy, Michael (2012). *Experiencing the World's Religions: Tradition, Challenge and Change*. 6th ed. New York: McGraw-Hill.
Moors, Annelies & Tarlo, Emma (eds.) (2013). *Islamic Fashion and Anti-Fashion*. London: Bloomsbury.
Morgan, David (2005). *The Sacred Gaze: Religious Visual Culture in Theory and Practice*. Berkeley, CA: University of California Press.
Narayanan, Vasudha (2004). *Hinduism*. New York: Oxford University Press.
Nasr, Seyyed Hossein (2003). *Islam: Religion, History and Civilization*. San Francisco: HarperSanFrancisco.
Neusner, Jacob (ed.) (2009). *World Religions in America: An Introduction*. 4th ed. Louisville, KY: Westminster John Knox Press.
Neusner, Jacob et al. (eds.) (2000). *Judaism and Islam in Practice*. London: Routledge.
Newman, Louis E. (2004). *An Introduction to Jewish Ethics*. Upper Saddle River, NJ: Prentice Hall.
Obayashi, Hiroshi (1991). *Death and Afterlife: Perspectives of World Religions*. New York: Praeger.
Oxtoby, Willard G. & Segal, Alan F. (eds.) (2011). *A Concise Introduction to World Religions*. Oxford: Oxford University Press.
Palmer, David et al. (eds.) (2012). *Daoism in the Twentieth Century. Between Eternity and Modernity*. Oakland, CA: University of California Press.
Parry, Jonathan P. (1994). *Death in Banaras*. Cambridge: Cambridge University Press.
Partridge, Christopher H. (ed.) (2005). *Introduction to World Religions*. Minneapolis: Augsburg Fortress.
Pauling, Chris (2004). *Introducing Buddhism*. 3rd ed. Birmingham: Windhorse.
Peters, F. E. (1996). *The Hajj*. Princeton, NJ: Princeton University Press.
Porter, Venetia (ed.) (2012). *Hajj: Journey to the Heart of Islam*. Cambridge, MA: Harvard University Press.
Powers, John (2008). *A Concise Introduction to Tibetan Buddhism*. Ithaca, NY: Snow Lion.
Prasad, R. C. (2014). *The Upanayana: The Hindu Ceremonies of the Sacred Thread*. New Delhi: Motilal Banarsidass.
Raz, Gil (2014). *The Emergence of Daoism: Creation of Tradition*. London: Routledge.
Reynolds, Frank E. & Carbine, Jason A. (eds.) (2000). *The Life of Buddhism*. Berkeley, CA: University of California Press.

Ridgeon, Lloyd (2003). *Major World Religions*. London: RoutledgeCurzon.
Riemer, Jack (ed.) (2002). *Jewish Insights on Death and Mourning*. Syracuse, NY: Syracuse University Press.
Rinehart, Robin (ed.) (2004). *Contemporary Hinduism: Ritual, Culture, and Practice*. Santa Barbara, CA: ABC-CLIO.
Rippin, Andrew (2013). *Muslims: Their Religious Beliefs and Practices*. 4th ed. London: Routledge.
Robinson, George (2001). *Essential Judaism. A Complete Guide to Beliefs, Customs and Rituals*. New York: Atria.
Robinson, N. (2004). *Discovering the Qur'an: A Contemporary Approach to a Veiled Text*. 2nd ed. London: SCM.
Robinson, Thomas A. & Rodrigues, Hillary (eds.) (2014). *World Religions: A Guide to the Essentials*. 2nd ed. Peabody, MA: Hendrickson.
Rosen, Lawrence (2004). *The Culture of Islam: Changing Aspects of Contemporary Muslim Life*. Chicago: University of Chicago Press.
Ruthven, Malise (2012). *Islam: A Very Short Introduction*. 2nd ed. New York: Oxford University Press.
Saeed, Abdullah (2008). *The Qur'an. An Introduction*. London: Routledge.
Saeed, Abdullah (2003). *Islam in Australia*. St Leonards, NSW: Allen & Unwin.
Sangharakshita (2004). *Ritual and Devotion in Buddhism*. 2nd ed. Birmingham: Windhorse.
Schauss, Hayyim (1996). *The Jewish Festivals: A Guide to their History and Observance*. New York: Schocken.
Scott, Jamie & Simpson-Housley, Paul (eds.) (1991). *Sacred Places and Profane Spaces*. London: Greenwood.
Segler, Franklin M. & Bradley, Randall (2006). *Christian Worship: Its Theology and Practice*. 3rd ed. Nashville, TN: B & H Publishing Group.
Sen Gupta, Subhadra (2003). *Chaar Dhaam: A Guide to the Hindu Pilgrimages*. New Delhi: Rupa.
Shariati, Ali (2005). *Hajj: Reflection on its Rituals*. Houston, TX: Free Islamic Literatures.
Sharma, Arvind (ed.) (2003). *The Study of Hinduism*. Columbia, SC: University of South Carolina Press.
Sherwin, Byron L. (2000). *Jewish Ethics for the Twenty-First Century: Living in the Image of God*. Syracuse, NY: Syracuse University Press.
Shirazi, Faegheh (2003). *The Veil Unveiled: The Hijab in Modern Culture*. Gainesville, FL: University Press of Florida.
Smith, Huston & Novak, Philip (2004). *Buddhism: A Concise Introduction*. San Francisco: HarperSanFrancisco.
Smith, Jane I. & Haddad, Yvonne Y. (2002). *The Islamic Understanding of Death and Resurrection*. Oxford: Oxford University Press.
Solomon, Norman (1996). *Judaism: A Very Short Introduction*. New York: Oxford University Press.
Stoddard, Robert H. & Morinis, E. Alan (eds.) (1997). *Sacred Places, Sacred Spaces: The Geography of Pilgrimages*. Baton Rouge, LA: Geoscience Publications, Louisiana State University.
Strassfeld, Michael (2001). *The Jewish Holidays: A Guide and Commentary*. 2nd ed. New York: Harper.

Swearer, Donald K. (2004). *Becoming the Buddha: The Ritual of Image Consecration in Thailand*. Princeton, NJ: Princeton University Press.

Sweetman, Will (2015). *Hinduism. An Introduction*. London: I.B. Tauris.

Tarlo, Emma (1996). *Clothing Matters: Dress and Identity in India*. Chicago: University of Chicago Press.

Teutsch, David (2011). *A Guide to Jewish Practice*. Wyncote, PA: RRC Press.

Turner, Victor Witter & Turner, Edith L. B. (1995). *Image and Pilgrimage in Christian Culture*. New York: Columbia University Press.

Want Yi'e (2006). *Daoism in China*. Portland, OR: Floating World.

Ward, Keith (2007). *Christianity: A Beginner's Guide*. Oxford: Oneworld.

Washofsky, Mark (2010). *Jewish Living. A Guide to Contemporary Reform Practice*. New York: UAHC Press.

Weaver, Mary Jo et al. (2008). *Introduction to Christianity*. 4th ed. Belmont, CA: Wadsworth.

White, James F. (2001). *Introduction to Christian Worship*. 3rd ed. Nashville, TN: Abingdon Press.

Wilkinson, John (2002). *From Synagogue to Church: The Traditional Design*. London: Routledge.

Witty, Abraham & Witty, Rachelle (2001). *Exploring Jewish Tradition: A Transliterated Guide to Everyday Practice and Observance*. New York: Doubleday.

Wong, Eva (2011). *Taoism. An Essential Guide*. London: Shambhala.

Woodhead, Linda (2014). *Christianity. A Very Short Introduction*. 2nd ed. Oxford: Oxford University Press.

Xun Liu (2013). *Quanzhen Daoists in Chinese Society and Culture, 1500–2010*. Berkeley, CA: Institute of East Asian Studies.

Young, William A. (2009). *The World's Religions: Worldviews and Contemporary Issues*. 3rd ed. Upper Saddle River, NJ: Prentice Hall.

Zhongjiang Wang (2015). *Daoism Excavated*. Honolulu: Three Pines.

Index

n

102 Extra Training Games

102 Extra Training Games

Gary Kroehnert

The McGraw-Hill Companies, Inc.

Sydney New York San Francisco Auckland
Bangkok Bogotá Caracas Hong Kong
Kuala Lumpur Lisbon London Madrid
Mexico City Milan New Delhi San Juan
Seoul Singapore Taipei Toronto

McGraw·Hill Australia

*A Division of The **McGraw·Hill** Companies*

Reprinted 2001, 2002, 2003, 2004

National Library of Australia Cataloguing-in-Publication data:

Kroehnert, Gary.
102 extra training games.

ISBN 0 07 470802 3.

1. Management games – Study and teaching. 2. Management games – Study and teaching – Australia. 3. Employees – Training of. 4. Active learning. I. Title. II. Title: One hundred and two extra training games.

658.312404

Published in Australia by
McGraw-Hill Australia Pty Limited
Level 2, 82 Waterloo Road, North Ryde, NSW 2113, Australia
Acquisitions Editor: Meiling Voon
Production Editor: Sybil Kesteven
Editor: Sarah Baker
Designer: R.T.J. Klinkhamer
Illustrator: Diane Booth, Di-Art Design
Cartoonist: Maria Mason, Southern Star Design
Typeset in 10/14 Bell Gothic by R.T.J. Klinkhamer
Printed on 80 gsm woodfree by Pantech Ltd. Hong Kong

Contents

Introduction

Welcome to my third book of training games. Many readers of the first two books, **100 Training Games** and **101 More Training Games**, contacted me asking when other books would be coming out. So for them, here is **102 Extra Training Games**. **103 Additional Training Games** is now under way.

As the introduction in **100 Training Games** and **101 More Training Games** is still current and relevant, I am using it again here with a few modifications. So if you've already read it, skip it, and go straight to the games section. The only point to be made before you skip ahead is to let you know that a new category of problem solving has been added. This category was used in **101 More Training Games**, but not in **100 Training Games**. This category has been added at readers' requests and now takes the total number of categories to ten: Icebreaker, Team building, Communication, Facilitator/presentation skills, Mid-course energiser, Problem solving, Learning, Perception, Evaluation and Self-management.

We have all seen and probably participated in various forms of training games, simulations, role-plays, brain teasers, case studies and other related activities. Just because we are aware of them doesn't mean that we can use them any time we wish to.

The use of these activities should allow the participant to discover outcomes, rather than be told everything without trying it. Most of the world's airlines, manufacturing plants, human resource companies, military establishments, small and large companies, private and public organisations now use these forms of structured exercises. The ultimate goal of using these structured exercises should always be improved learning.

Trainers and participants are changing. People attending training courses generally don't want to get involved with exercises that are too 'touchy feely'. Most of the trainers I know personally don't like using exercises where participants have to stare each other in the eye or start hugging each other. For that reason all the exercises included in this book are 'hands on' and 'down to earth'.

What these trainers and participants are generally interested in, on top of the information sessions, are structured experiences that they can apply, where no one feels very threatened or where they don't have to touch strangers. The other very important criterion that almost everyone agrees on is that the experience should be relevant to the training matter or relevant to the group's requirements.

All facilitators using structured exercises need to be aware that other things may come out in the use of games that normally wouldn't come out using other methods of instruction.

Games, simulations, role-plays, brain teasers, case studies and other related activities have been used successfully in countless numbers of training situations for many centuries by countless numbers of trainers. We can actually trace back the use of games and simulations thousands of years. Chess is an excellent example of this. Chess was developed by the military and was based on solving military problems.

Games, simulations, role-plays, brain teasers, case studies and other related activities have also been used **unsuccessfully** in countless numbers of training situations for many centuries by countless numbers of trainers.

For most of us, games, simulations and role-plays were part of the growing up process. If we think back to our earliest school days, we can remember playing games such as marbles or hide-and-seek. It is now recognised that these games are not only for fun, but also prepare the child for entry into the social system. If any of you took Home Economics, Woodwork or Metalwork at school you would probably call them a simulation of the real workplace. Some of us may also remember when we acted out roles in a game of 'Mothers and Fathers'—another form of role-play.

In a training situation we must be very selective in the use and timing of these methods of instruction. People become bored doing the same thing all the time, even if it is a 'mind-blowing experience' the first few times. If you intend using these methods effectively, plan them into your session notes or your outline.

This book and my previous books, **100 Training Games** and **101 More Training Games**, are aimed at giving both the new and the experienced trainer enough information, samples and sources to competently carry out their role as an adult trainer using these related training activities. They all focus primarily on games and brain teasers, as role-plays and case studies have to be designed by the individual trainer for each separate application. For the new trainer I would strongly suggest that they also spend some time looking at my training handbook, **Basic Training for Trainers**, Second Edition (McGraw-Hill Book Company, Sydney, 1994).

Today's trainer can simply walk down to the local shopping centre and purchase any number of games over the counter. It's worth mentioning now that even the simplest child's game can have a place in adult education if it's applied correctly.

Training games are now found in all sections of all kinds of education. It's important that the trainer realises, however, that a game is not played just because someone else has said, 'There should be a game played here.'

In **102 Extra Training Games** we will first look at the academic differences between games, simulations, brain teasers, role-plays and case studies. We will also address the problem of when to use training games. The largest (and most important) section of the book is a selection of favourite Australian training games and brain teasers. Last, an updated bibliography is included for new trainers to use as a resource and for their further reference.

It's worthwhile noting that trainers and facilitators these days tend to call all these activities 'structured experiences' or 'structured exercises'. So when you hear these terms being used you will know that they are still talking about the same things. I have mostly referred to games, simulations, brain teasers and role-plays as exercises or activities. To me the term is not that important as long as the trainer knows what the desired outcome is.

Most of the exercises are written as directions, rather than in the third person; however, where necessary I refer to the leader as the facilitator rather than as the trainer. In most structured exercises it's important for the leader not to be a dominant figure. Generally if you use the term 'facilitator' that lets the group know that they aren't going to be taught by a trainer but rather find out for themselves through experience.

With the exercises in this handbook I would suggest that the reader/user apply common sense to use the enlarging facilities on their photocopier to make appropriately sized overhead transparencies. This will save presentation time by reducing the writing required on the whiteboard, etc. All the overhead material has been shown in landscape format (i.e. wider than it is deep) as this has become the most common way of projecting overheads. It's also the easiest way for people to read them.

My policy for reproducing any material from this handbook is based on encouraging interprofessional networking. Therefore the material contained in this book may be freely reproduced for educational purposes or training activities. You are not required to obtain special permission for such uses. It is requested, however, that the following statement appear on all copies made:

Reproduced from:
102 Extra Training Games, Gary Kroehnert,
McGraw-Hill Book Company Australia, Sydney
Copyright 2000

Finally I would like to thank all the authors, game designers and publishers who have allowed me to use their material for the benefit of new trainers.

I have attempted to acknowledge the source wherever possible. Where a source hasn't been acknowledged, either the source is unknown to me or my colleagues, or it's an original game design. As it's next to impossible to find the source of a story or a game on most occasions, I will now apologise if I have not acknowledged the source, or if it has been acknowledged incorrectly.

If you have any games or exercises that you would like to share with other trainers, please send them to me for possible inclusion in future publications (as mentioned above, **103 Additional Training Games** is currently in production). Your name will be immortalised, as I **will** acknowledge the source. If possible, please try to use the same format as shown here. For those who are interested my contact details are shown below.

Before we start looking at the games, just remember what Confucius said around 450 BC:

'I hear and I forget,
I see and I remember,
I do and I understand.'

Have fun!

Dr Gary Kroehnert 2000

PO Box 3169
Grose Vale
New South Wales 2753
Australia

Phone: (02) 4572 2000
Fax: (02) 4572 2200
Email: doctorgary@hotmail.com

The Activities

THE DIFFERENCES BETWEEN THEM

Very few trainers agree on definitions for games, simulations and role-plays, case studies, and so on. The following definitions are very broad and have been included for a new trainer to use. The more experience a trainer gains, the more they can apply their own definitions.

By looking at some of the examples given here, you will be able to see that it's difficult to even categorise some exercises into one grouping. Chess, for example, isn't strictly a game or a simulation, it's a combination of both. Chess was developed in sixth century India and was designed to simulate a contemporary battle.

Games

A game is an exercise where participants are involved in a contest with someone else (or a group of people) with a set of rules imposed. Games normally include some type of pay off. Most training games are now aimed at having the individual trainee compete with themselves, rather than with another trainee. This avoids the situation where there are winners and losers.

The term 'games' includes psychomotor skills games, intellectual skills games and most games of chance. Some common types of games include darts, snakes and ladders, football, Scrabble, charades and most card games. Games in which individuals compete with themselves include solitaire, patience, crossword puzzles and even poker machines.

Simulations

A simulation is a mock-up of an actual or imaginary situation. Simulations are generally used to train future operators where it's impractical or too dangerous for these trainees to use real-life equipment or locations. Simulations are normally designed to be as realistic as possible so that trainees can learn from their actions without the financial worries of repairing or replacing damaged equipment.

Examples of simulations include flight simulators, driving simulators and war games.

Brain teasers

Brain teasers are in a class of their own. They are neither pure games nor simulations but puzzles that either keep participants' minds busy or highlight key points. Brain teasers generally don't have any rules, but they do allow the trainer to design their own rules to suit the individual training session.

Typical brain teasers include exercises such as joining the dots and most perception exercises.

Role-plays

Role-plays are used in training to see how participants react in certain situations before and after training sessions. Role-plays are very useful in getting participants used to dealing with other people in any given scenario. Even when the participant does it wrong, they still learn.

Case studies

Case studies are exactly what the name implies. A case (normally from the participants' workplace) is studied either by the group or by the individual. An in-depth study of a real-life or simulated scenario is undertaken to illustrate certain outcomes. When the group or the individual has the answer to the problem or situation it can be compared to what really happened and what the outcomes were.

WHEN SHOULD THEY BE USED?

Training exercises may be used at any time during the training as long as they are relevant, to the point or have been designed with a specific purpose.

The 'specific purpose' can be to keep the group occupied while waiting for stragglers, and to wake participants up after a lunch break. These purposes are okay as long as they are stated. It's not okay when they are simply used to fill in time or to make the facilitator look like a magician.

You can also use structured exercises as a means of channelling excess energy or to liven up the class. The activity can be a means of improving the learning atmosphere.

So these types of structured exercises should be selected and used on the basis of their usefulness, for reinforcing the instruction, or improving the learning environment.

A FACILITATOR'S RESPONSIBILITIES

Gone are the days when games and the like were not considered to be suitable as training methods. Training is a serious business, but we can and should use games, simulations, role-plays, brain teasers, case studies and other related activities in training situations.

War games (simulations) have been used by military personnel for many centuries and have proved to be very effective. Structured exercises are relatively new to training, and they are also proving to be very effective, if used properly.

Regardless of how good we are as presenters or lecturers, we can't fool ourselves into thinking that our whole presentation alone is going to keep everyone's interest for the whole period. Games, simulations, role-plays, brain teasers, case studies and other related activities are all applications of the principles of adult learning. You, the facilitator, must ensure that the participants do not become so involved in the activity that they actually miss the learning point. In addition, the facilitator must also realise that if the participants have too high a level of enthusiasm for the exercise they may become bored with 'normal' training. This isn't to say that we don't want high levels of enthusiasm, but we need to ensure we keep the participants interested with other methods of instruction as well.

The learning process can be sped up by the use of games, simulations, role-plays, brain teasers, case studies and other related activities. People learn better when they are enjoying themselves. So therefore we need to seriously think about creating or supplying the appropriate learning atmosphere.

You should always select the training method after setting the learning objectives. The method should respond to the participants' needs, not the facilitator's.

When you decide to use a structured exercise it is important that you practise the exercise at least once with a group of people not involved with the immediate presentation. This will help you see if the design is going to work, and in the expected way with the expected results. Like all types of training, these structured exercises must be evaluated for their worth and effectiveness. If they don't produce what is needed, you need to scrap them or modify them.

Do you have a responsibility for entertaining the group during any presentation? You have the responsibility for ensuring clarity and precision of information. You are also responsible for aligning the group and keeping them moving. Another responsibility is to keep yourself animated. (That could be considered the main entertainment value.) This is also what the participants may talk about later to their friends and colleagues. If the facilitator is in a situation where this type of feedback is required (such as an external trainer or consultant), then an assortment of training methods will be required. Games, simulations, role-plays and structured exercises will be of assistance.

It's your responsibility to pilot or test all new exercises or exercises that you haven't used in the past. Facilitators must realise that what works for some people doesn't always work for others. A lot of training exercises may have different outcomes every time you use them. So be prepared.

Trainers and facilitators must debrief all the exercises carried out during any type of training session. The purpose of debriefing is quite complicated. Without going into too much detail, there are two main reasons for conducting the debriefing session.

You have an obligation to put the players or participants back together when the exercise has finished. This means that if participants have bad feelings about the exercise they should be allowed to get things off their chest while still in the training room and also while things are still fresh in their minds.

Debriefing also allows the trainer and the participants to talk about the outcomes of the exercise. Was it what everyone expected? Would you do that in the real situation? What would you have done if this had happened? It also allows the trainer a time where mistakes can be corrected.

Put the participants back together if you shatter them, or scrape them off the floor.

Probably the most important point is that trainers must be completely honest and open with their participants. This includes not having any hidden agendas, not misleading participants, not setting anyone up, not deceiving any of the participants and not using the participants' efforts for your own gain.

WHERE CAN THEY BE USED?

Rather than fully catalogue these exercises and possibly limit their application, I have decided to use a coding system. Beside the name of the exercises on the following pages you will see one or some of the following letters and symbols. These letters have been placed there to give you suggested applications. These applications are only guides and can be modified to suit by the individual trainer.

Coding:

I Icebreaker
T Team building
C Communication
F Facilitator/presentation skills
M Mid-course energiser
X Problem solving
L Learning
P Perception
E Evaluation
S Self-management

A full breakdown of the exercises has been included on the next few pages of this handbook. First, each of the ten different categories has been given a detailed overview. The second list is an index of the 102 exercises included in this book, with full cross-referencing for each application for which they can be used.

I Icebreaker

Almost any exercise can be used as an icebreaker. The two main purposes of using an icebreaker are first, to allow the participants to introduce themselves to each other, and second, to lead into the topic matter. Participants often find that the topic matter is made clearer by the use of an appropriate icebreaker.

The exercises in this grouping are non-threatening introductory contacts. They are designed to allow participants to get to know each other a little and to lower any barriers that may exist. Experienced facilitators have found that the success or failure of a program may hinge on these two points.

The more comfortable participants feel with each other, the better the learning environment. If the participants are at ease with each other, they are more likely to participate and to generate new ideas.

While most facilitators won't see these exercises as too threatening, some participants may. If a participant does see an icebreaker as threatening, make sure they have a way out of participating. It's a wise decision to let people know at the very beginning of a program that they can pass on any exercise or activity they feel uncomfortable with. Obviously there will be exceptions to this. A trainee counsellor, for example, would not be expected to say that they feel uncomfortable talking with strangers and would prefer not to do any counselling role-plays. Common sense rules.

T Team building

Team-building exercises are used to improve the relationship of the individuals and sub-groups within a group. The term 'group' in team building normally refers to an established work group or a group which will be working together.

When using team-building exercises you, as well as the group, should be aware that the identification of conflict or problems between different parties or individuals may be the only outcome of some team-building exercises. However, a conflict or problem is much easier to solve or deal with after it has been identified. A team-building exercise should allow the participants to 'let their hair down' while they get to know each other.

It's very important that you thoroughly debrief team-building exercises to ensure that there isn't any build up of hostility, anger or frustration. Don't let the group break until this has been rectified.

C Communication

Exercises used for communication are designed to let the participants find out where certain communication skills may be improved. You, as the facilitator, have to be very aware of the exact purpose of some communication exercises as it is sometimes very difficult to sit back and say nothing while things start to go wrong for the participant.

You also need to be aware that you may be regarded by some participants as a role-model. While conducting a program on communication skills you must ensure that what you give out is correct. As feedback is a very important part of communication skills it must be used in all communication exercises. Feedback should be specific and aimed at observed behaviours that the individual has some control over.

F Facilitator/presentation skills

Facilitation skills activities are aimed at people who may need to develop or improve their up-front, or presentation, ability. The exercises in this category are designed to encourage the participants to think about particular aspects of their own presentation and facilitation skills.

While using any exercises to improve presentation skills you should take full advantage of the opportunity by using the individuals in the group wherever possible. This may mean getting some of them to run the exercises. It's important that you ensure the individuals are observed and debriefed by the rest of the group. By this simple observation, group members are able to see things that may or may not work for them. The more styles of presentation they see, the better.

Some of these exercises can be seen as very threatening to a few group members, so make sure you are prepared to offer your support and assistance if necessary.

M Mid-Course Energiser

Mid-course energisers can be used at any time you observe the group losing interest or falling asleep. Mid-course energisers are very similar in design to icebreakers, but they sometimes make the assumption that the members of the group know each other already. For this reason some of the exercises may appear a little threatening to some members of the group. If someone does not want to participate, let them sit back or act in an observer's role. You will normally find that they will join in as soon as they see how much fun the others are having.

These exercises are used to wake participants up, to get the blood moving, to keep participants from falling asleep after a lunch break, to simply get people back on line or to think about a new approach to a problem.

Experienced facilitators can also use these energisers to reduce tensions that may have built up with individuals or the group.

X Problem solving

Most of the problem-solving exercises have been designed to put participants, or small groups, in a situation where a solution is expected. These exercises are generally non-threatening.

The solutions that are given may not necessarily be the correct ones, so the facilitator must deal with this. The facilitator must also be aware that the solutions the individuals or groups put forward may actually be better ones than the facilitator originally had in mind.

Most of the problem-solving exercises also look at the use of synergy within the group. Synergy is where the total output of the group is more than the total combined output of the individuals.

All problem-solving exercises should be completely debriefed, so that everyone gets to hear other participants' ideas.

L Learning

These exercises are designed to let the participants see where their learning styles or attitudes need improvement. They tend to be more experimental in their application—that is, the participants are normally required to do something and come up with some kind of result or answer. After that phase of the exercise, the facilitator can normally draw out from the group better ways of doing the same thing with better results.

You must ensure that the whole exercise is totally debriefed and that every participant can see what the final results or methods should be. You should be aware that there are many different learning styles. Don't make the assumption that everyone in the group will learn the same way. Make certain you get plenty of feedback to check participant understanding.

P Perception

The perception exercises are generally fun for everyone to use. They are designed to see how participants perceive different situations or objects. The end result with most perception exercises is that participants are made aware of their need to use lateral thinking, to look at things in different ways, and to try to break down any preconceived stereotypes that they may be using.

As these exercises are fun to use, it is not uncommon to see them being used as icebreakers or mid-course energisers.

Some of the individuals in the group may have difficulty with perception exercises. If they do have difficulties, try to get the rest of the group to explain the different perceptions to them.

E Evaluation

Most of the evaluation exercises are designed so that participants can evaluate either themselves or the program. An important part of the evaluation process needs to be pointed out to the participants at the beginning of the exercise. This point is that any evaluation must be considered as constructive, not destructive. Things can be improved or rectified much more easily by using constructive evaluation. Destructive evaluation does nothing but leave some members with ill-feelings.

If any of these exercises are used for the purpose of program evaluation, it's a good idea to make sure the participants are told of the results, either verbally or in writing.

S Self-management

Exercises in the category of self-management allow the participants to find out where they can improve their own self-management techniques. These techniques are the same as time-management techniques, but with a different name. Here we look at improving participants' organisational skills.

Participants receive a lot of information and new ideas from other members within the group, so make sure that the whole group finds out what principles each participant used in the exercises.

Games Codes Grid

GAME NO.	NAME	PAGE	CATEGORY	Icebreaker	Team building	Communication	Facilitator/presentation skills	Mid-course energiser	Problem solving	Learning	Perception	Evaluation	Self-management
1	How Good Is Your Memory?	17	ITCFMXLP	●	●	●	●	●	●	●	●		
2	Colours of the Rainbow	22	ITCFMXLPS	●	●	●	●	●	●	●	●		●
3	Subjective Evaluations	25	CFLPES			●	●			●	●	●	●
4	$2^1/_2$ Minute Test	26	ITFMXES	●	●		●	●	●			●	●
5	Catawompus Sales	28	CFLS			●	●			●			●
6	Set Me Up	30	TCMXLPE		●	●		●	●	●	●	●	
7	Postage Stamps	31	IMX	●				●	●				
8	Who Went Where?	33	TCMXL		●	●		●	●	●			
9	Odd One	35	IMX	●				●	●				
10	Parallel Lines	37	IMP	●				●			●		
11	Arrows	39	IMLP	●				●		●	●		
12	Observations	41	MXP					●	●		●		
13	What Would You Do If...?	42	FXLS				●		●	●			●
14	Planets Apart	44	IMXL	●				●	●	●			
15	Stretching the Imagination	47	TMXPS		●			●	●		●		●
16	Missing Letter	48	TCMX		●	●		●	●				
17	Feather Race	50	TCMX		●	●		●	●				
18	Popcorn	51	TX		●				●				
19	Horse Races	52	TCMXL		●	●		●	●	●			
20	And the Next Figure Is?	53	IMX	●				●	●				
21	Which Program Am I?	55	ITMX	●	●			●	●				
22	Blindfolded Drawings	56	ICFMP	●		●	●	●			●		
23	The Magic Word	57	IC	●		●							
24	Money	58	ITE	●	●							●	
25	Auction	60	ITE	●	●							●	
26	Pass the Life Saver®	62	TMX		●			●	●				
27	Many Items	63	TCFMXLS		●	●	●	●	●	●			●
28	Kangaroo Races	64	TMX		●			●	●				
29	Ad Infinitum	65	TCFML		●	●	●	●		●			
30	Convincing Nonsense	67	CFS			●	●						●
31	Personal Inventory	69	ITMLS	●	●			●		●			●
32	Categories	71	TMX		●			●	●				

GAME NO.	NAME	PAGE	CATEGORY	Icebreaker	Team building	Communication	Facilitator/presentation skills	Mid-course energiser	Problem solving	Learning	Perception	Evaluation	Self-management
33	van Gogh	73	TCFMP		●	●	●	●			●		
34	Fancy Dress	76	T		●								
35	Positivity Raffle	77	IT	●	●								
36	Bloopers	79	TM		●			●					
37	The Worm	81	ITMXS	●	●			●	●				●
38	Give Me a Feel	84	ITCMXP	●	●	●		●	●		●		
39	20 Questions	86	TCMX		●	●		●	●				
40	Beyond the Call of Duty	87	ITXP	●	●				●		●		
41	Punctuality Check	90	IFLES	●			●			●		●	●
42	T-shirts #1	92	IT	●	●								
43	T-shirts #2	93	IT	●	●								
44	Brain Teasers #2	94	ICMXP	●		●		●	●		●		
45	Brain Teasers #3	96	ICMXP	●		●		●	●		●		
46	Formal Introductions	98	ITFLS	●	●		●			●			●
47	Earliest Thoughts	99	TL		●					●			
48	What Is It?	100	CFXLPS			●	●		●	●	●		●
49	Standing Ovation	101	IM	●				●					
50	Magnetic Fingers	102	IMP	●				●			●		
51	Popping Balloons	103	ITMLE	●	●			●		●		●	
52	A Model of Success	104	TCXPES		●	●			●		●	●	●
53	Motivators/Demotivators	105	TCXLPS		●	●			●	●	●		●
54	What Do You See #2?	107	CMP			●		●			●		
55	Foreign Goals	109	TCML		●	●		●		●			
56	Who Would It Be?	110	IM	●				●					
57	Mini Action Plan	111	ILS	●						●			●
58	Refrigerators	113	ITMXP	●	●			●	●		●		
59	Personality Styles	114	TCPS		●	●					●		●
60	Pin the Tail on the Donkey	117	TMLE		●			●		●		●	
61	Dumb Questions	118	ICLPE	●		●				●	●	●	
62	Must I Do It?	120	XLPS						●	●	●		●
63	Secret Sounds	122	ITMXP	●	●			●	●		●		
64	Who's the Leader?	124	TXS		●				●				●
65	3 Questions	125	IT	●	●								
66	Magic Ball	127	IMXP	●				●	●		●		
67	Training Name Tents	129	IL	●						●			

GAME NO.	NAME	PAGE	CATEGORY	Icebreaker	Team building	Communication	Facilitator/presentation skills	Mid-course energiser	Problem solving	Learning	Perception	Evaluation	Self-management
68	Learning Support Contract	131	LE							●		●	
69	Throw It Away	136	TMXLE		●			●	●	●		●	
70	Jackets and Ties	138	IMLPS	●				●		●	●		●
71	1089	139	IMP	●				●			●		
72	Which Group Am I?	140	ITF	●	●		●						
73	Shaky Start	142	F				●						
74	Contract with Me	143	LES							●		●	●
75	Top 20 Bloopers of Presenting	145	FLS				●			●			●
76	Toys	147	TXLPS		●				●	●	●		●
77	Creative Keys	148	TMXLPS		●			●	●	●	●		●
78	I'm Confused	150	ITMXL	●	●			●	●	●			
79	Jobs	152	TXLPS		●				●	●	●		●
80	What Are Your Answers?	153	IMLPS	●				●		●	●		●
81	Matchboxing	155	IMX	●				●	●				
82	Pass the Orange #1	156	ITMX	●	●			●	●				
83	Pass the Orange #2	157	ITMX	●	●			●	●				
84	Screen Savers	158	TM		●			●					
85	Suggestion/Question Box	159	IXE	●					●			●	
86	How Many Cubes?	161	IMXLP	●				●	●	●	●		
87	How Many Cubes This Time?	163	IMXLP	●				●	●	●	●		
88	X-Files	165	CMLS			●		●		●			●
89	The Good, the Bad and the Funny	167	PE								●	●	
90	Matches #3	169	IMXLS	●				●	●	●			●
91	What Comes Next?	172	IMXLPS	●				●	●	●	●		●
92	Levels of Knowledge	174	ILPS	●						●	●		●
93	Tossing Balls	176	ITMXPS	●	●			●	●		●		●
94	Follow Through	177	LES							●		●	●
95	1-2-5	179	IMLP	●				●		●	●		
96	Building Blocks	180	TXLPS		●				●	●	●		●
97	Flags	181	TM		●			●					
98	Reflections	182	LPE							●	●	●	
99	New Players	184	TCXL		●	●			●	●			
100	That's Torn It	185	IFMXLS	●			●	●	●	●			●
101	Stop Shop	186	ICMLP	●		●		●		●	●		
102	Hostage	187	TCXPS		●	●			●		●		●

The Games

1

How Good Is Your Memory?

ITCFMXLP

TIME REQUIRED	SIZE OF GROUP	MATERIAL REQUIRED
10–15 minutes.	Unlimited.	Four prepared overheads showing 'Number Sequence #1', 'Test #1', 'Number Sequence #2', and 'Test #2'. One sheet of paper and pen for each participant.

Overview

This exercise will show you how complicated material can be presented effectively and also be retained by the participants.

Goals

1. To show participants how complicated information can be linked to simple information to allow better retrieval.
2. To show one technique of improving memory recall.

Procedure

1. Advise the group that they are going to have a quick test. This test is to see how good their memories are.
2. Tell the group that you are going to show them an overhead with ten numbers and shapes shown on it. They will be required to memorise which shape goes with each number. They will have one minute to memorise this information.
3. Show the 'Number Sequence #1' overhead for one minute.
4. Ask each person to now get their pen and paper and write the answers to the equations shown on the next overhead.
5. Show the 'Test #1' overhead for one minute.
6. Show the 'Number Sequence #1' overhead and see how many correct answers each person had.
7. Ask the group why no one had a perfect score. This may lead into a quick discussion if relevant.
8. Ask if it would have been easier if they had been given additional information. Discuss.
9. Tell them that they are going to be given a second chance with the test, but this time the information will be shown in a slightly different way.
10. Show the 'Number Sequence #2' overhead for one minute.
11. Ask each person to now get their pen and paper and write the answers to the equations shown on the next overhead.
12. Show the 'Test #2' overhead for one minute.
13. Ask for results and then lead into a discussion on why the results were far better the second time around. Can we introduce 'patterns' into the information we need people to remember?

Discussion points

1. Why did everyone get much better results with the second exercise?
2. How can we apply this in the information we have to give to others?

Variations

1. Can be conducted as a small group exercise.
2. Handouts may be used instead of overheads.

Solution

Test #1 = 2, 6, 12, 20, 30
Test #2 = 20, 30, 42, 56, 72

TRAINER'S NOTES

Number sequence #1

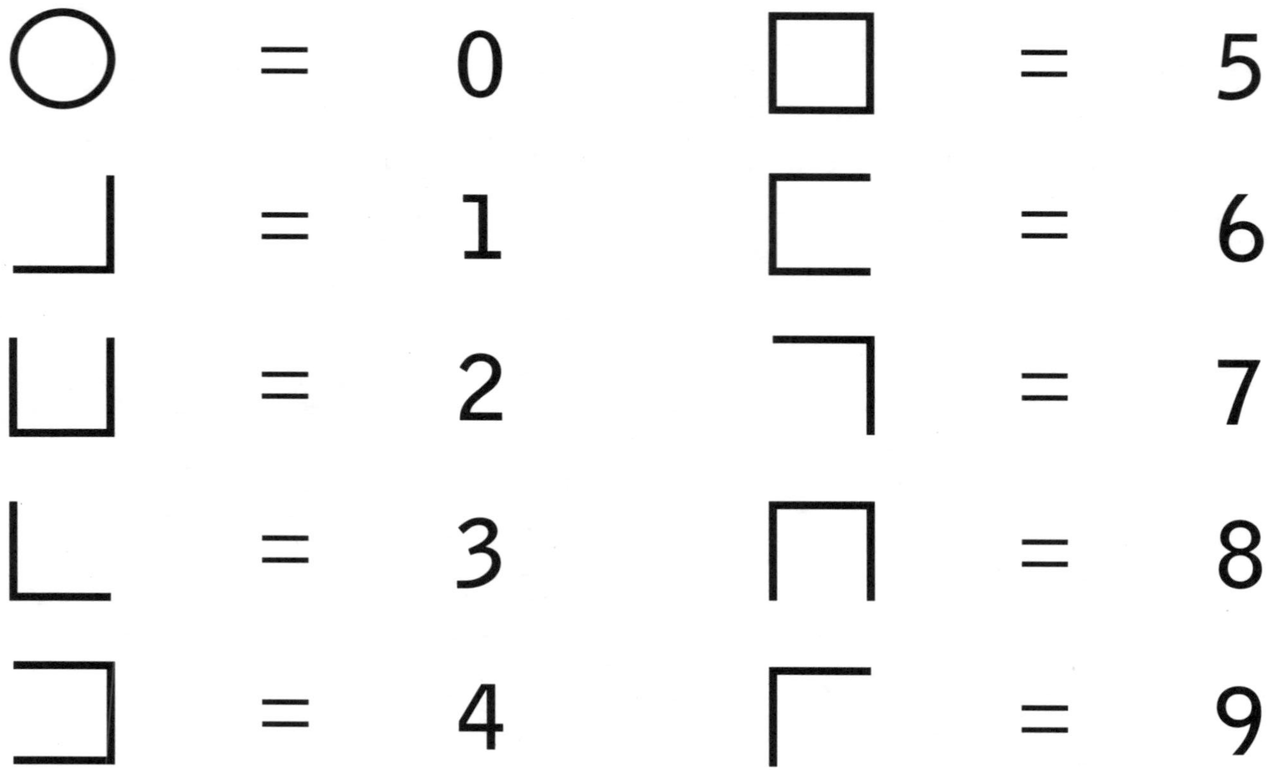

Test #1

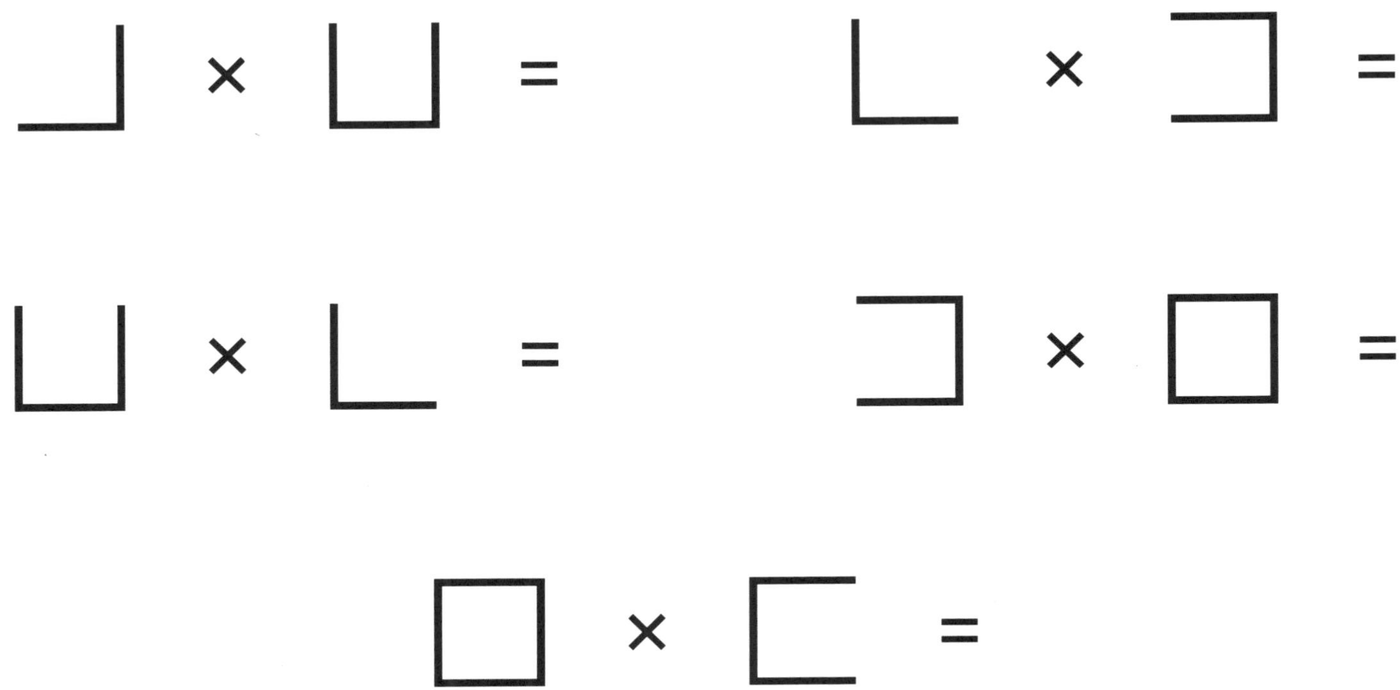

Number sequence #2

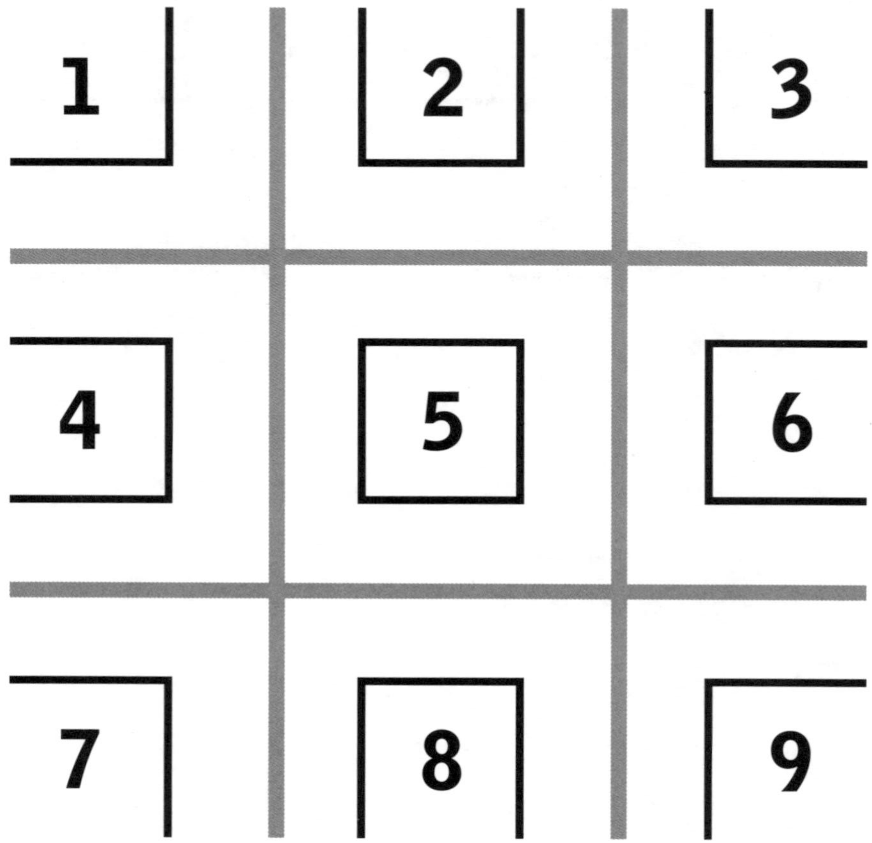

Test #2

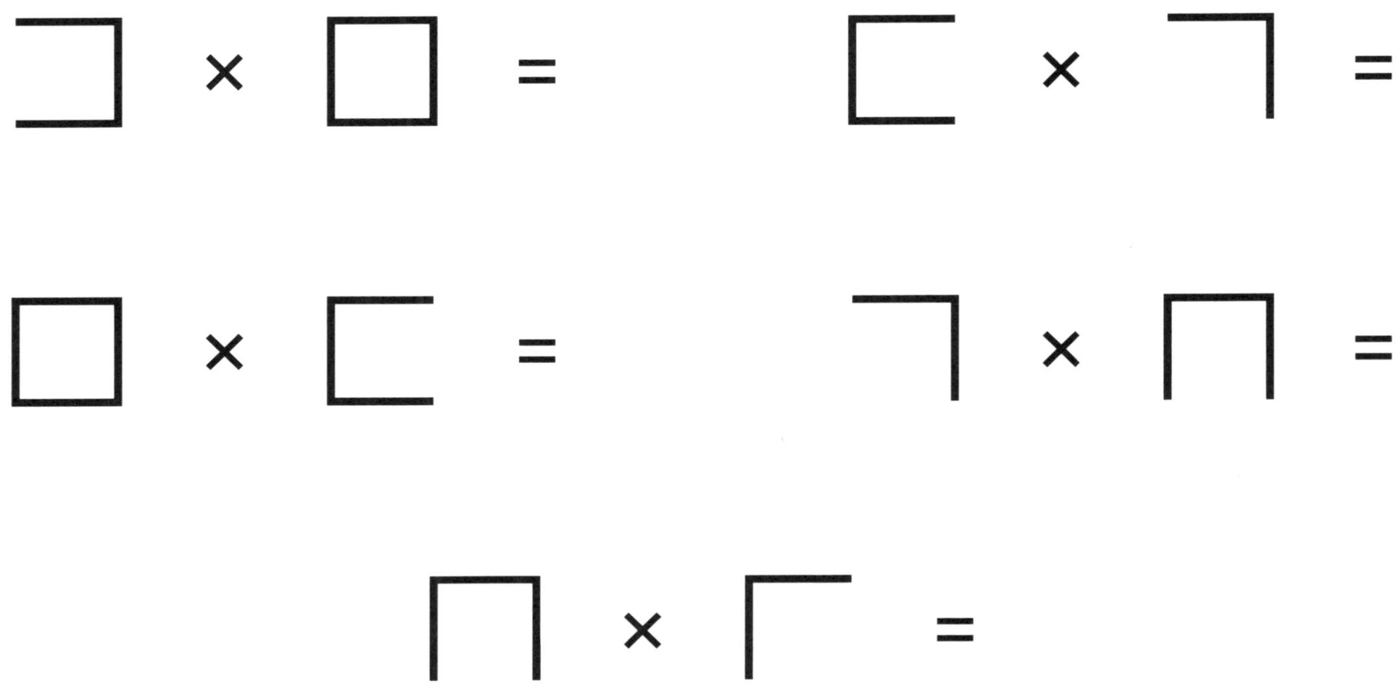

2 Colours of the Rainbow

ITCFMXLPS

TIME REQUIRED	SIZE OF GROUP	MATERIAL REQUIRED
10–15 minutes.	Unlimited.	Two prepared overheads showing 'Colours of the Rainbow' and 'Planets'. One sheet of paper and pen for each participant.

Overview

This activity will show participants an easy way to remember a series of facts or a sequence of information.

Goals

1. To show participants how to remember a list of items in the correct sequence.
2. To improve participants' test results.

Procedure

1. Ask the participants how good their memories are.
2. Then ask if they would like to be shown a way of improving their memories.
3. As a pre-test, ask the individuals to write the colours of the rainbow in the correct sequence. Allow about a minute for this.
4. Ask volunteers to read their lists out and compare results. It may add a bit of fun to ask how many people actually knew how many colours there were.
5. Tell them that you are now going to show them a way of remembering this list in the correct sequence using a mnemonic.
6. Show the 'Colours of the Rainbow' overhead.
7. After a couple of minutes of discussion, turn the overhead off and ask them to write the list again. Check the results.
8. Ask participants to now make their own mnemonic so they can remember the planets in our solar system in the correct sequence, starting with the planet closest to the sun.
9. Show the 'Planets' overhead and allow a couple of minutes.
10. Ask for volunteers to share their mnemonic with the group.
11. Lead into discussion if relevant.

Discussion points

1. How can we apply the use of mnemonics on this course?
2. How can we apply the use of mnemonics in our everyday lives?

Variations

1. May be done as a small group exercise.
2. Handouts may be used instead of overheads.
3. Lists of items that are common to everyone in the group could be used in addition to the others.
4. The group could be asked to create a mnemonic for the signs of the Zodiac, or the names of everyone in the group, in the correct seating order.

TRAINER'S NOTES

Colours of the Rainbow

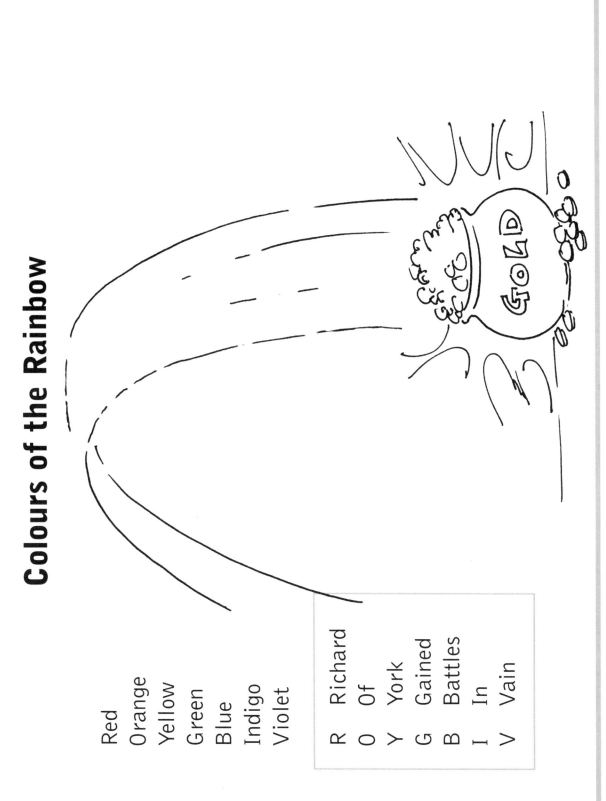

Red
Orange
Yellow
Green
Blue
Indigo
Violet

R	Richard
O	Of
Y	York
G	Gained
B	Battles
I	In
V	Vain

Planets

Mercury
Venus
Earth
Mars
Jupiter
Saturn
Uranus
Neptune
Pluto

3

Subjective Evaluations

CFLPES

TIME REQUIRED	SIZE OF GROUP	MATERIAL REQUIRED
10–15 minutes.	Unlimited.	One sheet of paper and pen for each participant.

Overview

This exercise will allow participants to give you some feedback as to how much they think they learnt from the course.

Goals

1. To allow participants the opportunity to give feedback on information gained from the course.
2. To give the facilitator feedback on the training.

Procedure

1. Ask the participants to list all the separate topic areas of the training course.
2. Then ask them to rank on a scale of 1–10 how much they think they gained from the training (1 being nothing, 5 being the amount they needed and 10 being far too much). Allow as much time as needed for this.
3. After everyone has completed their lists, encourage them to share their scores.
4. Group all the individual topic scores together and calculate the mean score for each. If the training has gone the right way, this should give an average score of somewhere between 5 and 7.

Discussion points

1. Which topics produced the best level of learning? Why?
2. Which topics produced the worst level of learning? Why?
3. Should we assume that everyone has the same level of knowledge before we start? Why, or why not?
4. Do some people require higher scores for a specific reason? If so, why?

Variations

1. You may have all the topic areas previously broken down and copied on to a sheet of paper as a handout.
2. After step 2, you could ask the group to calculate the average scores for each topic without you being present. After a predetermined time the group could then give feedback regarding the results. This should give more honest feedback.

TRAINER'S NOTES

4

2½ Minute Test

ITFMXES

TIME REQUIRED	SIZE OF GROUP	MATERIAL REQUIRED
5 to 10 minutes, depending on the group size and amount of discussion required.	Unlimited.	One '2½ Minute Test' handout and a pen for each participant.

Overview

This quick activity is designed to show how mistakes can be made, or how we can overlook things, if we rush things too much.

Goals

1. To demonstrate how mistakes can be made if we rush things.
2. To demonstrate how things can be overlooked if we rush.
3. To energise the group.
4. To have some fun.

Procedure

1. When appropriate, tell the group they are going to be given a quick test to see how they are going.
2. Give each person a copy of the '2½ Minute Test' handout. This should be placed face down in front of them.
3. Ask the participants not to commence until you give the signal. Tell them that this really is a quick test and that they only have 2½ minutes to complete it. Before any questions can be asked, look at your watch and say, 'Go'.
4. Count the time down to increase the pressure.
5. After the 2½ minutes ask them to stop.
6. Review each question one at a time, asking for their answers.
7. After you get the verbal answers, tell them the correct answers.
8. Ask who scored 8 out of 8? Then 7 out of 8, etc.
9. Lead into a discussion on the effects of rushing things.

Discussion points

1. How many people scored 8 out of 8?
2. What stopped everyone from getting a perfect score?
3. How does this apply to your training?
4. How does this apply in the workplace?

Variations

1. May be conducted as a small group activity.
2. Additional questions could be asked if necessary.

Answers

1. One hour. If you started at 8.00 am, your second would be at 8.30 and the final one at 9.00 am.
2. 70, because 30 divided by a half equals 60.
3. The match.
4. Two apples—remember, you took the apples.
5. All of them.
6. White. The house has to be on the North Pole, therefore the bear must be a polar bear.
7. None. Moses didn't have an Ark—it was Noah.
8. One hour. You had to wind up the alarm clock, therefore it was a mechanical one. It only works on a 12 hour cycle, not a 24 hour one.

TRAINER'S NOTES

$2\frac{1}{2}$ Minute Test

You have $2\frac{1}{2}$ minutes to complete this test. Therefore work as quickly as you can, making sure you attempt to answer all the questions.
Good luck!

1. If a doctor gave you three pills and told you to take one every half hour, how long would they last?
2. Divide 30 by a half. Add 10. What is the answer?
3. If you had only one match and entered a dark room where there was an oil lamp, an oil heater and some kindling wood, which would you light first?
4. Take two apples from three apples. What do you have?
5. Some months have 30 days, some have 31. How many months have 28 days?
6. Imagine that you built a house with four sides, and each wall had a southern exposure. If a bear went past one of the windows, what colour would the bear be?
7. How many animals of each species did Moses take on the Ark?
8. If you went to bed at eight o'clock in the evening, wound up the alarm clock and set it to get up at nine o'clock the next morning, how many hours' sleep would you get?

5

Catawompus Sales

CFLS

TIME REQUIRED	SIZE OF GROUP	MATERIAL REQUIRED
20–30 minutes, depending on the group size.	Works best with about 10 to 12 people. Larger groups can be used, but they will need to be broken into smaller groups for the presentations.	At least one 'catawompus' for each participant. A 'catawompus' can be any unusual object. The objects selected should be items that the participant is completely unfamiliar with. Each person may also require a pen and paper.

Overview

To show people how creative they can be when they need to.

Goals

1. To demonstrate how creative participants can be.
2. To give participants the opportunity to give a short presentation to the group.
3. To investigate ways of improved selling techniques.

Procedure

1. Let the participants know that they are going to be involved in a selling game. The object of the game is to try and sell your 'product' to the group.
2. Tell the participants that they will each be given an item before their presentation is due to start. They will have 1 minute to prepare for a 2 minute sales presentation. Let them prepare any notes they may wish to use.
3. After their 1 minute preparation, ask them to give their 'sales pitch' to the group.
4. At the conclusion of each presentation, the group should give feedback to the 'sales person'.
5. Before going on to the next person it may be appropriate to take a vote to see if the sales pitch worked. This will also make it a bit more light-hearted.
6. After all the presentations have been delivered, a list should be made on the whiteboard of all positive points raised in discussion.
7. This should now lead into a discussion on other techniques or whatever else is relevant.

Discussion points

1. How many people felt that they did a good job of selling their 'catawompus'?
2. Who felt nervous with the presentation? Why?
3. How can we overcome nerves?
4. How can we improve our sales techniques?
5. Who had the most creative 'catawompus'?

Variations

1. A prize may be given to the most creative person.
2. A prize may be given for the best presentation.
3. Let the individuals in the group draw a 'catawompus' on a sheet of paper. These sheets can be collected and folded. These 'catawompi' (that's the plural of catawompus) are then the items to be selected for the presentations.

TRAINER'S NOTES

Catawompus

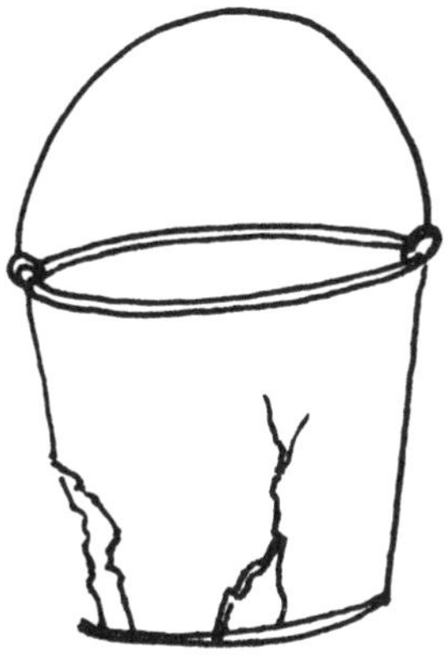

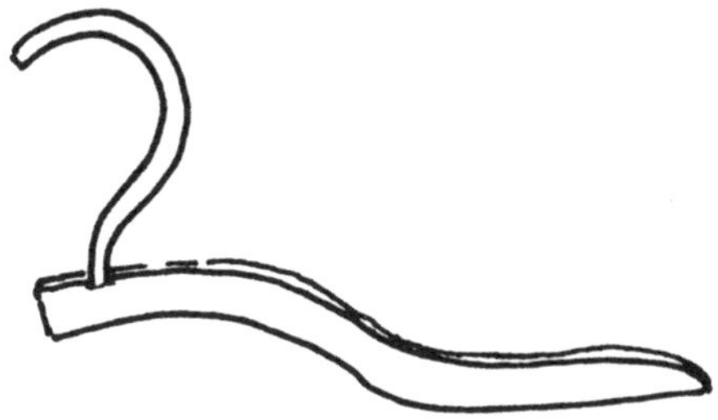

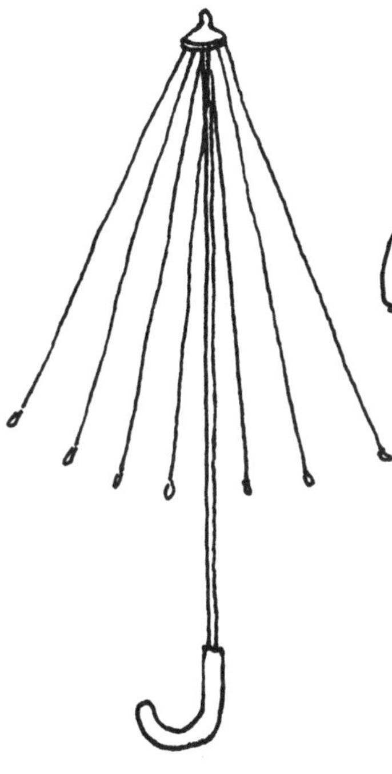

6

Set Me Up

TCMXLPE

TIME REQUIRED	SIZE OF GROUP	MATERIAL REQUIRED
10–20 minutes.	Unlimited.	None.

Overview

An activity to demonstrate how important constant feedback is and how frustrating it is when the feedback is withdrawn.

Goals

1. To demonstrate the positive use of feedback.
2. To demonstrate the negative use of feedback.

Procedure

1. Tell the participants that they are going to be given the opportunity to 'set up' the trainer.
2. Inform them that you will be leaving the room for a minute or two. During that time they are to pick something for you to do—something relatively easy, like running your fingers through your hair, or walking around the table. When you come back into the room, every time you make any action towards doing the 'task', they are to sing out 'yes'. This feedback has to be given with even the slightest movement in the right direction. Now have a quick practice. The other requirement is that they are not allowed to say anything else, not even 'no' if you are doing the wrong thing.
3. By only giving the word 'yes' as feedback, they are to get you to perform the 'task' three times.
4. Leave the room and ask someone to come and get you when they are ready.
5. Follow their directions until the 'task' has been performed three times. Lots of laughter generally follows.
6. Now tell them it's your turn to get even. Select a volunteer from the group (an outgoing person if possible). Let them know that they are going to be put through the same exercise, and then ask them to leave the room and wait to be called back in.
7. Now select another 'task' with the group.
8. Advise the group that they will be doing the same thing, but this time, after the 'task' has been performed three times, they are not to tell the person that they have completed the exercise. They are to remain silent and say nothing, just observe. This complete silence will last for 2 or 3 minutes. Ask them what they think our volunteer will do without the feedback.
9. Bring the volunteer back into the room and start the activity. Get them to perform the task and then watch and observe.
10. After closing off the exercise, thank the volunteer. Then ask them how they felt during the activity. This could lead into discussion about feedback, etc. Ask the group what they saw happening.

Discussion points

1. How did the volunteer feel during the first part of the exercise?
2. How did the volunteer feel during the last part of the exercise?
3. What happened after the positive reinforcers were removed?
4. What does this demonstrate about feedback?
5. How does this apply in the workplace?

Variations

1. You may arrange with the group that during step 9, the 'task' is to be changed after it has been performed twice.
2. This game can be played using a blindfold for a team-building activity.
3. This exercise may be videotaped for the debriefing.

TRAINER'S NOTES

7

Postage Stamps

IMX

TIME REQUIRED	SIZE OF GROUP	MATERIAL REQUIRED
1–2 minutes.	Unlimited.	Overhead, if required.

Overview

An exercise that can be used as a mid-course energiser.

Goal

To energise the group.

Procedure

1. Say to the group, 'Using only 19 and 25 cent postage stamps, what is the largest postal amount that cannot be made?'
2. Give the first person with the correct answer a prize.

Discussion points

1. Who worked out the answer first?
2. Why did some people not even try to solve the problem?

Variations

1. Use different stamp values.
2. Put up an overhead showing the two stamps.

Solution

$4.31

TRAINER'S NOTES

Postage Stamps

8 Who Went Where?

TCMXL

TIME REQUIRED

10–15 minutes.

SIZE OF GROUP

Unlimited, but large groups will need to be broken into smaller groups of 5 to 7 people.

MATERIAL REQUIRED

One prepared 'Who Went Where?' overhead and one sheet of paper and pen for each participant.

Overview

This exercise is designed as a problem-solving activity to show how teamwork can lead to better and generally faster results.

Goal

To demonstrate the benefit of teamwork in problem solving.

Procedure

1. Inform the participants that they are going to be involved in a problem-solving activity.
2. Ask them to form groups of 5 to 7 people.
3. You can now tell the participants that last week your company sent 5 people to 5 different places on 5 different days using different vehicles. Their task is to tell you who went where, on what day, using which vehicle. The boss needs to know as soon as possible.
4. Advise the groups that you are now going to show them an overhead full of information. From the information given they are to work out the answers. Before they ask, you can tell them that all the information they need is shown on the overhead. They will have 5 minutes to complete the task.
5. After the groups have finished, ask them how they went about getting the information together so that they could see the results. This could then lead into a discussion on teamwork or problem solving.

Discussion points

1. How many groups came up with the correct answers?
2. What helped the group arrive at the answers?
3. What hindered the group in arriving at the answers?

Variations

Substitute names and places can be used. These could be names and places that are familiar to the group. This could also add to the length of the activity as it may involve some 'gossip' between the participants.

Solution

Jones			
	Ansett Airlines	Australia	Monday
Brown			
	Singapore Airlines	UK	Wednesday
Smith			
	Qantas	New Zealand	Friday
Zoubari			
	British Airways	US	Tuesday
Wong			
	United Airlines	Hong Kong	Saturday

TRAINER'S NOTES

Who Went Where?

Jones flew with Ansett Airlines.
The Hong Kong flight was on Saturday.
British Airways flew to the US.
Brown went on Wednesday.
Smith went to New Zealand.
Qantas flew on Friday.
Zoubari went on Tuesday.
Singapore Airlines flew to London.
Wong went with United Airlines.
The Australian flight was on Monday.
Ansett Airlines flew on Monday.
Wong flew to Hong Kong.
Zoubari went with British Airways.
Brown went to the UK.

9

Odd One

IMX

TIME REQUIRED	SIZE OF GROUP	MATERIAL REQUIRED
1–2 minutes.	Unlimited.	One prepared 'Odd One' overhead.

Overview

This exercise can be used effectively as a mid-course energiser, or after a break while waiting for the latecomers to come back.

Goals

1. To energise the group.
2. To fill in some time.

Procedure

1. Show the group the 'Odd One' overhead and ask, 'Who can tell which is the odd name, and why?'
2. If they can't work it out, tell them the answer. This is a quick exercise, so don't try and draw it out.
3. If someone gives you the correct answer, give them a prize.

Discussion points

None.

Variations

You may find that you have various employee names or product names that would work in better with a group of people from the same company or industry.

Solution

Russell is the correct answer. All other names start with successive roman numerals: I, V, X, L, C, D, M.

TRAINER'S NOTES

Odd One

Ingrid
Victoria
Russell
Xavier
Lenny
Charles
David
Margaret

10 Parallel Lines

IMP

TIME REQUIRED
1–2 minutes.

SIZE OF GROUP
Unlimited.

MATERIAL REQUIRED
One prepared 'Parallel Lines' overhead.

Overview

This exercise shows how things can be easily modified to hide the facts.

Goal

To allow participants to see that their perceptions are not always correct.

Procedure

1. Project the 'Parallel Lines' transparency on to the screen and ask the group which horizontal line is longer, A or B?
2. After you have taken a vote on the 4 outcomes (A, B, both the same, or undecided), inform the group that they are both the same length. You may have to show some people that they are indeed the same length by using a pen lid or something similar as a measuring device.
3. Lead into a discussion on how some things are not as they seem.

Discussion points

1. How many people selected A?
2. How many people selected B?
3. How many people said they're both the same?
4. How many people are undecided?
5. Was anyone manipulated by the fact that they were actually asked to determine which line was longer? This statement obviously infers that one is longer.
6. Can everyone see that their initial perceptions may not have been correct?

Variations

May be used as a handout.

TRAINER'S NOTES

Parallel Lines

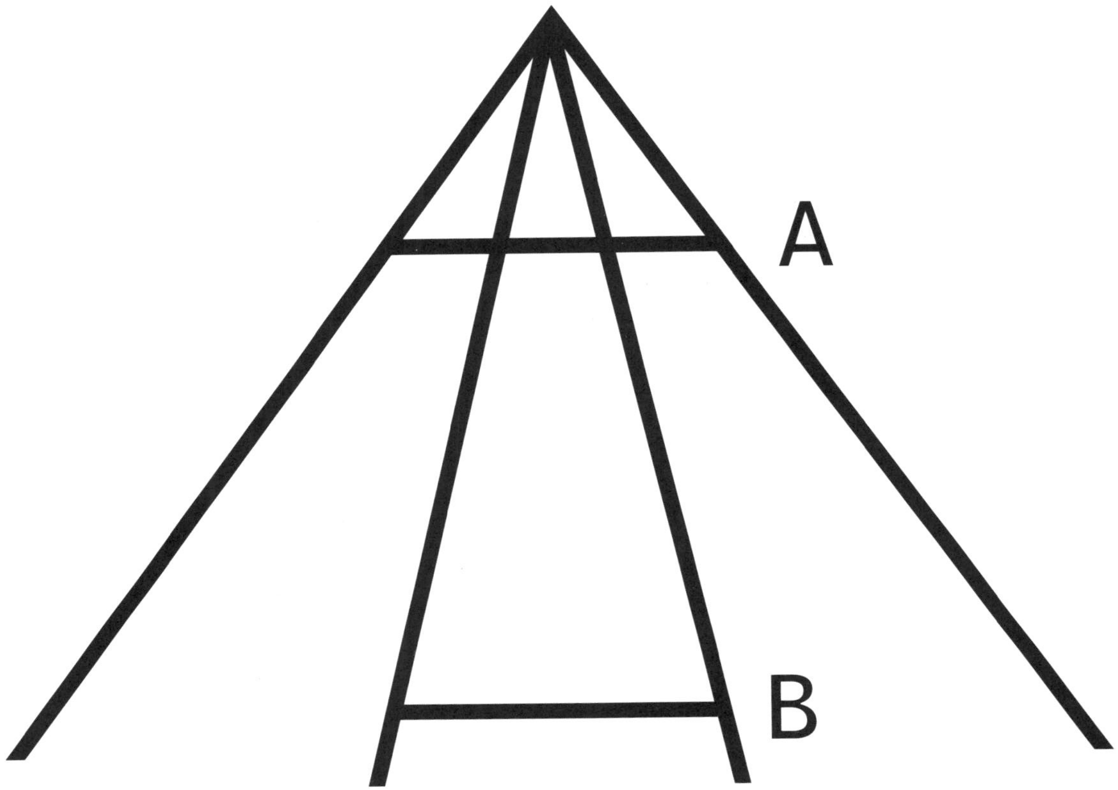

11

Arrows

IMLP

TIME REQUIRED	SIZE OF GROUP	MATERIAL REQUIRED
1–2 minutes.	Unlimited.	One prepared 'Arrows' overhead.

Overview

Another exercise to show how things can be easily modified to hide the facts. But if it is used after Game 10, it can demonstrate how learning may have taken place, or how we can now look closer at things.

Goals

1. To allow participants to see that their perceptions are not always correct.
2. To see if learning has taken place as a result of the previous exercise.

Procedure

1. Project the 'Arrows' transparency on to the screen and ask the participants which section of the line is longer, A to B or B to C?
2. After you have taken a vote on the 4 outcomes (A to B, B to C, both the same, or undecided), inform the group that they are both the same length. You may have to show some people that they are indeed the same length by using a pen lid or something similar as a measuring device.
3. Lead into a discussion on how some things are not as they seem.

Discussion points

1. How many people selected A to B?
2. How many people selected B to C?
3. How many people said they're both the same?
4. How many people are undecided?
5. Was anyone manipulated by the fact that you were actually asked to determine which line was longer? This statement obviously infers that one is longer.
6. If Game 10 was used beforehand, did learning take place?
7. Can everyone see that their initial perceptions may not be correct?

Variations

1. May be used as a handout.
2. May be used with Game 10, or by itself.

TRAINER'S NOTES

Arrows

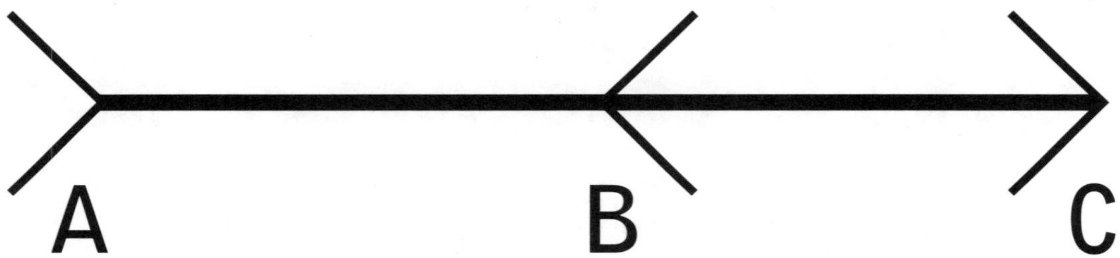

12 Observations

MXP

TIME REQUIRED	SIZE OF GROUP	MATERIAL REQUIRED
10–15 minutes.	Unlimited, but large groups will need to be broken into smaller groups of 5 to 7 people.	One sheet of paper and pen for each participant. One flipchart and pens for each small group.

Overview

A interesting activity to show how unobservant some people may be.

Goals

1. To demonstrate how unobservant some people are.
2. To demonstrate how combined thinking should come up with more accurate solutions.

Procedure

1. Select a person from the group. Ask them to leave the room (perhaps give them a task to do).
2. After this person leaves the room ask the rest of the group to get their pens and papers and write a description of what the person looked like, what they were wearing, etc. Allow a couple of minutes for this.
3. When people finish writing their descriptions, ask them to form teams of 5 to 7 people. Each team is now given a flipchart and pens, and asked to reach a consensus on the description.
4. Once they have completed the group work, ask them to report back on the group results.
5. When all groups have given their feedback, ask your volunteer to come back into the room, and then compare the results.

Discussion points

1. How many people had a perfect description?
2. How many groups had a perfect description?
3. Were the group descriptions more accurate than the individual descriptions?
4. Who had the most accurate description?
5. How can we improve our powers of observation?

Variations

You may ask a person not involved with the training to come into the room at the start of your presentation and hand you something. This would be done in front of the group. After they have left the room go straight into step 2.

TRAINER'S NOTES

13

What Would You Do If...?

FXLS

TIME REQUIRED

20–30 minutes, depending on the group size.

SIZE OF GROUP

Unlimited, but large groups will need to be broken into smaller groups of 5 to 7 people.

MATERIAL REQUIRED

A 'What Would You Do If ...?' handout and a pen for each participant. A cardboard box is also required.

Overview

A simple activity to allow individuals to identify problems without being 'put on the spot'. It can also allow the group to identify solutions to these problems.

Goals

1. To allow participants to identify problems they would like answers to.
2. To allow the group to devise solutions to identified problems.

Procedure

1. Inform the participants that they are now going to get a chance to pose problems they would like answers to.
2. Give each person a copy of the 'What Would You Do If...?' handout.
3. Now ask them to write on the handout at least one question they would like an answer to.
4. When they have completed this, ask them to fold their sheets in half and place them in the cardboard box.
5. After all the sheets have been collected, break the large group into smaller groups of 5 to 7 people.
6. Each group should then be given handouts from the cardboard box. They will be given the same number of sheets as there are members in their group.
7. Ask each group to work through the sheets one at a time and come up with as many solutions as they can to each problem. Allow as much time as necessary for this.
8. When all groups have completed their work, have each group report their findings to the large group.

Discussion points

1. Do we tend to limit ourselves when giving solutions? Why?
2. What is lateral thinking and how does it apply to this exercise?

Variations

1. You could collect all the sheets and summarise the questions for each group to deal with. This will take longer to prepare but it will help protect people's identities if that's important.
2. The groups may be asked to write their solutions on the bottom of the sheets. The sheets can then be spread over a table and during a break the individuals can collect them if required.
3. If used in conjunction with facilitation or presentation skills courses, the presentations would obviously be required as structured presentations.

TRAINER'S NOTES

What Would You Do If...?

Please take a minute to write down any questions you would like answered. These questions should relate to the training topic. Your name is not required on this sheet. These questions will be posed to other groups and solutions sought from them.

14

Planets Apart

IMXL

TIME REQUIRED

2–5 minutes.

SIZE OF GROUP

Unlimited.

MATERIAL REQUIRED

One 'Planets Apart' overhead and one 'Planets Apart: Solution' overhead.

Overview

An activity to test participants' logic. It can be used effectively as a mid-course energiser, or after a break while waiting for the latecomers to come back.

Goals

1. To test participants' logic.
2. To energise the group.
3. To fill in some time.

Procedure

1. Show the 'Planets Apart' overhead and ask the group the following question: 'If the planet Sram takes 4 years to orbit its Sun, and the planet Sunev takes 2 years, when will all three next be in line?'
2. After a minute or so has passed show them the solution on the second overhead.

Discussion points

1. Who got the right answer?
2. How did you work it out?
3. Who didn't even try? Why not?

Variations

1. Can be used as a handout, or as a small unobtrusive diagram in a workbook.
2. Instead of planet names, use the names of items or of people with which all the participants would be familiar.

Solution

2 years.

TRAINER'S NOTES

Planets Apart

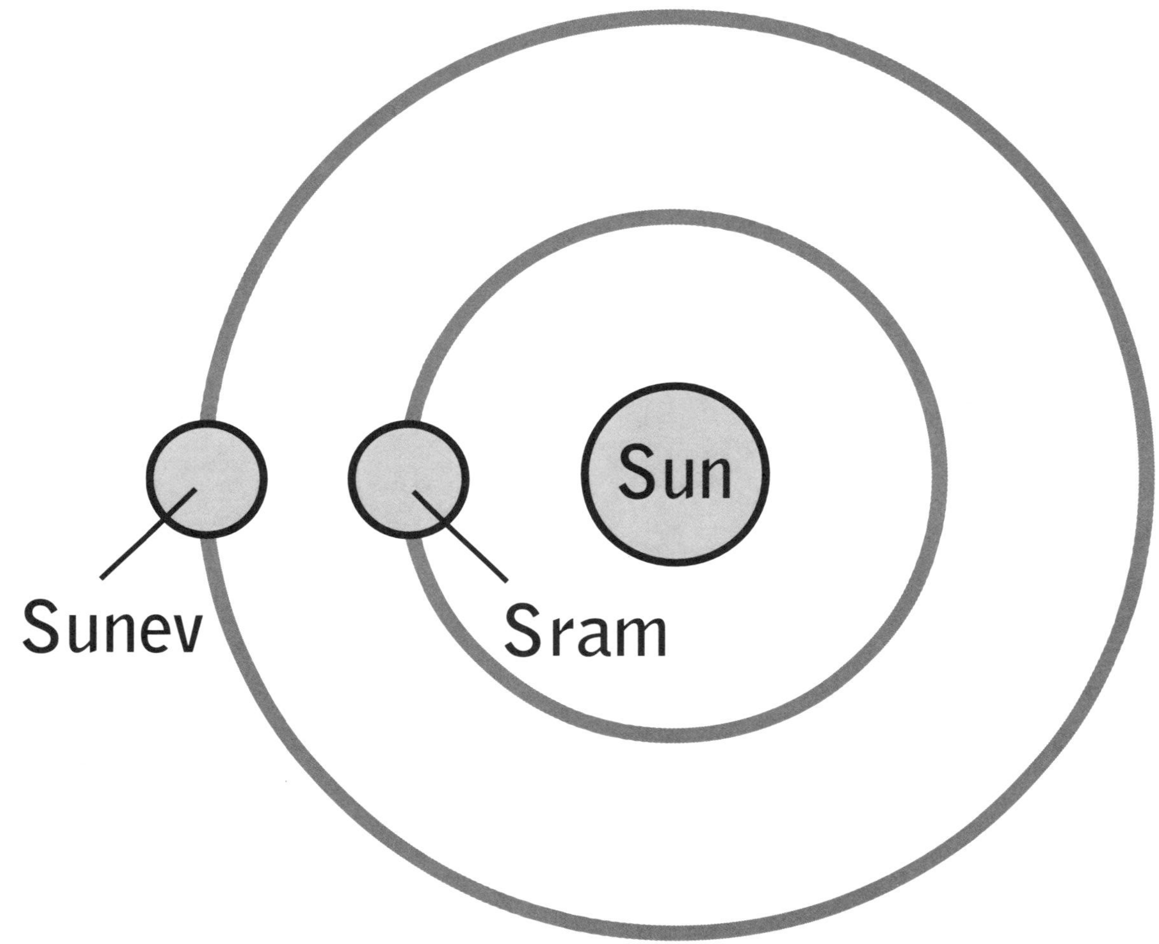

Planets Apart: Solution

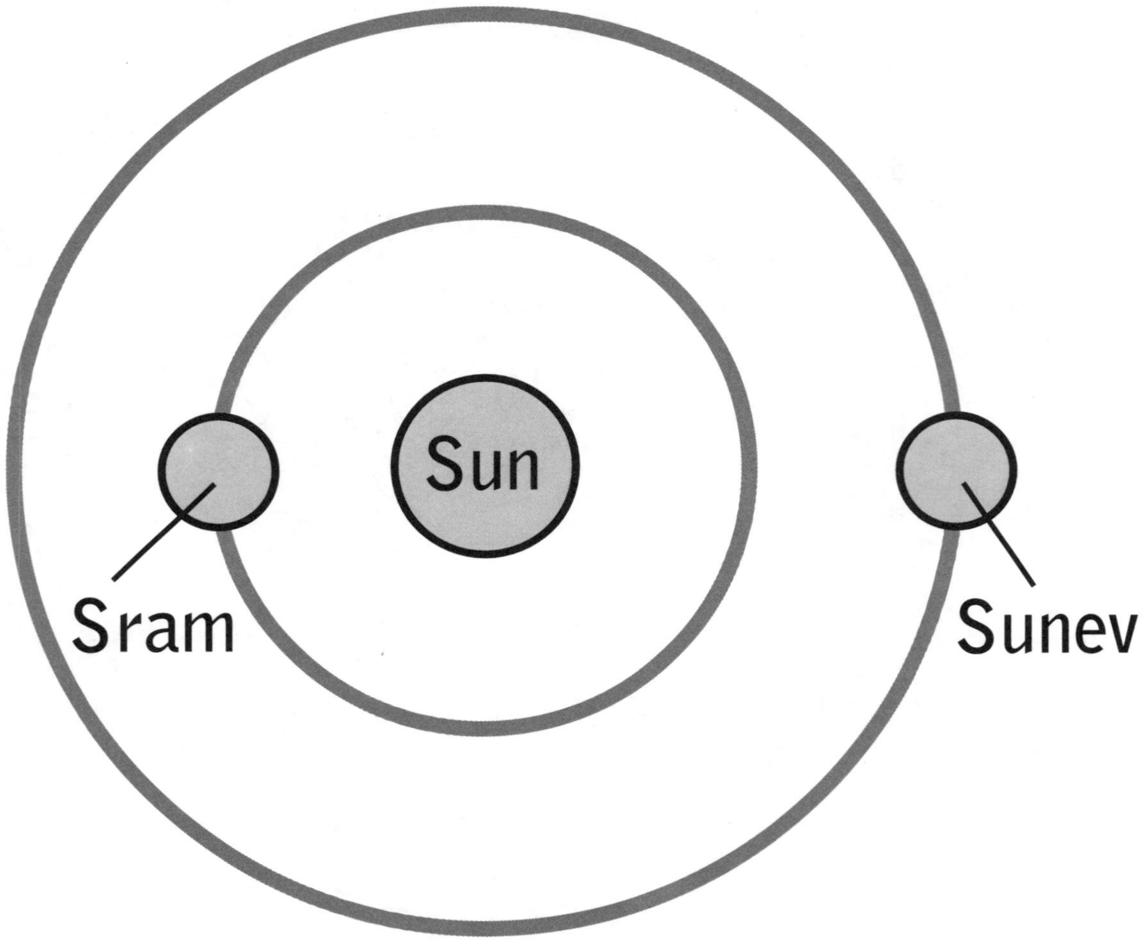

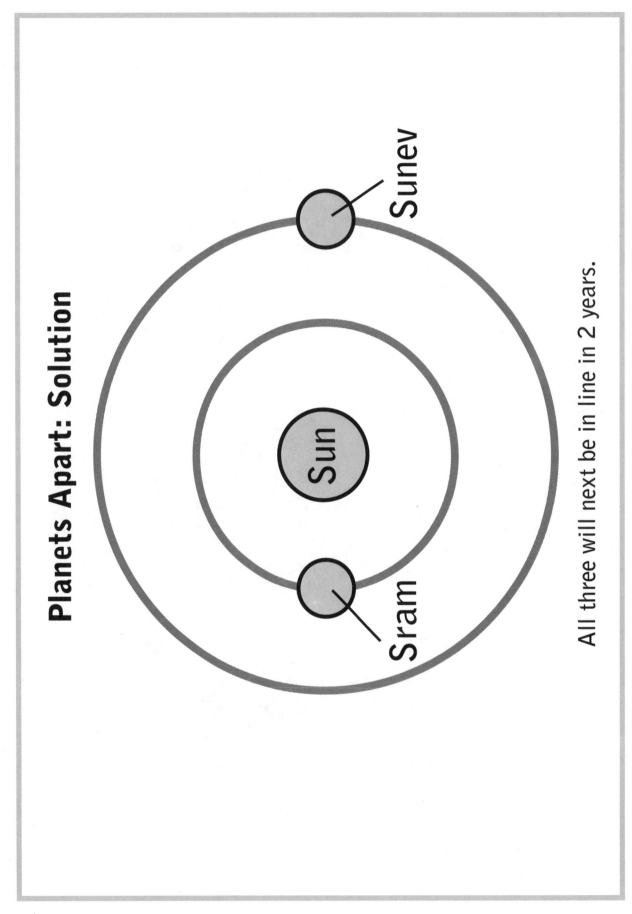

All three will next be in line in 2 years.

15 Stretching the Imagination

TMXPS

TIME REQUIRED
5–10 minutes.

SIZE OF GROUP
Unlimited.

MATERIAL REQUIRED
A roll of masking (or packing) tape, a balloon, a marking pen and a newspaper.

Overview

A simple activity designed to promote lateral thinking.

Goals

1. To get participants to use lateral thinking.
2. To allow the trainees to participate in a problem-solving exercise.

Procedure

1. Start this exercise by asking for a volunteer. Tell the volunteer they are going to be asked to solve a problem. The problem will be to retrieve a balloon off the floor using only the materials supplied to them.
2. While you are talking, blow up the balloon. Then make a square on the floor, using the masking tape so that everyone can see it. The square should be about 0.5 m x 0.5m.
3. Ask the volunteer to stand in the middle of the square. Give them the newspaper. Place the balloon about 3 to 4 m away from the edge of the square. Before putting the balloon on the floor it may add some fun to write something on it—such as 'extremely valuable', or '$$$', etc.
4. Now ask the volunteer to retrieve the balloon without moving from the square. They have 3 minutes to complete the task. The rest of the group is to observe only and not offer suggestions on how to solve the problem.
5. After the 3 minute time limit, ask the group for suggestions on how to solve the problem (assuming that your volunteer hasn't completed the task).
6. This could then lead into a discussion on problem solving, synergy, teamwork, etc.

Discussion points

1. How many people saw an answer to the problem?
2. How many other ways are there of solving this problem?
3. What rules do we tend to place on ourselves?

Variations

1. It's fun to put something inside the balloon (a couple of wrapped sweets, for instance). When the balloon is retrieved your volunteer can have these as their reward for participating.
2. This can be done as a small group exercise. Mark out a 1 m square on the floor using the masking tape. Have the small group get inside the square. They are to now retrieve the balloon using the same rules.

Solution

Here's one solution. Roll the newspaper up fairly tightly. Then start to pull the inside of it out at one end. This will create a rod. Then tear an end off the masking tape on the floor. This piece of tape can then be put on the end of the rod with the sticky side exposed. Touch the balloon with the sticky end and retrieve it!

TRAINER'S NOTES

16 Missing Letter

TCMX

TIME REQUIRED	SIZE OF GROUP	MATERIAL REQUIRED
10–15 minutes.	Unlimited, but large groups will need to be broken into smaller groups of 5 to 7 people.	One prepared 'Missing Letter' overhead and pen and paper for each participant.

Overview

A problem-solving activity that can be used for individuals or for groups. It has also been designed to help improve discussion within groups.

Goals

1. To allow participants to be involved in a problem-solving activity.
2. To allow participants to see the benefits of working together to solve problems—the use of synergy.

Procedure

1. Advise the participants that they are going to be involved in a problem-solving exercise.
2. Show them the 'Missing Letter' overhead.
3. Tell them that they have 2 minutes to tell you what the missing letter is and explain why that is the correct answer.
4. After the 2 minutes, organise the participants into groups of 5 to 7 people.
5. Now ask them to solve the problem as a group.
6. After a solution has been found, or a time limit has been reached, ask the participants what the purpose of the exercise was. This should lead into a discussion on problem solving.

Discussion points

1. How many people came up with the correct answer?
2. Is there more than one solution to the problem?
3. How does this apply in the workplace?

Variations

The 'Missing Letter' overhead can be used as a handout.

Solution

The missing letter is 'L'. The position of the letter in the middle is midway between the two letters shown above and below it.

TRAINER'S NOTES

Missing Letter

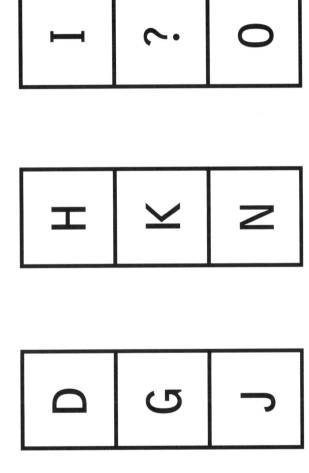

D	H	I
G	K	?
J	N	O

17

Feather Race

TCMX

TIME REQUIRED	SIZE OF GROUP	MATERIAL REQUIRED
10–20 minutes, depending on the size of the group.	Unlimited, but large groups will need to be broken into smaller groups of 5 to 7 people.	A roll of masking tape. One feather for each group.

Overview

This fun activity is a team competition. It allows for pre-planning time.

Goal

To demonstrate to participants how some pre-planning can help with most problem-solving activities.

Procedure

1. Break the large group into smaller groups of 5 to 7 people.
2. Ask the groups to stand at one side of the room.
3. Place a strip of masking tape about 1 m from the edge of the wall. This tape will run the full length of the room. Now ask the groups to stand between the tape and the wall.
4. Place another strip of masking tape about 1 m from the opposite wall. This tape will also run the length of the room.
5. Give each group one feather. Place it on the floor between the tape and the wall (next to the group). Tell them they are not to pick the feather up or to touch it.
6. Their task is to move the feather from their side of the room to the other side. The first team to get the feather across the line wins a prize. Allow 5 minutes planning time for this.

Discussion points

1. Who got the feather across first?
2. Who came up with the first solution?
3. How many solutions did each group get?
4. What helped generate ideas?
5. What hindered the idea flow?

Variations

1. This exercise can be conducted with a control group and an experimental group. One group is asked to get the feather across the line without any pre-planning time, while the other group is allowed the time to pre-plan. The results can then be compared.
2. Each group can be given other items to assist them with the exercise—items such as a calculator, an empty cup, or a whiteboard marker. Obviously these items are given to throw them off track.
3. If you tell the groups that their task is to get the feather from one side of the room to the other (not mentioning the word 'move'), the groups could be asked to devise as many ways as possible for solving this task. The winning group will be the one that has the most solutions.

Solution

This depends on the size of the room and the facilities/items available. It also depends on what types of constraints you place on the groups.

TRAINER'S NOTES

18

Popcorn

TX

TIME REQUIRED	SIZE OF GROUP	MATERIAL REQUIRED
5–15 minutes, depending on the group and the desired outcomes.	Unlimited, but large groups will need to be broken into pairs.	A bag or bucket of popcorn (fresh). One plastic spoon for each pair. One blindfold for each person.

Overview

A fun exercise to develop teamwork through a problem-solving approach.

Goals

1. To have participants take part in a team exercise.
2. To be involved in a simple problem-solving activity.

Procedure

1. Ask everyone to form pairs. Depending on the group, this pairing may be done on a voluntary basis, or you may already have lists drawn up.
2. Give each pair a plastic spoon and 2 blindfolds for the exercise.
3. Now ask them to put on their blindfolds.
4. Tell each team that they will be given 10 pieces of popcorn. Their task is for one person to feed the other the popcorn, one piece at a time, using the plastic spoon provided. They are to try not to drop any popcorn on the floor.
5. Once one person in each team has been given all their popcorn they are given the 'ready, set, go' to start the activity.
6. The first team to complete the exercise, dropping the fewest pieces of popcorn, can be given a prize—maybe the rest of the left-over popcorn!

Discussion points

1. Who fed the most pieces first?
2. If more than one round was conducted, ask if the 'scores' improved with each round.
3. How does this exercise relate to the workplace?

Variations

1. It may be of benefit to allow a minute discussion time between the team members before starting on step 4.
2. This activity can be done in 3 or 4 rounds. The first round as noted, the second round allowing a minute discussion, and the same for the third and any subsequent rounds. The results can then be compared and discussed. The results should show improving 'scores' for each round.

TRAINER'S NOTES

19

Horse Races

TCMXL

TIME REQUIRED

10–15 minutes.

SIZE OF GROUP

Unlimited, but large groups will need to be broken into smaller groups of 5 to 7 people.

MATERIAL REQUIRED

One sheet of paper and pen for each participant.

Overview

A quick activity that can be used for team building, communication and, perhaps, conflict resolution!

Goal

To demonstrate the benefit of teamwork in problem solving.

Procedure

1. Tell the participants that they will be going to the horse races on the weekend. Their problem is that they have to work out how many possible ways there are of picking the first 3 horses in a race containing 9 horses.
2. Ask the participants to try and work out the answer by themselves to start with. Allow 2 minutes for this.
3. Now break the larger group into smaller groups of 5 to 7 people, and ask them to work it out as a team. Allow as much time as necessary for this.
4. After at least one group has the answer, show the rest the calculation involved.
5. Then lead into discussion on the appropriate topic of team building, communication or conflict resolution, etc.

Discussion points

1. How many individuals got the correct answer?
2. How many groups got the correct answer?
3. Were the team results better or worse than the individual results?

4. If the team answers were incorrect, did any individual feel as though they were responsible for the wrong answer?
5. What happens when a team gets a wrong answer as opposed to an individual getting a wrong answer?

Variations

If horse racing isn't appropriate, suggest that it's a swimming contest, or something similar.

Solution

504 (9 x 8 x 7)

TRAINER'S NOTES

20

And the Next Figure Is?

IMX

TIME REQUIRED	SIZE OF GROUP	MATERIAL REQUIRED
1–2 minutes.	Unlimited.	One prepared 'And the Next Figure Is?' overhead.

Overview

A quick activity to test participants' logic. It can be used effectively as a mid-course energiser, or after a break while waiting for the latecomers to come back.

Goals

1. To test participants' logic.
2. To energise the group.
3. To fill in some time.

Procedure

1. Show the 'And the Next Figure Is?' overhead and ask the participants who can draw the next symbol in this series.
2. If anyone has the answer give them a prize.
3. If no one can answer, tell them what the next figure should be.

Discussion points

None.

Variations

None.

Solution

The next figure is 1. If held up to a mirror you would see the numbers 8, 4 and 2. The number to the right is half of the number on its left. Therefore the missing figure is 1.

TRAINER'S NOTES

And the Next Figure Is?

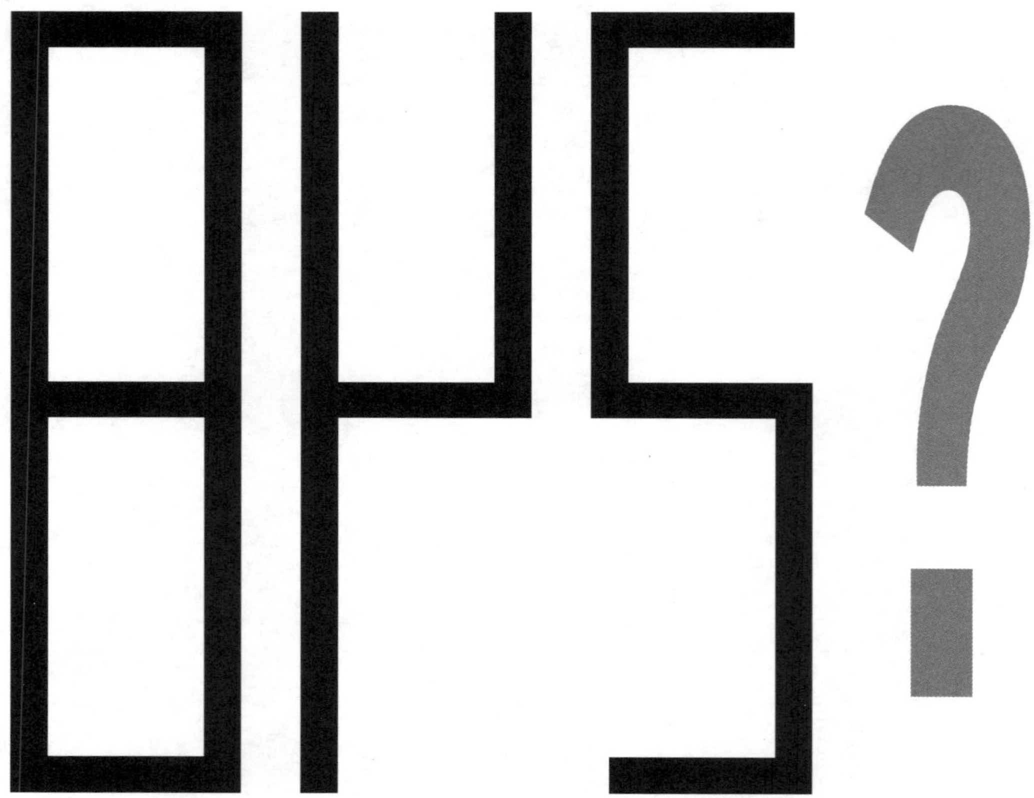

21 Which Program Am I?

ITMX

TIME REQUIRED

10–20 minutes, depending on the size of the group and how much fun they're having.

SIZE OF GROUP

Works best with groups of about 10 to 12 people. Larger groups can be used, but it may be better to have them broken into smaller groups.

MATERIAL REQUIRED

Large self-adhesive labels and marking pens.

Overview

A fun activity to get the group energised.

Goals

1. To energise the group.
2. To get participants laughing.

Procedure

1. Let the group know that they are now going to have some fun.
2. Give each person a blank self-adhesive label and a marking pen.
3. Now ask them to write the name of a television program on the label without anyone else seeing what they write.
4. After everyone has finished writing, ask them to stick the label on someone else's back without them seeing what's written on it. Everyone should finish up with 1 label on their back.
5. Ask them to form a circle.
6. One person starts by asking a question about the television program shown on their back. Tell the group that they can only answer the question by saying 'yes' or 'no'.
7. This process goes on around the circle.
8. After each person has asked their question, before going on to the next person, they are allowed one guess as to the name of the television program shown on their back.
9. The first person to guess the right program should be given a prize.

Discussion points

None.

Variation

Rather than using television program names, you may decide to use famous people's names, movie names, product names, etc.

TRAINER'S NOTES

22

Blindfolded Drawings

ICFMP

TIME REQUIRED	SIZE OF GROUP	MATERIAL REQUIRED
10–15 minutes.	Unlimited.	One blindfold for each person. Paper and marking pens for all participants.

Overview

A fun activity that can be used for communications skills, presentation skills or anything similar.

Goals

1. To demonstrate the difference between one-way and two-way communication.
2. To demonstrate how we get better results when all our senses are applied to a problem.

Procedure

1. Start by handing out the blindfolds. Each person is to put one on.
2. After they have their blindfolds in place, give them paper and a marking pen each.
3. Now ask them to draw a picture of their home (or anything else) without removing their blindfolds.
4. When all pictures have been completed, ask everyone to take their blindfold off and look at the results.

Discussion points

1. Why didn't the picture look like you intended?
2. What would have made it easier?
3. How does this apply to solving problems in the workplace?

Variations

1. Have each person put their name on the back of their sheet before putting on the blindfolds. After they finish their drawings, and before they take off their blindfolds, collect the pictures and hang them on the wall. Ask everyone to remove their blindfolds and try and select their own picture.
2. Rather than have everyone draw an object, give them a set of verbal directions to draw something specific. Give one direction at a time. After they finish, ask them to compare the pictures and discuss why they are all different.

TRAINER'S NOTES

23

The Magic Word

IC

TIME REQUIRED	SIZE OF GROUP	MATERIAL REQUIRED
None.	Unlimited.	A number of small prizes/rewards.

Overview

This is an activity that can be used throughout the training to promote questions and discussion.

Goal

To promote participants' questions and discussion throughout the training.

Procedure

1. During the initial opening of the training where rules are being set, inform the group that there is a series of 'Magic Words' that should be mentioned during the course of the training.
2. Each time you hear one of these words, a reward will be given to the person who used it.
3. You should have at least one word planned that they know will be used fairly early in the course. This will give immediate reinforcement. All other words should relate specifically to the topics concerned.

Discussion points

None.

Variations

1. Rather than give prizes, say you'll make coffee for the next person who uses the most 'Magic Words' between breaks.
2. Depending on the type of group and training, the words may need to be modified.

TRAINER'S NOTES

24 Money

ITE

TIME REQUIRED	SIZE OF GROUP	MATERIAL REQUIRED
None.	Unlimited.	Enough prepared pieces of 'Money'. Prizes if they are being used.

Overview

This will promote responses to questions asked.

Goals

1. To promote responses to questions asked.
2. To encourage interaction.
3. To have some fun.

Procedure

1. During the initial opening of the training, advise the group that they will be asked a number of questions during the day.
2. The first person to give a correct response will be given a piece of 'Money' (show one to the group).
3. They are to collect all of the pieces and, at the end of the training, you will tell them what they can do with it—for example, use it to purchase a product from the company at a discounted rate (5% for each coupon), use it for discounts on future training courses, etc.

Discussion points

1. Who collected the most 'Money'?
2. Why are most people more motivated by a reward at the end?
3. Do we always need a physical reward to be motivated? Why, or why not?

Variations

1. This can be done in teams. The teams are to collect as much 'Money' as they can during the training. The team with the most 'Money' receives a prize at the end.
2. This can be done as an auction. At the end of the training an auction is held where participants can use their 'Money' to bid on items supplied by the trainer.

TRAINER'S NOTES

5
FIVE
FIVE CREDITS
This certificate may only be used for
the purpose suggested by your trainer
FIVE CREDITS

5
FIVE
FIVE CREDITS
This certificate may only be used for
the purpose suggested by your trainer
FIVE CREDITS

5
FIVE
FIVE CREDITS
This certificate may only be used for
the purpose suggested by your trainer
FIVE CREDITS

5
FIVE
FIVE CREDITS
This certificate may only be used for
the purpose suggested by your trainer
FIVE CREDITS

25 Auction

ITE

TIME REQUIRED	SIZE OF GROUP	MATERIAL REQUIRED
10 minutes or so will be required at the end of the training to conduct an auction.	Unlimited.	Lots of prepared pieces of 'Auction Money'. A number of items to be auctioned off.

Overview

This is another activity that will promote responses to questions asked.

Goals

1. To promote responses to questions asked.
2. To encourage interaction.
3. To have some fun.

Procedure

1. During the opening of the training, advise the participants that they will be asked a number of questions during the day.
2. The first person to give a correct response to each question will be given a piece of 'Auction Money' (show one to the group).
3. They are to collect all the pieces, and at the end of the training they will be taking part in an auction. They can only make bids using the 'Auction Money' they have been awarded during the training.

Discussion points

1. Who collected the most 'Money'?
2. Why are most people more motivated when there is a reward at the end?
3. Do we always need a physical reward to be motivated? Why, or why not?

Variation

This can be done in teams. The teams are to collect as much 'Money' as they can during the training. The teams, rather than the individuals, will then be bidding at the auction.

TRAINER'S NOTES

The trainer must be generous giving out the 'Money' during the training. The more the better.

Auction Money

26

Pass the Life Saver®

TMX

TIME REQUIRED	SIZE OF GROUP	MATERIAL REQUIRED
5–10 minutes.	Unlimited, but larger groups may need to be broken into smaller groups.	A packet of toothpicks and a packet of Life Savers®.

Overview

A quick competitive activity to help develop teamwork within groups.

Goals

1. To develop teamwork.
2. To energise the group.

Procedure

1. Advise the participants that they are going to be involved in a competition.
2. Break the large group into smaller groups of 5 to 7 people.
3. Each team member is given a toothpick.
4. Each team is given a Life Saver®.
5. Tell them to form a line (or circle).
6. Ask each person to put their toothpick in their mouth. They are not allowed to take it out of their mouth until the game has finished.
7. The person at the beginning of the line is asked to slide the Life Saver® on to their toothpick.
8. Now tell them that they have to pass the Life Saver® along their line, one person to the next, and so on. They are only allowed to use the toothpicks. No hands allowed. If they drop the Life Saver®, they can only use the toothpicks to pick them up.
9. The first team to complete the task wins the prize—maybe a fresh packet of Life Savers®.

Discussion points

1. Who finished first?
2. What helped with this exercise?
3. What were some of the problems encountered? How were they overcome?
4. How does this exercise relate to the workplace?

Variations

1. The groups can be previously formed work teams.
2. This exercise can be repeated, say, 3 or 4 times with 1 or 2 minutes between each round. The time in between should be used for the teams to discuss various strategies. Each round can then be timed to demonstrate improved results.

TRAINER'S NOTES

27 Many Items

TCFMXLS

TIME REQUIRED	SIZE OF GROUP	MATERIAL REQUIRED
10–15 minutes.	Unlimited, but will need to be broken into smaller groups of 5 to 7 people.	A tray covered with about 20–25 items and covered with a cloth. The items could include things like a cotton reel, paper clip, box of matches, postcard, credit card, small novel, shoelace, fork, nail file, comb, etc.

Overview

A test of memory.

Goals

1. To test participants' memories.
2. To demonstrate the benefits of synergy.

Procedure

1. Start the activity by informing the participants that they are going to be involved in a memory test.
2. Bring out the tray of items covered with the cloth.
3. Before uncovering the tray, advise the participants that they are going to be shown the objects on the tray for a period of 1 minute. During this time they are to try and memorise as many of the items as possible. After the 1 minute period the tray will be covered over, and they will be required to write a list of the items they can recall. This list should be totalled and the amount noted.
4. Now organise the participants into groups of 5 to 7 people.
5. Show them the items in the tray for 1 minute.
6. Ask these groups to generate a list of the items that were shown on the tray. Allow as much time as needed for this.
7. After the groups have finished, ask them to total their items.
8. Show all the individual scores and group scores on the whiteboard.
9. Now lead into a discussion on why there is a significant difference between both sets of results.

Discussion points

1. Who listed all the items correctly?
2. Why couldn't everyone remember all of the items?
3. Would it be harder or easier using very unusual objects? Why, or why not?
4. Would it be harder or easier using very common objects? Why, or why not?
5. Why is it that the group results were significantly better than the individual results?
6. How could we make the results even better?
7. How does this apply in the workplace?

Variations

With a very large group, an overhead transparency can be used to show the objects.

TRAINER'S NOTES

28

Kangaroo Races

TMX

TIME REQUIRED	SIZE OF GROUP	MATERIAL REQUIRED
5 minutes.	Unlimited.	At least one balloon for every pair of participants.

Overview

A fun activity designed to liven up any group.

Goals

1. To energise the group.
2. To promote teamwork.

Procedure

1. Start this activity off by breaking everyone into pairs.
2. Give each pair a balloon.
3. One person (with the balloon) is to stand at one side of the room (touching the wall) while their partner stands against the opposite wall (also touching it). Have participants do this now.
4. Now ask the person with the balloon to place it between their knees. Once it is between their knees, they are not allowed to touch it with their hands.
5. Tell the participants that, on a given signal, the person with the balloon is to hop, like a kangaroo, across the room (while still holding the balloon between their knees). When they get to the other side and touch the wall, they are to pass the balloon on to their partner, again without either person touching the balloon with their hands.
6. Once the switch has been made, the second person is to hop back to the other wall.
7. The first team to complete the second leg will be determined the winners.

Discussion points

1. Who was back first?
2. What made this exercise difficult?
3. What made it easier?

Variations

Conduct this exercise as shown, then allow a minute or two before conducting it again. This will allow the pairs to discuss what they did last time, and how they can improve the result on the next round. If this variation is used, it may be worthwhile to record all 'finishing' times.

TRAINER'S NOTES

29

Ad Infinitum

TCFML

TIME REQUIRED	SIZE OF GROUP	MATERIAL REQUIRED
5–10 minutes, depending on the size of the group.	Unlimited, but works best with 10 to 12 people. Larger groups may need to be broken down.	None, but a copy of the 'Greatest Story Teller of Them All' award will add some fun.

Overview

A simple activity to promote creativity.

Goals

1. To promote creativity.
2. To develop presentation skills.
3. To get people to 'think on their feet'.

Procedure

1. Ask the participants to grab their chairs and form a circle.
2. Tell them that the objective of this exercise is to tell a continuous story.
3. One person will start to tell a story. After 30 seconds they are to stop, and the person sitting to their left will continue telling it. After 30 seconds they will stop, and the person on their left will continue, etc.
4. There are to be no pauses in the story telling, and no one is allowed to repeat any part of it in their 30 seconds.
5. If anyone pauses, or repeats any part, they are disqualified, and must drop out.
6. The last person left is given the 'Greatest Story Teller of Them All' award.

Discussion points

1. Why did some people find it easy?
2. Why did some people find this difficult?
3. What helps overcome the 'fear' that some of us have?

Variations

1. Story times can be reduced to 10 or 20 seconds for larger groups if necessary.
2. You may suggest a topic to start with.

TRAINER'S NOTES

You should participate in this game, but should probably make sure you are disqualified during one of the rounds. After all, the participants are the ones who need the encouragement! The participants also already know that trainers are good at telling stories!

AD INFINITUM AWARD

The Greatest Story Teller of Them All

Awarded to ______________________________
for being the best story teller of all time!

30

Convincing Nonsense

CFS

TIME REQUIRED
20–30 minutes, depending on the size of the group.

SIZE OF GROUP
Unlimited, but larger groups may need to be broken into smaller groups of 10 to 12 people.

MATERIAL REQUIRED
Prepared 'Convincing Nonsense Topics' slips and a bag to put them in.

Overview

The purpose of this exercise is to test the participants' ability to present information without any prior preparation.

Goals

1. To have participants give an impromptu presentation.
2. To define the structure of a presentation.

Procedure

1. After giving participants a presentation on 'How to Give Presentations', commence by advising them that they will be asked to give a short presentation themselves.
2. Tell them that they will be selecting a topic out of the bag, and that they have to talk on their topic for 2 minutes.
3. Ask one person at a time to come forward and pick a topic from the bag. Allow about 1 minute for them to prepare.
4. They now have 2 minutes to talk about their topic.
5. When they have finished, select the next person, and so on.
6. After all participants have given their presentations, it would probably be worthwhile to go back over the rules for structuring a presentation.

Discussion points

1. Who gave the most convincing presentation?
2. Who used the best presentation structure?
3. Do you think you might be able to effectively convince someone of a nonsense topic using good presentation skills? Why, or why not?

Variations

1. The preparation times in step 3 can be varied.
2. Have the structure shown on a whiteboard while they are giving their presentations.
3. Select your own nonsense topics.

TRAINER'S NOTES

Convincing Nonsense Topics

Teaching a blind person how to drive

Why it's best to read a book backwards

Teaching a bird how to swim

New uses for old toothpaste tubes

How to build a catawompus

Teaching a goldfish how to talk

How to make a time-machine

How to watch television without any power

Using a computer to mow your lawn

Why the number 5 is after the number 6

Who did kill Cock Robin?

What came first, the chicken or the egg?

How to succeed in business without really trying

What will we do once computers become obsolete?

How to drive a car without windows

How to run a petrol engine without petrol

31 Personal Inventory

ITMLS

TIME REQUIRED	SIZE OF GROUP	MATERIAL REQUIRED
20–30 minutes, depending on the size of the group.	Unlimited.	A prepared 'Personal Inventory' handout and a pen for each person.

Overview

This icebreaker can be used at the beginning of a course if participants don't know each other very well.

Goals

1. To encourage group participation.
2. To get to know each other.

Procedure

1. Hand out a copy of the 'Personal Inventory' and a pen to all participants.
2. Tell the participants they have 10 minutes to form pairs and then interview each other. That allows 5 minutes for each person to interview the other.
3. At the end of the 10 minutes the participants are then asked to introduce each other to the group and comment on the 3 most interesting things they found out about the other person.

Discussion points

Who had the most interesting piece of information?

Variations

1. Change the questions to suit the group.
2. Use an overhead of the 'Personal Inventory' rather than use the handout.

TRAINER'S NOTES

Personal Inventory

1. What was the best year of your life? Why?
2. What type of foods do you like? Why?
3. If you had the choice of any job, in any organisation, what would it be? Why?
4. What is your favourite song? Why?
5. If you could live anywhere, where would it be? Why?
6. If you were in charge of your company, what are some of the first changes you would make? Why?
7. What is your favourite book? Why?
8. If you could have dinner with any person, dead or alive, who would it be? Why?
9. What is your favourite movie? Why?
10. If you could be anywhere right now, where would it be? Why?
11. What is your favourite television show? Why?
12. What do you think about having to be here today?
13. If you could start a new company tomorrow, what would it do? Why?
14. What is your favourite colour? Why?
15. If you could have a free holiday anywhere in the world, where would you go? Why?

32

Categories

TMX

TIME REQUIRED

10–15 minutes.

SIZE OF GROUP

Unlimited, but will need to break participants into teams of 5 to 7 people.

MATERIAL REQUIRED

One copy of the 'Categories' handout and a pen for each person.

Overview

This activity can be used any time during training. It can be used to demonstrate teamwork, problem solving, or simply be used as a time filler.

Goals

1. To demonstrate teamwork.
2. To look at a problem-solving approach.
3. To fill in some time waiting for latecomers to arrive.

Procedure

1. Start this activity by telling everyone that they are going to play a game.
2. Ask the participants to form teams of 5 to 7 people.
3. After all teams have been formed, give each person a copy of the 'Categories' handout and a pen.
4. Tell the groups that they are going to be given a letter of the alphabet. Their task will be to write down a word starting with that letter for each category. Allow 5 minutes for this or as much time as necessary. After the teams have completed the task, ask the participants for their results. The team generating the most words, wins.
5. This could then lead into a discussion about teamwork, etc.

Discussion points

1. Which team obtained the highest score?
2. Could the rules have been interpreted a different way to give better results (i.e. combining with other teams)?
3. How does this apply in the workplace?

Variations

1. A prepared 'Categories' overhead could be used instead of the handout.
2. Can be conducted in pairs rather than teams.
3. The points system can be modified so that each word that a team generates, that hasn't been used by another team, could score double points.

TRAINER'S NOTES

Categories

Animal ______________________
Bird ______________________
Colour ______________________
Drink ______________________
Explorer ______________________
Food ______________________
God ______________________
Hero ______________________
Island ______________________
Jungle ______________________
King ______________________
Liquid ______________________
Movie ______________________
Novel ______________________
Ocean ______________________
Place ______________________
Queen ______________________
Rock Star ______________________
Sport ______________________
Televison Show ______________________
Union ______________________
Vegetable ______________________
Writer ______________________
Xmas Gift ______________________
Young TV Star ______________________
Zodiac ______________________

33

van Gogh

TCFMP

TIME REQUIRED	SIZE OF GROUP	MATERIAL REQUIRED
5–10 minutes each time used.	Unlimited.	A flipchart and pens, or whiteboard and pens. A series of prepared cards with one word or phrase shown on each of them (see the list of 'van Gogh: Words or Phrases'). A copy of the 'van Gogh Award'.

Overview

This exercise is based on a world famous game. It gives participants a chance to demonstrate their creativity and artistic skills. It can be conducted on a number of occasions during the training.

Goals

1. To develop creativity.
2. To energise the group.
3. To fill in time while waiting for latecomers to arrive.
4. To have some fun.

Procedure

1. Ask for a volunteer from the group.
2. Tell the volunteer that they are going to be given a word or phrase.
3. Their task is to get the group to guess what the word or phrase is. The rule here though is that they are not allowed to speak to the group or give any hand actions. They are only allowed to draw pictures. No words, letters or numbers can be drawn, only pictures. You will prosecute any offenders.
4. The person who attracts the fastest response during the course of the training will be determined the winner and given the 'van Gogh Award'.

Discussion points

None.

Variation

If appropriate, the words or phrases in the handout can be related directly to the training being given.

TRAINER'S NOTES

van Gogh: Words or Phrases

Emu Pie

Sheep Dog

River Punt

Pink Pencil

Clown Fish

Neighbours

Cotton Shirt

Raisin Toast

Windows '98

Up in Smoke

Ceramic Cup

Flower Power

War and Peace

Electric Calculator

Like Peas in a Pod

Duck-billed Platypus

2 Signs of the Zodiac

Mainframe Computer

Timber Picture Frame

Look Before You Leap

Yellow-crested Cockatoo

A Stitch in Time Saves 9

Too Many Cooks Spoil the Broth

The Early Bird Catches the Worm

Jack Be Nimble, Jack Be Quick, Jack Jump Over the Candle Stick

VAN GOGH AWARD

The Greatest Drawer of Them All

Awarded to ______________________________
for being the best drawer of all time!

34

Fancy Dress

T

TIME REQUIRED

15–30 minutes, depending on the size of the group and the resources supplied.

SIZE OF GROUP

Unlimited, but larger groups will need to be broken into smaller groups of no more than, say, 12 people.

MATERIAL REQUIRED

Lots of newspapers, magazines and pins.

Overview

An activity to promote bonding within teams.

Goals

1. To promote bonding within the group.
2. To have some fun.

Procedure

1. Start the exercise by breaking the participants into groups of, say, 10 to 12 people.
2. Give each group plenty of newspaper, magazines and pins.
3. Now ask them to dress one of their team members in a fancy dress costume using the materials supplied. They have 10 minutes to do this.
4. After all the teams have finished, instruct the models to have a parade (using appropriate gestures).
5. The other teams are to try and guess what each costume is.
6. The team creating the most ingenious costume should be given a prize.

Discussion points

1. Which team had the most ingenious costume?
2. Why don't we all apply this type of creativity in the workplace?

Variations

1. Other resources can be given to the teams.
2. Time limits can be shortened to increase pressure.
3. Smaller groups can be used effectively.
4. The groups can be previously formed work teams.

TRAINER'S NOTES

35 Positivity Raffle

IT

TIME REQUIRED

Two minutes or so will be required at the end of the training to conduct the drawing of the raffle.

SIZE OF GROUP

Unlimited.

MATERIAL REQUIRED

A book of raffle tickets and a suitable prize. If raffle tickets are not available, use a copy of the 'Positivity Raffle Tickets' sheet. Just copy it and cut it up. If more than 170 tickets are required, copy them on to different coloured paper. The final draw would then be 'blue ticket number 169', for example.

Overview

This activity will encourage people to take a positive attitude to training and to become more involved.

Goals

1. To encourage people to be more positive.
2. To encourage people to ask more questions.
3. To encourage people to become involved with the training.

Procedure

1. During the introductions let the group know that there will be a raffle at the conclusion of the training.
2. During the day give out raffle tickets to people who have a positive attitude, who ask relevant questions, who get involved, who are motivated, who participate, etc. You should be generous with the tickets during the course of the training, which should reinforce the positive outcomes.
3. At the conclusion of the training, put the tickets into a box, and ask one person to draw the winning ticket. Award the prize to that person and encourage a round of applause.

Discussion points

None.

Variations

1. Tickets may be forfeited for negative behaviours.
2. Other rules might be put in place.
3. Each group can be given a book of raffle tickets and they then become responsible for handing them out to worthy people.

TRAINER'S NOTES

Positivity Raffle Tickets

TICKET # 001	TICKET # 002	TICKET # 003	TICKET # 004	TICKET # 005	TICKET # 006	TICKET # 007	TICKET # 008	TICKET # 009	TICKET # 010
TICKET # 011	TICKET # 012	TICKET # 013	TICKET # 014	TICKET # 015	TICKET # 016	TICKET # 017	TICKET # 018	TICKET # 019	TICKET # 020
TICKET # 021	TICKET # 022	TICKET # 023	TICKET # 024	TICKET # 025	TICKET # 026	TICKET # 027	TICKET # 028	TICKET # 029	TICKET # 030
TICKET # 031	TICKET # 032	TICKET # 033	TICKET # 034	TICKET # 035	TICKET # 036	TICKET # 037	TICKET # 038	TICKET # 039	TICKET # 040
TICKET # 041	TICKET # 042	TICKET # 043	TICKET # 044	TICKET # 045	TICKET # 046	TICKET # 047	TICKET # 048	TICKET # 049	TICKET # 050
TICKET # 051	TICKET # 052	TICKET # 053	TICKET # 054	TICKET # 055	TICKET # 056	TICKET # 057	TICKET # 058	TICKET # 059	TICKET # 060
TICKET # 061	TICKET # 062	TICKET # 063	TICKET # 064	TICKET # 065	TICKET # 066	TICKET # 067	TICKET # 068	TICKET # 069	TICKET # 070
TICKET # 071	TICKET # 072	TICKET # 073	TICKET # 074	TICKET # 075	TICKET # 076	TICKET # 077	TICKET # 078	TICKET # 079	TICKET # 080
TICKET # 081	TICKET # 082	TICKET # 083	TICKET # 084	TICKET # 085	TICKET # 086	TICKET # 087	TICKET # 088	TICKET # 089	TICKET # 090
TICKET # 091	TICKET # 092	TICKET # 093	TICKET # 094	TICKET # 095	TICKET # 096	TICKET # 097	TICKET # 098	TICKET # 099	TICKET # 100
TICKET # 101	TICKET # 102	TICKET # 103	TICKET # 104	TICKET # 105	TICKET # 106	TICKET # 107	TICKET # 108	TICKET # 109	TICKET # 110
TICKET # 111	TICKET # 112	TICKET #113	TICKET # 114	TICKET # 115	TICKET # 116	TICKET # 117	TICKET # 118	TICKET # 119	TICKET # 120
TICKET # 121	TICKET # 122	TICKET # 123	TICKET # 124	TICKET # 125	TICKET # 126	TICKET # 127	TICKET # 128	TICKET # 129	TICKET # 130
TICKET # 131	TICKET # 132	TICKET # 133	TICKET # 134	TICKET # 135	TICKET # 136	TICKET # 137	TICKET # 138	TICKET # 139	TICKET # 140
TICKET # 141	TICKET # 142	TICKET # 143	TICKET # 144	TICKET # 145	TICKET # 146	TICKET # 147	TICKET # 148	TICKET # 149	TICKET # 150
TICKET # 151	TICKET # 152	TICKET # 153	TICKET # 154	TICKET # 155	TICKET # 156	TICKET # 157	TICKET # 158	TICKET # 159	TICKET # 160
TICKET # 161	TICKET # 162	TICKET # 163	TICKET # 164	TICKET # 165	TICKET # 166	TICKET # 167	TICKET # 168	TICKET # 169	TICKET # 170

36 Bloopers

TM

TIME REQUIRED	SIZE OF GROUP	MATERIAL REQUIRED
2 minutes.	Unlimited.	As many prepared 'Bloopers Award' certificates as required.

Overview

This award should only be used where the group members are well known to each other, and where it's known they all have a 'thick skin' and a sense of humour.

Goals

1. To reward people for saying silly things during the training.
2. To have some fun at the end of each training session.

Procedure

1. Silently keep track of 'bloopers' that people say during the training.
2. Before the training session closes, fill in the certificates as required.
3. Award the certificates to the appropriate people.

Discussion points

None.

Variations

1. You can recruit an observer to record the 'bloopers'.
2. During the opening of the training, you can tell participants about the 'Bloopers Awards', and that they will have to nominate group members during the course of the training should they overhear something worthwhile mentioning.

TRAINER'S NOTES

BLOOPERS AWARD

The Greatest Bloopers of Them All

Awarded to ____________________ for saying:

____

____

____

37

The Worm

ITMXS

TIME REQUIRED	SIZE OF GROUP	MATERIAL REQUIRED
5–10 minutes.	Unlimited, but will need to be broken into pairs.	One prepared 'Worm' overhead. One copy of the 'The Worm' handout for each pair and a pen.

Overview

This activity can be used any time during training. It can be used to demonstrate teamwork, problem solving, or be used simply as a time filler.

Goals

1. To demonstrate how competitive most people are.
2. To demonstrate teamwork.
3. To look at a problem-solving approach.
4. To fill in some time waiting for latecomers to arrive.

Procedure

1. Start this activity by telling everyone that they are going to play a game.
2. Ask everyone to select a partner and form pairs.
3. After all pairs have been formed give each pair a copy of the 'The Worm' handout and a pen.
4. Tell them that the person holding the handout at present is to draw one vertical or horizontal line on the handout and so join two of the dots together.
5. Their partner is then to draw a second horizontal or vertical line connecting to one end of the previous line.
6. Now ask the first person to draw another vertical or horizontal line connecting one end to the previous lines drawn, and so on.
7. Their task is to avoid drawing the line that will join the beginning of the worm to the end. Show the 'Worm' overhead if necessary and explain that the next move on this example will lead to the worm being joined to itself. Allow a set time frame of no more than, say, 2 minutes for this part of the exercise.
8. After everyone has completed the exercise, ask the group for their results. Someone during this debriefing will mention winning or losing or something similar. After this has been mentioned, ask them why they thought it was a competitive exercise, as this wasn't mentioned in the original briefing.
9. This should then lead into a discussion about assumptions, teamwork, etc.

Discussion points

1. Why did people assume this was a competitive activity?
2. Could we have had a result where both parties won?
3. How does this apply in the workplace?

Variation

Can be done in two teams using a whiteboard or prepared overhead.

TRAINER'S NOTES

Do not infer during the briefing that this is a competitive game: this is to be assumed by the players.

Worm

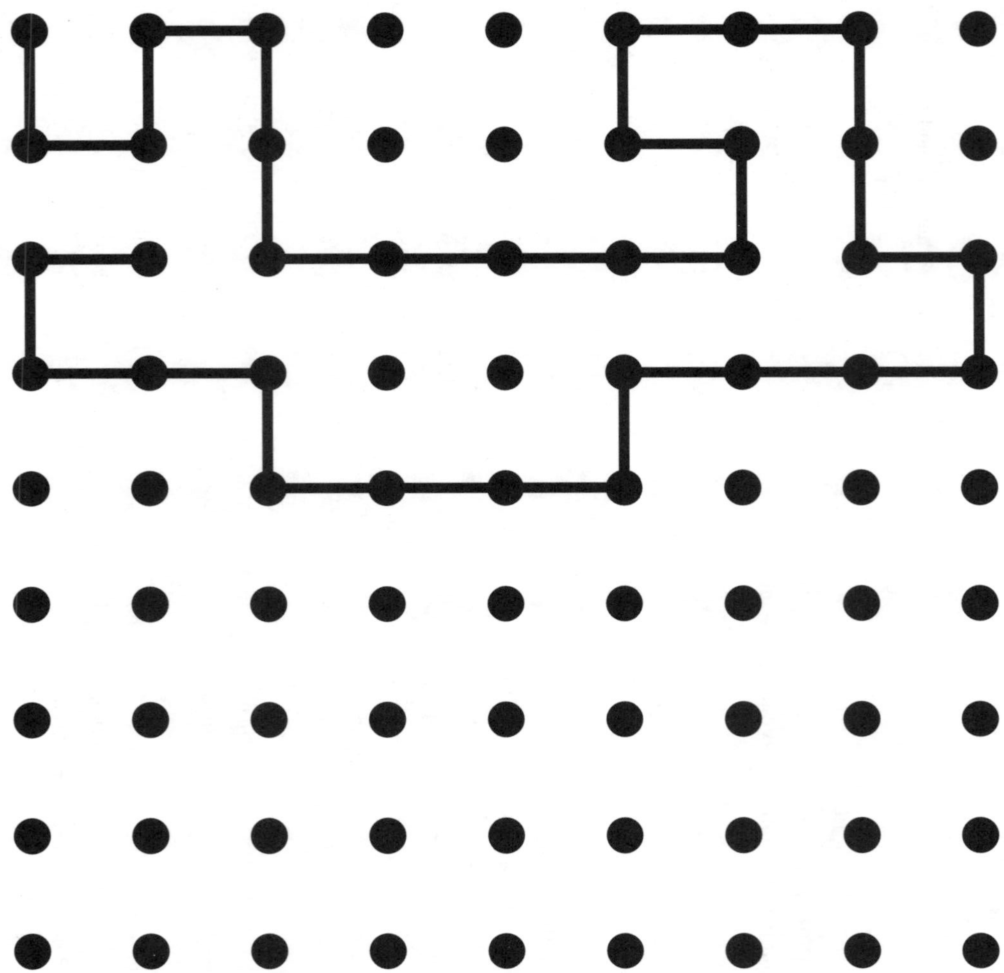

The Worm

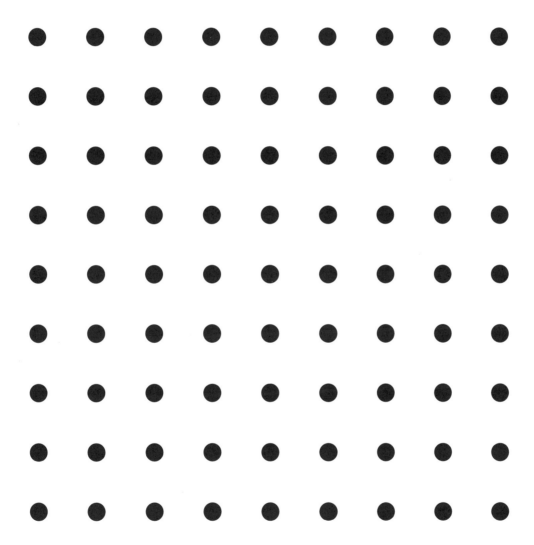

38

Give Me a Feel

ITCMXP

TIME REQUIRED

10–15 minutes.

SIZE OF GROUP

Unlimited.

MATERIAL REQUIRED

A pillowcase filled with an assortment of 15 strange objects (e.g. a Mickey Mouse keyring, or a cravat), or objects that might be similar in size and weight (e.g. a grapefruit is similar to an orange, or a diary is similar to a book). Each person will also require a pen and a copy of the 'Give Me a Feel' handout.

Overview

This exercise shows how people perceive things differently.

Goal

To allow participants to see that people perceive things in different ways.

Procedure

1. Before the training commences, put the assortment of objects into a pillowcase and tie the top up so that the participants can't see into it.
2. When appropriate, tell the participants that their powers of ESP are going to be tested.
3. Show the bag to the participants and tell them that it contains an assortment of objects. Their task is to come to the front of the room and feel the bag and its contents and then make a list of what they think the items are. Allow them 1 minute to come forward and feel the pillowcase.
4. Ask them to return to their seats and write their lists out.
5. After all the lists have been completed, ask them what they thought the individual items were.
6. At this point in time lead a discussion into the different perceptions people have generally.
7. After all suggestions have been taken, tell them what the items were. For each item they guessed correctly, they get 1 point. The person with the highest score is given a prize for being the best ESP person in the group.
8. Ask the winner to now see if they can read your mind to see what you want them to do next. If they can't, it's obviously time for a coffee break (or whatever is appropriate).

Discussion points

1. Who obtained the highest score?
2. How many objects were not guessed correctly by anyone? What were they? Why weren't they guessed?
3. Which object had the greatest number of different suggestions as to what it was? Discuss perceptions.

Variations

1. Don't give out the 'Give Me a Feel' handout until the participants sit back down ready to write their lists. That way part of the test is to see if they counted 15 items.
2. The number of objects can be varied.
3. With small groups the pillowcase can be passed around the group.

TRAINER'S NOTES

Give Me a Feel

1.

2.

3.

4.

5.

6.

7.

8.

9.

10.

11.

12.

13.

14.

15.

39

20 Questions

TCMX

TIME REQUIRED

10–20 minutes, depending on the size of the group.

SIZE OF GROUP

Unlimited.

MATERIAL REQUIRED

None.

Overview

This is based on a world famous radio game and is designed to improve communication and develop teamwork.

Goals

1. To improve communication skills.
2. To develop teamwork.
3. To have some fun.

Procedure

1. Start by asking for a volunteer from the group.
2. Ask the volunteer to think of an object without revealing what it is.
3. Now ask the volunteer to say whether their object is animal, vegetable or mineral.
4. Tell the rest of the group that they are allowed to ask up to 20 questions to determine what the object is. The questions being asked can only have a 'yes' or 'no' answer.
5. After the group have determined what the object is, or the 20 questions have been asked, keep going around the group.
6. The winner or winners will be the people who managed to not have their object discovered.

Discussion points

None.

Variations

1. This can be done in teams, where each team determines the object and answers questions asked by the other teams.
2. Objects can be pre-selected by the facilitator and written on cards. The cards would then be drawn at random and handed to the participant or team.

TRAINER'S NOTES

40

Beyond the Call of Duty

ITXP

TIME REQUIRED	SIZE OF GROUP	MATERIAL REQUIRED
30–60 minutes, depending on the size of the group.	Unlimited, but will need to be broken into groups of 5 to 7 people.	One copy of the 'Top 10 Rules of Good Customer Service' handout and a pen for each person. Each person should be sent a copy of the 'Customer Service Questionnaire' well before training commences.

Overview

This exercise has been designed for use in customer service training. It allows participants to reflect on experiences they have had and therefore requires some pre-work before attending the training.

Goals

1. To investigate what makes good and bad customer service.
2. To encourage interaction within the group.
3. To get the participants to identify the 'Top 10 Rules of Good Customer Service'.

Procedure

1. Send each person a copy of the 'Customer Service Questionnaire' several days before the training commences. Encourage them to fill in the questionnaire as it will relate directly to their training.
2. During the program, ask each participant to bring out their questionnaires and discuss them with their group. If groups haven't already been formed, break the large group into smaller groups of 5 to 7 people.
3. After everyone has told their story, ask them to think about what they've just heard. Tell them that as a group they are now to design a set of good customer service rules.
4. Give everyone a copy of the 'Top 10 Rules of Good Customer Service' handout and a pen.
5. After the teams have designed their rules, ask them to share them with the other groups.
6. The large group should now agree on a common list of 10 rules. These rules will become their Code of Practice after the training concludes.

Discussion points

1. How would you feel, as a customer, being looked after by someone applying these rules?
2. What do you think might happen in your workplace as a result of sticking with these rules?
3. What obstacles can you see? How can we overcome them?

Variations

The questionnaire could be given to some of your customers, both current and previous, to fill in.

TRAINER'S NOTES

Customer Service Questionnaire

A brief description of your encounter:

How efficient was the service?

How courteously were you treated?

Were your expectations met?

How would you rate the service overall?

Would you recommend this service/person/store to someone new to your suburb/city?

Top 10 Rules of Good Customer Service

Rule # 1 ______________________________

____

Rule # 2 ______________________________

____

Rule # 3 ______________________________

____

Rule # 4 ______________________________

____

Rule # 5 ______________________________

____

Rule # 6 ______________________________

____

Rule # 7 ______________________________

____

Rule # 8 ______________________________

____

Rule # 9 ______________________________

____

Rule # 10 ______________________________

____

41 Punctuality Check

IFLES

TIME REQUIRED	SIZE OF GROUP	MATERIAL REQUIRED
2 minutes or so will be required at the end of the training to conduct the drawing of the raffle.	Unlimited.	A book of raffle tickets and a suitable prize. If raffle tickets are not available, use a copy of the 'Punctuality Raffle Tickets' sheet. Just copy it and cut it up. If more than 170 tickets are required, copy them on to different coloured paper. The final draw would then be 'blue ticket number 169', for example.

Overview

Sick of people arriving late? This activity will encourage people to arrive back on time after breaks.

Goal

To encourage people to come back on time after breaks.

Procedure

1. During the introductions let the participants know that there will be a raffle at the conclusion of the training.
2. During the day give out raffle tickets to people who arrive back on time after a break. You should ensure that everyone who is in the room at the correct time gets a ticket.
3. At the conclusion of the training, ask everyone to put their tickets into a box, then ask one person to draw the winning ticket. Award the prize to that person along with a round of applause.

Discussion points

None.

Variation

Tickets already gained may be forfeited for late entrances.

TRAINER'S NOTES

Punctuality Raffle Tickets

TICKET # 001	TICKET # 002	TICKET # 003	TICKET # 004	TICKET # 005	TICKET # 006	TICKET # 007	TICKET # 008	TICKET # 009	TICKET # 010
TICKET # 011	TICKET # 012	TICKET # 013	TICKET # 014	TICKET # 015	TICKET # 016	TICKET # 017	TICKET # 018	TICKET # 019	TICKET # 020
TICKET # 021	TICKET # 022	TICKET # 023	TICKET # 024	TICKET # 025	TICKET # 026	TICKET # 027	TICKET # 028	TICKET # 029	TICKET # 030
TICKET # 031	TICKET # 032	TICKET # 033	TICKET # 034	TICKET # 035	TICKET # 036	TICKET # 037	TICKET # 038	TICKET # 039	TICKET # 040
TICKET # 041	TICKET # 042	TICKET # 043	TICKET # 044	TICKET # 045	TICKET # 046	TICKET # 047	TICKET # 048	TICKET # 049	TICKET # 050
TICKET # 051	TICKET # 052	TICKET # 053	TICKET # 054	TICKET # 055	TICKET # 056	TICKET # 057	TICKET # 058	TICKET # 059	TICKET # 060
TICKET # 061	TICKET # 062	TICKET # 063	TICKET # 064	TICKET # 065	TICKET # 066	TICKET # 067	TICKET # 068	TICKET # 069	TICKET # 070
TICKET # 071	TICKET # 072	TICKET # 073	TICKET # 074	TICKET # 075	TICKET # 076	TICKET # 077	TICKET # 078	TICKET # 079	TICKET # 080
TICKET # 081	TICKET # 082	TICKET # 083	TICKET # 084	TICKET # 085	TICKET # 086	TICKET # 087	TICKET # 088	TICKET # 089	TICKET # 090
TICKET # 091	TICKET # 092	TICKET # 093	TICKET # 094	TICKET # 095	TICKET # 096	TICKET # 097	TICKET # 098	TICKET # 099	TICKET # 100
TICKET # 101	TICKET # 102	TICKET # 103	TICKET # 104	TICKET # 105	TICKET # 106	TICKET # 107	TICKET # 108	TICKET # 109	TICKET # 110
TICKET # 111	TICKET # 112	TICKET #113	TICKET # 114	TICKET # 115	TICKET # 116	TICKET # 117	TICKET # 118	TICKET # 119	TICKET # 120
TICKET # 121	TICKET # 122	TICKET # 123	TICKET # 124	TICKET # 125	TICKET # 126	TICKET # 127	TICKET # 128	TICKET # 129	TICKET # 130
TICKET # 131	TICKET # 132	TICKET # 133	TICKET # 134	TICKET # 135	TICKET # 136	TICKET # 137	TICKET # 138	TICKET # 139	TICKET # 140
TICKET # 141	TICKET # 142	TICKET # 143	TICKET # 144	TICKET # 145	TICKET # 146	TICKET # 147	TICKET # 148	TICKET # 149	TICKET # 150
TICKET # 151	TICKET # 152	TICKET # 153	TICKET # 154	TICKET # 155	TICKET # 156	TICKET # 157	TICKET # 158	TICKET # 159	TICKET # 160
TICKET # 161	TICKET # 162	TICKET # 163	TICKET # 164	TICKET # 165	TICKET # 166	TICKET # 167	TICKET # 168	TICKET # 169	TICKET # 170

42
T-shirts #1

IT

TIME REQUIRED

30–40 minutes.

SIZE OF GROUP

Unlimited, but larger groups will need to be broken into smaller groups of 5 to 7 people.

MATERIAL REQUIRED

One large plain white T-shirt for each participant and a set of coloured laundry marking pens. These should be permanent markers.

Overview

This exercise can be used early in the program to help build a team atmosphere.

Goals

1. To allow participants to meet each other in their teams early in the program.
2. To get participants working together.
3. To develop a team atmosphere.

Procedure

1. After the initial introductions are completed, break the participants into groups of 5 to 7 people.
2. Give each person a plain white T-shirt.
3. Give each team a set of laundry marking pens.
4. Now tell the teams they have 20 minutes to design a logo for themselves and draw it on all their T-shirts.
5. When they have finished, ask them to model the T-shirts and explain their logos and why they selected them. You should encourage them to wear the T-shirts for the rest of the day. It's up to you whether you create one for yourself.

Discussion points

1. What is the logo?
2. Why was it selected?

Variations

1. A team name can also be included on the T-shirt.
2. For groups of people who may not be very artistic, ask them to select a team name and put that on their T-shirts.

TRAINER'S NOTES

43

T-shirts #2

IT

TIME REQUIRED

20–30 minutes, depending on the size of the group.

SIZE OF GROUP

Unlimited, but the larger group will need to be broken into its previously identified teams.

MATERIAL REQUIRED

This requires quite a bit of pre-work. You will need to design a team name (and perhaps a logo) for each team, then take these designs to a screen-printer and have the right number of T-shirts printed for each team. This can be done more economically by printing the design on to a special paper (e.g. Inject transfer paper). The design is then ironed on to the T-shirt. For programs of longer duration it would be worthwhile considering a couple of T-shirts for each participant.

Overview

This exercise can be used early in the program to help build a team atmosphere.

Goals

1. To allow participants to meet each other in their teams early in the program.
2. To develop a team atmosphere.

Procedure

1. During the initial part of the training organise the participants into teams.
2. Give each team its own set of T-shirts.
3. Ask each team member to introduce themselves to the rest of their group for a predetermined time.
4. After this introduction process, the teams could elect a team spokesperson who could now quickly introduce their team members to everyone else.
5. All participants should be encouraged to wear their T-shirts for the duration of the course.

Discussion points

None.

Variations

1. Use the same logo and name on all the T-shirts, but use different coloured T-shirts for each team. This saves considerably on time and money!
2. At the end of the course ask everyone to sign the other team members' T-shirts with a permanent marking laundry pen—they make great mementos.

TRAINER'S NOTES

44

Brain Teasers #2

ICMXP

TIME REQUIRED	SIZE OF GROUP	MATERIAL REQUIRED
5–10 minutes.	Unlimited.	A prepared 'Brain Teasers #2' overhead.

Overview

This activity was so popular in **100 Training Games** that another one has been included in this book.

Goals

1. To liven up the group after a break.
2. To see the basic idea of one of the brainstorming principles.
3. To keep the group occupied while waiting.

Procedure

1. Let the participants know that you are going to show them a series of brain teasers for them to solve.
2. Display the 'Brain Teasers #2' overhead and ask participants to call out what they believe the teasers indicate. You should process this exercise in a similar way to a brainstorming session.
3. When the correct response is given, move straight on to the next problem.

Discussion points

1. Who got most of them right?
2. Point out that we all tend to see things differently.
3. You may lead into techniques for brainstorming before moving on to the main session.

Variations

1. The 'Brain Teasers #2' overhead can be used as a handout instead of an overhead.
2. Give prizes for correct responses.
3. Break the large group into teams of 5 to 7 participants and have them compete to see which team can solve all the brain teasers first.

Solutions

1. Out of the question
2. Repeat after me
3. Female intuition
4. Actor's understudy
5. Anticlockwise
6. Growing older
7. Just a tick
8. Double or nothing
9. Treasonable
10. Night fall
11. Not up to it
12. Square deal

TRAINER'S NOTES

Brain Teasers #2

1 THE QESIN	2 AFTER ME ATFER ME	3 TUI♀TION	4 STUDY ——— ACTOR'S
5 A I N T	6 oLDER	7 ✓	8 OR O OR
9 YEW FIR ASH ELM ——— ABLE	10 SIR LAN CE LO T	11 T O 2 IT N	12 DE AL

45

Brain Teasers #3

ICMXP

TIME REQUIRED	SIZE OF GROUP	MATERIAL REQUIRED
5–10 minutes.	Unlimited.	A prepared 'Brain Teasers #3' overhead.

Overview

Yet another set of brain teasers that can be used at any time during training.

Goals

1. To liven up the group after a break.
2. To see the basic idea of one of the brainstorming principles.
3. To keep the group occupied while waiting.

Procedure

1. Let the participants know that you are going to show them a series of brain teasers for them to solve.
2. Display the 'Brain Teasers #3' overhead and get participants to call out what they believe they indicate. You should process this exercise in a similar way to a brainstorming session.
3. When the correct response is given, move straight on to the next problem.

Discussion points

1. Who got most of them right?
2. Point out that we all tend to see things differently.
3. You may lead into techniques for brainstorming before moving on to the main session.

Variations

1. The 'Brain Teasers #3' overhead can be used as a handout instead of an overhead.
2. Give prizes for correct responses.
3. Break the large group into teams of 5 to 7 participants and have them compete to see which team can solve all the brain teasers first.
4. Can be used as a follow-on from Game 44.

Solutions

1. Reverse gear
2. Topless swimsuit
3. Eiderdown
4. Beating around the bush
5. Profit before tax
6. Upside-down cake
7. Gross indecency
8. Paperback
9. Sideways glance
10. This afternoon
11. Milestone
12. Checkmate

TRAINER'S NOTES

Brain Teasers #3

1 RAEG	2 SWIMSUIT	3 E I D E R	4 B G the E N bush A 1 T
5 MOSES / TAX	6 CAKE	7 DEC144ENCY	8 REPAP
9 GLANCE	10 12:00 PM THIS	11 1760 YARDS 14 LB	12 M A T E

46

Formal Introductions

ITFLS

TIME REQUIRED

5–10 minutes, depending on the size of the group.

SIZE OF GROUP

Unlimited.

MATERIAL REQUIRED

None.

Overview

This activity will help people to remember the names of others in the group.

Goal

To be able to recall other participants' names.

Procedure

1. Ask the participants to stand in a circle.
2. Tell them they are going to be involved in an activity that will test their memories.
3. The rules are quite simple. One person will start by saying their name. The person on their left will follow with their name, and so on. Go around the group 3 times with this.
4. After the third round each person, in turn, is to go around the group and try giving the correct names.
5. The person with the best result should be acknowledged.

Discussion points

1. Why is it easier to remember some names and not others?
2. Is it important we do remember them?
3. How can we ensure that we remember names for the rest of this training?

Variation

Throw a ball around the group. As one person catches it, they sing out their name, and then they throw it on to someone else.

TRAINER'S NOTES

47 Earliest Thoughts

TL

TIME REQUIRED	SIZE OF GROUP	MATERIAL REQUIRED
A couple of minutes on top of the introductions.	Unlimited.	None.

Overview

This exercise can be used during the introductions at the start of training so participants can find out something unusual about each other. This is a revealing exercise and, as such, should lead to a closer team.

Goal

To create a team atmosphere.

Procedure

Before the participant introductions start, suggest to the group that while they are introducing themselves they tell the group what their earliest thought in childhood was.

Discussion points

None.

Variations

1. Any age could be used.
2. You could ask participants what they were doing when a specific event happened (e.g. on New Year's Day 2000).

TRAINER'S NOTES

48

What Is It?

CFXLPS

TIME REQUIRED	SIZE OF GROUP	MATERIAL REQUIRED
15–20 minutes.	Unlimited, but best suited for groups of around 10 to 16.	At least one unusual item (concealed in a bag) for each participant. The items should be things such as a box of orange chocolate sticks, small tin of sardines, picture of Elvis Presley, plastic butterfly, coloured condom, cigar cutter, etc. The harder the better for these items.

Overview

This is a simple exercise that can be used to demonstrate how important it is to give clear and accurate descriptions.

Goals

1. To demonstrate the importance of giving clear and accurate information.
2. To demonstrate that what may be obvious to one person, may not be obvious to another.

Procedure

1. Ask the participants how good they are at describing things.
2. Now tell them that they will have a chance to prove how good they are.
3. Tell them that they are each going to be given a bag containing an item. They are to look in the bag to see what it is, but they are not allowed to let anyone else see it.
4. Advise them that they are going to be given 10 seconds each (in turn) to stand in front of the group and describe the item inside their bag. They are not allowed to use the name of the item, or any other similar term. Their descriptions must be accurate and detailed. The other group members will write down what they think the items are.
5. After everyone has given their quick description and the guesses have been written down by everyone, all the items should be revealed.
6. When all the items have been shown, each person should score one point for each item they have guessed correctly. If the scores are high, congratulate the group on their efforts. If, on the other hand, some of the scores are low, you may lead into a discussion on how to give detailed and accurate information to others.

Discussion points

1. What made it easier to guess what the items were?
2. What made it harder to guess what the items were?

Variation

Putting more than one item in each bag makes it far more challenging.

TRAINER'S NOTES

49

Standing Ovation

IM

TIME REQUIRED	SIZE OF GROUP	MATERIAL REQUIRED
1–2 minutes.	Unlimited.	None.

Overview

A light-hearted activity to start the day.

Goals

1. To get the group moving at the very start of a program.
2. To demonstrate that the training will be fun.

Procedure

1. After the initial introductions have been made, ask everyone in the group to stand. Tell them they are going to start with an exercise to get the blood moving and stimulate their nerve endings.
2. Ask them to spread themselves out so that they are at least an arm's length from the person closest to them.
3. Now tell them to stretch their arms out from their sides (horizontal to their bodies).
4. When they have done this, ask them to bring their hands together rapidly and then take them apart.
5. Once they understand what is required, ask them to do it quickly 10 times in a row.
6. After they have done that, tell them that you don't know how they feel, but you feel great because that's the first time ever that you've started a training day with a standing ovation.

Discussion points

None.

Variations

None.

TRAINER'S NOTES

50

Magnetic Fingers

IMP

TIME REQUIRED	SIZE OF GROUP	MATERIAL REQUIRED
1–2 minutes.	Unlimited.	None.

Overview

A simple activity to show how powerful the mind is.

Goal

To demonstrate to participants how mental suggestion can sometimes cause physical movement.

Procedure

1. Start by asking everyone to clasp their hands together. When they have done this, ask them to extend their 2 pointer fingers. Ask them to keep the 2 fingers about 5 cm (2 in) apart.
2. Tell them to study the 2 pointers and imagine that there is an elastic band around them. The elastic band is tight, and they can feel the elastic band pulling their fingers closer and closer together. They are finding it difficult to keep them apart.
3. After the laughing has stopped (because you will find that over half the people will see their fingers getting closer), tell them that the purpose of the exercise was to show them that mental suggestion can cause physical movement, and therefore they should be paying a lot of attention to what's coming up on the course.

Discussion point

Why did that happen?

Variations

None.

TRAINER'S NOTES

51 Popping Balloons

ITMLE

TIME REQUIRED	SIZE OF GROUP	MATERIAL REQUIRED
5 minutes will be required at the end of training to play 'Popping Balloons'.	Unlimited, but if conducted as a team game, teams will need to be formed.	A number of 'balloon poppers' (numbered cards with a drawing pin stuck into them) and an equal number of numbered inflated balloons with slips of paper inside them showing what each prize is.

Overview

This activity is designed to promote interaction between participants. The 'balloon poppers' can be given out as prizes during training. If other games are being played during the training, and there are winners involved, they can be given a 'balloon popper' as a prize. The more 'balloon poppers' they collect during the day, the more prizes they get at the end.

Goals

1. To encourage participation.
2. To encourage the asking of relevant questions.
3. To encourage friendly competition.

Procedure

1. At the beginning of training advise the participants that there will be a chance to play 'Popping Balloons' at the end of the day.
2. Also tell them that the only way to get to play the game is to be awarded official 'balloon poppers' during the training.
3. Award 'balloon poppers' for all outstanding contributions. Obviously the person who gets the most 'balloon poppers' will finish up winning the most prizes.
4. At the conclusion of training all holders of official 'balloon poppers' now have a chance to play 'Popping Balloons'. The numbers on the cards match the numbers on the balloons: players must use the drawing pin on each card to pop the matching balloon.
5. The prizes are shown on the slips of paper inside the balloons. Books and sweets make great prizes.

Discussion points

None.

Variation

Can be used very effectively with teams.

TRAINER'S NOTES

52

A Model of Success

TCXPES

TIME REQUIRED

30–60 minutes, depending on the size of the group and how complex the model is made.

SIZE OF GROUP

Unlimited, but will need to be broken into smaller groups of 5 to 7 people.

MATERIAL REQUIRED

Several sets of children's building blocks. You will use some of these blocks to prepare a model and each group will also require a set of building blocks. Using different coloured blocks can be very effective.

Overview

This exercise will test the participants' ability to pass on a set of complex directions.

Goals

1. To test the participants' ability to pass on a set of complex directions.
2. To demonstrate how frustrating it can be when given a set of directions without being able to see the 'big picture'.

Procedure

1. Build the model before training commences. It should be reasonably complex, using about 40 to 50 blocks. You should keep the model outside where no one can see it.
2. At the appropriate time break the larger group into teams of 4 or 5 people.
3. Ask each team to elect a supervisor from their group.
4. Advise the groups that they will be required to build a model using the building blocks provided.
5. Give each team a set of blocks.
6. There are a couple of rules they must follow. Their supervisor is the only person from the team who is allowed to go outside and see the model you have already made. The supervisor is not allowed to use pens or paper to draw the model or to instruct in any way. All communication must be done verbally.
7. Now take the group supervisors outside to see the structure.
8. Tell the groups that they have 15 minutes to build a structure that is identical to the one outside.
9. After the construction phase, you can lead a discussion into the areas of teamwork, communication skills, delegation skills, etc.

Discussion points

1. Why were most models different to the original?
2. How did the supervisors feel about their instructions?
3. What did the group think about the instructions?
4. How did the group feel about the task?
5. How could it be improved next time?
6. How does this apply in the workplace?

Variations

1. Coloured shapes of cardboard could be used instead of the blocks.
2. In step 6, the instruction about only using verbal communication could be overlooked. This may lead into a discussion about certain assumptions people may have.

TRAINER'S NOTES

53 Motivators/Demotivators

TCXLPS

TIME REQUIRED	SIZE OF GROUP	MATERIAL REQUIRED
15–30 minutes.	Unlimited, but larger groups will need to be broken into smaller groups of 5 to 7 people.	One copy of the 'Motivators/ Demotivators' handout and a pen for each person.

Overview

An activity designed to identify things that motivate or demotivate people.

Goals

1. To identify individual motivators.
2. To identify individual demotivators.

Procedure

1. Give each participant a copy of the 'Motivators/Demotivators' handout and a pen.
2. Ask them to list the things that help or stifle their motivation—for example, management actions, their supervisors' actions, their colleagues' actions, or their own actions. Allow 5 minutes for this.
3. After the lists have been completed, break the participants into groups of 5 to 7 people.
4. Now ask them to discuss each of the items that have been noted, and try and find common themes. Allow 10 to 15 minutes.
5. After the groups have finished their discussions, have them share their findings with everyone else.
6. You can summarise the points as they are being made, and note them on the whiteboard. This can be the basis of a presentation on what tends to motivate or demotivate people.

Discussion points

1. Were common themes identified?
2. Would this set of 'rules' apply to everyone all the time?
3. How does this apply in your workplace?
4. What can you do to improve motivation?

Variations

With a small group it would work just as well to ask the group to note things straight on to the whiteboard.

TRAINER'S NOTES

Motivators/Demotivators

What does management do that **increases** my motivation?

What does management do that **decreases** my motivation?

What does my supervisor do that **increases** my motivation?

What does my supervisor do that **decreases** my motivation?

What do my colleagues do that **increases** my motivation?

What do my colleagues do that **decreases** my motivation?

What do I do that **increases** my motivation?

What do I do that **decreases** my motivation?

54

What Do You See #2?

CMP

TIME REQUIRED	SIZE OF GROUP	MATERIAL REQUIRED
5 minutes.	Unlimited.	A prepared 'What Do You See?' overhead.

Overview

This exercise shows how people perceive things differently.

Goal

To allow participants to see that people perceive things in different ways.

Procedure

1. Project the 'What Do You See?' transparency on to a screen and ask the participants to look at the image for a few seconds.
2. Ask them to raise their hands if they can see a distorted male face. Now ask them to raise their hands if they can see a naked woman. Finally, ask them to raise their hands if they can see both. You may have to show some people where both of them are.
3. Ask them to recall what they first saw. Did they see the distorted male face or the naked woman? This can now lead into a discussion about how people have different perceptions, and what one person sees clearly, the other may not.

Discussion points

1. Why do people perceive things differently?
2. Why can't everyone see both people in the picture?
3. How can we improve our perception skills?

Variations

If anyone can't see both people in the picture, have one of your group members show them where they are. This is useful if conducting this exercise in a presentation skills or training techniques course.

TRAINER'S NOTES

What Do You See?

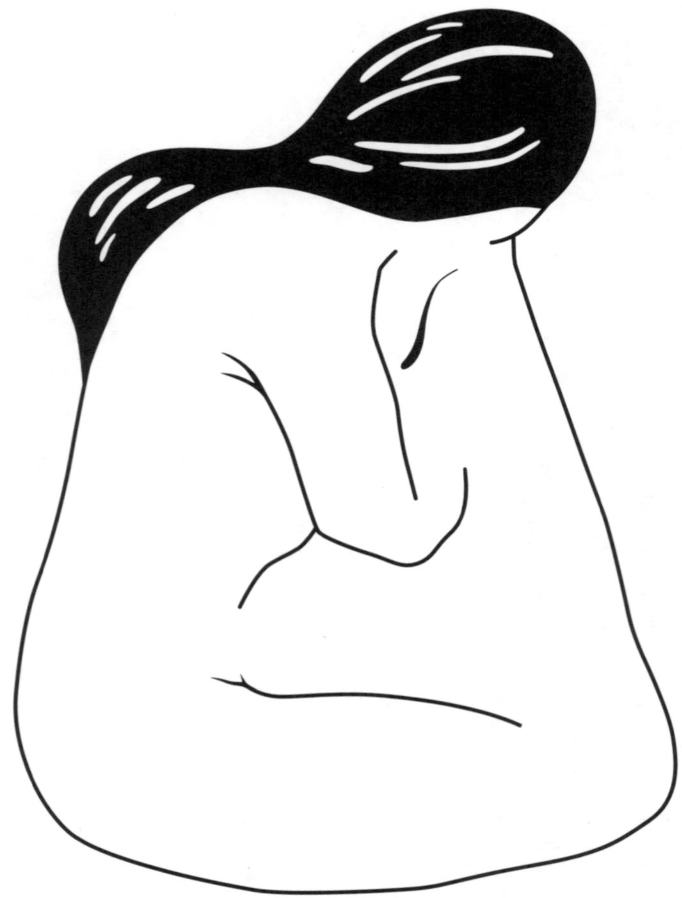

55

Foreign Goals

TCML

TIME REQUIRED	SIZE OF GROUP	MATERIAL REQUIRED
45–60 minutes.	12 to 16. Observers can be used effectively if you have larger groups.	Room furniture (e.g. tables and chairs), 2 identical assortments of groceries and 2 rolls of string.

Overview

An exercise to let participants feel what it may be like not to be understood.

Goals

1. To allow participants to design a new language.
2. To allow the participants to teach someone a new language.
3. To let participants feel what it may be like not to have their instructions understood.

Procedure

1. Ask the group to break into 2 teams.
2. Tell them that each team is going to have the experience of designing their own language. The language is not to have any more than 12 words and the words must not be from any established language—they must be made up. The words will be used to give someone directions to pick something up for you. All the team members must be able to speak this language within 40 minutes. They are to elect one of their members to be the person who will be receiving the instructions (the robot). Separate the 2 teams so that they do not disturb each other.
3. During the 30 minute design time, set up 2 'stores'. The stores are laid out on the floor using the string and the room furniture. Set out aisles and display the assortment of groceries. Both 'stores' are to be identical.
4. After the groups have designed and learnt their new languages, give them a briefing for the following exercise. Each team will be located at the front of the 'store' where they will be able to give their 'robot' verbal instructions. It is important that every instruction is given in their new language. They are not allowed to use any other form of communication. The object of the activity is to be the first group to use their robot to collect and return the items written down on a piece of paper (previously prepared by you).
5. Now comes the interesting bit! Tell them that they are now going to swap 'robots' with the other group and that they will have a maximum of 2 minutes to teach their new 'robot' their language.
6. After the 2 minute instructional period, ask the groups to start the exercise.
7. At the conclusion, a discussion can be led into the areas of communication, conflict resolution, etc.

Discussion points

1. How did the robots perform?
2. How easy/difficult was it to teach the robot?
3. How did the robots feel during the last part of the activity?
4. How does this exercise relate to the workplace?
5. How did the groups feel when their robots weren't functioning the way they should have?
6. How does this exercise relate to us and the way we deal with, or treat, others?

Variations

Any task can be used for this exercise, for example, turning on a computer and running a particular program, or going to the kitchen and making a cup of tea.

TRAINER'S NOTES

56

Who Would It Be?

IM

TIME REQUIRED

2–5 minutes.

SIZE OF GROUP

Unlimited, but larger groups may need to be broken into smaller groups of around 10 to 12 people.

MATERIAL REQUIRED

None.

Overview

A quick icebreaking activity that can be used during the initial introductions.

Goal

To encourage the participants to share information with others in the group.

Procedure

1. During the initial introductions, ask the group to imagine that they are going to a dinner party after the course finishes.
2. They are to ask 3 people as their guests. These people can be living or dead, fictional or real.
3. They are now to say who their guests would be, and why they were selected.

Discussion points

None.

Variation

Rather than inviting these guests to a dinner party, they may be inviting people to be guest speakers for today. Who would they be and what would they be asked to talk about?

TRAINER'S NOTES

57 Mini Action Plan

ILS

TIME REQUIRED	SIZE OF GROUP	MATERIAL REQUIRED
2 or 3 minute blocks during the training.	Unlimited.	A copy of the 'Mini Action Plan' and a pen for everyone. The 'Mini Action Plan' can have sub-topics already shown if required. Multiple copies may be required.

Overview

This is a good way to get participants to focus on action plans during training, rather than at the end.

Goals

1. To allow participants to develop their own action plans as they progress throughout the training.
2. To increase the trainee's accountability in applying their learning back in the workplace.

Procedure

1. At the beginning of training let the group know that it's important that everyone develop their own action plan based on what they will learn during the training.
2. Also explain that, at the end of training, an action plan is generally seen as overwhelming, and that it's sometimes very difficult to remember everything that's been covered. So here is a tool they can use during the training.
3. Give everyone a copy of the 'Mini Action Plan' and a pen.
4. Advise them that at specific times they will be asked to get these sheets out and write down any relevant points they feel will have an impact on them when they get back to work. This is not to say that this will be the only time they can write on them—it will just be a friendly reminder.
5. At the end of the training, ask all participants to get their sheets out and expand on, or summarise, the main points, and look at ways of implementing these ideas back at work.

Discussion point

Would you like to discuss the action items with others in the group?

Variations

1. Can be done in small groups.
2. Copies can be taken at the end for you to follow up.

TRAINER'S NOTES

Mini Action Plan

What have I learnt? What are the important points for me?	How can I apply this after training? How can I ensure that I use this?

58

Refrigerators

ITMXP

TIME REQUIRED	SIZE OF GROUP	MATERIAL REQUIRED
15–20 minutes.	Unlimited, but larger groups will need to be broken into smaller groups of 5 to 7 people.	Flipcharts and pens for each group.

Overview

This is a problem-solving activity that is team oriented.

Goals

1. To look at group strategies for problem solving.
2. To see how competition affects the problem-solving process.
3. To demonstrate to participants the effect of synergy.
4. To energise the group.

Procedure

1. Break the large group into smaller groups of 5 to 7 people.
2. Give each team a flipchart and pens.
3. Tell them that they have done an incredible deal with the local Junk Shop. They have been able to purchase 10 000 used refrigerators for almost next to nothing.
4. Their task is to list as many possible uses as they can for these items.
5. You could reward the group with the longest or most creative list with a prize.

Discussion points

1. How many ideas did each group have?
2. How were the ideas arrived at?
3. Which is the best idea?
4. Did each group see this as a competitive exercise? Was that part of the initial brief?

Variations

1. If flipcharts are not available, you can use paper and pens.
2. Any item, not just refrigerators, could be used.

TRAINER'S NOTES

59

Personality Styles

TCPS

TIME REQUIRED	SIZE OF GROUP	MATERIAL REQUIRED
30–60 minutes, depending on the size of the group and the time available.	Unlimited.	A 'What Colour Are You?' handout, a 'Four Styles' handout and a pen for each person.

Overview

This exercise can be used to quickly identify personality types within the group.

Goals

1. To identify participants' personality types.
2. To show the different needs of each of the 4 basic groups.

Procedure

1. Start by informing the group that there are 4 basic personality styles and that the next exercise will identify which style they are.
2. Give each person a copy of the 'What Colour Are You?' handout and a pen.
3. Now instruct them to read through the characteristics shown on the handout and place a tick beside any they think describes them best.
4. After everyone has finished, ask them to total the number of ticks in each area.
5. Advise them that the colour category that has the most ticks in it will indicate their personality style at present.
6. You should now give a copy of the 'Four Styles' handout to everyone, and ask them to read through it. This could then lead into a discussion on the likes and dislikes of each of the four styles.

Discussion points

1. Which was your predominant colour?
2. What are the things that we like and dislike?
3. What do we do that other colours would dislike?
4. How does this apply in the workplace?

Variations

1. Can be conducted as a small group exercise.
2. After step 4, 4 groups can be formed. Each group will have members of the same colour. They can then discuss as a group what their strong and weak points are. After the discussion, they should report back to the other 3 groups.

Source: Adapted from 'Personality Styles' by Linda Urquhart in Carolyn Greenwich, **The Fun Factor**, McGraw-Hill, Sydney, 1997.

TRAINER'S NOTES

What Colour Are You?

Tick the characteristics that best describe you.

Blue

Decisive
Independent
Tends to be dominant
Strong willed
Wants immediate results
Causes action
Likes power and authority
Likes freedom from control
Dislikes supervision
Outspoken
Wants direct answers
Restless
Competitive
Adventurous
Assertive

Green

Orderly
Performs exacting work
Likes controlled circumstances
Likes assurance of security
Uses critical thinking
Follows rules
Reads and follows instructions
Prefers status quo
Dislikes sudden or abrupt change
Tends to be serious and persistent
Cautious
Diplomatic
Respectful
Agreeable
Checks for accuracy

Red

Optimistic
Tends to be exciting/stimulating
Generates enthusiasm
Often dramatic
Talkative
Open and friendly
Likes working with people
Likes participating in groups
Desires to help others
Wants freedom of expression
Wants freedom from detail
Likes change, spontaneity
Persuasive
Appears confident
Likes recognition

Yellow

Patient
Accommodating
Good listener
Shows loyalty
Concentrates on task accuracy
Likes security and stability
Needs good reasons for change
Home life a priority
Expects credit for work done
Likes traditional procedures
Dislikes conflict
Neighbourly
Considerate towards others
Important to perform good work
Pleasure in sharing and giving

Four Styles

Blue

Blue is the colour of the sky and the ocean. It is also seen as the colour of authority. Explorers have long been pioneers of the land, the ocean and in space and their characteristics match this style. They enjoy looking at the 'big picture'—that is, being in charge—and are comfortable taking appropriate risks for themselves and their groups. They are goal oriented people and like to have their fingers in many pies. They are generally motivated by challenge and like competition. People of other 'styles' get frustrated with these 'blues' because they see them as sometimes impatient and abrupt people, selective listeners, but they appreciate the strong leadership qualities that they display.

Green

Green is the colour of the dollar and was one of the original colours on computer screens. Of all the styles greens are most comfortable where accuracy and numbers are important. Perfectionism is inherent in their style. 'If a job's worth doing, it's worth doing it right—the first time' might be their motto. They are willing to take the time to get the job done right. They are the best of the four styles at critical thinking and planning. They make the best administrators as they like order, structure, following guidelines and plans (especially if they inititiate them). Other styles complain that the greens are too rigid, too slow at making decisions, too 'picky', but value their planning and problem-solving skills.

Red

Red is the colour of blood and Valentines, and tends to connote passion and enthusiasm, which sounds a lot like the reds. Reds are happiest when they are influencing or entertaining other people. Like the blues, they are comfortable taking risks and enjoy trying new things. They get bored if they have to do the same old thing all the time. They are the charming, playful, spontaneous, talkative types who are energised by being the centre of attention. They are motivated by recognition—they want to be liked! Other styles see them as unfocused procrastinators who make up the rules as they go along, but appreciate their talents as great promoters who can sell anything.

Yellow

Yellow is the colour of the sun and yellows are like a ray of sunshine when they enter a room with their warm and caring style. Family is their number one priority. They tend to be most concerned with the needs of others. They are the best team builders, always listening to, encouraging and bringing out the best in others. They are motivated by appreciation for work done and have a strong need to please others. Like the greens, they dislike confrontation and will give in to others to avoid conflict. Other styles see yellows as too soft, not hard-nosed enough, indecisive (they can see all sides of an issue) and resistant to change. They are often the 'glue' that holds a group together.

60 Pin the Tail on the Donkey

TMLE

TIME REQUIRED

5 minutes will be required at the end of training to 'Pin the Tail on the Donkey'.

SIZE OF GROUP

Unlimited, but if conducted as a team game, teams will need to be formed.

MATERIAL REQUIRED

A 'Pin the Tail on the Donkey' game. Either buy one from a toy shop or make it.

Overview

This activity is designed to promote interaction between participants. The 'tails' can also be given out as prizes during training. If other games are being played during the training, and there are winners involved, they can be given a 'tail' as a prize. The more 'tails' they collect during the day, the greater their chance of 'pinning the tail on the donkey'.

Goals

1. To encourage participation.
2. To encourage friendly competition.

Procedure

1. At the beginning of training advise the participants that there will be a chance to play 'Pin the Tail on the Donkey' at the end of the day.
2. Also tell them that the only way they can play the game is to gain 'tails' during the training.
3. 'Tails' will be awarded for all outstanding contributions. Obviously the person who gets the most 'tails' has the greatest chance of winning.
4. At the conclusion of training all holders of 'tails' now have a chance to 'Pin the Tail on the Donkey'.
5. The player who gets their 'tail' closest to the correct spot wins the ultimate prize.

Discussion points

None.

Variation

Can be used effectively with teams rather than individuals.

TRAINER'S NOTES

61
Dumb Questions

ICLPE

TIME REQUIRED

5–10 minutes.

SIZE OF GROUP

Unlimited, but more time may be required for larger groups.

MATERIAL REQUIRED

One copy of the 'Don't Be Afraid to Ask Dumb Questions' handout to be used as a sign.

Overview

This is an activity designed to encourage questions from participants during the course of training.

Goals

1. To encourage questions from participants.
2. To increase interaction.

Procedure

1. During the initial introductions, put a copy of the 'Don't Be Afraid to Ask Dumb Questions' sign at the front of the room.
2. As you put the sign on the wall, tell the group that there is no such thing as a dumb question. Every question has value.
3. To get participants involved in this, ask each person to ask one dumb question when they introduce themselves. You should start this off by asking the first question—for example, something like: 'Are your chairs comfortable?', 'Do you think the colour of the walls is appropriate?', or 'How long do we have at the break times?'

Discussion points

None.

Variations

1. May be used after the first break.
2. Can be done in pairs.

TRAINER'S NOTES

Don't Be Afraid to Ask Dumb Questions

62

Must I Do It?

XLPS

TIME REQUIRED

5 minutes.

SIZE OF GROUP

Unlimited.

MATERIAL REQUIRED

A prepared 'Must I Do It?' overhead.

Overview

This exercise will give participants a tool to use when they feel overwhelmed by tasks at work.

Goals

1. To help participants make a decision on what to do with extra tasks that they are being assigned during the work day.
2. To reduce stress levels.

Procedure

1. If the situation arises where participants need to know what to do with extra tasks that are imposed on them during the work day, put up the 'Must I Do It?' overhead.
2. Tell participants that they need to ask themselves (and perhaps the person making the request) these questions when put in that situation.
3. If they answer 'yes' to the first question they go on to the next one, and so on. If they answer all 4 questions 'yes', then tell them just to smile and get on with the job. The sooner they finish the sooner they can get back to their other set priorities.

Discussion points

1. Why do some people think that everything is important?
2. What is the difference between urgent and important?
3. Can we tell the boss that we are too busy to do something that they have asked us to do?
4. Can we tell the boss that we have something else that is more important to work on?

Variations

None.

TRAINER'S NOTES

Must I Do It?

1. Must it be done?
2. Must it be done now?
3. Must it be done by me?
4. Must it be done their way?

63

Secret Sounds

ITMXP

TIME REQUIRED	SIZE OF GROUP	MATERIAL REQUIRED
10–15 minutes.	Unlimited, but large groups will need to be broken into smaller groups of 5 to 7 people.	A 'Secret Sounds' handout and a pen for each person. A prepared audio tape with 5 unusual sounds on it (e.g. a bucket being slid across a tile floor, or a page being torn out of the phone directory, or an electric razor being turned on and off, etc.).

Overview

A fun activity that can be used at any time during training to fill in time or as a team problem-solving activity.

Goals

1. To have participants take part in a fun problem-solving activity.
2. To fill in time while waiting for latecomers to arrive.
3. To encourage interaction.
4. To energise the group.

Procedure

1. Break the participants into groups of 5 to 7 people.
2. Tell the teams they are going to listen to an audio tape with 5 different sounds on it.
3. Give each team member a copy of the 'Secret Sounds' handout and a pen.
4. Play the sounds.
5. Give everyone 1 minute to write down their own ideas.
6. After the 1 minute time frame, ask them to discuss with their group what everyone else thought it was. Now ask the groups to generate a list of suggestions. More than one suggestion is allowed, and should be encouraged. Allow a few minutes for this.
7. When the groups have finished, ask for their answers and list them on the whiteboard.
8. After you have taken all the answers from the groups, give them the right answers if they haven't already given them.
9. Each team receives 20 points for each correct guess. The winning team is given a prize.
10. You can lead a discussion into the area of problem solving, teamwork or perceptions.

Discussion points

1. Which team received the highest score?
2. Did people find this difficult? Why, or why not?
3. How does this apply in the workplace? (See Step 10.)

Variations

1. The last of the 5 sounds could be something that is extremely common to the group. That should then lead into a discussion on creativity as lots of suggestions should be made as to what it is. In fact the obvious may be overlooked.
2. If time permits, allow each team to record its own 'Secret Sound' before the activity is due to commence.

TRAINER'S NOTES

Secret Sounds

1.

2.

3.

4.

5.

64 Who's the Leader?

TXS

TIME REQUIRED	SIZE OF GROUP	MATERIAL REQUIRED
1–2 minutes.	Unlimited.	None.

Overview

If your groups need to select a leader, this activity will let them do it quickly.

Goal

To select a leader quickly.

Procedure

1. Break the participants into the group sizes required.
2. Tell everyone to point one finger into the air.
3. Then tell them that on the count of 3 they are to point to the person they would like to see as the group leader.
4. The person with the most fingers pointed at them is now elected the group leader.

Discussion points

None.

Variations

Lots of variations can be used here. The leader may be the person with their birthday being the closest to today's date, or the person with the longest length of service, or the person who lives the furthest away. Some of these can be a lot more fun if done as a non-verbal exercise.

TRAINER'S NOTES

65

3 Questions

IT

TIME REQUIRED	SIZE OF GROUP	MATERIAL REQUIRED
15–20 minutes, depending on the size of the group.	Unlimited, but large groups will need to be broken into smaller groups of 8 to 12 people.	A copy of the '3 Questions' handout and a pen for everyone.

Overview

An activity to be used as an icebreaker with participants who don't know each other very well.

Goal

To find out more information about each other.

Procedure

1. During the introductory part of the course, break the participants into groups of 8 to 12 people.
2. Give everyone a copy of the '3 Questions' handout and a pen.
3. Ask each person to answer 3 of the questions in the handout and share that information with the rest of their group.
4. After the groups have finished, ask each group who had the most interesting answers.

Discussion points

None.

Variations

1. The questions can be modified to suit the group, the course content, or the specific workplace.
2. This may be done as an individual exercise with each person sharing their 3 answers with everyone else.

TRAINER'S NOTES

3 Questions

My 3 favourite books are:

My 3 favourite movies are:

My favourite food is:

If I could buy any car it would be a:

The best part of my job is:

The worst part of my job is:

In high school I was considered:

I really enjoy doing this outside work:

The best boss I ever had was:

If I could live anywhere in the world it would be:

66

Magic Ball

IMXP

TIME REQUIRED	SIZE OF GROUP	MATERIAL REQUIRED
5 minutes.	Unlimited, but if used as a group activity, larger groups will need to be broken into smaller groups of 5 to 7 people.	A 'Magic Ball' handout for everyone.

Overview

An exercise that can be used at any time during training.

Goals

1. To demonstrate the use of teamwork to solve problems.
2. To fill in time while people come back from breaks.
3. To energise the group.
4. To have some fun.

Procedure

1. Before the course spend some time preparing the 'Magic Ball' handout. Use a word-processing package that has a special effects tool for text.
2. Select, say, 3 lines of text and make each one into a separate ball, stretching the text. You will also need to rotate 2 of the balls. Then layer the 3 balls on top of each other (see the handout, for example). To be able to read the text you need to lay the page flat and hold it at eye level, so that you are looking along the page. You must rotate the page to be able to read all 3 blocks of text.
3. When appropriate, give out a copy of the previously prepared 'Magic Ball' handout.
4. Ask each person to solve the puzzle.
5. After an appropriate amount of time, small groups should be formed. Now ask the groups to solve the problem.
6. After the solution has been found, you can lead the group into a discussion on problem solving.

Discussion points

1. Why was it difficult to find the solution?
2. What made it easier to find?

Variations

1. Use appropriate text for the group.
2. To make this more difficult, it can be shown as an overhead only.

TRAINER'S NOTES

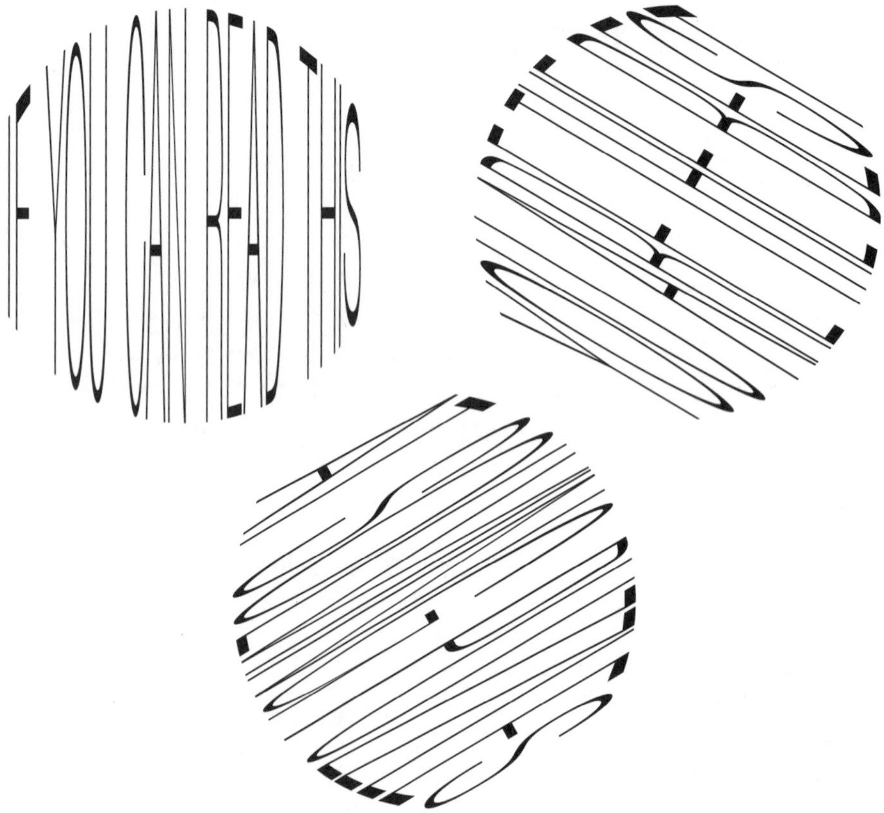

3 separate blocks of text

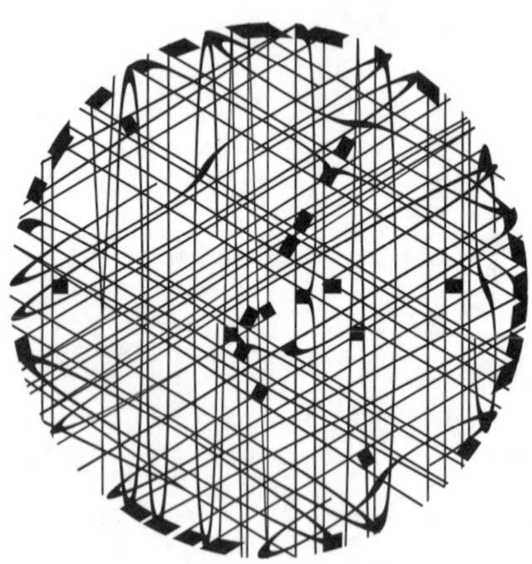

All 3 blocks of text on top of each other

67

Training Name Tents

IL

TIME REQUIRED	SIZE OF GROUP	MATERIAL REQUIRED
1–2 minutes.	Unlimited.	A 'Training Name Tents' handout for each person. At least one marking pen.

Overview

A name tent that can be used to set the rules for training.

Goals

1. To allow participants to see the rules for the training course.
2. To allow participants to see everyone else's name.

Procedure

1. During the introductions give a 'Training Name Tent' handout to everyone.
2. Ask each person to write their name (legibly) on the front of the tent, and to read the rules on the back of it.

Discussion points

None.

Variation

You can write all the names on the tents before the training starts.

TRAINER'S NOTES

Training Name Tent

Take part constructively in all discussions.
Remarks should be relevant to the topic being discussed.
Appreciate the other person's point of view.
Indicate what you really think.
Note all ideas that may be useful to you.
Improve your knowledge, listen alertly.
No private conversations please during course discussions.
Give freely of your experience. It's of value to all of us.

Take part constructively in all discussions.
Remarks should be relevant to the topic being discussed.
Appreciate the other person's point of view.
Indicate what you really think.
Note all ideas that may be useful to you.
Improve your knowledge, listen alertly.
No private conversations please during course discussions.
Give freely of your experience. It's of value to all of us.

68

LE

Learning Support Contract

TIME REQUIRED	SIZE OF GROUP	MATERIAL REQUIRED
10 minutes during training and 20 minutes after training.	Unlimited.	A 'Learning Support Contract' handout and a pen for each participant.

Overview

This will help increase participant/supervisor accountability for learning back in the workplace. It will also give you feedback after the participants have gone back to work.

Goals

1. To have participants identify their training objectives before they start the course.
2. To have participants identify what it is they've learnt during training.
3. To have participants identify what they will do differently as the result of the training.
4. To have participants identify what support they require to achieve point 3.

Procedure

1. At the beginning of training give everyone a copy of the 'Learning Support Contract' handout and a pen.
2. Ask each participant to fill in parts 1 and 2 of the 'Learning Support Contract' and then put it away.
3. At the completion of training ask participants to fill in parts 3 and 4 of the contract.
4. Ask the participants to take these contracts back to work and discuss them with their immediate supervisor. Together with their supervisor, they should fill in part 5 of the contract.
5. After part 5 is completed, they are to take a copy of the contract and send it back to you.
6. You can read through the information and, if relevant, have this copy attached to each participant's job folder or similar.

Discussion points

None.

Variations

1. After step 2, you could ask each participant to share their objectives with everyone else.
2. After step 2, you could ask each participant to discuss their objectives with a partner.
3. Parts 1 and 2 can be completed before attending the training.

TRAINER'S NOTES

Learning Support Contract

fold here when finished

Please return completed copy to:

▼ staple here ▼

▼ staple here ▼

Learning Support Contract

Part 1

Participant's Name: ______________________________

Training Attended: ______________________________

Telephone Number: ______________________________

Part 2

Workshop Objectives

Write down your objectives for the course

1. ______________________________

2. ______________________________

3. ______________________________

4. ______________________________

5. ______________________________

6. ______________________________

Signed: ____________________ Participant

____________________ Supervisor/Manager

Learning Support Contract

Part 3

At the conclusion of training write down the things you learnt:

1. ______________________________
____

2. ______________________________
____

3. ______________________________
____

4. ______________________________
____

5. ______________________________
____

6. ______________________________
____

7. ______________________________
____

8. ______________________________
____

The participant has demonstrated or identified opportunities to demonstrate learning.

Signed: ______________________ Participant

______________________ Training Facilitator

Learning Support Contract

Part 4

Write down what you will do differently on the job as a result of the training you have just done:

1. ______________________________
2. ______________________________
3. ______________________________
4. ______________________________

Part 5

Write down what support you will require to achieve the above:

1. ______________________________
2. ______________________________
3. ______________________________
4. ______________________________

Signed: ______________________ Participant
______________________ Supervisor/Manager

69

Throw It Away

TMXLE

TIME REQUIRED
30–45 minutes, depending on the size of the group and the types of questions being asked.

SIZE OF GROUP
Unlimited, but will need to be broken into smaller groups.

MATERIAL REQUIRED
A 'Question? Problem? Concern?' handout and a pen for everyone. One clean rubbish bin.

Overview

This activity can be used to get groups to answer participants' individual questions.

Goals

1. To allow participants to identify one question they would like answered.
2. To get the groups working together.

Procedure

1. At any relevant point during training, you can give everyone a copy of the 'Question? Problem? Concern?' handout and a pen.
2. Ask everyone to write at least one question, problem or concern they have right now that is relevant to the topic.
3. After they have done this, ask them to crumple up their papers and throw them into the bin provided.
4. After all papers have been thrown in, break the large group into smaller groups. Then ask each group to take out of the bin one piece of paper for each person in their group.
5. Give them 15 minutes to write as many answers or solutions as they can for each piece of paper they have taken out of the bin.
6. When all groups have finished, a spokesperson for each group should give a verbal summary of the questions, problems and concerns they were given, along with their suggested answers or solutions.

Discussion points

1. Were any new areas raised that should be looked at?
2. Were any common themes identified?

Variations

1. Can be done in pairs rather than groups.
2. For small groups this can be done as an exercise for individuals rather than teams.

TRAINER'S NOTES

Question? Problem? Concern?

Please take a minute to write down any question, problem or concern you have at this point in time that is relevant to the training. After this has been done, please crumple this piece of paper and throw it in the bin provided. Your trainer will then tell you what to do next.

70 Jackets and Ties

IMLPS

TIME REQUIRED
5 minutes.

SIZE OF GROUP
Unlimited.

MATERIAL REQUIRED
None.

Overview

A quick activity to demonstrate how it is sometimes difficult to do something a different way.

Goals

1. To demonstrate to participants how it is sometimes difficult to change the way we do things and how this may interfere with the learning process.
2. To get the group moving around.

Procedure

1. Ask everyone to stand up and form pairs.
2. Ask each pair to face each other.
3. Depending on what the participants are wearing, ask them, one person at a time, to take off their jacket, cardigan, tie, or something else. While they are taking it off, they (and their partner) are to observe how they take it off.
4. When they have done this, ask them to put it back on. Again both people should observe how this is done.
5. When they have put the item back on, ask them to take it off and put it on again, but this time using the opposite hands or arms. That is, if they took their jacket off by taking their right arm out first, they are to now take out their left arm first. And if they put their right arm in first when putting it back on, they put their left arm in first this time.
6. After they have all tried this, ask them how they felt and what their partners saw happen.
7. You can now lead into a discussion on barriers to learning or something similar.

Discussion points

1. How many people felt comfortable doing it the new way?
2. When watching your partner, what did you see (or hear)?
3. How does this apply to the training you are about to go through?
4. How does this apply back in the workplace?

Variations

1. Ties or scarves can be used, but the game will take a lot longer.
2. Ask participants to take off their watches and put them back on the opposite hand.

TRAINER'S NOTES

71

1089

IMP

TIME REQUIRED	SIZE OF GROUP	MATERIAL REQUIRED
5 minutes.	Unlimited.	A prepared card or folded sheet of paper with the number 1089 written on it in bold text. This is to be kept out of sight until the appropriate time. Also required is a flipchart and pen.

Overview

An activity that can be used to let the group know that you don't have all the answers and that you don't know what they are thinking.

Goals

1. To encourage the participants to ask questions.
2. To energise the group at the beginning of training.

Procedure

1. To demonstrate a point about the powers of extrasensory perception, ask for a volunteer from the group.
2. Ask your volunteer to come to the front of the room with you.
3. Tell the group that you are now going to demonstrate your powers of extrasensory perception.
4. Position yourself behind the flipchart so that you cannot see what's about to be written.
5. Ask your volunteer to write any 3 digit number. The only stipulation here is that the number is not to be a mirror image type number (e.g. 696).
6. Then ask your volunteer to reverse the number and then subtract the lower number from the higher number. If they have any zeros in their number they are included in the reversal (e.g. 200 would become 002).
7. Once they have the answer, ask them to reverse this number and add it to their previous answer.
8. As your volunteer completes the calculation you can now reveal your previously hidden card or folded sheet.

Discussion points

1. Are we able to read people's minds?
2. How does this exercise relate to our training?

Variations

1. None.

Solution

If done correctly the answer will always be 1089.

321	300	782
– 123	– 003	– 287
198	297	495
+ 891	+ 792	+ 594
1089	1089	1089

TRAINER'S NOTES

72

Which Group Am I?

ITF

TIME REQUIRED	SIZE OF GROUP	MATERIAL REQUIRED
1 minute each time.	Unlimited. The more the better.	Prepared name tags or name tents with the 'codes' already shown on them.

Overview

An easy way to get large groups to break into smaller groups and to have them mixing in different ways each time.

Goals

1. To get participants to break into smaller groups.
2. To have participants mix with different people every time they have to form a new group.

Procedure

1. Organise as many name tags or name tents as you need for the training.
2. 'Code' each name tag or name tent before the training commences. Sample codes are shown on the 'Which Group Am I?' handout for a group of 20 being broken into groups of 5 for 6 different exercises.
3. If you require the large group to break into groups of 5 on 4 separate occasions during training, then 4 lots of information would be shown (e.g. '1, Red, Square, B'). For this example the words and letters could be written, or perhaps a red square could be drawn in the corner and '1B' written inside it.
4. Then every time you require the group to break, ask them to form according to the code (e.g. all the Reds get together, or all the squares get together).

Discussion points

None.

Variations

1. Different categories could be used, according to what is appropriate for the group (e.g. product names, materials or locations could be used).
2. You may need more combination charts for larger groups or different group sizes.

TRAINER'S NOTES

Which Group Am I?

Participant name	Numbers	Colours	Shapes	Letters	Animals	Fruits
	1	Red	Square	A	Cat	Orange
	2	Green	Triangle	B	Dog	Apple
	3	Blue	Circle	C	Cow	Banana
	4	Yellow	Rectangle	D	Horse	Pear
	5	Pink	Star	E	Bird	Grapefruit
	1	Green	Circle	D	Bird	Pear
	2	Blue	Rectangle	E	Cat	Banana
	3	Yellow	Star	A	Dog	Apple
	4	Pink	Square	B	Cow	Grapefruit
	5	Red	Triangle	C	Horse	Orange
	1	Green	Circle	D	Bird	Pear
	2	Blue	Rectangle	E	Cat	Banana
	3	Yellow	Star	A	Dog	Apple
	4	Pink	Square	B	Cow	Grapefruit
	5	Red	Triangle	C	Horse	Orange
	1	Green	Circle	D	Bird	Pear
	2	Blue	Rectangle	E	Cat	Banana
	3	Yellow	Star	A	Dog	Apple
	4	Pink	Square	B	Cow	Grapefruit
	5	Red	Triangle	C	Horse	Orange

73

Shaky Start

F

TIME REQUIRED	SIZE OF GROUP	MATERIAL REQUIRED
5 minutes.	Unlimited.	A prepared script, handful of old papers, lectern, pair of glasses, poorly designed overhead and any other item that may assist with the 'show'.

Overview

A great way to start a presentation skills course.

Goals

1. To show participants what not to do when giving a presentation.
2. To start the course in a fun way.
3. To demonstrate that the facilitator is prepared to look silly in front of the group.

Procedure

1. Before training commences you'll need to prepare for the 'show'. The intention here is to give a demonstration of a very bad presentation; however, the group doesn't know this in advance.
2. Prepare or copy a script that is close to the topic, but not too close. The more boring and academic the script, the 'better' it will be.
3. Place this script on top of a handful of old papers.
4. As you walk nervously out in front of the group, avoid eye contact with anyone. Drop the handful of papers and appear to put them back together in the correct sequence (obviously it's only the script that needs to stay on top).
5. Turn on the overhead projector, which will have nothing on it. Make sure it's out of focus before you start.
6. You should place all the papers on the lectern in a random and nervous manner. You must avoid eye contact at all costs.
7. As you fumble with your glasses you drop them on the floor. Pick them up, put them on, grab the lectern with both hands tightly, and start to read in a low monotonous voice, avoiding any enthusiasm for the subject.
8. Fiddle with the glasses case, or something else, while you continue to read your script.
9. You could place an overhead on the projector at this point. You should put it on crookedly and leave it out of focus.
10. After 10 or 15 seconds look back at the overhead and see that it's out of focus. Make a quick, nervous and unsuccessful attempt to fix this.
11. As people start to fidget and perhaps get ready to walk out of the room, stop and 'get serious' with the group. Let them know it's all an act, and that's not what they will be doing when they finish the training. After the introductions, this could lead into a discussion on the worst things they've seen people do in presentations—The Top Bloopers of Presentations.

Discussion points

1. What did you see?
2. How did you feel?
3. What could be improved?

Variation

1. Props could be changed to suit the venue, etc.
2. Straight after your 'act', you could ask the group to list 10 suggestions for improving your presentation style.

TRAINER'S NOTES

1. You need to prepare for this well before training commences.
2. The presentation must be as bad as possible.
3. You must be as nervous as possible.
4. After the 'show' take a few deep breaths to get yourself back under control. The adrenaline flows and the pulses race with this exercise.

74 Contract with Me

LES

TIME REQUIRED	SIZE OF GROUP	MATERIAL REQUIRED
10 minutes at the conclusion of training.	Unlimited.	Two copies of the 'Contract with Me' handout and a pen for everyone.

Overview

This exercise will help people to apply their learning back in the workplace. It will also allow you to follow up with participants.

Goals

1. To encourage participants to apply their learning back in the workplace.
2. To allow the facilitator to follow up with participants and see if learning has been applied back at work.

Procedure

1. At the conclusion of training, you may say that it's important that people look at ways of applying their learning back at work as soon as possible.
2. Give everyone 2 copies of the 'Contract with Me' handout and a pen. Ask them to fill in the forms, sign them, have them witnessed by someone in the group, and then give you one of the copies.
3. Advise the group that you will contact them shortly after the contract date to see how they went.

Discussion points

None at the time, but lots during the follow-up:

1. What worked?
2. What didn't work?
3. What problems were encountered?
4. What helped with the application?
5. What would you suggest for others doing the training?

Variations

Rather than giving everyone 2 copies of the handout, you could collect all the completed forms and photocopy them. You could then return the copies to the participants.

TRAINER'S NOTES

Contract with Me

To: ________________________________ (your name)

From: ______________________________ (your name)

Date: ______________________________ (today's date)

Re: Contract with me

The three most important things I have gained as a result of this training are:

1. ____

2. ____

3. ____

These are the things I am going to do in the next 2 weeks to apply these ideas:

1. ____

2. ____

3. ____

These ideas will be implemented by: ________________ (date 2 weeks from today)

Signed: ______________________________________

Witnessed: ___________________________________

75

Top 20 Bloopers of Presenting

FLS

TIME REQUIRED	SIZE OF GROUP	MATERIAL REQUIRED
15–20 minutes.	Unlimited.	A prepared 'Top 20 Bloopers of Presenting' overhead. A copy as a handout and a pen for everyone.

Overview

This activity can be used at any stage during a presentation skills course or training techniques program.

Goals

1. To have participants identify their top 'turn-offs'.
2. To have participants make a commitment with themselves not to do any of these things.

Procedure

1. When appropriate lead a discussion into the area of bloopers that presenters or trainers make. This exercise works well when it follows on from #73.
2. Show the 'Top 20 Bloopers of Presenting' overhead and discuss each item.
3. Hand everyone a copy of the 'Top 20 Bloopers of Presenting' handout and a pen and ask them to tick off the things that really turn them off.
4. After everyone has finished, ask them to write this statement at the bottom of the page: 'I will never ever do any of these things in my presentations.'
5. Have them sign the page, and have it witnessed by someone in the group to make it legal.

Discussion points

1. What turns you off when watching someone give a presentation?
2. What are the things you like?
3. How can we ensure we only use the positive things?

Variation

This type of list can be used for lots of topics—for example, 'The Top 20 Bloopers of Driving', 'The Top 20 Bloopers of Safety', 'The Top 20 Bloopers of Report Writing'.

TRAINER'S NOTES

Top 20 Bloopers of Presenting

1. Not being prepared	☐	**11.** Too basic a presentation	☐
2. Misreading your audience	☐	**12.** Information overload	☐
3. Being late	☐	**13.** Offensive or inappropriate humour	☐
4. Lack of eye contact	☐	**14.** Over- or underdressing	☐
5. Lack of enthusiasm	☐	**15.** Turning your back on your audience	☐
6. Not delivering the goods	☐	**16.** Failure to practice	☐
7. Not dealing with questions	☐	**17.** Poor pacing	☐
8. Not using the media available	☐	**18.** Boring the audience	☐
9. Poorly planned visual aids	☐	**19.** Lack of conclusion	☐
10. Distracting visuals and verbals	☐	**20.** Running overtime	☐
		Total	____

Statement: ______________________

____

____

Date today: ______________________

Signature: ______________________

Witness: ______________________

76

Toys

TXLPS

TIME REQUIRED

15–20 minutes.

SIZE OF GROUP

Unlimited, but the group will need to be broken into 2.

MATERIAL REQUIRED

A table with a partition in the middle of it. A box of about 15 to 20 toys (the more the better). A pen and paper for everyone.

Overview

An activity to demonstrate how our creative ideas can be stimulated.

Goal

To demonstrate how creative ideas might be stimulated.

Procedure

1. Start this activity by asking the group to split into 2 smaller groups, preferably of equal size.
2. Now tell them that they are going to be given the job of creating a range of new toys to be launched for next Christmas.
3. Ask each group to take their chairs and sit on opposite sides of the room.
4. Place the table, with the partition in the middle of it, in between the 2 groups.
5. Open the box of toys (which has been kept out of sight) and place it on one side of the table behind the partition so that only one group can see the items. Spread out the toys so that one group can see them and the other one can't.
6. Advise both groups that they have 10 minutes to come up with their list of new toys for the Christmas range. This is to be done as an individual exercise (i.e. no talking).
7. After 10 minutes, ask both groups to give you the number of new toys shown on their lists. These individual scores for one group should be shown on one side of a whiteboard, and the scores for the other group shown on the other side. It may be necessary to calculate the mean score for both groups.
8. The result of this calculation should then lead into a discussion on why one group had a higher score than the other (see the note below).

Discussion points

1. Why did one group have a higher score than the other?
2. Did the group who could see the toys have an advantage? Why, or why not?
3. How do visual stimuli improve creativity?
4. How does this apply in the workplace?

Variations

1. Rather than use a table with a partition, it may be easier in some cases to simply send the 2 groups into different rooms.
2. If the toys are difficult to get, use a handout with pictures on it for one group. Check your mail box for a department store catalogue and copy the toys page.
3. Pictures of different toys can simply be stuck on one side of the partition.

TRAINER'S NOTES

The group who were able to see the toys should have a higher mean score than the group who were unable to see them.

77

Creative Keys

TMXLPS

TIME REQUIRED

30–45 minutes.

SIZE OF GROUP

Unlimited.

MATERIAL REQUIRED

A chair, set of keys on a ring, mop or broom, roll of masking tape and a number of other items (e.g. flower pot, cup, packet of biscuits, book, newspaper, etc.).

Note: The ring on the set of keys should be about 2.5 cm in diameter so that the broom or mop handle will not quite fit inside it with the keys attached on the ring. The broom or mop should be the type where the handle screws into the broom or mop head.

Overview

This activity can be used to show a problem-solving strategy and to develop lateral thinking.

Goals

1. To look at a problem-solving strategy.
2. To demonstrate how creative ideas can be encouraged.

Procedure

1. Start by asking for 2 volunteers.
2. Ask both volunteers to leave the room for the time being.
3. Now set up the props. Place the chair in the centre of the room, or another suitable location. Place the set of keys with the ring sticking up on the chair. Place a length of masking tape on the floor about 2 m away from the chair so that it forms a circular border about 4.5 m in diameter around the chair.
4. Ask the first volunteer to come back into the room.
5. Tell them that their task is to get the set of keys from the chair. The only rules are that they are not allowed to cross over the tape boundary, they can use only the broom as a tool to assist and that the keys are not allowed to touch the floor.
6. Give them the broom and ask them to carry out the task. The rest of the group are observers.
7. After they fail at the obvious solution of trying to spear the ring on the bunch of keys with the broom tip, they will start to look at other ways of solving the problem. They might place the broom head behind one of the chair legs so that they can drag the chair with the keys over to the tape border.
8. After they have solved the problem congratulate them, but now tell them that's not the solution you were looking for. Reset the chair and keys and ask them to try again.
9. Keep them going until they arrive at the solution you are after, which is to unscrew the handle from the mop or broom head, and use this tapered end to fit into the key ring.
10. After this has been completed, ask the second volunteer to come back into the room.
11. Reset the props and give the second volunteer the same set of instructions, except this time tell them that they can use the flower pot, cup, packet of biscuits, broom or mop, etc. (In other words, don't specify the broom or mop as the only tool they can use—it's one of many.)
12. Keep going until they arrive at the required solution. It may take some time, but they will get there eventually.
13. You can now lead the discussion into predictability, frustration, lateral thinking, etc.

Discussion points

1. Were the first solutions predictable? Why, or why not?
2. How did both people feel during the exercise?
3. What did the group observe?
4. How did the volunteers feel when they arrived at a solution only to be told it was wrong?

5. Was it unfair to give a lot of irrelevant material to the second volunteer? Does this happen in the workplace?
6. How does this activity relate to our work environment?

Variation

Use other items for the second volunteer.

TRAINER'S NOTES

78

I'm Confused

ITMXL

TIME REQUIRED

5–10 minutes.

SIZE OF GROUP

Unlimited, but the group will need to be broken into pairs.

MATERIAL REQUIRED

A prepared 'I'm Confused' overhead.
A pen and paper for everyone.

Overview

An activity to be used with pairs to show how answers can come from confusion.

Goal

To demonstrate how a feeling of confusion can be part of the problem-solving process.

Procedure

1. At the beginning of training ask the group to break into pairs.
2. Give each person a paper and pen.
3. Show the 'I'm Confused' overhead, and ask them to find the three out of place words. No other instructions need to be given.
4. Congratulate the first pair to get the 3 correct words.
5. Ask the group how they felt at the start of the activity. Was there uncertainty or confusion? Explain that even with this uncertainty and confusion the correct answers were achieved.
6. Discuss how this may relate to the training you are about to start.

Discussion points

1. Why was there confusion?
2. How can we overcome, or minimise, this confusion?
3. How can this relate to our training?

Variations

1. A handout may be used instead of the overhead.
2. This activity may be conducted in small groups.

Solution

1. (a) Stool
   (b) **Spoon**
   (c) Table
   (d) Desk
   (e) Chair
2. (a) Eagle
   (b) Canary
   (c) Sparrow
   (d) **Horse**
   (e) Hawk
3. (a) Train
   (b) Educate
   (c) Learn
   (d) Knowledge
   (e) **Paint**

TRAINER'S NOTES

I'm Confused

1. What word does not belong here?
   (a) LOTOS
   (b) NOPOS
   (c) BATLE
   (d) KEDS
   (e) RACIH

2. What word does not belong here?
   (a) AGEEL
   (b) ACRYAN
   (c) AWSRROP
   (d) SOREH
   (e) KAHW

3. What word does not belong here?
   (a) RANIT
   (b) UCEEDAT
   (c) NELAR
   (d) NEWKEGDOL
   (e) NAIPT

79 Jobs

TXLPS

TIME REQUIRED

15–20 minutes.

SIZE OF GROUP

Unlimited, but best for groups of around 12 to 24.

MATERIAL REQUIRED

A chair for every person. 6 sheets of paper and 6 pens.

Overview

Another activity to demonstrate how our creative ideas can be stimulated.

Goal

To demonstrate how creative ideas may be stimulated.

Procedure

1. Start this activity by asking for 6 volunteers.
2. Tell the 6 volunteers to take their chairs to the front of the room.
3. Tell them to place the chairs and themselves so that 3 people are directly facing the rest of the group, and the other 3 are facing the back wall (which is preferably blank). The 3 chairs facing the back wall should also be angled away from each other so that the people sitting in them can't see the audience or each other. All they can see is a blank wall in front of them.
4. Give each of the 6 people pen and paper.
5. Now tell them that they are going to be given the job of creating or inventing new job titles. The boss of the company needs to know what kind of job titles may be needed in the future. This information is needed in the next 10 minutes. This is to be done as an individual exercise (i.e. no talking).
6. After the 10 minutes ask both groups to give you the number of new job titles they have on their lists. These individual scores should be shown on a whiteboard, in 2 separate groups—one for the group who could see the audience and the other list for the group who couldn't. It may or may not be necessary to calculate the mean score for both groups.
7. The result of this calculation should then lead into a discussion on why one group had a higher score than the other (see the note below).

Discussion points

1. Why did one group have a higher score than the other?
2. Did the group who could see the audience have an advantage? Why, or why not?
3. How do visual stimuli improve creativity?
4. How does this apply in the workplace?

Variations

1. It may be useful to give the audience another exercise to do while the 6 volunteers are creating their lists.
2. With larger groups more volunteers can be used.

TRAINER'S NOTES

The group who were able to see the audience should have a higher mean score than the group who were unable to see them.

80

What Are Your Answers?

IMLPS

TIME REQUIRED	SIZE OF GROUP	MATERIAL REQUIRED
5 minutes.	Unlimited.	A prepared 'What Are Your Answers?' overhead. A pen and paper for each person.

Overview

A quick activity that can be used effectively to show how some things are totally predictable.

Goal

To demonstrate to the group how predictable some things are.

Procedure

1. Tell the group that they are going to be shown an overhead with 5 questions on it.
2. Their immediate task is to answer the questions as quickly as they can and write their responses on the sheet of paper provided. Emphasise how important it is to write their answers quickly.
3. Show only the questions column of the 'What Are Your Answers?' overhead.
4. After everyone has written their answers, show them the 'correct' responses by revealing the other half of the overhead.
5. Ask those who scored 3 or more correct answers to put up their hands.
6. You can now lead into a discussion on predictability.

Discussion points

1. How many people scored over 3 correct answers?
2. Why is it that most people had lots of 'correct' answers?
3. How will this affect the training?
4. How does this apply in the workplace?

Variation

Can be done as a handout exercise if required.

TRAINER'S NOTES

What Are Your Answers?

1. Name a piece of furniture.	Chair
2. Name a flower.	Rose
3. Name a colour.	Red
4. Select a number between 1 and 4.	3
5. Name an animal from the zoo.	Lion

81 Matchboxing

IMX

TIME REQUIRED	SIZE OF GROUP	MATERIAL REQUIRED
5–10 minutes.	Unlimited, but larger groups may need to be broken into smaller groups.	The outer hollow part of a matchbox for each team.

Overview

A quick competitive activity to help develop teamwork within groups.

Goals

1. To develop teamwork.
2. To energise the group.

Procedure

1. Advise the group that they are going to be involved in a competition.
2. Break the large group into smaller groups of 5 to 7 people. All sub-groups should be of equal size.
3. Give each team the outer part of a matchbox.
4. Now tell them that they are to form a line (or circle).
5. Ask the person at the beginning of the line to put the outer section of the matchbox on their nose.
6. Now tell them that they have to pass the matchbox along their line, nose to nose, one person to the next, and so on. They are only allowed to use their noses. No hands allowed.
7. The first team to complete the task, wins a prize.

Discussion points

1. Who finished first?
2. What helped with this exercise?
3. What were some of the problems encountered? How were they overcome?
4. How does this exercise relate to the workplace?

Variations

1. The groups can be previously formed work teams.
2. This exercise can be repeated, say, 3 or 4 times with 1 or 2 minutes between each round. The time in between should be used for the teams to discuss various strategies. Each round can then be timed to demonstrate improved results.

TRAINER'S NOTES

If it's obvious that some people will be uncomfortable with this type of activity, suggest that each group should only have so many people in the line. This will let the others become observers.

82

Pass the Orange #1

ITMX

TIME REQUIRED	SIZE OF GROUP	MATERIAL REQUIRED
5–10 minutes, depending on the size of the group, and how much fun everyone is having.	Unlimited, but larger groups may need to be broken into smaller groups.	One orange for each team.

Overview

Another quick competitive activity to help develop teamwork within groups. This is an intimate activity and afterwards the participants should feel as if they've known each other for years!

Goals

1. To develop teamwork.
2. To break down any barriers within the group.
3. To energise the group.

Procedure

1. Advise the participants that they are going to be involved in a competition.
2. Break the large group into smaller groups of 5 to 7 people. All sub-groups should be of equal size.
3. Give each team an orange.
4. Now tell them that they are to form a line (or circle).
5. Ask the person at the beginning of the line to put the orange under their chin and hold it in place without using their hands.
6. Now tell them that they have to pass the orange along their line, chin to chin, one person to the next, and so on. They are not allowed to use their hands for this activity.
7. The first team to get the orange to the end of their line wins a prize.

Discussion points

1. Who finished first?
2. What helped with this exercise?
3. What were some of the problems encountered? How were they overcome?
4. How does this exercise relate to the workplace?

Variations

1. The groups can be previously formed work teams.
2. This exercise can be repeated, say, 3 or 4 times with 1 or 2 minutes between each round. The time in between should be used for the teams to discuss various strategies. Each round can then be timed to demonstrate improved results.
3. May be followed immediately by Game 83.

TRAINER'S NOTES

If it's obvious that some people will be uncomfortable with this type of activity, suggest that each group should only have so many people in the line. This will let the others become observers.

83

Pass the Orange #2

ITMX

TIME REQUIRED

5–10 minutes, depending on the size of the group, and how much fun everyone is having.

SIZE OF GROUP

Unlimited, but larger groups may need to be broken into smaller groups.

MATERIAL REQUIRED

One orange for each team.

Overview

Another quick competitive activity to help develop teamwork within groups. This is an intimate activity (even more intimate than the last one) and afterwards the participants should feel like they've known each other for decades!

Goals

1. To develop teamwork.
2. To break down any barriers within the group.
3. To energise the group.

Procedure

1. Advise the participants that they are going to be involved in a competition.
2. Break the large group into smaller groups of 5 to 7 people. All sub-groups should be of equal size.
3. Give each team an orange.
4. Now tell them that they are to form a line (or circle).
5. Ask the person at the beginning of the line to put the orange between their knees and hold it in place that way without using their hands.
6. Now tell them that they have to pass the orange along their line, knees to knees, one person to the next, and so on. They are not allowed to use their hands for this activity.
7. The first team to get the orange to the end of their line wins a prize.

Discussion points

1. Who finished first?
2. What helped with this exercise?
3. What were some of the problems encountered? How were they overcome?
4. How well did you get to know the person either side of you?
5. How does this exercise relate to the workplace?

Variations

1. The groups can be previously formed work teams.
2. This exercise can be repeated, say, 3 or 4 times with 1 or 2 minutes between each round. The time in between should be used for the teams to discuss various strategies. Each round can then be timed to demonstrate improved results.

TRAINER'S NOTES

If it's obvious that some people will be uncomfortable with this type of activity, suggest that each group should only have so many people in the line. This will let the others become observers.

84

TM

Screen Savers

TIME REQUIRED

30–40 minutes.

SIZE OF GROUP

Unlimited, but larger groups will need to be broken into small groups of 5 to 7 people.

MATERIAL REQUIRED

Flipcharts and coloured marking pens for each group.

Overview

This exercise is designed to get teams working together towards a common goal.

Goals

1. To get participants working together.
2. To have participants identify the company's mission/vision statement.

Procedure

1. Break the participants into small teams of 5 to 7 people.
2. Give each team a flipchart and a set of coloured marking pens.
3. Now tell the teams that they have been asked to design a new 'screen saver' for the company's computers. The only stipulation is that it must reflect the theme of the company's mission/vision statement. At the end of the design phase they will be required to give a presentation to the rest of the group showing what they have designed and what it means. Allow 20 minutes for this.
4. After the designs have been completed, have each team give a short presentation on what they have designed and why they chose it.
5. You can hold a vote to decide the best screen saver, and award a prize to the winning team.

6. Leave the 'screen savers' on display for the rest of the training.

Discussion points

1. What is it?
2. Why have you chosen that?
3. Does it really reflect the company's philosophies?

Variation

Instead of designing a screen saver with a mission/vision statement, the teams can design whatever they like.

TRAINER'S NOTES

85

Suggestion/Question Box

IXE

TIME REQUIRED	SIZE OF GROUP	MATERIAL REQUIRED
A couple of minutes before each break and some time after to deal with them.	Unlimited.	A 'Suggestions?/Questions?' handout and pen for each person. One 'Suggestion/Question Box'. Cut each handout into quarters before the session so that each person has a slip for every break.

Overview

An idea to elicit suggestions or questions from everyone in the group, even the quiet ones.

Goals

1. To encourage more suggestions from the group.
2. To encourage more questions from the group.

Procedure

1. During the opening of the training, give out copies of the 'Suggestions/Questions' handout. Each person should have one slip for each break during the training.
2. Tell the participants that just before each break they will be asked to get out one of the slips and write something on the back if they want. Even if they don't want to write anything they should be asked to fold their paper and place it in the 'Suggestion/Question Box' on their way out. This will encourage the quieter ones to write something as they won't feel conspicuous putting something in the box.
3. During the break you should read all the slips and deal with the suggestions and questions at the appropriate time.

Discussion points

None.

Variations

None.

TRAINER'S NOTES

Suggestions?/Questions?

Please take a minute to note any suggestions or questions you may have at this point in time. Fold the paper when you have finished and place it in the box provided. All suggestions and questions will be dealt with as appropriate.

Suggestions?/Questions?

Please take a minute to note any suggestions or questions you may have at this point in time. Fold the paper when you have finished and place it in the box provided. All suggestions and questions will be dealt with as appropriate.

Suggestions?/Questions?

Please take a minute to note any suggestions or questions you may have at this point in time. Fold the paper when you have finished and place it in the box provided. All suggestions and questions will be dealt with as appropriate.

Suggestions?/Questions?

Please take a minute to note any suggestions or questions you may have at this point in time. Fold the paper when you have finished and place it in the box provided. All suggestions and questions will be dealt with as appropriate.

86

How Many Cubes?

IMXLP

TIME REQUIRED

2–3 minutes.

SIZE OF GROUP

Unlimited.

MATERIAL REQUIRED

A prepared 'How Many Cubes?' overhead.

Overview

A very quick activity to demonstrate how well some people can visualise or how well they can use their visual cognitive skills.

Goals

1. To test visual cognitive skills.
2. To energise the group.
3. To fill in a little time while people come back into the room.

Procedure

1. Ask the participants how good they think they are with their visual skills.
2. Show them the 'How Many Cubes?' overhead and ask them to write down how many single cubes are contained in the large cube.
3. After 10 or 15 seconds ask people to show their hands if they have the solution.
4. Ask these people how they arrived at the solution.

Discussion points

1. Why do some people find this easier to do than others?
2. How does this apply in the workplace?

Variations

1. Change the number of squares.
2. Ask how many cubes of size 2 x 2 x 2 could be contained inside the larger cube. This is much more difficult. Solution = 343 (7 x 7 x 7).

Solution

512 (8 x 8 x 8)

TRAINER'S NOTES

How Many Cubes?

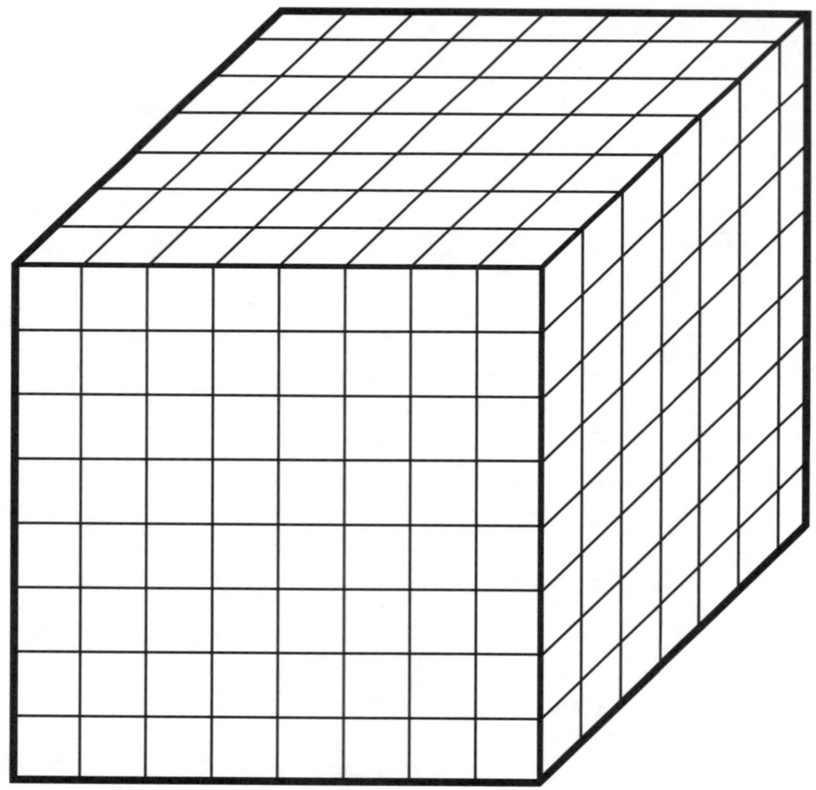

87

How Many Cubes This Time?

IMXLP

TIME REQUIRED	SIZE OF GROUP	MATERIAL REQUIRED
2–3 minutes.	Unlimited.	A prepared 'How Many Cubes This Time?' overhead.

Overview

This activity can be used as a follow-on from Game 86, again to demonstrate how well some people can visualise or how well they can use their visual cognitive skills.

Goals

1. To test visual cognitive skills.
2. To energise the group.
3. To fill in a little time while people come back into the room.
4. To see if learning from the last activity has taken place.

Procedure

1. Ask the participants how good they think they are with their visual skills.
2. Show them the 'How Many Cubes This Time?' overhead and ask them to write down how many single cubes are contained in the diagram assuming there are none hidden behind.
3. After 10 or 15 seconds ask people to show their hands if they have the solution.
4. Ask these people how they arrived at the solution.

Discussion points

1. If Game 86 has been used previously, ask if the group had better results this time.
2. Why do some people find this easier to do than others?
3. How does this apply in the workplace?

Variation

Change the diagram to make it easier or more difficult.

Solution

43.

TRAINER'S NOTES

How Many Cubes This Time?

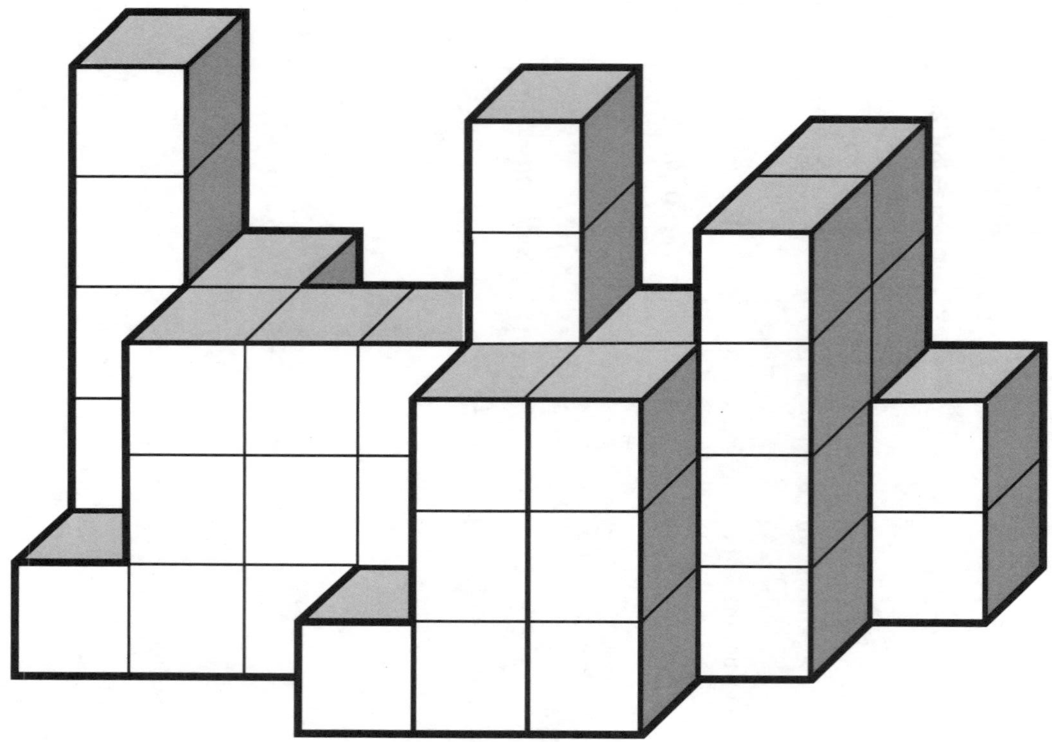

88

X-Files

CMLS

TIME REQUIRED	SIZE OF GROUP	MATERIAL REQUIRED
30–45 minutes, but depends on how much discussion is required.	Unlimited, but larger groups will need to be broken into smaller groups of 5 to 7 people.	One prepared 'X-Files' overhead. One 'X-Files' handout for each person.

Overview

This exercise can be used as the basis of discussion for a customer service training course.

Goal

To identify the things that are important in exceptional customer service.

Procedure

1. Start a discussion about what makes exceptional customer service.
2. After many ideas have been collected from the group and noted on the whiteboard, you can say that an 'X-File' that guarantees exceptional customer service has been discovered. Its secrets will now be revealed.
3. Show and discuss each item on the 'X-Files' overhead.
4. After the discussion has been completed, give all participants a copy of the 'X-Files' as a handout.

Discussion points

As appropriate.

Variation

The ideas collected in step 2 can be used for a small group exercise if required.

Source: Adapted from 'The X Factor' in Carolyn Greenwich, **The Fun Factor**, McGraw-Hill, Sydney, 1997.

TRAINER'S NOTES

X-Files

Xceed customer's Xpectations
Xercise discretion
Demonstrate the Xception, not the rule
Xamine why things are done in a certain way
Xhaust all avenues to help the customer
Be an Xpert at something
Don't Xclude the customer
Don't make Xcuses
Xcel at speed of service
Xchange pleasant greetings
Provide Xact information
Xpress yourself clearly
Xhibit a positive outlook
Xpand on ideas
Go that Xtra mile
Xplain features and benefits
Don't Xecute the customer
Xplore problems thoroughly
Xtend yourself beyond the norm
Give Xactly what's required
Don't Xaggerate
Xtract as much information as you need
Give Xamples
Offer Xcellent service
Master Xcellence
Don't get Xitable
Xit politely
Don't Xorcise the customer
Xpect them to be friendly
Don't use Xpletives
Xplode after 5.00 pm

89 The Good, the Bad and the Funny

PE

TIME REQUIRED	SIZE OF GROUP	MATERIAL REQUIRED
10–15 minutes.	Unlimited.	A 'The Good, the Bad and the Funny' handout and a pen for each person.

Overview

A simple evaluation that can be used at the end of training where in-depth information is not required.

Goals

1. To gain some subjective feedback at the end of training.
2. To review the funny things that have happened during the training.

Procedure

1. At the conclusion of the program, give 'The Good, the Bad and the Funny' handout and a pen to everyone.
2. Give the participants a couple of minutes to write at least one entry in each of the three sections of the form if they can.
3. Quickly go around the group and ask what people have written in each area or, for larger groups, collect the forms and just read out the 'funny' sections.

Discussion points

1. Which part of the course was the best?
2. Which was the worst part of the course?
3. What was the funniest thing that happened?

Variations

1. You can hold a vote to find out what people thought was the funniest thing that happened. A prize should be given to the person/s involved.
2. Can be conducted in small groups with the groups giving a verbal summary of their results.
3. Can be used before all breaks if required.

TRAINER'S NOTES

The Good, the Bad and the Funny

Which part of the course was the best?

What was the worst part of the course?

What was the funniest part of the course?

90

Matches #3

IMXLS

TIME REQUIRED

5–10 minutes.

SIZE OF GROUP

Unlimited, but large groups need to be broken into teams of 5 to 7 people.

MATERIAL REQUIRED

5 matches for each group. A 'Matches #3' handout and a pen for everyone. A copy of the 'Matches #3 Solution' as an overhead.

Overview

A lateral thinking and problem-solving activity.

Goals

1. To allow participants to experience an exercise in problem solving.
2. To highlight the value of synergy in a team situation.
3. To have some fun.

Procedure

1. Break the participants into teams of 5 to 7 people.
2. Tell the teams that they are going to be involved in a problem-solving activity.
3. Give each person a 'Matches #3' handout and a pen.
4. Give each team 5 matches.
5. The teams' task is to break the circle into 14 pieces by placing the matches inside the circle. They are not allowed to break or split the matches.
6. The first team to arrive at the correct solution receives a prize.
7. Show the 'Matches #3 Solution' overhead to the other groups.
8. You can now lead a discussion into the area of problem solving or teamwork.

Discussion points

1. Why did some teams find this easy?
2. Why did some teams find this hard?
3. What helped solve this exercise?

Variations

1. Can be done as an individual exercise, but then it obviously won't relate to teamwork.
2. May be modified by using drinking straws instead of matches.

TRAINER'S NOTES

Matches #3

Your task is to break the circle into 14 parts using only the five matches provided.

You are not to break or split the matches.

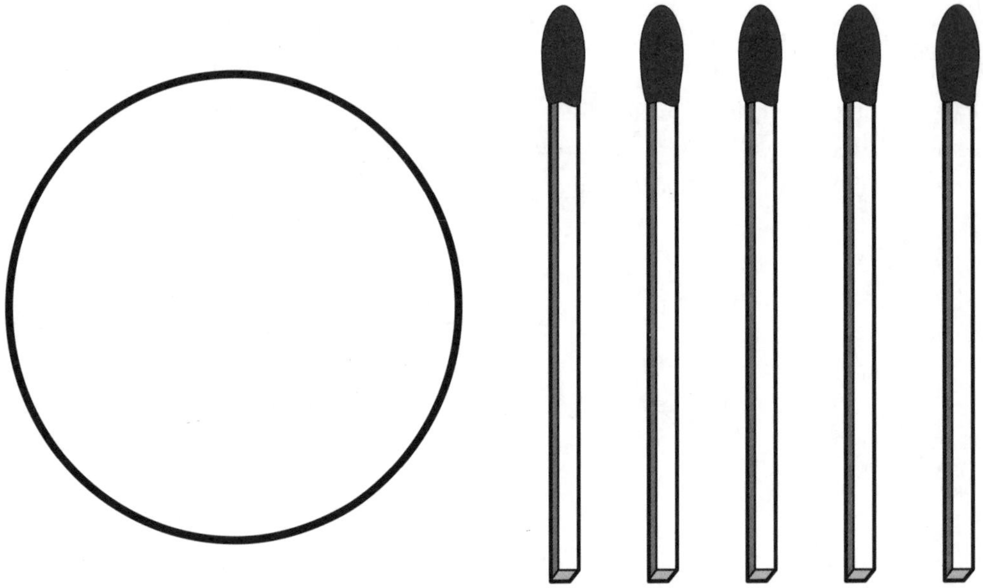

Matches #3 Solution

91

What Comes Next?

IMXLPS

TIME REQUIRED
2–3 minutes.

SIZE OF GROUP
Unlimited.

MATERIAL REQUIRED
A prepared 'What Comes Next?' overhead.

Overview

A quick problem-solving activity.

Goals

1. To allow participants to experience a problem-solving activity.
2. To look at lateral thinking.
3. To fill in some time while waiting for latecomers to arrive.
4. To have some fun.

Procedure

1. Show the 'What Comes Next?' overhead and ask the group the question, 'What comes next?'
2. The first person to give the correct answer receives a prize.
3. This may lead into a discussion on lateral thinking or problem-solving techniques.

Discussion points

1. Who arrived at the right answer?
2. How did you arrive at it?

Variation

Can be done as a small group exercise if required. Allow more time for this.

Solution

10 would come next, as the numbers are arranged in alphabetical order.

TRAINER'S NOTES

What Comes Next?

18, 57, 5, 92, 6, 67, ?

10 or 2? Why?

92

Levels of Knowledge

ILPS

TIME REQUIRED
5–10 minutes.

SIZE OF GROUP
Unlimited.

MATERIAL REQUIRED
A prepared 'Levels of Knowledge' overhead.

Overview

This activity shows us how we develop our learning processes.

Goal

To show the process of learning.

Procedure

1. Show the 'Levels of Knowledge' overhead.
2. Ask the participants to think of an experience where they didn't know that they needed a specific skill, but later they realised they did. Driving a car is a good example to use for this.
3. When we were much younger we didn't know that we needed to learn how to drive a car. At this level we were 'Unconsciously Unskilled'. We didn't know that we didn't know how to do it.
4. As we grew older, we realised that we knew we didn't know how to do it, so we had to learn. This is the 'Consciously Unskilled' level.
5. After we learnt how to drive, we were at the 'Consciously Skilled' level. We knew how to do it but we still had to think about what to do (e.g. how to park the car, or how to turn on the headlights).
6. After many months or years of practice we achieved the 'Unconsciously Skilled' level. This is where we do something without even thinking about it.
7. This now leads into a presentation on how to apply, and persevere with, these new ideas back in the workplace until they become 'Unconsciously Skilled'. Get participants to acknowledge that they generally go through all levels with any new skill, and this training will now be the same.

Discussion points

1. How can you use this back in the workplace?
2. How can you ensure you take these new skills to the 'Unconsciously Skilled' level?
3. What barriers can you see?

Variation

The 'Levels of Knowledge' material may be used as a handout instead of an overhead.

TRAINER'S NOTES

Levels of Knowledge

Unconsciously - Unskilled

Consciously - Unskilled

Consciously - Skilled

Unconsciously - Skilled

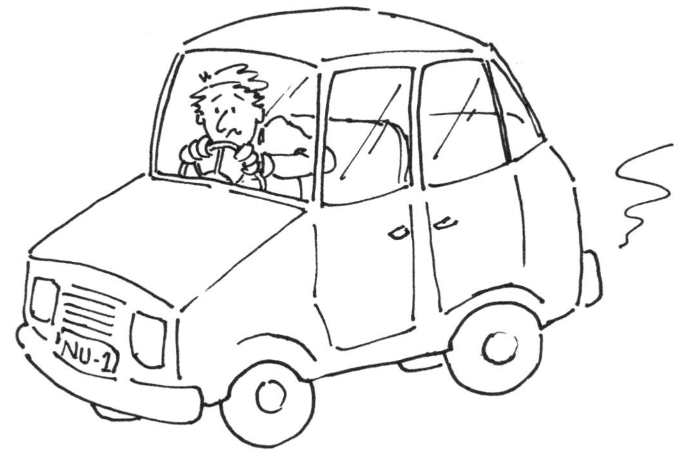

93

Tossing Balls

ITMXPS

TIME REQUIRED	SIZE OF GROUP	MATERIAL REQUIRED
10 minutes.	Unlimited, but large groups may require more (or perhaps less) time.	A tennis ball.

Overview

An activity to demonstrate a team approach to problem solving.

Goals

1. To allow the group to participate in a simple problem-solving activity.
2. To energise the group.

Procedure

1. Start this activity by asking everyone to stand up and form a circle.
2. Ask one person to be a volunteer time keeper.
3. Ask the time keeper to time how long it takes to pass the ball around the group.
4. Now throw the ball to the person on your left.
5. When the ball gets back to you, ask the the time keeper how long it took.
6. Now tell the group that they will be doing the exercise again, but this time it must be done faster.
7. Repeat steps 3, 4 and 5.
8. Again tell the group that they will be doing the exercise again, but this time it must be done faster than the second attempt.
9. This process is kept going until the group achieves its fastest time, which is generally when someone suggests getting as close together as possible and just handing the ball to the next person.
10. This may lead into a presentation on how we need to work as a team and listen to, and encourage, other people's ideas.

Discussion points

1. Why did it take so long to arrive at the best solution?
2. How does this apply to the training we are about to start?
3. How does this apply in the workplace?

Variation

For a newly formed group, every time a person gets the ball they may be asked to call out their name. If this activity goes for several rounds (as it normally does) it will help people remember other people's names.

TRAINER'S NOTES

94
Follow Through

LES

TIME REQUIRED	SIZE OF GROUP	MATERIAL REQUIRED
10–15 minutes.	Unlimited.	A 'Follow Through' handout and a pen for everyone.

Overview

An activity to encourage the application of new ideas back in the workplace.

Goals

1. To encourage participants to apply their new ideas gained from training back in their workplace.
2. To increase participant accountability in the training process.

Procedure

1. At the conclusion of the training, give everyone a copy of the 'Follow Through' handout and a pen.
2. Now ask the participants to think about this scenario. They have been made part owners of this company or organisation. They are now to write down the evidence which proves that this training has been worth the resources put into it. In other words, how can the people attending this training prove to you that it's been worthwhile?
3. After everyone has completed this list, tell them that's what they have to do after leaving here.

Discussion points

None.

Variations

1. Can be done as a small group exercise.
2. You could take copies of all the completed 'Follow Through' handouts before everyone leaves, and actually follow up on all the attendees within a set time frame.

TRAINER'S NOTES

Follow Through

Imagine that you have been made part owners of this company or organisation. You are now required to write down the evidence that this training has been worth the resources put into it. In other words, if people attend this training, how can they prove to you that it's been worthwhile?

95

1-2-5

IMLP

TIME REQUIRED

5 minutes.

SIZE OF GROUP

Unlimited.

MATERIAL REQUIRED

A large prepared sheet with the numbers 1, 2 and 5 written boldly on it (this should be folded and placed out of sight or covered over). 3 sheets of flipchart paper stuck side by side on the wall, and 3 marking pens. 3 sheets of paper and 3 pens.

Overview

This activity will show the group your powers of extrasensory perception.

Goals

1. To allow the group to participate in a non-threatening exercise.
2. To demonstrate to the group how people can be easily manipulated.
3. To let the group know in advance that you may not have all the answers.

Procedure

1. Start this activity by asking for 3 volunteers from the group.
2. Ask each volunteer to move to one of the flipchart sheets stuck on the wall. Give each a pen and paper to work with.
3. Now ask them to think of a number between 1 and 100. They are to keep this number to themselves; however, they may write it on their small sheet of paper (not allowing anyone to see it).
4. Then ask them to double their numbers. Again they are to keep this number to themselves. They can use the sheets of paper for these calculations if required, but these sheets should not be shown to anyone.
5. Ask the first person (facing them, that's the one on the left) to add 2 to their number.
6. Ask the second person to add 4 to their number.
7. Ask the third person to add 10 to their number.
8. Now ask all 3 volunteers to divide this number by 2.
9. After this has been done they are to subtract their original number from the one they've just arrived at.
10. Give each of the 3 people a marking pen and ask them to write the answer on their piece of flipchart paper.
11. When this has been done, take the previously prepared piece of folded paper and open it to show the group. If all 3 volunteers have done their calculations correctly, the numbers on the flipchart sheets should be 1, 2 and 5 in that same sequence.

Discussion points

1. How did they finish up with the same numbers—1, 2 and 5?
2. How does this relate to the upcoming training?

Variations

None.

TRAINER'S NOTES

96

Building Blocks

TXLPS

TIME REQUIRED	SIZE OF GROUP	MATERIAL REQUIRED
20–30 minutes.	Unlimited. Resources may be the limiting factor with this activity.	A prize and about 30 wooden blocks (30 mm cubes) for each person. Odd size blocks may be used as long as everyone gets an identical set. Everyone will require a flat and smooth work area.

Overview

This activity is designed to see if participants place self-imposed limits on themselves.

Goals

1. To see if people place self-imposed limits on themselves.
2. To see if participants are setting themselves realistic goals to work with.

Procedure

1. Give each person a set of wooden blocks by placing them in piles in front of them.
2. Ask the participants to estimate how many of the blocks they could stack on top of each other without the column falling over. They are to do this without touching the blocks. They should keep the estimate to themselves for the time being.
3. Now ask them to try and build the column using the number of blocks they estimated.
4. Ask them to take the blocks apart.
5. For the next part of the activity ask them to estimate, based on their previous experience, how many blocks they can now stack on top of each other without the column falling over. This will be a competitive exercise and the person who completes the highest column, as per their estimate, will win a prize.
6. Show all these estimates on the whiteboard or flipchart beside the participants' names.
7. The exercise is now carried out.
8. The person with the highest estimate and who completes their column successfully is given their prize.
9. You can now direct a discussion on why some people underestimate their ability while others overestimate it. You can also look at the value of external motivators (the prize), group pressure, willingness to assume risks, etc.

Discussion points

1. Why do some people underestimate their ability?
2. Why do some people overestimate their ability?
3. How does this apply to us as individuals?
4. How does this apply in the workplace?

Variations

1. A third round could be conducted as a team exercise.
2. If you can't obtain the right sort of wooden blocks, use playing cards, coins or matchboxes. Any smallish stackable item that you can get in large quantities will be OK.

TRAINER'S NOTES

97

Flags

TM

TIME REQUIRED	SIZE OF GROUP	MATERIAL REQUIRED
30–40 minutes.	Unlimited, but larger groups will need to be broken into small groups of 5 to 7 people.	Flipcharts and coloured marking pens for each group.

Overview

This exercise is designed to get teams working together towards a common goal.

Goals

1. To get participants working together.
2. To have participants identify the company's mission/vision statement.

Procedure

1. Break the large group into small teams of 5 to 7 people.
2. Give each team a flipchart and a set of coloured marking pens.
3. Now tell the teams they have been asked to design a new flag for their company. The only stipulation is that it must reflect the theme of the company's mission/vision statement. Allow 20 minutes for this.
4. After the designs have been completed, ask each team to give a short presentation on what they have designed and why they have chosen it.
5. Hold a vote to decide which flag the large group prefers, and award a prize to the winning team.
6. Leave the flags on display during the training.

Discussion points

1. What is it?
2. Why have you chosen that?
3. Does it really reflect the company's philosophy?

Variations

Instead of being constrained by the mission/vision statement, the teams can design whatever they like.

TRAINER'S NOTES

98

Reflections

LPE

TIME REQUIRED
10 minutes.

SIZE OF GROUP
Unlimited.

MATERIAL REQUIRED
A copy of the 'Reflections' handout and a pen for everyone.

Overview

A quick activity to get participants to identify the most important things they gained from the training.

Goals

1. To allow participants to reflect on the training.
2. To get participants to identify the most important things they gained from it.

Procedure

1. At the conclusion of the training give everyone a copy of the 'Reflections' handout and a pen.
2. Ask everyone to take 9 or 10 minutes to reflect on what they have done over the training period and identify the 5 most important things they learnt. These points are to be written on the 'Reflections' handout.
3. After all the sheets have been completed, ask them to take another minute to prioritise these points in order of importance, with 1 being the highest priority.
4. Now go around the group and ask everyone what they have written.
5. Take notes here to identify the most common points raised. This can then be used as a final summary to recap the main points.

Discussion points

1. Were there lots of common areas listed by the participants?
2. What appeared to be the most important point for most people?

Variations

1. Steps 1 and 2 may be conducted in small groups with the groups required to report back.
2. In step 5 get the participants to give you a summary of the main points.

TRAINER'S NOTES

Reflections

Please take 9 or 10 minutes to reflect on what you have done over the training period and identify the 5 most important things learnt. Write down these points below. After you have identified the points, take another minute to prioritise these points in order of importance, with 1 being the highest priority.

1.

2.

3.

4.

5.

99 New Players

TCXL

TIME REQUIRED
30–40 minutes, depending on the size of the group.

SIZE OF GROUP
Unlimited, but will need to be broken into 2 separate groups for the exercise.

MATERIAL REQUIRED
A pen and paper for everyone.

Overview

This activity has been designed to demonstrate how teams operate in a changing environment.

Goals

1. To allow participants to take part in a team activity where new team players keep coming in.
2. To see if a changing team is better or worse then a static team.

Procedure

1. During a presentation on teams and teamwork you may incorporate this activity. The first task is to get 4 volunteers. These people are taken from the main group.
2. Break the rest of the group into 2 separate groups of the same size.
3. Send both groups to different rooms to perform a set task. Their task is to conceive a new product for their organisation and come up with a name for it. They will have 15 minutes to complete this task.
4. Send one group from the room to start on their task, but before they go you should tell them that they must work as a team from the very start of this activity. It's up to them to elect a leader, and so on, if they want to.
5. Once the first team is out of the room tell the second group that they will have 5 minutes to work on this as an individual exercise before they have a go as a group.
6. After 5 minutes send the second group to another room to complete the task as a group. They are also asked to work as a team and advised they have 10 minutes left to complete the task.
7. After 2 minutes send one of the 4 volunteers in with the second group. Tell the group that this person has been appointed as a new member of the team.
8. After another 2 minutes send in the second volunteer. After 2 more minutes send in the third, and after another 2 minutes send in the fourth.
9. After the total 15 minutes call both groups back into the room.
10. Ask for feedback on their results, and then discuss why one group appeared to have better results than the other. The second group should have much better results.

Discussion points

1. Why did one group, the second group, appear to gain better results?
2. Was the 5 minutes of individual activity given to the second group an advantage or disadvantage?
3. Does a changing work team usually get better results? Why?
4. Is this what normally happens in the workplace?

Variation

1. Groups can be given a different problem to work on.
2. More volunteers can be used and sent in more frequently.
3. As you send in the volunteers, you may ask someone else to leave the group to keep the numbers the same.

TRAINER'S NOTES

100

That's Torn It

IFMXLS

TIME REQUIRED

5 minutes.

SIZE OF GROUP

Unlimited.

MATERIAL REQUIRED

A prepared index card for everyone. Each card is to have 2 cuts in it as shown below.

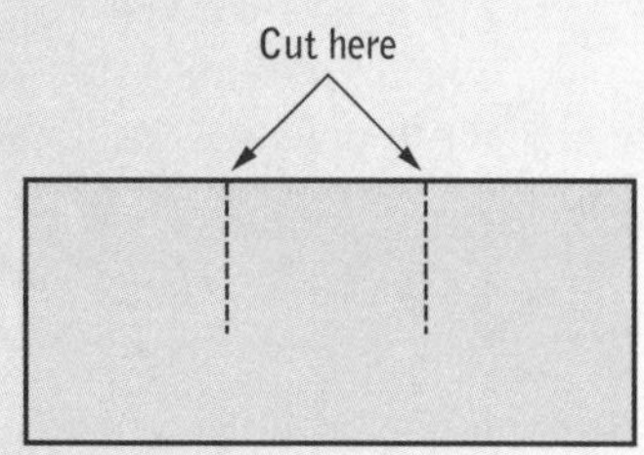

Overview

This simple activity has been designed to show how to manage with limited resources.

Goals

1. To allow the group to participate in an activity to be completed with limited resources.
2. To demonstrate that we tend to limit ourselves with known resources.
3. To develop lateral thinking.

Procedure

1. Give everyone in the group a card (as shown above).
2. Now ask the group to grab the card in both top corners with their fingers.
3. They have to tear the card into 3 pieces without moving their fingers.

Discussion points

1. Who did it?
2. How was it done?
3. Was that the only way of doing it?
4. How many people thought that there weren't enough resources to do this?
5. Why do we sometimes overlook the obvious?

Variations

None.

Solution

Hold the top left-hand and right-hand corners with your fingers. Then grab the top centre piece between your lips. You can then tear the sheet into three separate pieces.

TRAINER'S NOTES

101

Stop Shop

ICMLP

TIME REQUIRED	SIZE OF GROUP	MATERIAL REQUIRED
1-2 minutes.	Unlimited.	None.

Overview

A very simple activity to show how subliminal suggestion works.

Goal

To allow participants to see the power of subliminal suggestion.

Procedure

1. You may start by asking how many people believe in hypnosis or subliminal suggestion.
2. To prove a point, ask for a volunteer.
3. Ask the volunteer to spell the word 'shop'. Ask them to repeat the spelling to confirm what was said.
4. Now ask what they would do if they came to a green light. After they say 'stop', ask them how they are going to get home today, because everyone you know would go at a green light.

Discussion points

1. Why do most people say 'stop'?
2. How does this affect our training?

Variations

Other stories can be used—for example, ask the person to spell 'silk' and then ask them, 'What do cows drink?' Most people would then say milk rather than water.

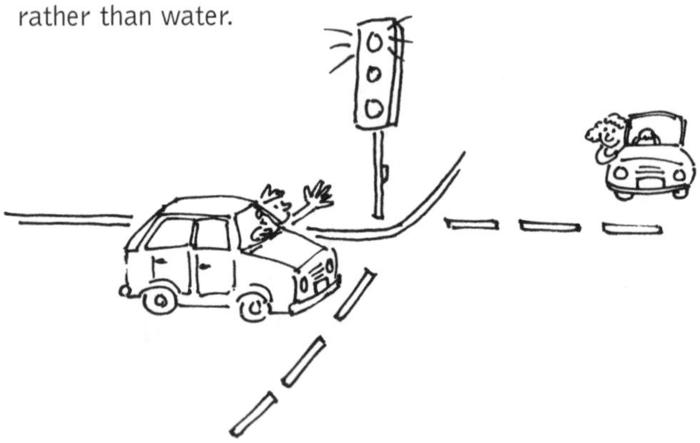

TRAINER'S NOTES

102 Hostage

TCXPS

TIME REQUIRED

45–60 minutes.

SIZE OF GROUP

Unlimited, but the group will need to be broken into teams of 3 or 4 people.

MATERIAL REQUIRED

A 'Hostage' handout and a pen for everyone.

Overview

This activity allows team discussion and problem-solving activities.

Goals

1. To allow participants to become involved in a problem-solving activity.
2. To allow participants to see how important communication in this type of activity is.
3. To let the group see how synergy creates a better solution for the majority of the people involved in the decision-making process.
4. To demonstrate how a team approach to problem solving shares the responsibility so that no one person is held responsible for the result.

Procedure

1. Start this activity by advising the group that they are going to be involved in a problem-solving exercise.
2. Break the group into teams of 3 or 4 people.
3. Now give everyone a 'Hostage' handout and a pen.
4. Read out the opening set of instructions on the handout and ask participants to take 10 minutes to do their own individual rankings. There should not be any discussion.
5. After the individual exercise has been completed, advise the teams that they have 20 minutes to reach a group consensus.
6. These rules are to be highlighted:
   - Everyone in the team must agree with the choice.
   - No voting or compromise is allowed.
   - The final decision must be acceptable to everyone in the team and a decision must be reached within 20 minutes.
   - The leader of the group must be able to give reasons for their selections.
7. After the time has expired each team reports back to the other groups with its results. These results can be displayed for everyone to see.
8. This can then lead into a discussion on teamwork, problem solving, personal values, conflict resolution, etc.

Discussion points

1. What were the principal criteria used in ranking the people?
2. How far did the group's criteria line up with your own?
3. How uncomfortable did you feel about making this kind of decision?
4. How did the team members feel about the responsibility placed on them?
5. What behaviours helped the group in arriving at a final decision?
6. What behaviours hindered the group in arriving at a final decision?
7. How does this apply to the workplace?

Variations

1. This exercise may be conducted effectively with larger teams.
2. All discussion points can be used as a handout for discussion. This is very effective.

TRAINER'S NOTES

The exercise must be completely debriefed as some people take this exercise very seriously. After step 7 you should state the fact that this was only an exercise and allow participants to talk about any points they would like to discuss before moving on to step 8.

Hostage

You are part of a Hostage Unit Negotiation Team (HUNT). Your complete team consists of the people in your group. Your team has just been called to a specific situation and you are sitting together inside the HUNT van. Unfortunately, you are in control of this operation. Ten people are being held hostage by an unknown number of people in a high-rise building across the road.
This is the situation. The people holding the hostages are armed and dangerous. They have given you a set of demands that will take at least 45 minutes to comply with, perhaps longer; they may in fact take several hours. They are not interested in listening to your reasons for the delay. They want their demands met now. They have said that to prove their point they are going to execute one hostage every 30 minutes until their demands have been met. This means the first hostage will be executed 30 minutes from now.

They have also told you that you will be responsible for choosing the first victim, the second, third and so on. The hostages have agreed to this themselves as they are not prepared to make this decision.

They have stopped all communication with you and have said unless their demands are met within the next 30 minutes the executions will start. They will call you in 30 minutes for your complete list of names indicating your selected order.

The only information you have is the information collected by the other people who arrived on site before you. This information is shown on the other side of the handout.

Please show your choices below.

Choices

Order of execution	Name (your selection)	Name (group selection)
1.		
2.		
3.		
4.		
5.		
6.		
7.		
8.		
9.		
10.		

Hostage details

Name	Age	Sex	Occupation	Other details gained
Robert	25	M	Accountant	Married to Samantha, also being held hostage. Senior partner in his firm. Born in US. Holds position as Mayor of the local Council.
Michelle	22	F	Novelist	Has just started her career as a novelist. Divorced with 2 young children. Very attractive. Has just become engaged. Born in England.
Jobe	67	M	Biochemist	Born in Central Africa. Married. Has written many books on biochemistry. Gained PhD at 22 years of age. Has 11 children. Convicted twice for indecent exposure.
Yung-Fu	35	M	Police officer	Engaged. Has lived in numerous countries. He is a Youth Adventure Leader who devotes much of his time and energy to helping young people.
Jennifer	58	F	Medical researcher	Single with 4 adolescent children. Currently researching deadly virus strains. Recognised as a world authority on the treatment of AIDS. Born in India.
Samantha	26	F	Accountant	Married to Robert, also being held hostage. Pregnant with first child. Born in Australia. Both parents and sister killed in car accident last year.
Joe	19	M	Medical student	Member of the Communist Party. Just returned from a trip to Russia. Is also studying religion. Last year raised over $1 000 000 for the church. Single.
Danny	45	M	Unemployed	Formerly an officer in the army. Spent part of his service in Vietnam. Received a special commendation for undercover work done. Has a drinking problem.
Selina	55	F	Unemployed	No information available.
Ingrid	21	F	Model	Highly successful model. Born in Sweden. Has one young child. Is having a relationship with Robert, also being held hostage. Today is her birthday.

Sample Observer's Sheets

The attached 'Observer's Sheets' are to be used as sample designs. They have been included as reference for you to design your own 'Observer's Sheets'. It is important when you use observers that they know exactly what it is they are supposed to be observing.

By using a properly designed observation sheet you are ensuring consistency. You are also ensuring that all the points you want raised will be covered in the final discussion phase.

Observer's Sheet No. 1

It is your task to record what happens in chronological order. Record the time in the left-hand column, your observation in the centre column and who was involved in the third column.

Do not take part in the exercise, pass any comment or make any suggestions. The information you provide after the exercise will assist the whole group to discover things that are directly relevant to the way in which they operate.

Time	Observation	Name

Observer's Sheet No. 2

It is your task to record appropriate points under the headings listed below.

Do not take part in the exercise, pass any comment or make any suggestions. The information you provide after the exercise will assist the whole group to discover things that are directly relevant to the way in which they operate.

Was the exercise planned?

How was it planned?

Were people organised?

…ources used?

…ed?

…d?

…take?

…communication?

…recording?

Observer's Sheet No. 3

It is your task to record appropriate points under the headings listed below.

Do not take part in the exercise, pass any comment or make any suggestions. The information you provide after the exercise will assist the whole group to discover things that are directly relevant to the way in which they operate.

How was the exercise analysed?

Were people organised?

Were objectives set?

Were tasks properly delegated?

Were all available resources used?

How was the group led?

Were problems solved?

How effective was the communication?

How were alternatives discussed and evaluated?

What else was worth recording?

Observer's Sheet No. 1

It is your task to record what happens in chronological order. Record the time in the left-hand column, your observation in the centre column and who was involved in the third column.

Do not take part in the exercise, pass any comment or make any suggestions. The information you provide after the exercise will assist the whole group to discover things that are directly relevant to the way in which they operate.

Time	Observation	Name

Observer's Sheet No. 2

It is your task to record appropriate points under the headings listed below.

Do not take part in the exercise, pass any comment or make any suggestions. The information you provide after the exercise will assist the whole group to discover things that are directly relevant to the way in which they operate.

Was the exercise planned?

How was it planned?

Were people organised?

Were objectives set?

Were all available resources used?

Was the time controlled?

How was the group led?

What roles did people take?

How effective was the communication?

What else was worth recording?

Observer's Sheet No. 3

It is your task to record appropriate points under the headings listed below.

Do not take part in the exercise, pass any comment or make any suggestions. The information you provide after the exercise will assist the whole group to discover things that are directly relevant to the way in which they operate.

How was the exercise analysed?

Were people organised?

Were objectives set?

Were tasks properly delegated?

Were all available resources used?

How was the group led?

Were problems solved?

How effective was the communication?

How were alternatives discussed and evaluated?

What else was worth recording?

Further Reading

Below is a list of publications that can be used as sources for more training games. This list also includes publications that contain some theoretical background behind training and the use of games.

All of the publications are valuable, but some are more relevant than others. The symbols shown to the left of the titles have been included to give the reader a guide as to the relevance of these books to our topic of training games. The key to the symbols is shown below.

Reference key

✪ Read this one and put it in your library; it's a great training games resource.

★ Read this one if you need more information or ideas on training games or other associated areas.

☆ Read this one if you've got nothing else to do.

While some of these titles are fairly old, remember that a game designed in sixth-century India (chess), can still be very useful, and a lot of fun. Training games never die, they just get modified.

☆ BAKER, Pat, MARSHALL, Mary-Ruth, **More Simulation Games**, The Joint Board of Christian Education of Australia and New Zealand, Melbourne, 1977.

☆ ——, **Using Simulation Games**, 2nd Edition, The Joint Board of Christian Education of Australia and New Zealand, Melbourne, 1982.

✪ BISHOP, Sue, **Training Games for Assertiveness and Conflict Resolution**, McGraw-Hill, Inc., New York, 1977.

✪ BURNARD, Philip, **Training Games for Interpersonal Skills**, McGraw-Hill, Inc., New York, 1992.

✪ CARLAW, Peggy, DEMING, Vasudha, **The Big Book of Customer Service Training Games**, McGraw-Hill, Inc., New York, 1999.

★ CARRIER, Michael, **Take 5: Games and Activities for the Language Learner**, Harrap Limited, London, 1983.

✪ CHRISTOPHER, Elizabeth M., SMITH, Larry E., **Leadership Training Through Gaming**, Nichols Publishing Co., New York, and Kogan Page Limited, London, 1987.

★ CONNER, Gary, WOODS, John, **Sales Games and Activities for Trainers**, McGraw-Hill, Inc., New York, 1997.

☆ EITINGTON, Julius, **The Winning Trainer**, Gulf Publishing Company, Texas, 1984.

☆ ELLINGTON, Henry, ADDINALL, Eric, PERCIVAL, Fred, **A Handbook of Game Design**, Kogan Page Limited, London, 1982.

☆ **ELT Documents: Games, Simulations and Role-Playing**, The British Council English Teaching Information Centre, London, 1977.

★ FLUEGELMAN, Andrew (ed.), **More New Games**, Doubleday, New York, 1981.

✪ FORBESS-GREENE, Sue, **The Encyclopedia of Icebreakers**, University Associates, California, 1983.

✪ GREENWICH, Carolyn, **The Fun Factor**, McGraw-Hill, Inc., New York, 1997.

✪ HARSHMAN, Carl, PHILLIPS, Steve, **Team Training**, McGraw-Hill, Inc., New York, 1996.

★ HONEY, Peter, **The Trainer's Questionnaire Kit**, McGraw-Hill, Inc., New York, 1997.

✪ KIRK, James, KIRK, Lynne, **Training Games for the Learning Organisation**, McGraw-Hill, Inc., New York, 1997.

✪ KROEHNERT, Gary, **100 Training Games**, McGraw-Hill Book Company Australia, Sydney, 1991.

✪ ——, **101 More Training Games**, McGraw-Hill Book Company Australia, Sydney, 1991.

★ ——, **Basic Presentation Skills**, McGraw-Hill Book Company Australia, Sydney, 1998.

✪ ——, **Basic Training for Trainers**, 2nd Edition, McGraw-Hill Book Company Australia, Sydney, 1994.

★ ——, **Taming Time: How Do You Eat an Elephant?**, McGraw-Hill Book Company Australia, Sydney, 1998.

★ MILL, Cyril R., **Activities for Trainers: 50 Useful Designs**, University Associates, California, 1980.

✪ NEWSTROM, John W., SCANNELL, Edward E., **Games Trainers Play**, McGraw-Hill, Inc., New York, 1980.

✪ ——, **The Big Book of Team-Building Games**, McGraw-Hill, Inc., New York, 1998.

☆ **Oddities in Words, Pictures and Figures**, Reader's Digest Services Pty Limited, Sydney, 1975.

☆ ORLICK, Terry, **The Cooperative Sports and Games Book**, Pantheon Books, Canada, 1978.

☆ ——, **The Second Cooperative Sports and Games Book**, Pantheon Books, Canada, 1982.

✪ PFEIFFER, J. William, JONES, John E., **A Handbook of Structured Experiences for Human Relations Training**, Volumes 1–10, University Associates, California, 1975–85.

★ ROHNKE, Karl, **Cowstails and Cobras II**, Kendall/Hunt Publishing Company, Iowa, 1989.

★ ——, **Silver Bullets**, Kendall/Hunt Publishing Company, Iowa, 1984.

✪ SCANNELL, Edward E., NEWSTROM, John W., **More Games Trainers Play**, McGraw-Hill, Inc., New York, 1983.

★ ——, **The Big Book of Presentation Games**, McGraw-Hill, Inc., New York, 1998.

★ SILBERMAN, Mel (ed.), **The 1997 McGraw-Hill Team and Organisational Development Sourcebook**, McGraw-Hill, Inc., New York, 1997.

★ ——, **The 1997 McGraw-Hill Training and Performance Sourcebook**, McGraw-Hill, Inc., 1997.

★ TUBESING, Nancy Loving, TUBESING, Donald A., **Structured Experiences in Stress Management**, Volumes 1 and 2, Whole Person Press, Duluth MN, 1983.

★ ——, **Structured Exercises in Wellness Promotion**, Volumes 1 and 2, Whole Person Press, Duluth MN, 1983.

✪ TURNER, David, **60 Role-plays for Management and Supervisory Training**, McGraw-Hill, Inc., New York, 1992.

☆ VAN MENTS, Morry, **The Effective Use of Role-play**, Kogan Page Limited, London, 1983.

✪ VILLIERS, Peter, **18 Training Workshops for Leadership Development**, McGraw-Hill, Inc., New York, 1993.

✪ WOODCOCK, Mike, **50 Activities for Teambuilding**, Gower Publishing Company, England, 1989.

☆ WRIGHT, Andrew, BETTERIDGE, David, BUCKBY, Michael, **Games for Language Learning**, Cambridge University Press, Cambridge, 1979.

TRAINING INFORMATION

We offer a comprehensive range of training services around the world. If you would like more information on our training services, please complete the information below and forward it to us by mail, fax or email.

Name: ______________________________

Position: ______________________________

Company: ______________________________

Address: ______________________________

____

____

Phone: ______________________________

Fax: ______________________________

Email: ______________________________

I would like more information on:

- ☐ In-house Presentation Techniques Skills Seminar
- ☐ Public seminar information for Presentation Techniques Skills Workshops
- ☐ In-house Training Techniques Workshops
- ☐ Public seminar information for Training Techniques Workshops
- ☐ In-house Time Management Seminars
- ☐ Public seminar information for Time Management Seminars
- ☐ Public seminar information on other subjects

Post to: Gary Kroehnert
Training Excellence
PO Box 3169
Grose Vale, NSW 2753
Australia

Or fax to: (02) 4572 2200

Or email: doctorgary@hotmail.com